JOHN A.

John A. Macdonald (*c. 1863*) *by William Sawyer, based on an earlier photograph. Here this Kingston artist projects a sensual quality unmatched in any other portrait of Macdonald.*

RICHARD GWYN

John A

THE MAN WHO MADE US

The Life and Times of John A. Macdonald
VOLUME ONE: 1815–1867

RANDOM HOUSE CANADA

Library and Archives Canada Cataloguing in Publication

Gwyn, Richard, 1934–
John A. : the man who made us : the life and times of John A. Macdonald /
Richard Gwyn.

Includes bibliographical references and index.
Contents: v. 1. 1815–1867.
ISBN 978-0-679-31475-2 (V. 1)

1. Macdonald, John A. (John Alexander), 1815–1891.   2. Canada——History——
19th century.   3. Canada——Politics and government——19th century.
4. Prime ministers—Canada—Biography.
I. Title.
FC521.M3G89 2007   971.05'1092   C2007-903422-5

Printed and bound in the United States of America

10 9 8 7 6 5 4 3 2 1

To Carol
My wife, and my love

Contents

Introduction

The spirit of past ages never dies—
It lives and walks abroad and cries aloud.
Susanna Moodie, *Victoria Magazine*, 1847

If an international competition were ever to be staged to identify the world's most complex and contradictory country, Canada would be a serious contender. The winner, surely, would be India, with its sixteen official languages and more than two hundred local languages, its sacred cows and cutting-edge computer software, its combination of being both the world's largest democracy and the only nation-state with a caste system. Canada might well come in second. It's become a commonplace to describe the country as "the world's first postmodern country," given its unparalleled ethnic diversity, its decentralization (exceeded, if at all, only by Switzerland and Belgium), the in-rush of immigrants (the largest proportionately among developed nations), the expanding population of Aboriginal peoples (second only to New Zealand), and the ever-increasing number of "nations" within the nation-state—Quebec as the latest to join the list.

In quite a few ways, we were postmodern before we ever became modern. That was the way we were in John A. Macdonald's time. In 1884, Goldwin Smith, the leading political commentator of his day, summarized Macdonald's lifelong mission as "to hold together a set of elements, national, religious, sectional and personal, as motley as the component patches of any 'crazy quilt,' and actuated each of them by paramount regard for its own interest." Here, Smith identified exactly Macdonald's supreme talent—that he knew how to herd cats.

No one else in Canada came close to Macdonald; after him, perhaps only Mackenzie King did, his paramount art being that of doing as little as possible for as long as possible. At the time, few others anywhere could match him. Even without the spur of chauvinism, any reasonable ranking of nineteenth-century democratic leaders would be Abraham Lincoln, Benjamin Disraeli, William Gladstone, John A. Macdonald. (Otto von Bismarck, no democrat, would otherwise rank near to the top.) Macdonald happened to perform on a stage that was small and threadbare. But in the primordial political tasks—the managing of men (then, only them) and the winning of their hearts and minds, and so their votes—contemporary equals are not easy to identify. Nor were there many nation-builders like him in his day: Bismarck, Giuseppe Garibaldi and Simón Bolívar. His achievement may have been the more demanding because none of the others had to create a country out of a crazy quilt.

Within the range of Macdonald's accomplishments, there are sizable gaps. The largest, surely, is that, unlike Lincoln, he never appealed to people's "better angels." He was a doer, not a thinker, although highly intelligent and omnivorously well read. He lacked the certitudes of a moralist, instead taking human nature as he found it and turning it to his purposes. He was, that is, a very Scottish Scot. He of course drank too much. And although he was in no way the first to use patronage and election funds for partisan purposes—a cherished and well-embedded Canadian tradition (which still thrives)—Macdonald gave the practice credibility and durability by his masterful exercise of it. That's a shoddy legacy for the father of a country to leave behind.

Yet his accomplishments were staggering: Confederation above all, but almost as important, if not more so, extending the country across the continent by a railway that was, objectively, a financial and economic insanity. Also, the National Policy of tariff protection, which endured in one form or other into the 1980s. And the RCMP or, more exactly, its precursor, the North-West Mounted Police. The first immigration from outside the British Isles, and Canada's first labour legislation. On the ledger's other side, he was responsible for the CPR scandal, for the execution of Louis Riel and for the head tax on Chinese workers.

He's thus not easy to scan. His private life was largely barren. Yet few other Canadian leaders—Pierre Trudeau, John Diefenbaker for a time, Wilfrid Laurier—had the same capacity to inspire love. One MP—a Liberal—wrote in a magazine article of Macdonald's hold on his supporters: "They would go through fire and water to serve him, and got, some of them, little or no reward. But they served him because they loved him, and because with all his great powers they saw in him their own frailties." The novelist Hugh MacLennan, in his *Scotchman's Return*, caught many of the layers within him: "This frail-looking man with the immense and rueful patience of a Celt. . . . This utterly masculine man with so much woman in him . . . this lonely man flashing gay out of his inner solitude . . . this statesman who understood that without chicanery statesmanship is powerless." Macdonald was as complex and contradictory as his own country.

Add a last, lesser, legacy of Macdonald's to the list. In writing this book, I have made a host of spelling "mistakes," but have paid them no heed. Each has been signalled clearly by a red line that my computer's U.S. text system inserts beneath the offending word. The mistakes aren't really mine, though; they are

Macdonald's. He had an order-in-council passed directing that all the government's papers be written in the British style, as with "labour" rather than "labor."

Discoveries of this kind have been for me one of the chief delights of writing this book, and even more so of researching it. All historians, professional or freelance like myself, are keenly aware that these small epiphanies are the joy that more than compensates for the later pain of trying to transfer from mind to computer screen whatever it is one wants to say. The discovery, for instance, that, at least in parts of nineteenth-century rural Canada, unmarried mothers were often regarded far less as sinners than as a "species of heiress"; as one observer noted, their condition both confirmed their fecundity and, as dowry, they brought children who would soon be able to work on the farm. The discovery, one of slightly grander moment, that the principal reason the Confederation Fathers spent almost no time discussing the respective powers of the national and provincial governments—the obsession of our politicians ever since—was that most Canadians then were self-sufficient farmers (even making their own clothes and soap and candles) and didn't want governments to do much for them or to them. The discovery, most substantial of all, that the single most important decision Canadians made in the nineteenth century was not to become a confederation, but, rather, not to become Americans. And the discovery that the National Policy, a phrase always applied only to Macdonald's policy of tariff protection for Canadian manufacturers, began instead with Confederation itself, with tariff protection as a later sub-policy, together with other highlights such as his building a transcontinental railway.

Macdonald made us by making a confederation out of a disconnected, mutually suspicious collection of colonies, and by later magnifying this union into a continental-sized nation. He could not have brought off Confederation without the others of the "Big Four"—George-Étienne Cartier, George Brown and Alexander Tilloch Galt. Among them, though, the irreplaceable man was Macdonald. He understood as well something more fundamental. The United States had emerged from its Civil War as a putative superpower. Britain, the global superpower, wanted to pull back from North America in order to attend to its empire. For Canada to survive on its own, it had to demonstrate that it possessed the will and nerve it took for a nation to survive. Confederation was the essential means to that end. What Macdonald understood as no other, excepting perhaps Galt, was that Confederation was only a means, not an end.

I began work knowing precious little about Macdonald and his times. What I knew was negative—that while Macdonald was the most important of all our prime ministers, the last full-scale, critical, biography of him had been written more than half a century ago. It is the greatest biography in Canadian historiography—Donald Creighton's two volumes *The Young Chieftain* and *The Old Politician*, published in 1952 and 1955. They are magisterial and encyclopedic, composed with narrative flair. But times move on, new evidence emerges, attitudes and assumptions change and open doors—maybe trap doors—to new interpretations of old givens. Anyway, why should the United States, where history was once dismissed as "bunk," each year publish up to a half-dozen biographies of historical figures or major studies of past doings that attempt to extract contemporary lessons from long-ago events, while Canada settles for so few—precariously close to none at all? Our history, as we know perfectly well, lacks the drama of revolutions and civil wars, of kings and queens losing their heads. But it is our history. It is us. It's where we came from and, in far larger part than often is recognized, it is why we are the way we are now, no matter all the transformational changes since—demographic, economic, technological, lifestyle. Moreover, as was always Macdonald's core conviction, human nature itself changes little.

I came to this biography sideways. This book started out to be a slim one, then threatened to grow obese, then was sliced into two more or less manageable halves. This is to say that I began boning up on Macdonald for a Brief Life series on historical figures for another publisher. Out of this cramming came one, to me, unarguable conclusion: Macdonald deserves a new full-scale biography, and Canadians deserve the chance to rediscover him. With quite considerable daring—in Canada, history really is often now treated as "bunk"—Random House of Canada accepted the challenge, eventually taking the double dare that an originally planned single volume should be divided into two. This book is the result of that dare.

A last note on my work habits. Early on, Carol, my wife, found a large poster of Macdonald created originally to promote Macdonald's cause in CBC-TV's *The Greatest Canadian* contest. She installed it in my attic office. Throughout my labours, he's looked down, quizzically and mischievously.

ONE

Lairds Ourselves

~

Mark my words, John will make more than an ordinary man.
Helen Macdonald's judgment on her eldest son

Where John A. Macdonald was born and when he was born are unknown. Or, rather, are not known exactly. About the essentials of his beginnings, there are no doubts whatever. He was born in the Scottish industrial city of Glasgow in 1815.

There were historical dimensions to both place and date. Glasgow was the lustiest child of Britain's Industrial Revolution: a sleepy town of only twenty thousand in 1791, its shipyards along the Clyde, its engineering works and factories and its "dark Satanic mills" had sent the town's population soaring above one hundred thousand by the time of Macdonald's birth, less than a quarter-century later. As well, 1815 was the year of the Battle of Waterloo. That cataclysmic military clash didn't so much ensure Napoleon's defeat (which was inevitable eventually, anyway) as ensure that Britain, its strength multiplied by its long industrial lead over all its rivals, would become the global powerhouse of the nineteenth century. By pure happenstance, Britain's global reach created a possibility that its leftover colonies in North America, strung across the top half of the continent like widely spaced and oddly sized beads, and having little in common other than their mutual Britishness (for the most part), might yet— just—remain independent from their overwhelming neighbour, the coming hegemon of the twentieth century. For that to actually happen, however, required the arrival of a leader who could cajole and bluff and bully these colonies into becoming a whole larger than the sum of their parts. In 1815, little of this was of the slightest interest to anyone in the British Isles. Yet it was in Glasgow in that year that Canada's future began to take shape.

The minutiae of Macdonald's birth need to be cleared up. Throughout his life and for the near century and a quarter that has followed his death, his birthdate has been commemorated as January 11, 1815—as in the joyous celebratory dinner staged each year in Kingston, Ontario, for example, and in the inscriptions on all the plaques and statues that honour him. But this particular day may be a mistake. The January 11 date is taken from the entry for his birth made by his father, Hugh Macdonald, in his memorandum book. The entry recorded in the General Register Office in Edinburgh, though, is January 10.* Similarly, precision about where specifically Macdonald was born, while a matter of lesser consequence, is as difficult to determine. The delivery may have taken place at 29 Ingram Street in Glasgow or, not far away, at 18 Brunswick Street, both on the south side of the Clyde River, because the family moved between these locations around the time of his birth. To pick at a last

---

*Hugh Macdonald recorded the birthdates of all his children in the 1820 edition of his memorandum book.

unknowable nit, Macdonald's father recorded the moment of birth as 4:15, without specifying afternoon or early morning.

The other defining attributes of Macdonald's birth are known beyond argument. His parents were middle class, if precariously so. They were Scots, and so of course was he. And soon after his birth, they chose to immigrate to Canada rather than take the advice of Samuel Johnson about the most attractive prospect that any Scotsman could ever come upon and follow the usual road to London.

Immigration always happens for one of two reasons or for both simultaneously: either individuals or families are pushed out from their homeland by poverty, oppression, failure or plain bad luck, or they are pulled towards a new country by the tantalizing promise it holds for new beginnings and new opportunities. Both factors applied to the Macdonalds, but in distinctive ways, when they set out across the Atlantic in 1820. John A. himself was then five years old. An early biographer described him as having "a bright eye, a lively manner and a head of curly brown hair which darkened into black as he grew up." At least supposedly, he showed early promise of having the gift of the gab, once giving a speech to a gathering of relatives by mounting a table, from which, as his gestures became ever more dramatic, he projected himself to the ground.

As soon as the Napoleonic wars ended, England was gripped by a depression that cut most deeply into its farming counties; the same outwards push existed in Scotland, given force there by the clearances of people from the land to make way for sheep—as often, despite later myth, by Scottish landowners as by English ones. The great migration from the British Isles to both Canada and the United States dates from this period, although it remained relatively small until the 1830s, later multiplying exponentially through the 1840s as the Irish fled from the horrors of their Great Famine. To magnify the force of the outwards push, the British governments of the day accepted the thesis of Thomas Malthus that population growth would always outpace the growth in food production. To avoid social unrest, perhaps even the ultimate horror of a revolution of the kind from which Napoleon had sprung, successive governments encouraged the "idle poor" to move elsewhere.

The Macdonalds, though, were not a family of farmers. And although hard up, they weren't poor, not in the sense of their being malnourished and in rags. The force that pushed them out was failure—quite unnecessary failure, and the product almost entirely of the fecklessness of Macdonald's father, Hugh.

Before Hugh Macdonald is introduced, it's necessary to go backwards one further genealogical step to Hugh's own father, John Macdonald. Although he never left Scotland, John Macdonald set the family on its transatlantic journey. When he came down from the Highlands—pushed out by the clearances implemented by his laird, the Duke of Sutherland—he went first to a little village in the Strathfleet Valley and then on to the Sutherlandshire town of Dornoch, where he set up as a shopkeeper. John Macdonald was widely liked—a contemporary described him as having "a tender nature, full of humour, a quick and winning manner, with a bow and smile for everyone he met." Many of those qualities would pass to his grandson, as did his longevity, for he died at the age of eighty-six. John Macdonald's most distinctive legacy to his grandson was his head of abundant but curiously crinkly hair. His most important legacy to his heirs, though, was to get them out of the beautiful but bleak Highlands into a settled community, and to raise them there to at least the lower rungs of the middle class.

Hugh Macdonald squandered the greater part of what had been

handed down to him. Born in Dornoch,* he moved in early adult-hood to the growing city of Glasgow and there owned and operated a succession of small enterprises—one, for instance, making bandanas. Their common characteristic was that they all failed. Hugh was known as a decent, amiable man, good in conversation and impossible to dislike. This quality served him well: after one bankruptcy, when he was at serious risk of being sent to a debtors' prison, he was allowed not only to remain free but to keep his library and household effects, later selling them to pay for the tickets for his transatlantic passage. Two attributes that Hugh passed on to his son were that he had a hot, Celtic temper, and that he drank a lot.

Hugh Macdonald's most considerable accomplishment during his relatively short life was to marry Helen Shaw. It happened in 1811, when she was at the relatively advanced age of thirty-four and he at the comparatively tender one of twenty-eight. Helen was an exceptional woman, the rock upon which the small tribe took its stand facing outwards to the world, arms linked. She kept the family going through thin and thick. A surviving por-trait of her, done in at least middle age, depicts accurately her rock-like qualities of strength and determination. "She was a little above the medium height, large limbed, and capable of much endurance," commented the contemporary biographer E.B. Biggar.† "Her features were large, and as some considered coarse; but there beamed through her dark eyes a depth of apprehension mingled with such graciousness and good will." She

---

*A small town, then and now, Dornoch has one claim to fame as the site of the last judicial execution for witchcraft in Britain: in 1727, a court ruled that a Janet Horne had turned her daughter into a pony.

†E.B. Biggar's *Anecdotal Life of Sir John Macdonald*, hurried into print in 1891, the year of his death, is the source of most of the best-known anecdotes about him. The first biography of Macdonald, *The Life and Times of the Right Honourable Sir John A. Macdonald*, published as early as 1883, was written by J.E. Collins, an

Helen Macdonald. She was determined that her son would make his mark in life.

read widely, and as Biggar wrote, "had she possessed the advantages of a high education, and the opportunities some get in life, she would have been a noted woman."

While the portrait of Helen Macdonald suggests the depth and liveliness of her eyes, it betrays little hint of the most attractive of her qualities—her capacity for gaiety. She and John A. loved to trade stories and jokes, his being the racier. Biggar commented, "She appreciated a droll saying or a droll situation." Once, when Macdonald ascended to the social height of being elected president of Kingston's St. Andrew's Society, he led a gathering preceded by a piper to her house; when she heard the wail of the bagpipe, Helen came downstairs and danced a jig in the street.

She was wholly Scots, and above all a Highlander. Her preferred language was Gaelic. Her father fought for Bonnie Prince Charlie at Culloden, and afterwards, as did many Scots, joined the British Army. She could be stonily stubborn, a quality that repeatedly taxed Macdonald's talents once he became the de facto head of the family. She possessed an exceptional memory—a gift she passed on to her son—and functioned as the family historian and the teller of Highland tales.

---

expatriate Newfoundlander. By a curious coincidence, Collins also wrote the first biography of Louis Riel as well as a bodice-ripper of a novel, *Annette, the Metis Spy: A Heroine of the N.W. Rebellion.* He died in New York, of drink, in 1892.

Of her children—two boys and two girls at the time of leaving Glasgow—there was never any doubt that her favourite was her elder son, John Alexander. "Mark my words, John will make more than an ordinary man," she said on many occasions.

⁓

Besides the push of failure at home, there were more positive attractions pulling the Macdonald family to Canada. Of these, the most apparent was that Hugh Macdonald, unlike the great majority of immigrants,* possessed the priceless asset of connections. In and around Kingston, the town where they were headed, there was a cluster of Macdonald relatives and cousins. That most were distant relatives mattered not the least; they all belonged to the same clan. The most important person by far was Colonel Donald Macpherson, who was married to Helen Macdonald's stepsister. The colonel, who twice fought for King and Country against the Americans (during the War of Independence and the War of 1812), retired afterwards to the garrison town of Kingston, built a large stone house called Cluny (meaning "meadow") and settled down as one of the community's principal citizens. Before leaving Glasgow, Hugh Macdonald knew that Colonel Macpherson would find space in his house for him and his family for at least a transition time, and that afterwards Macpherson would help with advice and contacts as Hugh set up his first business.

How much Hugh Macdonald knew about Canada before he left is unknowable. Information was available, however, in book-

---

* Immigrants were then commonly referred to as "emigrants," because the significant point was that they were leaving Britain rather than that they were coming to Canada.

lets such as *The Emigrant's Guide to the British Settlements in Upper Canada and the United States of America*, published the same year that the Macdonalds left. In some ways, Canada was distinctly unappealing. Its total population was only a little more than half a million, the great majority being French-speaking Canadiens. The particular part of Canada where they were headed—Upper Canada (now Ontario)—had fewer than two hundred thousand people; mostly, the land was untouched, primeval forest broken here and there by the crude log shacks of pioneer settlers. All of Canada was incomparably poorer and less developed than any of the thirteen American colonies.

Yet Canada possessed two considerable attractions. Land itself was free to most settlers. To the Macdonalds, this bounty was irrelevant, since they were headed for a town and not for a clearing in the wilderness. The country's second general attraction, that there were no class divisions, was a derivative from the first and exactly fitted the ambitions, however muddled, of Hugh Macdonald. As the Scottish settler George Forbes wrote to his brother back in Aberdeenshire: "We in Canada have this glorious privilege that the ground we tred is our own and our children's after us." And he went on to describe the fundamental difference between Canada and any part of Britain, or indeed anywhere in Europe. "Here, we are lairds ourselves."

Had John A.'s parents moved from Glasgow to somewhere else in the British Isles, the upwards drive that Macdonald eventually undertook would have butted sooner or later against the steel ceiling of the British class system. In Canada, by contrast, there was no aristocracy at all other than a few fragments within the Family Compact—the small clique who, as politicians, public officials and judges, ran the country on behalf of the governor general. (Lower Canada, or Quebec, was markedly more hierarchical.) Instead, the vast majority of Canadians were either middle class or believed that they could become middle class, or, since the term "middle class" wasn't yet used, they were "respectable" citizens—law-abiding, churchgoing, debt-free, or attempting diligently to be all three.

The idea of classlessness was lodged deep in the Canadian consciousness from its very beginnings. In *Roughing It in the Bush*, Susanna Moodie noted crossly of her servants, "They no sooner set foot upon the Canadian shores than . . . all respect for their employers, all subordination is at end." She went on to record, though, that "with all their insolent airs of independence, I must confess that I prefer the Canadian to the European servant."

In fact, a respectable claim can be made that in one vital respect, the country Macdonald's parents were taking him to was more democratic even than the United States, that great experiment in egalitarianism. In the South and in parts of New England, there was an aristocracy, and, in the North, a class of self-made millionaires who cascaded their wealth upon their heirs. Above the border there was virtually no over-class, but no under-class either. There were no slaves in Canada, they having been liberated by Governor John Graves Simcoe's decree of 1793,* and there was no equivalent of the proletariat now developing rapidly in the great northern cities of the United States. Almost all Canadians were indeed "lairds," in possibility and in self-perception, if not in actual fact. They could rise as high as their talent, ambition and luck might take them.

It's unknowable whether Hugh and Helen Macdonald had any idea of the benefit they were conferring on their elder son by bring-

---

* While Simcoe's legislation ended the slave system, it did not immediately end slavery: owners of existing slaves were allowed to hang on to their "property," although almost all were released within a few years. By gaining legal equality, blacks in Canada did not in any way gain social and economic equality.

ing him to a society where, compared with almost any other society in the world, there were fewer barriers to whatever upwards rise he might attempt. But that's what they did by not taking the well-travelled road down to London and, instead, taking a ship to a far-away country in which there were just about no roads at all.

TWO

A Boy's Town

~

Remember, oh remember, the fascination of the turkey.
John A. Macdonald, to a girl he owed a dance

When the Macdonalds came up the St. Lawrence River from the Gulf in 1820, they would have seen the same strangely foreign prospect, at first impressive but after a while depressing, that Catharine Parr Traill described in *The Backwoods of Canada* a few years later: "I begin to grow weary of its immensity . . . we see nothing more than long lines of pine-clad hills with here and there white specks that they tell me are settlements." At long last there was a real town—Quebec City. There, their ship, the small, 600-ton *Earl of Buckingham*, discharged its six hundred passengers, the Macdonalds included. Behind them, at last, were six weeks of the appalling food,* overcrowding, incessant lice and rats and complete lack of privacy that everyone in steerage

---

* To minimize the cost of feeding their passengers, some captains were known to supply them on the first day with large helpings of porridge and molasses, making them so sick that, thereafter, they seldom demanded their full rations.

Quebec City. A thriving port, a British garrison town and the oldest city, by far, in Canada. This view is a steel engraving from a painting by William Bartlett prepared for his book Canadian Scenery Illustrated *(1842)*.

experienced, along with the constant damp and seasickness that even those in cabin class endured. They must have been delighted to see the end of this decaying vessel—indeed, two years later it drifted into Galway Bay and broke up in pieces.

Left on the dock at Quebec City was the small tribe of Macdonalds, as well as their orphaned cousin Maria Clark, who had accompanied them on the voyage. It numbered Hugh and Helen Macdonald, both now in their forties, and their four children: Margaret, the oldest at seven, nicknamed Moll; then John A. and James, one year younger; and lastly two-year-old Louisa, known as Lou. (A fifth child, the first-born William, had died back in Glasgow.) Scots, unlike the English and even the Irish, to a lesser extent, almost never sent a single family member ahead to scout the terrain but moved any distance as a complete family.

They would have been amazed by the scene that greeted them once they entered the port: endless lines of log rafts with a crude shack at their centre, stretching out for miles along the river and waiting to load the pontoons of huge, squared timbers they had brought all the way from the Ottawa Valley onto one of the same sailing ships that had just transported the immigrants. Their stop at Quebec City would have been exciting—lots of familiar redcoats and Royal Navy tars, but also the unfamiliar language of most of the local inhabitants. And they would have taken a little time to look over the sights—the massive hulk of the Citadel, the steep bank soaring upwards from the St. Lawrence over which Wolfe's Highlanders had scrambled, the imposing churches and nunneries and the low stone houses packed together along narrow streets as in some Breton town.

By now, the Macdonalds had completed barely half their journey. Beyond Quebec City there were no roads, or none that anyone would risk trying by stagecoach. Canada's entire highway system was made up then of its rivers and lakes. (The one great cross-country trip, undertaken just for show, was Governor General Lord Sydenham's amazing 1840 journey from Toronto to Montreal in a sleigh with a bed in it, completed in just thirty-six hours, a record that stood until the railways came along.)*

Their second voyage lasted some four weeks, first from Quebec City to Montreal, then on to Kingston. It would have been as uncomfortable as their ocean crossing. They made their way first in a bateau and then in a Durham boat, each open to the elements, moving slowly up the St. Lawrence, sometimes pushed by sail-power, sometimes pulled by oxen and by oars, but often both pulled and pushed by the male passengers as they jumped into the chill water to squeeze the boat past shallows and between rocks.

---

* The real hero of this feat wasn't so much Sydenham as a stagecoach operator in Toronto (York), William Weller, who organized the relays of horses needed to maintain an average speed of fifteen miles an hour. For his contributions, Weller received four hundred dollars and a gold watch.

On August 13, 1820, the family made it to Kingston. In Colonel Macpherson's house, packed in with his own family, they could at last rest, eat properly, clean their clothes and, most important, begin to learn about their new country.

~

Of all the towns in early Upper Canada where Hugh Macdonald might have gone, Kingston was perhaps the best possible place for an imaginative boy to grow up. With a population of around four thousand people, it was the biggest centre in the colony, even larger than York (to be renamed Toronto in 1834). Above all, it encompassed within its boundaries an uncommonly wide range of human experience.

It had a military garrison of red-coated British soldiers, who regularly emerged from Fort Henry to march through the streets to the beat of drums and the peep of pipes. It was a port. Tied up alongside its finger piers jutting out from the shore, throughout the summer and into the fall, were thirty to forty sailing ships, from three-masters to fore-and-aft schooners, and, later, steamships belching columns of smoke as they prepared to chug off to York and Montreal, Oswego and Niagara. To the north, the dense, forbidding forest came close to the town's limits; inside it, almost always hiding out of sight, were Indians. From spring to fall, waves of immigrants arrived in Kingston; after a few weeks' rest and burdened down by provisions, the newcomers would head on, either westwards to the softer, richer country beyond the town of York or, by turning right at some point along Lake Ontario, plunge northwards into the forests to try their luck at some isolated spot as pioneers—in the manner of Susanna Moodie and Catharine Parr Traill and their unhardy husbands. Kingston itself lacked a rural hinterland because the Precambrian

Shield came right to the town, but farmers did well in the good soil of Prince Edward County some forty miles to the west and supplied the growing town with food.

The Kingston of those days was rude and rowdy and raunchy rather than scrubbed and neat and dignified as today. It was also exceedingly dangerous. Immigrants often arrived riddled with disease, touching off a typhoid epidemic in 1828, a cholera epidemic in 1832, a truly terrible typhus epidemic in 1847 (during which 1,200 immigrants and townsfolk had to be buried in a mass grave) and yet another cholera outbreak in 1849. Soldiers and sailors brawled with each other and with the locals in incomparably rougher versions of the occasional town-gown confrontations of today.

Kingston's one constant has always been its history. Whoever occupied it commanded the entry point to the chain of Great Lakes as well as the exit point from the interior, on down the

Kingston. When the Macdonalds arrived in 1820, it was Upper Canada's largest town, with some four thousand people. It was also an important transshipment point for goods going up or down the St. Lawrence. Again, a view by William Bartlett.

St. Lawrence River to the Atlantic. The French built Fort Frontenac as far back as 1673. The Loyalists arrived in 1784, laid out a plan of streets and housing plots, and drew lots for the best of them. The town's importance as a transfer point for cargo and people would soon be enhanced by the construction, eastwards, of the Lachine Canal to Montreal and, northwards, of the Rideau Canal, snaking its way up to Bytown (later Ottawa). The starting point was the mouth of the Cataraqui River, which formed Kingston's harbour.

Later, a major share of Kingston's historical aura would derive from its association with Macdonald. No other Canadian leader has ever been as intimately connected to any place as he was to Kingston. A boy when he arrived, he was educated and established himself in business there; he represented the town for the greater part of his political career, winning thirteen elections there; and he is buried in its Cataraqui Cemetery. Kingston still commemorates him on two occasions each year—the anniversaries of his birth and his death. Above all, Kingston provided Macdonald with the raw material for the greatest of his political gifts—his matchless understanding of life as it is actually lived and of people as they actually live it, with all their faults and follies, interspersed with occasional spasms of altruism and even idealism. Charles Dickens, who came through in 1842, dismissed Kingston as "a very poor town"; had he stopped for a while, Dickens would have found it a microcosm of the human condition.

Cows and sheep, pigs and chickens ran freely through Kingston's streets, which, when it rained, were deep in mud, dirty and pungent from the leavings of animals—and sometimes of humans too. The only means by which a pedestrian could make it from one planked sidewalk to the opposite side of the road without sinking into the gummy, stinking mass was by using the occasional narrow crosswalk of flagstones or cobbles. The Precambrian Shield lay just below the surface, so the sewer system was primitive, with shallow and odiferous "privy pits." In winter, workers carried the night soil onto the ice in the harbour, to slide to the bottom once spring arrived. Of course, all these things were standard in British North American towns in the early nineteenth century, their one aesthetic advance over today being the absence of any overhead tangle of telephone and hydro wires.

Rural Canadians, who made up more than four in five of all Canadians, lived lives that for a great many were nasty, brutish, short and bitterly cold. Alexander Tilloch Galt, who would work alongside Macdonald in the battle for Confederation, provided a first-rate summary of country life in a report to his London bosses in a British land-settlement company: "A settlement in the backwoods of Canada, however romantic and pleasing may be the accounts generally published of it, has nothing but stern reality and hardship connected with it," he wrote. "Alone in the woods in his log cabin with his family, tired from his day's work and knowing that the morrow brings but the same toil, the migrant will find but few of his fancies realized . . . for the first years, the emigrant to succeed must work as hard and suffer perhaps greater privations than had he remained in Great Britain."

Unlike today, though, conditions in the towns were, if anything, worse than those in the countryside—except, perhaps, for women, who suffered terribly from the loneliness of pioneer life. In towns and villages, women at least had companionship and some kind of support networks. But townies were much more likely than their country kin to succumb to diseases caused by everything from epidemics to poor or non-existent sanitation. Unlike pioneer settlers, they were self-sufficient neither in food nor in wood for winter fuel. In the towns, a great many jobs ended in early November; the ports closed because of ice, and all public works and construction were halted. At the same time that the price of food and firewood soared, the wages of those still at work in small manufacturing plants, stores and offices were often cut by a third or even half. As the winter wore on, workers spent as much as a fifth of their miserable wages on wood to keep themselves warm. The cost of bread typically went up by as much as 50 per cent. Commonly, those who had jobs went straight to bed when they returned to their barely heated lodgings. Some practical types even committed crimes so they would be sent to a partially heated jail. The late spring, when food and fuel prices were at their highest, was known as "the pinching season."

Yet, as historian Judith Fingard has noted, there was a conspicuous "absence of mass demonstrations and violent crime amongst the poor during the winters of greatest suffering."* The poor were kept quiescent by exhaustion, by the bitter cold and, far from least, by a deep and seldom-questioned respect for the law. Macdonald learned all about this real, unromantic, urban Canada while he grew up in Kingston, and from his boyhood stays with his roving family in nearby Prince Edward County he gained an understanding of rural Canada as well.

Kingston was actually better off than other towns in Upper Canada. An 1837 guide for emigrants called it "perhaps the finest-built town in the Province," while T.R. Preston, an English visitor at around the same time, said it "resembled an English village but somewhat stragglingly built, though it possessed in its substantial parts some very substantial homes." Kingston possessed

---

* The source is Fingard's study "The Winter's Tale: The Seasonal Contours of Pre-Industrial Poverty in British North America, 1815–1860."

one invaluable urban asset: lots of limestone. When the Macdonalds arrived, most houses were constructed of logs or hewn lumber—a motley array of dwellings often destroyed by fire. With the completion of the Rideau Canal, though, a lot of Scottish stonemasons were suddenly looking for work, and by the 1840s Kingston had begun to acquire more substantial buildings made of the local stone.*

A few of the leading citizens commissioned remarkable houses in the delicate Adamesque style and began to install beautiful mouldings and chimney pieces in their mansions. Some major public buildings, far grander than the small town itself, were constructed during these years—a hospital, a penitentiary, a lunatic asylum, a courthouse and, later, a superb town hall. Kingston even became important enough for a stagecoach to make a twice-weekly trip between it and Montreal—a bone-shattering experience, for sure, but with the benefit that, unlike in England, highwaymen were rare.

The Kingston of Macdonald's day even encompassed some of the finer things of life. It had a lending library and two newspapers. Occasionally, travelling theatre groups performed for a night or two, and in the churches there were organ recitals and, on Sundays, sonorous, scary sermons. Band concerts were particularly popular, and for the active, so were cricket matches, fox hunts and horse races—all made possible by the military garrison stationed in the town. The military, moreover, made one major cultural breakthrough: on the frozen lake, members of the Royal Canadian Rifles developed, by hit and miss and bump and grind, a new game using skates, field hockey sticks and a lacrosse ball.

The most intense competition in Kingston revolved around

---

* In the absence of any zoning regulations, grand houses, shacks, stores and grog shops all jostled against one another.

the sexes, as Dickens would have noted had he lingered. The highest ambition of the wives of successful merchants and farmers was to marry off a daughter to a bachelor English officer. Few fulfilled this aspiration, because, in the cruel comment of one witness, they all "still smelt of bread and butter." Nevertheless, the young officers praised the way Kingston chaperones were less watchful than those back in England.

The underside of life flourished here too. One visitor described the streets as "swarming with drunkards and prostitutes"—the inevitable consequence of so many soldiers and sailors and immigrants passing through. Kingston's Common Council, or town council, reported in 1841 that there was a drink shop for every seven or eight men, ranging from taverns or pubs to "low dram shops" or shebeens. In counterpoint, a local temperance society was started up; it suggested, among other things, the installation of a treadmill as the best way to deal with drunkenness and better "the morals of the lower classes."

If Kingston was in many ways a brutal society, so at the time was all of British North America and, indeed, just about the entire world. Drunken soldiers and sailors were easy marks for muggers. Soldiers often deserted across the nearby American border; those caught were flogged at a triangular wooden frame, to the beat of a drum. Punishments everywhere were brutal: inmates in the penitentiary in Kingston included a child of eight who began his three-year sentence with a flogging by the cat; another inmate, ten years old, received 102 strokes of rawhide. Hangings were a public attraction—one steamer brought in two hundred "tourists," including children, to watch an execution. A man was hanged for stealing a cow.

After three months of living jammed up in the Macpherson home, Hugh Macdonald moved his family out on its own. He opened a store in the centre of town, and the six of them lived in the rooms above. Besides a mix of foodstuffs and hardware, he offered customers "groceries, wines, brandy, shrub [a cordial], vinegar, powder and shot, English window-glass and putty, etc." The enterprise failed quickly. Hugh opened another general store in another location. It soon failed too.

Amid these setbacks, the family had to come to terms with an almost unimaginable trauma: the second son,

NEW GOODS

THE Subscriber begs leave to inform his friends and the public, that, in addition to his former Stock of dry goods, he has received an assortment of FANCY GOODS, suitable for the season.

The Subscriber has also, always on hand, a supply of Groceries, Wines, Jamaica Spirits, Brandy, Gin, Shrub and Vinegar, Powder and Shot, English Window Glass and Putty &c. &c. all of which he is now selling on the most reasonable terms.

HUGH MACDONALD.

Kingston, 3d July 1821.

Hugh Macdonald's ad in the Kingston Chronicle *of July 27, 1821, showed, for him, a rare business sense as the only one in the paper to carry an illustration of his wares.*

James, was killed at the age of five and a half by a family servant named Kennedy. It's impossible to be certain what happened. One day, Hugh and Helen went out, leaving John A. and James at home in Kennedy's care. The servant was a secret drinker. In one account, Kennedy got angry with James for crying for his parents and lashed out at him with a stick. In another, he lunged drunkenly at him and James slipped, hitting his head on an andiron. Whatever the cause, the young boy died while seven-year-old John A. witnessed his murder or manslaughter. The May 3 issue of the Kingston *Chronicle* in 1822 carried this sad obituary: "On Monday the 22 ult., James, second son of Mr. Hugh Macdonald, Merchant of this town, aged five years and six months."

That newspaper notice was the family's entire recorded response. No charge was ever brought against Kennedy. Hugh entered no record of the death in his memorandum book of family events, though John A. later added it to the chronology. No

burial place for the boy has ever been identified; he is not listed among those interred in the family plot at Cataraqui Cemetery.*
Nor is there any reference to the tragedy in any of the family letters that have been preserved. At the time, the most common reference likely to be mentioned in family correspondence would have been to a locket or brooch containing a circle of the lost child's hair, commonly worn for years afterwards by a bereaved mother. Yet no surviving letter contains any mention of such a commemorative object.

This silent reaction can be attributed far more readily to acceptance than to callousness. Then, death was part of life, and as any stroll through any old cemetery will confirm, to be young then was to be close to death. A survey done in Montreal in 1867 found that two out of every five children never reached the age of five. As well, grief may have been generally subdued because it amounted to an expression of doubt about the existence of an afterlife. Religion provided healing; a loved one who had died was often referred to as one who "went before"—to a place where the others would later join the departed.

The single certain consequence of this tragedy was that, henceforth, the Macdonald family's entire hopes rested on the shoulders of John Alexander—the last surviving male heir among the original three.

After his second enterprise in Kingston had failed, Hugh decided to change his location entirely. In 1824, four years after their

---

* This plot was purchased by John A. Macdonald in 1850. The remains of Hugh Macdonald, who had been buried in the old "Lower" Burial Ground, were brought there, but not, apparently, the remains of James Macdonald.

arrival, he moved the family out to Hay Bay, on the lakeshore to the west of Kingston, where he opened yet another store. Young John, by now nine years old, continued with his schooling in the nearby village of Adolphustown.

Each day he walked three miles to school and, in the late afternoon, three miles back. This commute was entirely ordinary. His sisters, Margaret and Louisa, made the same walk with him. The three of them played well together, often as soldiers in a game where he was always the officer, and they got into the usual scrapes. As the only boy now, and anyway his mother's favourite, John was spoiled rotten. Margaret, small and delicate, possessed an aptitude for seeming vulnerable. Louisa, by contrast, was tall, with a stern face and a long, thick nose. At best she could be called plain; in later years she protested that someone had compared her to her brother, "the ugliest man in Canada." Independent and stubborn like her mother, she was John A.'s pal.

One of the most surprising comments Macdonald ever made was to his confidential secretary and biographer, Joseph Pope: "I never had a boyhood. From fifteen I began to earn my living." It is Macdonald's rare lapse into unguarded bitterness that makes this admission so surprising. More astounding still, his complaint was quite untrue. Macdonald did indeed have to quit school at the age of fifteen, when he began his legal career, but this pattern was almost universal then. The phenomenon of adolescence had yet to be discovered (or invented); a survey done in 1871 found that one in four boys aged eleven to fifteen were working in some kind of a job. Typically for the times, Egerton Ryerson, the great Canadian educator, espoused the proposition that children were small men in need of greater instruction than older siblings. In any case, Macdonald's boyhood was more agreeable than that of most boys. At home, he experienced no shortage of love, and he benefited from the kindliness of an extended family. While the family was pinched for money, that was not in the least unusual, and of little concern to a boy.

The explanation for Macdonald's bitterness may reside in another comment he made to Pope. "If I had had a university education," he reflected, "I should probably have entered the path of literature and acquired distinction therein." Looking back from a time near the end of his life, Macdonald may have been expressing an uneasy sense that politics hadn't stretched his intellect enough and that he had missed out on opportunities to express the creative and imaginative side of his character.* Perhaps he was thinking enviously of British prime minister Benjamin Disraeli, his ideological and physical look-alike, who, amid the grinding pressures of politics, had found time to write no fewer than twenty novels, *Tancred* and *Endymion* the best received among them.†

While at school—the length of his tenure there being entirely average—Macdonald received an education that was well above the norm. The schools he attended, first in Kingston and then in Adolphustown, were the typical one-room schools where children of all ages sat at a raised board that ran around three sides of the room and served as their desk. They faced the fourth, open side, where the teacher had a smaller desk. The only other

---

* In 1830 there were only two universities in British North America—Dalhousie and McGill. Sending Macdonald to either of them would have been quite beyond the family's financial capacity.

† Macdonald, who closely followed news from Britain, would also have been aware that Disraeli eventually commanded advances of an amazing £10,000, more even than Dickens or Trollope—a reflection, naturally, more of his appeal as a celebrity than of his skill as a novelist.

pieces of furniture were a pail of water and a stove. Most teachers in the region were Scots, each known as a "dominie"—an apt phrase because of the strap they always carried. Books and paper were rare. For most children, this schooling was their entire education. In Ontario, school was not compulsory until 1874—and then for a minimum of only four months a year—a rule that was regularly ignored by farmers' sons.

Macdonald mostly had a grand time at school. Boys liked him because he could tell stories and knew tricks, and because he wasn't afraid of the masters. They also had a wary respect for his Scottish temper. Girls liked him, even though they teased him as "Ugly John"—as he most certainly was, with his absurdly crinkly hair and outsized nose. But they would have noted with approval, certainly with interest, that he was a bit of a dandy, with a taste in gaudy waistcoats. Wit more than compensated for his lack of looks. At one dance, Macdonald forgot he was due to partner a particular girl in a quadrille. She rejected his abject apologies until he flung himself at her feet, proclaiming manically, "Remember, oh remember, the fascination of the turkey." With her uncontrollable laughter came forgiveness. He did all the customary boyish things, getting into scrapes and, at the age of thirteen, writing florid poetry to a pretty cousin. Although he seldom took part in sports, he was good at running barefoot, at skating and at dancing. Early on, he showed some skill at mathematics, an unusual accuracy in spelling and an insatiable appetite for reading.

Two factors pushed Macdonald onto a life's arc different from that of most of his fellow students: he was a Scot, and he had a mother who was determined that he would be more than an ordinary man.

After a couple of years of making the long daily walk to the school in Adolphustown, John was sent by his parents to Kingston to attend the Midland District Grammar School. It was run by a graduate of Oxford University, the Reverend John Wilson. Annual tuition fees were seventy pounds, representing a steep sacrifice for the family. Here, Macdonald learned Latin and French as well as English and mathematics. (His French grammar book, dated May 28, 1825, still survives.) He stayed with the Macphersons, where he was thoroughly petted and spoiled. Years later, his nephew, John Pennington Macpherson, recalled in a slight biography of his famous relative how Macdonald would read compulsively, quite untroubled by the noisy antics and quarrels of the large family around him. In the summers he went back to the Bay of Quinte area—to Glenora, where his father had moved to run a grist mill. It, again, soon failed.*

In 1829, the fourteen-year-old Macdonald moved to a new establishment for "general and classical education" run by a recent newcomer, the Reverend John Cruickshank. There were some twenty pupils, from six to sixteen years old; among them was Oliver Mowat, later a Father of Confederation along with Macdonald and later still premier of Ontario. The school's standards were high, the local Scots having decided that the Midland District School was inadequate to give their children a quick start in life. What really set this grammar school apart was that it was coeducational, one of the first in Upper Canada. At the risk of reading too much into it, Macdonald's coeducational experience, reinforced by the female-centred household he grew up in, may explain one of the qualities that set him apart from most men of his day—and of a good many still. In the company of women, Macdonald was always wholly at his ease. He was never awkward or shy or predatory with them. He could flirt and play the gallant, but he never patronized women.

---

* The stone mill, little changed, still stands in Glenora, Prince Edward County.

As is common enough, Macdonald was his own principal teacher. He read omnivorously—history, biographies, politics, poetry, geography. His most remarked-upon scholastic skill was his handwriting—clear, large, even and fluid. (His letters would be a delight to later scholars.) Cruickshank was always proud to show Macdonald's compositions to new students, and he kept them for years afterwards as models of penmanship.

Macdonald's preparation for life ended in his fifteenth year. From then on, he began to live it. But he'd already learned a great deal about life's essence—the ways and the whys of how people behave.

THREE

The Right Time to Be a Scot

A man's a man for a' that.
Robert Burns

John A. Macdonald placed his first foot on life's ladder by apprenticing to an established Kingston lawyer. To qualify for this post, he had first to go to Toronto, to the offices of the Law Society of Upper Canada, and, before a panel of benchers, sit an exam that involved some Latin and some mathematics. He passed, paid the fee of fifteen pounds, and returned to Kingston as he had come, by steamboat. There was then no formal training for lawyers or any law degree. Now just short of sixteen, he worked long days as a law clerk, running errands and putting newly written letters through a letter press to squeeze out copies on onion-skin paper before the ink was dry; at night he crammed through textbooks.

To become a clerk to an established lawyer constituted a substantial step forward. The one taken by Macdonald was more like a leap. No matter how junior his post, he had gained entry to what was probably the most sought-after legal premises in Kingston—the office of George Mackenzie. Although only thirty-five, Mackenzie was already one of the town's most successful and highly regarded lawyers.

The crucial introduction to Mackenzie had come to Macdonald as a gift from the family's patron, Colonel Macpherson. Mackenzie would also have been well aware of the quality of the education his clerk had received at Reverend Cruickshank's school. A couple of years later, Macdonald's budding legal career benefited from his being asked by another relative, Lowther Macpherson, to fill in temporarily, with Mackenzie's permission, in his Prince Edward County law office while he himself was away trying to recover from an illness; Macdonald thereby gained management experience at the earliest age. While in Kingston, he made his first adult friendships, most particularly with a bright and attractive young man called Charles Stuart. The preceptor of St. Andrew's Church there took a liking to Macdonald and, while teasing him as "a free thinker of the worst kind," engaged him in biblical discussions that gave the young law clerk valuable practice in how best to organize his arguments. Moreover, around this time, Hugh Macdonald was rescued from his uninterrupted business failures by a relative, Francis Harper, who slipped him into a secure if lowly sinecure post as a clerk in Kingston's newly established Commercial Bank of the Midland District.

To all these individuals who enabled Macdonald to make his first career steps a good deal more quickly than he would have otherwise, and to others like them who later provided similar assistance as his trot quickened into a canter, there was one obvious and defining characteristic. Each of them was a Scot. Had Macdonald not been a Scot himself, he wouldn't have moved up nearly as fast. His own talents mattered a great deal, of course. But it mattered critically that other Scots were prepared to help him because he was one of their own; it mattered as much that they themselves were doing well enough to be able to provide real help. Before Macdonald's ascent is tracked, it's necessary first to place him in the context within which he operated. As he moved upwards, he did so as a member of a distinct and uncommonly successful ethnic group.

~

Macdonald came by his Scottishness through his parents, of course. The benefits of this gift to him were multiplied many times over by another happenstance—one of timing. Macdonald was a Scot when it was the best time in history to be a Scot.

Early in the nineteenth century, the Scots exploded outwards from a small, poor, backward society to become, collectively, one of the most admired and respected of all societies of the day; more remarkable yet, a great many of them had gone on to become the first "citizens of the world." Through the greater part of the century, Scots accomplished more in more places around the globe than did any other people. Nowhere was this more true than in British North America, the country to which Macdonald's parents had just brought him.

Until about the middle of the eighteenth century, Scots were regarded generally as rude and crude at best, and at worst as outright savages. They were brave, of course, with the special allure of a fiercely proud, freedom-loving people, but backward, self-enclosed, impossible to comprehend. (Indeed, they were not dissimilar to the Métis of the prairies, with whom Macdonald would later so tragically find it difficult to come to terms.) The Scots all knew how to eat porridge properly (standing up, with salt) and how to position exactly the *skein dhu* dagger (in the stocking, just below a kilt-clad knee). Suddenly, before the eighteenth century ended, all this parochialism was replaced by intellectualism and internationalism. Of the transformation, Voltaire would declare,

"It is to Scotland that we look for our idea of civilization."

In a transformation that has few national equivalents, a poor, quasi-feudal society turned almost overnight into a society of ideas and creative energy. The catalyst of change was the Scottish Enlightenment, which, during the period from 1740 to 1790, made the small capital of Edinburgh into an intellectual and cultural rival of any other city of the time, only London and Paris excepted. The two superstars of the Scottish Enlightenment were David Hume, the first modern philosopher, and Adam Smith, the first modern economist. At the time, a cluster of others were as well regarded as these two, among them Lord Kames, Francis Hutcheson, Adam Ferguson, William Reid and William Robertson.

This extraordinary story has been told lovingly and adroitly by Arthur Herman in his book *How the Scots Invented the World*, subtitled, with only a slight exaggeration, *The True Story of How Western Europe's Poorest Country Created Our World and Everything in It*. Herman's thesis is that Edinburgh attained "a self-consciously modern view" that is now "so deeply rooted in the assumptions and institutions that govern our lives that we often miss its significance, not to mention its origins." In fact, Herman never resolves satisfactorily why this achievement should have happened in the particular society of Scotland, so small and backward. The nearest he comes is to argue that, after union with England in 1707, Scottish intellectuals had to cope with the challenge, today common, of "deal[ing] with a dominant culture that one admired but that threatened to overwhelm one's own heritage and oneself with it."

Those Scots were grappling with some of the most intractable of challenges of our own time, such as how to exploit the benefits of capitalism without destroying society's ethical framework, and how to balance the aspirations of the individual against the needs of the collectivity. Hutcheson decreed that

society's ultimate purpose was "the greatest good of the greatest number." In *The Wealth of Nations*, Smith unveiled one of
the most liberating of modern ideas—that the interests of the
community could be advanced better by the self-interest than
by the "benevolence" of the butcher, the baker and all the
other upwardly clambering capitalists.* Hume decreed that
"Liberty is the perfection of society," but believed equally that
"authority must be acknowledged as essential to its [freedom's]
very existence." Two observations by Ferguson could have
been minted as mantras for Macdonald: "Man is born in society
and there he remains" and, even more so, "No government is
copied from a plan: the secrets of government are locked up in
human nature."

These Scots were all progressive conservatives. They believed
in natural democracy and in meritocracy, and because they were
intensely practical men they believed in education. A 1694 law
decreed that each parish in Scotland had to have its own school;
England wouldn't catch up until the end of the nineteenth century.
Scots' churches (except for the Catholic ones) elected their own
pastors. Yet the people were skeptical about the fashionable new
doctrine of political democracy—and they were outright hostile
to revolution. More than a fifth of the Loyalists, for example, were
Scots, among them Flora Macdonald, the Scottish heroine who hid
Prince Charles from the English soldiers after his defeat at
Culloden, and who eventually made her way back to the Isle of
Skye by way of Nova Scotia. A cause for this skepticism was their

---

* One observation by Smith in *The Wealth of Nations* of more direct interest
to Canadians was that Britain should let go its North American colonies, both
to escape from the cost of "supporting any part of their civil or military estab-
lishments" and, more urgently, from a cause as sure to be lost, in his view, as
had the thirteen American colonies.

disbelief in the perfectibility of human nature. Ferguson warned, "The individual considers his community only so far as it can be rendered subservient to his personal advancement and profit." Common sense was their golden rule, not least in the Philosophy of Common Sense, which would play such a part in the development of higher education in Canada.

These enlightened Scots most certainly believed in progress, including technological progress. James Watt developed the steam engine, for example, and John McAdam, hard-surfaced roads. They also believed in the ability of a society to improve itself; otherwise, all that education and that unleashing of enlightened self-interest would be in vain. Yet they were very conservative. As Lord Kames put it, "Without property, labour and industry were in vain."

The Scottish Enlightenment had run its course before Macdonald was born, and as a young child he moved thousands of miles away from Scotland. Yet in Kingston most of his teachers were Scots. His mother's love of reading, which he inherited and which was so rare among his peers in those early years in Canada, came directly from the respect for knowledge that the Enlightenment implanted in all Scots. All kinds of echoes of the ideas initiated in Edinburgh can be found in Macdonald's own thinking—his disbelief in the possibility of human progress, his belief in the possibility of causing a society to progress (why else throw a railway across a wilderness?), his indifference to political democracy and yet his inherently democratic nature, as you'd expect for someone coming from a society whose national poet laureate had proclaimed "A man's a man for a' that." No less so, Macdonald would have accepted Robbie Burns's skepticism, so quintessentially Scottish: "The best-laid schemes o' mice an' men / Gang aft a-gley, / An' lea'e us nought but grief an' pain, / For promised joy." Macdonald wasn't a product of the Scottish Enlightenment, but he was, because of it, an enlightened man.

Macdonald's most direct debt to the Scottish Enlightenment was cultural. The Scots who produced all those ideas weren't solitary geniuses sharpening quill pens in attics. They thought collectively, amid company, and over dinners that ended with lots of broken crockery, or in pubs and taverns amid arguing and shouting and brawling. Even the brainiest among them put on no airs, nor suffered any in others. Their interest in ideas was how to get things done, not to talk about what should and might be done. As them, so Macdonald.

Benjamin Disraeli once remarked that although he had been in many countries, "I have never been in one without finding a Scotchman, and I never found a Scotchman who was not at the head of the poll"—that's to say, on top. This outwardness was one of the most remarkable after-effects of the Scottish Enlightenment. Commonly, minorities react to defeat and occupation by turning in on themselves; the Scots, a century after Culloden, burst out all over the world. The men from the Orkneys joined the Hudson's Bay Company—the joke went—to get warm. Their sheer hardiness as northerners, their conversion to modernity ahead of everyone else, and the excellence of their education (out of a population of 1.4 million at home, twenty thousand people earned their living through writing and publishing) gave them a confidence, a resilience and a distinctive sense of self. So did two other factors. The Enlightenment had changed everyone's image of the Scots. Any society that could produce a David Hume and an Adam Smith could not be a society of barbarians. Their reputation now went before them and opened doors to them.

In their own separate ways, a monarch and a novelist presented a second gift to the Scots. Early in the nineteenth century, Queen Victoria and Sir Walter Scott rediscovered the romance of the Highlands, or, more accurately, invented it. In truth, the Highlands were a brutal place; the standard of living there was lower than that of the Plains Indians of North America. But just as the film *Braveheart* was irresistible, so were Scott's novels and the tartans that Victoria made everyone wear at Balmoral. One of Macdonald's distinguishing characteristics among nineteenth-century Canadians was that, whenever he went to London and moved among "the greats" (whether by office or by birth), he held his own dignity. He never exhibited the least sign of "colonial cringe" or felt any need to apologize for being a colonial.

The Scots of the nineteenth century were by no means perfect: they were clannish, hot-tempered, parsimonious and they drank an incredible amount—"the most drunken nation on the face of the earth," according to *The Scots Magazine*. As the century progressed, Scottish culture turned increasingly inwards, judgmental and holier-than-thou. Macdonald, influenced by earlier attitudes, was a product of Scottish culture at its best.

For the Macdonalds, when they moved to Canada, the immediate benefit of being Scots was that they weren't alone in this strange, hard land but were enveloped by a clan. Besides the many Macphersons, the Macdonalds could claim ties of kinship to Shaws, Grants, Clarks and Greenes. In Kingston itself there were institutions like the St. Andrew's Society and the Celtic Society to provide the young Macdonald with contacts, social connections, insider gossip and information about upcoming business deals. Clannishness could hurt as well as help. As Pope wrote in his biography, Macdonald could never bring himself to trust fully a Campbell, even though one member of that clan, Alexander Campbell, was his later law partner and political organizer, simply because the Campbells had massacred the Macdonalds in the Pass of Glencoe in 1692.

As Macdonald moved upwards, the circles of Scots ready to let him through their doors kept widening. Among the first directors of the Bank of Montreal—*the* bank, by a wide margin— eight were Scots; Canada's entire banking system was modelled on Scotland's. Almost every member of the original Canadian Pacific Railway syndicate was a Scot, including the founder-president, George Stephen. So was the country's greatest railway engineer, Sandford Fleming, the inventor of standard time. By 1880, even though numbering just one in seven European Canadians, half of Canada's industrial leaders would be Scots or the sons of Scottish immigrants. In Montreal, the country's financial and industrial capital, the city's business leaders included a McGill, a MacTavish, a Redpath. At the country's largest corporate enterprise in the nineteenth century, the Hudson's Bay Company, four in five employees were Scots. The country's biggest and best newspaper, the Toronto *Globe*, was owned and edited by a Scot, George Brown. All three of Canada's first universities—McGill, Dalhousie, Toronto—were founded by Scots; in *The Scot in America*, published in 1896, Peter Ross reckoned that "the entire educational system of the country, from the primary school to the university, is more indebted to the Scottish section of the community than to any other."

As for politics, once Macdonald got there, he would be crowded around by fellow countrymen. Both he and Canada's second prime minister, Alexander Mackenzie, were Scots; so were the first two premiers of Ontario, John Sandfield Macdonald and Oliver Mowat. Of the "Big Four" among the Fathers of Confederation, all but George-Étienne Cartier would be Scots— Macdonald, Brown and Alexander Tilloch Galt.

Macdonald naturally played the advantage of Scottishness for all it was worth. When he met his first governor general, he did so wearing the "fine Macdonald Soft Tartan Kilt with Green Riband Rosette . . . [and] a silk Velvet Highland Jacket" that he'd bought in Edinburgh as part of his trip around Britain in 1842. He would drop Scottish sayings into speeches, such as "He'll cool in the same boots he got warm in."

Yet he didn't sound much like a Scot. His burr was far less pronounced than that of at least two other Scottish-born political personalities of his time, George Brown and Alexander Mackenzie. Alexander Campbell, who knew him well and was himself from Kingston, wrote in an undated memoir that Macdonald was "in tone of voice & manner as thoroughly a Bay of Quinte boy as if he had been born there."* A complicating factor here is that, as is often the case with good storytellers, Macdonald was an excellent mimic. Yet Campbell was on to something. In speech, as well as in many other ways, Macdonald was far more a Canadian than he was a Scot. One journalist wrote of Macdonald, "It was long a moot question where he was born." In a couple of substantial ways, he wasn't that much of a Scot: during all his many visits to England, he went only once to Scotland—on his first trip; also, he never had himself photographed looking like a Scot by wearing his tartan.

As a politician, Macdonald benefited in one last critical way from his Scottishness. For the most part, the four principal European ethnic groups in nineteenth-century Canada—English,

---

* An excellent article on Macdonald's speech patterns, from which some of this material is drawn, is Ged Martin's piece of splendid title in the *British Journal of Canadian Studies* (2004), "Sir John Eh? Macdonald."

French, Irish and Scot—thoroughly disliked each other, while the Irish (Protestant and Catholic) disliked their own countrymen, if anything, even more. Within these discontents, though, there was one striking exception: the French and the Scots got on exceedingly well. It made a great difference that the man who made us, and who did so primarily by connecting together, politically, Canada's two great ethnic solitudes, should have been a Scot.

In the light of what he would achieve as a man, one aspect of Macdonald's youth is surprising. No one who knew him then recalled his having ever displayed any vaulting ambition or recounted any anecdote about Macdonald describing some hero he planned to emulate or to exceed. True, his mother predicted great things for him, but many mothers say that about their children. Several of his boyhood contemporaries, as well as some of his teachers, expected him to do well. No one, though, forecast that he would do better, by far, than anyone in the country had ever done. They hadn't misjudged his talents; they had failed to take account of his capacity for growth and, no less, his inexhaustible competitiveness.

FOUR

Horse Dealing, Tavern Keeping and the Law

⁓

Say nothing on business without receiving a fee in advance.
Fellow lawyer's advice to John A. Macdonald

The suggestion that Macdonald should aim for a career in law had actually come first from his father. Hugh Macdonald pointed out that "the province was yet only in its infancy, was rapidly growing, and would soon need a horde of professional men." For Hugh, such acuity in financial matters was rare, but this time he was absolutely right. Although clearly unusually intelligent, Macdonald had no money, so the attraction of a legal career was obvious: law required no start-up capital and no training at a university. Once the apprenticeship was served, the profession guaranteed at least modest prosperity to all but the indolent or the inebriated. As John Langton, Canada's first auditor general, remarked, "I know of no money-making business in Canada except the law, store-keeping, tavern-keeping and perhaps I might add, horse-trading."

Practising law came as easily to Macdonald as breathing. He soon showed himself deft at mastering briefs, remembering and using detail to good effect and, most effective of all, having a talent for reading judges and juries. By the age of twenty-three he was already defending men on trial for their lives against some of the best-known counsels in the province. A few years later he was well on the way to establishing himself as a leading commercial lawyer. Had he stayed with the law, Macdonald would surely have made a great deal of money and, as did others, eventually used it to buy himself a knighthood and retire to leisurely comfort in England.

When George Mackenzie took Macdonald as an apprentice in 1830, Mackenzie specialized in corporate law, handling the accounts of local farmers, businessmen and merchants. Intelligent and amiable, he was one of Kingston's leading lawyers and would soon be nominated as the Conservative candidate for Frontenac. As a mark of his special regard for his clerk, Mackenzie invited Macdonald to board at his own house in Kingston. There the young man began to learn something about the graces in life, such as the joys of a fine dining room and an ample library.

From Mackenzie, Macdonald picked up two of the most valuable of all legal lessons. The first was to "say nothing on business without receiving a fee in advance." The other amounted to an admonition to remember that, in law, personality counts for a good deal more than knowing the statutes. Mackenzie, after hearing that his junior was acting in a standoffish manner with clients, warned him, "I do not think you are so free and lively with people as a young man eager for their good should be. A dead-and-alive way with them never goes." Later, in a third gift to his junior, Mackenzie sent Macdonald to the countryside to open a branch office for him in the town of Napanee, thereby providing independent responsibility and experience.

Hallowell (later Picton) is the Prince Edward County town where Macdonald filled in at the law practice of an ailing relative.

To a remarkable extent, good luck quickened the pace of Macdonald's advance as a lawyer, one of the comparatively few occasions in his career when he didn't have to create most of his own good fortune. Its source was the bad luck of several other lawyers. Macdonald's first stint on his own occurred when he temporarily replaced his sick relative, Lowther Macpherson, returning to Mackenzie's office when Macpherson died at sea after receiving treatment in England. In 1834 his own employer, Mackenzie, was struck down by the cholera epidemic of that year. Once he had set up his own shingle, Macdonald took over some of Mackenzie's accounts. Lastly, the sudden death in 1839 of another prominent Kingston lawyer, Henry Cassady, would enable Macdonald both to take over much of his business and to succeed him to the prime post of solicitor of the Commercial Bank of the Midland District.

Mostly, he advanced in his own way. From Mackenzie he had acquired the ambition to become a corporate lawyer. To do that, Macdonald opened his own office in Kingston in 1835. He posted a notice in the Kingston *Chronicle* that "John A. Macdonald, attorney, has opened his office . . . where he will attend to all the duties of the profession. Kingston, 24 August, 1835." At the time, he was only twenty years old, still a year short of being entitled to claim to be an attorney. He achieved that rank the next year when, after passing the necessary examination in Toronto, he was called to the bar. Soon afterwards, Macdonald himself took on two students of law. They were a remarkable pair. One was Alexander Campbell, later a cabinet minister under Macdonald and eventually lieutenant-governor of Ontario. The other was his one-time schoolmate Oliver Mowat, later a member of the legislature and, several years on, Macdonald's most relentless and effective political opponent as premier of Ontario. Macdonald came to loathe Mowat, remarking, in a reference to their schooldays together, "The one thing I have always admired about Mowat is his handwriting." ⌣

Macdonald set up his first office in rented quarters in Kingston's Quarry Street. A year later, early in 1836, both he and his entire family moved into a substantial house, two and a half storeys high and of roughcut limestone, on Rideau Street.* Within this residence, he had both his bedroom and his study in the attic, confirming that he was already a success as a lawyer and was now effectively the head of the family, in place of the diminished and scarcely more than tolerated Hugh Macdonald.

Three years later, Macdonald moved both his office and the family home to the more fashionable Queen Street. In this office, helped by his clerks Campbell and Mowat, he busied himself with lucrative

---

* This house, at 110 Rideau Street, still stands and has been converted into an exquisite small museum about Macdonald by its present owners, Donna Ivey and Norma Kelly. On a wallboard in the attic, the initials "L.M." have been carved, perhaps standing for Macdonald's sister Louisa, but more probably for his cousin Lowther Macpherson.

but tedious work, such as chasing down unpaid bills and searching titles. And then, abruptly, he gave it all up—not the law itself, but the kind of law he was engaged in. For two years, from 1837, Macdonald devoted himself entirely to the practice of criminal law.

His reasons for the switch can only be guessed at, because no record of his motive remains. However, a plausible explanation is easy to construct. As a criminal lawyer who took on dramatic cases, Macdonald got himself noticed well beyond the narrow confines of the Kingston business community. He was operating now in the arena where he would spend by far the greatest part of

A youthful Oliver Mowat, later Macdonald's implacable opponent as premier of Ontario, but at this time a clerk in his law office.

his life—the court of public opinion. And while there he was learning the arts of argument and of persuasion that would serve him all his political life. For a lawyer new in practice and still aged only twenty-two, he was taking a short-term gamble on a long-term goal, particularly given that he lost almost as many cases as he won.

Macdonald's first case involved William Brass, the son of a respected Loyalist accused of the horrendous crime of rape of an eight-year-old girl.* The sentence for such a crime was death.

---

* A prime source for the material in this section has been the excellent master's thesis "A Dead and Alive Way Never Does," by William Teatero for Queen's University in 1978.

Working with an experienced courtroom lawyer, Macdonald offered a triple defence: Brass was not guilty; he was the victim of a conspiracy; or he had been insane at the time the crime was committed. His legal opponent was William Draper, then solicitor general and later premier of the United Province of Canada. While Macdonald lost the case, the Kingston *British Whig* reported that "Mr. John A. Mcdonald [sic] . . . made a very able defence in favour of the unhappy prisoner." At Brass's execution, the rope proved to be too long and the wretched man fell to the ground from the gibbet, landing in his own coffin. He screamed out, "You see. I am innocent; this gallows was not meant for me." The sentence was nevertheless carried out, the second time with a rope of the proper length.

Macdonald won his next case. Peter Anderson was charged with the murder of a friend, James Cummings, whom he had followed into the woods with a rifle after a quarrel between them. Later, Cummings was found dead from a rifle wound. Macdonald handled this case alone. After extensive cross-examination of Crown and defence witnesses, he was able to argue that Anderson had been seen two miles from the scene of the crime at the time it was committed. To the surprise of the local newspapers, the jury rendered a not-guilty verdict. The *British Whig* praised Macdonald for "an excellent address." Campbell, who was then Macdonald's student at law, later observed in his memoir that Macdonald had won the jury over by his "humour and strong liking for anecdote more than for his professional knowledge."*

---

* There was always an edge to Campbell's comments about Macdonald. "He never became in my judgment a good lawyer," he said, "but was always a dangerous man in the courts." One cause, despite their long relationship, was very likely Campbell's resentment that Macdonald dropped him from the plum portfolio of minister of justice in 1882.

His third case attracted much wider attention. In 1837 William Lyon Mackenzie rose up against the colonial administration and staged a brief tragicomic uprising in the capital of York. In Kingston, eight of his supporters assembled with a few weapons, but when they realized that no one else was going to join them they returned home. Still, they had taken up arms against the King. Macdonald took the bold course of appealing directly to the judge for an acquittal of the rebels on the grounds that the self-incriminating affidavits the defendants had signed after their arrest had been executed illegally by a police magistrate. The judge agreed and directed the jury to acquit the eight accused.

Less dramatic in its legal consequence but of considerable political consequence was Macdonald's next case involving a prison warden, John Ashley, who had been arrested without a warrant and held for eight hours by Colonel Dundas, the commander of Fort Henry, on suspicion that he had provided the tools that had enabled fifteen rebel prisoners to escape by burrowing through the jail's four-foot-thick stone walls. On being released, Ashley brought a thousand-pound suit for damages. Macdonald argued that nothing justified Ashley's being arrested in this way and, in any case, that he was innocent. There was some evidence to show that other people had provided the tools. The judge instructed the jury to take account of the fact that the colonel had, at the time, acted in good faith. The jury disagreed and awarded Ashley damages of two hundred pounds. This time the Kingston *Chronicle* judged that Macdonald had displayed "much ingenuity and legal knowledge."

The case that in retrospect reveals the most about Macdonald's attitudes to the law occurred early in 1839, when he took up a cause that directly threatened any future political interests he might have. The 1837 rebellion had stirred up support in the United States, particularly along the northern border of New York State after Mackenzie fled there for safety. American citizens eager to liberate Canadians from political oppression set up a number of so-called Hunters' Lodges to work for the cause. In November 1838 a contingent of Hunters boarded the steamship *United States*, with two schooners in tow behind it, and set off for Prescott on the Canadian side. Some 180 of them landed at Windmill Point not far from Prescott. After assuring his men that a much larger force was right behind them, the expedition's leader got into a small boat and sped away across the lake. Those remaining took possession of a stone windmill and, led by Nils Gustaf von Schoultz, dug in there and waited for developments.

Schoultz was a mysterious figure. By origin a Swede, he'd fought with the Poles defending Warsaw against the Russians, was captured and then escaped (some said in exchange for becoming a Russian spy). He made it to Italy, where he married the daughter of a British general, then abandoned her and fled to the United States, entering into relationships with at least two other women who didn't know he was already married. After reading about Canadians' need to be liberated from British oppression, Schoultz joined the Hunters. He was attractive and brave, but befuddled. The local militia and British regulars soon surrounded the windmill. For two days the invaders remained untouched behind the stones walls of their redoubt. Then heavy cannon were brought up, forcing them to surrender. The death of a Canadian lieutenant in an early attack on the windmill, and the rumour that his body had been deliberately mutilated, made it difficult for the soldiers to protect their prisoners as they marched them to jail through Kingston.

Legally, the prisoners were without hope. Their trial was to be a military court-martial on the grounds they had made an invasion into Canada, and as a consequence no civilian defence lawyer could argue on their behalf. Worse, because of the roused public opinion, no local lawyer wanted even to advise the prisoners on how best to defend themselves. In a display of personal courage and out of a conviction that everyone deserved a defence, Macdonald stepped forward to help the first two men to be tried, Schoultz and Daniel George, the expedition's paymaster. Macdonald suggested a series of arguments to George, one being that there was no proof he had ever fired a gun. George was nevertheless found guilty. Schoultz, for his part, declared himself guilty. Standing stiff and proud before his fellow officers, he explained that the lieutenant's body had been mutilated by pigs, not by his men; that wounded Canadian soldiers had been cared for; and that he now realized Canadians were not oppressed. The one thing Macdonald could do for Schoultz was help him compose his will; when Schoultz said he wanted to include in it a payment for the service, Macdonald refused the offer. The two prisoners died bravely.

One aspect of the case had lasting relevance. Schoultz and the others were tried under a 1352 statute of Edward III that defined as treason an act committed by a non-citizen who "most wickedly, maliciously and traitorously, did levy and make war against our Said Sovereign." Macdonald tried to defend his clients against the application of that law. Almost exactly fifty years after the Hunters' case, this archaic statute would be deployed once again in Canada. On that occasion, the allegedly treasonable act was committed by a Canadian who had become an American citizen. The person responsible for the decision to prosecute the offence under the old statute was the prime minister. He was Macdonald, by then Sir John A. The defendant was Louis Riel.

Macdonald's last appearance as a defence lawyer occurred late in 1839, when he represented a Mohawk Indian, Brandt Brandt, charged with murdering a fellow Mohawk. Macdonald defended him with the aid of an interpreter. He cross-examined the Crown's principal witness, showing that the deed had been done in a house in the dark, when everyone there was drunk, making it impossible to be certain who had wielded the knife. The judge directed the jury that the facts could not sustain a verdict of manslaughter, so a conviction for murder was the only option. The jury nevertheless decided on manslaughter, and the judge sentenced Brandt to just six months in jail. Again, the *Chronicle* judged Macdonald's defence as "ingenious."

Macdonald never again appeared in the courts, except in civil actions. The immediate reason was the sudden death, on September 10, 1839, of the prominent lawyer Henry Cassady, who was also mayor of Kingston and solicitor to the Commercial Bank of the Midland District. At the age of just twenty-four, Macdonald took over many of Cassady's accounts and was chosen to succeed him in the prime post of solicitor for the bank. It's also easy to guess that, by now, Macdonald judged he had gained all the attention and publicity he needed for his legal career—or for another one.

Henceforth, Macdonald concentrated entirely on corporate matters. Though a major part of his legal work derived from the Commercial Bank accounts, he began to extend his reach to nearby towns such as Belleville and, eventually, to the financial centre of Montreal. Initially, most of his work involved debt collection and the foreclosure of mortgages, but he began to develop new lines of business. As early as 1842, he went into real estate, buying and selling lots and parcels of land in Kingston; he did well at first, but later all his gains were wiped out by a real estate crash. He eventually became a director of no less than a dozen Kingston companies, involved in everything from insurance to canals. In 1842 he used the opportunity of a trip to Britain to make legal and commercial contacts there; they eventually paid off in his becoming solicitor for the London-based Trust and Loan Company of Upper Canada.

In 1841 his father died, at the comparatively young age of fifty-nine. He was now officially head of the family and responsible for the financial security of his mother and two sisters, both unmarried. The strain took its toll. Beginning in 1840, and off and on through 1841, Macdonald was stricken by some ailment that, while never really identified, as was common then, left him weak and listless. His doctor thought that a long holiday, beginning with a sea trip, might do wonders for his health. That could mean only Britain; much more probably by coincidence rather than calculation, the prescription worked.

Macdonald sailed from Boston in January 1842 in the company of two friends, Thomas Wilson and Edward Wanklyn. Before leaving Kingston, he got into a high-stakes card game known as loo with some business associates and, over three nights, won the astounding sum of two thousand dollars. Afterwards, he vowed never again to gamble—and he never did, except once, when he made a throwaway bet at a horse-race and won.

Macdonald's stay in Britain, which eventually extended to six months, proved to be the most important holiday he ever took in his life. During it, he fell in love with the woman who would become his first wife. He also fell in love with England. More exactly, he came to understand the reasons for the love he already possessed for British culture, style and accomplishments. And radiant and compelling they were: a glowing young woman now sat on the throne; the glory of the defeat of Napoleon still reverberated in the recent past; the Royal Navy policed the seven seas;

London, with its incredible population of more than two million, was easily the largest and richest city in the world; British parliamentary and legal systems were regarded as models just about everywhere—except in France, and, as didn't really count, in the United States. Macdonald's anglophilia did not begin on this trip, but what he saw and experienced during his months there at the still-impressionable age of twenty-seven deepened his lifelong conviction that whatever was British was best—both in itself and also for Canada.

Of all the letters Macdonald wrote over the years to members of his family (of which, sadly, comparatively few have survived),* the letter he sent to his mother from London on March 3, 1842, stands apart from the rest by its sheer, uninhibited joy. He's excited and dazzled by the city, by its gargantuan buildings and affluence, and by himself. He's like the clever boy not quite certain of his gifts and aching for the approval of the one person whose applause, or censure, he really cares about. So he tells her everything.

"You would be surprised at the breakfasts I eat," he wrote. "Wilson laughs as he sees roll after roll disappear and eggs and bacon after roll. My dinners are equally satisfactory to myself. . . . Now only fancy, my commencing my dinner with a sole fried, with shrimp sauce, demolishing a large steak, and polishing off with bread and cheese and a quart of London Stout." He told her he was getting on well with the girls. Through a Lord De La Warr he had obtained "an order to see the Queen's private apartments" at Windsor Castle. He didn't go alone: "I had a very pretty girl, Margaret Wanklyn [a relative of his other companion from

---

* All these surviving letters, together with an excellent introduction, are contained in Keith Johnson's *Affectionately Tours: The Letters of Sir John A. Macdonald and His Family.*

Canada], on my arm, to whom the scene was also new," he enthused, "so we were agreeably engaged in comparing our impressions. Our ideas *sympathized wonderfully*." He also described his networking successes. "I have formed acquaintances and dined with two or three lawyers here by whose assistance I have seen all the great guns of the law." Among them, as he looked down from the gallery in the House of Lords, were "the great Law Lords, Lyndhurst, Brougham, Campbell and Cottenham. At the Guildhall, I saw Lord Denman and Sir Nicholas Tindal." Later, he went to the House of Commons, where he spotted "Peel, Goudham, Lord John Russell, Lord Stanley, O'Connell, Duncombe, Walkley." He had plans to go on to the Tower and dine with two members of Parliament. Still, he hadn't forgotten his domestic commitments: he would buy, as requested, damask, and "paper hangings and some chimney ornaments."

Macdonald gave to and received from his mother, Helen, pure unconditional love, right up to her death and then beyond; he was buried beside her in Kingston's Cataraqui Cemetery. In different ways, their lives were hard, and they both deserved this pure intercourse between them.

Yet, as so often with Macdonald, nothing was ever simple. He worshipped his mother, but he didn't copy her. She was deeply pious; he most certainly was not. She came from a long line of military men; he, as was most unusual among public figures of the day, never held an officer's commission in the militia and always regarded the military with a distinct skepticism. In the end, Macdonald did his own thing in his own way.

During his long stay in Britain, Macdonald travelled widely: to Manchester (where he bought wallpaper and the damask, and also a kitchen stove and iron railings); over to Chester to see a son of the family's now-deceased patron, Colonel Macpherson; on up to Scotland; and then a side trip to the Isle of Man to see yet more relatives. It was fully summer by the time he returned home.

Macdonald went back to the grind of law. His Kingston properties did exceptionally well for a time, until the real estate crash. Confident of his business skills nevertheless, Macdonald eventually bought and sold land all over the province, in Guelph and Toronto and Peterborough and as far away as Sarnia. At one time, he and Campbell jointly owned a steamship, though it promptly sank. Macdonald did better with a steam yacht that he managed to resell at a profit. Surprisingly, in view of his future history, Macdonald almost never invested in railways.*

Even as he was trying to become a tycoon, though, friends noticed a distinct change in the line of his interests. He asked one of them what he should do to prepare himself for political office should he ever seek it. Back came the reply, "Join the Orange Lodge and become an alderman." He asked Tom Wilson, his companion on the trip to Britain, about the financial side of political life. Back came the sound advice: "Secure a handsome independence first and then give as much attention as you please to the public weal."

---

* The authority on Macdonald's business affairs is the historian Keith Johnson, most particularly in his "John A. Macdonald, the Young Non-Politician," Canadian Historical Association, *Historical Papers*, 1971.

FIVE

A Conservative in a Conservative Country

~

In a young country like Canada, I am of the opinion that it is of more consequence to endeavour to develop its resources and improve its physical advantages than to waste the time of the legislature and the money of the people on abstract and theoretical questions of government.

John A. Macdonald

Macdonald took the advice and joined the Orange Lodge; to cover all bases, he later joined the Masonic Lodge and the Oddfellows. In February 1843 he announced that he would contest a vacant seat for alderman in Kingston's Fourth Ward. Helped by the *Chronicle*'s praise for his "well-known talents and high character," he won easily. As word of his new diligence in civic duties spread, he was elected president of Kingston's influential St. Andrew's Society. He was also an active supporter of the campaign to establish a university, Queen's, at Kingston.

He applied the same diligence to the task of sorting out his business affairs. For several years, Alexander Campbell had served him exceptionally well as a law clerk. Macdonald now promoted him to junior partner. Their agreement gave Campbell a third of the profits of the general business, excluding those generated by Macdonald from his own work as solicitor of the Commercial Bank. The deal was well structured: the practice would continue to provide him with a salary, but Macdonald no longer needed to be there all the time.

He closed the contract with Campbell on September 1, 1843. That same day he entered into another contract, a lifelong one. Macdonald married the woman with whom he'd fallen in love.

It had happened during his holiday in Britain the year before. It's just possible that the "very pretty" Margaret Wanklyn who had toured Windsor Castle on his arm had set him to thinking about the pleasures of the permanent company of a woman with whom he "sympathized wonderfully." On the Isle of Man, he had gone to call on his cousin, Margaret Greene, who was living in a farmhouse near the small capital of Douglas. Born a Clark in the same Highland site of Dalnavert where Macdonald's mother had been born, Margaret had crossed the Atlantic to live with an uncle in Georgia. There she had married a John Ward Greene, the descendant of a hero of the Revolutionary War, but had been widowed a few years later and retreated back across the Atlantic to the Isle of Man to stretch out her finances. She was living comfortably but carefully with her two unmarried sisters, Jane and Isabella.

Isabella Macdonald (née Clark), probably close to the time of her marriage. Her wan, girlish vulnerability helped get her in under Macdonald's radar screen.

Macdonald and Isabella clicked almost immediately. By the time he left, Macdonald had secured from Isabella a commitment to come to

Kingston the following year, ostensibly to visit yet another of her sisters, Maria, now the wife of John Alexander Macpherson, a son of Colonel Macpherson. Isabella made the journey. As was by now inevitable, a proposal was made and was accepted. And so on that September morning, they exchanged vows and matching gold wedding rings in St. Andrew's Church in Kingston. Right after the wedding, Macdonald hurried over to his law office to sign his agreement with Campbell. By marriage, and thereby the acquisition of respectability, Macdonald had cleared the last hurdle to his political candidacy.

No election date had yet been announced, but it was now only a year away.

Because Macdonald would go on to become so successful a politician, it has often been taken for granted that his motive for getting into the game was to get to the top as soon as possible and, once there, to remain at the top for as long as possible. In fact, it's wholly possible that Macdonald's principal motive for entering public life was to make money.

The professions of law and politics are joined at the hip. They always have been: in particular, lawyers are practised in the arts of debating and oratory, two political skills of immense esteem in the nineteenth century. Of the eleven prime ministers back to Louis St. Laurent just over a half-century ago, all but three (Lester Pearson, Joe Clark, and Stephen Harper) have been lawyers. Lawyers are good at spotting loopholes in legislation and regulations, and at attitudinizing—projecting shock and disbelief—at the arguments of their opponents. Lawyers who leave politics can return more easily to their practices than can members of almost any other profession; there are more, and better, post-politics prospects for lawyers, from the bench to boards of public enterprises to commissions of inquiry.

Two pieces of evidence suggest that short-term practical considerations were indeed Macdonald's purpose. When asked why he had stood as a candidate, Macdonald answered, "To fill a gap. There seemed no one else available, so I was pitched on." Many years later, his minister of justice of that time, Sir John Thompson, asked Macdonald if it was proper for a friend to run for Parliament for only a single term. Macdonald replied bluntly, "Those are the terms on which I came into public life." In this strictly private conversation, he had no reason to dissemble.

As further evidence that Macdonald's motivation for entering public life was more to make money than to make a name for himself, not a single companion or friend, nor any member of the family, ever claimed to have heard him say during his early years that he planned to become a great man. By contrast, his closest contemporary British prime minister, Benjamin Disraeli, proclaimed uninhibitedly, "I love fame. I love reputation," while Pierre Elliott Trudeau, who comes closest to Macdonald in his hold on the Canadian imagination, wrote in a journal he kept as a youth, "I must become a great man . . . a future head of state or a well-known diplomat or an eminent lawyer."

John A. Macdonald as a young man— alert, active and, as so often, very clearly amused.

It's thus entirely possible that Macdonald initially saw politics as an opportunity to gain a quick understanding of government and to accumulate contacts that he could then deploy on behalf of old and new clients. Only later, as he realized how good he was at it, would politics become his life, fame his spur, and power his addiction.

As always with Macdonald, little is certain. He prepared himself with the focused rigour of someone girding for a marathon, not a sprint. Once elected, he set out systematically to turn Kingston into a political citadel from which he could sally out knowing he had a secure base to retreat to. And, of course, once in, Macdonald stayed on, and on and on.

The call came in the spring of 1844. A group of leading Kingston citizens asked him to run in the election that was coming due. They asked him to stand as a Conservative—he being conservative by nature, Kingston being Loyalist, and all those worthy types looking for someone sound and sensible to represent them. Macdonald agreed to their request and then told them exactly what they wanted to hear: that all politics is local—today it's a cliché, but at the time it came to Macdonald instinctually.* He promised he would address "the settlement of the back township district, hitherto so utterly neglected, and to press for the construction of the long projected plank road to Perth and Ottawa." He also said that he intended to get things done in the way they themselves would do it—by being practical: "In a young country like Canada," he declared, "I am of the opinion that it is of more consequence to endeavour to develop its resources and improve its physical advantages than to waste the time of the legislature

---

* The "all politics is local" aphorism is generally attributed to "Tip" O'Neill, the powerful Democratic House leader in the United States from 1977 to 1987.

and the money of the people on abstract and theoretical questions of government."

Macdonald and his supporters (all men of property, they being the only ones with the right to vote) were as one. That curious but occasionally insightful book *The Canadian Commercial Revolution, 1845–1851* contains a good description of the typical Canadian voter of the time: "They were energetic, progressive and materialistic . . . they were strong and shrewd men, disdainful of theories, and interested chiefly in the material realities of life."* In one respect, these unsentimental types might have wondered just what they were getting into. Part of Macdonald's reply to his petitioners had a decidedly teasing, over-the-top quality to it: "With feelings of greater pride and gratitude than I can express . . . [t]he mode in which I can best evince my high sense of the honour you have done me is, *at once*, to lay aside all personal considerations and accede to your request."

For the actual election, in the fall of 1844, Macdonald issued his own proclamation in the Kingston *Chronicle*. It repeated his local ambitions and dealt with a topic that concerned most voters in the staunchly Loyalist town, no less so than Macdonald himself: "I, therefore, scarcely need state my firm belief that the prosperity of Canada depends upon its permanent connection with the Mother Country and that I shall resist to the utmost any attempt which may tend to weaken that union."

The balloting—each elector casting his vote not by marking an X on paper but in the "manly" manner of shouting his choice out loud—took place on Monday, October 14, and throughout the next day. Macdonald won easily, by 275 shouts against just 42 for his opponent, Anthony Manahan. As was far from always the case,

---

* *The Canadian Commercial Revolution* was published in 1936 by the historian Gilbert Norman Tucker. It was his doctoral thesis.

the casting of the votes and their counting were conducted "in a most peaceful and orderly manner," according to the *Chronicle*.

But one thing had gone wrong for Macdonald. He had always assumed he would be serving as a member in a legislature that met in his home town of Kingston. Lord Sydenham, the first governor general of the new United Province of Canada, which had just replaced the separate provinces of Upper and Lower Canada, had announced in February 1841 that Kingston would be the capital of his domain. This town of some five thousand souls had gone into an instant and ecstatic boom—as had Macdonald's law practice. Civil servants streamed in, along with the governor general and his mini-court. Construction was soon under way for at least four hundred new houses. Town officials took delighted note of the fact that a grand new town hall was being constructed which just happened to have, in its second storey, two high-ceilinged chambers ideal for the Legislative Assembly and the

Kingston, c. 1863. Some fine two-storey buildings by now, and horses and carriages, but still a street of deep, foul-smelling mud.

Legislative Council, or upper chamber. Until this building was completed, the Assembly met in a newly built but empty hospital, with eighty-four overstuffed armchairs equipped with an attached writing tablet hurried in for the eighty-four legislators.

If Kingstonians were pleased, few others shared their enthusiasm. French-Canadian members complained loudly that, compared with Montreal or Quebec City, this new capital was dull and, worse, homogeneously English; one of the French members referred to "cet enfer de Kingston." The demands of the French, headed by the emerging leader Louis-Hippolyte LaFontaine, could not be denied. In September 1843 a new governor general, Sir Charles Metcalfe, announced that Kingston's brief hour of glory was over and, perhaps initiating the tradition of resolving national problems by displeasing everyone more or less equally, that the seat of government would henceforth rotate every three years from Montreal to Quebec City to Toronto.* Macdonald's inaugural appearance in the legislature thus was in its new temporary quarters in St. Anne's Market in Montreal. There, he would begin to learn for the first time about the "other" Canada.

In nineteenth-century Canada, the observation that all politics is local would have been treated not as an insight but as a banality. With occasional exceptions, such as the campaign to achieve Responsible Government or, later, Representation by Population, almost all politics was about local issues. Debates that engaged the general public were almost always those inspired by sectarianism—

---

* A few years after Kingston's fall from grace, an English visitor noted that the town had "a rather dreary appearance" and that many streets were "over-run with grass."

French versus English, Catholic versus Protestant, and sometimes Protestant versus Protestant, as between Anglicans and Methodists. Just about the only non-religious exception to the rule of the dominance of localism was the issue of anti-Americanism; it was both widespread and, as was truly rare, a political conviction that promoted national unity because it was held as strongly by the French as by the English.

Almost all politics was local for the simple reason that almost everyone in Canada was a local: at least 80 per cent of Canadians were farmers or independent fishermen. Moreover, they were self-sufficient farmers. They built their own houses. They carved out most of their implements and equipment. They grew almost all their own food (tea and sugar excepted) or raised it on the hoof. They made most of their own clothes. They made their own candles and soft soap. Among the few products they sold into commercial markets were grain and potash. Few sent their children to school. They were unprotected by policemen (even in the towns in Upper Canada, police forces dated only from the 1840s). For lack of ministers or priests, marriages were often performed by the people themselves. Even the term "local" conveys a false impression of community: roads were so bad and farms spaced so far apart that social contact was limited principally to "bees"—barn and house raising, stump clearing and later, more fancily, quilting.

Government's reach in Canada was markedly more stunted than in England. While there had been a Poor Law there from 1597, the first statute of the Legislature of Upper Canada provided specifically that "Nothing in this Act . . . shall introduce any of the laws of England concerning the maintenance of the poor."* The churches were responsible for charity, and in some

---

* The Maritimes, then quite separate colonies, had both Poor Laws and Poor Houses.

areas for education.* It was the same for that other form of social activism, the Temperance Societies, commonly brought into being by the Methodist, Presbyterian and Baptist churches. The unemployed were "the idle poor," and no government had any notion that it should be responsible for their succour. Governments collected taxes (almost exclusively customs and excise duties) and were responsible for law and order, maintaining the militia, and running the jails, where the idea of rehabilitation as opposed to punishment was unknown. But without any income tax, there was comparatively little the government could do even if it wished. Consequently, the total spending on public charities, social programs and education amounted to just 9 per cent of any government's revenues. To most Canadians in the middle of the nineteenth century, government was as irrelevant to their day-to-day lives as it is today to the Mennonites, Hutterites and Amish.

Because Macdonald was an avowed conservative, he was little different from almost everyone else; the other major party, the Reform Party (which changed its name over time to the Liberal Party), was at least as conservative as the Conservatives. Later, the populist Clear Grits arose in Upper Canada to advocate such disturbing American notions as the secret ballot and direct democracy. In mid- to late-nineteenth-century Canada, though, conservatism was as widely held a political attitude as liberalism would become a century later. It took a long while for things to change. In one post-Confederation debate, in 1876, held during an economic depression, a Liberal MP argued that the government should assist the poor. Another MP rounded on him to declare, "The moment a Government is asked to take charge and feed the

---

* The first legislation in British North America to establish free education was in Prince Edward Island in 1852. Nova Scotia followed in 1864, and Ontario only after Confederation.

poor you strike a blow at their self-respect and independence that is fatal to our existence as a people." The shocked second intervenor was also a Liberal, as was the government of the day.

Amid this emphasis on the local, there was, nevertheless, one broad national dimension. Governments were remarkably ready to go into debt—proportionately more deeply than today—to build up the nation itself. Here, Conservatives were actually greater risk-takers than the Reformers. Bishop John Strachan, a leading member of the arch-conservative Family Compact, held that "the existence of a national debt may be perfectly consistent with the interests and prosperity of the Country." In the early and middle part of the century, mostly Conservative governments bankrolled major public projects—first canals, such as the Welland, the Lachine and the Rideau—and then a spiderweb of railways, nearly all of them money-losing. These Conservatives were, of course, undertaking projects that benefited their supporters, but they were also building the country.

Politicians performed one social program of vital importance—patronage. When Macdonald first entered the legislature, though, relatively little patronage was available for politicians to distribute. Purity wasn't the cause: impotence was. In the early 1840s, patronage was allocated almost entirely by the governor general. The fight through the decade for Responsible Government, or for the transfer from London to Canadians of responsibility over almost all internal or domestic matters, would really be a contest between the governor general and Canadian politicians over who should get to dish out patronage.

Although they did a good deal less than today's politicians do, nineteenth-century legislators performed with a good deal more flourish. Speeches, delivered in the long, declamatory cadences of high rhetoric, could last two, three, even five hours. Among epithets used commonly in the province's Parliament were "poltroon," "blackguard," "traitor," "infamous traitor," "coward," "cur," "jackal." Here, as recorded by newspaper reporters,* are the exchanges in a debate on May 8, 1846:

> Mr. Deblurey[†]: "Mr. Chairman, if you are absolutely unable to keep the hon. Member in order, I will cross the floor and make him observe the respect due to a member addressing this House."
>
> Mr. Aylwin, (clenching his fist and extending his arm over his desk): "Take care. Take care. Take care." (Great excitement). Later, Mr. Aylwin again (shaking his fist): "Come over here, if you dare, your scoundrel." (Mr. Deblurey attempted to go over but was prevented by two of the members).
>
> Mr. Hall: "Are we in a Canadian legislature to be bullied and browbeaten?" (The whole house was on its legs in a moment. Some cried, "Leave the chair," some, "Call the Speaker," others "Clear the gallery," and several gentlemen went to the gallery to tender assistance to the ladies, who were, of course, greatly alarmed).
>
> Macdonald then intervened, declaring: "He would pull Mr. Aylwin's nose."

The newspapers did a great deal to raise the political temperature. The Toronto *Globe* once described one member, Dr. John Rolph, as "a sleek-visaged man with cold grey eyes, treacherous mouth and lips fashioned to deceive," and as "dark, designing, cruel, traitorous."

---

* No official Hansard record existed during these years. In an inspired project, the Parliamentary Library has assembled a "virtual Hansard" by collating the near-verbatim reports of debates as published in the newspapers of the time on the basis of accounts sent in by shorthand reporters. The post-Confederation series is all but complete; that for the pre-Confederation Legislative Assembly, though, extends only up to 1856. One editorial challenge is that newspapers often gave short shrift or no shrift at all to members of parties they opposed.

[†] His actual name was De Bleury.

The assaults went beyond the verbal to the physical, particularly during the evening sessions as the intake of liquor increased. During an 1849 debate on an especially contentious issue, Macdonald first denounced a speech by a Reform minister, William Blake, as "most shameful," then sent him a note challenging him to a duel. Blake accepted, but the sergeant-at-arms managed to head them off. George-Étienne Cartier and a Lower Canada (Quebec) member followed up a comparable shouting match by actually arriving at a duelling ground; nothing happened, because their seconds had "forgotten" to bring any ammunition.

Macdonald came into the legislature quietly. During his first session he made not a single speech, asked not a question, made not a single interjection. He spent a great deal of time in the Parliamentary Library, boning up on the rules and precedents, reading speeches, figuring out the jousting techniques involved in asking questions of ministers and responding to their replies. He sat in the back row—and he still got himself noticed.

He did so by the classic device of being different. He was clean-shaven at a time when the legislature and the courts were a thicket of muttonchop whiskers, hedge-sized moustaches and full, patriarchal beards. He wore his ties loose, in a carefree Byronic manner; his clothes, colourful, almost foppish, shouted out the message "Notice Me." A vivid description of Macdonald's appearance and demeanour at this time was provided by one of his early biographers, E.B. Biggar, in his *Anecdotal Life of Sir John Macdonald:* "His walk, then, as ever, was peculiar. His step was short, and when he went to a seat, there was something in his movement which suggested a bird alighting in a hesitating way from flight. His quick and all-comprehending glance, and that peculiar jerking of the head, bore out the comparison in other respects." Shrewdly, another early biographer, J.E. Collins, compared Macdonald's posture and choice of clothes to those of "an actor." As a further advantage, Macdonald's frizzy hair and large, bulbous nose—"qui faisait toute sa gloire," in the wonderful phrase of François-Xavier Langelier, who for long sat across from him as an opposition MP—made him stand out from the crowd.

Much as is the case with Parliament today, the legislature was essentially a large club. Members hurled insults at each other but behind the curtains turned into convivial friends, because they were all in the same, adrenaline-charged, winner-take-all game. Few, if any, members of that assembly would have been as "clubbable," in the British phrase, as was Macdonald. People liked him because he liked them. It helped materially that he wasn't moralistic, whether about drink or anything else, but was a man of the world, unshockable and unjudgmental. Also, he was funny.

Macdonald found his voice during his second session, in 1845. He spoke, in these first efforts, not merely like a voice from the past but like one from an antediluvian past. In February he took part in a debate on a motion calling for reform of the law of primogeniture, which required that, when a property owner died intestate, all his holdings went to his eldest son. Macdonald was appalled that some share of such estates might instead be reserved for younger sons. "The law of primogeniture was the great bulwark between the people and the Crown and the Crown and the people," he declared. "It was the younger sons of England that had made it great in peace and war. What would have been the younger Pitt or Fox if, instead of being sent forth to seek their fortunes, the estate of their father had been divided: they would have been mere country squires." He cited the example of the Duke of Wellington, almost penniless, but "left with his sword in his hand." To pass a motion "merely because it would please the people" would be an "act of madmen," Macdonald concluded. The motion was defeated.

In May of the following year, Macdonald made an interjection on a bill, moved by Reform leader Robert Baldwin, to change on a trial basis the practice of electors shouting out their vote choices at the balloting stations in Montreal, where there had been violence in some places. Once again, Macdonald was appalled. He admitted that proposals for a secret ballot had been made in the British Parliament, but only to "prevent the landlord's influence over the tenant." In Canada, where so many citizens were landowners, there was "no one exercising an illegitimate influence over them." So, concluded Macdonald, "every man in Canada would, and did, make public his opinion." The public ballot was retained. That same session, Macdonald also showed that he had a temper. He provoked a member of the High Tory Boulton family to challenge him to a duel. Macdonald refused to back off, but other members intervened and heads, on both sides, cooled down.

Most of the time, Macdonald applied himself to strictly local matters. He introduced a bill to incorporate the Wolfe Island, Kingston and Toronto Railroad Company, and as well a petition for a Catholic college, Regiopolis, to be established at Kingston. He attracted the attention of journalists—one in the *Montreal Transcript* described him as "very popular . . . I should say he is 'a rising man' and not likely to disappoint the expectations of his friends." At the very least, he had by now made Kingston into a citadel for himself.

SIX

Going Headlong

The rod cannot always be smiting.
John A. Macdonald

In 1843 Margaret Greene, the sister of Macdonald's wife, Isabella, left the Isle of Man, where she had introduced the couple, and moved back to Georgia—to the ancestral estate of her late husband's family, which she had now inherited. She and Macdonald exchanged letters, he at times offering her advice on legal and real estate matters. On July 11, 1845, he wrote Margaret a letter utterly different in nature.

This letter, sent less than two years after John and Isabella had married, and one year after he became a member of the legislature, was the saddest and most fateful he would ever write. Although he did not yet know it, his life was about to change totally and irreversibly.

"My Dear Sister," Macdonald began, "Isabella has been ill—very ill—with one of her severest attacks. She is now just recovering and I hope has thrown off for the time her terrible disease. Still, this is not certain, and at all events it has left her in the usual state of prostration that follows every attack." Clearly this was not the first "attack" Isabella had suffered. He had planned for them to go to New York, as they had done the previous year—exactly why and for how long, Macdonald doesn't say—but that was now doubtful. "It may be days—nay weeks—before she has rallied sufficiently to attempt any journey. What to say or do, I know not."

Just one day later, Macdonald wrote again to his sister-in-law. His mood had deepened into despair. "Her pain has in a great measure left her, but her debility is in the greatest degree alarming. She is weaker than

Margaret Greene, Isabella's elder sister and Macdonald's confidante as he tried to cope with his wife's illness.

she has ever been, and there are symptoms, such as an apparent numbness of one limb, and an irregularity in the action of the heart, that made me send for Dr. Sampson, altho' against Isabella's wish. He saw her this morning and says he cannot relieve her, and I ought not, my beloved sister, to disguise from you, that he thinks her in the most precarious state." He praised Margaret Greene for her "strength of mind" and, his despair now bringing him close to the point of abandoning all hope, wrote that "unless God in his infinite mercy works an immediate change for the better, it is impossible for her to remain in her exhausted state for many days." Isabella in fact didn't die; neither, though, would she ever recover.

There were a great many bonds between Macdonald and Isa, as Isabella was often called. They were cousins. They both were Scots. She was thirty-three when they married and must have been well aware both of the ticking of her biological clock and of the sparseness of marital opportunities in the rural Isle of Man. For him, on the eve of entering politics, having a wife meant that voters need not worry that he might misbehave and embarrass them. That their ages were inverted—he a mere twenty-eight on their wedding day—wouldn't have struck Macdonald as unusual, because there was a similar gap between his own mother and father. He was a good catch, although by no means a great one—he was still building his law practice and his background was barely middle class. His looks, to the extent they mattered, were odd, but not alluringly ugly in the manner of, say, his contemporary Thomas D'Arcy McGee.

Isabella, for her part, possessed a certain pale prettiness, but in no way was she beautiful. The first known portrait of her was done around the time of her marriage. A second was done around 1852 by the same Kingston artist William Sawyer who painted the distinctive portrait of Macdonald that is the frontispiece of this book; a locket version of Isabella's image appears later in this chapter. As well, in 2006 another portrait, either of Isabella or much more likely her sister Margaret Greene, was purchased by the Agnes Etherington Art Centre in Kingston.* The Sawyer portrait shows Isabella with a high forehead, her mouth slim but determined, her hair dark and thick, her nose long and delicate, her eyes a bright, pale blue. Isabella seems not to be wholly there but withdrawn and passive, as though observing herself rather than being on display for the benefit of observers.

---

* This portrait is of the correct period—the 1840s—and comes from the Kingston area. The woman in it has dark eyes, though, rather than the light-blue eyes Isabella was known to have.

Isabella may have possessed some ineffable quality now impossible to pin down, or she may have been an enigma without a riddle. In the mysterious way of these things, she connected to some romantic core hidden deep within John A., composed in part no doubt of the traditional male urge to protect. Her means for achieving this bond was spontaneity. She was open, vulnerable, breathy: "*You* know how *headlong* I ever go," she wrote in a letter to Margaret. Macdonald was never cynical, but he most certainly was unsentimental and fully capable of being hard. With Isabella, he expanded his emotional range to that of love. The use of that word to describe his feelings for her can only be speculative. The fact is that when Isabella began to reveal the extent of her frailty, Macdonald demonstrated an exceptional tenderness towards her and, a good deal rarer among husbands, a durable tolerance for her weakness.

The full nature of their relationship can only be guessed at. Just two of Isabella's letters survive, both of them to her sister. We thus have no record of Macdonald's and Isabella's voices when they were talking to each other.* Her own voice comes across as, well, "headlong": people and subjects are all jumbled together. The first of these letters was written on June 11, 1845, a month before Macdonald's anguished letter. She is a bit cross, because Margaret had apparently delayed a planned visit to Kingston: "I have of course countermanded yr bonnet dearest sister. But it was to have been lovely. An exquisite lavender satin & blonde but you will do penance in yellow stockings for it as I thought we have been so becoming & sweet. Jane shall shall [sic] wear her *purple* if it *were at night*—for I wont let *her* off. Bye

---

* The paucity of surviving letters by Isabella is striking because, being frequently away from Macdonald for extended periods, she must have written often to him and to other family members.

the way, Mama has bought a London cap to send you. Mrs. Abbott had just received it when M. saw & pounced on it. But I'm so mad about that bonnet I won't tell you what it is like, & I don't think I'll be satisfied till I get a red petticoat for you to wear with the yellow stockings." The rest of the letter continues this girlish, gushing tone.

Isabella's second extant letter, of 1848, also written to Margaret, is even gushier. "Gush," though, is a misleading descriptor. What we are reading now is the cry of someone sensing that she is drowning. By this time indeed Isabella was struggling, growing ever weaker, against an illness that was reducing her to a hollow shell. This letter begins by referring to one of Margaret's friends, a Mrs. Biddle: "I sincerely sympathize in your leaving dear, dear Mrs. Biddle & most precious Husband. Full well I know your spirit *must* be born down by the hourly *yearning* for her society. . . . My dear, dear Mrs. Biddle. How I reverence her! How my weary, *weary*, spirit bows before her. May God's holiest, richest mercies *rest, now & ever, abidingly,* on her and hers." She names another of Margaret's friends: "I rejoice you are with Mrs. Field. Dear beautiful, *Porcelain* Mrs. Field, so different from the *gilt delf* of every day life. I really would dread seeing her often, my own darling precious sister, *you* know how *headlong* I ever go & I much fear I would love her but too fondly."

She was, surely, writing far less about Mrs. Biddle and Mrs. Field than about herself.

John and Isabella Macdonald were married for fourteen years. For the first two years or so, they were wholly happy. For another dozen she was a bedridden invalid, struck down by an illness no doctor could diagnose or cure, interspersed initially by occasional brief and unpredictable respites that, over time, became rarer and briefer. Her doctors could prescribe just one effective medicine. It was opium, in ever larger quantities.* It brought her relief, but it also took her ever further from her husband and from real life. During this long, empty period, Macdonald would hurry home from the legislature or his law office, often to dine alone because she was too weak even to accompany him by sitting up in bed. The house was silent most of the time because the noise of guests would give her a headache. Inevitably, they had less and less to talk about, and less and less in common. Also inevitably, he took to drink.

The first two years of his marriage to Isabella would be the single span of time in John A. Macdonald's entire adult life in which he experienced a normal marriage and family life. In place of the small daily epiphanies of any couple, whether they are in love or are merely companionable, Macdonald's entire life would be politics. This was one reason—the tragic one—why he became so good at it.

⌒

There was a particular cause for Macdonald, in his letters to Margaret Greene of July 11 and 12, 1845, to be so close to utter despair. In the previous few months his mother had suffered two strokes. As hardy Highlanders do, she recovered, but for the rest of her life she would need permanent care. As head of the family,

---

* Opium was widely available in the mid-nineteenth century and a common ingredient in patent medicines, such as Winslow's Soothing Syrup, Godfrey's Cordial and McMunn's Elixir of Opium, all of which could be bought without a prescription at drugstores. In its most common form, especially favoured by women, it was sold as laudanum.

Isabella's downstairs bedroom at Bellevue House in Kingston. It was from here, while bedridden, that she ran the household like "the Invisible Lady."

Macdonald was now responsible for ensuring that his mother was looked after, for making similar arrangements for his wife as she too became an invalid, and for the financial and other needs of his two unmarried sisters. While doing all this, Macdonald was at the same time trying to advance his career in politics and to maintain his law practice, now under the strain of his many absences on personal and political business.

Many would have buckled. Macdonald just got down to doing what he could. He conceived the idea—presumably on the advice of doctors—of taking Isabella to Savannah in the Deep South, where she might better regain her strength by escaping the long blast of a Canadian winter. Before leaving, he had to sort out a family dispute caused by his own sister Margaret (Moll) refusing to accompany Isabella partway southwards, as she'd undertaken to do, because she had to remain behind to watch over their mother. Eventually, Margaret agreed to go with them as far as

Oswego, New York, and Macdonald then set off. It was a night-mare journey. Transportation systems were rough and ready; accommodation for travellers was spartan. On July 18 he wrote to Margaret Greene from Oswego: "We arrived here this morning at about one o'clock my dearest sister. The exhaustion produced by carrying Isabella down to the boat was dreadful to witness. We thought she would die on the dock. . . . The weather was so stormy, that all our party were sick, Isabella dreadfully so, and yet strange to say her health and strength seemed to return to her." They went on to Syracuse, and then, by train, to Philadelphia, where "her fatigues were very great and she was obliged to subdue pain by opium, but still she kept up her spirits & at about four o'clock we arrived at this House. Only think what a journey she had. First to be carried down a narrow stair at Jersey & over to the cars; 2nd a journey in the cars for about 70 miles to Bristol; 3rd To be carried in a chair from the cars to a steamboat, 4th a voyage of 22 miles to this city, and lastly and worst of all a quarter of a mile's drive in a hack over rough streets. . . . She from fatigue and opium combined slept from 10 o'clock last night until the morning and is now easy and in good spirits. She never speaks of it, but I am perfectly conscious of how much she suffers."

A few days later, still in Philadelphia, in another letter to Margaret, Macdonald recounted, first, that Isabella "exerted her-self too much, so that in the evening she was a good deal exhausted, and was threatened by tic, so that she had recourse to opium," and then reported, "She has had a good day today, has walked a good deal & eaten pretty well." In early November they reached Baltimore, where they had reserved rooms in a hotel near the railway station, but finding them wholly unsatisfactory they moved to another establishment. "The consequence of all this was great exhaustion and great suffering by Isabella. She was in great agony all night, and was obliged to have recourse to opium, externally and internally in great quantities." On a brighter note, Macdonald reported that "Isa . . . says she does not anticipate suffering from our today's journey, as the weather is calm."

At the small town of Petersburgh, he wrote, "The house we stayed in was dirty, the food badly dressed and the beds overrun by ants." They hurried on the 160 miles to Wilmington: "She bore it like a *Shero** as she is, but as you may well believe dreadfully exhausted by the exertion. She passed a miserable night and continues today to pay the penalty for her extra exertions." On a cheerier note, Macdonald reported they had passed their time reading a "strange mélange" of books, among them *The Bible in Spain*, Thomas Carlyle's *Life of Schiller*, Bishop Moore's *Sermons*, and were about to "take up Lord Mahon's *History of England.*"

They pressed on, by steamer, reaching Savannah on November 20 after a calm journey—"There was scarcely a curl on the sea." There they rented two "quiet" rooms. Isabella, though, "has been very miserable since our arrival. The tic encouraged by her weakness from fatigue has made a furious attack upon her which she is *manfully* resisting with the assistance of the blister and the pill-box." Now that he was in the Deep South and it was late November, Macdonald appreciated the benefits of being there. "The weather here is so fine & warm that I cannot fancy it winter at all." He would have loved to stay, rather than going back "among the frosts & snows of Canada, sucking my paws like any other bear." Political duties compelled him to return, though. He made an adroit appeal to Margaret Greene to enable him to slip

---

* Macdonald's use of *Shero* poses a tantalizing mystery, perhaps an insolvable one. None of the standard etymology dictionaries consulted by the author cite any uses of the word in the nineteenth century; rather, "shero" is a modern neologism (s-hero) minted by the feminist movement. It seems that Macdonald either invented it as a tease or overheard it, perhaps from his strong-minded and highly intelligent mother.

away: "I need not say however that it would afford me great pleasure to reflect that you were near her, when I am far away."

Macdonald's manipulation achieved its purpose. In a letter sent from Kingston on February 27, 1846, he told Margaret, "I am sanguine in my hopes and belief, that in the fine climate she [Isa] now enjoys, and under your affectionate and judicious care she may yet be restored to me, in health, strength and spirits."

~

No such recovery occurred. Instead, a miracle did. After a reunion late in 1846, Isabella let Macdonald know that she was pregnant. He moved her to New York, where medical standards were higher (and a great deal more expensive). On April 5, 1847, he wrote to Margaret Greene from New York—"this American Babylon"—to report: "Doctor Washington still says she is in very critical condition arising from the continued attacks of uterine neuralgia. These attacks, he apprehends, may bring on a premature confinement. . . . Still he is not without hopes of being able to prevent an abortion. She is quite calm & resolute, and is much encouraged by Maria's presence." (Maria was yet another of Isabella's sisters, of whom there were four in all.)

That summer, Macdonald's mother suffered a third stroke. He wrote encouragingly to her that "such attacks are not uncommon in aged people." He then switched to some role-reversing nagging: "These illnesses should have the effect of inducing you to be more particular in keeping your system in order, and conquering your antipathy to medicine."

But soon it was time for an exultant letter. On August 2, 1847, Macdonald was able to write to his mother from New York that Isabella had gone into labour and a specialist, a Dr. Rodgers, had come to administer "the *Lethean* or somnific gas," although able to risk only a small dose because of her weakness. "She suffered dreadfully all night and about 8 this morning was so weak that the Doctors determined to use the forceps, as she was quite unable to deliver herself. They succeeded to a miracle, and I am delighted to tell you that she was delivered of a healthy & strong boy." The child instantly dominated their lives. Macdonald reported triumphantly to Margaret Greene that "his eyes are dark blue, *very large & nose* to match. When born his length was 1 foot 9 inches & very strong and healthy, though thin, but as Maria told Dr. Washington, that was not to be wondered at, seeing he had been living on pills for so long." Isabella, at the end of her "head-long" letter to Margaret Greene, for once found the words to express what she truly wanted to say: "My very soul is bound up in him. God pardon me if I sin in this. But did I not purchase him dearly?" They named their baby son John Alexander.

By September, Macdonald was back in Canada—and back in politics. "Our poor Isabella was a good deal agitated at my leaving her," he tells Margaret Greene in a letter written from Montreal. "The *Boy* is flourishing like a *Green bay Horse* so writes Margaret [his own sister Margaret, who'd gone down to New York], and that he is becoming strong & fat." Isabella remained in New York that winter, cared for by her sister Maria, while Macdonald's sister Margaret returned to Kingston to look after their mother. Macdonald himself was now alone, in Montreal, where the government had moved. He told Margaret Greene, "I feel quite solitary & miserable living in lodgings alone. I would spend a pleasant winter if Isabella were only here."

In the late spring of 1848, Isabella came back from New York to join Macdonald in Kingston. They moved to Bellevue, an airy Tuscan-style villa with large, well-landscaped grounds. Its usual nickname was the Pekoe Pagoda, but Macdonald called it the Eyetalian Willar. (It is now a National Historic Site of Canada.) A

particular attraction of the house for
Isabella was its distance from the
noise of the town, which always
upset her. A far greater attraction,
of course, as Macdonald wrote to
Margaret Greene, was "the society
of her boy. At first he was shy and
uncomfortable in her room, which is
to some degree darkened and as she
could not handle him, or toss him
about, which the young gentleman
insists upon from all who approach
him." But "he is now however great

*A miniature of an oil portrait of Isabella by
William Sawyer, dated 1852.*

friends with her, and sits most contentedly in the bed with her,
surrounded by his toys which he throws about, much to her
inconvenience I am sure, tho' she will allow it."

If the spirit was now willing, the flesh was soon assailed
again. On August 1, 1848, Macdonald informed Margaret that
Isabella was consistently coughing. "On her route & after her
arrival [home], there were occasional appearances of blood from
her lungs. . . . [Dr. Hayward] discerns no symptoms of ulceration
or permanent affection—but I fear, I fear." A few days later, he
confirmed the alarming new symptom. "The chief cause of
uneasiness is the occasional appearance of blood in her handker-
chief when she coughs." A fortnight later, Dr. Hayward told him
that "the cough & the blood of course indicate something wrong,
some cause of irritation. And yet she has none of the evidence on
which a medical man could state there was any ulceration." Still,
the baby John Alexander was there to lift her spirits: "He sits by
the hour now with his Mother as contentedly as possible, and
smiles & crows away from one end of day to the other."

Three weeks later, a nurse went to check on John Alexander in his room next door to Isabella's on the ground floor. He was still and cold in his cot. "Convulsions" was the explanation given; it may have been sudden infant death syndrome. He was buried in the Garrison Burial Ground near the grave of the grandfather he'd never seen, Hugh Macdonald.

In those days, the death of young children was common. This infant, though, had been brought into the world amid excruciating pain, and during his brief life he had given to his mother and father a joy they had never dared imagine they might possess. He was never forgotten.

In 1865, the remains of the infant John A., as well as those of Hugh Macdonald, originally interred in the old Garrison Burial Ground that was by now in a state of disrepair, were removed to the new Cataraqui Cemetery (of which Macdonald was a founding subscriber) and there placed in the family's burial plot. Many years later, Macdonald's second wife, Agnes, came upon a small dusty box while cleaning the attic of Earnscliffe, their house in Ottawa. Inside it were some odd wooden objects. When she showed them to her husband, Macdonald explained they were John Alexander's toys; through all the many moves he had made from city to city and from house to lodging house to bachelor quarters and back again to a house, Macdonald had kept with him these relics of his lost son.

Thereafter, Macdonald's marriage became "a grey, unrelieved tragedy," in the fine phrase of his principal biographer, Donald Creighton. From then on, and until his life was over, he applied all his passion to politics.

SEVEN

New Guys with New Ideas

> The British people of the North American Colonies are a people on whom we may safely rely, and to whom we must not grudge power.
>
> Lord Durham, in his report of 1839

By luck, Macdonald began his political career in 1844, at the best possible time for a newcomer to arrive at least in the wings of the political stage. Shortly before he got there, the Canadian political system had been decisively shaken up and had set off in an entirely new direction. Shortly afterwards, the system was galvanized by the introduction into it of a new, almost revolutionary, idea in governance. The decisive change was caused by a new constitution that joined the two previously separate colonies of Upper and Lower Canada (today, Ontario and Quebec) into the United Province of Canada; for the first time, the country's two European peoples, French and English, were brought into direct political contact. The almost revolutionary idea was that of Responsible Government: it called for the colony's government to be responsible to the elected legislature, not, as before, to the governor general. Under the old system, the governor general exercised unchallengable authority as the personal representative of the monarch; he selected and appointed all the ministers, who then functioned as his ministers rather than as those of the legislature and the voters. Transferring responsibility to elected ministers who commanded a majority in the legislature effectively ceded to the colony full self-government in domestic affairs. Only Confederation, still two decades away, would change the country as radically as these two measures.

For the politicians, whether Macdonald or anyone else, the effect was like that of a comprehensive spring cleaning. As Creighton observed in *The Young Politician*, almost all the leading political figures of the era before Responsible Government "failed, with astonishing uniformity, to survive very long in the new political atmosphere." Macdonald thus joined the system at the very moment when it was time for new guys with new ideas. Except that Macdonald did not—yet—have any new ideas. He survived, nevertheless, because he was street-smart and a quick learner. Still, he contributed nothing to the transformational changes themselves, and it took him time to figure out how to take advantage of the extra space at the top that had just been opened up for someone like him.

Macdonald also had to cope with practical constraints. During his first term, from 1844 to 1848, he was a backbencher, literally as well as figuratively, because he chose to sit in the very back row. His appearances on the actual stage itself were in the junior cabinet posts of receiver general and commissioner of Crown lands, in each instance briefly. During his second term, from 1848 to 1852, he sat in opposition, because the Conservative government had lost to the Reform Party. Mostly what he did during this time was to listen and learn, to make useful contacts and to acquire insider know-how, all of which would be highly useful, whether he chose to give politics up for the law or try clambering up the ladder.

As an even more practical constraint, Macdonald was having problems with his law practice. Campbell complained, justifiably, that he was being underpaid, particularly because Macdonald was often absent on political business. In 1846 they rewrote their original agreement, this time dividing the general profits equally between them, giving Campbell a third of the Commercial Bank business and allowing him a lump payment of £250 a year to compensate for Macdonald's absences. This arrangement tightened Macdonald's finances at the very time he had to look after a permanently invalided wife as well as his mother, who kept suffering strokes even while recovering from the latest, and provide for the financial needs of his unmarried sisters, Margaret and Louisa.

Before we carry on with the chronicle of Macdonald's career, it's necessary—anyway, it ought to be useful—to describe the new political environment within which Macdonald now found himself operating.

Here, all readers to whom this mid-nineteenth-century period of Canadian politics is a well-annotated book should jump ahead to the next chapter. However, their ranks may be relatively thin. A great many Canadians have come to assume that their country began on July 1, 1867, not least because we celebrate each year that anniversary of Confederation. But Confederation wasn't the starting point of all that we now have and are. It developed from its own past, and that past, even if now far distant from us, still materially affects our present and our future.

The most explicit description of the continuity of Canadian politics across the centuries is made by historian Gordon Stewart in his book *The Origins of Canadian Politics*. There he writes, "The key to understanding the main features of Canadian national political culture after 1867 lies in the political world of Upper and Lower Canada between the 1790s and the 1860s."* His argument, one shared fully by this author, is that all Canadian politics, even those in our own postmodern, high-tech, twenty-first-century present, have been influenced substantively by events and attitudes in the horse-and-buggy Canada of our dim past.

One key example would be the role of political patronage in Canadian politics. Except on rare occasions, our two mainstream parties have either no ideology at all or only fragments of it. Their distinguishing difference is not in their titles, Liberal and Conservative, but in the fact that, at any one time, one party is in and the other is out. Without patronage, it would be just about impossible for either organization to function as a national party. Other motives, of course, attract individuals to join one or other of the mainstream parties, which alternate, rather irregularly, in office: idealism, the attraction of public service and, no less, the adrenaline high that is generated by the fierce competitiveness of the political game. But the prospect of good, high-status jobs matters as critically—in effect, no patronage, no national political parties. (Regional parties have in their very regionalism a substitute for ideology, as do the rarer ideology-driven parties like the New Democrats and the Greens.) Two international comparisons may confirm the point: in Britain, from which we originally copied a great deal, there is relatively little patronage but a considerable difference in ideology between Labour and Conservative; in the United States, always our principal comparison, there is about as much patronage as there is north of the border, but Democrats and Republicans differ in their ideology or, perhaps more particularly these days, in their cultural

---

* Stewart, an expatriate Scot, teaches at Michigan State University.

assumptions. Patronage really is as Canadian as maple syrup.

Another example, this one unique to Canada, is the effect on our political system of the ongoing alliance of convenience between the French and the English, or now, more accurately, of francophones and English-speaking Canadians. No less so before Confederation than after it, whichever party has been able to forge a partnership with francophone Quebecers has almost automatically become the government and remained in power for a long time. Few of Macdonald's political insights were as perceptive as his recognition early on that a sta-

Lord Durham, known as "Radical Jack." He found "two nations warring in the bosom of a single state" and set out to assimilate the second one—les Canadiens.

ble national government would be impossible without abundant amounts of patronage and a close, mutually self-interested apportionment of the spoils (including that generated by government spending) between the French and the English.

Now to go back to our future, this of course being also Macdonald's present.

⌐

The catalyst of fundamental change in pre-Confederation politics were the rebellions in 1837–38 by the Patriotes in Lower Canada led by Louis-Joseph Papineau, which was a serious uprising, and by the rebels in Upper Canada led by William Lyon Mackenzie, which was more of a tragicomedy. Both uprisings provided a warning to London that, as had gone the American colonies a half-century earlier, so the colonies of British North America might also go. To deal with the crisis, the Imperial government sent out one of its best and brightest.

John George Lambton, Earl of Durham, arrived accompanied by an orchestra, several race horses, a full complement of silver and a cluster of brainy aides, one of whom had achieved celebrity status by running off with a teenage heiress and serving time briefly in jail. Still in his early forties, "Radical Jack" was cerebral, cold, acerbic and arrogant. After just five months in the colony, he left in a rage after a decision of his—to exile many of the Patriotes to Bermuda without the bother of a trial—was countermanded by the Colonial Office. Back home, he completed, in 1839, a report that was perhaps the single most important public document in all Canadian history.* Lord Durham himself died of tuberculosis a year later.

Parts of Durham's report were brilliant; parts were brutal. The effects of each were identical: they both had an extraordinarily creative effect on Canada and Canadians. The brutal parts of Durham's diagnosis are, as almost always happens, much the better known. He had found here, he declared, "two nations warring in the bosom of a single state . . . a struggle, not of principles, but of races."† The French Canadians, *les Canadiens*, had to lose—for

---

* The only serious competitor for the title of "most important" would be the Rowell-Sirois Report of 1940, from the commission established originally to equip the federal government with the tools to cure the Great Depression of the previous decade. When this mission was fulfilled anyway by the economic boom generated by the Second World War, the commission's report was used to justify transferring jurisdictional responsibilities and revenues to the federal government in order to transform Canada into a welfare state.

† Durham's use of the word "race" will strike contemporary ears as odd. It was used then to describe people now usually referred to as "ethnic groups."

their own sake. They were "a people destitute of all that could constitute a nationality . . . brood[ing] in sullen silence over the memory of their fallen countrymen, of their burnt villages, of their ruined property, of their extinguished ascendancy."

. In fact, Durham was almost as harsh about the English in Canada. They were "hardly better off than the French for the means of education for their children." They were almost as indolent: "On the American side, all is activity and hustle. . . . On the British side of the line, except for a few favoured spots, all seems waste and desolate." He dismissed the powerful Family Compact as "these wretches." Still, he took it for granted that Anglo-Saxons would dominate the French majority in their own Lower Canada. "The entire wholesale and a large portion of the retail trade of the Province, with the most profitable and flourishing farms, are now in the hands of this dominant minority." All French Canadians could do was "look upon their rivals with alarm, with jealousy, and finally with hatred."

The only way to end this perpetual clash between the "races," Durham concluded, was for there to be just one race in Canada. The two separate, ethnically defined provinces of Upper Canada and Lower Canada should be combined into the United Province of Canada. As immigrants poured in from the British Isles, the French would inevitably become a minority. To quicken the pace of assimilation, the use of French should cease in the new, single legislature and government. To minimize the political weight of Lower Canada's 650,000 people, compared with Upper Canada's 450,000, each former province, now reduced to a "section," should have an equal number of members in the new legislature.*

---

* Officially, Upper Canada now became Canada West, and Lower Canada became Canada East. In fact, almost everyone continued to refer to the new sections by

Montreal. Place d'Armes, with a view of Notre Dame church, c. 1843. It was Canada's only real city, the first to install such technology as gas lights and the horse-drawn omnibus.

Durham's formula worked—but backwards. Quebec's commitment to *la survivance* dates less from Wolfe's victory over Montcalm (after which the Canadiens' religion and system of law were protected by British decree) than from 1839, when Durham told French Canadians they were finished. The consequence of this collective death sentence was an incredible flowering of a national will to remain alive.*

In the years immediately following 1839, a sociological miracle occurred in Lower Canada: a lost people found themselves.

their old titles, and for simplicity's sake this older terminology to describe today's Ontario and Quebec is used throughout this text. (In fact, the legislature relegalized the use of the old Upper and Lower Canada terms in 1849.)

* A parallel exists with the publication in 1965 of George Grant's *Lament for a Nation*, predicting Canada's inevitable absorption by America. In response, English-Canadian nationalists suddenly stood on guard for their country.

Historian François-Xavier Garneau, the poet Octave Crémazie, and Antoine Gérin-Lajoie, author of the patriotic lament *Un Canadien Errant*, created the beginnings of a national literature. Étienne Parent, a brilliant journalist, wrote a long series of articles calling for sweeping social, educational and religious reforms. The *Instituts canadiens* were founded as a means of generating intellectual inquiry and speculation and as a form of adult education. Montreal's Bishop Ignace Bourget, an ultramontane,* or right-wing Catholic, attracted major orders of priests—the Jesuits and the Oblates—and four orders of nuns to staff the new *collèges classiques*, from which a new and educated middle class would soon graduate. In 1840 there was just one priest for every two thousand parishioners; by 1880 there was one for every five hundred. As historian Susan Mann Trofimenkoff wrote in *The Dream of Nation*, "the clergy was as much a means of national unity as the railroad." The culmination of this new surge in national self-assertiveness, the Société St-Jean-Baptiste, was established in 1843.

Few in Upper Canada noticed. Their attention was focused on the other part of Durham's report, one calling for a totally different kind of Parliament. It was to be a responsible Parliament, with a cabinet composed of members of the majority party rather than chosen at the pleasure of the governor general. In a phrase of almost breathtaking boldness, Durham wrote, "The British people of the North American Colonies are a people on whom we may safely rely, and to whom we must not grudge power."

Durham almost went right to the constitutional finish line. He recognized the advantages of Confederation: "Such a union

---

* The term *ultramontanism* meant "over the mountains" to Rome. The movement began as a reaction, led by Pope Pius IX, to the ascendant liberalism sweeping across Europe; it was defensive but also reformist.

would . . . enable all the Provinces to cooperate for all common purposes," he said. "If we wish to prevent the extension of this [American] influence, it can only be done by raising up for the North American colonist some nationality of his own." At the last instant, Durham drew back from specifically recommending Confederation because he doubted that Canada possessed politicians of the calibre needed for so ambitious an undertaking.

At the time, Durham's report attracted little applause either in Canada or in Britain. A century passed before it came to be recognized by some as "the greatest state document in British imperial history." His recommendation for Responsible Government began a fundamental reordering of the Empire, and it set the political maturation of the British North American colonies in motion. Had that precedent—and its logical successor of Confederation—been applied to Ireland, as William Gladstone attempted in his Home Rule Bill in 1886, thousands of lives could have been saved.

Embedded in the proposal for Responsible Government was a fundamental illogicality. The colonial secretary, Lord John Russell, spotted it immediately: it would be "impossible," he wrote his cabinet colleagues, "for a Governor to be responsible to his Sovereign and a local legislature both at the same time." To stop Responsible Government, the British government sent out another of its best and brightest, Lord Sydenham, then in the cabinet as president of the Board of Trade. Still in his thirties, multilingual, highly professional and confident to the point of cockiness, Sydenham was one of the ablest of governors general— and one of the most dashing. Described as "worship[ping] equally at the Shrine of Venus and at the Shrine of Bacchus," he died following a fall from his horse after a visit to his mistress. He was also one of the more corrupt. The election of 1841, which he ran single-handedly, has few equals in Canadian history for chicanery, gerrymandering, vote-rigging, bribery and the systematic use of violence. Sydenham's candidates won handily.

To implement the part of Durham's program that the British government found wholly acceptable—the assimilation of the French—Sydenham moved the seat of government to Kingston, its attraction being that it was entirely English-speaking. All the legislative documents were unilingual; and the Throne Speech, read by Sydenham himself, was in English only. Following his death a year later, his successor, Sir Charles Bagot, quickly recognized that Britain had positioned itself on the wrong side of history. "Whether the doctrine of responsible government is openly acknowledged or only tacitly acquiesced in, virtually it exists," Bagot wrote home in 1842.

In fact, Britain ceded Responsible Government with remarkable readiness. The quite separate colony of Nova Scotia actually gained it two months ahead of Canada, in 1848. But it had been allowed effectively in 1846, when Britain adopted free trade and abolished its protectionist Corn Laws and Navigation Laws. Thereafter, Canada and several other colonies were free to make their own trading arrangements, thereby exercising de facto self-government.

The fight for Responsible Government mattered, though. It entered Canadian political mythology as a sort of non-violent version of the Boston Tea Party. And the struggle brought together one of the most important and appealing of all Canadian

---

* The initiation of the new legislature of the United Province of Canada was accomplished through the swearing in of Sydenham as governor general in Montreal on February 10, 1841. Proclamations in both languages were posted on the main streets, but they were all ripped down overnight.

Robert Baldwin. He won Responsible Government, or self-government, for the colony of Canada. High-minded and single-minded, he was known as the "Man of the One Idea."

political partnerships, one that would provide Macdonald with a template of the way to fashion and sustain a political alliance between the country's two principal European races.

One of these partners was Robert Baldwin. The son of a successful lawyer, William Baldwin, who had originated the idea of Responsible Government, Robert came from the same social circles as the Family Compact. He was highly intelligent and of irreproachable integrity. Robert took over the cause from his father and, in January 1836, sent a letter to the Colonial Office. In it, he made a case for Responsible Government on the politically shrewd grounds that it was essential for "continuing the connection" with Britain. Durham's advocacy of the idea can be dated to this letter.

The other partner in the emerging alliance was Louis-Hippolyte LaFontaine. He was the prototype of the commanding *le chef* figure whom Quebecers have so often followed. Grave in manner and exuding gravitas, LaFontaine was blessed with a resemblance to Napoleon that he assiduously fostered. As a one-time Patriote, he had nationalist credentials that were unimpeachable.

Soon after the formal creation of the United Province of Canada, LaFontaine spotted an opening for himself and for his Canadiens. Skilfully used, the new configuration could lead not merely to *la survivance* in defiance of Durham's assimilation program but to substantive economic benefits for his people. He saw that an alliance between his bloc of French members and the Reform group led by Baldwin would form a majority in the legislature. Baldwin would get the Responsible Government he so desired (even if it was of small interest to LaFontaine, who, by inclination, was a conservative). In exchange, LaFontaine would get the keys to the patronage treasure chests that Responsible Government would transfer from the governor general to the Canadian politicians in

Louis-Hippolyte LaFontaine. With Baldwin, he forged a French-English political alliance that turned Durham's policy upside-down.

power. Though a partnership of convenience, the alliance was also one of principle and of personal trust. In the election of 1841, with LaFontaine badly in need of a winnable seat, Baldwin found one for him among the burghers of the riding of Fourth York in Upper Canada. A year later, LaFontaine returned the compliment by handing to Baldwin the equally unilingual riding of Rimouski. (And at the personal level, Baldwin sent all four of his children to French schools in Quebec City.)

To move the Imperial government over to the "right" side of history took a new governor general, Lord Elgin. Exceptionally able, he was Durham's son-in-law and, later, viceroy of India— the top position on the Imperial ladder.* The key year was 1848, when an election returned a majority for Baldwin and

---

* Lord Elgin was the son of the British ambassador in Athens who spirited away the Elgin Marbles to the British Museum.

Governor General Lord Elgin, with his wife, Mary Louisa, her sister and an aide. Unusually able and far-sighted, he ended Durham's assimilationist policy by reading the Throne Speech in English and then, for the first time ever, repeating it in French.

LaFontaine. Acting on the principle of the sovereignty of the people, Elgin accepted the result and invited the pair to form the first biracial ministry. (Technically, LaFontaine, the leader of the largest bloc of members, was the premier. In practice, Baldwin functioned as co-premier, a system followed throughout the life of the United Province of Canada.) At the opening of that year's session of the Legislative Assembly, Elgin read the Throne Speech in English, as all his predecessors had done, and then, after a fractional pause, read it again in French. Canadien members burst into wild applause and song; one so forgot himself that he rushed up and kissed the governor general on both cheeks.

The main immediate beneficiaries of the change were the graduates now pouring out of Lower Canada's *collèges classiques.* Historian Jacques Monet has memorably described what happened in his essay "The Political Ideas of Baldwin and Lafontaine": "With a kind of bacterial thoroughness it [Quebec's emerging middle class] began to invade every vital organ of government and divide up among its members hundreds of posts." Monet went on to remark that Canadiens "came to realize that parliamentary democracy could be more than a lovely ideal: it was also a profitable fact."

Elgin accepted this downgrading, for himself and for his successors. In a dispatch to the colonial secretary he remarked that, henceforth, governors general would have to depend on "moral influence," adding, surely without really believing it, that this could "go far to compensate for the loss of power consequent on the surrender of patronage." Even Baldwin, himself skittish about patronage, declared stoutly in a legislature speech that "if appointments were not to be used for party purposes, let those who thought differently occupy the treasury benches."*

As always in government, some of the consequences of Responsible Government were unanticipated. The transfer of power from the governor general to elected politicians meant that Canadians hereafter placed blame for the mistakes that all governments make no longer at the entrance to their governor general's residence but at the doors of their cabinet ministers and premiers. Certainly, the tone of Canadian politics worsened from this time on. Sectarianism, or the injection into politics of the rivalries, suspicions and hatreds between religious groups, now became the dominant issue in Canadian politics. No less significant, once the premiers occupied the shoes of the governors general, they began to acquire some of the quasi-dictatorial habits of those who had run the country before the change to Responsible Government in 1848. Cabinet ministers now became the premiers' ministers, just as they had once been ministers of the

---

* In the nineteenth century, the customary term for patronage was the much more descriptive one of "jobbery." It had, in fact, an honorable intellectual parentage. Adam Smith, in his great *Wealth of Nations*, argued that the loss of the American colonies might have been prevented had only some of their leaders been offered "the great prizes which sometimes come from the wheel of the great state-lottery of British politics." Perhaps what the Founding Fathers were really after was less liberty than patronage.

Crown's representative. The ascent to an imperial prime ministership—best described by Donald Savoie in his *Governing from the Centre*—began very early in this country's history; it happened, moreover, far earlier here than in the United States, occurring there largely because the United States acquired immense foreign responsibilities—always quasi-imperial in their nature—which was not at all the case here. An imperial prime minister is another political attribute that is as Canadian as maple syrup.

These were epochal changes to Canada's political makeup. Yet Macdonald's contribution to them was almost non-existent. He made a few somewhat critical but carefully noncommittal comments about Responsible Government as a potential threat to the connection with Britain. For the most part, though, he simply listened and learned. It wasn't long, now, before the era of Responsible Government would be replaced by the era of government by Macdonald.

EIGHT

A Short Time before the Long Game

My plan thro' life is never to give up; if I don't
carry a thing this year, I will next.
John A. Macdonald

Macdonald's appointment by Conservative premier William Draper to the junior cabinet post of receiver general on May 22, 1847—roughly equivalent to being minister of revenue today—constituted a respectably rapid promotion. By then he'd been in the legislature for just three years and was only thirty-two years old. The Toronto *Globe*, the champion of the Reformers, dismissively advised its readers that he was "a harmless man" who, during two sessions of the legislature, had "barely opened his mouth." The *Montreal Transcript* was more positive, describing Macdonald as "a rising man." Nevertheless, there was more to the *Globe*'s judgment than partisanship.

Macdonald's public record was certainly thin. In each legislature session he'd seldom delivered more than one speech, and his contributions had almost all been on secondary issues. He still seemed undecided whether to make politics or the law his primary career. Indeed, Macdonald had been offered his first cabinet position—as solicitor general—as early as the winter of 1846–47 but turned it down because "it would make me too dependent on Govt and I like to steer my own course." During his ten months in the two junior portfolios that he did accept (the second being the somewhat more substantial one of commissioner of Crown lands), he made no great impression. Late in 1847, Macdonald introduced a bill to amend the charter of King's College in Toronto in a manner that would square the interests of the founding Anglicans with those of other religions, notably Catholics, then excluded from the college. His attempt at conciliation failed, and he had to withdraw the bill.

A sharper observer would, nevertheless, have marked Macdonald as a legislator with potential. From the start, he was a popular member of the cosy club that all parliaments become. He sat through the interminable debates, cheering on fellow Conservatives and heckling opposition members—principally the loose group of Reformers—with teasing quips. He spent many hours studying in the library. He schmoozed and chaffed and drank with the best of them, and for as long as any of them. And while he seldom spoke, his speaking style was fresh and effective. Rather than the hours-long orations then the convention, Macdonald's speeches were short (seldom more than thirty minutes in duration) and conversational in tone, as though he were talking to each member across a dinner table.

As a politician, Macdonald suffered from one serious defect, especially in those days when oratory mattered and there were no microphones to add body and timbre to a speaker's voice. Even his highly laudatory biographer Joseph Pope admitted that Macdonald "could not be called a great speaker" and that his voice, "while pleasant, was not strong, nor remarkably distinct." Journalists covering the debates complained constantly that his low voice and manner of delivery—"careless utterance, irregular inflections of voice and general disregard for acoustic effect," in the phrase of one—caused them to miss parts of his speeches. The leading journalist Hector Fabre (later a senator and diplomat) noted that "he is languid at times at stating his case and rather gropes through his opening sentences."

Macdonald rarely prepared his speeches in advance but felt his way along, testing out arguments and lines that might get through to his audiences, and chopping and changing them until he was hitting the mark. Pope, with a tone of amused resignation, recalled that Macdonald often wrote down the topic headings for his speech on the back of an envelope, which he then "not infrequently contrived to mislay." As a consequence, despite some disorganization, he kept that vital ingredient of spontaneity. There may have been defects in his speeches in conventional terms, but Macdonald consistently held his audiences. Even in his earliest years he pulled members into the House because he put on such a good show. Fabre remarked on the "matchless tact" with which Macdonald crossed swords with opponents, scoring points but never drawing blood, because, as he put it, Macdonald was "too clever and too well-versed in the knowledge of mankind to be cruel: his executions are always amusing; they extort a smile even from the gloomiest victims." Above all, his listeners knew that at one point or other Macdonald would make them laugh—and that often he would make them laugh at themselves.

Macdonald possessed another invaluable asset that made him difficult to outpoint in extemporaneous debates: he had an exceptional memory. He possessed, as many successful politicians do, an uncanny ability to remember names and faces. The examples are endless. J.P. Reeves, once a resident of Kingston, met Macdonald after an absence of more than twenty years when he was a member of a guard of honour in Belleville. "Hello, Reeves. Stand at ease," said Macdonald, after which they talked about old times. A Mr. Munroe, whom Macdonald had met once at a convention in Kingston in 1849, he remembered by his correct name when they met again thirty-three years later in St. Thomas. Either in jousts in the legislature or in contests with hecklers on the stump, Macdonald repeatedly gained an advantage by tossing out extracts from documents he had read long before, including statements once made by his opponent of the moment. The combination of his memory and his constant reading left him never short of quotations from British authors such as Trollope and Dickens. His journalist friend T.C. Patteson once got into a literary argument with colleagues and, to settle it, wrote a letter to Macdonald asking what line followed "Ye gentlemen of England who sit at home at ease." Back instantly came the answer, written on the reverse of Patteson's note, "Ah, little do you think upon the dangers of the seas."

Perhaps the most striking example of Macdonald's memory concerns a newspaper article that he scanned quickly in 1840 and then, forty years later, referred to while giving a speech in the Commons. In the speech, Macdonald recalled that "an Indian once said to myself, 'We are the wild animals; you cannot make an ox of a deer.'" He then used this example to support his argument that "you cannot make an agriculturalist of the Indian." The original article, written by an Anglican missionary to a Mohawk community at Napanee, near Kingston, described how an Indian chief had told him that God had made all kinds of different animals, from the wily fox to the industrious beaver, and also all kinds of different men. "Now you cannot teach the fox to live like the beaver, nor can you make the Indian work and live like the white man," reasoned the chief. "I have a farm and could live by it, but when the season comes for game or fish . . . I am tempted to go and look for it, even to the neglect of sowing and gathering my crops." With such a memory bank to draw on, Macdonald was not an easy opponent to outwit.

Behind the scenes, Macdonald's aptitudes and talents were beginning to get recognized. William Draper, an able man but lacking in the political skills needed to be a successful premier, began to regard him as a protégé. In March 1847 he summoned Macdonald to Montreal to help him brief the new governor general, Lord Elgin—in particular to make sure that Elgin understood the party sufficiently well not to "mistake ultra Toryism for Conservatism (i.e., selfishness for patriotism)." Elgin later described Macdonald in a dispatch home as "a person of consideration," although, for reasons not entirely clear, relations between the two men were never cordial.

Yet Macdonald remained an on-again, off-again politician. He had ample personal reasons for his ambivalence. Home was now either a silent house in which the prostrate Isabella waited for him to return to inject life and energy into it, sometimes silently turning accusatory eyes towards him when he arrived late, or, ever more often, the bleak anonymity of a boarding house in whichever city—Montreal, Toronto, Quebec—the legislature had rotated to. He had to worry about his mother, who, as she suffered a succession of twelve strokes, was looked after by his sister Louisa. "Poor Mama

Helen Macdonald in the 1860s. Hardy and strong, she survived eleven of twelve strokes. Her preferred language was Gaelic.

has again been attacked with another apoplectic affliction, and only the most prompt and vigorous measures have restored her," he wrote to Margaret Greene on September 18, 1847. In that same letter he spelled out the range of his personal problems: "Isabella is struggling for strength enough to join me in Canada this winter. I doubt much whether she will be able to muster vigour enough to do so, and I fear that neither Margaret nor Louisa will be able to go to New York to look after matters." Isabella did come back the following spring; that summer their infant son, John Alexander, died in his crib.

All that was left to Isabella now was Macdonald himself. Yet the demands of his cabinet portfolio and, at the same time, of ever-mounting difficulties at his law practice kept pulling him away from her. The more he moved away, the more frantically she tried to hold on to him. "She is just putting the finishing stitch to a new waistcoat for me, which I am to sport as a winter vest." Late in 1848, Macdonald wrote to Margaret Greene to report: "I returned last week from Toronto, my dearest sister, where I had been for the fortnight previous, attending the sittings of the Court of Queen's Bench," to find that Isabella "had been practising sitting up for a few minutes daily in my absence in order to be able to surprise me by coming to dinner which she effected. We had our little table brought to her bed room, and there we dined in State." He would leave the house at nine each morning, returning around six, and he admitted that "her time passes very monotonously out here."

Isabella did have some duties to occupy herself. "She had as much to do as she is able for, in directing the household affairs, managing her servants etc., and I can assure you, such is her attention and method that confined to the room though she may be, she makes a capital housekeeper," he told Margaret Greene. Everything was kept neat and tidy, and "*my* dinner, the great event of each day, about which poor Isa takes the greatest pains, is served up as well as one could wish." Even when confined to bed day after day, as was increasingly the case, she still struggled to keep connected to him—just. "She is like the 'Invisible Lady' that used to exhibit, not 'show' herself some years ago," he told Margaret Greene. "The invisible Lady's voice orders & behests are heard and obeyed all over the house & are carried out as to cupboards which she never sees & pots & pans that have no acquaintance with her. Not a glass is broken or set of dishes diminished, but she knows of, and calls the criminal to account for."

Politics, though, kept demanding his attention. He had to go to Montreal, "but not for long," and yet, "the idea of my going distresses her so much that I would not go, were it not a matter of necessity."

In a letter Macdonald sent to Margaret Greene in January 1850, he sounds like someone feeling himself pulled apart by horses charging in different directions. "Since September last I have been alone and without a [law] partner," he wrote. "Isa says I work too hard, & in truth I begin to feel that I do, but like a thief on the treadmill, I *must* step on, or be dragged."

Macdonald's reference to his being without a partner derived from his difficulties with Alexander Campbell. Macdonald's constant absences, and the fact that he sometimes dipped into the firm's funds to cover his political expenses, had made Campbell

Alexander Campbell, Macdonald's first law partner, later his political Mr. Fix-It and then a cabinet minister. No one worked more closely with Macdonald for a longer period, but they were never real friends.

more and more dissatisfied with their partnership arrangement. Their bank account was overdrawn, and the firm was eighteen hundred pounds in debt. Campbell wrote him crossly, "Your absence from home and your necessities have been I think the *main* although not by any means the only cause of the annoyances that have arisen." In reply, Macdonald assured him, "I think I have hit on the *only* mode by which we can prevent inextricable confusion." He offered a new arrangement of a fifty-fifty split of all revenues, including those from the Commercial Bank, and the assurance that, "when in Kingston, Macdonald to attend to business." Campbell initially accepted the arrangement. He wrote reassuringly to Macdonald that he was "anxious that your political career should not be cut short at this point." Later, Campbell changed his mind. Their partnership was dissolved in September 1849, with Macdonald buying back Campbell's share for £1,250. Macdonald engaged other partners, but never again one as competent as Campbell. Yet despite their business breakup, Macdonald and Campbell maintained their close political partnership.

In the meantime, Macdonald found himself increasingly pinched for money. "I am more than usually *tight* now," he wrote to a friend, reminding him of a debt of "five pounds for books, besides some interest." In a later letter to another friend he used the expressive phrase "I haven't got a shilling to jingle on a tombstone."

Given all the costs Macdonald was covering—Isabella and her servants, his mother, his unmarried sisters, his own expenses—it was no surprise that he should be financially strapped. But he ought not to have been as short of revenues as he in fact was. As a member of the legislature, he'd made useful new business contacts in addition to the networks he'd already developed in Kingston and Montreal, and extended across the Atlantic to

England. His political responsibilities were a major distraction, but the root cause of his money problems was that he simply wasn't a very good businessman. A friend and fellow Conservative, the Hamilton businessman Isaac Buchanan, once wrote in affectionate censoriousness, "I would not have supposed it possible that a man of so much intellect and general versatility could on this one matter [finance] be such a child." No doubt he was exasperated as well as amused by Macdonald's overconfidence in his financial capabilities, as when he wrote to Buchanan, who was himself highly successful, "I thoroughly understand that business and can invest without chance or risk of loss." In truth, Macdonald never applied himself consistently to the task. There was something of his father in him: he was much the smarter and the more purposeful, but in financial matters he too was dreamy and, in the end, not at all as interested in making money as in spending it.

By this time, Macdonald had undergone one other major change in his circumstances. In the election held early in 1848, he won easily in Kingston, but the Conservatives were voted out of office and lost half their members.* A new Reform government took office, run jointly by Baldwin and LaFontaine. Macdonald and his colleagues were beached on the Opposition benches.

For a time, there was a real possibility that Macdonald would never get back to the government side of the chamber, or even to the chamber itself. In August 1849 the Kingston *Chronicle* ran a story

---

* Macdonald's patron, Draper, had managed to avoid the firing line ahead of this debacle by getting himself appointed to the bench.

that he had made up his mind to resign, and it went on to speculate about possible successors. Two days later the anonymous author of a letter to the newspaper called on fellow Conservatives to persuade Macdonald to stay. Throughout his long career, Macdonald regularly mused out loud about resigning, and sometimes specifically threatened to do so. Most times he did this to discipline his supporters or to vent his own frustrations. On this occasion, he may well have meant it. Campbell, in a letter written to him several years later, referred to these times: "You will remember that throughout your long and apparently hopeless opposition [1848 to 1854] I always deprecated your retiring from parliament, as you often threatened to do." A threat made to someone as close to him as Campbell was almost certainly a serious one; it's entirely possible that Campbell leaked the information to the *Chronicle* to head him off—as it turned out, successfully.

Macdonald's political letters during this period provide indirect evidence that he was serious about quitting. Almost always, they brim with mischievousness, energy and guile, such as when he recommends arguments that candidates could use on the stump and then dismisses his own concoctions as "bunkum arguments." But most of the political observations he made to correspondents through the late forties and early fifties are bland and routine. Their tone was that of someone disengaged from what he was doing.

In the end, despite the vacillations, Macdonald decided to remain a full-time politician. Somehow, along with his work, he would juggle both his family responsibilities and his financial obligations. He described his political strategy as playing "the long game." He was resilient, tenacious, indefatigable. As he said in one speech, "If I don't carry a thing this year, I will next." His favourite phrase for minimizing setbacks and miscalculations was the old saying "There's no use crying over spilt milk."

So he continued to play the long game. Macdonald remained an active local member, lobbying for legislation to benefit home-town institutions such as Queen's University, Regiopolis College and the Kingston Hospital. His reward was a repeat victory in the 1851 election, his third in a row, not only for himself but this time also for three other Conservative candidates in the surrounding Midland District. He had earned, now, not just a local but a regional base. That the Reformers continued their hold on power, and the Conservatives did poorly elsewhere, only increased his stature.

At this same time, he began gathering around him one of the most useful of all political assets—a stable of close friends who would be reliable, long-term allies. Campbell functioned as Macdonald's local campaign manager and as a general "fixer" throughout Upper Canada, recruiting candidates, handling election funds, distributing patronage to pro-Conservative newspapers. Another member of Macdonald's Kingston mafia was Henry Smith, a fellow lawyer who had helped him found Kingston's Cataraqui Club "for the discussion (under proper restrictions) of the various subjects which ought to interest society." They were so close that Macdonald asked Smith to intervene for him in an "affair of honour" arising from a nasty exchange in the House with an opposing member—an episode that could have led to a duel between them.

The most important member of the network that Macdonald was building systematically was a fellow Scot, John Rose. After earning a degree at the University of Edinburgh, he had immigrated to Montreal in 1836. There, Rose quickly became one of city's leading corporate lawyers; later he moved to London,

John Rose, a highly successful Montreal lawyer who became a substantial financial and social figure in London. He and Macdonald were exceptionally close, intellectually as well as personally.

England, where he became an insider in financial and political circles, serving on two royal commissions, and, as a friend of the Prince of Wales, a society leader. Although fascinated by the political game, Rose was only twice, briefly, an active politician in Canada, as a junior minister in 1857 and, for two years, as Macdonald's first post-Confederation finance minister. They respected each other's intelligence and enjoyed flouting convention; once, while young, they crossed the border and pretended to be strolling entertainers, Rose as a bear and Macdonald playing some instrument. Macdonald's secretary, Joseph Pope, reckoned that of all his intimates, "personally, he was most attracted to Rose."

Ogle Gowan was another important member of the network, though in a very different way: with him came votes. Gowan was the grand master of the Orange Lodge. In hindsight, those Orangemen are seen today as anti-Catholic and anti-French fanatics. Many were. Many, though, joined only for the business and social contacts the lodge provided. Gowan himself was a moderate. He forged an alliance with Irish Catholics in Upper Canada and lost his position when hard-liners decided he had "sold out to the Pope." It was only after Gowan's defeat as grand master that the organization took on its full anti-French colour. He and Macdonald became friends in the mid-1840s when they were working together to replace Family Compact Tories with moderate Conservatives, largely because the old Tories looked down on

Orangemen as not respectable. Nevertheless, Macdonald always held Gowan at a certain distance and never gave him the high-level government posts he sought. Their friendship ended in 1862 when Gowan was charged with the rape of a serving girl: although he was acquitted, his political career was ended. Macdonald's last contact with Gowan was to appoint him to the minor post of inspector of money orders in the post office.

Quite different was another Gowan, James Gowan, a cousin, who, when appointed to the bench in 1843, was the youngest judge in the British Empire. Sophisticated, intelligent and an outstanding judge, although refusing all promotions

Ogle Gowan. As grand master of the Orange Lodge—a moderate later pushed out by hardliners—he brought to Macdonald the greatest of all political assets: votes.

(during his long career on the bench only two of his judgments were overruled), Gowan exchanged letters with Macdonald over the decades on everything from politics to literature. Near the end of his life, Macdonald appointed Gowan to the Senate, where, although nominally a Conservative, he functioned as an independent.

⌐

Macdonald gave at least one strong signal that he still wasn't really committed to politics. At the close of the 1840s, Canadian politics were dominated by a crisis that touched directly on the subject that most commanded Macdonald's heart—Canada's connection to Britain. Yet he had almost nothing to say about this defining issue.

In the mid-1840s, the British prime minister, Robert Peel, adopted free trade. One objective was to reduce the cost of importing food, so as to help the starving Irish through the potato famine. The main reason was that Manchester free-traders such as Richard Cobden and John Bright had won the argument that Britain, as the world's leading economy, would gain by opening wide its doors to raw materials while exporting its cornucopia of manufactured goods.* No nation was more affected by the abandonment of Imperial Preference than Canada. Within a few years, all the protective tariffs that subsidized its exports to Britain—principally of lumber and flour—vanished. A few years later the Navigation Laws, which gave an advantage to colonial shipping, were repealed. Wheat exports dropped by more than 50 per cent, and flour exports by 40 per cent. Cheaper and better wood began to be shipped to Britain from the Baltic. In 1849 Governor General Elgin estimated that "property in most Canadians towns, and most especially in the capital [Montreal], has fallen 50 percent in value . . . three-fourths of the commercial men are bankrupt."

Across Canada there was widespread anger and a sense of abandonment. To magnify this discontent, the Imperial government had refused the demands of Tory Conservatives to disallow

---

* The most approving comment about Britain's adoption of free trade came from across the Atlantic, from Andrew Carnegie, the Scot expatriate now well on his way to fame and fortune in the United States. Trade didn't follow the flag, declared Carnegie; rather, "trade follows the lowest price current. If a dealer in any colony wished to buy Union Jacks he would order them from Britain's worst foe if he could save sixpence."

a Rebellion Losses Bill introduced by the co-premier, LaFontaine. The bill provided compensation for property damaged during the Rebellion of 1837–38, and many of the beneficiaries would be those Lower Canadians who had actually rebelled against the Crown. On April 25, 1849, riots instigated by local Conservatives broke out in Montreal. That night, the rioters (all of them English-speaking) broke into the Parliament Buildings and put them to the torch; the buildings were burned to the ground, and almost all the books and collections in the parliamentary library were destroyed.

In response, Montreal businessmen and financiers organized a petition condemning British policy. Eventually, the document carried more than one thousand signatures, among them two Redpaths, three Workmans, two Molsons, a future prime minister (John Joseph Abbott) and three future cabinet ministers of Canada. In October, a mass meeting in Montreal approved a manifesto calling for "a friendly and peaceful separation from the British connection and a union upon equitable terms with the great North American Confederacy of Sovereign States"—in other words, for annexation.

Macdonald kept almost completely silent about this direct challenge to the British connection, though he helped to organize a meeting in Kingston of a new British America League. After roundly rejecting annexation, the league argued instead for some form of reciprocity pact or cross-border free-trade deal with the United States to replace the lost British market. The Kingston meeting attracted few other leading politicians, excepting Macdonald, a home-towner. He did not make a speech or play any role in drafting the communiqué. By the time the league ceased to function, towards the end of 1850, Macdonald had already cut his association with it.

In fact, with the ending of a worldwide depression in 1850,

most of the lost prosperity quickly returned. Montreal businessmen and financiers abandoned their temporary interest in
protest and transferred their allegiance to the cause of reciprocity with the United States. Elgin exercised some brilliant diplomacy to arrange a pact between the two countries in 1854. The
real political significance of what had happened was that during
the turmoil Macdonald had scarcely stirred.

Two factors may have caused Macdonald to make up his mind
sometime in the early 1850s that politics, and not the law, would
be his life's work. The first was that, late in 1849, Isabella told him
a second miracle was about to occur in their married life: although
now forty years old, she was pregnant again. On December 9,

*Hugh John as a baby, c. 1852. He was the
only child of Macdonald and Isabella to survive. His mother was too ill to care for him,
and he and Macdonald later became
estranged. The artist is Sawyer.*

1849, Macdonald informed Margaret
Greene, with mixed hope and fear,
that "Isa views her coming trials with
great fortitude & from her courage &
patience I have every hope of a happy
issue. Still she prepares for the
worst." A month later, he reported
that "all arrangements have long
been made, and she now awaits for
the issue with patience and fortitude.
She has given me many directions
about herself and her offspring,
which any evil happen, & having
done all that she can do, is now content." But Macdonald was not able to
focus only on his wife and unborn
child. A fortnight earlier, he told his

sister-in-law in another letter that his mother, following yet another couple of attacks, was "perfectly resigned to her probable fate and sudden exit."

By early February 1850, Macdonald was writing that Isabella's "immediate confinement is much to be desired, this continuance of suffering wears down her strength." A few days later he reported again that "the struggle has exhausted her very much, but she has kept up her spirits." Finally, on March 13, 1850, Macdonald declared in triumph, "We have got Johnnie back again, almost his image." The baby was less "delicate" than the brother he would never meet, but "born fat & coarse." He was called Hugh John, names that connected him to both his father and his grandfather.

The second explanation for Macdonald's decision about his career was that, sometime early in the decade, he realized that he could get right to the top. He was, still, a relatively new guy, and he had at last begun to frame in his mind a genuinely new idea. As well, his mother, still watching over him despite her repeated strokes, had always told him that he was destined one day to be "more than an ordinary man."

NINE

Enlarging the Bounds

~

If a Lower Canada Britisher desires to conquer, he must "stoop to
conquer." He must make friends with the French; without sacrificing
the status of his race or lineage, he must respect their nationality.
John A. Macdonald

Almost without exception, almost every party that
has formed the government in Canada has embodied
two defining characteristics: it has been a centrist
coalition, and it has been a French-English alliance.
These ruling principles of Canadian politics were invented by
Macdonald. In this sense, he can lay claim to a second "Father of"
title—as the architect and builder of Canada's political Big Tent.

In February 1854, while still in opposition, Macdonald wrote
a long letter to James McGill Strachan, a Toronto lawyer, alderman and Conservative supporter, in response to his criticism that
their party was habitually ineffectual. Macdonald began by
admitting that Strachan was quite correct, saying, "We are a
good deal hampered with 'old blood.'" He reassured Strachan
that the party's leader, Sir Allan MacNab, whom Macdonald
always referred to with mixed exasperation and affection as "the
Gallant Knight," will "not be in our way." MacNab, he continued, was "very reasonable and requires only that we should not in

his 'sere and yellow leaf' offer him the indignity of casting him aside." In case the doubts he had expressed about his leader should ever get back to MacNab, Macdonald added that he himself "would never assent to" MacNab's being dumped, "for I cannot forget his services in days gone by."

The preliminaries done, Macdonald got down to the point he wanted to make to Strachan: the Conservative Party could be, and had to be, radically reorganized and re-energized. "My belief is there must be a material change in the character of the new House. I believe also there must be a change of Ministry after the election, and from my friendly relations with the French, I am inclined to believe my assistance would be sought." As for other changes after the election, "There would be a new House & new people to choose from, and our aim should be to enlarge the bounds of our party so as to embrace every person desirous of being counted as a 'progressive conservative.'"

In those few sentences, Macdonald sketched out a formula to create a different kind of Conservative Party—an entity quite unlike any other party then functioning in Canada. He was proposing that the Conservatives stretch themselves in two directions they had never gone before or had seldom ever thought about: first, to reach out to French members to try to form an alliance with a group among them.* And, simultaneously, to open themselves—"to embrace," as Macdonald put it—all voters who were prepared to be progressive about some issues, even while being conservative about others. There would be a cost to this dual expansion: certain ridings would have to be reserved for candidates who were not themselves Conservatives, and, by

---

* William Draper, Conservative leader and premier when Macdonald entered politics, made some attempts to reach out to Canadien members, but he lacked the skills to make it happen.

extension, some cabinet posts also. Patronage would likewise have to be divvied up to accommodate more than party members. Another complication, potentially even greater, was that quite a few Conservatives, above all those who were members of the Loyal Orange Lodge, were decidedly hostile to French Canadians. They would have to be persuaded that finding space among themselves for a bloc of Canadien members was a worthwhile price to pay to achieve power—principally on the grounds that this was the only way for the Conservatives to ever do so.

Macdonald had come to his Conservatism without having given it much thought, if any at all. Being a Conservative was of course a virtual precondition for getting elected in Loyalist Kingston. All his friends and business partners were Conservatives. They favoured what he favoured—loyalty to the Crown, hostility to the universal franchise, deep suspicion of anything American, a great respect for law and order and an abiding skepticism about change as a virtue in its own right. In the middle of the nineteenth century, little in this litany of attitudes and assumptions made the Conservative Party in the least unusual. The Reformers, now in government, were about as conservative in their views, and even more timid than the Conservative Party about spending money on nation-building projects such as railways and canals. The pro-clerical *bleus* in Lower Canada were more conservative still. The only exceptions were, in Upper Canada, the populist Grits and, in Lower Canada, the liberal *rouges*, who opposed the right-wing conservatism of Montreal's ultramontane Bishop Ignace Bourget.

In fact, this kind of taxonomy of parties and groupings in mid-nineteenth century Canada is far too neat and tidy. In the contemporary sense of the term, parties scarcely existed then. Many members, no matter on what label they gained election, performed thereafter as "loose fish," as the term went. They voted, this is to say, not with their party but as they judged best, in their own and their constituents' interest; nor were they penalized for their lack of discipline. Indeed, party discipline of the contemporary kind was widely condemned as "partyism"; the ideal, if seldom achieved, was that the legislature should function as a debating chamber somewhat like a Greek *agora* or a New England town hall. As a consequence, and as one of the most striking differences between politics then and now, premiers (or co-premiers, as a further complication) functioned roughly as leaders of a permanent minority government, always at risk of defeat and having forever to bargain with groups of members or with individuals for their temporary support. This challenge applied no less to the Reformers, who were more often in office, than to the Conservatives. Thus, after Baldwin and LaFontaine retired, a leading Reformer, Francis Hincks, became premier. An able man but forever dogged by scandal, Hincks led a fragile government that depended on the support of a small group of Canadiens led by a fellow Reformer, Augustin-Norbert Morin.

Just one party had about it some of the attributes of modernity (in an ideological sense rather than an organizational one): those intriguing newcomers to the Canadian political scene, the populist Grits. Early in 1850, a number of high-minded types gathered at the Toronto offices of a young lawyer turned journalist, William McDougall, to form an association of what one of them called "only men who are Clear Grit." The name stuck, and the new movement spread rapidly in Toronto and through the rich farmlands to the west and south. The old rebel, William Lyon Mackenzie, returned from exile to join it. In many ways, the Grits prefigured by more than a century the populist Reform Party of the 1980s and 1990s. They advocated direct democracy (including the election of many office holders), the open ballot, fixed parliamentary terms and Representation by Population (although not the universal franchise). They produced a lively newspaper, the *North American*, edited by McDougall. The movement's most important qualities were energy and purposefulness. In the short term, its principal political effect was to split the non-Conservative vote in Upper Canada.

In many ways the political system was often downright amateurish, certainly by contemporary standards, if in some respects engagingly so, because nineteenth-century politicians often said what they meant rather than what they thought their party wanted them to say. And the "partyism" we now take for granted as the way parties should function is indeed thoroughly bureaucratic. But then it was all quite chaotic and intensely local, with petty and immediate issues repeatedly trumping national ones.

Macdonald now began to plot a way through this congenial chaos towards some political order. In no way was he seeking order for the sake of implementing particular policies, national or otherwise. He was seeking it for the sake of power, because he had come to realize, by some combination of instinct and experience, that the precondition for power, for gaining it and even more for holding it, was order and organization. Feeling his way along, and without any precedents to guide him (none existed in Britain at this time),* Macdonald was working his way towards turning the Conservative Party, with all the "loose fish" swimming inside it or every now and then darting towards and then away from it, into an entity that roughly constituted a precursor to Canada's national political parties of today.

He was out to reorganize the Conservatives in three radical respects. First, he wished to make it a centrist party, so that its

---

* The first, modern-style, organized political party in Britain can be dated to Gladstone's Liberals of the 1880s.

members wouldn't repeatedly charge off on their own pet crusades. To do this, he wanted it to be filled with "progressive Conservatives" rather than the old bewhiskered crowd of Family Compact Tories. They, he wrote cuttingly, had "little ability, no political principles and no strength in numbers," adding, in case anyone doubted his feelings, that they had "contrived . . . to make us and our whole party stink in the nostrils of all liberal-minded people." In one particularly graphic phrase, Macdonald denounced those he called "pre-Adamite Tories"— those who hadn't evolved much beyond the dinosaurs. He would quit, he wrote to a Conservative friend, "rather than have anything to do with such a reactionary party." Second, Macdonald wanted to make it a true national party. This required forging an alliance between the Conservatives and a bloc of Canadien members. LaFontaine and Baldwin had already followed this route, but their alliance had lasted only a few years, with both leaders retiring soon after they had achieved their goal of Responsible Government. By contrast, Macdonald wanted to create a French-English union that would be the foundation of a permanent governing party. Lastly, he aimed to use patronage not just to reward supporters but to attract newcomers into the party, and to keep supporters loyal when particular actions by their party might otherwise have caused them to waver.

The consequence of all this work would be power, for the Conservatives and for Macdonald. This power, though, would be in the hands of moderate men, both French and English—"moderate" being one of his favourite words. This new, organized coalition would be made up of three groups: his own Conservatives, with the "pre-Adamite Tories" among them kept firmly in check; a bloc of Canadiens, the obvious ones to target being the *bleus*; and, finally, a number of "loose-fish" Reformers who would hop abroad the bandwagon as it rolled towards power.

From this mélange emerged as oddly named a party as any that ever made it to the Canadian political stage: the Liberal-Conservative Party. (The name had to have been Macdonald's, but no specific evidence of its authorship exists.) To a substantial extent, the new nomenclature was pure illusion. The party's so-called Liberal wing comprised just a few Reformers whom Macdonald seduced into joining him by promising them cabinet posts. Their presence, though, discomforted his Reform opponents and, no less usefully, diminished the influence of the new party's outright Tories. At the same time, Macdonald's concoction had substance. Combined with the bloc of *bleu* members, the coalition would have a quasi-permanent majority in the legislature and, thereby, a firm hold upon power. The result would be Canada's first stable government—giving it at least the possibility of administrative professionalism. Moreover, because this government would be composed of both French and English Canadians, the two sides would learn about each other—and about accommodation and compromise.

In trying to get all these factions heading in the same direction, Macdonald faced one distinctively Canadian problem. If a Liberal-Conservative alliance was imaginable, so too was its mirror image of a Conservative-Liberal alliance—or an alliance between the Reformers and "progressive Conservatives." The leading Reformer was George Brown, owner and publisher of the Toronto *Globe*. The same idea had, in fact, occurred to him. "Between the great mass of the Reformers of Upper Canada and this largest or liberal section of the Conservatives, there is little difference of opinion," he said in a statement reported in his newspaper on February 27, 1854. "Not one great principle divides them. Nothing but old recollections of antagonism."

In the contest between them, Macdonald had one decisive asset. As he had written to Strachan, he enjoyed "friendly relations with the French." By contrast, Brown had far too often denounced "French domination," either personally or through the pages of his *Globe*, and the Grits were even more virulent in their criticism of the French. Macdonald saw this door of opportunity opening before him, and through it he slipped.

Where Baldwin and LaFontaine had left off, Macdonald now took over. In part, his plan was of course pure opportunism. It was also, though, the product of an idea about Canada's very nature that was uncommonly imaginative and generous. Indeed, it's not easy to identify any leading English-Canadian politician, all the way down to the 1960s (when the rise of separatism in Quebec caused everyone's mind to focus wonderfully), who came close to matching the vision of the country that Macdonald expressed at this time.

Macdonald didn't go in for grand ideas or for the "vision thing." He expressed his understanding of Canada's nature in colloquial language in a private letter, one written to a correspondent who disagreed with almost everything he was saying. There was no benefit to Macdonald in this exercise, therefore. He wrote it in order to think out what it was that he actually believed.

This remarkable statement, often quoted but most times only in summary form, is contained in the letter Macdonald wrote in January 1856 to Brown Chamberlain, the editor of the Montreal *Gazette*. Typically, he began with a joke. He had been lax, he admitted, in replying to Chamberlain's earlier letters, so "I have hunted up your old letters, so that you see I *cherish* them, if I do not reply." Next came some gossip. Then, without any peal of oratorical trumpets, Macdonald set out some of the most insightful passages in all Canadian political prose.

> The truth is you British L[ower] Canadians never can forget that you were once supreme, that Jean Baptiste was your hewer of wood and drawer of water. You struggle like the protestant Irish in Ireland, like the Norman invaders in England, not for equality but *ascendancy*. The difference between you and those interesting and amiable people is that you have not the honesty to admit it. You can't and won't admit the principle that the majority must govern. The Gallicans may fairly be reckoned as two-thirds ag-st one third of all the other races who are lumped together as *Anglo-Saxon*. Heaven save the mark! Now you have nearly one-third if not quite of the representat-n of Lower Canada, & why is it the misfortune of your position that you are in a minority & therefore can't command the majority of votes. The only remedies are immigration and copulation and these will work wonders.
>
> . . . No man in his senses can suppose that this country can for a century to come be governed by a totally unfrenchified Gov-t. If a Lower Canada Britisher desires to conquer, he must "stoop to conquer." He must make friends with the French; without sacrificing the status of his race or lineage, he must respect their nationality. Treat them as a nation and they will act as a free people usually do—generously. Call them a faction and they become factious.
>
> Supposing the numerical preponderance of British in Canada becomes greater than it now is. I think the French would give more trouble than they are now said to do. At present, they divide, as we do, they are split up in several sections, & are governed more or less by defined principles of action. As they become smaller and feebler, so they will be more united, from a sense of self-preservation they

> will act as one man & hold the balance of power. . . . So long as the
> French have 20 votes, they will be a power & must be conciliated.

Then came some political gossip, followed by his customary jaunty ending. "I scarcely think you can read this scrawl. It is written by the light of one dip & my eyes are rapidly becoming irascible. Good night to you."

Even all these decades later, after such an overflowing abundance of books, of learned articles and speeches and conferences and colloquia, all explaining what it is that Quebecers really want, it is hard to identify an analysis that comes nearer to understanding the way Canada is defined by the political dynamic between a threatened minority and a casually confident majority than this exposition, written late at night by a guttering candle and tossed into the mail without a single word or sentence altered. Much that is in it—the invocation to "respect their nationality" as an obvious example—is as relevant today as it was then. Such a capacity for understanding and generosity would be uncommon under any circumstances, but especially in an unsentimental and pragmatic power-seeking politician. A comment about Macdonald by Pope is relevant here, namely that there was "an entire absence of prejudice in his large and liberal mind." He took people as they were, with all their faults and frailties, and almost never judged them or moralized about their failings.

Macdonald also exploited people for his own partisan purposes when their religion or culture or language might be of use to him. His goal wasn't to preserve the French fact in Canada for its own sake, but rather to achieve national harmony so the government could get on with its business—and, as doesn't need to be added, to gain and retain power. In mid-nineteenth-century Canada, though, it took an unusually large and liberal mind to conceive that government itself had to function so as to accommodate, year in, year out, the inescapably conflicting interests of the two European peoples—or nations—who made up the national political community.

There was another, seldom-appreciated reason why Macdonald understood French Canadians so readily. He wasn't an English Canadian himself. He was a Scottish Canadian.

Macdonald himself was a member of a small, threatened people. Between Scots and French there had been the Auld Alliance of the two of them against the English; but that was now history. Current, though, was the fact that the Scots, like French Canadians, had their own religion, their own educational and legal systems, and even, if growing weak, their own language. So they were at ease in each other's company. French-Scottish marriages were common, in contrast to their scarcity among the English and the Irish. André Siegfried, who came over from France to survey Canada much as de Tocqueville did in America, wrote in his 1907 work, *The Race Question in Canada*, "They [Scots] manifested a real goodwill towards the French, and the latter were the first to recognize it." And Wilfrid Laurier once said, "Were I not French I would be honoured to be a Scot."* It's hard to doubt that when Macdonald looked at Lower Canada, he sometimes saw Scotland.

About Macdonald's personal command of the French language itself there is uncertainty. The evidence is mixed. George-Étienne Cartier's assistant, Benjamin Sulte, wrote in his memoir

---

* Laurier actually spoke English with a slight Scots accent, having learned the language in the Lower Canada settlement of New Glasgow—an area originally settled by Scots.

that "Macdonald was fond of reading French novels—he always kept them close at hand." No supporting evidence for this claim exists, and Sulte may have chanced upon a French novel on Macdonald's desk that actually belonged to his second wife, the creditably bilingual Agnes. The historian Ged Martin has reported that a unilingual Canadien member, François Bourassa, claimed to have had a number of conversations in French with Macdonald while the two whiled away the time in the legislature.* Yet the Montreal lawyer and journalist François-Xavier-Anselme Trudel commented in an article published in 1887 that Macdonald knew not a word of French. The probability is that Macdonald in fact spoke very little French (the Bourassa story may just have been family myth) but could read it comparatively well—not to the level of being able to enjoy French novels but sufficiently to comprehend the letters that, for instance, Étienne-Paschal Taché, twice his co-premier, regularly sent him in French.

The Big Tent that Macdonald was out to erect was thus to be held up by four supports: Conservatives willing and able to be reasonably progressive; Reformers looking for a sanctuary; a dependable bloc of Canadiens; and Macdonald himself, as master builder and circus barker. Once set up and shown to be durable, this became the political edifice that almost every one of Macdonald's successors down to today would attempt to emulate.

* Ged Martin unearthed the François Bourassa story in Roger Le Moine's 1974 book, *Napoléon Bourassa l'homme et l'artiste*. The French novel Macdonald supposedly was reading was *Le Diable boiteux* [The Devil on Two Sticks] by Alain-René Lesage. It's about romantic misadventures involving greybeards marrying young girls, and bankrupt heiresses marrying fortune hunters. It's hard to believe it would be to Macdonald's taste.

In the fall of 1853, the Hincks-Morin government entered its death throes. Hincks became the subject of press stories that he and the mayor of Toronto had refinanced the city's debt by a private manoeuvre that earned them each ten thousand pounds. The press hounds kept on sniffing and came up with reports about railway stock that Hincks had picked up for a song and some bargain-priced government land he had profited from.

The inevitable election finally came in June 1854, after Hincks had lost two successive confidence votes in the legislature. In the election, Macdonald, for the first and only time in his career, made the corruption of his opponents his central theme, coining the phrase that Hincks and his ministers were "steeped to the lips in corruption"—an exercise in verbal cleverness he would come to regret because it would be quoted back at him. He won handsomely in Kingston. Across Upper Canada, though, the Conservatives did comparatively poorly, in part because Macdonald was known to be friendly towards the French—the Orange Order, had, by this time, turned against his key Orange ally, Ogle Gowan. As an additional handicap, the Conservative leader for whom people were actually being asked to vote was not Macdonald but Sir Allan MacNab—a decent old duffer and military hero of the 1838 Rebellion, but indiscreet enough to say "all my politics are railroads" at the same time that he was president of the Great Western Railway and leader of the opposition. MacNab was a figure out of the past. "The party is nowhere, damned everlastingly," Macdonald wrote despondently to Alexander Campbell after the election. At that very point, Hincks lost yet another confidence vote and suddenly resigned.*

---

* Apologists claimed that Hincks had clung to office only to prevent Brown from replacing him with a ministry from which all French Canadians would be excluded. This effort may account for his being rewarded in 1856 with an appointment by the British government as governor of Barbados and the

MacNab was now called in by the governor general to form a new government. A lot of baling wire went into its assembly. All the Canadien ministers who had served under Hincks were kept in their posts. There were six newcomers—three Conservatives, with MacNab at their head, and three Reformers, to give some credence to the Liberal-Conservative label. Macdonald, as the new attorney general for Upper Canada, held the cabinet's most important portfolio. And of these two principal figures, MacNab was for show and Macdonald was for real.

As attorney general, Macdonald now had a quite comfortable income of £1,250 a year. He was able to sort out without strain many of the responsibilities that fell to him as head of the family. In 1852 a most unexpected family event had occurred: his sister Margaret, aged thirty-nine, married James Williamson, a professor of science at Queen's University.* It was a successful marriage, and Macdonald developed a high regard for Williamson, who, although bookish and humourless, was well liked by colleagues and students. Macdonald's nickname for Williamson, an ordained Presbyterian minister, was the affectionately teasing term "the Parson."

Margaret's marriage left Louisa isolated as the remaining unmarried sister. Macdonald arranged for her to move into the

---

Windward Islands. He later returned to Canada as Macdonald's post-Confederation minister of finance.

* Macdonald actually missed the wedding because he was detained in Quebec City on legislature business. He got Louisa to buy his present for the couple: "I wish that Moll should have a good kit, & I wish you to spend £25 for her on such things as you like. Don't say anything to her about it."

Margaret Macdonald. To everyone's surprise (not least to Macdonald, who missed her wedding), she suddenly married a Queen's University professor, James Williamson. They became the de facto parents of Hugh John.

James Williamson, dour and humourless, yet well liked by his students, other professors and Macdonald. (This photo, as well as the photos of Margaret and Louisa, is from Lady Macdonald's personal album.)

Williamson household with their mother, Helen, for whom she had been caring. Showing the Macdonald streak of stubborn independence, Louisa insisted that she not go there as a dependant. Macdonald's solution was inventive and perhaps unique. He rented the house—Heathfield—that the Williamsons owned, naming Louisa as his representative. This arrangement ensured that, technically, the Williamsons were now boarding with Louisa in their own house. Louisa was entitled to sit at the head of the table, except when Macdonald visited and she moved to one side. As the "tenant," Louisa had the right to invite friends to visit, rather than merely joining gatherings arranged by the Williamsons. She also rented (again with Macdonald's financial aid) a portion of the garden, where she grew her own flowers and vegetables; Professor Williamson had his own vegetable plot

and charged the general household
for any produce consumed by the
group. The real hero of this arrangement was Margaret: she understood, as few chatelaines would do,
Louisa's fierce determination not to
become a kind of paying guest in her
sister's house.

Nothing, though, could change
the state of Macdonald's own marriage. There was one small ray of
hope. In 1855, when the government
moved from Quebec City to Toronto,
the national capital for the next four
years, Isabella decided to join him,
and she made the journey from

Louisa Macdonald. Difficult, fiercely inde-
pendent, a lifelong spinster, but also
Macdonald's favourite sister.

Kingston by train that October. They rented an apartment in a
boarding house on Wellington Street, near the city's western outskirts. Hugh John, now five years old and living more often with
his surrogate parents, Margaret and James Williamson, than with
the invalid Isabella, was brought up to Toronto to join his father
and mother.

By this time, Toronto had suddenly taken off as a community.
New immigrants poured into the city, swelling its population to
forty thousand. (Kingston's population, meanwhile, remained
unchanged at five thousand.) Toronto's own manufacturing
plants and the success of the farmers to the southwest brought it
prosperity. Substantial buildings such as the St. Lawrence Hall,
the Mechanics' Institute and St. James' Cathedral had been completed, while the University of Toronto was starting to grow.
The city itself stretched in long blocks from the Don River to
Bathurst Street and north all the way to Gerrard Street.

Yet, sadly, the three Macdonalds could not turn themselves into a real family. Most of the time, Isabella remained secluded in her darkened sickroom, constantly complaining about the light and the noise. Macdonald's reports to family members about her condition continued through the depressing cycle of "Isabella has been very, very ill," then, hopefully, that "she is evidently on the mend," then, mournfully, that she was "desperately ill all last week." Only rarely could Isabella even leave her bed to play with her son. Hugh John was regularly sent off to stay at the homes of friends and relatives in the new city. The ever-optimistic Macdonald reported to his mother that in these houses "there are young people, well brought up, so that he has the advantage of a good companionship." When back home again, Hugh John would play with his father. "He and I play Beggar My Neighbour," Macdonald wrote, "and you can't fancy how delighted I am when he beats me." In another letter to his mother, Macdonald made, perhaps intentionally, perhaps by accident, a most revealing comment about his son's reaction to the stress being imposed on him: when he asked Hugh John where he would prefer to live, in Toronto or in Kingston, the child replied, "I like Kingston best because my Grandmother lives there." Effectively, the boy had told his father that he would be happier living away from his permanently sick mother.

That same stress, a compound of guilt, repressed anger and bleak hopelessness, applied no less to Macdonald. As attorney general, he often had to work late or go on trips, duties that gave him an excuse to absent himself from the gloomy apartment. One letter to his mother in January 1856 captures the magnitude of the strain between him and Isabella: "I get lots of invitations here. I was asked out for every day last week, but declined of course on account of Isa's illness. Next week, or rather this week, is the same thing. But I am obliged to refuse."

In all his letters to his relatives, Macdonald seldom strayed beyond family matters into politics. The letter he wrote to his mother on March 17, 1856, contains a striking exception. After news about Isabella and Hugh John, Macdonald suddenly exploded into rage: "I am carrying on a war against that scoundrel George Brown and I will teach him a lesson that he never learnt before. I will prove him a most dishonest, dishonourable fellow."

In all of Canada's political history there has never been a personal contest like that between Macdonald and Brown. No other two rivals were so clearly above the ordinary. They were at odds about the fundamentals of the country itself and about the nature and purposes of politics. Their personalities and styles were near opposites, except that each was combative, competitive and quick to anger. On one occasion they came close to blows in public, and for eight years they said not a word to each other, even though they crossed paths regularly in the legislature building. Yet it would be their joint partnership during the critical years of 1864 to 1866, teeth gritted and tempers tamped down, that would bring about Confederation.

Brown is the great might-have-been of nineteenth-century Canadian politics. He possessed the intellect, charisma and strength of character to match Macdonald's more subtle talents. The difference between them was, in the strictly political realm and in the famous formulation of the philosopher Isaiah Berlin, that one of them was a hedgehog and the other a fox. Brown was Berlin's hedgehog: he was seized of one great idea—Representation by Population, the basic democratic principle that each person's vote should be equal. Macdonald, the fox, was at ease with a multiplicity of ideas, some contradictory, as he constantly changed course and doubled back (including on himself), never accepting defeat as permanent or regarding victory as anything but temporary. Above all, Macdonald was almost infinitely adaptable: "The great reason I have always been able to beat Brown," he wrote, "is that I have been able to look a little ahead while he could on no occasion forgo the temptation of a temporary triumph."

Despite Brown's exceptional talents, Macdonald would forever dance ahead out of his reach. "A campaign," *Globe* editor Sir John Willison remarked astutely in his *Reminiscences*, "is George Brown in the pulpit and John A. making merry with the unrepentant on the outskirts of the congregation." (By an uncanny coincidence, almost exactly the same kind of contest between two out-of-the-ordinary political leaders was in progress in Britain at the time, where the rivals were William Gladstone and Benjamin Disraeli. Again, moralist contended with worldly-wise realist, professor of ethics with student of human nature, hedgehog with fox, and, least consequential of all, Liberal with Conservative. The transatlantic difference was that, in Canada, it would be Macdonald who trounced Brown, while in Britain the outcome in terms of longevity in office—the only measure that counts in politics—would be Gladstone over Disraeli.)

Brown was a formidable and attractive figure. His most obvious attribute was sheer physicality. Six foot two, large and immensely strong, he had flaming red hair and radiated energy: he ate fast, rode fast, took steps two at a time—and sometimes four. He was intellectually capacious and fearless. He immigrated to New York with his father to help him run a newspaper. In 1843 he came north to edit a Free Kirk paper. Soon after settling in Toronto, Brown leaped into publishing on his own. The first edition of the *Globe* appeared in 1844, the same year Macdonald was elected to the legislature. Its editorials were forceful and trenchant, its news up to the minute, and its pages were printed on the new, highly efficient Hoe rotary press. Brown published the paper first as a semi-weekly, then a tri-weekly, and, in 1853, a daily. Its circulation soon topped an amazing twenty thousand, as the new railways extended its reach. It was easily the largest, most influential and most profitable newspaper in the country.

George Brown, founder/publisher of the Globe, *easily Canada's most influential newspaper, and a Reform leader. The rivalry between him and Macdonald has no equal in Canadian politics. He had a fine mind, but was narrow and bigoted.*

Intellectually and morally, his most attractive cause was the abolition of slavery. One of his speeches on the subject attracted praise from the great philosopher John Stuart Mill.* As well, and far ahead of his time, he called for reforms in penitentiaries, urging that convicts be treated as human beings who might be capable of change. Although not a textbook democrat—no different from Macdonald, Brown opposed universal suffrage, fearing it would lead to American-style demagoguery—he staged Canada's first mass political convention.

Yet there were flaws in Brown of narrowness, intolerance and intellectual and moral arrogance. One of the ablest journalists of the time, Edward Farrer, wrote of him, "He was a good, and in his way a great man, but Scotland never sent forth a more bigoted son of the manse." Another exceptional journalist, George Sheppard,

---

* Brown condemned the slavers with the vivid phrase "men-stealers," describing them as "a disgrace not only to Americans but to the whole world."

an editorial writer with the *Globe*, similarly judged, "Take him on the ground of abuses . . . and he is the strongest public man in Canada. . . . But off this ground he is an ordinary man." Brown personally, and the *Globe* on his behalf, railed regularly against "French domination" and "Priestcraft." He could never understand that his campaign for Representation by Population (Rep by Pop) was at one and the same time self-justifying and destructive: it would fulfill the individual rights of English Canadians by matching their representation to their ever-increasing numbers, but it would do so at the cost of threatening the collective rights of French Canadians. Brown could not understand that, while for one people the issue was justice, for the other it was survival.

Brown contested the 1851 election in two constituencies, as was then permissible, losing one to William Lyon Mackenzie but winning the other. He soon emerged as the effective leader of the Reformers. The battle between him and Macdonald was quickly joined. In his first speech, in September 1852, Brown argued for the separation of church and state on the basis of the "voluntary principle," which decreed that separate schools should be supported by their own faithful rather than by the state. Macdonald responded with the kind of wilful exaggeration he knew would drive Brown to sputtering fury: if the rule was to be that "every man should support his own religious teacher by his own means," he declared, then this surely had to mean that "the Indians and heathen ought to support their own missionaries." It was a glib, if temporarily effective, response to Brown's essential argument that "the law shall know no man's religion."

The angriest confrontation between them was not about principle. It was a squalid affair, revealing on Macdonald's side a capacity for narrowness and vengefulness, magnified in this instance by sheer hot-headedness. Back in 1849, Baldwin, as premier, had set up a commission to inquire into allegations of mistreatment by

Henry Smith, the warden of Kingston Penitentiary. He had chosen Brown as secretary of the inquiry, and the resulting report was largely Brown's work. Its findings were devastating. As many as forty men and women were being flogged each morning; one had received 168 lashes in twenty-eight days; boys as young as ten had been lashed for laughing and whistling; and the convicts were perpetually half-starved. The commission, on Brown's urging, recommended a series of reforms. In the event, other than Smith's dismissal, few recommendations were implemented—principally because Macdonald repeatedly denounced the report. He took this position because Warden Smith was the father of his friend and fellow Conservative Henry Smith; mostly, though, because Brown was the principal author of the report.

Over the next half-dozen years, Macdonald four times raised the commission report in the legislature, twice moving a resolution for it to be made the subject of a legislature inquiry—unsuccessfully, both times—and repeatedly accusing Brown of personal bias. On the last occasion, in 1855, Macdonald flatly accused Brown of having fabricated evidence, shouting out "Liar" when Brown rejected the charge. For a time it seemed that the two men would come to blows on the House floor. Brown called for a legislature committee to investigate Macdonald's allegations. While the evidence was overwhelmingly against Macdonald, the committee's Conservative majority found words to exonerate him. The affair petered out, leaving a residue of unrestrained hatred between the two men.

Their most substantial confrontation was over Rep by Pop. Year after year, Brown moved resolutions calling for an amendment to the constitution of the United Province of Canada so that Upper Canada's ever-growing population could be matched by a corresponding number of seats. Macdonald's reply, in March 1853, was succinct: "If there is one thing to be avoided, it is meddling with the constitution of the country . . . [it] should not be altered till it is evident that the people are suffering from the effects of the constitution as it actually exists."

The statistics were on Brown's side. Once published, the census for 1851 showed that Upper Canada's population had edged ahead of Lower Canada's for the first time—952,000 to 890,000. Immigration was certain to widen this gap rapidly. Nor was politics on Macdonald's side: a number of his own Conservatives now agreed with Brown.*

Brown had another advantage. If his tone was angry, the answering voice from Lower Canada was no less furious but incomparably less effective. The ascendant new order in Lower Canada was ultramontanism, or right-wing Catholicism, narrow, defensive, authoritarian, all amplified by the personality of its leader, Montreal bishop Ignace Bourget. Opposition to him did exist, from the anti-clerical *rouges* and the intellectually progressive *Instituts canadiens*. But Bourget dominated the scene. His political power would grow to the point where he could inform the faithful, "It is the duty of electors to give their votes only to those who will comply entirely with the teachings of the Church"—the *bleus*, or the Conservatives' allies. That kind of voice grated harshly on the ears of other Canadians. There was thus a ready public echo for Brown when he thundered that Rep by Pop was "the question of all questions—it lies at the foundation of all reforms."

Sectarianism, once contained by the Baldwin-LaFontaine concord, was now unconstrained. Brown's equivalent to Macdonald's

---

* "Rep by Pop" was a most persuasive slogan, although what Brown really had in mind was rep by section—namely, that Upper and Lower Canada should have seats in proportion to their respective total populations. As was most curious, throughout the long Rep by Pop debate, little notice was ever taken of the fact that Upper Canada's own constituencies were even more unbalanced, varying as widely as from 4,100 for Brockville to 80,000 for Huron-Bruce.

Toronto, c. 1856. The stately Osgoode Hall stands in the background, showing that Toronto is becoming a city. Note the width of the streets, the lack of trees and the many wooden buildings.

"Treat them as a nation" letter was one he sent late in 1852 to selected Reform supporters: "What has French-Canadianism been denied? Nothing. It bars all it dislikes—it extorts all its demands—and it grows insolent over its victories." Brown admitted that his insistence on Rep by Pop might help the Conservatives by compelling the *bleus* to persist in supporting them. Here, the moralist turned into a dogmatist: "And what if they did?" Brown asked rhetorically. "It is our duty to act uprightly and leave consequences in higher hands. Should we do evil that 'good' may come? And such 'good'—a base vassalage to French-Canadian Priestcraft." The *Globe* said it all again in public: "We lie helpless at the feet of the Catholic priests of Lower Canada" and "Let the Pope put plaster on his mouth once and for all."

Viewed in the hindsight of the secularized, post-Christian Canada of today, the strength of sectarianism in the mid-nineteenth century isn't easy to comprehend. In fact, the cause was the most obvious of all: religion mattered a great deal to almost everyone then. At the University of Toronto, for example, all students were required to study metaphysics and ethics during each of the four years it took to earn their degree.* Not only did people care deeply about their particular faith, but it defined what they supported and whom they opposed. The resulting religious tensions were then magnified by race: Protestant English versus French Catholic in Lower Canada; Orange Ulster Irish versus Green southern Irish in Upper Canada. And because there was no explicit separation between religion and the state, as there was in the United States, there were no barriers to sectarianism. The shrewdest comment on the relationship between the state and the churches in Canada at this time was made by W.L. Morton in *The Shield of Achilles:* "Church and state could not really be separated, because religion dominated the state."

In the end, the greatest surprise about sectarianism in nineteenth-century Canada is not that it existed and was divisive, but that it was so seldom violent. Ireland's civil war never crossed the Atlantic.

These problems were now Macdonald's. After the muddle that followed the drawn election of 1854, the so-called Liberal-Conservative Party had backed into office. MacNab was the premier; the man with the power was Macdonald. Power came to him because he was remaking the party in his own image. And also because, as attorney general for Upper Canada, he held the single most important portfolio. After a decade in politics, Macdonald was now just one rung—a very short one—from the top. He also, for the first time, had a real job.

---

* One of the might-have-beens in the development of Canadian intellectual life is Thomas Huxley, the great champion and popularizer of Darwin's theory of evolution, who applied for and almost secured in the mid-1850s the post of professor of natural history at the University of Toronto. The slot was filled, instead, by the brother of Premier Sir Francis Hincks.

TEN

Forms Are Things

〜

It is of the very last importance that the administration of the
affairs of the country should be according to the law.
John A. Macdonald

To single out the two defining characteristics of
Macdonald's term as attorney general is easy: he
loved the job, and he held on to it for as long as he
could. He snapped up the portfolio when he was
first offered the position in 1854. He kept it during all the years
he was premier of the United Province of Canada (whether as
premier in actual title or, initially, as de facto leader behind
MacNab). Post-Confederation, by then holding the title of prime
minister, Macdonald continued to reserve for himself the successor portfolio of minister of justice for another full decade.*

---

* Before Confederation and after it for several decades, premiers and prime ministers functioned at the same time as a regular cabinet minister. The practice
eventually died out, although John Diefenbaker was both prime minister and
minister of external affairs for a time in the years 1957 to 1959. A rough contemporary equivalent would be that deputy prime ministers, largely a symbolic
title, always hold a departmental portfolio.

Any attempt to describe Macdonald's performance as the Crown's principal law officer has to adopt an unfamiliar perspective: rather than the usual one of him as political leader and schemer, it has to be of him as an administrator, or of someone doing a particular job. As an administrator, Macdonald performed in a way almost unknown today: he worked entirely by himself. Just about all leading politicians did that then; Macdonald, though, worked harder at more things than almost anybody else. For a start, he wrote, or more often delivered extemporaneously, all his own speeches, only occasionally asking a supporter or aide to help him with some preliminary research. He wrote all his own letters, in longhand, from lengthy policy memorandums to the governor general to governmental minutiae: "You will see by the enclosed that Hopkirk highly commends acting landing waiter Kidd for an increase say to 6/sh a day," he scrawled. "If you see no objection I would be glad to see Kidd get the increase." As campaign organizer of the Conservative Party, he sent a stream of letters containing comments such as, "I shall have all the Crown prosecutors appointed this week, if possible. We must as *perhaps* we are on the eve of an election, take political considerations only into our minds," or, "I am told there are a dozen [Conservative] candidates in the field for West Middlesex & that the consequence will be a Grit triumph. Now my dear fellow, set your wits to work, & choke off as many of them as possible."

After becoming premier in title in 1856, Macdonald effectively performed in three jobs—as premier, as attorney general and as Conservative Party organizer and manager. It wasn't until 1864, though, that he took on Charles Drinkwater as his first full-time secretary, or "stenographer clerk," a post he then made permanent in his office.* At the time he engaged Drinkwater, Macdonald had

---

* Before Drinkwater, R.A. Harrison, later chief justice of Upper Canada, and

taken on a fourth job: he appointed himself minister of militia.

These multiple duties encompassed only his political and governmental affairs. He needed at the same time to make enough money from his law practice to meet the expenses of an invalid wife, a growing son, an ailing mother, an unmarried sister and himself. He kept on trying to earn extra money by land speculations, acquiring extensive property in Guelph and Toronto and holding on to undeveloped "wild land" that might tempt some optimistic immigrant, but he seldom made money on any of these ventures. His burden lightened a little once Margaret married Professor James Williamson and they willingly took care of Hugh John as their surrogate son. As

By the mid-1850s, Macdonald had become attorney general and, effectively, Conservative leader. He'd also emerged as a political strategist, turning the old Tory Party into a centrist party for, in his words, "progressive conservatives."

another relief, in 1854 he took on a bright young attorney, Archibald Macdonnell, to replace Campbell as his law partner.

Macdonald was able to do so much because he worked hard in furious bursts, made decisions easily and confidently and absorbed files at remarkable speed; also, far from least, he approached life with a cheerful and hopeful disposition. He never doubted that he could overcome every challenge, even if some time had to pass before he figured out a solution.

Hewitt Bernard, later his brother-in-law, functioned as Macdonald's private secretary while also performing other departmental duties.

Generally, historians have given Macdonald low marks as an administrator. A major cause for this judgment was the outcome of his most closely scrutinized performance—the land and other claims of the Métis, first in Manitoba, then in Saskatchewan, both of which ended in the twin disasters of the Riel uprisings. Another reason was that, every now and then, Macdonald got things thoroughly botched up because he had drunk too much.

Other more recent historians, as well as some well-qualified contemporaries, gave Macdonald at least a passing grade as an administrator. The only study dedicated specifically to this subject—a thesis written by Joyce Katharine Sowby, "Macdonald the Administrator: Department of the Interior and Indian Affairs, 1878–1887"*—reached the opposite conclusion: "Contrary to the claims of the Liberal politicians and press of the time and of many historians since, [Macdonald] was actively involved in the administration and policy-making of his two departments. He gave close attention to the day-to-day work of the departments: evolving policy; dispensing patronage and consulting about personnel matters; reorganizing duties and providing additional staff and space for his burgeoning departments." The historian Keith Johnson reaches a similar conclusion in his long essay on Macdonald in *Pre-Confederation Premiers: Ontario Government Leaders, 1841–1867*: "He took these duties seriously and performed them conscientiously and well. He worked hard, though not always to a regular schedule, and he expected industry and efficiency from

---

* Sowby's master's thesis, an exceptional one, was written in 1984 for Queen's University.

his staff." Auditor General John Langton, a highly capable, politically neutral colleague, said of Macdonald in 1855, "He can get through more work in a given time than anybody I ever saw, and do it well." *

Macdonald shared this laudatory view of his own administrative capabilities. He wrote to one correspondent, "I have infinitely more to do in my own legitimate sphere than any one man ought to have to do, and if it were not that I am a quick worker I should have been hopelessly in arrears." He would also brag—with some justification—that he could lay his hands on every letter of consequence he'd ever received and on copies of his replies.† Indeed, this orderliness is the reason why the archival record of Macdonald's correspondence is so voluminous.‡ Joseph Pope wrote of his own experiences with Macdonald, "He attached great importance to his correspondence, and made a point of answering all letters addressed to him as promptly as circumstances would permit." He recalled also that Macdonald "was exacting in his demands. He required all a man's time. The thought of holidays never entered his mind."

Later doubts about Macdonald's administrative competence may have been caused by the difficulty commentators had in accepting that anyone so jaunty and theatrical and consumed

---

* Langton developed a system of reporting the budget accounts in the 1850s that remained Ottawa's standard system down to the 1970s.

† He did not keep *all* copies of his own letters or of incoming ones. At the end of an 1856 letter to Brown Chamberlain of the Montreal *Gazette* in which he had made some frank political observations, Macdonald advised, "I hope you burn my letters. I do yours." In fact, Chamberlain kept the letter.

‡ Even his bitter opponent, Sir Richard Cartwright, admitted that Macdonald could "generally lay his hand on any document he wanted, even after a long lapse of years."

with partisan politics, besides being occasionally inebriated, could keep his desk clean and his paper moving. Yet that is what Macdonald did, particularly when he was new to the government grind. He actually improved the bureaucracy a bit: soon after becoming receiver general in 1848, he revised the hours of work in government offices and forbade absences on personal business. When he became attorney general in 1854, he reorganized the department so that legal and penitentiary matters were dealt with separately. Among his acts as premier was the appointment of Langton as the first auditor general and, in 1857, the enactment of the Civil Service Act, patterned on the one in Britain, which introduced competitive examinations for positions, although in practice it didn't have much effect on patronage appointments.

Over the years, Macdonald's interest in administration dwindled. He remarked that when new to office he had been "the devil of a departmental reformer"—implying that, in hindsight, he had concluded that all his worthy attempts to improve the bureaucracy had accomplished little.

About some administrative niceties, Macdonald was a good deal less than fastidious. On one occasion, when his personal affairs required him, as the Canadian president of a British company, to secure a charter for it from the legislature, he properly recused himself from involvement because he was then the attorney general. Instead, he gave his long-term deputy minister, close friend and sometime apartment-mate, Hewitt Bernard, a commission to secure the franchise.

While Macdonald was attorney general for Upper Canada, with another member carrying the title of attorney general for Lower

Canada,* no one doubted that he was the senior law officer of the
Crown; for most Canadians he was *the* attorney general. The zest
and enthusiasm that Macdonald brought to his job comes ring-
ingly through in a letter he wrote to the provincial secretary on
April 17, 1856:

"The Justices of the Peace had no power to arrest Lanton[†] for
a crime [horse-stealing] committed in the United States, unless
under the Statute 12 Vic., Cap. 19, & then only on a specific
application for the extradition of the prisoner. . . . In this case it
appears that the man Lanton was illegally arrested & improperly
put into the hands of the pursuing parties. There is too much reason to fear that Lanton, a man of colour, fugitive from the United
States, was the victim of a scheme to kidnap him. The conduct of
the Magistrates, even if it was caused by their ignorance, is
highly reprehensible . . . & I respectfully recommend that they
be discharged."

This particular letter confirms a cardinal characteristic about
Macdonald's approach to the law. The fact that it shows a
Canadian politician acting to protect an escaped American slave
was, while gratifying to contemporary readers, not the point.
Rather, the point was that, to Macdonald, it was the law itself
which had to be protected. As went the law, in his view and in
that of most Canadians, so went society itself.

When Macdonald insisted, as he did repeatedly, that Canada
had to remain British, he really meant that it had to remain in
and under the British system of law, written and understood,
from the presumption of innocence to the acceptance that a

---

* Officially, their titles were those of attorneys general for Canada West and
Canada East, or for each of the new "sections" within the United Province of
Canada, but the old Upper and Lower Canada titles were widely used.

† Archy Lanton was an escaped American slave who had made it across the border.

man's house was his castle, to immunity from arbitrary arrest, to trial by a jury of peers, to the equality of all before the law (and thereby equality for an escaped slave who wasn't even a Canadian), to judicial impartiality, to the gradual evolution of the law by the technique of precedent. The core reason Macdonald was loyal to Britain throughout his life was that he was fiercely loyal to British law, never having the least doubt it was far superior to that of any other nation, not least that of the United States, with (in his mind) its ill-considered innovations such as elected judges.

Macdonald liked the law for the uncomplicated reason that he was good at it. During his brief stint as a trial lawyer, he had won several cases by identifying or inventing loopholes through which his client could escape. It was because he had spent years studying parliamentary rules and procedures, as few members bother to do, that he would be able to pull off one of his most brilliant (also one of his least scrupulous) political tricks—the famous "double shuffle" of 1857, by which he tumbled a Reform government out of power just two days after it had gained office.

Most directly, Macdonald loved the law for its own sake. One of his most self-revelatory comments was "Forms are things"; that is to say, the way something is done matters as much as what is done. He never questioned that unless the law remains majestic, it can look like an ass.

He loved the law almost as much as he loved politics. An early post-Confederation deputy minister, Edmund Meredith, recorded in his diary that his minister had suggested to Macdonald that he might consider taking the post of chief justice of the planned new Supreme Court of Canada. Macdonald replied, "I'd as soon go to Hell."

Macdonald's duties as attorney general covered a great swath of territory. Besides his general responsibilities for the nation's laws and their improvement, he had to make recommendations to the governor general about the resolution of death sentences and possible revisions of lesser sentences. He appointed all the judges. He had charge of the penitentiaries. A whole range of other matters came within his purview, from the incorporation of companies and municipalities, to labour disputes, to the choice of county towns, to a host of militia matters such as determining eligibility for pensions in compensation for service in the conflicts of 1812 and of 1837–38.

The most significant example of the range of Macdonald's duties as attorney general occurred in 1857.* The year before, a royal commission had been established to recommend "the best mode of so managing Indian property as to secure its full benefit to the Indians without impeding the settlement of the country." The objective was to avoid the succession of murderous— literally—Indian wars that erupted continually in the United States. The commission recommended measures to protect the Indians from "contamination by the white settlers" and to enable them to "assimilate the habits" of the white men. Macdonald translated these recommendations into the Gradual Civilization Bill of 1857 and steered it through the legislature. Essentially, it confirmed the policies followed for the preceding hundred years by British authorities. Any adult Indian male judged to be of good character, educated and free of debt could apply and, after a

---

* Much of the material for this section is drawn from the research done by historian Donald Smith of the University of Calgary and reported in his long article "John A. Macdonald and Aboriginal Canada," published in *Historic Kingston*, 2002.

three-year trial period, achieve outright ownership of fifty acres of reserve land. Such Indians would gain the franchise and become full citizens of Canada, while at the same time ceasing to be Indians in the official sense of that term. The policy combined paternalist protection with explicit assimilation; it accepted that Aboriginal people were "wards" of the government, but to gain the benefits of the white man's "civilization" they had to cease being Indians.

The new act was approved by the legislature without amendment, with little debate and by a margin of 72 to 1, the single naysayer being the old William Lyon Mackenzie who asked querulously, "Why should we wish to civilize them?" One member, Benjamin Robinson, who had negotiated several Indian treaties, protested that Indian chiefs had not been consulted. He told the legislature members, "At their Council meetings, the Indian chiefs deliberated quite as sensibly as honorable members did in this house, and sometimes even more so." The Gradual Civilization Act set the stage for the complete handover of responsibility for Indians from Britain to Canada in 1860.

Macdonald's own views about Indians were the same as those of most Canadians at this time: they should be protected from whites but assimilated into white society. In two respects he differed from the general opinion. The letter of the law itself and the treaties negotiated with the Indians were of cardinal concern to him. Macdonald consistently rejected requests by individuals, including Conservative supporters, for permission to buy reserve lands that they had persuaded bands to sell them.

As well, Macdonald had personal knowledge of Indians that was unusual among politicians and officials of the time. While running a law office in Napanee in 1832–33, he had got to know some members of the nearby Mohawk Band in Tyendinaga Township by singing in the choir of the Anglican missionary there. He also knew some members of a band of Mississauga in the Bay of Quinte area. He became friends with the remarkable Reverend Peter Jones (his real name was Kahkewaquonaby, meaning "Sacred Feathers"), who had converted to Christianity and had married an Englishwoman, Eliza Field, a marriage the Kingston *Chronicle* denounced as "improper and revolting." By contrast, Macdonald approved of marriages between Indians and non-Indians as a way to speed the process of assimilation.*

The Reverend Peter Jones (Kahkewaquonaby). He was one of a number of Indians whom Macdonald, as was unusual for the times, knew personally. Highly intelligent, Jones shocked some contemporaries by marrying a white woman.

Two other aspects of his work as attorney general reveal his particular attitude to the law: sentencing and judicial appointments.

About sentencing, Macdonald was stern but scrupulous; every now and then, though, he could be remarkably progressive. In nineteenth-century Canada, the criminal law was not only about crime and punishment but also about morality, or at least many people thought it should be. Indictable offences included "sabbath-breaking," "blasphemy" and the "seduction" of an unmarried female. Upper Canada's leading criminologist, Israel Lewis, proclaimed that "all Criminal Law should be considered a

---

* Macdonald was friendly also with John Cuthbertson, the son of a Scottish fur trader who had married a Mohawk woman.

transcript of the Divine Law." Macdonald didn't agree with that view—his opponent, George Brown, probably did—but the notion that the law ought to serve some higher purpose exercised wide appeal.

At the same time as the law was, at least sometimes, moral, it was often brutal. Executions were public and frequently treated as occasions for a family outing. Children as young as ten years of age were sent to penitentiaries and could be flogged there. Debtors' prisons and duels continued in Canada long after they'd been proscribed in Britain, and the list of crimes punishable by execution was far more extensive.

Macdonald's ambivalence about all these aspects of the law shows in his attitude towards sentencing, that part of the legal system where he had the greatest operational influence. Just a month after becoming attorney general, he wrote to the provincial secretary to declare that a five-year sentence for rape, notwithstanding a plea for mitigation by a member of the legislature, "was altogether an inadequate punishment for the offence." Not long after, he took the same view about a five-year sentence for horse stealing. He accepted the point that public opinion could be a part of the sentencing process: a six-month term imposed on two soldiers who had attempted to commit sodomy while drunk was too lenient and "would have, in my opinion, a bad effect to have it known among the soldiery and by the public generally that so heinous and demoralizing a crime" should have received only "a punishment often inflicted for mere assault."

Still, youth and gender did bring out his kindlier side. When a girl of thirteen was sentenced to three years in a reformatory (her crime is not recorded), Macdonald said this punishment would "only be a means of further contamination," and he urged that her sentence be reduced. He argued to the provincial secretary that while imprisonment for life was the legally correct

sentence to be imposed on a Samuel Ross for the offence of stealing from the mails, yet "this sentence may with propriety be
commuted" to three years, because of "the youth of the prisoner
. . . and especially to relieve the anxiety which has injured the
health and threatens the life of his mother." However, in another
instance, "the ground of poverty of the petitioner alleged as a
reason for the remission of the sentence of her husband [seven
years, for manslaughter] is in my opinion insufficient."

Macdonald believed in at least the possibility of rehabilitation. Of a convicted arsonist he wrote, "As he is a young man, six
years of compulsory labour may wean him from his degrading
habit and make him a useful member of society." But fundamentally he was skeptical that criminals could be rehabilitated. He
warned the Kingston Penitentiary warden, John Creighton,
"Your natural kindness of disposition may lead you to forget that
the primary object of the Penitentiary is punishment, and the
incidental one, reformation," adding, "there is such a thing as
making prisons too comfortable and prisoners too happy." Always
insightful about human nature, Macdonald understood that
reformers could be deceived by the behaviour of certain prisoners: "The most brutalized man is commonly the most insensible,
or rather insensitive and therefore the most docile," he once
observed to the chief justice, while "the man of quick and sensi-
tive feeling is fully alive to the shame of his position and frets
against the prison restraints." A striking difference remains
between Macdonald's consistent skepticism about reform and
rehabilitation and George Brown's idealistic call that prisons not
remain "the moral tomb of those who enter them." Macdonald
may have been a product of his times; Brown was ahead of them.

If indeed at times stern, he seldom deviated in his scrupulous-
ness. The law itself, in its exactitude, equality and clarity, was
Macdonald's abiding concern. When G.C. Reiffenstein, a confiden-

tial clerk in the receiver general's department, was arrested for for-
gery, convicted and sentenced to four years in the penitentiary, a
great many respectable people lobbied on his behalf for clemency.*
Macdonald yielded not an inch. "The first duty of a Government is
to administer even-handed justice; the second, is to satisfy the
public that it has been so administered. Now there are many poor
and ignorant men in the Penitentiary who committed no greater
crime than Reiffenstein, and should therefore receive no greater
punishment." Reiffenstien served three years of his sentence, was
paroled, and to the horror of fellow civil servants went right back
to Ottawa. Macdonald's response, as recorded by Deputy Minister
Edmund Meredith, was succinct: "Cut him dead like any other
felon." (In fact, Reiffenstein managed to restore his reputation and
made a new and successful career as an insurance agent.)

Macdonald so revered the law that in one respect he gave it precedence over politics—not always, but with reasonably respectable
frequency. Less than a year after becoming attorney general, he
had to fill an impending vacancy in the post of chief justice of
the Court of Common Pleas. He wrote to an attractive candidate,
"We are satisfied that these requirements are to be found in yourself and that no more worthy successor to Mr. Macaulay could be
found." The candidate was Robert Baldwin, the former premier
and leader of the Reform Party, which was now in opposition. In
the event, Baldwin turned down the offer.

"My only object in making Judicial appointments, is in the
efficiency of the Bench," Macdonald informed one cabinet minister.

---

* Reiffenstein's actual arrest, in 1869, was the talk of Ottawa, primarily because
the police came to his house and arrested him at his own dinner table.

He later told a Nova Scotia supporter that his test was "to consider fitness as the first requirement for judicial appointments . . . political considerations should have little or no influence." He was protesting too much, but not entirely. Richard Cartwright, who loathed Macdonald, conceded in his *Reminiscences*, "Sir John was always anxious, as far as political exigencies would permit, to maintain the dignity of the Bench." Pope, more predictably, wrote of his "solicitude for the high character of the Bench."

A good example of Macdonald's practising what he preached was his appointment of Samuel Hume Blake to the prime judicial post of vice-chancellor of Ontario. He was the brother of Edward Blake, then the most prominent and effective of his Liberal opponents. To a colleague, Macdonald admitted that "Blake's politics make his appointment difficult," but he alone was "of heavy enough metal to preside in the court." As striking was his promoting William Johnston Ritchie as chief justice of the Supreme Court, a man who not only had been a Liberal but, in Macdonald's own words, "an anti-confederate and a strong one." As he had done with Blake, Macdonald justified his choice on the grounds that "the Supreme Court is weak, and we can only feed it from above."

Inevitably, Macdonald did not always practise what he preached about judicial appointments. As he explained to one supporter, the fact that Judge Ross of Toronto was a well-known Liberal made him highly desirable: "He is a Grit and it would be a good answer to the allegations of our opponents that only Tories are appointed."

Macdonald could also be concerned about the dignity of the bench. Post-Confederation, after appointing Lewis Wallbridge, a Liberal, to be chief justice of Manitoba, he commented, "He will be a good judge. . . . It is so seldom one can indulge one's personal feeling with due consideration for public interest." Macdonald remained concerned, however, that the new appointee's blackened and stumpy teeth would impair his gravitas, and he asked a colleague to prevail on Wallbridge to get himself a new set of teeth.

Macdonald's interest in the law never slackened, and it extended to just about every aspect of it. He was particular about the details of the law. "Certainty of punishment, and more especially certainty that the sentence imposed by the Judge will be carried out, is of more consequence in the prevention of crime than the severity of the sentence," he advised his friend, Warden John Creighton. He was as particular about the generality of the law. During the 1865–66 invasions of Canada by Fenians, or Irish Americans, public pressure developed for individuals to be arrested on mere suspicion of supporting the Fenians. Macdonald rejected the demands: "This is a country of law and order," he said, "and we cannot go beyond the law."

Without question, Macdonald loved the law. Politics, though, he worshipped. And that is where his thoughts and talents now turned.

ELEVEN

The Double Shuffle

Ah John A., how I love you. How I wish I could trust you.
Reform-Liberal member during conversation with John A. Macdonald

To clamber the political ladder's last, short rung, Macdonald needed to ease his own leader, Sir Allan MacNab, from the top spot. His challenge, though, was a good deal more complicated than that. Given the rule that whoever commits regicide almost never succeeds to the throne, Macdonald needed to dispatch MacNab while leaving no impression of his own footprints on his departing leader's back.

MacNab, "the Gallant Knight," had the round, red face and white whiskers of Charles Dickens' Mr. Pickwick. He was also a proud man, certain to react strongly against any suggestion of betrayal. Macdonald's solution was to get others to do the deed for him. In the spring of 1856, all three Reform ministers in the Liberal-Conservative cabinet resigned, claiming that the government no longer commanded their confidence. Shortly afterwards, Macdonald and the single other remaining Conservative minister resigned, ostensibly to maintain solidarity with their former

Premier Allan MacNab, the Conservative leader whom Macdonald eased out so he could get to the top. He was famous for declaring, unapologetically, "all my politics are railroads."

colleagues. MacNab was left with no choice but to resign himself. Racked by gout and in acute pain, he had himself carried into the chamber on a stretcher to cast his vote against his own demise. Immediately afterwards, a new Liberal-Conservative ministry was formed. Nominally, its premier was a Canadien, Étienne-Paschal Taché. Beside him, still in the attorney general portfolio he had held since 1854, was Macdonald. No one had any doubt that Auditor General John Langton had it right when he described Macdonald as "the recognized leader."

Macdonald protested his innocence. "Heap as many epithets and reproaches on me as you like," he told the House, "but this I contend, that having performed my portion of the contract, having stuck to my leader, having tried every means of keeping the cabinet together, I had a right as a gentleman and a man of honour to go into a new government with a Speaker of the Legislative Council, or anyone else."* Taché, by creating the illusion that a new government had been created, had allowed Macdonald to switch leaders with a certain, minimal, decency. In a letter to Henry Smith, though, Macdonald dropped the pretence: "I might, as you know, have been Premier, & insisted on Taché's claims lest it be said that in putting McNab [sic] out I was exalting myself."

---

* The Legislative Council, of which Taché was a member, was the pre-Confederation equivalent of the Senate.

However he had got there, Macdonald was now at the ladder's top.

⟡

The heights suited Macdonald. He performed there with a political skill never seen before on the Canadian political stage. It was from this time on that he set out systematically to develop the kind of organized centrist party that he had sketched out in his letter to John Strachan two years earlier about the need for a "material change" in the party to bring in "'progressive' Conservatives" and Canadien members. By today's standards, the Liberal-Conservative Party was neither organized nor disciplined, and the tripod on which it rested—of Conservatives, *bleus* and fair-weather Reformers—was decidedly wobbly. Yet it was a genuinely centrist party and, by its interweaving of French and English, a genuine national party, the first since Baldwin and LaFontaine.

This Big Tent party would soon demonstrate that it possessed a quality then exceedingly rare in Canadian politics—durability. The Liberal-Conservative Party had this attribute because it was a distinctively Canadian political party. It was, that is to say, a party of compromise, of endless accommodation between its constituent groups, of wheeling and dealing, horse-trading, temporary alliances and pacts, disagreements and splits, and broken deals—most of which unravelled at some time or other and then had to be reassembled laboriously.

In this sense, what was most remarkable about Macdonald's achievement was not that he should have become Canada's first prime minister, on July 1, 1867. It was, rather, that long before then he should have become the country's first truly *Canadian* prime minister (or premier, as he was called then). Macdonald fashioned a mould into which almost all successful Canadian political leaders have fitted themselves and their parties.

At the time, very few people appreciated the magnitude of Macdonald's achievement in keeping together, and maintaining on a more or less even keel, a party that encompassed such disparate elements as Conservatives and Tories, French and English, Orange Irish and Green Irish, Catholics and Protestants (and among the latter, the Anglicans who believed they were, and certainly should be, the established church, as well as grittier denominations like the Methodists). Most who followed politics in those days loathed "partyism," or the notion of an organized, impersonal and bureaucratic political machine. Few appreciated then that in so inchoate and dispersed a country a national political party was one of the few instruments available to give it a spine. The journalist Goldwin Smith understood what was going on: while he abhorred what he saw as Macdonald's corruption of Canadian politics, he could not hide his admiration for Macdonald's irreplaceable skill in keeping together what Smith called a "crazy-quilt" of a country. (Wilfrid Laurier also understood, which was why, when his time came, he governed like a francophone Macdonald.)

Patronage; abundant and endlessly inventive political deviousness and guile; an exceptional understanding of human nature; a natural tolerance for the inescapable intolerances of groups and individuals—these were Macdonald's essential operating tools. Add to them another quality as critical as any of the rest: likeability. Some opponents—Brown, Cartwright, later Edward Blake—hated Macdonald with a ferocious intensity. But a vast number of people of all kinds—supporters and opponents, legislature members and rank-and-file Conservatives, voters and non-voters—liked him and gave him the benefit of the doubt even when he didn't deserve it. Other politicians were admired and looked up to: Robert Baldwin, George Brown and the Patriote leader Louis-Joseph Papineau. But Macdonald alone was widely liked, and by quite a few was loved.

A great many people never called him "Macdonald." Rather, it was "John A."—even to his face—a signal of ease, familiarity, trust. Maybe he was a rogue, but he was *their* rogue. Among other Canadian leaders, only Diefenbaker gained the same familiarity, as "Dief," and in his case the diminutive came almost as often from anger as from affection.

Macdonald worked hard at being liked, most especially by his own supporters. "I dare say you are very busy from night until morning, and again from noon 'til night," Alexander Campbell, his ex-partner and now political crony, wrote to him. "That drinking with the refractory members is in your department, I take for granted. Another glass of champagne and a *story of doubtful moral tendency* with a little of the Hon. John Macdonald's peculiar 'sawder' are elements in the political strength of a Canadian ministry not to be despised." Macdonald distributed his "sawder" to all points of the compass. The best anecdote involves a passerby noticing Macdonald and a Reform-Liberal sitting together outside the chamber, with the opposition member's head resting on Macdonald's shoulder, as he remarked mournfully, "Ah John A., how I love you. How I wish I could trust you." The best description of Macdonald's seductive allure was made—later— by a Liberal MP, W.F. Maclean, who, in a magazine article, wrote that Macdonald "had a wonderful influence over many men. They would go through fire and water to serve him, and got, some of them, little or no reward. But they served him because they loved him, and because with all his great powers they saw in him their own frailties."

The importance of all the other assets that Macdonald deployed to keep together his coalition should not be underestimated. He was above all a politician who enjoyed politics immensely and who went at it with a zest and dedication matched by no other Canadian leader of his time.

Unique to Macdonald also was the fact that he loved the political game, absolutely revelled in it, for its own sake. He just had fun. The failing of one Conservative member, he complained to another, was impatience: "He destroyed one or two marvellous good plots of ours by premature disclosure." And he counselled a supporter he was trying to recruit as a candidate (in the end, successfully) that conversations with the governor general, Sir Edmund Head, "will do you good, as you have a great game to play before long."

From this time on, Macdonald sent out a stream of political letters—an absolute torrent of them. He gave advice to the editor of the pro-Conservative *Hamilton Spectator* on how to execute a reversal in policy: "It's a damned sharp curve, but I think we can make it." He showered upon members and supporters what he called "good bunkum arguments" on how to deal with such dangerously popular issues as Rep by Pop. He kept in close touch with Conservative newspaper editors, often accompanying his comments with references to likely advertising and printing contracts. "Splits," or more than one Conservative candidate running in the same riding and so dividing the vote, kept him in a state of constant agitation. In one letter to a supporter, Macdonald raged, "We are losing everywhere from our friends splitting the party. If this continues it is all up with us." As well, he scouted for candidates, gave them advice and sometimes provided campaign funds (at times from his own pocket), although men standing for office were expected then to cover their own electoral costs. He kept in touch with important non-Conservatives such as the education reformer Egerton Ryerson, who might be able to influence Wesleyan Methodists to vote

Conservative (he did), and the leading Reformer Sidney Smith, whom he hoped to persuade to join the Liberal-Conservative cabinet (he did). And when elections approached, his advice to candidates was candid: "Canvass steadily and vigorously, yet quietly—get your own returning office, a true man selected."

The fairy dust that Macdonald sprinkled over everything was, of course, patronage. There was nothing new in this. Patronage has fuelled Canadian politics from its earliest days. Macdonald's oldest preserved letter, dated November 22, 1836, was about patronage. "I am infinitely obliged to you for the hint respecting the clerkship of the peace," the young lawyer wrote gratefully to a Macpherson cousin. He would remain silent, Macdonald wrote, until the incumbent had committed himself to leaving, "in which case I shall call upon you to exert your kind endeavours on my behalf." As Macdonald's letter suggests, patronage flourished because, as is the case in all underdeveloped countries, secure, white-collar jobs were scarce, and because no criteria existed to determine who merited them, other than political favouritism. The political scientist S.J.R. Noel has used the term "clientelism" to describe the condition of mutual dependency that patronage involved—the client needing anything from a land grant to a railway charter to a soft job, and the patron needing votes, or perhaps just deference.* Moreover, as Noel observed, clientelism was "long assumed to be a normal part of the political process because it was a normal part of practically everything else." Patronage was a major issue in the Rebellions of 1837–38; it was also the prime issue in the fight for Responsible Government. The railway boom, which began shortly before Macdonald's political career, attracted extensive offers of patronage

---

* In Noel, *Patrons, Clients, Brokers: Ontario Society and Politics, 1791–1896*.

simply because of the huge sums of capital involved. The promoter of the Great Western Railway, Samuel Zimmerman, claimed that at any time more members could be found in his apartment than in any room in the legislature.

While Macdonald was doing nothing in the least new by distributing patronage, he used it in a radically new way. He employed it systematically as a tool to build and nurture the Conservative Party as an effective and ongoing institution. Unlike amateurish predecessors in all parties, he aimed not simply to please supporters by dishing out jobs, contracts, appointments and emoluments, but to make more Conservatives, both by solidifying the gratitude of those who were already members of the party and by attracting newcomers. He distributed patronage in sophisticated ways that derived from his understanding of human nature. He urged one candidate to "keep the Whitby Post Office [position] open until after the election" because "it may be valuable to have the office to give away." He urged another to make the same kind of appointments before the election to make gratitude certain, but with no public announcements and the winners being told "they will be appointed immediately after the elections" so as to encourage them to "work harder for your return." Over time, he became progressively more adept. Local members had to give their approval to patronage choices; those favoured had to have proof of having worked for the party; and no one could get a post by displacing an incumbent.

Perhaps what was most original about Macdonald's system was that he was entirely open, and entirely unapologetic, about what he was doing. He made little attempt to pretend that his purpose was good government rather than the good of the party. And he made certain that his own supporters understood his rules. When party members in Toronto complained they weren't getting their share of goodies, Macdonald retorted, "As soon as

Toronto returns Conservative members, it will get Conservative appointments."

It wasn't all crass. If patronage was not about good government, in the sense of getting the best people in the right posts, Macdonald did care about the well-being of individuals. Some of his choices really amounted to charity. He wrote to one official, "De L'Armitage is dying of congestion of the liver or some such devilry and is obliged to give up his Rifle Company. He wants much to retain his rank. Pray do this for him & break his fall." And, to a cabinet minister, "I have a letter from Noel wanting the Notaryship of the Bank. Can you give it to him[?] Poor fellow, he wants it badly enough."

In truth, Macdonald didn't so much systematize patronage as personalize it. For his system to work, he always had to be there at its centre, with his winning personality, his remarkable range of contacts, his exceptional memory for names and deeds, his incomparable knowledge of politics and the governmental apparatus, and, far from least, his uncommon ability to work extremely hard at high speed. At the same time that he was creating a national, centrist party, he was creating a Macdonald party.

Besides doing all this, Macdonald had yet one more substantial job: he had to run the country. For all practical purposes he had being doing that since mid-1854, when he functioned behind the facade of MacNab, just as he now functioned behind the facade of Taché. Within a few years of reaching the top, Macdonald had concocted solutions to two deeply divisive sectarian disputes that had bedevilled Canadian politics for more than a decade—the Clergy Reserves and separate schools. He then went right on to dispose of a third, entirely new issue that was almost as polarizing as the first two—the location of a permanent capital. All three involved an exercise in accommodation and compromise for the sake of national harmony.

The first of the conflicts to develop concerned the Clergy Reserves. By virtue of the Constitutional Act of 1791, one-seventh of all the land in Upper Canada had been reserved for "the clergy," with the revenues allocated to the established Anglican Church and, later, to the Church of Scotland (by coincidence, Macdonald's own church). All other churches, the Roman Catholic and the newly expanding Protestant denominations, were exceedingly unhappy to be excluded from this support. Brown in particular was outraged, because this system violated his cherished "voluntary principle"—that each church should be supported entirely by its own believers. Proposals for reform had always splintered on the rock of opposition from Tory Conservatives, the great majority of whom were Anglicans.

Macdonald's solution gave something to everybody. The Clergy Reserves would be secularized, and the funds allocated to municipalities for the support of public schools. The incumbent clergy of the Anglican Church and the Church of Scotland, though, would continue to receive payments until they died. When Macdonald first introduced legislation to deal with the Clergy Reserves, in October 1854, his strongest critics were his own Conservatives. But Brown, in a speech of exceptional generosity, agreed that a genuine advance had been made, even if it was still insufficient. The Tories who protested were now isolated.

Macdonald's two speeches in support of this legislation are among his most expressive. In a rare departure from the practical and the immediate, he used them to speak directly about the public interest and how it should be advanced. He was shrewd enough to say little about the details of how he proposed to dispose of the Clergy Reserves fund, talking instead about how the political process itself ought to work. Macdonald talked, that is to say, about the art of compromise.

He made his first comments on October 27, 1854, during a debate about a private member's bill to regulate religious holidays. After Brown delivered a strong speech criticizing what he saw as special treatment for Roman Catholics, Macdonald addressed the wider issue of religious tolerance. "It was of the very greatest importance for the mutual comfort of the inhabitants of Canada to agree as much as possible," he declared, "and the only way they could agree was by respecting each other's principles, and as much as possible even each other's prejudices. Unless they were governed by a spirit of compromise and kindly feeling towards each other, they could never get on harmoniously together."*

Ten days later, Macdonald spoke directly on the Clergy Reserves legislation. His bill had been attacked, he remarked, both by those who opposed any changes to the existing system and by those who opposed continuing payments to incumbent clergy. The effect, he said, would be "that the agitation will still be kept up. On the one hand, the 'drum ecclesiastic' will be beaten at every election, the worst feelings would be excited . . . whilst others would be constantly attacking the charge of paying the salaries of these 'drones' as these people would be called."

Compromise was the only solution. "There is no maxim which experience teaches more clearly than this, that you must yield to the times. Resistance may be protracted until it produces rebellion." Macdonald continued, "I believe it is a great mistake

---

* As is the case with most early newspaper reports of parliamentary debates, the language of this quotation is curiously stilted, with Macdonald appearing to have spoken in the past tense. No Hansards were published before Confederation.

in politics and in private life to resist when resistance is hopeless. I believe there may be an affected heroism and bravado in sinking with the ship, but no man can be charged with cowardice if, when he finds the ship sinking, he betakes himself to the boat." He then returned to his theme: "I call on the hon. gentleman [Brown] and upon the Church whose interests he advocates, to yield. I call on them to cease this agitation. They may smart under a sense of wrong and may feel they are deprived of rights, but . . . one thing is clear that the blow must fall, that secularization must take place. Why then resist against all hope? Why continue to agitate the public mind? Why not yield to inevitable necessity?" Macdonald won this battle against sectarianism by a comfortable margin of 62 to 39 votes. With the Clergy Reserves of Upper Canada settled, Macdonald moved on to deal with Lower Canada's issue of its quasi-feudal seigneurial system, which gave the seigneurs ownership of the land and left their *censitaires* as landless tenants. Other legislation in 1854 abolished the seigneurial system.*

Another year, another battle. The issue this time was separate schools. Pressure for them to be supported by public funds came from the Irish Catholics, whose leader was the newly appointed bishop of Toronto, Armand-François Charbonnel, a hard-line ultramontane. Macdonald crafted legislation that met the bishop roughly halfway. The largest bloc of Upper Canada members were now the populist Grits, deeply mistrustful of anything Catholic and ardent believers in what was known as the "double majority" parliamentary convention—that no legislation affecting Upper Canada should be passed unless it was

---

* That Lower Canada's agricultural productivity was at most one-fifth of that of Upper Canada was widely attributed to its antiquated seigneurial system.

approved by a majority of Upper Canadian members. (Likewise for Lower Canada, in reverse.)

Securing legislative approval would be difficult. To manoeuvre himself into position, Macdonald concocted a clever and partially plausible argument. "He should be sorry," he told the House, if a legislature, "the majority of whose members were Protestants professing to recognize the great Protestant principle of the right of private judgment, should yet seek to deprive Roman Catholics of their power to educate their children according to their own principles."

Nevertheless, the legislature's majority of Reform and Grit Protestants had every intention of doing just that. Macdonald, though, had spotted a loophole in the "double majority" rule that gave these members their de facto veto. This was that while Upper Canada members had to approve legislation affecting their own territory, no one had ever said that this opinion needed to be expressed by the majority of all elected Upper Canada members rather than just the majority of those in the House when the vote was called. Macdonald waited until the final days of the 1855 session, and as soon as many of the Reformers and Grits had left for home he introduced a bill to extend the privileges of separate schools, much as Bishop Charbonnel had demanded. To the belated fury of the now shrunken opposition, the measure was brought quickly to a vote. It passed by a clear majority of the members present, many of them being Canadien members in alliance with Macdonald.

Macdonald subsequently justified his tactic on the grounds that the alternative was to withdraw all public funds from an established institution, the separate schools. Such a draconian solution could work only "if they [the opposition] could make the world all of one way of thinking . . . yet he doubted very much if things would go on one bit better on that account." This was gamesmanship: Macdonald had won, but the cost of his victory was to further inflame sectarian rage.

⁓

Macdonald experienced more success with another issue that was potentially sectarian rather than explicitly so—the choice of a single permanent capital.* One point was certain: whichever city or hamlet was chosen, either the English Protestants of Upper Canada or the French Catholics of Lower Canada would be furious. Indeed, feelings on the issue were so strong that more than two hundred votes on it were taken in the Legislative Assembly.

There are two particularly good stories about how Ottawa got picked: that Queen Victoria threw a dart at a map, or that Lady Head, the governor general's wife, made a sketch of the view from what is now Parliament Hill and showed it to an impressed Queen. Common to both stories is the point that the Queen made the choice—and she, of course, could do no wrong. In fact, Macdonald concocted the Queen's intervention in conjunction with Sir Edmund Head. He and Head had become close, in part because their Toronto houses were near each other, but more because Head, an academic, found in Macdonald an intellectual kin rare in the colony. Head, who favoured Ottawa on the grounds that it was "the least objectionable" of all the contenders, first sent a message to the Colonial Office that "it would not be expedient that any answer be given for 8 or 10 months." Only after a delay that cooled everyone's tempers did the Palace send its reply:

---

* The capital by this time rotated between Toronto and Quebec City, Montreal having lost the honour as a result of the burning of its parliament buildings in 1849 by a Conservative-organized mob.

Ottawa was indeed Her Majesty's choice. Macdonald got the deed done while appearing to have had no part in it.

He wasn't yet finished with it, though. On July 28, 1858, while the House was debating an address to the Queen on the subject, a Canadien member moved a cleverly worded motion that opposed not the choice of Her Majesty—an unimaginable act—but the objective suitability of Ottawa. Most of the customarily tame bloc of *bleus* broke away from their alliance with Macdonald, and the errant motion was passed 64 to 50. This defeat put the life of the Taché-Macdonald government in peril. Brown, overexcited, moved a motion of adjournment to give everyone time to think. The *bleus* realizing now how they could make up for their disloyalty, streamed into the House to vote en masse against Brown's routine motion. Macdonald's hold on power was thus restored. One day later, however, on what he chose to call "an insult offered to the Queen," Macdonald and his ministers resigned.

Governor General Head now invited Brown to form a government. He agreed and did so. Just two days later, though, Brown was out and Macdonald was back again in power. These events were so unprecedented, and so surreal, that a legend grew that Macdonald had planned all along to lure Brown into a trap and there to crush him. Brown indeed was crushed, but he trapped himself; Macdonald had merely closed the gate over Brown's prone body.

Brown's miscalculation was that once he'd agreed to replace Macdonald's government, the parliamentary rules of the day required all the incoming ministers to resign and regain their seats in by-elections. While his ministers were temporarily absent, Brown would lose his majority in the House. To survive, he had to have an election, which, under the circumstances, he was virtually certain to win. However, as Head had warned

One of the earliest Canadian newspaper cartoons (c. 1858) mocking Macdonald's politi-cal trickery in the "double shuffle." Signed "H.R. in Toronto," it may have been drawn by the English cartoonist John Doyle—whose grandson, Arthur Conan Doyle, created Sherlock Holmes.

Brown when he first called on him, the preceding election had taken place only seven months earlier; to avoid back-to-back elections, Head advised Brown that he had to reserve the right to invite the just-resigned Macdonald to try to form an alternative new government. On Monday, August 2, Brown lost a vote in the House. He asked Head for a dissolution so an election could be called. Head refused. Brown resigned immediately, a bare two days after having taken office.

All observers now assumed that the same cycle would drag down Macdonald as soon as he attempted to form a cabinet. Macdonald, though, had already found his loophole. He had all his old ministers re-sworn again, but each in a new portfolio. (Macdonald's new post was postmaster general.) A day later, he switched his ministers back to their original portfolios, thereby avoiding the need for any of them to resign. No Reform lawyer was able to find any specific illegality in this double shuffle.

As Macdonald later said teasingly about Brown, "Some fish require to be toyed with. A prudent fish will play around with the bait some time before he takes it, but in this instance the fish scarcely waited till the bait was let down." The consequences of this political *commedia dell'arte* were that Macdonald got Canadians a capital that began its life behind the protection provided by the Queen, Brown got humiliated and Macdonald came away with a reputation for political knavery.* While absurd in itself, the incident marked the start of Macdonald's ascent to the status of a political legend. At this instant he gained another political asset at least as valuable: he secured the most important ally he would ever have: George-Étienne Cartier.

When the paths of Macdonald and Cartier first crossed, Macdonald paid him little attention. In a letter to a friend on January 27, 1855, he mentioned, in a review of his Canadien members, that "[Joseph-Édouard] Cauchon will prove a valuable man from his energy & talent" and that "[François-Xavier] Lemieux brings the whole strength of the Quebec district with him." Of Cartier, he said only, "He will represent the Montreal section . . . which was wholly without a representative." In his next reference, in February, Macdonald was somewhat more positive: he reckoned that Cartier was well suited to his portfolio of provincial

---

* Many years later, when Macdonald was sent a copy of Collins's 1883 biography of him—the first—he didn't bother to read it but "turned," as he put it in a letter to a friend, to just two sections: one, understandably enough, was the Canadian Pacific Scandal; the other was the "double shuffle."

George-Étienne Cartier. Macdonald praised him as "bold as a lion." Their French-English alliance revived that of Baldwin and LaFontaine. It was the foundation on which Confederation was built.

secretary, "which only requires industry and method, both of which he has to a remarkable degree." He still described Cauchon as "the ablest French-Canadian in the House"; a few days later, his skepticism returning, Macdonald described Cartier as "active—too much so."* A guess at why they didn't click immediately would be that Cartier, who could be full of himself, may have failed to give Macdonald due deference in their earlier encounters.

Cartier was exactly what Macdonald needed as French lieutenant: he commanded a disciplined bloc of French-Canadian members and was a national figure in his own right. As important, he quickly became Macdonald's principal link with Montreal's powerful community—overwhelmingly anglophone—of businessmen and financiers.

Cartier has slipped to the margins of Quebec historical consciousness: the one-hundredth anniversary of his death, on May 21, 1973, passed almost without notice.† It didn't help that Cartier once described himself as "an Englishman who speaks French." He bought all his clothes in London; he subscribed to

---

* Cauchon eventually crossed the floor to join the Liberals, becoming a minister in Alexander Mackenzie's government.

† There is a bust of him (in a Roman toga) in the Quebec City legislative building, and in Montreal, besides parks and schools, he is commemorated with an eighty-seven-foot-high statue inscribed with his cry, "Avant tous, je suis Canadien."

ten English magazines, but none from France. He was a passionate monarchist, declaring that the Conquest "saved us from the
misery and shame of the French Revolution" and naming one of
his daughters Reine-Victoria. Anglophilia aside, it is a fact of life
that Quebecers generally lose their hearts to wounded heroes,
such as Henri Bourassa or René Lévesque, rather than to
winners—Cartier, Laurier, Trudeau. Yet Cartier was wholly and
completely a Canadien. He was never happier than when belting
out voyageur songs at his regular and raucous *conversations;* when
introduced to the Prince of Wales, he broke into a French-
Canadian chanson. In 1834 he was the first secretary of the new
Société St-Jean-Baptiste, of which the slogan was "Nos institutions, notre langue, nos droits." He was one of the Patriotes during the 1837–38 uprising.

Cartier's near disappearance from the memory of his own
people isn't justified by the legacy he left them. Montreal in the
mid-nineteenth century was Canada's most important city—
really its only one. Nevertheless, Toronto posed a substantive
threat to Montreal's dominance. It had an incomparably richer
hinterland in the dark soil of southwestern Ontario, attracted
many more immigrants and was close to booming American cities
such as Buffalo, Rochester and Syracuse. Yet Montreal would
keep ahead of Toronto as Canada's metropolis for a full century
after Cartier's death—until the 1970s, when the respective population counts of the two cities at last switched around. This lead
was based on a political-industrial alliance, for which Cartier
largely created the template. In his fine biography *George-Étienne
Cartier: Montreal Bourgeois*, Brian Young writes that "his career
demonstrates the power of railways in 19th century Montreal,"
and he goes on to describe Cartier as playing a leading role "in the
transformation of Montreal civil society and in the imposition of
fundamental social, economic and legal institutions."

Intuitively—he was in no way an intellectual—Cartier understood that the Empire of the St. Lawrence no longer depended on
the great river and chain of inland lakes but on the newfangled railways, those slim, arrow-straight, year-round transportation systems. "The prosperity of Montreal depends upon its position as
the entrepôt of the commerce of the West," he said. "We can only
maintain that position if we assure ourselves of the best means of
transport from the West to the Atlantic." The Grand Trunk, then
the world's longest railway line, had its headquarters in Montreal.
The company was there, bringing with it Canada's first wave of
industrialization, because Cartier was the Grand Trunk's solicitor
for eighteen years. During most of that time, he was also a senior
cabinet minister. Cartier piloted the Grand Trunk's charter
through the legislature in 1854; later, he functioned as the company's lobbyist, protecting it from what were called "the evils
of competition." As a result, Montreal became the country's
industrial and financial centre, with the Bank of Montreal as its
fiscal fulcrum. Above all, it had Ottawa as its patron. It would take
separatism to turn Montreal into a second-tier city.*

Born in 1814, a year ahead of Macdonald, Cartier came from a
family, for three generations, of merchants. He himself became a
lawyer. He had excellent connections (including in the Catholic
Church) and considerable charm. He drank enough to be convivial
but with none of Macdonald's escapist intensity. He could also be
intimidating: he was known to bully servants and he issued several challenges to duels. On one occasion, he and his opponent
actually fired shots, both missing—almost certainly deliberately.

---

* Over succeeding years, a succession of transportation and communications
enterprises, all either government agencies or dependent on government support, would locate in Montreal—Canadian National Railways, the National Film
Board, Telefilm Canada, Telesat Canada.

Cartier was a force of nature. He was short (five foot six inches), stocky, immensely strong, indefatigable (he often put in fifteen-hour days, and one of his speeches lasted seven hours in English, after which he repeated it in French). His self-confidence was boundless. When a Conservative member criticized him for not consulting widely, he answered, "That is quite correct, I do not consult anybody in making up my mind." When another member observed that Cartier "never sees a difficulty in anything," he answered, "And I have been generally pretty correct." He was fastidious about his dress, usually wearing a long black Prince Albert coat and a silk hat. He flirted a lot. "Feo" Monck, the sister of the governor general, recorded in her diary that when she asked Cartier his favourite occupation, he answered, "The activity of the heart." His mistress, Luce Cuvillier, a smoker of cheroots and, even more daringly, a wearer of trousers, was a great admirer of Byron and George Sand. She and Cartier lived openly together and travelled together, most often to London. In his will, he praised Luce's "sagesse et prudence" and left her six hundred dollars—a sizable sum—in his will.*

First elected in 1848, he joined the cabinet in 1855. After Taché retired, the government became the Macdonald-Cartier administration, with Cartier as attorney general for Lower Canada. As part of the contortions that ended the 1858 "double shuffle," the supposed new government was titled the Cartier-Macdonald ministry. Macdonald described the bloc of Canadien members who kept him in power as his "sheet anchor."

---

* His wife, Hortense, was deeply pious. A family friend remarked that she would have been happiest as a nun—provided she was the Mother Superior. After Cartier's death she moved to Cannes with her two daughters, dying there in 1898. One daughter, Hortense, lived on in Cannes until 1940, when she left hurriedly as the Germans approached. She died in London in 1941 at the age of ninety-three.

Character drew Macdonald and Cartier together. Both were bold—"as bold as a lion" was Macdonald's own description of Cartier. Neither was daunted by difficulties or defeats. Both loved Britain: Cartier's retirement plan was "to settle myself in London." Both feared the United States. About patronage and election funding, their views were identical, with Cartier being the less restrained of the two by a wide margin. He was well known for paying ten dollars for a vote, although for Irish votes he offered "a barrel of flour apiece and some salt fish thrown in for the leaders."

If Macdonald and Brown were a pair of rivals for whom few, if any, equivalents exist in Canadian history, Macdonald and Cartier were a pair of allies with few peers. They fought together for just under twenty years, 1854 to 1873; had they not stood side by side, there could have been no Confederation.

Politics, though, had not, yet, become Macdonald's whole life. His other life, his personal one, was dipping down now to one of its lowest points.

TWELVE

Isabella, Hugh John and Daisy

Tell Hugh that I am extremely pleased at the
report of Mr. May [his teacher].
John A. Macdonald's rare praise for his son

The "grey, unrelieved tragedy"—in Creighton's phrase—Macdonald had been living through for twelve years came to its final, inevitable end in the very last days of 1857. He'd long given up any hope, or pretence, that Isabella might recover. He no longer sent out letters that said, as they once had, "Isabella is not worse than she was yesterday." He no longer composed elaborate explanations to family members or to the increasingly comatose Isabella about why he had to stay late at the office or leave for some trip on political business.

In the summer of 1857 Macdonald went to England as part of a delegation seeking to raise capital for a new railway to the Maritimes. (The mission failed.) There, in his spare time he ordered a Highland dress outfit for Hugh John, to enable him to "bare his bottom with due Celtic dignity." Once back, Macdonald went first to Kingston, where Isabella was being looked after by his sister Louisa, and then on to Toronto, the seat of the government. Late in December (which meant he'd skipped spending Christmas with Isabella), Macdonald hurried back to Kingston, either because he had been warned or because he had a premonition that the ultimate crisis had arrived. For three days he sat beside Isabella's sickbed. On December 28 she died. No cause was given, but she was by then so weak that almost any ailment would have been enough.

On December 29 a notice in the Kingston *Daily News* invited "friends and acquaintances" to attend a funeral at the house his mother now lived in with Louisa. Isabella was buried in the family plot in Cataraqui Cemetery alongside her father-in-law, Hugh, and her infant son, John Alexander.

⌒

The exact nature of Isabella's prolonged ailments cannot be identified with any certainty. An argument can be made that many of them were located in her head.

The most extensive examination was that made by Dr. James McSherry, reported in two articles in *The Canadian Bulletin of Medical History* and the magazine *Historic Kingston*. His basic diagnosis was that "the probabilities are Isabella had pulmonary tuberculosis, a hysterical personality, complicated migraine and opiate dependence." He wrote that everything that is known about her "does not fit any recognizable medical pattern." And he added, "One can only wonder at John A. Macdonald's patience and kindness."

The "tic" to which Macdonald often referred was not a facial tic, as the term would be understood today, but, McSherry believed, "a generalized pain in the head." Much of her weakness may have derived, as might not have been fully appreciated at the time, from atrophy caused by prolonged bed rest. In one letter,

Macdonald described how, following an attack, "her bed had not been made for ten days, but this evening I managed to have her shifted to the sofa & she has now got back, much fatigued by the change, but is now, of course much more comfortable."

As is inevitable when the evidence is so old and so fragmentary, some of the medical puzzles do not yield to easy explanations. Isabella was weak, obviously; yet she remained strong enough to give birth twice and suffered no reported miscarriages. In frank puzzlement, McSherry writes, "It is difficult to imagine any medical condition which would produce such gross deterioration in physical well-being while preserving menstrual function and fertility."

The diagnosis of tuberculosis—then known as "consumption"—seems highly persuasive. Tuberculosis, though, can be transmitted by intimate contact, and she and Macdonald engaged in conjugal relations; as well, neither of her sons suffered from the disease. A medical friend of the author, Dr. Bryon Hyde of Ottawa, agrees with McSherry's primary diagnosis of pulmonary tuberculosis but reckons that the more likely cause was either of two comparable diseases, bovine tuberculosis or brucellosis; these, while similar to tuberculosis, are much less readily transmittable between humans and were prevalent in Georgia, the state where Isabella lived for several years. Hyde makes another interesting point. From today's perspective, the quantity of opium prescribed to Isabella is shocking, but, in fact, it made substantial sense because it significantly reduced her coughing and so minimized her loss of blood.

McSherry opens up an important non-medical aspect of Isabella's tribulations. He writes of "the frankly manipulative appearance of much of [her] behaviour. Any time Macdonald was about to leave, her condition worsened; as soon as he returned, it improved. Her calmness and courage while he was around would certainly have encouraged him to linger." McSherry speculates that Isabella may have capitalized on a genuine illness as a way of putting distance between herself and the intimidating, female-dominated Macdonald household—his two sisters and most particularly his formidable mother. Separated from her own relatives and in a strange land, Isabella may have been suffering a form of "culture shock." It's easy to guess that these hardy, practical Scots women would have regarded her as soft and gushy, not at all the right chatelaine for their John A.

It's impossible to know whether Macdonald actually loved Isabella. Most likely he did, at least in the earliest years of their marriage, and it may have been her flightiness and fragility that initially attracted this unsentimental, worldly man to her. The emotional cost to Macdonald of seeing his gay, girlish wife turn into a pain-racked, stupefied wreck of a human being, and then linger in that condition for a dozen years, can only be guessed at.

All that can be said with reasonable confidence is that if Macdonald did once lose his heart to Isabella, he never lost it again—or never again in the same way. Many years later, his son, Hugh John, fathered a daughter who was always known in the family by her nickname Daisy. These Macdonalds lived in Winnipeg, but as a young girl Daisy stayed with her grandfather in Ottawa while she went to school there, and she spent several summer vacations with him. They adored each other. Daisy's real name was Isabella.

~

Isabella's great gift to Macdonald was to give him a son and heir, Hugh John. Yet Macdonald all but "lost" him. When Hugh John was born, Macdonald's cry had been, "We have got Johnnie back again, almost his image." Hugh John would never know this, of course, but as he grew up he must have sensed that he was competing with an opponent he could never beat—his own, long-dead, infant brother. The relationship between father and son was never relaxed or close, and quite often it was strained.

There was the practical fact that the demands of politics on Macdonald made him a virtually absent father. He did try: he sent Hugh John that Highland dress, arranged for a tutor to come to the house when the child was ill and bought him a Shetland pony and a "waterproof" to wear while he was out riding; later, Macdonald sorted out the complications when Professor James Williamson's servant balked at having to look after the pony and its sleigh and harness. And once, early in 1861, Macdonald sent to Hugh John, by way of Louisa, the kind of message any son would ache to hear from his father: "In the first place, tell Hugh that I am extremely pleased at the report of Mr. May [his teacher]." Macdonald then added, "Tell him that I am quite proud of it and that I have shown it to all my friends." No doubt Hugh John would have far preferred to have heard those words directly from his father.

Hugh John. By now a young lad, he regarded Macdonald's sister Margaret and her husband, James Williamson, as his surrogate parents. (This photo is also from Lady Macdonald's album.)

By then, Hugh John had become, all but formally, the son of Macdonald's sister Margaret and her husband. They had brought him up at their home in Kingston from his earliest years, with occasional exceptions, such as when he joined his family in Toronto. It's not quite true, though, that Hugh John was a surrogate son to a comparatively elderly couple who could not have a child themselves. True for Margaret, who had married on the cusp of forty, but not for Williamson. Before coming to Canada, he had been a minister in Scotland with a wife and son. When his wife died, soon after giving birth, Williamson decided to immigrate to Canada. He left behind the boy, James, to be brought up by his sister-in-law. In *Private Demons: The Tragic Personal Life of John A. Macdonald*, Patricia Phenix describes how young James tried frantically to maintain contact with his father, writing him pleading letters to be allowed at least to visit, but almost never getting a reply. The dereliction may have been more Margaret's than Williamson's. She, having come to regard Hugh John as her own son (he was after all her nephew), may well have feared that James, once in Kingston, would have competed with Hugh John for the attention of the man who was in fact his biological father. It's also possible that Macdonald himself was secretly glad to have so easy an out from the responsibilities of single fatherhood.

Isabella's death made Macdonald a middle-aged widower—and therefore once again a bachelor. From now on, he lived in boarding houses or in apartments. Often he roomed with other legislature members and with his principal civil servant, Hewitt Bernard. Inevitably, he drank a great deal more than before, spending longer hours in the Smoking Room of the Legislative Assembly. From this point on it becomes more difficult to know what Macdonald actually meant when he reported to his sister Margaret, as in a March 1858 letter, "I was very unwell last week so as to be confined to bed for three days and was hardly able to crawl to the House." Most likely he was afflicted with some combination of both illness and inebriation.

In some ways, Macdonald's personal life improved. He could go places when he wanted to, and no longer needed to feel guilty for having invented some excuse to avoid hurrying back to Isabella's side. His mother, Helen, continued to suffer strokes, yet she remained indomitable. She now lived with the Williamsons, but in her stubborn way she insisted on paying Macdonald rent, including a small sum for the use of the garden and yard and a share of the cost of the male servant. At the same time, Macdonald's law practice seemed to be in exceptionally good shape under his energetic young partner, Archibald Macdonnell.

Macdonald even managed to survive unscathed a near-death experience. In July 1859 he boarded the steamer *Ploughboy* for an excursion to Sault Ste. Marie. The ship's engine failed and the vessel began drifting towards the rocky coastline amid ever-rising wind and waves. Only when it was near shore did the anchors finally catch, after having dragged for close to twelve miles. "None of the party will be nearer to their graves until they are placed in them," Macdonald wrote to Louisa, adding, "The people behaved well, the women heroically."

Without Isabella and without Hugh John, Macdonald no longer had anything to distract him from "the long game." From now on, his personal life provided him with so few emotional demands or outlets for affection that he was free to apply all his abundant energy and passion exclusively to politics.

THIRTEEN

Double Majority

~

Is it a decree of destiny that Mr. Macdonald shall be the everlasting
Prime Minister? We must face issues.
The Colonist, June 19, 1858

As the decade of the 1850s drew to its end, Macdonald was approaching a political peak. He had outmanoeuvred Brown over the "double shuffle" with all the ease of a feral cat toying with a mouse. The bloc of *bleu* members who followed faithfully behind Cartier assured him of a semi-permanent majority in the legislature. His Liberal-Conservative Party, while shaky in several places, hugged the vital centre of the political spectrum, with the Tories in its ranks lapsing into sullen silence. As the de facto premier since 1854 and as co-premier in title since 1856, he'd held that post longer than had anyone in the life of the United Province of Canada. He'd deployed his tactics of compromise and accommodation to dispose successfully of long-standing issues such as the Clergy Reserves, the seigneurial system and separate schools, and had managed to select a single capital for the nation. Encomiums about Macdonald that floated across the Atlantic from the upper reaches of the Colonial Office described him as "a distinguished statesman" and "the principal man" in Canada. It's always easier, though, to stumble when standing on a peak than on flat ground.

The warning to Macdonald came from an inconsequential source. On June 29, 1858, a small newspaper, the *Colonist*, ran a startling editorial titled, "Whither Are We Drifting?" After citing examples of national drift, it asked, "Is it a decree of destiny that Mr. Macdonald shall be the everlasting Prime Minister? We must face issues. Worse can happen than a ministerial defeat." What was truly startling was the fact that the *Colonist* was a pro-Conservative newspaper—and that it was on to something. A disconnection had opened up between the governed and the governing; a disconnection, that is, between reality and politics.

Early in 1858, a letter proposing an extravagant idea crossed Macdonald's desk. In it, Walter R. Jones of Kingston suggested that the government should encourage the formation of a company to build a railway "through British American territory to the Pacific." The next step should be "a line of steamers from Vancouver Island to China, India, and Australia." Although the historical record contains nothing more about Jones, his letter catches perfectly the spirit of the times.

The years from the late 1850s to the mid-1860s were either the best that Canadians experienced throughout the entire nineteenth century or a close second-best.* Everything was booming. The economy was benefiting triply: from the Reciprocity Treaty

* The rival time span occurred near to the century's close and continued into the next, prompting a new prime minister, Wilfrid Laurier, to predict that the twentieth century would belong to Canada.

(a free trade deal) with the United States, a general upturn in world trade, and the special demands created in Britain by the Crimean War and the closing of the rival lumber trade from the Baltic. Immigration was booming, at the same time as outmigration to the United States had slowed substantially. Towns such as Toronto and Quebec were acquiring some of the characteristics of cities, while Montreal, with close to one hundred thousand inhabitants, was not that far behind Boston. Promising new manufacturing towns were taking shape, including Hamilton and Brantford; London, in just the last half decade of the fifties, tripled its population to fifteen thousand.

The word "progress" was on almost everyone's lips. In *The Shield of Achilles*, edited by W.L. Morton, the historian Laurence S. Fallis notes that there was "an almost total absence of a literature of pessimism in the Province of Canada." Optimism was generated by the abundance of jobs and by rising wages. By no coincidence, a great many of the country's finest and boldest buildings, most spectacularly the Parliament Buildings in Ottawa, but also churches, cathedrals and public halls such as Toronto's St. Lawrence Hall, date from this period. One other agent of change affecting Canada more decisively than any other country in the world was the steam engine, and the parallel lines of steel that stretched out beyond the horizon.

Initially, Canadians went timidly into the Age of Railways. In 1844, a decade and a half after George Stephenson's famous Rocket made its first run in England, there were just fifty miles of track in the entire country. Then Canadians embraced the new age of transportation totally and extravagantly: by 1854 there were eight hundred miles of track; by 1864 there would be more than three thousand, including the Grand Trunk, reputedly the longest line in the world, stretching all the way from Quebec City to Sarnia. Soon, there were lines all over the place, built by the

Great Western, the Northern Railway, and the St. Lawrence and Atlantic. In fact, almost all these companies lost money and had to be subsidized by government. Often the railways disappointed; their underpowered locomotives repeatedly broke down and could be halted by even minor snowdrifts.

Railways were by no means the only catalyst of change. Canada's Pioneer Age was beginning to pass. The last parcel of "wild land" in the Bruce Peninsula was sold in 1854; the first "macadamized" roads were being built; and a few towns even boasted street lights. In some homes, parlour organs broadened the means of entertainment beyond fiddles and squeeze boxes. People had begun to realize that each new mechanical advance was not a fluke but the product of a system that would forever produce more and more marvels, from the mechanical harvester and the sewing machine to the telegraph. Many of these inventions brought

Poster for the Grand Trunk Railway, the longest railway in the world. The illustration shows the tubular iron Victoria Bridge, which spanned the St. Lawrence River. It was completed in 1859 and, the next year, was opened officially by the visiting Prince of Wales. Both railway and bridge reflected the emerging expansionist and confident Canada.

further radical changes, such as the division of labour and the elimination of distance. During this period, no change would be more transformational than the publication in 1859 of a massive, near-unreadable tome—Charles Darwin's *On the Origin of Species by Means of Natural Selection*. Decades would pass before the

One Canadian sage compared the transformational effect of the railways to that of the invention of printing. They made a huge difference, although the small-engined locomotives had a hard time pushing through the snow on the Grand Trunk rails.

"melancholy, long withdrawing roar"* of the loss of faith would reach Canada, but a defensive response came early when the curriculum of the required courses at the University of Toronto was altered to incorporate natural theology and "evidences" of the validity of Christianity.

Nothing, though, changed Canada more than did the railways. In 1849 the Montreal engineer Thomas Coltrin Keefer, a kind of nineteenth-century Marshall McLuhan, published a pamphlet, *Philosophy of Railroads*, in which he proclaimed, "Steam has exerted an influence over matter which can only be compared with that which the discovery of Printing has exercised upon the mind." A century later, the historian Michael Bliss revisited this idea in his book *Northern Enterprise:* "Steam conquered space and time. It

---

* From Matthew Arnold's "Dover Beach," published in 1867.

seemed to liberate communities from the tyrannies of geography and climate. . . . Steam changed the land itself, for wherever the rails went, they gave the land value." From now on, Canadians were less and less immured in their villages and small towns. They could reach out to each other to exchange everything from goods to ideas. Newspapers—the Toronto *Globe* most particularly—ceased to be purely local; business, from nail-makers to insurance companies, began to operate on a province-wide basis. Goods became more diverse and more competitive, and food became fresher and more varied. Mrs. Beeton's monumental cookery book became available in 1860. Time became standardized—by Sandford Fleming. In short, Canadians began to become a single community.

This was the environment, optimistic and expansive and ever more agreeable, in which a great many Canadians lived during the last years of the 1850s and the first of the 1860s. Keefer proclaimed, "Ignorance and prejudice will flee before advancing prosperity." The magazine *Canadian Gem and Family Visitor* told its readers: "Canada is destined to become one the finest countries on the face of the globe." The geologist and surveyor of the west, Henry Youle Hind, in his book *Eighty Years Progress of British North America* predicted "a magnificent future . . . which shall place the province, with the days of many now living, on a level with Great Britain herself, in population, in wealth, and in power." That the nineteenth century would belong to Canada seemed obvious; the politicians, though, were talking quite differently.

The changing circumstances did effect political change. Railways gave politicians a whole new range of power: they could decide who would win a charter to build and operate a company, and where its line should go. It could also give them personal profits—Premier MacNab as president of the Great Western; Cartier as solicitor for the Grand Trunk; and Hincks, the ex-premier, as a major shareholder in the same company. A British lobbyist for the Grand Trunk remarked, "Upon my word, I do not think that there is much to be said for Canadians over Turks when contracts, places, free tickets on railways or even cash was in question." Put simply, there was now incomparably more money than ever before rattling around inside the Canadian political system. Keefer described the period as "the saturnalia of nearly all classes connected with railways." Surprisingly, Macdonald himself never seems to have benefited personally from this first railway boom, and the only shares he appears to have bought were a modest number in the Great Southern Railway. But Canadian politics had undergone a sea change from its glory days of fighting for Responsible Government.

Macdonald ought to have been thoroughly enjoying him-self. The boom made people happy, and happy voters are grate-ful voters. Yet time and again, Macdonald's naturally sunny nature seemed clouded by an undertone of dissatisfaction—as if he himself was wondering, "Is that all there is?" The frustra-tion came through in comments he wrote to friends: "I find the work and annoyance too-much for me," and, "*Entre nous,* I think it not improbable that I will retire from the Govt." He even let down his guard enough to allow some of his pessimism to creep into letters to his family. To his sister Margaret, he wrote, "We are having a hard fight in the House & will beat them in the votes, but it will, I think, end in my retiring as soon as I can with honour"; and to his mother, "We are getting on very slowly in the House, and it is very tiresome." In 1859 the rumour spread that Macdonald intended to retire. Joseph Pope wrote of Macdonald, "I believe, [he] had fully made up his mind to get out." The entreaties of Conservatives eventually kept Macdonald at his post, but, as Pope wrote, "sorely against his wishes."

Macdonald expressed much the same sentiments in public. At a formal dinner given for him in Kingston in November 1860, he lapsed into quite-out-of-character self-pity. "When I have looked back upon my public life," he said, "I have often felt bitterly and keenly what a foolish man I was to enter into it at all (Cries of 'No, no'). . . . In this country, it is unfortunately true, that all men who enter the public service act foolishly in doing so. If a man desires peace and domestic happiness, he will find neither in performing the thankless task of a public officer."

One factor exacerbating Macdonald's pessimism was sheer loneliness. He lived in boarding houses, as, for example, jointly with a Mr. Salt on Toronto's Bay Street. In 1861 he wrote to his sister Margaret about his new apartment-mate, an Allan McLean: "He is a very good fellow but rather ennuyant and I will be glad when he goes. I am now so much accustomed to live alone, that it frets me to have a person always in the same house with me."

His natural optimism was rubbed down further by the progressive weakening of his beloved mother, Helen. She died on October 24, 1862. Alerted by Louisa, Macdonald was at her side through her last days. She too was buried in the family plot at Cataraqui Cemetery. Of his own family, only Margaret and Louisa remained; also Hugh John, but by now he had become a detached son. From this time on, Macdonald had less and less reason to go to Kingston, and, inevitably, he became increasingly distanced from his own childhood and youth.

While Macdonald was subject to occasional depressions, this general mood of listlessness and pessimism was alien to him. His usual philosophy of life is set out in a reply he wrote to a friend who had complained about financial problems. "Why man do you expect to go thro' this world with trials or worries. You have been deceived it seems. As for present debts, treat them as Fakredden [sic] in Tancred treated his—He played with his debts, caressed them, toyed with them—What would I have done without those darling debts said he." Macdonald then described his creed: "Take things pleasantly and when fortune empties her chamberpot on your head—Smile and say 'We are going to have a summer shower.'"

Not until later did Macdonald—by now without any real confidante—reveal a major cause of his sense of alienation and purposelessness. The occasion—to cite it here requires slipping out of the straitjacket of chronology—was a dinner in Halifax in September 1864, right after the close of the first Confederation conference in Charlottetown. During his speech, Macdonald turned confessional in a way that was most unusual for him. "For twenty long years I have been dragging myself through the dreary wastes of Colonial politics," he told his audience. "I thought there was no end, nothing worthy of ambition, but now I see something which is worthy of all I have suffered in the cause of my little country." By that vivid phrase—"twenty long years . . . through the dreary wastes"—Macdonald was coming very close to saying that his entire career had been an exercise in pointlessness.

Macdonald loved power for its own sake, and he loved the political game for itself, so it would be far too sweeping to conclude that he meant literally what he was saying. But there is hard truth in that analysis. Macdonald had not come into politics with any grand goal or vision, and after two decades in politics, a good half-dozen of them at the top of the ladder, he had yet to accomplish much that would linger after he left. During this time he had missed out on several chances to make real money or to have a normal family life. Most particularly, Macdonald was failing in politics itself. Rather than the national harmony that should have resulted from his turning the Conservative Party into a centrist group, by forging a French-English alliance and by settling long-standing disputes, what had grown stronger over these same years was disharmony, division and sectarianism.

Religion was the "other" of these times. Almost every topic of public debate was dominated by and deformed by sectarianism. It was Canada's equivalent to the division then rapidly taking hold in the United States between the slave-owning South and the anti-slavery North. The Orange Order, its membership constantly augmented by new Irish Protestant immigrants, was becoming ever more explicitly anti-Catholic, and the moderate Ogle Gowan was steadily losing ground to the hard-liner John Hillyard Cameron. At the same time, the Catholics in Lower Canada were becoming ever more ultramontane, or authoritarian. In Toronto, Bishop Armand-François Charbonnel declared that any Catholic who possessed the vote but failed to use it to elect candidates committed to expanding separate schools was guilty of a mortal sin. Differences in religion multiplied those of race, and the reverse equally.

In particular in Upper Canada, there was an ever-rising anger at the political power exercised in the national legislature by Lower Canada's Canadiens, this in important part because of the very alliance that Macdonald had forged with Cartier and his bloc of *bleus*. As was rare, Macdonald's political antennae failed to function. He dismissed Representation by Population as "too abstract a question [for the public] to be enthusiastic about." Rather, and as always in politics, appearance mattered far more than fact, and the appearance here was that the minority—a defeated one, moreover—was now in charge.

The responses went far beyond mutterings in the various Orange Lodges. The *Globe* laid it out explicitly: "Our French rulers are not over particular, we are sorry to say, and we are powerless. Upper Canadian sentiment matters nothing even in purely Upper Canadian matters. We are slaves. . . . J.A. Macdonald may allow his friend to buy an office, he may even take a thousand pounds of plunder, if he likes; so long as he please Lower Canada, he may rule over us." George Brown was even more intemperate: he railed in the *Globe* against "a deep scheme of Romish Priestcraft to colonize Upper Canada with Papists . . . a new scheme of the Roman hierarchy to unite the Irish Roman Catholics of the continent to a great league for the overthrow of our common [public] school system."

Macdonald was by no means without sin himself. While he deplored sectarian strife with a vigour few other English-Canadian politicians matched, he also exploited it. In a letter to education reformer Egerton Ryerson, after mentioning a grant to the university that Ryerson favoured, Macdonald urged, "The Elections will come off in June, so no time to be lost in rousing the Wesleyan feeling in our favour." He wrote to Sidney Smith, a Reformer he was trying to lure into his cabinet, "We must soothe the Orangemen by degrees but we cannot afford now to lose the Catholics." It was in this letter to Smith that Macdonald laid down his often-quoted maxim of how to rule: "Politics is a game requiring great coolness and an utter abnegation of prejudice and personal feeling."

Two solutions existed. One was Macdonald's policy of compromise, endlessly and exhaustingly pursued by guile, skill, outright deviousness and a sizable portion of self-interest. He still had Gowan on his side, and he had bought off the *bleus*, a great many them right-wing ultramontanes, by patronage. Despite its patches and outright holes, the Liberal-Conservative Big Tent still stood.

A second solution existed. Known as the "double majority," it amounted to a mechanical device for keeping Upper Canadians and Lower Canadians apart from each other politically. Up to a point, this system could work for regional matters, but national or province-wide measures became virtually impossible to put into effect. The solution merely papered over the problem, at the cost of making government paralysis all but inevitable and permanent.

Macdonald began by refusing to accept the double-majority rule. Gradually, he came to apply the rule he himself had spelled out in his legislature speech of 1854, of "yielding to the times" rather than engaging in "affected heroism or bravado"—and, also, of saving his political skin. He now proclaimed, "In matters affecting Upper Canada solely, members from that section claimed the generally exercised right of exclusive legislation, while members from Lower Canada legislated in matters affecting only their own section." This compromise ceded the double majority in fact, if not officially. It worked, but at the cost of making the legislature largely unworkable.

Paralysis was never absolute, of course. Work began in Ottawa in 1860 on the construction of a complex of Parliament Buildings of exceptional grandeur—and cost. In 1859 Macdonald's finance minister, Alexander Tilloch Galt, enacted higher tariffs on British imports to preserve Canada's vital Reciprocity Treaty with the United States. British manufacturers protested furiously, but the Colonial Office endorsed Galt's schedule. Effectively, London thereby added full economic self-government to the political self-government already ceded to Canada. And the term "world class" began to be applicable to Canada. Besides the Grand Trunk as the world's longest railway, the Victoria Bridge, spanning the St. Lawrence at Montreal and a marvel of tubular iron, was the

The Parliament Buildings under construction, c. 1862. They were huge, dramatic and extraordinarily ambitious for so small a colony. They were also the one thing in Ottawa that everyone liked.

world's longest; completed in 1857, it was opened officially in 1860 by a visiting royal prince.

But the dominant, all-consuming issue in Canadian public life remained sectarianism. To increase the tension, Brown's call for Representation by Population had become unanswerable. The census for 1861 showed that Upper Canada now had 285,000 more inhabitants than Lower Canada. More and more Conservatives were coming to accept that Upper Canada had to be given more seats in the legislature, in proportion to its population. Cartier— naturally—was adamantly opposed to any change in the balance of seats between Upper and Lower Canada, and Macdonald had to stand in solidarity with him or lose his *bleu* supporters. Yet rejecting Rep by Pop only magnified the fury in Upper Canada.

A yet-more-radical solution now began to be proposed—to disassemble the Province of Canada and recreate its two original provinces. Each province could then have whatever number of constituencies it wanted, because the two legislatures would be quite separate. But Canada itself would be no more.

Brown, who had begun to assert his authority over both the moderate Reformers and the radical Grits, took up this notion of sundering the nation. An editorial in the *Globe* threw down the gauntlet: "The disruption of the existing union" was needed to remove Canadien influence over Upper Canada. This would satisfy Lower Canada by giving it "a position of comparative independence." The alternative would be to "sweep away French power altogether."*

Macdonald's response was defiant. "I am a sincere unionist," he declared. "I nail my colours to the mast on that great principle." There had to be both union with Britain and "union of the two Canadas," he said. "God and nature have joined the two Canadas and no faction should be allowed to sever them." He had an obvious self-interest in keeping a Canadien bloc onside to compensate for the paucity of Conservative members in Upper Canada. His problem was that a call for compromise and accommodation had none of the mobilizing power of Brown's war cry for Rep by Pop.

There was only so much that Macdonald—or anyone—could do about sectarianism itself. Any real solution would have to wait for the time when Canadians cared less deeply about their religion, and about the religion of others. On a personal level,

---

* This near declaration of race war was written not by Brown but by his able and extremist chief editorial writer, George Sheppard.

though, there was something that Macdonald could do about his sense of malaise, of being unfulfilled, of feeling he was making no mark that he would leave behind: to find a woman to marry who could fulfill him.

In no way did Macdonald take advantage of his widowerhood to gain a reputation similar to that which would later earn his cabinet colleague Charles Tupper the nickname "the Ram of Cumberland." In the engagingly eccentric book *Kingston: The King's Town* (1952), Queen's University professor James Roy declared flatly that Macdonald "was known to have an amorous disposition," but provided not a scintilla of proof. As for sex specifically, Macdonald's prevailing attitude appeared to be that of worldly amusement. Apprised of one minister's marital misdemeanours, Macdonald responded by quoting the maxim, "There is no wisdom below the belt." As could be expected, the evidence of Macdonald's amorous activities as a widower is scanty. Most accounts pass over it in silence. Enough evidence exists, though, to suggest that during this period Macdonald may have had some kind of a relationship with at least five women, and in one instance to have come very close to an offer of marriage.

There's no question whatever that Macdonald liked women and, as is considerably less common, that he was entirely at ease in their company. In the very practical and rather prosaic Canadian society of the mid-nineteenth century, this alone would have made him a considerable catch. About that society, the visiting Englishwoman Anna Jameson observed, astutely and tartly, "I have never met with so many repining and discontented women as in Canada. . . . They seem to me perishing of ennui, or from the want of sympathy which they cannot obtain."

To any woman of spirit, Macdonald, by contrast, would have been catnip. There was his Windsor Castle companion of 1842, Miss Wanklyn, with whom he "*sympathized* wonderfully." Later on that same trip, he spent the considerable sum of seven pounds fifteen shillings on a riding whip as a present for an unnamed lady, very likely the same Miss Wanklyn. In 1845, while taking Isabella to Georgia, he sent one letter to Margaret Greene that captures his delight in female company: "I forgot to tell you that Mrs. Robinson, a sweet pretty woman, called on Saturday & I went to find her out today, but the directory was vague & I was stupid and & so did not see her again, much to Isabella's delight, who says she does not like me taking so much to your lady friends." That confidence committed to paper, Macdonald became bolder. "I always considered you a *Charming Woman*, but I did not calculate for all your friends being so. From those I have seen, I have only to say that you will confer a great favor* on me by sitting down & writing me letters of credence to *every one* of your Yankee friends, and it will go hard but I [will] deliver most of them." It would appear that Isabella had good reason to be glad that Macdonald had failed to say "Hey" to Mrs. Robinson.

That Macdonald understood how to charm women is confirmed by the extraordinary St. Valentine's Day ball that he organized for February 14, 1860, while living in Quebec City. It was held in the Music Hall of the St. Louis Hotel, the city's grandest. The chamber was packed with large garlands of roses and graced by busts of Queen Victoria and the Prince of Wales (who was booked to visit the colony later in the year). The walls

---

* Macdonald's spelling of "favour" in the American style of "favor" was unusual; he may have picked it up osmotically because he was writing from south of the border.

St. Louis Hotel, Quebec City. It was here, in 1860, that Macdonald staged the splendid, if extravagant, St. Valentine's Day ball that featured a huge pie from which emerged twenty-four blackbirds.

were adorned with new mirrors everywhere and thirty small wreaths of artificial flowers stitched by the Sisters of Charity. A fountain splashed out eau de cologne. The bill for food and drink came to an incredible $1,600, and the list included sparkling Moselle, sherry, port, ale, porter, and both red and white wine. Close to one thousand guests were invited, and on arrival each lady was presented with a valentine on which Macdonald had penned "very, pretty remarks." There was music throughout the evening, and dancing far into the night. As a highlight, when an exceptionally large pie was carried into the centre of the room, four and twenty blackbirds flew out from it once it was opened. Macdonald never organized another gala like it again. He was premier, after all, and he had no need to stage an extravaganza to impress local society. In this instance, given the day he chose for the party, it's entirely possible that he was trying to impress a particular woman.

In fact, after Isabella's death, Macdonald wouldn't have had to work hard to impress. His looks remained odd, but he was growing into them. He was self-assured, clever, funny, a delight for any woman to find seated beside her at a dinner table. He also possessed the aphrodisiacal allure of power. His one glaring defect was that he drank far too much—and this may have deterred the woman he came closest to proposing to during this period. She was Susan Agnes Bernard, the daughter of a wealthy Jamaican sugar planter and the sister of Hewitt Bernard, Macdonald's own top civil servant. They met once by accident in Toronto, then by Bernard's design in Quebec City, where Susan Agnes was living with her mother. They met there several other times, and it was reported that Macdonald asked her to marry him. Nothing came of it in the end, but Susan Agnes will make another appearance in these pages.

The most intriguing case of a might-have-been involves Elizabeth Hall, herself a widow. Macdonald and her late husband, Judge George B. Hall, had become friends when both of them were freshmen legislature members after the 1844 election. Hall died in 1858, and as a favour Macdonald wound up his estate and set up a trust fund for his children. Macdonald described Hall as "a warm, personal friend," and Hall, just before he died, wrote to Macdonald to say, "Have had a hard tussle with grim death. . . . If I don't see you again may we meet in Heaven." While settling his friend's legal affairs, Macdonald saw Elizabeth Hall often. Their relationship continued, and on December 21, 1860, she wrote him a letter that, between some bits of business information, positively aches with her longing for him.

"My loved John," she began, and then discussed the sale of some of her effects, the progress of the railway being built to Peterborough and the condition of the mails. She used this point to reach right out to Macdonald: "No hope now till I return from the backwoods where I only intend to stay a week & you will have no letter for that time—if that is a privation to *you* what must *I* feel if a fortnight without hearing from you. I cannot bear to think of it." Next came a description of a visit to neighbours, with her added comment: "A lady who was there made a set at me to find out if I was to be married in [the] Spring & I told her it was rumour, & my mother advised me when setting out in life to believe 'nothing I heard & only half of what I *saw*.'" Finally, she noted that the horses were being readied to take her for a drive, followed by a confident—or perhaps an overconfident—"Goodbye my own darling—love from loving Lizzie."

Unquestionably, something was going on between Macdonald and Elizabeth Hall. Most commentators have assumed that it was principally in Elizabeth's mind and that she made the mistake of pressing Macdonald too hard and lost him. Perhaps not, though; perhaps the opposite happened. What is truly fascinating about Elizabeth's letter is that it should exist at all. Macdonald kept very few personal letters, and none at all from either of his wives or from his mother. That he should have kept this one, hanging on to it for more than a quarter-century, suggests some recognition of a lost chance. Perhaps nothing happened because, with several children to bring up, Elizabeth Hall had too many dependants for him to cope with. She would, though, have already been well aware of his drinking "vice," and she possessed the invaluable asset of experience as the wife of a public man. So perhaps Macdonald let happiness slip through his fingers out of ineptitude or timidity.

Two of the other women are only wraithlike figures. There were rumours that the sister of a Prince Edward Island politician might marry him, but nothing came of the affair. And, at the close of a routine October 29, 1861, letter to one Richard William Scott, Macdonald added the tantalizing postscript: "P.S. You can make love to Polly." Here, Macdonald appears to have been telling

Scott that whatever may once have passed between him and the semi-anonymous Polly, the way was now open for Scott to press his own suit.

Then there is Eliza Grimason. Two writers, Patricia Phenix, the author of *Private Demons*, and more tentatively Lena Newman, the author of the excellent 1974 coffee-table book *The John A. Macdonald Album*, have suggested that a physical relationship may have existed between Macdonald and the lady. Eliza Grimason was a remarkable woman, and there's no question she adored Macdonald. No beauty by even the most generous estimate, but strong and confident, she owned and man-

Eliza Grimason, owner of the tavern in Kingston that Macdonald frequented. Rumours of a relationship between them were almost certainly untrue, but, even though they were from totally different social backgrounds, they were lifelong close friends.

aged Grimason House, Kingston's leading tavern.* She performed this role with such aplomb that, having started as an illiterate Irish immigrant, she went on to own properties with the handsome value of fifty thousand dollars. When they first met, she was just sixteen and he had turned thirty. Her husband, Henry, bought the property that became the tavern from Macdonald; when Henry died eleven years later, Macdonald did not press her for the balance of the payments, knowing she had three children to bring up.

Under her management, Grimason House became the most popular place in the town. It also became Macdonald's unofficial

---

* The tavern, now called the Royal Tavern, still exists, at 344 Princess Street in Kingston.

campaign headquarters. In one description, admittedly from the suspect source of James Roy, it was "the shrine of John A.'s worshippers with Mrs. Grimason as high priestess." The place was crowded, raucous, rowdy and raunchy. Macdonald went there regularly, bantering with the customers (mostly Conservatives), watching the cockfights (though not himself betting on them) and drinking a great deal. Election nights were his night. Eliza Grimason reportedly controlled one hundred votes, and she made her van available to take Conservatives to the polls, held "open house" for workers and voters and contributed to his campaign funds. According to Macdonald's early biographer Biggar, "when the returns were brought in, she would appear at Sir John's committee room, and walk up among the men to the head of the tables, and, giving Sir John a kiss, retire without saying a word." On the one occasion he lost, she was devastated. "There's not a man like him in the livin' earth," she said.

Many years later, Eliza Grimason came to Ottawa as Macdonald's guest at the opening of Parliament. He toured her round the buildings. Then she went to Earnscliffe to have tea with Lady Macdonald, whom Eliza judged "a very plain woman" but doing the job that needed to be done, because "she takes very good care of him." It's just not credible that Macdonald would have taken a former mistress around Parliament and then handed her on to have tea with his wife. The kiss she gave him in his committee rooms after he won each election must have been innocent, or the half-tipsy Conservative ward-heelers would have been shocked and, incomparably worse, they would have talked.

Macdonald's character, though, gave his friendship with Eliza Grimason a dimension that was far less common and far more interesting than any illicit relationship between them would have been. Their friendship was an extraordinarily democratic one. Macdonald, the nation's most powerful man, and a highly intelligent and well-read one to boot, was the true friend of a rough countrywoman who earned her living running a grungy tavern. Their friendship was so close, and so unaffected, that Macdonald in later years kept a framed photograph of Mrs. Grimason on his desk, beside one of his mother. It was because Macdonald knew people like Mrs. Grimason and her customers that he knew Canada better than any succeeding premier or prime minister ever did.

Maybe, post-Isabella, Macdonald could not allow himself to be close to another woman. One chronicler, the historian Keith Johnson, has written that Macdonald seemed to have a "central, emotional dead spot." That's too strong an assessment; all his life he could be extraordinarily tender with children and wholly at ease with them. But except for Isabella during their first few years together, he never again really let down his guard with a woman.

Here, as always with Macdonald, there is a glaring contradiction—although perhaps only an apparent one. Women adored him. That was the judgment of that sophisticated observer Sir John Willison, the editor of the *Globe*, who wrote in his *Reminiscences* that "because women know men better than they know themselves and better than men ever suspect, there was among women a passionate devotion to Sir John A. Macdonald such as no other political leader in Canada has inspired." (Since Willison was a confidante of Laurier, this was high praise indeed.) Willison ends, with the gallant flourish, "No man of ignoble quality ever commands the devotion of women."

One other aspect of Macdonald's relations with women deserves some attention, if cautiously so. In an essay on Macdonald in the 1967–68 edition of the *Dalhousie Review*, the historian Peter Waite first remarks that "his liking for human beings was genuine" and then goes on to make the intriguing comment,

"It is not too much to say that he often liked men as much for their bad qualities as for their good." A readiness to like people for their faults, or at least an acceptance that such failings are an integral part of the human condition, is more a female trait than a male one. In his own person, Macdonald was thoroughly masculine: he drank a lot, told bawdy stories, had a nasty temper and was highly competitive. But there was also a female side to his nature—an aspect of him caught by the novelist Hugh MacLennan's comment quoted in the introduction, "This utterly masculine man with so much woman in him." Whatever his own nature, he took people as they came and worked with their faults and shortcomings, rather than trying to reform them or to improve them. As well, the failings of human beings provided him with invaluable raw material for the endless anecdotes by which he gently tugged self-doubting opponents into his web.

Whatever his qualities, Macdonald, during the years on either side of 1860, succeeded neither with women nor with sectarianism. Perhaps he did win one signal victory over the latter challenge, though proof is impossible. A fascinating document exists that captures the essence of the policy of compromise and accommodation that Macdonald deployed to try to resolve the deeply divisive issue of sectarianism that so disfigured Canadian politics through the 1850s and early 1860s.

In a long dispatch to the colonial secretary in June 1857, the governor general, Sir Edmund Head, wrote, "If it is difficult for any statesman to stem their [sic] way amid the mingled interests and conflicting opinions of Catholic and Protestant, Upper and Lower Canadian, French and English, Scotch and Irish, constantly crossing and thwarting one another, it is probably to the action of these very cross interests and these conflicting opinions that the whole united province will, under providence, in the end owe its liberal policy and its final success." Head added, "In such circumstances, constitutional and parliamentary government cannot be carried on except by a vigilant and careful attention to the reasonable demands of all races and all religious interests."

To that analysis of Canada's essential nature, there was not a word Macdonald would have wanted to add. He may indeed have helped to compose many of them. He and Head had several long, private conversations when the government was located in Toronto. Pope wrote in his biography that Macdonald was "never so intimate with any Governor-General as with Sir Edmund." Moreover, the governor general needed to learn from Macdonald; when he first arrived in 1855, Head caused an uproar among Canadiens by commenting to an Upper Canadian audience on "the superiority of the race from which most of you have sprung."

If Head learned from Macdonald, the reverse was not true. In another dispatch home in 1858, Head suggested a federation of all the British American colonies. To Macdonald, such an idea was but an intellectual abstraction—perhaps nice, but irrelevant because undoable.

By this time Macdonald was well aware that something was fundamentally amiss in Canadian politics and governance. But he still had no idea what to do to cure the malaise. Around him, though, the times had begun to change.

FOURTEEN

The Shield of Achilles

~

*I see within the round of that shield, the peaks of the Western
mountains and the crests of the Eastern waves.*
Thomas D'Arcy McGee

The change in Canada that most affected Macdonald
at the beginning of the 1860s was the size of the
country. Not literally, of course. The United
Province of Canada remained just as it had always
been—an elongated oblong extending from the mouth of the
Gulf of St. Lawrence to just beyond the western edge of Lake
Superior, and encompassing only about half of today's Ontario
and Quebec; an oblong, moreover, blocked from the sea except
during the near half of the year that the St. Lawrence River was
free of ice. Even though it took up an impressive amount of space
on any map of the North American continent, it was a strangu-
lated community.

The change in Canada's size was psychic. In the years immediately before 1860 a consciousness began to stir among
Canadians that they were occupying the antechamber of a vast
empire. They began to realize that their own United Province
was only a part of the territory that existed above the forty-ninth
parallel. Elsewhere in the immense, intimidating expanse of land
there were no fewer than five other British colonies—to the east,

Nova Scotia, New Brunswick, Prince Edward Island and Newfoundland, and almost an unimaginable distance away to the west, the tiny colony of Vancouver Island, clinging to the edge of a second vast ocean. As well, roughly in the continent's middle, there was a small settlement out on the prairies in a place called Red River, which was administered—sort of—by the Hudson's Bay Company. Almost all this land was entirely empty except for Indians. All of it, though, was British.

Macdonald's interest in this additional territory varied from negligible to non-existent. Between sectarianism and the tensions dividing English and French in the United Province and, most immediately challenging of all, the gradual shift of opinion among his own Conservatives in favour of Rep by Pop, he had more than enough to cope with. About the West, as he later described his sentiments, he was "quite willing personally to leave that country a wilderness for the next fifty years." As for the Maritimes, although there were occasional proposals for a railway to connect quasi-inland Canada to tidewater at the ice-free port of Halifax, the costs would be horrendous, and no bank or financier in London showed the least interest in advancing the capital needed for such a project.

Yet change was happening in people's minds. It was very tentative and not at all well informed. But a shift in self-awareness about Canada's possibilities had begun that would, before many years, cause Macdonald to undertake the single most radical political project of his life.

One catalyst of change can be traced back to Montreal and to the middle of 1857. A new tri-weekly literary journal, the *New Era*, appeared there. As its opening attraction, it published a series of editorials on the topic "The Future of Canada." The ideas expressed in these essays were lively and novel. One declared that although Canada possessed the central spine of the St. Lawrence, it lacked the essential "one-ness of political life." After asking, "Who reads a Canadian book?" and noting that almost no one did, the journal threw out a challenge: "Come, let us construct a national literature for Canada, neither British nor French nor Yankeeish . . . borrowing from all lands, but asserting its own title." The journal questioned whether Canadian trade policy should be "unconditionally and absolutely in the hands of the Colonial Secretary" and urged the appointment of a Canadian "representative" in Washington. The solution to the country's general political problems, it declared, had to be "a Federal compact" within which each province would have its own Parliament while "conceding to the federal authority such powers as are necessary for the general progress and safety." A new federal constitution, though, was not enough: "The federation of feeling must precede the federation of fact."

What was happening here, as happened so rarely in the pragmatic, provincial world of mid-nineteenth-century Canadian politics, was original thought and unleashed imagination. The author was a newly arrived immigrant, Thomas D'Arcy McGee. He possessed, as was even rarer in Canada, the voice of a poet or, since the florid verse he scribbled out was scarcely poetry, then at least the voice of a romantic.

Irish, of course, born in 1825 in County Louth and the son of a coast guard, McGee got involved with the revolutionary Young Ireland movement, fled the island disguised as a priest, and made his way to Boston and later New York, earning his living as a journalist. He proclaimed, among a good many other bravura ideas, that the United States would eventually stretch "from Labrador to Panama" and that "either by purchase, conquest, or stipulation, Canada must be yielded by Great Britain to this Republic." Yet McGee grew restive in that country. Its practice of slavery disgusted him, as did, more personally, the anti-Irish bigotry of the anti-immigrant Know Nothing movement. McGee came north to Montreal in 1857 and to his astonishment found there, after all his years of fighting the English, "far more liberty and tolerance enjoyed by those in Canada than in the U.S." Besides his capacity for passion, McGee attracted attention by two qualities: he had great charm, and he was exceptionally ugly. He was short, swarthy, with a sort of squashed-up face. His wife, Mary, when asked whether she ever worried he might stray during his many trips away from home, responded, "Sure, I've got great faith in his ugliness."

Besides his editorials in the *New Era*, McGee developed a set speech that commanded ever-larger audiences. It was a hymn to a wider, bolder Canada: "I see in the not remote distance, one great nationality bound like the shield of Achilles, by the blue rim of the ocean . . . I see it quartered into many communities, each disposing of its internal affairs but all together by free institutions, free intercourse and free commerce. I see within the round of the shield, the peaks of the Western mountains and the crests of the Eastern waves . . . I see a generation of industrious, contented moral men, free in name and in fact." McGee was Canada's first nationalist.

D'Arcy McGee. Passionate, eloquent, hard-drinking, he was Canada's first nationalist, and, effectively, Confederation's poet laureate. His wife expressed her "great faith in his ugliness."

Nationalism was enough to put him at odds with Macdonald, so suspicious of any innovation that might weaken the British connection. Even more irritating was that McGee, when he got into politics, did so as a Reformer. In the *New Era*, he damned Macdonald's government as "one of expedients, a succession of make-shifts." McGee took a ministerial post in George Brown's two-day "double-shuffle" government, and afterwards enraged Macdonald by writing articles accusing Governor General Head of having colluded with Macdonald to oust Brown. Macdonald was annoyed enough to declare, "Never did a man throw away a fine career as he [McGee] has by his violence, falsehood & folly." From their first encounter, though, Macdonald and McGee saw something in each other. After McGee made his maiden speech in the legislature damning Macdonald's "timid, makeshift policy," Macdonald ambled over, extended his hand and congratulated him. McGee remarked afterwards how "ready and dextrous" the older man was, and how "good humour is his most apparent characteristic." No doubt that was just Macdonald's "soft sawder."

Over time, though, their early recognition of a connection between them would blossom into a partnership, both of political allies and of drinking buddies. Perhaps Macdonald saw in McGee, ten years younger, the kind of protege men in power often like to have around to mentor. Perhaps Macdonald responded to the romantic in McGee, aware in his inexhaustibly subtle way that a dreamer is as much a part of public affairs as is a doer. It is tempting to call Macdonald, Cartier and McGee the three musketeers of Confederation, but it would not be true: Cartier never liked McGee, perhaps because, with his quick wit and marvellous singing voice, he was more popular at parties.

With McGee, the idea of Canada as something larger than the sum of its parts entered the public discourse. It was an idea, moreover, that all those who crowded in to hear McGee's speeches applauded wildly, no matter whether they were Conservatives or Reformers or Grits, or entirely indifferent to all politics.

⁓

Another voice addressing itself to the possibility of a wider Canada also began to be expressed at about this same time—from Alexander Tilloch Galt. Its nature was quite different from McGee's, more precise, less flowery, more attuned to accounting than to poetry. But still, it was a voice able to inject credibility and solidity into the vague notion of a wider Canada.

One of Macdonald's most glaring political weaknesses was that, while he had many members in the legislature, the ranks of his ministers were conspicuously thin in the vital ingredient of talent. Galt was an obvious potential new recruit for the cabinet, except that he displayed great wariness about Macdonald. Luring Galt to his side now became Macdonald's principal project.

Born in 1817, just two years after Macdonald, and like him a Scot, Galt was the son of John Galt, a writer who once travelled with Byron through Asia Minor. He was well educated and exceptionally bright. He grew up tall, lean and hardy, once walking thirty-six miles in six hours. His father immigrated to Canada to manage a British-financed scheme for colonization in the area of Sherbrooke in Lower Canada. Galt joined his father, who soon returned to Britain. The young Galt rose quickly in the business: when he was just twenty-six he was sent back to London to become commissioner of the Canadian operations of the British American Land Company. He returned to Sherbrooke, did well and, as was common at the time, went into the legislature, as an Independent.

Once Macdonald had become premier, he was in a position to place an alluring bait in front of Galt. Cannily, he offered nothing at all; instead, he engaged in tantalizing teasing: "You call

Alexander Galt. The fourth of the four "Super-Fathers" of Confederation and its financial brain, he shared Macdonald's fear that Britain wanted to rid itself of Canada.

yourself a *Rouge*. There may have been at one time a reddish tinge about you, but I could observe it becoming by degrees fainter. In fact you are like Byron's Dying Dolphin, exhibiting a series of colours—'the last still loveliest'—and that last is 'true blue,' being the colour I affect," Macdonald wrote in a letter to Galt in 1857. "So pray do become true blue at once: it is a good standing colour and bears washing."

Galt preserved his virtue for another year and then joined the cabinet—but at a high price to Macdonald. By this time Galt had become convinced that the only solution to Canada's governmental inertia was to form a federation of all the British American colonies. He sketched out his idea in impressive detail, including a supreme court to settle jurisdictional disputes. In fact, neither Macdonald nor Cartier was in the least persuaded by Galt's ideas, but they both accepted fully the political credibility he could bring to the government. They offered him the finance portfolio, and he joined the cabinet in July 1858. Galt then exacted his price. In a long speech to the House, he set out on behalf of the government his idea for a federation of British North America. The response made right afterwards by Macdonald and Cartier was striking: after Galt had finished speaking, neither of them said a word.

As a further part of his price, Galt had secured from Macdonald approval for him to go with Cartier to London that October to try to sell his federation idea to the Colonial Office.

The response of the colonial secretary, Sir Edward Bulwer-Lytton,* was dismissive, principally because of London's skepticism that Canadian politicians were up to so ambitious a task, but also because the reaction to the idea in the Maritimes was negative.

Galt and Macdonald were never close. Macdonald once described him as "unstable as water, and can never be depended upon to be of the same mind for forty-eight hours together." This assessment wasn't off the mark; before advocating Confederation, Galt had advocated annexation with the United States. Nevertheless, he succeeded for the first time in actually discussing a possible federation with the Colonial Office and, however nominally, secured a commitment for that notion to be added to the grabbag of policies that belonged to the Liberal-Conservative Party. As important for the way the future would unfold, Galt, with his well-known competence for accounting on a grand scale, was now working alongside Macdonald.

A third voice could be heard musing out loud about the need for a wider Canada. It was that of the Toronto *Globe* owner and publisher, George Brown. A grand federation held few charms for him. Instead, the catalyst for Brown's interest was his realization that, with the new immigrants having settled on the last "wild" land in Upper Canada, this province—Brown's province—needed new worlds to conquer. The *Globe* expressed this expan-

---

* In his day, Bulwer-Lytton was far better known as a popular writer—as of the romantic novel *The Last Days of Pompeii*—than as a politician. Today, he's best known as the inspiration for the annual Bulwer-Lytton Fiction Contest for bad writing, which takes off from his famous opening line, "It was a dark and stormy night." This association is a bit unfair, given that Bulwer-Lytton also minted the aphorism that writers love to quote, "The pen is mightier than the sword."

sionist concept best in an epistle to its Toronto readers on December 26, 1856: "If their city is ever to be made great—if it is ever to rise above the rank of a fifth-rate American town—it must be by the development of the great British territory lying to the north and west."

The *Globe*'s reference was to the North-West Territories, stretching out all the way from Lake Superior to the Rockies. It was bald, empty prairie, except for the Indians and a small cluster of Métis and a few Canadian settlers at the bend in the Red River. The rest of the territory served as a gigantic trapping ground for the fur traders of the Hudson's Bay Company and as a killing ground of the buffalo. Commonly called the North-West, it was also known as Rupert's Land—after Prince Rupert of the Rhine, the dashing cavalry general and cousin of Charles II, who in 1670 had secured a monopoly charter over the territory for himself and a group of British financiers and businessmen.

By the late 1850s the members of the governing board of the Hudson's Bay Company had come to realize that their exercise of absolute rule over a land that was now desired by nearby British North Americans was anomalous and ultimately unsustainable. They continued to protest that the land of the North-West was arid and useless. At Red River, though, as the settlers there knew well, the soil was black and deep. One of Macdonald's ministers, Joseph-Édouard Cauchon, the commissioner of Crown lands, wrote a memorandum to cabinet arguing that the "Red River and Saskatchewan Country" could attract to Canada many of the immigrants now passing straight through to the United States.

Another possibility—a distinctly alarming one—was that the Americans might come into the North-West first. In fact, they were almost there already. By now a railway line had reached St. Paul, Minnesota. From there, by oxcart and by boat along the winding Red River, it was incomparably easier to send goods to and from the settlement of Red River than it was for Canadians to make the long, brutal slog westwards across the Pre-Cambrian Shield above Lake Superior. To heighten the threat, a scientist at the Smithsonian Institution, Lorin Blodgett, issued a report in 1857 describing the land beyond the forty-ninth parallel as "perfectly adapted to the fullest occupation by a civilized nation." In response, two surveying expeditions to the West were dispatched from Canada the following year, one headed by Captain John Palliser, a Britisher, and the other by Henry Youle Hind, a graduate of Cambridge who had settled in Toronto as the professor of chemistry and geology at Trinity College. To heighten the sense of cross-border rivalry and threat, Minnesota was elevated from a territory to a state in 1858.

Macdonald's response to all this expansionism was cautious to a degree. About a possible federation he said nothing at all. About territorial expansion he said as little as possible, influenced by the warning of his friend John Rose, a Montreal lawyer, that it would be expensive to protect "such an extent of territory, even if it is given up to us for nothing."

Britain, in the person of the colonial secretary, Henry Labouchere, nevertheless felt that something had to be done to regularize the situation in the North-West. At Westminster, a select committee of the Commons was set up to recommend on the future of the Hudson's Bay Company charter, including whether the territory should be offered to Canada and at what price. The company adroitly countered with an offer that it would accept a takeover in return for a payment of one million pounds. To present Canada's case to the Commons committee, Macdonald established a commission headed by his former leader William Draper, now a judge.

Very little came of any of this. Draper told the select committee that Canada "must assert her rights" in the North-West, but in the absence of clear instructions from Macdonald his presentation to the British MPs was vague and legalistic. The committee made only one innovative recommendation—for a second Crown colony to be established on the Pacific Coast, to be named British Columbia. By oversight (or perhaps by design), the Hudson's Bay Company charter was allowed to lapse of its own accord in 1859. A group of British businessmen bought up the company, calculating shrewdly they would make an easy profit once they were forced to resell it to Canada. The Hudson's Bay Company continued to rule over its land, but less and less to govern it. Among those who came increasingly to control their own lives were the Métis of Red River, a change in their sense of themselves that no one outside the settlement took any notice of.

For the first time, though, ordinary Canadians had become aware of the open territory to their west. Indeed, because of a gold rush at the Fraser River, they appreciated now that this immense territory stretched all the way to the Pacific. An eventual takeover seemed more or less inevitable, if in no way imminent. Canada's own version of Manifest Destiny beckoned.

That expansionary thought precipitated others. If Canada were to be extended to the Pacific, then logically it should be extended as well to the east, to the Atlantic. Yet if Canada proper were to be augmented by both the North-West and the Lower Provinces (as the Maritimes then were called), the population balance would tilt decisively against the Canadiens—everyone taking it for granted that the West would be colonized by settlers from Upper Canada and by new immigrants from the British Isles. The Canadiens, though, would oppose any such radical change in Canada's demographic character as a violation of the agreement between the two groups when the United Province had been formed; more to the point, they could forestall it by exercising the de facto veto they possessed through the double-majority convention. When Cartier and Galt went to Britain for their meetings in 1858, Cartier warned Colonial Secretary Sir Edward Bulwer-Lytton that, if forced to, he would exercise this veto. Nothing was resolved, but for the first time politicians were giving thought to the kind of problems that would emerge as soon as any serious attempt was made to add to Canada some or all of the other pieces of British North America.

Here, Macdonald allowed himself for the first time to express some views about a possible wider Canada. In the debate that followed the announcement that Draper would represent Canada's views on the North-West to the British Parliament, Macdonald made an intriguing comment quite different from his earlier cautious utterances on the topic of Canada's future. "The destiny of this continent," he told the House, could depend on the results of the parliamentary inquiry in London. "Upon that action may depend whether this country remains confined to its present boundaries or swells to the dimension of a nation; whether we are to be annexed to the neighbouring Republic or extend the boundaries of this country itself."

Macdonald was allowing the wheels of his mind to turn in public. Earlier he had dismissed the western territory as useless, and on one occasion expressed concern that Canada could be weakened by spreading out its settlers too thinly. Now he was declaring that adding the West to Canada could transform what was still only a province into something resembling a nation. While the word "federation" had not yet crossed his lips, Macdonald was here using the word that had always held talismanic importance to him—"annexation"—in the sense of stressing the need to make certain it never happened.

Proposals for a federation of the British North American colonies, or for a confederation of them—the terms were used interchangeably at this time—were not in themselves in any way new. The number of different proposals made for some form of federation or confederation before McGee and Galt took up the cause has been estimated at eighteen in all. The first person to advocate it—three-quarters of a century earlier—was Major Robert Morse, a British army engineer who, after surveying the Bay of Fundy in 1784 for possible settlements following the loss of the American colonies, suggested that all the colonies still remaining under the Crown should be banded together for their own protection. The same thought was expressed a few years later by two leading Loyalists, William Smith, later chief justice of Quebec, and Jonathan Sewell, who, in 1807, published a pamphlet about his idea: *Plan for a General Legislative Union of the British Provinces in North America.** In the late 1830s in Britain, a Canadian-educated British MP, James Roebuck, proposed it at Westminster; Lord Durham came very close to recommending it in his famous report; and the Colonial Office later drafted a report on how it might be constructed.

A major obstacle—one common to most transformational ideas—was that potential losers could count their losses before they experienced them, while gains for likely winners were futuristic. The Maritimes, all of which were separate colonies

---

* The most unorthodox version of confederation, submitted to the legislature of Upper Canada in 1825 and advocating a loose federation, was by Robert Gourlay, who turned out to have written it while in a lunatic asylum in England. Gourlay was an engaging eccentric and an agrarian radical. His most considerable accomplishment was, at the age of eighty, to contest a riding in Upper Canada and to marry his twenty-eight-year-old housekeeper. However, he lost both.

that had already won Responsible Government for themselves, had little interest in giving up London as their protector in favour of Ottawa. Upper Canada had little interest in offering the one lure Maritimers might respond to—a railway to Halifax—because it would be the principal payer of the scheme, while Montreal, where the headquarters of this intercolonial railway would be located, would be the chief beneficiary. As for the Canadiens, it was difficult to offer them any greater protection than the virtual veto over Canadian national affairs they already exercised.

This combination of indifference and skepticism among so many of the British North Americans had been more than enough to convince Bulwer-Lytton to give Galt and Cartier a dusty, evasive answer when they came looking for British support for Galt's federation concept. Further, the colonial secretary was sharp enough to guess that Macdonald's real motive for sending over the mission was "the convenience of the present Canadian administration"—in other words, to make certain that Galt joined his cabinet.

Yet again, inertia won the day. What was needed to make something actually happen was a crisis, one that would shake everyone from his own fixed position. Also needed at that moment of opportunity would be a political leader who knew how to herd cats.

Some commentators, the most influential among them Donald Creighton, have attempted to situate Macdonald among the early advocates of Confederation, as if to mingle his lustre with that of the cause of union itself. The weight of evidence is otherwise: even the inclusion of support for Confederation in the Liberal-

Conservative policy from 1858 onwards was strictly tactical. The most persuasive negative evidence comes from Macdonald himself—in his own words.

In advance of the impending next election—it actually happened in the summer of 1861—Macdonald published an *Address to the Electors of the City of Kingston* of some three thousand words in which he set out his policies on all the central issues of the day, including a bankruptcy law, university reform, the Grand Trunk Railway, law reform and Representation by Population. About this last, controversial, topic, Macdonald penned the evasive phrase "This is not a party question, and ought not to be made one."

About his thoughts on Confederation as he held them in mid-1861, Macdonald wrote, "The Government will not relax its exertions to effect a Confederation of the North American Provinces. We must however endeavour to take warning by the defects in the Constitution of the United States, which are now so painfully made manifest, and to form (if we succeed in a Federation) an efficient, central government." That was all he had to say. To have said less would have been difficult. His disinclination to commit himself to any "vision thing" came out of the policy of governance he was committed to. Back in 1844, in advance of his first election, Macdonald had promised Kingston's voters that he would not "waste the time of the legislature and the money of the people on abstract and theoretical questions of government."* After two decades of practical political experience, the abstract and the theoretical still left him cold.

About constitutions, Macdonald was at all times particularly

---

* Creighton's case for Macdonald as an early champion of Confederation rests primarily on a speech he gave in the House in April 1861 calling for "an immense confederation of free men, the greatest confederacy of civilized and intelligent men that has ever had an existence on the face of the globe." All those golden phrases, though, were simply Macdonald at his "buncombe" best.

wary. They should not be fiddled with, he believed, unless "the people are suffering from the effects of the constitution as it actually exists," as he had said in a legislature speech in 1854. Anyway, the substance of constitutions could be changed without an *i* or a *t* of them being amended. Canada had, after all, gained Responsible Government, although its constitution had been drafted specifically to exclude it; and the double-majority principle had entered into legislative life without any legal sanction. Britain, Macdonald's political ideal, had won and was now administering the world's second-greatest empire on the foundation of no written constitution at all. Put simply, Confederation at this time was, to Macdonald, an impractical irrelevancy.

But that left him with no governing principle at all—at the time when Brown's governing principle of Rep by Pop kept gaining ever more legitimacy and support. Even Antoine-Aimé Dorion, the leader of *rouges*, who were loosely allied to the Reformers, felt compelled to suggest in the legislature a possible trade of his agreement to Rep by Pop for disentangling the United Province of Canada into a loose federation of two provinces with some minimalist central government.

Macdonald was reduced to advising Conservative candidates who supported Rep by Pop how best to express their opinion without appearing to be splitting from the party. He wrote to a sitting member, George Benjamin, to "go for Rep by Pop as strongly as you like, but do *not* say that it must be granted if a majority of U.C. members say so. Say that the principle is so just & equitable that it must prevail and that you have no doubt it will eventually." He went on to urge Benjamin, "As you are situated, *do not put yourself in opposition to the French.* . . . The French are your sheet anchor."

Macdonald was being forced to perform like a gymnast edging his way along a high wire that someone else was jiggling. Of the six Upper Canada ministers in his government, all but one would eventually go public as supporters of Rep by Pop—the lone exception being Macdonald himself. At the same time, his French Canadians were becoming increasingly concerned that Macdonald could not forever forestall Rep by Pop. So, some *bleus* began to wonder, why not switch over to the winning side—that of Brown and the Reformers—and thereby keep hold of the perks of patronage? Moreover, while Macdonald had spotted the possibility that he might be reduced to an opposition rump by a loss of *bleu* support, so had Brown.

After the humiliation of the double shuffle—and the taunt that he had headed "His Excellency's most ephemeral Administration"—Brown's career had gone into decline. He seemed even to have lost power at the *Globe*, where the editorials were being determined by the editor, George Sheppard. The anti-French Sheppard repeatedly called for an end to "French domination" and demanded that the problem be solved by an outright dissolution of the Union that would release Upper Canada from "Romish" and "Jesuitical" scheming.

Brown began his march back to leadership by organizing a huge Reform convention for the fall of 1859 in Toronto; its six hundred delegates made it easily the largest Canada had seen. Sheppard delivered a powerful speech and moved a resolution calling for the "unqualified dissolution" of the United Province of Canada. Brown's turn came a day later. He agreed with Upper Canada's complaints about the dominance of its smaller partner,[*]

[*] The imbalance wasn't simply one of political representation in proportion to population. About three-quarters of all Canada's tax revenues came from the Upper Canada "section."

admitted that dissolving the union might resolve the problems, but then offered a brighter alternative: "What true Canadian can witness the tide of immigration now commencing to flow into the vast territories of the North West without longing . . . to make our own country the highway of the traffic to the Pacific." The one way to achieve this was to keep the United Province together, so that it "may at some future date readily furnish the machinery of a great confederation." Brown had found for himself a new voice as a moderate advocate of Confederation.

Brown, though, was no politician. After the convention, one Reform member recalled meeting his leader several times and never being recognized; a few days later, he had encountered Macdonald, who grasped his hand, slapped him on the back and declared how glad he was to see him. Brown's ideas remained remote, abstract—and confusing. The resolution eventually passed by the Reform convention called for a federation composed only of the two existing "sections" of the United Province, Upper and Lower Canada, each separating to form new provinces, with, over them, "some joint authority." The populist Grits rejected such a scheme as tame, and, far worse, as failing to be certain of ridding them of the French Canadians. By the summer of 1860, Brown's hold on the party had weakened again, and he began to talk about resigning.

At the same time as Brown was losing control over his own party, so was Macdonald over his group. Besides having to tug back into line the ever-growing number of Conservatives now openly supporting Rep by Pop, he had to cope with rising disaffection with his leadership among the Orange Order, which had always provided him with a large number of his electoral foot

The young Prince of Wales, Canada's first royal visitor. On the far left is Governor General Sir Edmund Head, a great admirer of Macdonald's. John Rose organized the prince's tour.

soldiers. The divisive force here was that, in the summer of 1860, a spectacular royal tour of Canada—the first ever of its kind—had been made by Queen Victoria's son Albert Edward, the Prince of Wales, at the request of Macdonald's government. While the prince's progress had been overwhelmingly successful, it had been marred by one jarring confrontation involving the Orange Order.

Only eighteen years old, Prince Edward was generally judged to be handsome in the way, then as now, a special indulgence is always extended to royal princes. He had the reputation of being a good dancer and a stylish dresser—too stylish perhaps, because Victoria's consort, Prince Albert, complained that his eldest son took "no interest in anything but clothes. Even when out shooting, he is more occupied with his trousers than with the game."

But no matter—parades, pageantry and pomp always please the masses. For the colony to put on its best show—as Macdonald observed, "Our administration is more familiar with cocktails than cocked hats"—he picked his friend John Rose, at this time the minister of public works. And it went splendidly. The colonials were ecstatic and awed. There was one terrible gaffe, in London, where an overeager citizen had the audacity to "seize the hand of his Royal Highness and shake it like a pump-handle." More generally, as the *Ottawa Citizen* reported, "Ottawa appeared lovely and anxious as a bride awaiting the arrival of the bridegroom to complete the joy." Everywhere, there were triumphal arches, red, white and blue bunting, patriotic banners, fireworks and illuminations achieved by the new marvel of gas. And there were newly minted ditties: "For hark, the trumpets / hark, the drums / The Princely Heir of England comes!"*

Then it all unravelled in Macdonald's hometown of Kingston. It was the most loyal town in the country, not only because of the Loyalists but even more because the Loyal Orange Order was so strong there. To greet their prince who had come over the water, Kingston's Orangemen built two large arches of firs, which they covered with their own regalia and symbols. Then they gathered en masse to await him. Premonitions of trouble came from complaints by Kingston's Catholics that the prince should not and could not be welcomed by a sectarian political organization that was banned in England itself. To stir things up, the *Globe* pointed out that when the prince began his tour in Quebec City, he had not only been greeted in French but visited Roman Catholic

---

* In his *Royal Spectacle: The 1860 Visit of the Prince of Wales to Canada and the United States,* from which much of the material in this section is drawn, Ian Radforth observes that one problem for the tour's organizers was that the towns and cities of then underdeveloped Canada lacked any of the "grand avenues and parade grounds" so necessary for ceremonial spectacles.

The prince's tour was a huge success, with one exception. In Kingston, the Orange Order massed to greet "their Prince." Because the Lodge was banned in England, he refused to come ashore and walk beneath their triumphal arch.

institutions such as Laval University and the Ursuline Convent. To head off a confrontation, Macdonald met with the colonial secretary, the Duke of Newcastle, who was accompanying the prince.* Macdonald argued that Upper Canadians felt that the Catholics "had had it all their own way in Lower Canada" and that the same courtesy should be extended to Upper Canada's Protestants. Newcastle replied that there was no comparison between the Catholic artifacts in Quebec City, "which were emblematical of a faith," and the paraphernalia of Orangemen, "which were those of a rancorous party."

On the afternoon of Tuesday, September 4, 1860, the prince entered Kingston Harbour aboard the steamer *Kingston*. It drew

---

* Newcastle thus became the first colonial secretary to visit the most important of the colonies he was responsible for, and the only one to do so during the nineteenth century.

close to the official landing place, where the Orangemen had massed—some fifteen thousand of them—in their costumes and with their banners. At the last minute, the ship changed course and moved off into mid-harbour. The standoff continued into the next day, with the Orangemen refusing to leave, but making no disturbances other than singing such songs as "Water, water, holy water. / Sprinkle the Catholics everyone. / We'll cut them asunder and make 'em lie under." Late in the morning of the 5th, despite last-minute appeals by Macdonald, the *Kingston* weighed anchor and chugged off to the prince's next engagement in Belleville, and then on to Cobourg.

The incident earned Canada an international black eye, including the comment in the *New York Times* that nowhere in Canada could the prince find "a rational population before reaching the American frontier." The *Globe* put it all down to Macdonald's hypocrisy and incompetence. In fact the blame rested principally with the Duke of Newcastle, who, concerned only with domestic British politics, ignored the fact that the Orange Order was a legal organization in Canada. In the United States, where he next went, the prince had no problems: newspapers pronounced him a "heart smasher," and many of the young ladies at balls and receptions wrestled each other to get near to him. In Philadelphia, a production of *La Traviata* came to a halt because "the leading ladies on stage could not keep their eyes off the royal youth."*

---

* Years later, the Prince of Wales encountered a Canadian MP in London who answered the prince's inquiry by saying that he came from Kingston. "Ah," replied Edward in a deft reference to his aborted visit, "it looks very well from the water." Later still, on Queen Victoria's death in 1901, he succeeded to the throne as Edward VII. Throughout his life, he remained exceptionally close to a great many ladies.

To recover from this fiasco, which had left him furious with British officials at the same time as the Orangemen were angry with him, Macdonald resorted to a political innovation that served as a response to Brown's mass convention of the summer before, as well as a platform for him to tell his side of what the newspapers were calling "The Siege at Kingston." He embarked on a cross-country speaking tour.

No one had done that before—except Americans. Stump speeches were exceedingly rare then, as Canadian politicians limited themselves to orations in the legislature, to church congregations and dinners organized by businessmen. Manifestos like Macdonald's *Address* were the standard way of spreading the word. In one critical respect, Macdonald was quite unlike most politicians of the time: he was entirely at ease with ordinary people. He dealt with people not by lecturing them or by orating at them but by talking colloquially with them, telling stories, exchanging repartee—all in everyday language.

Not for many decades would Canadians again encounter a politician so completely at ease with ordinary people. Once, after Macdonald had clambered onto a piece of farm machinery to better address a gathering, word was passed to him that he was actually standing on a manure spreader. His instant reply: "This is the first time I've stood on the Liberal platform." When a passerby stopped him on Toronto's King Street to tell him that a friend had said Macdonald was "the biggest liar in all Canada," he looked gravely at his interlocutor and answered, "I dare say it's true enough." Mostly, people—even those intending to vote against him—clustered around Macdonald at his meetings for the uncomplicated reason that he was fun.

So off he went on his speaking tour, travelling from town to town—first in Brantford, and then in a succession of meetings, from Toronto to Hamilton to St. Catharines, from St. Thomas to

London to Guelph, from Belleville to Simcoe to Kingston. At times, the crowds topped eight hundred listeners. Usually there was a dinner or lunch, typically of six or more courses. There were speeches and toasts, jokes and stories, and more speeches— typically eight or ten speakers. Macdonald frequently was funny, but in a way that got across a message. He referred to the "some joint authority" resolution passed at the Reform convention and asked, "Is it a legislature, or is it a bench of bishops?" He set out his case: "I am a sincere Unionist. I nail my colours to the mast on that great principle." He used the flag to salute two masters at the same time: "I say that next to the Union with Great Britain, next to having our Queen as ruler, I look to the Union of the two Canadas as most essential." He turned maudlin: "Whatever may have been the antecedents of any man in Canada, whether he has acted with me or against me, if he becomes a disunionist, I disown him; and I don't care what may have been the antecedents of another, though he may have struggled fiercely against me, if he enters himself as a supporter of the union with England . . . and of the union of the two Canadas, I hail him as a brother. God and nature have joined the two Canadas, and no factious politician should be allowed to sever them." The argument didn't make much sense, but it abundantly served its purpose: Macdonald had put Brown and the Reformers on the defensive as would-be dividers of the nation and of the Empire, and he had positioned himself as the protector of the nation and, better yet by far, of the Queen.

As for the recent royal tour, Macdonald took credit for its overall success: "It had called the attention of the world to the position and prospects of Canada." He admitted that although the prince's visit "had been a source of great pleasure to the people, it had been accompanied in some respects with disappointments, in some degree with heart burnings, in some degree with mistakes." The fault lay with the Duke of Newcastle for interfering in a way that upset Canada's careful balance between French and English, Catholics and Protestants. It was an adroit defence, and a courageous one, given that he was directly criticizing no less a power than the colonial secretary.

Macdonald delivered his most important speech in Caledonia. There he addressed directly the central issue of the coming election and of the Canadian political system. "It has been said that I and my Upper Canadian colleagues sacrificed the interests of Upper Canada to Lower Canada; and that we hold to our Lower Canadian colleagues simply for the sake of office. They say we are traitors to our race; that we knuckle to the Frenchmen; that we are faithless to our religion; and that we are under Roman Catholic influences." Then he offered his reply. He and Cartier had attempted, "in our humble way, to advise the head of the Government for the good of the whole country and the equal interest of all." In itself, his argument was unremarkable. What was remarkable was that Macdonald, in the heartland of English-speaking Protestantism, could tell his audience that much of what they were thinking was wrong in itself and, equally, wrong for the country.

Afterwards, Macdonald told a friend that he had found this pre-campaign swing "wearisome beyond description." But not so wearisome that he didn't add jauntily, "I never took to the stump before, & find that I get on capitally." Macdonald's legend as a man of the people had begun to take root.

Impending elections focus the minds of politicians as, to all others, the prospect of being hanged is said to do. Any frustration felt by Macdonald or any intimation of attenuated accomplishment immediately vanished. From early 1861 on, he became a whirlwind of energy. He bombarded Hamilton businessman Isaac Buchanan with arguments why he shouldn't step down as a member (Buchanan stayed on). He dispatched confidential letters to candidates tipping them off to the date of the election. He encouraged (successfully) Sidney Smith, a friend, to remain as a Reformer, so that a shred of substance would adhere to the label Liberal-Conservative. And he wrote to Egerton Ryerson—"No time must be lost in calling on the Wesleyan Methodists in every constituency"—to try to swing those of his faith to come over (quite a few did).

The results of all this activity could not have been better. Through the summer of 1861—elections were then held over several months—Macdonald won his first ever (and only ever) Conservative majority in Upper Canada. The simultaneous loss of a few seats by Cartier's *bleus* was, by comparison, a minor setback. Most admirable of all, Brown lost in his own riding.

In fact the election result changed nothing. The Rep by Pop challenge still remained to be dealt with. The double-majority convention still stalled national action. No sooner was the election over than Macdonald was complaining in a letter to a supporter about "violent Tories who are fools enough to think that a purely Conservative Gov-t can be formed. Now I am not such a fool as to destroy all that I have been doing for the last 7 years."

In fact, Macdonald's world, as well as Canada's, had already changed beyond recall.

⌒

Four months before that election was held, a single mortar shot fired on the morning of April 12, 1861, had signalled the start of the bombardment of the small federal garrison in an unfinished fort, Fort Sumter, at the mouth of Charleston Harbor, South Carolina. A day and a half later, the garrison's commander, Major Robert Anderson, surrendered to the Confederate commander, Brigadier General P.G.T. Beauregard. One of the most bloody, brutal and tragic of civil wars in history had begun. It would go on for four relentless years. Out of it would come a totally different America, pulsating with energy, confidence and drive, never pausing on its way first to industrial supremacy and thereafter to military and geopolitical supremacy. Out of it too would come a radically different Canada. The crisis that could dislodge everyone from their fixed positions had happened at last.

Interior of the badly damaged Fort Sumter by John Kay (1863). From out of the Civil War came a transformed United States and also a transformed Canada.

FIFTEEN

Canada's First Anti-American

~

Long may that principle—the Monarchial principle—prevail in
this land. Let there be "No Looking to Washington."
John A. Macdonald

For the premier of a country whose next-door neighbour had just been convulsed by a murderous domestic conflict, Macdonald's reaction to the start of the
American Civil War was remarkably calm. Through
the balance of 1861, he made no comments about the war in any
of his letters. For quite a time, his principal concern was only the
war's potential effect on Canadian politics. In his June 1861
Address to the Electors of the City of Kingston, Macdonald put forth
this analysis: "The fratricidal conflict now unhappily raging in
the United States shows us the superiority of our institutions
and of the principle on which we are based. Long may that
principle—the Monarchial principle—prevail in this land. Let
there be 'No Looking to Washington,' as was threatened by a
leading member of the opposition."

As was by no means always the case, there was actually some
validity to Macdonald's accusation. In the legislature, a leading
Grit, William McDougall, had blurted out that unless Rep by Pop

was enacted, he and other populists might look southwards for support. A jugular having been offered up to him, Macdonald went straight for it. During that summer's election, a crowd of six hundred Conservatives at Whitby burned McDougall in effigy, as the figure's straw-filled hand held up a placard reading, "Look to Washington." The Conservatives hurried out a pamphlet warning of "Clear Grit treason."

The start of hostilities at Charleston came as no great surprise to Macdonald. Close observers of the U.S. scene—so far as Canadians were concerned that really meant the British ambassador in Washington—had long regarded Southern secession as all but inevitable, particularly since the Supreme Court's famous, and infamous, 1857 Dred Scott ruling in favour of the legality of slavery. Overwhelmingly, Northerners refused to accept this judgment. The remaining issue became whether the North would allow the South to secede. This choice was determined by the victory in the November 1860 presidential election of the comparatively little-known Republican candidate Abraham Lincoln, who, although not prepared—yet—to free the slaves, was committed to an "indivisible union." Soon after Lincoln's election, Southern senators and congressmen streamed out of Washington. The new Southern Confederacy was proclaimed on February 11, 1861. Lincoln dismissed the secession as "legally void" and declared that the federal government would maintain control over all military installations throughout the country. Lincoln's policy was blown to pieces by the Confederate guns at Fort Sumter.

During this period, Macdonald expressed no opinions about Lincoln in his private correspondence. (In a later letter, of November 1864, he referred to Lincoln as "a beast," but in a jokey way, his full comment being that, for Canada's sake, "Abe Lincoln, beast as he is, should be elected.") The prevailing Canadian view about Lincoln was conveyed by the *Globe*'s dismissal of him as "a fourth-rate lawyer."* Canadian insiders, though, regarded Lincoln as a plus. That wasn't because of Lincoln's as-yet-untested qualities, but rather those of William Seward, the politician who, most unexpectedly, had lost the Republican presidential nomination to Lincoln. Seward, a former New York senator, able and supremely confident, a man likened to "a huge bird chiseled in stone," now became secretary of state rather than president. He was also an unabashed annexationist—and an astute one. He espoused the "ripe fruit" doctrine,

William Seward, U.S. secretary of state. A strong annexationist, he believed that Canada would sooner or later join the United States peacefully and passively, like a "ripe fruit."

which held that Canada would fall naturally from Britain's grasp into the handily available and incomparably more attractive basket of the United States.† Once the Civil War began, Seward searched for ways to speed the process by provoking Britain into some intemperate action that could justify a retaliatory invasion of Canada. Macdonald's concerns about Canadians who looked to Washington seemed justified.

The summer of 1861 witnessed repeated alarms and excursions. In June the British prime minister, John Russell, sent a

---

* The unofficial official British view of Lincoln was even wider of the mark. Lord Lyons, the ambassador (minister) in Washington, informed London that Lincoln was "a rough westerner of the lowest origin and little education."

† Seward had formed this view as a result of an extensive trip he made in 1857 across the British North American colonies, even north to Labrador.

coded telegram to Governor General Head warning that "a sudden declaration of war by the United States against Great Britain appears to me by no means impossible." The *New York Times* declared that Canada's union with the North was a certainty, and the New York *Herald* reassured readers there would be "no necessity for hostilities," because Canadians themselves overwhelmingly favoured annexation. Offstage, Massachusetts senator Charles Sumner, chair of the Senate Committee on Foreign Relations, talked up the advantages to the North of letting go the South in exchange for getting Canada. Ambiguous evidence exists suggesting that, in London, William Gladstone, then the chancellor of the Exchequer, may have been considering the same kind of swap to head off a possible war between Britain and the United States.* The ire of Americans had been raised by Britain's declaration of neutrality, meaning that it treated the South as a legitimate belligerent.

About the Civil War itself, Canadian public opinion was deeply divided. Taverns became meeting places for either pro-Northerners or pro-Southerners. (One bar in Montreal served mint juleps.) Anti-slavery sentiments were strong, led by George Brown, who penned denunciatory editorials in the *Globe* and donated generously to organizations that looked after runaway slaves. The historian Sidney Wise has observed astutely that Canadians didn't so much favour one side or the other, but rather were either anti-South or anti-North. The South was slave country, yet it had a British social quality to it and was a safe distance away. Canadians knew the North quite well, many had worked

---

* The evidence is questionable. In a book published in 1904, Goldwin Smith claimed that Gladstone had written to him during the war proposing that "if the North thought fit at this time to let the South go, it might in time be indemnified by . . . Canada." Smith said that he had later destroyed Gladstone's letter because it might "prove embarrassing."

there, and some forty thousand enlisted in the Northern armies, for the pay or for the excitement.* It was the North, though, that threatened Canada. A song sung by Union soldiers to the tune of "Yankee Doodle" included the lines: "Secession first he would put down / Wholly and forever, / And afterwards from Britain's crown / He Canada would sever."

As a conservative and a believer in hierarchy, and one who was always silent on the slavery issue, Macdonald appears to have favoured the South. At the war's start, he expected the South to succeed in its attempt to break away: "If they [Americans] are to be severed in two, as severed in two I believe they will be," he said in the legislature in his first post–Fort Sumter speech on April 19, 1861, "they will be two great, two noble, two free nations [that] will exist in the place of one." And his principal concern was always the North. He wrote to a friend that all the Canadians who had joined the Northern armies "will return to Canada sadder and wiser men, with a good deal of military experience that they may perhaps be able to use hereafter against their teachers." His public stance, though, was always strict neutrality. When, early on, some Conservative members cheered the news of the Southern victory at the First Battle of Bull Run, Macdonald angrily silenced them.

By the fall of 1861, it appeared that the cross-border threat had passed. The North, now losing engagement after engagement, could not risk a wider war. As well, Britain that summer hurried over an extra two thousand troops, deliberately doing so in the most public possible way by transporting them in *Great*

---

* More than half of these Canadian volunteers were Canadiens. Mass migration from Quebec to the United States during the nineteenth century dates from the Civil War years, in large part because of the classic "pull" factor in migration— those who've already gone to or already know a new country always attract others to follow them.

Eastern, the world's largest steamship.* As always, the unexpected then happened.

On November 8, 1861, the U.S. warship *San Jacinto* came upon the Royal Mail steamship *Trent* in the Bahamas Channel. On information received from federal spies in Havana, its last port of call, but without any orders from Washington, the *San Jacinto*'s commander, Captain Charles Wilkes, forced the *Trent* to stop and sent marines aboard; they found there, and brought back to their own ship, two Confederate officials who were on their way to England to order supplies and arrange for them to be brought back by blockade runners. This action was outright piracy on the high seas. The Northern newspapers, delighted to have even a small victory to report, cheered, and Wilkes was celebrated at public dinners. Canadian newspapers, naturally loyal to Britain, answered with outrage. Even if limited in itself, the affair was the most serious diplomatic incident between the United States and Britain since the War of 1812. As the giants glared at each other, Canadians, caught in between, could only blink nervously.

Sometimes, bad communications can lead to good decision making. The news took three weeks to reach London. Another three weeks passed before the British government's official response—a demand for the release of the prisoners and for a formal apology—reached Washington. By this time, heads in the White House had begun to cool. After fierce cabinet debates,

---

* *Great Eastern* raced across the Atlantic in a new record of eight days and six hours, going full speed through icefields—as would, less successfully, another "world's largest ship" a half-century later.

Lincoln ruled, "one war at a time." With deft timing, the Confederate pair was released around Christmas, when the newspapers were distracted; just as deftly, the Imperial government "forgot" that it had ever called for an apology. By luck, Alexander Tilloch Galt, Macdonald's finance minister, was then in Washington to discuss trade matters; he got an unexpected call to come to the White House; there, Lincoln reassured the visiting Canadian that he and the Northern government had no hostile intentions towards their neighbour. The assurance only partially reassured, because both Macdonald and Galt remained worried that public opinion might yet force Lincoln to take precipitate action.

That risk did exist. The New York *World* pronounced, "The simple fact is, Canada hates us." More threatening still was the Cleveland *Leader*'s declaration that, in a reference to the vast Northern Armies, "six hundred thousand men will want something more to do" once they had done with the South. To placate his public, Lincoln ruled that all visitors to the United States would henceforth have to carry passports, a rule that hit Canadians by far the hardest. Fortunately, American public opinion cooled quickly, and the passport regulation was quietly lifted.

On first hearing the news of the *Trent* crisis, the British cabinet had decided that a show of force had to be made. Some eleven thousand additional redcoats were rushed out. By the time the ships had reached the St. Lawrence, the freeze-up had begun. The boats hurriedly swung round to Saint John, where the soldiers disembarked. Using a kind of snowshoes called "creepers," they marched over the snowbound, hilly roads of New Brunswick to the St. Lawrence River. Britain had done its bit; it was now Canada's turn.

Responsibility for the defence of Canada rested at the time not with its premier and his government but with the governor general. Responsibility for Canada's doing what it could to help rested with its minister of militia. It was a new portfolio, created by Macdonald on December 18, 1861, in the midst of the *Trent* crisis. He appointed himself to the position, thereby making himself, already attorney general and premier, a triple minister.

In some ways Macdonald's assumption of this role was questionable. He had no military experience whatever, other than in 1837, when, as a member of the Sedentary Militia, he took part in the attack on Montgomery's Tavern in the countryside north of Toronto which crushed William Lyon Mackenzie's rebellion. Macdonald never fired a shot himself, claiming only to have "carried my musket." More intriguingly and reflective of his attitude towards the military, a half-century passed before Macdonald mentioned to anyone that he had actually seen action.* He learned from the brief experience that a soldier's lot was not an easy one. As he recounted, "The day was hot. My feet were blistered. I was but a weary boy and I thought I would have dropped with weight of the old flint musket which galled my shoulder, but I managed to keep up with my companion, a grim old soldier who seemed impervious to fatigue." More surprisingly still, unlike many in public life, Macdonald had never sought a commission as an officer in the militia for the sake of the status. If anything, he was actively suspicious of the military; Macdonald would later discourage his son, Hugh John, from following a military career. And he wrote back to an

---

* Not until 1887, in a conversation with his friend Judge Gowan, did Macdonald disclose for the first time his front-line experience, or, more accurately, his near to the front-line adventure. His company was placed safely behind the artillery that levelled the tavern and killed eleven of the hapless rebels.

inquirer, "There is no chance of there being any such thing in this country for a long time as a Profession of arms."

This indifference is a bit puzzling, given that the military was British and hierarchical—two of Macdonald's favourite qualities. He seemed to have a distaste for warfare itself. In no way was he a pacifist (as, then, almost no one was), but he never evinced any interest in the lives of heroes like Caesar or Napoleon. Although he loved the Empire, he was in no way an imperialist, and he later rejected appeals from London for Canadian troops to be sent to this or that patch of Imperial sand or rock.

In other respects Macdonald's self-appointment was well merited. He knew more about British politics, as was now of critical importance, than anyone else in Canada. He was also well regarded by Britain's representative—Lord Monck, who had just succeeded Head as governor general, was an admirer of Macdonald, although far from an uncritical one. Macdonald had already acted as virtual militia minister before creating the portfolio, sending regular memorandums to Monck suggesting, for instance, an increase in militia strength from 5,000 to 7,500 and proposing that railway workers be excluded from militia service, because "the withdrawal of any of them would weaken our lines of communication." Once minister, Macdonald poured out memorandums on all kinds of militia topics and early in 1862 set up a high-level commission with himself as chair to recommend ways to improve the country's defences.

~

For Canadians in the early 1860s, defence meant resisting any cross-border incursion. Yet, as few people had begun to recognize, the real threat was not that vast numbers of grey-uniformed Union soldiers might one day march across the border and, in the words of the New York *Herald*, "overrun the Province in three weeks"—as, most certainly, they could have done. It was, instead, that as soon as the Civil War was over, a transformed and powerful United States would emerge from the carnage.

The first appearance of this new United States was in its military guise. On the eve of the opening cannon-shot at Fort Sumter, the total U.S. army strength was nominally about thirteen thousand, but effectively was a good deal less, because the desertion rate was high and many soldiers were tied down by wars against the Indians. By comparison, there were then about four thousand redcoats in Canada, incomparably better trained and experienced. The odds were pretty even, particularly since more redcoats could be dispatched from elsewhere in the Empire. Less than two years later, the Federal Army had grown to more than eight hundred thousand—larger than any of Napoleon's armies. It would grow eventually to more than two million men, well provisioned and with excellent weapons. Militarily, this United States was unbeatable within North America. And that was only the start. Given the power and energy it was displaying in the Civil War, the new United States would not only rearrange the geopolitical order on the North American continent but extend its reach far overseas. A new world order was taking shape, and Canada was going to be the first country to have to figure out how to accommodate itself to it.

Canada was no longer situated next door to a larger, richer neighbour. It was huddled alongside a colossus in the making—a colossus of unprecedented dynamism which, while waging the largest civil war in history, could still take in vast numbers of immigrants and begin to build a transcontinental railway. Soon after the war ended, all this dynamism would be applied to extending the country westwards to the Pacific, and a few decades later to building it up towards the sky. All this energy, much of it generated by a new entrepreneurial form of capitalism, would never flag: within half a century, the United States would be the world's leading industrial power.

Macdonald was slow to appreciate the scale of the change. Unlike other Canadian leaders such as Brown and McGee, he had never worked in the United States. As a young lawyer, he had gone on holidays in northern New York State with clients, and he had carried Isabella on that long pilgrimage to Savannah. But all his political, commercial and social contacts were in London rather than in Washington or New York.

This orientation was the real limitation to Macdonald's southwards gaze. He saw the United States through British eyes. During that 1845 trip south with Isabella, he went to a political meeting in Savannah at which a U.S. senator spoke. Afterwards he recounted to Margaret Greene, "He is evidently an able man, with great fluency and force of expression, but has the great fault of American speakers . . . of being too theatrical in his manner and turgid in his style." Consistently, he saw just about any bottle south of the border as half-empty. As he commented to a friend, "one soon tires of Yankee humour—except in a book when you can lay it down if it wearies you." About major matters, Macdonald could be crashingly wrong—as in his view of the presidency: "By the election of the President by a majority and for a short time, he is never the sovereign and chief of the nation," he declared. "He is never looked up to by the whole population as the head and fount of the nation. He is at best but the successful leader of a party."

By comparison, the British (and Canadian) system was near perfect, to Macdonald: "We shall have a Sovereign who is placed above the region of party. . . . Representatives of the Sovereign [the governors general] can act only on the advice of his ministers, those ministers being responsible to the people through

Parliament." He took for granted that just about anything British had to be the best: "I do not think there is anything in the world equal in real intellectual pleasure to meeting the public men of England. Their tone is so high and their mode of thinking is so correct that it really elevates one." As for the equivalent Americans, "the standard of excellence is far lower than the English one."

Macdonald did sometimes look clearly across the border. From the start of the Civil War onwards, he repeatedly described the U.S. Constitution as "defective" because it was so decentralized, treating its member states as if they were sovereign and thereby giving legitimacy to the South's secession. But he also appreciated that something out of the ordinary was being attempted there. "It has been said that the United States is a failure," he said in one major speech. "On the contrary, I consider it a marvellous exhibition of human wisdom. It was as perfect as human wisdom could make it, and under it the American states prospered until very recently; but being the work of men, it had its defects." Yet he could not help noticing all the defects below the border. American conventions to elect party leaders were "immoral" and "horrid," resulting in presidential candidates being chosen "by cliques of the lowest politicians." To reinforce his conviction of British superiority, many of the recent presidents produced by that system during his time—Millard Fillmore, Franklin Pierce, James Buchanan—had indeed been nonentities.

To Macdonald, the United States was Canada's "other"— the alien, the threat, or to put it most simply, the enemy. To him, Britain was Canada's elder brother, at once protector and role model.

To appreciate the magnitude of what was happening south of the border required an observer with the imagination of a poet, or at least with the trend-spotting capabilities of an alert journalist. D'Arcy McGee saw straight into the future: "It is not the figures [of soldiers] which give the worst view. . . . It is the change which has taken place in the spirit of the people of the Northern states themselves. If we do not desire to become part and parcel of this people, we cannot overlook this, the greatest revolution of our times. . . . We run the risk of being swallowed up by the spirit of universal democracy that prevails in the United States."

Macdonald and McGee disagreed on the way Canada could best accommodate itself to the challenge of living and surviving beside a colossus. McGee was now calling for "a new nationality," or for common social and cultural characteristics that would make Canadians a distinct people. Macdonald's solution was more narrowly political: Canada should remain as British as possible.

This disagreement was about means, not about the end they sought. Macdonald and McGee, who had started out as opponents, were now well on the way to becoming political allies and personal friends. Politically, they were both anti-Americans. Macdonald, because of his incomparably greater power, merits the title of Canada's first anti-American; before Macdonald, lots of Canadians had disliked and feared the United States, but none, like him, raised it to the level of his principal political policy. What is really striking about Macdonald's anti-Americanism was that the overwhelming majority of Canadians agreed with him.

In the mid-nineteenth century, anti-Americanism was one of two forces that held this "crazy-quilt" country together. The other, to be discussed later, was the mirror-image force of loyalty to Britain.

Anti-Americanism was one of the very few things that Canadians then agreed on—English Protestants no different from Canadien Catholics.* Its comprehensiveness defied common sense. A great many in Upper Canada were in fact Americans, not just the Loyalists but the ordinary settlers who early in the century constituted three-quarters of the province's population. There were also many Irish, whose only pre-Canadian experience of the English had been of them as oppressors and occupiers. Yet the loyalty of these Americans and French and Irish never wavered—not even among the Green Irish, many of whose kin across the border were enlisting in the Federal Army to acquire military skills to be exercised later, either in Ireland or in Canada. At the same time, the idea of Canada uniting with the United States attracted astonishingly little support, given that it would obviously benefit Canadians economically. Only in the extremities, in British Columbia and in New Brunswick, was there any substantial support for annexation, and even there only by a minority.

The historic roots of anti-Americanism were straightforward. The Americans were revolutionaries who had rebelled against their King. They had tried twice to tear Canadians away from their loyalty to the Crown—in 1775, at their start of their Revolutionary War, when armies led by Generals Benedict Arnold and Richard Montgomery invaded Quebec, capturing Montreal and besieging Quebec City; and again, and within living memory, during the War of 1812. Thomas Jefferson never entirely accepted the drawn outcome of the 1812 war, holding out in the peace negotiations for annexation to "liberate" Canada.

---

* The most powerful expression of Canadien sentiment about Americans was Premier Taché's famous prediction that "the last cannon which is shot on this continent in defence of Great Britain will be fired by the hand of a French-Canadian."

Memories of the 1812 War had a powerful effect on Canadians' consciousness. In the 1820s, soon after the Macdonald family arrived, strong public pressure developed to designate all American immigrant settlers, even those who had fought on Canada's side during the war, as "Aliens" ineligible to run for office or to hold property. A watered-down Naturalization Act was finally passed in 1828, granting citizenship to all Americans who had settled in the country before 1820 but requiring an oath of allegiance from all newcomers.

The increased confidence in the loyalty of Americans living here wasn't matched by any waning of suspicions about the intentions of America itself. The most forceful expression of this view was McGee's: "They coveted Florida, and seized it; they coveted Louisiana, and purchased it; and then picked a quarrel with Mexico, which ended by their getting California. They sometimes pretended to despise these [British North American] colonies as prizes beneath their ambition; but had we not the strong arm of England over us, we should not have had a separate existence."

Some of the sources of mid-nineteenth-century anti-Americanism in Canada would surprise and disconcert those in the twenty-first century who harbour the same views. Then, few felt any need to justify their attitude by attributing it to the doings of a particular president. Few felt any need to deny being anti-American themselves—particularly at a time when public debate was so decidedly ungenteel that explicit accusations of "traitor" were hurled routinely across the floor of the legislature.

One of the root sources of the shock and horror on this side of the border was Canadians' concern about Americans' lack of religiosity. Many Canadians—especially the Canadiens—regarded with deep misgivings the absolute division of church and state in the United States. There, no public money could be used to support faith-based schools. Deeply unsettling, further, was the fact that several of the Founding Fathers, Jefferson among them, had expressed doubts about the divinity of Christ. Most shocking was the discovery of the questionable Christianity of President James Polk.* On Polk's death in 1849, the New York press reported that he had received a last-minute baptism. The *Church* magazine of Toronto commented: "For four years the neighbouring republic was governed by an *unbaptized* President. . . . The anomaly must bring disgrace with it, and possibly something worse, to a nation professing to honour Christianity at all. . . . What would be thought of the Monarch of the British Empire, if he or she had never been baptized? Could such a thing happen in our Monarch, or in any other Christian Kingdom in the world? No!" Then there was Archdeacon A. N. Bethune of York, who declared in a sermon that republicanism meant "the extravagant wanderings and never-ceasing cravings of an unbridled ambition," while monarchy meant "the inestimable blessings of law, order, quiet and true religion."

There was also lively concern in Canada about the experiment in multiculturalism being attempted south of the border. The Nova Scotia humorist Thomas Haliburton, author of the highly successful Sam Slick series, put into the mouth of one character a complaint about the "human refuse" in American cities. And, near the century's end, the popular historian George R. Parkin wrote in disgust about "those pouring into the United States. Who were they? Icelanders, Greeks, Armenians, Bulgarians, the Latin races of the South. People unaccustomed to self-government."

As is more familiar, Canadians worried that Americans were inherently violent. Canadians were aghast at the gangs in U.S. cities, at the lynchings of Negroes, at the wars against Indians. It

---

* Polk's name still lingers among Canadians as the author of the slogan "Fifty-Four Forty or Fight," meaning that the border should be pushed way up north from the forty-ninth parallel.

was widely held by Canadians that Americans were licentious, the far greater frequency of divorce there being blamed on an excess of female independence. The cross-border differences were real; on its northern side there was no equivalent, even remotely, to the slaughter by the U.S. Army of forty-five thousand Indians during the nineteenth century; nor was there any equivalent to the slave system. (In Canada's early years there had been some slaves, brought in by Loyalists or held over from the French regime, but the system was abolished in 1793,* two-thirds of a century ahead of the United States.)

The cardinal attitude of Canadians towards Americans in this century was crystal clear: they took for granted that they were morally superior. They also took for granted that their political and legal systems were superior. About other matters, from commerce to trade to education to scientific invention to the arts, they talked rather less. Not that all the talk north of the border was glib: the journalist Nicholas Flood Davin wrote shrewdly that, in an egalitarian democratic community, "where there is nothing to differentiate one man from another but wealth, nothing to aim at but wealth, character becomes materialized."

This Canadian conviction of moral superiority is the answer to one of the most puzzling questions about nineteenth-century Canadians. It was posed by Sydney Wise and Craig Brown in their book *Canada Views the United States*. In it they described as "a seeming contradiction of nature, environment and proximity" the fact that "the bulk of Canadians, standing on the very threshold of liberty, were so little susceptible to American institutions."

Not only were nature and the environment identical on both

---

* In 1793 Governor Simcoe prohibited the importation of slaves into Canada. Existing owners were allowed to retain their slaves, but most were freed not long afterwards.

sides of the border, so were the people themselves. In the mid-nineteenth century, Canadians and Americans were almost exactly the same people: both were overwhelmingly Anglo-Saxon, except for the large number of black slaves in the United States. They were not just the same people but were often of the same families. Few Canadian families did not have a relative south of the border (in Macdonald's own case, his cousin Margaret Greene). Many, including many Canadiens, had lost a son or nephew or cousin to migration across the border in search of a better job; in reverse, most of the Loyalists and the American settlers had left kin behind. Most Canadians, therefore, for all their protestations of loyalty to the Queen and genuine belief in the superiority of British law and British politics, were perfectly well aware that the United States was incomparably richer, more advanced and developed, possessed a far superior education system (Harvard University dated back to 1636), and boasted grander buildings, roads, canals, railways.

To gain all the abundant benefits of being American, Canadians then needed to do little more than to declare collectively, "We want in." Britain wouldn't have stood in their way, its leaders having declared repeatedly that they would accept Canadians' choice of independence. The succeeding step would have been, sooner or later, that of a "ripe fruit" dropping, passively and effortlessly, into the Union. But it never happened.

Macdonald did stand in the way. He possessed an instinctual understanding that the choice would be determined by passion, not by reason. That was why he so often escalated the emotional content of the public debate on the subject by accusing opponents not just of being wrong but of "treason" and even of "veiled treason"—this phrase being almost his trademark, although in fact its actual author was Disraeli. In the early 1860s, though, Macdonald was only the latest in a line of leaders, rather than the iconic, national leader he would become. The X factors that decided the issue were Canadians' certitude of moral superiority and, as much, their certitude that British was best. These attitudes did stand in the way of annexation; neither of them, though, could have stopped an army.

⌒

Describing Macdonald as an anti-American, although it evokes a contemporary echo, doesn't position him properly. Ultimately, the United States was simply irrelevant to him, except on the occasions when it specifically threatened Canada. In the huge library that he eventually accumulated at Earnscliffe, his home in Ottawa, there were almost no American books. Except for his early sorties to Upper New York State, he always holidayed in Rivière-du-Loup, or in Prince Edward Island, or in England. During all his post-Confederation years as prime minister, he went only once to Washington on government business, and to no other city. He met only one president, Ulysses S. Grant, by accident at a reception. He took no interest in U.S. politics. He never showed any understanding that one reason many Americans favoured annexation was far less expansion for its own sake—although obviously an imperative—than that they believed, genuinely, that Canadians would be better off once Americans; Richard Cartwright, in his *Reminiscences*, was much closer to the mark when he observed that Americans "have always found it very hard to believe that we honestly preferred our own institutions to theirs." As well, Macdonald was oddly unwilling to accept the legitimacy of, and most certainly the consequences of, American anger with Britain (and by extension with Canada) for the way that, during the Civil War, Confederate commerce raiders were allowed to be built under contract in British yards and then cross the Atlantic to sink Federal merchant ships. To

Macdonald, the United States was a *terra incognita* about which he had no desire, and felt no need, to learn anything.

Rejecting the United States didn't make him British. It made him a British-American, at a time when the descriptor "Canadian" was seldom used—other than by Canadiens. It made him, in other words, wholly British and at the same time wholly North American. While Macdonald went often to England, he never considered moving there, as many Canadians like him did, once they had retired—including the two first presidents of the Canadian Pacific Railway, George Stephen and Donald Smith; his political rival of the 1870s and 80s, Edward Blake; and, in his plans for the future, his own close ally Cartier. To them and to many other Canadians for quite a while yet, Britain was "home." To Macdonald, although he loved to visit London, Canada was home.

For Canada to remain his home, it had to remain British. Had Canada ever become American during his time, it's just about certain that Macdonald would have left for the other side of the Atlantic.

The leitmotif of Macdonald's career and life was to preserve Canada's un-Americanness. To him, the perpetuation of its Britishness was essential to that cause. So too would be the Confederation project. The handily available tool he used to lever himself towards both these objectives was anti-Americanism.

That most Canadians thought the same way made his task that much easier—up to a point. Being Canadians, the fact that they overwhelmingly rejected the United States didn't prevent huge numbers of them from voting for it with their feet. By the end of the nineteenth century, one in five Canadians would be living in the United States.*

---

* There was a small reverse flow, mostly of Northern draft dodgers, or "skeedadlers" as they were called, but most of them returned home once the Civil War was over, as did most of the runaway slaves. Late in the century, after

Besides stirring up the underlying anti-Americanism, the *Trent* crisis stimulated a pan-Canadian consciousness. Nova Scotia was then a separate colony, and especially emotionally close to Britain, because it was protected by the Royal Navy. Yet in the winter of 1861–62, Nova Scotians enlisted in their militia in proportionately greater numbers than did Canadians. The crisis also prompted the first serious debates about a long-discussed railway—the Intercolonial—to connect the Maritimes to inland Canada. (These discussions had been going on, entirely fruitlessly, since 1851.) The railway's justification was that it could be used to rush British reinforcements to Canada in winter rather than have them plod through the backwoods.* The Imperial government now began to consider the possibility of guaranteeing the loans needed to build a railway that in itself would be uneconomic. The crisis marked the first instance of all British North Americans reaching out to each other.

It was Macdonald himself who helped abort this nascent pan-Canadianness. He did so by botching a piece of major legislation and then seeming not to care about the consequences—one of which was the defeat of his own government.

The previous March, the commission on defence that he had

---

the Midwest was filled up, American farmers moved north in search of land, particularly in Alberta.

* A further defence problem revealed by the *Trent* crisis was that the telegraph line from Halifax to Montreal was being tapped by the Americans.

set up and chaired handed in its report. The findings were startling: there should be "an active force of 50,000 men of all arms,
with a reserve of the same kind." This goal was extraordinarily
ambitious. More startling still, the commission recommended
that if voluntary enlistments proved insufficient, conscription
should be instituted. During the *Trent* crisis, that might have
been acceptable. But with that alarm well past, everyone,
Macdonald included, took it for granted that Canada was secure
until at least the Civil War was over.

Macdonald drafted legislation to implement his commission's
recommendations. In the House, though, he came across as confused, at times offering different estimates of the costs. The best
estimate amounted to a staggering one-tenth of Canada's entire
revenues. To make these costs even more unacceptable, Macdonald
was, at the same time, having to explain a nine-hundred-thousand-
dollar overrun in the cost of the Parliament Buildings in Ottawa.

His defeat was determined by his own *bleu* supporters, many of
whom bolted rather than share ownership of a measure that might
result in conscription, however limited in its extent. The vote was
held on May 20, 1862, and the Militia Bill was defeated 61 to 54. A
day later, Macdonald and Cartier resigned. He "took the matter
very quietly," reported Edward Watkin, general manager of the
Grand Trunk Railway, who knew him well. "I am at last free,
thank God, and can now feel as a free man," Macdonald wrote to
his sister Margaret. "I have longed for this hour & only a sense of
honour has kept me chained to my post . . . I have now fulfilled my
duty to my part & can begin to think of myself." After Macdonald
had stepped down, the governor general invited his namesake,
John Sandfield Macdonald, a Reformer, to form a new government.

One good reason existed why defeat was the best possible outcome for Macdonald at this time. In the middle of the debate on
his Militia Bill, the *Globe* had broken one of the unwritten rules of

nineteenth-century journalism by informing its readers on May 15 that Macdonald "has had one of his old attacks."* The newspaper was entirely correct. Claiming illness, Macdonald was absent from the legislature for more than one week of the debate on his Militia Bill, and Galt had to substitute for him.

The *Globe*'s use of the phrase "old attacks" signalled its readers that Macdonald had been in the same condition—drunk, that is—before. A few days later, the paper renewed the attack: "It must be confessed that Mr. Macdonald's 'illnesses' occur at very convenient times." At the same time, Governor General Monck, in a confidential dispatch home, did his duty and informed the colonial secretary that Macdonald had been absent from the House for an entire week during the critical militia debate, "nominally by illness, but really, as everyone knows, by drunkenness."

There had in fact been quite a few earlier "attacks." The previous April, Macdonald had a heated exchange with a leading Reformer, Oliver Mowat, in the House in which he had threatened to "slap your chops." That fall, a visiting Englishwoman who met him at a dinner party at the governor general's residence, wrote afterwards, "The cleverest man of the lot, distinguished himself by getting completely drunk." After the *Globe*'s reports, Macdonald's secret was known not merely to insiders but to just about everyone in the colony.

Macdonald's "vice," as it was called then, has become since one of the best-known facts about him, almost as well known as his role in Confederation or his achievement in spanning the country with a railway. It's time to hold up this particular aspect of his life story to closer inspection.

---

* The *Globe*'s first reference to Macdonald's habit, in February 1856, was in the correct, coded form of describing him as speaking in the legislature "in a state of wild excitement."

The first recorded instance of Macdonald's drinking to excess occurred back in 1839 when a legal client and relative, Alan Macpherson, left a note on his door: "I called at your office twice on Tuesday but could not gain admittance. I suppose you were doing penance for the deeds of the previous day." That incident was nothing but a young man's boisterousness. During the years since, however, Macdonald had gained a reputation as one of the legislature's most convivial members, staying up as late as anyone in the Smoking Room and topping all of them with his repartee and anecdotes—and by his taste for champagne.

Macdonald's loss of control during the critical Militia Bill was quite different: it provoked, as Macdonald had to have known it would, highly critical comments from senior British ministers as well as a blistering editorial from the influential *Times* (London): "If Canada will not fight to protect its independence, neither will England. . . . If they are to be defended at all, they must make up their minds to bear the greater part of the burden of their own defence. This will be the case if they separate from us. This will be the case if they remain by us." The difference, very simply, was that Macdonald had by now really lost control over his drinking.

Both friends and enemies identified the same period as the time his behaviour changed—the time when it had become obvious that Isabella would never recover and that he was condemned, whether she lived or died, to bleak solitude. His secretary, Joseph Pope, wrote in his biography that Macdonald's lapses were "particularly true for the period of his widowerhood, between 1857 and 1867." Richard Cartwright, originally a Conservative and later a Liberal minister, wrote in his memoir that Macdonald was "leading a very dissipated life from 1856 to 1863, and afterwards."

Isabella's illness and death didn't cause his drinking; her condition intensified a pre-existing inclination. From Macdonald's earliest years, it was always probable that he would drink a lot. His father did. So did many Scots, and many politicians. George-Étienne Cartier was a heavy drinker, and D'Arcy McGee drank even more than Macdonald. The behaviour of these men, and a great many others like them in all occupations in Canada, was in no way out of the ordinary.

In the middle of the nineteenth century, drinking heavily was as common in Canada as smoking would be in the middle of the twentieth century. An 1842 municipal survey in Kingston counted 136 taverns for a population of fewer than five thousand people. In his 1846 book *Canada and the Canadians*, Richard Bonnycastle described Canada as "a fine place for drunkards; it is their paradise." Rotgut whisky cost 25 cents a gallon; in many houses a pail of whisky stood handy in the kitchen, much like a pail of water, for any visitor to ladle out however much he wanted At the end of a ride in a horse-drawn cab, it was common to "treat" the driver with a shot of whisky—a substitute for today's practice of tipping, which didn't then exist. At elections times, "treating" was a near-universal practice.

Few social sanctions existed to inhibit anyone from drinking heavily in public. As Susanna Moodie noted in *Life in the Clearings*, "Professional men were not ashamed to be seen coming from the bar-room of a tavern early in the morning." Her sister, Catharine Parr Traill, observed that heavy drinking was more prevalent among the "better classes" than among ordinary people. Drinking didn't mean then, as in today's "social drinking," a few glasses of wine spaced out over an evening; it meant getting totally, stupidly, drunk. Being an important public figure was no bar to getting inebriated in public. Indeed, of the U.S. presidents who were Macdonald's contemporaries, two, Franklin Pierce and Ulysses S. Grant, were well known as drunkards. Formal occasions provided no restrictions. The senior civil servant Edmund Meredith recorded in his diary, "Captain Sparks was hopelessly drunk while escorting the Governor General to the House: he fell off his horse while essaying to draw his sword." Lady Monck, the wife of the governor general at the time of Confederation, wrote home about a cousin having his coattails "nearly torn off" at a grand ball in Quebec City and reporting, "such drunkenness, pushing, kicking and tearing he says he never saw."*

As for Macdonald's own lack of inhibition about getting drunk on the most inappropriate occasions, he once got blind drunk while waiting for one newly arrived governor general's ship to dock, and an another occasion told the aide to another governor general sent to check on his prolonged absence from official duties either to "go to hell" himself or to tell the Queen's representative to go there.

At the time that Macdonald's "vice" became general public knowledge, the only real alternative to heavy drinking was total abstinence. Temperance organizations—the leading one, based in the United States, was the Order of the Sons of Temperance—lobbied fiercely against any drinking at all. Their crusade was justified: a Legislative Assembly committee reported, "One-half of all the crime committed . . . three-fourths of all the pauperism, are ascribable to intemperance." So, of course, was a great deal of the domestic violence and family breakdown.

It needs to be remembered here that the Victorian Age, in the sense we now use that term—repressed, dark, overstuffed—didn't spring into existence in 1837 when the young Victoria

---

* Even the term "alcoholic," applied to a person, didn't exist then. It was not coined until 1891, the year of Macdonald's death.

ascended to the throne. Much as the 1960s' "Peace and Love" era didn't really get going until the middle of that decade, the Victorian Age really only took hold around the 1870s. Over time, Macdonald fell behind the times. When he started out, though, his behaviour was closer to that of the preceding Regency era— incomparably freer in all respects. Lord Kimberly, the colonial secretary, was undoubtedly thinking of this time lag when he remarked of Macdonald, "He should have been in the good old times of two bottle men, when one of the duties of the Secretary of the Treasury is said to have been to hold his hat on occasion of the First Lord when 'clearing himself' for his speech."

But while Macdonald, for a time, was one of the crowd, he was always one of a kind. He was always a public drunk, in that term's exact sense. Macdonald's manner of drinking was unique to him. Increasingly, from his widowerhood on, it became uninhibited, ugly, out of control. The decisive change was in his openness. Henceforward, Macdonald would get drunk on the most public and the most important occasions without any apology or self-consciousness or shame. It became as much a defining fact about him as his crinkly hair or his inexhaustible wiliness. From this time on, and for quite a time, heavy drinking *was* Macdonald.

He never made the least attempt to hide his drinking— unlike, say, his contemporary William Gladstone, with his sallies across London to save prostitutes, or Mackenzie King, with his crystal-ball gazing. Not only was Macdonald entirely unashamed about his behaviour but he actually drew attention to it. Once, when a heckler at a public meeting accused him of being drunk, he responded, "Yes, but the people would prefer John A. drunk to George Brown sober." And indeed they did. They applauded his deft recovery from throwing up on the platform at an all-candidates' meeting by saying, "Mr. Chairman, I don't know how it is but every time I hear Mr. X speak, it turns my stomach."

There was no hypocrisy in Macdonald's makeup, and no fear.

Macdonald wasn't so much a heavy drinker as a binge drinker; he could go for long periods without a drop. Once he had started, though, it often took complete insensibility for him to stop. A common trigger for this kind of "tear" was some combination of pressure and tiredness; actual political setbacks or disappointments, though, appeared to have little effect on him. Macdonald thus didn't so much drink to relieve a fear of failing but more to relieve the tensions generated by his attempts to succeed. The best single comment about the nature of his drinking was made by the visiting governor of the Hudson's Bay Company, Sir Henry Northcote, who recorded in his diary, "People do not attribute his drinking to vice, but to a state of physical exhaustion which renders him obliged sometimes to have recourse to a stimulant, and which gives the stimulant a very powerful effect. When he once begins to drink he becomes almost mad and there is no restraining him till the fit is over."

Here is as good a place as any to clarify the record that although he was a Scot, Macdonald's favourite choice for something that would get him drunk was not Scotch, except in his earliest years, but champagne, claret, port and brandy.

⁓

As soon as Macdonald stepped down, Canadian newspapers speculated eagerly that he might carry right on and leave politics entirely. The easiest of all outs for him appeared just at this time, when the positions of chief justice and chancellor of Upper Canada fell vacant. Yet Macdonald refused them both. In a revealing letter to a supporter, he explained why he'd stepped down so quickly as premier rather than attempt some variation on his old double-shuffle escapade: by stepping down, he wrote, "we have shown that we do not wish to cling to office for its own sake." He wanted to make an elegant exit, that is to say, to make it easier for himself to slide right back in again.

That fall, Macdonald took ship to England, for the first time in twelve years. He was made an honorary member of the Athenaeum Club, met with the colonial secretary and the Duke of Newcastle, and was generally favoured and petted. In February 1863 he was back again in Canada, "in very good health and spirits, and eager for the fray." So eager indeed was Macdonald that year that he went to the extreme limit of joining the Sons of Temperance in Kingston. It probably won him some votes but had no discernible effect on his drinking.

SIXTEEN

The Will to Survive

~

For the sake of securing peace to ourselves and our posterity, we
must make ourselves powerful. The great security for peace is to
convince the world of our strength by being united.
John A. Macdonald

A fter his return from England in February 1863,
Macdonald set to work to ease his namesake out of
office and return himself to the premiership. The
deed was done just over a year later: on March 21,
1864, John Sandfield Macdonald resigned in advance of certain
defeat on a non-confidence vote. The intervening months were
probably the least useful of any in the United Province of
Canada's parliamentary history: no legislation of consequence
was passed; a second attempt to enact a Militia Bill failed;
Canadien members became more and more suspicious that Rep
by Pop was going to be imposed on them no matter what they
did; and an election in mid-1863 changed nothing at all—Cartier
won back some of the *bleus* he had lost in 1861, but Macdonald
was reduced to just twenty supporters in Upper Canada, in large
part because of suspicions he was "soft" on the French.

In an attempt to avoid yet another election, Governor General
Monck invited in succession two senior legislature members to try

to form a government. Both reported failure. Next he turned to Macdonald, who approached his former co-premier, Étienne-Paschal Taché. Between the two of them they cobbled together a bare majority in the legislature. Two months later, the Taché-Macdonald alliance lost a confidence vote. Another election was unavoidable.

Within the space of less than three years, there had now been four governments and two inconclusive elections, with a third one due. Canada's political system had degenerated into paralytic deadlock.

⌒

Amid the gathering gloom there were a few points of light. One was that Macdonald's old opponent George Brown had got married—at the mature age of forty-three. His bride, Anne Nelson, the daughter of an Edinburgh publisher, was a woman of substance. They met when he had gone north to Scotland during a trip late in 1862. Anne was intelligent, sophisticated, well travelled (she was fluent in French and had studied in Germany), calm and confident, and the marriage proved to be one of unalloyed love. Whenever he was away from home, Brown wrote to Anne almost every day—and repeatedly with unabashed affection. "Already I long to be back with you," he penned on one occasion, "and will grudge every day I am kept from your side." In the winter of 1863, when Anne informed him she was pregnant,

Anne Nelson Brown. After he married her, Brown turned into a moderate. Had she been round earlier, he might have won his contest with Macdonald.

Brown pronounced himself as "frisky as a young kitten."

Brown got himself back into politics at a by-election early in March 1863 and soon re-established himself as the leader of the Reformers. His former angry moralism had mellowed. Phrases such as "French domination" dropped from his speeches, to be replaced by softer musings about the need for "constitutional reform." Brown's biographer, J.M.S. Careless, described Anne Brown as "the Mother of Confederation,"* meaning that she so influenced Brown to view the world more even-handedly that, provided some nation-saving crusade was at stake, it actually became possible that he and Macdonald might be able to work together in a partnership—temporarily. At the time, Brown's most important political supporter and ally, Oliver Mowat, wrote that under Anne's influence, "the softer side of his nature has been developed." To Brown, she was "the best wife that ever lived." No story is ever perfect. While she may have been Confederation's mother, Anne disliked the child itself. "You must never speak of settling down here for life," she wrote to Brown, "The idea of being buried here is dreadful to me." (After Brown's early death, Anne moved back to Scotland.)

Brown's new attitude of moderation showed that some movement had begun beneath the hardened crust of Canadian politics. Macdonald made two attempts to find out what Brown was up to, one with the assistance of a Liberal-Conservative member who had connections to both camps, and the other by making use of Charles Brydges, the new general manager of the Grand Trunk Railway. In his meeting with Brown, Brydges offered him the bait

---

* The first to make this observation was Frank Underhill. In a paper he presented to the Canadian Historical Association in 1927, Underhill, in the terminology of those less-evolved times, described Anne Brown as "perhaps the real father of Confederation."

of the chair of the Canada Board of the Hudson's Bay Company, stirring up some interest in Brown. The reports of both intermediaries suggested that Brown was looking for what Brydges called an "omnibus arrangement," or some kind of comprehensive new political rearrangement. By no means, though, had he lost his suspicions of his old rival. During the 1863 session, Brown got off a splendid shot at Macdonald, calling him a "grimalkin" crouched "at the door of the pantry, watching for mice to come in and out."

Movement had begun elsewhere as well. By now, Macdonald and McGee were allies. In a key by-election early in 1863, they campaigned and caroused together; one of the songs they bawled out in taverns went, "A drunken man is a terrible curse / But a drunken woman is twice as worse." The Conservative candidate won handily. McGee brought Macdonald a lot of Catholic Irish votes; he also brought with him his passion for Confederation. In a series of articles that summer, McGee put forward his argument for a "new nationality." Later he toured the Maritimes—the first Canadian politician to do so—to tell audiences in Halifax and Saint John about "the fortunate genius of a united British America." When Macdonald formed his March 1864 government with Taché, McGee became its minister of agriculture.

The most significant change in the Canadian political scene took place in the early summer of 1863, but outside the country. That June, General Robert E. Lee followed up a sweeping victory at Fredericksburg, Virginia, by sending the seventy-five-thousand-strong Army of Northern Virginia swinging up into the Shenandoah Valley. At the hamlet of Gettysburg, Pennsylvania, Lees' troops met the ninety-thousand-strong Army of the Potomac. The two vast forces clashed on July 1. Two days later, Lee turned his shattered army back towards Virginia, followed almost immediately by the surrender of Vicksburg, the last Confederate fort on the Mississippi. The Confederacy was now cut in two. Gallantry and dash could no longer overcome numbers and industrial productivity. The South hung on, despite Lincoln's expectations of its collapse, but the war's eventual outcome could no longer be doubted. Once that happened, the question would then become, what would happen to Canada?

During the months after Gettysburg, Macdonald plotted his way through all the post–Civil War possibilities. They encompassed everything from an actual cross-border invasion, to nothing happening at all but with the U.S. colossus completely overshadowing the small and poor Province of Canada, to Britain reassessing its position on the North American continent and withdrawing its troops. The *Times* (London) commented, perceptively but embarrassingly, that the redcoats stationed in Canada were "numerous enough to irritate but not numerous enough to intimidate or to defend." Macdonald revealed the product of his ponderings in a remarkable speech—more exactly, a remarkable portion of a speech dealing mostly with other matters—that he gave in the fall of 1864, a year and a bit after Gettysburg.

To describe the key section of this speech here involves fast-forwarding past a cluster of political events in which Macdonald played a critical part, and afterwards winding back to recapture the skipped-over parts. This, though, is the only way to make sense of the sequence of events and to understand why Macdonald should have abruptly abandoned his long indifference to Confederation and then gone on to become first its main cheerleader and then its impresario.

The date of this speech was Tuesday, October 11, 1864. By then, the Confederation process was already well under way. Macdonald spoke at the start of a conference in Quebec City at which delegates from all the colonies of British North America debated whether to create a new, pan-Canadian government and how best to do it. Macdonald used part of his speech to explain why success at the conference mattered so much. The issue, he argued, was not a new constitution, important and indeed essential as that obviously was. Rather, it was Canada's survival. Macdonald was expressing here the leitmotif of his life—to ensure that Canada did not become American.

From Macdonald's perspective, Confederation and the new constitution that would go with it were means to an end. That end was Canada's survival as a distinct, un-American society in North America. To remain distinct, Canada had to remain British. To keep the British connection, Canada had to impress a doubting Britain by an expression of its national will to survive. And the way to do that was Confederation, because it involved a commitment to national unity across British North America on a scale never before attempted.

In trying to communicate such thoughts to an audience, Macdonald was hobbled by his customary and considerable handicap. As a debater, he was quick, skilled and often lethal; as a speaker, though, he was little better than average. He had little aptitude for, and was actually suspicious of, oratory or eloquence. Unlike Lincoln, he never attempted to summon up "men's better angels." Most times, Macdonald preferred to act rather than talk, expressing himself by deeds rather than by words. He did, however, possess one highly effective oratorical device: every now and then he would use candour to get people to pay attention. This device sent out a signal that whatever he was saying, he actually meant. So people listened.

"It is stated [by some opponents of Confederation], that in England . . . federalism will be considered as showing a desire for independence," Macdonald began this part of his speech at the conference. He himself didn't believe that, he continued, but rather that "the people of England are strongly bent on keeping her position as a mighty empire, which can only be done by helping her colonies." Yet, he admitted, "the value of the colonies has never been fairly represented to the people of England." He cited some of the important British figures who publicly questioned the worth of the colonies—for instance, the influential journalist Goldwin Smith, then still a professor at Oxford. Many of the delegates, few of whom ever looked much beyond their own county or town, would have been surprised and shocked to hear their most senior politician admit openly that doubts existed in high places in England about the value of holding on to Canada. Macdonald hammered home his point: "Our present isolated and defenceless position is, no doubt, a source of embarrassment to England." He speculated that "if it were not for the weakness of Canada, Great Britain might have joined France in acknowledging the Southern Confederacy."

Having identified the problem—Canada's weakness might motivate England to pull back from North America—Macdonald then presented his solution: "We must, therefore, become important, not only to England but in the eyes of foreign states. And most especially to the United States. . . . For the sake of securing peace to ourselves and our posterity, we must make ourselves powerful. The great security for peace is to convince the world of our strength by being united."

Macdonald was using these passages in his speech to appeal to Canadians to send out a clear, collective signal of their will to survive. Doing this—by Confederation—would give a message that would be noticed and respected in the two places that mattered to Canada—London and Washington.

What Macdonald was telling the delegates in Quebec City was, as most of them must have recognized, the truth itself, harsh and unvarnished. U.S. power was the new continental reality. Britain could still help and would continue to do so, but increasingly from a distance. Ultimately, Canada was on its own. Either it made a convulsive effort to survive or it just might vanish.

When and how Macdonald underwent such a eureka moment has to remain a mystery—indeed, no proof exists that he ever experienced it. He left no writing describing it; no colleague ever claimed later to have been there when he blurted out, "Now I see!" Intellectual epiphanies were not, anyway, his style; Macdonald favoured action, not angst. And to him action included the seeming inaction of waiting for the exact moment when all the stars were aligned. That Macdonald eventually committed himself to Confederation at about five minutes to midnight doesn't mean that he had not recognized its necessity a good deal earlier. What mattered is that, once he had intuited that the moment was ripe, Macdonald hurled himself into action, never again glancing back. We were made, this is to say, by a man who, once he knew what do to, knew how to get it done.

Other commentators have argued for different interpretations of the sequence of events. To some, Donald Creighton above all, Macdonald moved stealthily towards Confederation for years before he committed himself to it publicly. The predominant view is that he took up Confederation's cause only when he realized that unless he joined the project he would put at risk his own and his party's future. That interpretation is, of course, far from being wholly wrong. But it amounts to a one-dimensional analysis of a leader with a multilayered mind—something akin to treating as the complete Lincoln the very limited leader that Lincoln amounted to at the start of the American Civil War.

That speech by Macdonald at Quebec City was the first time Canada's politicians had been told the truth about the "double" threat that Canada faced from across the Atlantic and from across the border. It's uncertain how many of his contemporaries understood what Macdonald was attempting to do. Galt did, as a later letter of his will show. And so did Goldwin Smith, who at the time wrote that the only way to defend Canada was "to fence her round with the majesty of an independent nation." What was happening, though, was that the Confederation stakes were being transformed from merely those of finding a way to end a political deadlock to that of finding a way for Canada to survive.

⌒

That Britain might, if not actually abandon Canada, then gently but firmly pull itself back from a close embrace in order to position itself nearer to the United States, challenges the generally presented view of Canada as the nineteenth-century linchpin of the British Empire. After all, without Canada, the Empire would no longer stretch around the world in an unbroken chain on which the sun never set. At the time, though, such a gap would not have mattered that much—simply because the Empire did not matter that much to the British themselves.

The British Empire of the mid-1860s was not at all the Empire of bugles and banners and thin red lines that has been handed down in the history books. These flummeries existed then, but the Empire itself did not really exist. It did physically, of course. Britain was the global hegemon: it accounted for one-third of the world's industrial output; its Royal Navy policed the seas; and London was easily the world's largest and richest city. Moreover, the British Empire possessed the aura of having defeated Napoleon (a glory now fading fast) and the moral aura of having deployed the Royal Navy to sweep slavery from the high seas.*

---

* In counterpoint to whatever credit Britain gained by its abolition of slavery in the Empire in 1833, it incurred the off-setting discredit of initiating the Opium Wars at about the same time, employing the Royal Navy to blast open China's ports to the opium trade.

But it didn't exist psychically. Rather than an empire, what Britain owned then was an agglomeration of territories acquired or conquered or bought or swapped or stolen "in a fit of absence of mind," to use the famous phrase.* The British Empire, in the term's ordinary meaning—the one it took Canada until the Statute of Westminster of 1931 to gain full independence from— didn't come into being until the 1870s. Its birth is commonly dated to Disraeli's purchase of the Suez Canal shares in 1875, although a better date might be 1872, when Disraeli turned imperialism into Britain's political litmus test—and not coincidentally won power for himself—by attacking the Liberals, and his arch-rival Gladstone, for seeking "the disintegration of the Empire of England."†

Before this time, the British were quite uncertain whether they wanted to have an empire. The country was divided between "Big Englanders" like Disraeli and "Little Englanders," who reckoned that any empire imposed far greater costs on Britain than benefits. Intellectually, the Little Englanders made all the running; they won a key argument over free trade in the 1840s, after which Britain's trade no longer followed the flag but chased after profits anywhere. Disraeli himself spoke at times in the tones of a Little Englander; in 1852 he described the colonies

---

* Accident played a large part in determining that nineteenth-century Canada was among the blotches of red on the map. In the negotiations for the Treaty of Paris of 1763, Prime Minister Pitt the Elder came close to handing Canada back in exchange for France's sugar-rich islands of Guadeloupe. In the end, he held on to Canada largely out of fear of public outrage at the abandonment of the conquest for which the dauntless hero General James Wolfe had given his life.

† In 1872 Disraeli made imperialism the central tenet of Conservative Party policy. He was drawn to this stance because he had realized that working-class Britons, newly enfranchised by the 1867 Reform Act, were strong supporters of the Empire, perhaps as a source of colour in their hard lives.

as "a millstone around our necks." As late as 1866 he reasoned from the emergence of a united Germany and a rising Russia that "power and influence we should exercise in Asia, consequently in Eastern Europe, consequently in Western Europe; but what is the use of these colonial deadweights *which we do not govern?*" (The peak of the Little Englanders came in 1868–72, when such views were held not just by Gladstone, then the prime minister, but also by his chancellor of the Exchequer, the foreign secretary and the colonial secretary.)

Little Englanders made the economic case—men including Manchester School Liberals such as Richard Cobden,* John Bright and Goldwin Smith. The press fired more shots, as in the *Edinburgh Review*'s description of the North American colonies as "productive of heavy expense to Great Britain, and of nothing else." Such opinions were common among the most knowledgeable Britons of all—those in the Colonial Office. In 1864 John Taylor, one of the influential officials there, dismissed all the British North American colonies as "a sort of *damnosa hereditas.*" Taylor and the top official, Sir Frederic Rogers, were "separatists" who believed that the best solution was to gently nudge the colonies towards independence.

Those who wanted the Empire retained evoked glory and honour. Prime ministers in particular held this view: Lord Melbourne proclaimed that "the final separation of these colonies might possibly not be of material detriment. . . . But it is clear it would be a serious blow to the honour of Great Britain"; Sir Robert Peel's

---

* Cobden could lay a claim to be the father of the "Narcissism of small differences," that practice whereby some Canadians stare intently across the border to identify differences between themselves and their neighbouring Americans. After a tour of the two countries in 1859, he proclaimed that Canadians "looked more English than those on the other side of the American frontier—they are more fleshy and have ruddier complexions."

view, specifically about "the Canadas," was that "the tenure by which we hold [them] is most precarious, & that sooner or later we must lose them"; Lord John Russell warned that "the loss of a great portion of our Colonies would disrupt our imperial interests in the world, and the vultures would soon be getting together"; and Lord Palmerston felt that "it would lower us greatly, for 'if reputation is strength' then the reverse would weaken us much." Until Disraeli won the day, the Big Englanders' case was defensive: while no particular colony might be worth keeping, a domino effect might precipitate the loss of all the rest. (The real concern of those who wanted to keep the colonies was that if Canada went, so, sooner or later, would Ireland.)

It was only *after* Confederation that the British really embraced their empire, and so embraced Canada. During the earlier years, Macdonald had no assurance that his own loyalty and that of other Canadians would be reciprocated. Indeed, it was during this period of uncertainty that he made some of his sharpest comments about Canada-British relations: he pronounced that Canada had the right "to raise revenue in [its] own fashion," that is, to impose whatever tariffs it saw fit on British goods; he protested strongly to the governor general, as "a matter of the gravest importance . . . directly affecting the independence of our Courts and of our people" and as "an unseemly and irritating conflict of jurisdiction," the decision of a British court to issue a writ of habeas corpus to protect an accused person in Canada.* Macdonald praised the action itself as done for "praiseworthy motives" but insisted that "the English Courts of Justice

---

* The accused was a runaway slave charged with murder in the United States whom the British Anti-Slavery Society was seeking to protect from being extradited from Canada.

shall have no jurisdiction in Canada, and that no writ or process from them shall run into it."

The possibility of a split should not be exaggerated. The British aristocracy and political class always supported the Empire—it created jobs for those troublesome younger sons. Some did so for high-minded reasons: Edward Cardwell, the colonial secretary, argued in a January 1865 speech at Oxford University that while "lynx-eyed logicians" might dismiss the colonies, in contrast to other empires that had clung on to their holdings, "it has been given to England alone to be also the mother of great and free communities."* There was also the powerful emotional argument that imperialism's real purpose was to create converts to Christianity; prime ministers always wanted to keep the colonies, because none of them wanted to go down in the history books as the leader who had "lost" them. And at no time did anyone ever suggest giving up India, that jewel in Britain's crown, or naval bases such as Gibraltar and Malta—or Halifax.

Support for keeping all the other colonies, though, remained suspect until the 1870s—particularly Canada, because with it came the risk of a clash with the United States. The Colonial Office itself was a second-rank portfolio and remained so until almost the end of the century.† Its staff was tiny; its offices—at 14 Downing Street—were crumbling and so damp that fires had to be kept going all year round to prevent the files from going mouldy. Colonial Office clerks passed their time playing darts with pen-nibs attached to literal red tape.

---

* *The Times* went on to comment sourly, "We put no great trust in the 'gratitude' of colonies."

† The earliest first-rate colonial secretary—to everyone's amazement, and even more so because he had insisted on the portfolio—was Joseph Chamberlain—but he didn't take office there until the post-Macdonald year of 1895.

Among the colonies, Canada, while the richest and most advanced politically, attracted little sentiment. "Who is Minister, at Quebec City or any other seat of British government in America, we none of us know," observed the *Times*. "If we knew today, we should forget tomorrow." New Brunswick's lieutenant-governor, Arthur Gordon, described Canada as "a last resort for people who have ruined themselves at home." According to the *Times*, Canada came second to Australia, because those going there came from "a wealthier and more completely English class"—by which it meant that, blessedly, few Irish went to Australia. Outside politics, Canada could count on few friendly voices or pens: the novelist Anthony Trollope had his eponymous hero Phineas Finn declare, "Not one man in a thousand cares whether the Canadas prosper or fail to prosper."* Mind you, a number of Canadians— Macdonald conspicuously absent from their ranks—felt the same, in reverse. A legislature member, Philip VanKoughnet, wrote home from London that he "felt himself like a cat in a strange garret." George Brown, while in England on the trip during which he met Anne, wrote home that "after all I have seen, I say now as earnestly as I can—Canada for me!" Still, there was that crushing, dismissive judgment of the authoritative *Times* that whether Canadians opted for independence or not was hardly "considered a matter of great moment to England."

From this conflicting raw material, Macdonald had to forge a counterweight to the colossus next door. Two comments capture the outer limits of the possibilities available to him. One was by the colonial secretary, the Duke of Newcastle. The other was by an unknown editor of a backcountry weekly. While in

---

* Trollope had his finger on the public pulse. He had Phineas Finn go on to say that the British did care "that Canada not go to the States because although they don't love the Canadians, they do hate the Americans."

Wilfrid Laurier. As the editor of a small rural newspaper, Laurier dismissed the argument that Confederation would secure Canada from invasion by comparing its effect to trying to stop a bullet with an eggshell.

Washington at the end of 1860, following the Prince of Wales' North American tour, Newcastle sought out the future secretary of state, William Seward. They talked about the possibility that Canada, just by being there, might accidentally precipitate a Britain-U.S. conflict. Seward said he couldn't believe Britain would risk so much for so little. "Do not remain under such an error," answered Newcastle. "Once touch us on our honour, and you will soon find the bricks of New York and Boston falling about your heads"*—in other words, the Royal Navy would use the Atlantic ports of the United States for target practice. The other comment was contained in a small Lower Canada newspaper, *Le Défricheur*, in an editorial about whether, as Macdonald and many others claimed, a confederation of the British North American colonies would actually improve Canada's military security. Such dependence on a piece of paper, wrote the young editor, would be like being "armed with an eggshell to stop a bullet." The editor's name was Wilfrid Laurier.

The duke in private and the country editor in an unknown newspaper were saying what Macdonald had told the Quebec

---

* Back home, Newcastle gave a level-headed analysis of the implications of what he had said to Seward: "The injury to our own trade of burning New York and Boston would be so serious we ought to be as reluctant to do it as to destroy Liverpool and Bristol," he reported. He added, though, "but they know we must do it if they declare war."

City delegates. There was only so much that Britain could or would do for Canada. It would do even that almost entirely for the sake of its honour, and do it on its own terms. Canada really was on its own.

———

Credible or not, useful or not, some sort of attempt to improve Canada's military security had to be made, if only as a gesture. In 1863 Britain sent out a Lieutenant-Colonel William Francis Drummond Jervois to recommend improvements for defence. Jervois's report, made public early in 1864, touched off a political storm because he had quite clearly concluded that Upper Canada was indefensible. Hope remained only for those places the Royal Navy could reach, such as Halifax, Quebec City and perhaps Montreal. The effect of his report, said Macdonald, had been to create "a panic" in Upper Canada. Jervois later turned in a second, more optimistic report calling for heavy spending on fortifications and, to reassure Upper Canadians, for a fleet on Lake Ontario. The Canadian legislature approved the spending of one million dollars, though little work was actually done. Macdonald refused to take the plans seriously. After two years, he forecast, "a hole may be made in the mud opposite Quebec, and the foundation of single redoubt built." Implicitly, Macdonald agreed with Laurier.

———

Something else was needed. What it might be, Macdonald as yet had no idea. But he did understand the nature of the problem that had to be solved—Canada had to find a gap, no matter how narrow and twisting it might be, between the opposed risks of "forcible annexation and abandonment by Britain," as he phrased it in a letter to a Maritime supporter. What Macdonald could not know was that Queen Victoria had been discussing the very same conundrum with her ministers at the same time. This was, as she recorded, "the impossibility of our being able to hold Canada, but we must struggle for it; and by far the best solution would be to let it go as an independent kingdom under an English prince."* The problem was defined. The next step, long overdue, was to define a solution and then implement it.

---

* A rough precedent existed in the creation of Brazil, which broke away from Portugal in 1822 and remained an independent kingdom, under Pedro I and Pedro II, until it became a republic in 1899.

SEVENTEEN

Irreplaceable Man

~

Everybody admits that the union must take place some time. I say
now is the time. If we allow so favourable an opportunity to pass, it
may never come again.

John A. Macdonald

T he political minuet that followed the defeat of
Macdonald's government on June 14, 1864, was well
practised. After he had lost the non-confidence
vote, Macdonald called on Governor General
Monck at Spencer Wood, his residence in Quebec City, where the
government was now located, to ask for a dissolution of the legislature so an election could be held. This Monck agreed to. Here,
though, the familiar ritual was halted; it was interrupted first by
George Brown, and soon afterwards by Monck himself.

A month earlier, the resolution Brown had moved at the start
of the session—for a legislative committee to look at all the alternative proposals for some form of federation—had at last come to
a vote; to general surprise it passed, 59 to 48. Those opposed
were mostly Canadien *bleus*, but they also included John A.
Macdonald, Alexander Tilloch Galt and George-Étienne Cartier,
all of them suspicious of what Brown was up to. On May 20 the
committee assembled—Macdonald as a member—to begin its

work. To make certain that all present stayed and really worked, Brown strode over to the door, locked it, and told the group, "Now gentlemen, you must talk to me about this matter, as you cannot leave this room without coming to me." Another seven meetings followed, with Cartier playing an active part—an unusual role for him when constitutional changes were being discussed.

By a fluke of fate, the committee's report was finished on the same day, June 14, that Macdonald's government fell. Brown read out its conclusion to the House: "A strong feeling was found to exist among members of the committee in favour of changes in the direction of a federative system, applied either to Canada alone or to the whole British North American Provinces." Its sole recommendation—opposed by just three of the twenty members, among them Macdonald—was that yet another committee look again at the matter. This was tepid stuff.

Late that night, though, Brown spoke to two Liberal-Conservative members. Could the crisis not be used to address directly the great constitutional questions? he suggested. The pair asked if they could pass this comment back to Macdonald and Cartier. Brown agreed. The members hurried off.

The next morning, there was a slight alteration in the customary steps of the minuet. Macdonald asked the House for an adjournment to give him time to consult the governor general. When Macdonald and his delegation arrived, Monck assured them that his approval for a dissolution and an election still stood. He asked, though, why they did not talk to the opposition leaders to see whether an all-party government might be formed to address the constitutional options. One day later, members of the legislature were astonished to see Brown and Macdonald having a brief, urgent yet seemingly amicable conversation in the chamber's centre aisle. They were discussing when and where

Macdonald and Galt should meet Brown to talk about a possible coalition government.

The challenge before the old enemies was to agree on what such a government should stand for and, scarcely less consequential, who should be in its cabinet. They met, at one in the afternoon on the 17th, in Brown's room in the St. Louis Hotel, overlooking Quebec City's harbour. For Macdonald and Galt, harking back to their own agreement of 1858, the new government's first priority had to be a pan-Canadian federation. For Brown, it had to be Representation by Population. The differences between them had to be fudged, and getting there took time and immense care by both sides as they struggled not to look back at old battles and wounds. The fudge proved to be that Brown, no less than Macdonald and Galt, was committed to the "federative principle"—a term that conveniently could mean almost anything and could also be applied as easily to the United Province of Canada alone, as Brown wanted, or to all of British North America, as was Macdonald and Galt's choice. They were still arguing about details when they had to hurry back to the chamber for Parliament's three o'clock opening.

Macdonald spoke first. His government had initiated negotiations with a leading opposition member, he disclosed, and as a result of progress in these talks the dissolution of Parliament was being delayed. After a pause to heighten the suspense, Macdonald revealed that the opposition member he was negotiating with was "the member for South Oxford"—Brown. There were gasps of disbelief. Then Brown spoke. He had never imagined himself negotiating with such a government, but "the repeated endeavours year after year to get a strong government formed have resulted in constant failure." Out of this crisis, he continued, a chance had been created "to consider the interests of both sections of the Province, and to find a settlement of our differences." With great grace, Brown singled out Cartier as having done "a most bold and manly thing" by agreeing to the project. The chamber rang out with cheers, shouts, exclamations, slaps on the back. At one in the morning, alone at last in his hotel room, Brown wrote home to tell Anne all about it: "You never saw such a scene . . . but as the whole thing may fail, we will not count our chickens yet." The *Canadien* newspaper expressed its opinion that the Macdonald-Brown accord "comptera parmi les plus memorable de notre histoire parlementaire." In the town now known as Kitchener, the *Berliner Journal* expressed, in the primary language of the people of that area, its delight that the project could lead to the incongruity: that "George Brown mit John A. Macdonald, Cartier und Galt Hand in Hand zu gehen—daran nätte, gewiss Niemand in Traume gedacht."*

It was the most dramatic instance of political reconciliation in Canada's parliamentary history since 1848, when Governor General Lord Elgin had followed his reading of the Throne Speech in English with, for first time, a re-reading in French. As on that earlier occasion, some Canadien members rushed up to Brown to kiss him on both cheeks—a challenging feat given his height of more than six feet. Brown and Macdonald had fought over everything from Rep by Pop to the double majority to the choice for Canada's capital. Besides their multiple combats, they shared a mutual animosity, thickening towards contempt, matched only a century later by that between Prime Ministers John Diefenbaker and Lester Pearson. Yet here they were, doing what they had promised never to do—joining hands with each other.

---

* A rough translation, provided by a bilingual friend, would be: "Certainly no one would have dreamed of Brown walking hand in hand with Macdonald, Cartier and Galt."

The explanation each gave at the time was "deadlock." That was true enough: the journalist Goldwin Smith would later describe deadlock as having been the "true Father of Confederation." The Canadian political system had become stale and sterile. The Conservatives and the Reformers were like punch-drunk fighters, still upright only because they each propped the other up, too depleted now to take more than the occasional swipe at each other over stale quarrels.

Brown in particular was displaying an out-of-character generosity for which Anne Brown surely deserves a share of the credit. The newspaper owner had a first-rate mind, but as a politician he was of the third rank; yet he was now putting himself into Macdonald's supple and deviously articulated hands.

Macdonald's own explanation for embracing Brown and Confederation, given in a letter to a Conservative supporter two years later, was straightforward: "As leader of the Conservatives in Upper Canada, I then had the option of forming a coalition government or of handing over the administration of affairs to the Grit party for the next ten years." That admission of opportunism is persuasive—Macdonald's political circumstances were indeed parlous. His count of Conservative supporters was down to twenty. He had misjudged until the very last moment the readiness of politicians in all corners of the House to find a way out of the legislative inertia made unavoidable by the double-majority rule.

An entirely new political threat also confronted him. Now that Brown had stopped denouncing "French domination," an alliance between Brown and Cartier's *bleus* became a real possibility. Brown could bring to such a grouping many more elected members than remained with Macdonald. The "mini-confederation" that Brown favoured, of separating Upper and Lower Canada into autonomous provinces with some minimal "joint authority" over them, would give Cartier what he most wanted—protection against Rep by Pop. And Macdonald knew it would be far easier merely to reshape the existing government in this way than to recreate the entire country as he now wanted to do.

It fact, though, Brown had for too long said too much that was hateful for Canadien members ever to fully accept him. His "mini-federation" would be far more difficult to bring off than it might seem at first glance. It would leave the English in Lower Canada (now one-quarter of Montreal's population) isolated in a quasi-separate province dominated by the French. Cartwright wrote in his *Reminiscences* that he thought the English in Lower Canada would have responded by seeking union with the United States (as they had advocated in 1849). To prevent such an unhinging of all its British North American colonies, the Imperial government would almost certainly have intervened to disallow the "mini-federation."

Yet something was going on between Brown and Cartier, and if it ever came to anything, the victim would be Macdonald. Cartwright wrote later that there existed at this time a perfectly good understanding between Mr. Cartier and Mr. Brown about forming "a new ministry"—and he claimed that Governor General Monck had told him this. In the end, all this backstage plotting came to nothing, except that thereafter Macdonald and Brown circled each other even more warily.

Nevertheless, a transformational change had taken place. Macdonald and Brown had reversed their roles. Brown, the impatient moralist, was now the cautious conservative. The scheme he was advocating amounted only to a rejigging of the existing system. Macdonald, the scheming opportunist, had turned visionary. He had not only committed himself to Galt's 1858 plan for a new Confederation extending to the Maritimes but had added to it an entirely new goal of stretching this new nation west to the Pacific. His leitmotif of maintaining Canada as an un-American nation was at work. As Macdonald expressed it in a letter to British railway promoter Edward Watkin, "If Canada is to remain a Country separate from the United States, it is of great importance that they should not get behind us by right or force and intercept the route to the Pacific." Not only was Macdonald now calling for a much more ambitious federation than that proposed by Brown but he was calling also for a much more ambitious national government than Brown's minimalist "some joint authority." Of the pair, one wanted only to spring clean the existing house, while the other wanted to build an entirely new mansion.

It was this formula for national survival that, six months later, Macdonald would lay before the delegates at the Quebec Conference when he challenged them to "convince the world of our strength by being united."

In the immediate future, the boldest of the three was Cartier. He was risking the bird he already had in his hand—the effective veto on national affairs exercised by his *bleu* members—on a good-faith assumption that Quebec's distinctiveness would continue to be respected even when it was surrounded by an entire transcontinental flock of English-speaking fowl. Between Macdonald and Brown, though, there was no question who now was the bolder. Indeed, Brown at times seemed curiously self-doubting. Asked how he saw the way ahead, he replied, "I am not so well informed as to all the bearings on the question of a union of all the British North American Provinces that I could at once pronounce a final option on that question." Brown's *Globe* echoed his timidity: "Efforts are to be made to induce the Lower Provinces [the Maritimes] to join confederation, but the success of the scheme, so far as Canada is concerned, is not to be contingent on their assent."

A timeout is needed here to justify the argument being presented that Macdonald, despite the judgment of most historians, was acting strategically as well as tactically for the sake of his own partisan advantage. True, Macdonald seldom went in for big ideas or "visions." But that's not the same as saying—as has been said many times—that he had no ideas at all.

The world over, politics then had precious little to do with ideas. There were exceptions, of course, such as the daring ones that came out of the French and American revolutions, ideas that found their source in the eighteenth-century Enlightenment. But the sweeping economic and social concepts that lay ahead—Karl Marx published the first volume of *Das Kapital* in the Confederation year of 1867—were prompted largely by the search for a response to the human dislocations caused by the Industrial Revolution and the growth of huge, impersonal cities, neither of which had happened yet in overwhelmingly rural Canada. Other than going to war or, the Canadian equivalent, trying to build a nation, governments did precious little. Only the most occasional politician—the high-minded Gladstone in Britain or Bismarck in Germany—thought much about social change and reform. As Goldwin Smith, the Regius Professor of History at Oxford before he transplanted himself to the colony, wrote in sad resignation about Canada, "In this country, what is there for Conservatives to conserve, or for Reformers to reform?"

Macdonald's Scottishness should never be discounted: Scots didn't go in for intellectualizing or for attitudinizing. Essentially, they get on with the job at hand. Inside almost every Scot, though, there is, somewhere, an urge handed down across the generations to behold the Hebrides in dreams. Confederation, while about such practical matters as ending political deadlock, was at its core an absurdly romantic project. Its end objective was to create a new nation that might actually survive in North America without becoming American. At some level that Macdonald would never allow himself to show, man and mission had to be as one.

Some of Macdonald's often-expressed contempt for the utility of ideas was a pose. He read far too much, from literature to philosophy to politics to history, to have been in the least timid about ideas in themselves. It's a rare reader who does not think.

Yet Macdonald has usually been portrayed as having no political ideas at all: the two historians who studied this specific part of his record—T.W.L. MacDermot in 1931 and Peter Waite in 1968—reached this conclusion.* The single contrary view is that of political scientist Rod Preece, who in a 1980 article made a spirited argument that Macdonald did have a political philosophy. He traced Macdonald's philosophy to Edmund Burke, writing that "Macdonald practised the Burkean principles of prudence and experience combined and it is these which have been confused with pragmatism by Macdonald's numerous commentators." In one especially fine phrase, Preece writes: "What distinguished Macdonald from the commonplace political leader was that he understood in a philosophical manner why he should be expedient."

Waite, the leading post-Creighton scholar on Macdonald, doesn't in any way dismiss him as merely an opportunist. "For Macdonald, the supreme test of any policy was in the results. . . . No Canadian politician, except perhaps [Mackenzie] King, had

---

* In one article, MacDermot criticized Macdonald for failing to show any awareness of having read, among others, "the Fabians." Since the Fabian Society was formed only in 1884, this seems a critical reach too far. In fact, the Fabian leaders Sidney and Beatrice Webb did come to Canada, in 1897, and didn't much like what they saw: a "complete lack of thinking" about social problems in a "nation of successful speculators in land values."

such a grasp of the art of the possible." He goes on to discuss the central characteristic about Macdonald's concept of the exercise of political power: "For Macdonald, the word 'reform' was largely devoid of political significance. . . . He distrusted the reforming temperament; he distrusted the view of society, which sees in changes of institutions or of laws, the panacea for the problems of human society. . . . The reason for that assumption was his view of human nature. Human beings do not change, and since they do not, the root character of human life cannot change much either. Reform this, or reform that; but human beings will find holes in any system."

Waite's analysis is brilliant and is absolutely correct. In fact, Preece was saying much the same thing in describing Macdonald as the embodiment of Burkean prudence and experience. Both are different ways of saying that politics is about people, not about ideology—and that, of course, is an ideology in itself.

Besides his belief in the cardinal values of prudence and experience, and his idea that politics is about the nature of human beings writ large, Macdonald had a second line of consistent thought. This thought was about Canada itself. Today, Canadianness has acquired a kind of cult status. Contemporary politicians and all those involved in public life in any way compete to be more Canadian than anyone else, to be more passionate about the nation's potential than others. Some end their speeches with the words, "God bless Canada." In the mid-nineteenth century, few people loved Canada. Their love was for Britain (or, for Canadiens, for Quebec). The constitution that the Confederation project eventually gave birth to was not the Constitution of Canada but the British North America Act.

Whatever the constitution's formal title, its defining characteristics were that it was a British-inspired document crafted for an un-American Canada. It would be only one step of many that

Macdonald would take to preserve the un-Americanness of Canada—the National Policy of protecting domestic manufacturers, the building of a railway from sea to sea, and his unceasing opposition to cross-border free trade. What is so striking about these policies is their consistency. Macdonald committed himself to this course with his first declaration on entering politics in 1844; his last war cry a half-century later was "A British subject I was born, a British subject I will die." Among Canadian leaders, perhaps only Trudeau matched his consistency. Macdonald, though, unlike Trudeau, never paraded his intellect before the crowd like a cape. Rather, he went out of his way to appear to have no ideas: "I am satisfied to confine myself to practical things . . . I am satisfied not to have a reputation for indulging in imaginary schemes and harbouring visionary ideas . . . always utopian and never practical," he said during the Confederation Debates of 1865. He sent out to ordinary Canadians the reassuring signal that he was just like them, and to his opponents the equally reassuring signal that they didn't need to worry about overestimating his intellect.

He just got on with the job, occasionally smiling sardonically at those who preferred merely to talk about the job. In Creighton's fine phrase, "he thumped no tubs and he banged no pulpits." In his *Reminiscences, Globe* editor Sir John Willison gave a wonderful description of Macdonald keeping himself at a distance from ideology: "For the evangelical school of reconstructionists who would remake the world in their own image and reform mankind by legislation, he had only a complacent tolerance." Except that Macdonald then went ahead and reconstructed Canada in his own image.

Macdonald seldom allowed his feeling about Canada to show through his pose of unruffled pragmatism. It happened once in the small Upper Canada town of St. Thomas during his speaking tour in November 1860. There he said, "I am like those who hear me, a Canadian heart and soul. I heard the gallant officer who returned thanks for the army and navy say he was. That, I believe, is the feeling that exists in every breast here; and though I have the misfortune, like my friend the deputy adjutant-general, to be a Scotchman, still I was caught young and was brought to this country before I was very much corrupted. [Laughter] Since I was five years old, I have been in Canada. All my hopes and dreams and my remembrances are Canadian; not only are my principles and prejudices Canadian but what, as a Scotchman, I feel as much as anyone else, my interests are Canadian. [Applause]"

Not until Laurier would another Canadian leader talk with such feeling about his country, and, after Laurier, there was a long gap until Diefenbaker.

It's time now to return to the story itself.

The backroom bargaining about the policies and composition of the new coalition government went on for another week. Brown made a last attempt to secure a commitment that the new government would work for an immediate federation of the Province of Canada alone, but yielded to Macdonald's insistence that a pan-Canadian federation had to be considered first. Incomparably more difficult was the bargaining over cabinet posts. Macdonald insisted that the six Upper Canada portfolios be split evenly between Conservatives and Reformers, even though Brown's party was far larger. He insisted also that Brown himself fill one of those coalition posts. "I have the offer of office for myself and two others to be named by me," Brown wrote to Anne. "I am deeply distressed at having this matter thrust on me now—but dare not refuse the responsibility with such vast interests at stake. How I do wish you had been here to advise me." During the bargaining, Macdonald at one point offered to step aside himself if this would induce Brown to come in; the offer was rejected, as Macdonald undoubtedly knew it would be. Brown, before making his final decision, consulted his caucus and the governor general and read all the letters that came pouring in. One from D'Arcy McGee advised, "How *can* you hope to secure the settlement without your own personal participation?" Monck similarly told Brown that success or failure "depends very much on your consenting to come into the Cabinet." Finally, on Wednesday, June 22, Brown made up his mind, explaining to Anne, who had been hoping he would return home to Toronto, "There was no help for it—and it was such a temptation to have possible the power of settling the sectional troubles of Canada forever."

That day, Macdonald informed the House that a new government had been formed—the Great Coalition it would come to be called—for the specific purpose of attempting a confederation of all the British American colonies, and, if that failed, of the United Province of Canada alone. The new premier was—again—Sir Étienne-Paschal Taché, by now close to seventy years old and serving in the Legislative Council. Taché's Upper Canadian ministers would be Macdonald, Alexander Campbell and McGee, and, from the Reformers, Brown, Oliver Mowat and William McDougall. His Lower Canadian ministers would be led by Cartier and would include Galt. The only group not represented was Antoine-Aimé Dorion's *rouges*.

Relations between Macdonald and Brown were never easy. Just six weeks after the coalition was formed, Brown was complaining about overspending on the new Parliament Buildings, exactly as he had done repeatedly from the Opposition benches but now, as a minister, fully informed that "it will cost half the revenue to the province to light them and heat them and keep them clean. Such monstrous folly was never perpetrated in the world before." More smoothly, that same August, Macdonald advised an inquiring newspaper editor that "Brown and myself are going to sit down immediately to arrange the names of the newspapers deserving of Government patronage."

Convincing Conservatives and Reformers to work together after years of clawing at each other was a constant trial. As early as July, Macdonald had to plead with a supporter "that I may call on you to lay aside, for the present at least, party feeling . . . and to ask you to support Mr. McDougall, and will feel very much obliged by your doing so." To McDougall, one of Brown's supporters now in the cabinet and running in a by-election, Macdonald wrote reassuringly that he shouldn't "suspect McGee of acting against you merely because he was seen talking to his countryman and co-religionist Moylan [an old opponent of McDougall's]." Macdonald added that Brown, by saying that the Great Coalition was only "a temporary junction for a temporary purpose, which being attained[,] old party lines would be re-drawn," had made many Conservatives unwilling to "dissolve their organization and be powerless at the next general election." The Conservatives followed their chief, but reluctantly. "I scarcely know where I am or who I am," one wrote plaintively to Macdonald.

The work that mattered, of drafting proposals for a confederal constitution, did get done, nevertheless, and at remarkable speed. Luck helped, by confining these internal debates, carried on in the cabinet offices in Quebec City, to an inalterable deadline. It so happened that the Maritime provinces were already scheduled to meet, in just over two months, in Charlottetown, on

September 1. Their agenda was to discuss Maritime Union, a scheme being pushed on them by the Colonial Office. Monck asked London whether a Canadian group could come down and add its ideas to the mix. London said yes, and the request to attend was made and accepted.

Over a span of less than six weeks, the cabinet ministers discussed, and made decisions about, what they would say about federalism to the Maritime politicians, along with the specific proposals they would make about a confederation of British North America. No record survives of how they accomplished this task, or of any disagreements among them and how they resolved them. There certainly were difficult moments. Macdonald, with the extreme pressure and ongoing exhaustion as factors, was now hitting the bottle hard. As Brown recounted to Anne, a key meeting set for noon was delayed until three, when Macdonald finally arrived, "bearing symptoms of having been on a spree." Having at last joined the others, who were waiting impatiently, Macdonald promptly went over to the lunch table and poured himself one glass of ale after another, until he was "quite drunk." Yet somehow the discussion began and the business got done.

There were also easier times: Macdonald and Brown went together to a party at the governor general's residence and, as Brown reported to Anne, "John A. and I were the only civilians—we had a very good fun." The driving force behind them all was the sense of history. As Brown told Anne, "For the first time in my political life, I indulged in a regular chuckle of gratified pride. . . . It will be a tremendous thing if we accomplish it. . . . There is no other instance of a colony peacefully remodelling its own constitution—such changes have always been the work of the parent state."

A distinctively Canadian attribute of the process by which Confederation was achieved was that the motivating force which enabled it to happen was, as often as not, that of separating Canadians as of uniting them. Thus, the United Province of Canada was to be disassembled into its two original provinces— soon to be renamed Ontario and Quebec—in order to separate English Protestants from French-Canadian Catholics. London's foremost interest, though never stated in public, was that Confederation would give Britain an excuse to separate itself militarily from North America. To the Maritimers, a determining attraction of Confederation was that it would keep them separate from each other rather than compacting them together into a Maritime Union. The Colonial Office strongly advocated this scheme, but Arthur Gordon, New Brunswick's lieutenant-governor, understood Maritime culture better. He reported home: "The different counties [of New Brunswick] hate each other, and they all unite in hating Halifax."*

On August 29, seven senior ministers, among them Macdonald, Cartier, Brown, Galt and McGee, and also three secretaries (including Hewitt Bernard, Macdonald's principal civil servant), boarded the government steamer *Queen Victoria* for the sail down the St. Lawrence to Charlottetown, Prince Edward Island. *Queen Victoria* was a gay little ship of two hundred tons and with a three-hundred-horsepower engine.

Fortunately, for this part of the story, an insider's report on Confederation does exist. It deals not with politics but with

---

* During the century and a half since, Maritime Union has remained a topic of academic interest, but of none whatever to Maritime people and politicians.

A twentieth-century painting by Rex Woods of the ship Queen Victoria, *which brought the Canadian delegates to the Charlottetown Conference. Macdonald stands on the landing at the top of the ladder.*

people. In his almost daily letters to Anne, Brown described how the voyage downstream was a succession of sunny, calm days, with the delegates relaxing under an awning, reading, playing chess and backgammon, and sometimes taking saltwater baths. The *Queen Victoria* arrived at Charlottetown on September 1 and lowered its two boats, each packed with ministers accompanied by four oarsmen and a boatswain. They were met by a single oyster boat, flat-bottomed and with a barrel of flour in the bow and two jars of molasses in the stern, and, in between, the Prince Edward Island provincial secretary, William H. Pope. He reported that no official reception was immediately possible, because everyone was attending a performance of Slaymaker and Nichols' Olympic Circus. Because of this attraction, all the hotels were filled. Most of the Canadians, Macdonald included, had to sleep on their own boat.

Brown described to Anne the "shake elbow, and the how-d'ye-do" of their first encounter with the Maritime delegates, who immediately informed them that Maritime Union was being held over for later so that Canada's Confederation proposal could be first on the conference agenda. All business was then set aside until the next day, which included a state dinner given by the island's governor, followed by dancing. Brown sat outside as he wrote, telling Anne about "the sea washing up gently to the very door" and how "there is something to the sea."

The next day, in the small red-sandstone building that housed the island's Parliament, the real work began. Cartier started, making a general case for Confederation. Macdonald followed with a long exposition on the benefits of union and the different types of federalism, along with their faults and virtues. That evening there was a buffet that, according to the Charlottetown *Islander*, included "substantials of beef rounds, splendid hams, salmon, lobster . . . all vegetable delicacies peculiar to the season, pastry in all its forms, fruits in almost every variety." All these dishes were generously washed down with the ample supplies of liquor, principally champagne, that the Canadians had cagily brought with them on their boat.

The next day Galt delivered a closely argued analysis of the finances of federalism, laying special stress on how the new central government would compensate the Maritime provinces for their revenue losses—primarily from giving up their tariffs on entering Confederation. There followed a long lunch aboard *Queen Victoria* at which, in Brown's description, "the ice became completely broken, the tongues of the delegates wagged merrily." That night, PEI's premier, Colonel John Hamilton Gray, gave a dinner, followed by dancing. To his astonishment, Brown found himself talking there to one lady who, in her entire life, had never crossed to the mainland; he later advised Anne that

In this cabinet room in Charlottetown's Parliament Buildings, the two sides agreed on the principles of Confederation. Macdonald took time out to sign his name as a "Cabinet maker" in the visitors' book.

Prince Edward Islanders were, nevertheless, "amazingly civilized." After the break on the Sunday, Brown spoke about the division of powers and the new national judiciary.

By Tuesday, the Canadians were done. On Wednesday, the Maritimers gave their answer. "They were unanimous," a delighted Brown wrote home, "in regarding Federation of all the Provinces to be highly desirable—*if the terms of union could be made satisfactory.*" To celebrate their success, they gathered together for a grand ball at Province House. John Ross of *Ross's*

Weekly described the closing gala: "The fascinating dance goes merrily, and the libidi[n]ous waltz with its lascivious entwinements while in growing excitement; the swelling bosom and the voluptuous eye tell the story of intemperate revel." Ross may have been getting a bit intemperate himself.

Macdonald would have been too canny to get overexcited while still in the company of the Maritimers. But he must have been as pleased as Brown was with their progress. To augment his pleasure, he had acquired in Charlottetown a political asset that would prove invaluable in the future. Among the Canadians, no one knew the Maritimes as well as McGee did. In addition to all his visits, he had that summer organized and led a tour of approximately one hundred Canadian businessmen, journalists and politicians around the principal Maritime cities. He would have briefed Macdonald that both of the two most important Maritime premiers, Nova Scotia's Charles Tupper and New Brunswick's Leonard Tilley, were strong Confederates. In Charlottetown, Macdonald began developing friendships with these powerful regional figures as potential recruits for the Liberal-Conservative Party.

The wind was blowing full in the sails of the Canadians. The Maritimers had not only agreed in principle to Confederation but had also agreed to attend a second conference to be held in Quebec City just one month later. There, they and the Canadians, and as well delegates from Newfoundland, would attempt to draft an actual constitution for a confederation. Moreover, while the agreements reached at Charlottetown had been only an agreement in principle, those there had in fact settled on many draft clauses that could go on for final approval at Quebec City.

During one of the breaks in the conference, when Macdonald took a tour of Province House, the island's legislature building, he came upon the visitors' book. He signed his name and, in the column for occupation, wrote "Cabinet maker."

From Charlottetown, the delegates went on as planned to Halifax, some by train and others, Macdonald among them, by the *Queen Victoria*. The press commentary was highly laudatory. As the Halifax *Witness* remarked, almost in bewilderment at the change in Maritimers' attitude towards the Canadians, "There is less aversion to Canada. Indeed, there seems to be a positive desire for union."

At a dinner in the Halifax Hotel on September 12, Premier Tupper proposed a toast to "Colonial Union." In his reply Macdonald talked about his twenty long, dreary years in provincial politics. He mentioned the distance that Canada and the Maritimes still had to go to form a real nation: while all were part of the Empire, he said, "there was no political connection, and we were as wide apart as British America is from Australia. . . . We had only the mere sentiment of a common allegiance, and we were liable, in case England and the United States were pleased to differ, to be cut off, one by one." He outlined the mistakes that the American constitution makers had made in giving too much power and sovereignty to the constituent states—an arrangement that, in his view, had made the American Civil War, or dissolution, inevitable. He claimed that the makers of Canada could avoid these dangers, "if we can agree upon forming a strong central government—a great central legislature—a constitution for a union which will have all the rights of sovereignty except those that are given to the local governments."

He talked, again with the almost unnerving frankness he sometimes employed, about the Intercolonial Railway, that great lure to attract the Maritimes to Confederation; the truth here, said Macdonald, was that "as a commercial enterprise [it] would be of comparatively little advantage to the people of Canada. Whilst we have the St. Lawrence in summer, and the American ports in time of peace, we have all that is requisite for progress."* But, Macdonald went on, this railway would provide for a common defence, and, once the West was opened up, "all [its] great resources will come over the immense railways of Canada to the bosom of your harbour." He described how the new nation would be "a great British monarchy, in connection with the British empire, and under the British Queen." And he said the time to do all this nation-building had to be now: "Everything, gentlemen, is to be gained by union, and everything to be lost by disunion. Everybody admits that the union must take place some time. I say now is the time. If we allow so favourable an opportunity to pass, it may never come again."

The cheers went on and on and on. Three months earlier, Macdonald had been a defeated premier leading a dwindling band of Conservative members. He was now British North America's irreplaceable man.

---

* In fact, the Intercolonial enabled Canadian manufactures to capture the Maritime market from local companies. At the time Macdonald spoke, though, the Reciprocity deal with the United States had made east-west traffic incidental to the huge flow of north-south traffic.

EIGHTEEN

A Pact of Trust

In giving ourselves a complete government we affirm our existence
as a separate nationality.
La Minerve (Montreal)

F our weeks after the close of the Charlottetown
Conference, the *Queen Victoria* was again chugging
around the Gulf of St. Lawrence, this time to Pictou
and Shediac and once again to Charlottetown to pick
up the Maritime delegates to transport them to Quebec City for
the second Confederation conference. The return trip, unlike the
downriver one, was stormy and cold; they arrived on October 6,
amid an unseasonably early snowstorm. The conference's purpose
was to move beyond pleasantries and generalities by drafting a
constitution, which would be sent over to London for enactment
by the Mother of Parliaments.

A little more than two weeks later, between October 10 and
October 27, with only two days off for rest, the deed was done.
Seldom can so much work of this kind have been done so quickly.
By the end of the conference, the delegates had agreed to
seventy-two resolutions spelling out the rules of governance for a
new nation, down to minutiae such that the "general government"

would be responsible for "quarantine" but the "local" ones for immigration. With remarkably few changes (for example, to make immigration and agriculture joint jurisdictions), these resolutions would be translated into the clauses of the British North America Act that established Confederation. To this original constitution, no substantial change would be made until 1982, when

The Quebec City Conference. In less than three weeks, the Canadians and Maritimers agreed on seventy-two resolutions that, with few changes, became Canada's founding constitution. Macdonald emerged as the clear leader.

Pierre Trudeau's new Constitution Act[*] added to it the Charter of Rights and Freedoms. In a fundamental sense, all of Canada's prime ministers have functioned as managers of the estate that Macdonald created, Trudeau alone expanding it significantly.

D'Arcy McGee later credited Macdonald with the authorship of fifty of these seventy-two resolutions. Macdonald himself claimed to a friend, "I ha[d] no help. Not one man of the Conference (except Galt on finance) had the slightest idea of Constitution making." Warming to his theme, he wrote, "I must do it all alone as there is not one person connected with the government who has the slightest idea of the work."[†] Both were exaggerating, but not by that much. Macdonald was the gathering's orchestra conductor, cheerleader, bookkeeper (of the law, not the finances), entertainer and diplomat. At times, he performed as a clown, cooling tempers by his antics: "Feo" Monck, the governor general's sister, who was visiting from Ireland, recorded in her diary, "He is always drunk now, I am sorry to say, and when someone went to his room the other night, they found him in his night shirt with a railway rug thrown over him, practicing Hamlet."[‡]

The best description of Macdonald's performance was made later by the Colonial Office's top official, Sir Frederic Rogers. He made these comments about the last of the Confederation confer-

---

[*] As a consequence of the 1982 Constitution Act, the BNA Act was renamed the Constitution Act, 1867.

[†] To improve his own knowledge, Macdonald in this letter asked for a copy of a standard work, G.T. Curtis's *History of the Origin, Formation, and Adoption of the Constitution of the United States.*

[‡] In the published edition of Feo Monck's journal, Macdonald's name was left a discreet blank, but her original page contains the handwritten note "Macdonald afterwards Premier."

ences, held in London at the end of 1866, which he attended and where Macdonald once again did just about everything except cut the sandwiches for the luncheon breaks. They provide an excellent insight into how he operated throughout the entire Confederation project: "Macdonald was the ruling genius and spokesman, and I was very much struck by his powers of management and adroitness," wrote Rogers. "The French delegates were keenly on the watch for anything that weakened their security; on the contrary, the Nova Scotia and New Brunswick delegates were very jealous of concessions to the *arrière province;* while one main stipulation in favour of the French was open to constitutional objection on the part of the home government. Macdonald had to argue the question with the home government on a point on which the slightest divergence from the narrow line already agreed on in Canada was watched for—here by the English, and there by the French—as eager dogs watch a rat-hole; a snap on one side might have provoked a snap on the other; and put an end to all the concord. He stated and argued the case with cool, ready fluency while at the same time you saw that every word was measured, and that while he was making for a point ahead, he was never for a moment unconscious of the rocks among which he had to steer."

The clear, deep water beyond the shoals towards which Macdonald was steering the delegates at the Quebec Conference was Confederation itself. Just getting the deal on the constitution mattered far more than its specific legal arrangements. As Macdonald wrote to Matthew Crooks Cameron shortly after the conference, on December 19, 1864, "I am satisfied that we have hit upon the only practical plan. I do not mean to say the best plan, but the only practical plan for carrying out the Confederation." About the value of constitutional rewrites in order to solve fundamental political and economic problems,

Macdonald had always been deeply skeptical. A constitution, he told the Quebec City delegates, "should be a mere skeleton and framework that would not bind us down. We have now all the elasticity which has kept England together." He wanted the best possible constitution, and he wanted a strongly centralized one. But just gaining a constitution itself would be the declaration of will that Canada needed to make to become a nation that others would respect as a nation.

Luck helped. Chilly rain fell day after day, leaving the delegates with nothing better to do than get on with the work. As a further inducement to stay indoors, the delegates soon found that while Quebec City was charming and historic, its streets were new and horrible. "Bump-thump-jump you go from one stick to another— out of one deep hole into another till you are well nigh shaken to pieces," was the account of a ride in a horse-drawn calèche by a reporter from Halifax's *Morning Chronicle*. The work itself was done in a plain, three-storey, grey-stone building, originally intended as a post office and used temporarily as a parliament building after the original one had burned down.* The second-storey parliamentary reading room, now crowded with a huge table, had been refashioned into a conference chamber. The incessant rain was hard to take; for some reason the pitch of the roof, combined with three awkward skylights, magnified the noise of the rain to a constant drumming. What made up for this was the conference's location: through the windows of their chamber, the delegates could look down at the St. Lawrence River, at the rafts

---

* Within a year, as the government moved to the new, permanent national capital in Ottawa, Quebec City would lose even its temporary parliament building.

of logs a little upstream, and then the shipyards and docks, and then the river flowing eastwards, past thin strips of farms on either bank, the magnificent Montmorency Falls as a white wisp in the distance, and the water gradually becoming ever more saline as, now out of sight, it widened into the Gulf, there to wash against all four of the Lower Provinces now represented at the conference. The delegates worked exceedingly hard, initially from 11 a.m. to 4 p.m., and soon through two full sessions each day, the first from 10 a.m. to 2 p.m., and the second from 7:30 on, sometimes to midnight. Lunches, usually so leisurely, lasted just fifteen minutes. The Canadians worked harder still, meeting each day at 9 a.m. to discuss tactics and, again, from 4 to 6 p.m. After the close of the conference sessions, Canadian ministers retired to their rooms to catch up on their correspondence and go over their draft resolutions.

Careful planning and several dollops of canniness helped as well. In advance of the arrival of the Maritimers in Quebec City, the Canadians leaked to the *Morning Chronicle* a summary of most of their intended resolutions, thereby minimizing the surprises while leaving themselves free to deny authorship should controversy break out over any of them. They paid for all the hotel expenses (totalling some fifteen thousand dollars) of the delegates, and of their wives and daughters. To keep everyone amiable, there were constant balls and dinners and receptions, principally hosted by the governor general but also by railway lobbyists. Mercy Coles, the daughter of a Prince Edward Island delegate, recorded in her diary that her father returned home from one of these balls "with every stitch of clothing wringing wet with perspiration." Feo Monck wrote of Cartier flirting with her, saying that his favourite occupation was "the *activity* of the heart." (Neither woman paid the least attention to the work of the conference itself.) The Prince Edward Island delegate Edward

Whelan sent regular stories to his newspaper, the *Examiner*,
informing readers that "the Cabinet ministers—the leading ones
especially—are the most inveterate dancers I've ever seen" and
that "the French ladies here give a delightful tone to society. . . .
They make no difficulty in falling in love—or appearing to do
it—with a dozen gentlemen at a time."

As with Charlottetown, a good deal more is known about who
danced with whom at Quebec City than who bargained what with
whom. The sessions were closed, and no briefings were held for
the press. (Among the journalists were a half-dozen from Britain
and the United States.) All that was ever made public were the
texts of the seventy-two approved resolutions. Official minutes
were kept by Macdonald's deputy minister, Hewitt Bernard, but
they were prosaic and terse. Unofficial and abbreviated notes
were taken by a Prince Edward Island delegate, A.A. Macdonald,
who did record the snippet that Newfoundland delegate
Frederick Carter had expressed the hope that Confederation
might encourage wealthy fish merchants not to "retir[e] to the
Old Country to spend their fortunes."

After a brief formal opening by the premier of the United
Province of Canada, Étienne-Paschal Taché, Macdonald took the
floor. He delivered a speech that said little that was new—
Confederation should not repeat the American mistake of being
too decentralized, and all residual or unspecified powers should
revert to the federal government, not to the states, as had happened south of the border—but he said it persuasively. When
Macdonald finished, those outside the chamber could hear a
burst of applause from inside. His speech done, Macdonald
moved the first general resolution, to establish a "federal union"
with a government based on the British system and with the
monarch as its head of state. The actual work now began.

In hindsight it is remarkable how much the delegates accomplished—and also how little they did. Issues that have dominated Canadian politics ever since, such as the division of powers between the two levels of government, were barely discussed at all; Macdonald suggested a list of federal powers, and Oliver Mowat a list of provincial ones, and both were passed quickly with little argument or debate. Matters fundamental to the functioning of any federal system, such as how to amend the constitution, were not debated. A satisfactory explanation has never been constructed for the absence of so vital a piece of constitutional machinery. Speculatively, Macdonald may have worried that an amending system, which merely by existing implied that the constitution might need improving later on, might open the way for critics calling for changes before the constitution was carved into legislative stone, but whose real purpose was delay for its own sake. What is remarkable is that no one in Quebec City commented on the absence of an amending formula, even though one existed in the United States and was known to be working well. The Nova Scotia anti-Confederate Joseph Howe (who was not present at Quebec City) was one of the few in the entire country to raise the issue.

Premier Étienne-Paschal Taché. He served as the titular leader whom both Macdonald and Brown could accept.

What interested the delegates most was the Senate. One full week was spent on a debate (which came close to breaking up the conference) about how many senators* each section (Upper Canada, Lower Canada, the Maritimes) should have. "Everyone here has had a fit of the blues," reported the Toronto *Globe*. At Charlottetown, it had been agreed that every section would have twenty-four senators. The possible addition of Newfoundland meant that the Maritime colonies as a whole would end up with fewer senators than either of the Canadas. Eventually Macdonald concocted a compromise—Newfoundland would get four senators all of its own, if and when it joined. That said, the work resumed.

It was now October 19, and progress had been slow. From this point on, as Prince Edward Island delegate Edward Palmer reported in a newspaper article, "the current seemed to set with the Canadians." Contentious matters remained: Prince Edward Island asked for a special grant of £200,000 to buy up the extensive holdings of absentee landlords (mostly British) but was refused, and its delegates thereafter effectively dropped out of the discussions. Mistakes were made: on New Brunswick's behalf, Leonard Tilley managed to get an extra $63,000, but Charles Tupper forgot to ask for a matching amount for Nova Scotia.

The turn of the tide towards the Canadians meant a turn at the same time towards the strong central government that Macdonald had always called for. Words like "unity" and "nation" gained a magical quality. During a debate about criminal law, Mowat declared, "I quite concur in the advantages of one uniform system. It would weld us into a nation." A quote from a popular pamphlet, *The Northern Kingdom*, written by S.E. Dawson—"Never was there such an opportunity as now for the birth of a nation"—was reprinted in a Quebec City newspaper

---

* The term used then was Legislative Council, but for simplicity's sake, Senate and senators are here used throughout.

and commented on by many delegates. When a New Brunswicker, E.B. Chandler, protested that the provinces would be reduced to "merely large municipal corporations," he was almost shouted down. Macdonald was now so confident of success that he was able to dismiss as invalid another delegate's claim that the provisions of New Zealand's 1842 constitution, which had ended with the provinces there being abolished, could be used in Canada. A Newfoundland delegate, Ambrose Shea, caught the mood of many when he said the scheme would enable British North Americans to escape from the "wretched broils of our colonial life." Out of Quebec City came the first sense of Canada as a national community.

On Wednesday, October 26, the conference held its final full sessions—which extended until midnight. They met again on Friday to tidy up the details. That evening there was a huge ball, attended by one thousand guests. For the first time in history, a band of colonists had drafted a constitution for themselves. The deed was done.

The first reward of this constitutional success was financial. "The immediate effect of the scheme was such on the public mind that our five per cents [government bonds] rose from 75 to 92," Brown reported to Anne.

The new draft constitution was in fact an unrelievedly prosaic document, more like a car repair manual than a prescription for building a nation. The London *Times* commented, unkindly but accurately, on its "practical and unpretending a style." Only one resolution contained even a hint of poetry. It called for Canadians to move ahead by means of "the perpetuation of our connection with the mother country and the promotion of the best interests of the people of these provinces [who] desire to follow the model of the

British constitution," with, since this was a Canadian document, the closing qualifier "so far as our circumstances will prevail."

Macdonald understood the significance of what had been achieved. During the brief debate on the division of powers, he intervened to say that if the mix was too decentralized, a "radical weakness" would be introduced into the constitution that would "ruin us in the eyes of the civilized world." To gain respect and acceptance, the new nation had to let the world know, and its own people know, that it was united and capable of being daring. To do that took a strong central government. By contrast, Brown's understanding was much more parochial: "Constitution adopted—a most credible document—a complete reform of all the abuses and injustices we have complained of," he wrote to Anne right after the conference's close. He then added, "Is it not wonderful? French-Canadianism is entirely extinguished." (He meant by this that French Quebecers would no longer be able to intervene in the politics of English Ontarians.)

To be fair to the Quebec City delegates, they had to cobble together a federal constitution at the very time when the world's best-known federation had dissolved into a horrendous civil war. The temptation was strong to assume that federations were inherently flawed and that only a "legislative union," or a unitary state like Britain, could work. They were also hemmed in by circumstances. The United States' solution to the challenge of representing the regions at the centre—two senators from each state, no matter their size—was indeed well known in Canada. But Canada was too oddly sized for such a system to work here. The three Maritime provinces together contained only a fifth of the total population; a U.S.-style equal allocation of Senate seats would give them a majority in that chamber, growing to a two-to-one majority once Newfoundland joined. This said, any solution would have served better the need for a national balance than the one the delegates settled on—a Senate supposed to represent the regions, but with all its members appointed by the federal government.

There was, nevertheless, a fair amount of shrewd sense in the delegates' preference for the pedestrian. Thus, the Canadiens were conspicuous by their silence about the rights of French Canadians outside Quebec, in particular entirely ignoring the interests of New Brunswick's Acadians. Any vocal defence of the pan-Canadian interests of French Canadians, though, would have triggered demands for extra protections by English Canadians in Quebec. The silence was unbrotherly, and even cowardly, but it preserved for Quebec's Canadiens what they wanted.

To contemporary eyes, the aspect of the Quebec City resolutions most difficult to comprehend is that the delegates took almost no interest in the respective powers of the federal and provincial governments. Ever since, there have been long periods when the only matter of consequence in Canadian politics seems to be which level of government is responsible for what, and who should pay for it. While unsatisfying, the explanation for this constitutional amnesia is easy: governments then did so little because people wanted them to do little. Pre-Confederation, the share of government revenues expended on what are now the principal activities of government—education, public charities and social services—was just 9 per cent of the total.* Neither governments themselves nor ordinary Canadians expected them to do much more. Then, some 80 per cent of Canadians were farmers and fishermen, and they looked after themselves and their families.

---

* Today, the equivalent share of government spending on education, health and social programs would be around 70 per cent.

Also, there was a general assumption that setting down lists of federal and provincial responsibilities would pre-empt all the jurisdictional problems. This attitude was odd, given that delegates were familiar with the contortions that had bedevilled the quasi-federation of the United Province of Canada. But the naïveté about federalism was widespread. Macdonald would later proclaim, "We have avoided all conflict of jurisdiction and authority." The *Globe*, in that tone of plaintive exasperation at the follies of others so distinctive to editorial writers, would ask with unconcealed impatience, "We desire local self-government in order that the separate nationalities of which the population is composed may not quarrel. We desire at the same time a strong central authority. Is there anything incompatible in these two things? Cannot we have both? What is the difficulty?"

The delegates were practical men, not visionaries or scholars. Just one of the thirty-three Fathers of Confederation at Quebec City—Nova Scotia's Charles Tupper—had a university education, in his case in medicine from the University of Edinburgh.* By contrast, of the fifty-five at Philadelphia in 1787, more than half were university trained or had studied at the Inns of Court in London. The composition of the Senate interested the delegates for the sake of regional balance, but scarcely less so for their personal career prospects.† Few had bothered to study federal

---

* To confirm the indistinguishable interconnectedness of law and politics, of the thirty-three Fathers, two-thirds, or twenty-one, were lawyers, but, like Macdonald, lawyers who had learned the trade on the job.

† The interest the delegates took in the Senate would have reached fever pitch had they known that serious consideration would be given later to granting to all the Confederation senators "the rank and title of Knight Bachelor." Macdonald scotched this idea by pointing out to the colonial secretary that quite aside from the possibility of an errant senator lowering the tone of knighthood, it "would entail a title on his wife, which might not in all cases be considered desirable."

systems. The proceedings of those American colonists were available at the conference, and Macdonald had brought along his well-annotated copy of James Madison's *Debates in the Federal Convention of 1787*, which included Alexander Hamilton's *Draft of a Constitution for the United States.* But really only Macdonald, Galt, Mowat and, less so, Brown understood the complexities and subtle tradeoffs inherent in any federal system.

Practical men—even pedestrian ones as most of them were—the Quebec City delegates did one thing that was more imaginative than anything attempted at any federal-provincial conference since: most of the delegations were composed of representatives of both the government and the opposition in the home colony, as Christopher Moore pointed out in his excellent book *1867: How the Fathers Made a Deal.* (The one exception was the opposition *rouges*, who refused to take part.) Also, half hidden beneath all the workaday clauses of the resolutions, there was one radical new notion that was little appreciated by most of the drafters: in the new nation, linguistic and cultural differences would be protected.* This promise had never been made before, not even in the constitution of the original Swiss federation, which, if only by historic circumstance, was based on cantons that were all linguistically and ethnically German.

⌒

Here resides one of the great mysteries of the achievement of Confederation. It was built on the understanding of a pact between Canada's two founding races. Yet this fundamental

---

* No protection was provided for French Canadians as such or for any ethnic group, Aboriginal people excepted. The protections were all to religion and to language.

building block of the national architecture was, for all practical purposes, never discussed.

The extent of this pact is not at all easy to decipher. The actual provisions for bilingualism agreed on at Quebec City were exceedingly limited. There was no ringing proclamation of the equality of the two languages: the Quebec Resolutions merely declared, permissively, that "both the English and French languages may be employed by the general parliament . . . and also in the federal courts." There was no mention of bilingualism in the federal government, or anywhere in Canada outside Quebec.

Just once did Macdonald appear to accept that French should be a national language rather than one limited, outside Quebec, to Parliament and the federal courts. During the Confederation Debates that immediately followed the Quebec Conference, Macdonald said that "the use of the French language should form one of the principles upon which the Confederation should be established." Here, he linked French to Confederation itself rather than only to the new central government. This statement, though, was made only during a debate; he made no similar statement (so far as is known) during any of the conferences at which the new constitution was drafted. And his phrase "the use of" was imprecise. Yet the *bleu* members were satisfied. More striking, because Confederation could never have been implemented without his approval, Cartier was satisfied.

Cartier's confidence wasn't misplaced. Much would be gained by Confederation: the Canadiens would have their own legislature and government. In them, the dominant language would of course be French, in a return to the situation that existed before the Conquest. To reinforce the sense of assurance so gained, there was also the force of rising expectations. The eventual British North America Act would be the sixth constitutional construct by which French Canadians had been ruled—the earlier five being the Military Government of 1760, the Royal Proclamation of 1763, the Quebec Act of 1774, the Constitutional Act of 1791 and the Act of Union of 1841. Whatever the particular constitutional system, French Canadians had found ways to use it not merely to survive but progressively to enlarge their self-rule, gaining recognition of their religion, their language and their right to a full share of the patronage of the national government. If this much had been won already, why not more, later, by other constitutional changes and rearrangements?

These ambitions were expressed quite openly. *La Minerve* (Montreal), a strong supporter of Cartier, used the evocative phrase "maîtres chez nous" to describe what Confederation would accomplish for the francophones of Quebec. *Le Journal de Québec* said that French Canadians "can and must one day aspire to being a nation," adding that premature independence would lead to annexation by the United States. Other than "nation," probably the most common word in the commentaries on the Confederation project in Quebec newspapers was that of "separation." The most explicit declaration was in *La Minerve*, which in its issue for Confederation Day, July 1, 1867, advised readers, "As a distinct and separate nationality, we form a state within a state. We enjoy the full exercise of our rights, and the formal recognition of our national independence." The magazine *Contre-poison* wrote that Quebec was to be "completely separated from Upper Canada" and praised the leaders who had "turned us over into our own hands, who have restored our complete autonomy." And *La Minerve* observed, "In giving ourselves a complete government we affirm our existence as a separate nationality."

Quebecers—as they soon would be called—were saying to each other, or at least were being told by their newspapers and political leaders, that Confederation's purpose was not to create some new Canadian nation but to create a political system in which they could not only continue to be what they always had been but grow into something larger—perhaps, to quote *La Minerve* again, into a "state within a state," or, eventually, into "national independence." And their understanding of Confederation itself was quite different from that of English Canadians. At the same time, English Canadians were being told by leaders such as Macdonald and Brown that Confederation's purpose was to create a "new nation." *Le Canadien*, by contrast, informed its readers that Confederation's purpose was to create "un certain nombre d'États souverains, déléguant une partie définie de leurs droits et leurs pouvoirs à un gouvernement central."

Few if any English Canadians, in Upper Canada or the Maritimes, read any of these commentaries. In the mid-nineteenth century, the two solitudes were wholly disconnected from each other and wholly self-absorbed. But for this mutual ignorance, the bliss of Confederation, such as it is, simply could not have been achieved.

To some extent, the use of terms such as "separation" and "nationality" in *bleu* newspapers was just a tactic to reassure Quebec francophone voters. Some of it was wish-fulfillment. A large part of it, though, was real. It was an expectation about the future that arose directly out of the past and the present.

The concept of Canada as a political pact between the two races derived from the alliance years between Robert Baldwin and Louis-Hippolyte LaFontaine. Macdonald and Cartier had picked it up a decade later, and so it had remained in the public discourse. The Confederation pact itself was now Macdonald and Cartier's pact. Once it was achieved, both of them would still be there to implement it. Many Canadiens must have taken for granted that the pair of them could, and would, make it work. It wasn't a legal compact but rather a pact of trust.

Nothing was ever said about this pact during any of the Confederation conferences, and no evidence exists that Cartier and Macdonald ever discussed the nature of the pact between them. Whether they even sketched out a deal is unknowable. Most of Cartier's personal papers were destroyed after his early death in 1873, almost certainly deliberately to protect him (and Macdonald) from any further disclosures about Canadian Pacific Railway funds being used in Conservative election campaigns. Macdonald and Cartier were so close, though, that they would hardly have needed to commit to paper any agreement between them about Confederation's future.

Macdonald, nevertheless, is on the public record as committing himself to a pact with both Cartier and *les Canadiens*. In reference not to Confederation but to its predecessor, the United Province of Canada, he said in a speech he gave in Toronto, which was quoted in the Toronto *Leader* on April 30, 1861, that union had been "a distinct bargain, a solemn contract." During the Confederation Debates of 1865, Macdonald again used the term "Treaty of Union" to refer to the practices followed in the legislature of the United Province, and he intriguingly admitted that, although a single unit according to its constitution, it had been, "as a matter of fact . . . a Federal Union"—or little different in its reality from what the proposed Confederation would be.

Legally, no such treaty or contract between the French and English ever existed. But in Macdonald's mind, and equally in Cartier's, a "distinct bargain, a solemn contract" existed between them, and so between the English and the French. Confederation didn't create this bargain between the two founding peoples, as has often been claimed. Instead, it arose out of a pact of trust that predated Confederation and had, by the time of Confederation, been made into part of Canada's DNA by Macdonald and Cartier.

Between Cartier and Macdonald there was one dramatic Confederation-era public exchange that revealed how they understood their respective roles. In March 1864, on the eve of the formation of the Great Coalition government, Macdonald, then not yet committed to Confederation, spoke briefly on Brown's motion to set up a legislature committee to consider all federal options. "The sad experience on the other side [the United States]," Macdonald said, "proved that it must not be merely a federal one; that instead of having a federal one, we should have a Legislative Union, in fact, in principle, and in practice." Sitting beside him, Cartier interjected grimly, "That is not my policy," meaning he would never accept a unitary state in which his Canadiens would have no government of their own to protect them. Just a few days later, Macdonald showed that he understood Cartier's objection, and that he accepted it, by coming out in support of a pan-Canadian federal union. The mutual trust between these two men was the unwritten pact that made Confederation possible.

At Quebec City, there was one revealing public discussion of this existential issue between French and English, though it involved neither Macdonald nor Cartier. It occurred right at the start of the conference, and it's very likely that only Macdonald among the English-speaking delegates understood the significance of what was being said. Sir Étienne-Paschal Taché made a brief opening statement in his role as nominal premier of Canada. After pleasantries, he informed the delegates that Confederation would be "tantamount to a separation of the provinces, and Lower Canada would thereby preserve its autonomy together with all the institutions it held so dear." Not one member of the "other" solitude rose to challenge or inquire about what the words "separation" and "autonomy" meant; by their silence, English Canadians sealed the pact.

Here is the place for a footnote too important to be tucked away at the bottom of the page. Taché, avuncular in his appearance and genial in his manner, was highly regarded by his English counterparts as one of the gatekeepers between themselves and the near-invisible Canadiens. But Taché was also a passionate patriot. He showed this side of himself in a remarkable 1858 letter to a fellow Canadien politician. "The important thing to remember is that the unity we have just consolidated in Lower Canada ensures that *we are the de facto rulers of the entire province* [of Canada]," he wrote. "It may come that, in their impotent rage, we will soon be hearing weeping and gnashing of teeth from the Upper Canadians. . . . All the blustering of our enemies will vanish into thin air, while we go forward, *govern*, progress. . . . And we will do more: we will safeguard our institutions and preserve them from impure contact." Fortunately for Macdonald, and for Canada, neither Brown nor the *Globe* ever learned about this other side of their gatekeeper.* Equally fortunately for Canada, no Canadien leader learned of Brown's triumphant declaration to Anne that Confederation's great accomplishment was that French Canadianism had been extinguished.

Macdonald achieved all he really wanted just in getting the Confederation deal itself at Quebec City. Prince Edward Island pulled out from the pact later, as did Newfoundland, neither of these island colonies having any interest in the Intercolonial Railway or any fear of Americans attempting to invade by running the gauntlet of the Royal Navy. The approval of the Nova

---

* This revealing letter is reproduced in full in Alastair Sweeny's *George-Étienne Cartier: A Biography*.

Scotia and New Brunswick delegates, though, meant that Macdonald had in his hand one-half of a continental-sized nation that would stretch to the Atlantic; the addition of the second half, stretching all the way to the Pacific, was specifically provided for in the Quebec Resolutions.

Macdonald didn't get what he had said on several occasions he personally would prefer to a confederation or federation—a "legislative union." Such an arrangement was highly attractive to Britain, itself a "legislative union," or unitary state, and one that had forged a "Union" with Scotland and had rejected repeatedly, and violently, any attempts at Home Rule, or self-government, in Ireland. Midway through the conference, Macdonald wrote to the businessman-politician Isaac Buchanan, "My great aim is to strengthen the general Legislature and Govt. as much as possible, and approach as nearly to a Legislative Union as is practicable." Shortly after the conference ended, he wrote to a supporter, Malcolm Cameron, "If the Confederation goes on, you, if spared the ordinary age of man, will see both local Parliaments and Governments absorbed in the General Power." Macdonald added, as hardly needed to be said, "But of course, it doesn't do to adopt that point of view in discussing the subject in Lower Canada."

While Macdonald kept on saying this kind of thing, he may not have meant it. He may have been playing another set of his "long game." He once even showed his hand in public. In the Confederation Debates in the Canadian legislature that followed the Quebec Conference, Macdonald engaged in an intriguing exchange with the High Tory M.C. Cameron, who challenged Macdonald that he would have "better shown [his] patriotism by waiting a little longer to accomplish it." Macdonald interjected,

"Accomplish what?" Cameron answered, "A legislative union of all the provinces." Macdonald then gave his colleague a lesson in *realpolitik*. "I thought my hon. friend knew that every man in Lower Canada was against it, every man in New Brunswick, every man in Nova Scotia,* every man in Newfoundland and every man in Prince Edward Island. How, then, is it to be accomplished?" The "long game" that Macdonald thus was playing was to position himself at a constitutional extreme from which he could gracefully retreat, while using his concessions to gain in exchange yet more bits and pieces of a highly centralized federal system.

That in fact is exactly what happened. Before the Confederation project was completed, Macdonald won a succession of important additions to the central power. Immigration and agriculture became joint jurisdictions rather than exclusively provincial concerns, and Ottawa gained the right to appoint the provincial lieutenant-governors, officials considered so powerful at the time that Macdonald described them as "chief executive officers." Moreover, during the negotiations at the Quebec Conference, even though many delegates favoured a legislative union rather than a confederation—Brown[†] and Galt among the Canadians, and, among the Maritimers, Tupper and some senior men—Macdonald made no attempt to win approval for a legislative union. By not attempting seriously the impossibility of a legislative union, he got the possible—namely, as he expressed it

---

* Macdonald was exaggerating for effect. Tupper, Nova Scotia's premier, denounced the "absurdity" of provinces claiming any sovereignty and said that Confederation would instead make Nova Scotia "a large municipality under the Central Government; but just as clearly a municipality as the City of Halifax now is under our Provincial Government."

† Brown so doubted the usefulness of provincial governments that he said they "should not take up political matters."

and believed he had achieved, that "the Central Government assumes towards the local governments precisely the same position as the Imperial Government holds with respect to each of the provinces."

The constitution that emerged from Quebec City, and that went on to become the BNA Act, was almost certainly the most centralized constitution for a federation or confederation that's ever been assembled. Macdonald secured all the four centralizing measures Alexander Hamilton had attempted to insert into the U.S. Constitution at Philadelphia in 1787—appointment of senators for life; federal appointment of state governors; the federal right to disallow state laws; and the granting of residual powers to the federal government. He also secured one centralizing authority, over "banking, incorporation of banks, and the issue of paper money," that Hamilton never even thought of.

Macdonald's "long game" had another objective, one far more critical to his purpose than creating a strong central government for the sake of governmental efficiency. Confederation's prime purpose was to impress Britain and the United States by a statement of national will; gathering together the British North America colonies was merely a means to that end. A central government that possessed, as he put it, "all the powers which are incident to sovereignty" would impress as the government of a nation rather than of some upgraded province or colony. To impress further, it would avoid what Macdonald saw as the "fatal error" that had almost sundered the United States—that of "making each state a distinct sovereignty, and giving to each a distinct sovereign power." In the nation-state he was creating, therefore, sovereignty would reside, as in all real nation-states, at its centre.

As it turned out, Macdonald would lose this part of his "long game"—in later sets. Quirky decisions by the Judicial Committee of the Privy Council in London during the latter part of Macdonald's post-Confederation term were an early cause. The underlying reason was that Canadians themselves wanted a decentralized confederation rather than Macdonald's centralized one. Another reason was the most obvious one of all: immense distances kept the people of British North America apart from each other and turned them to their own local governments and away from the remote national one. Above all, Canadiens, soon to become Québécois, located their true national government not in Ottawa but in Quebec City. As to the future of federal-provincial relations, rather than Macdonald's benign confidence about federal dominance, the shrewdest guess was the one made by that unnervingly perceptive critic Christopher Dunkin: the "cry" of the provinces, he predicted in 1865, "will be found to be pretty often and pretty successfully—'Give, give, give.'"

A closing note about the Quebec Conference. The most famous painting in Canadian historiography is Robert Harris's *The Fathers of Confederation*. Macdonald dominates the picture— because he's in the centre, he's standing rather than sitting, he's tall (at five foot eleven he was above the average height for the time), he's wearing a dashing white waistcoat inside his black frock coat, and, in contrast to the ponderous gravitas of most of the others, his posture is alert, watchful, purposeful. Harris painted it in 1884. By that time the building in which the event had taken place had burned down, and Harris improved the vista by painting in delicate arched windows in place of the square wooden casements of the original.

This painting was lost in the 1916 fire that destroyed the Parliament Buildings in Ottawa. Harris, by then seventy, refused a second commission but did touch up his original cartoon, or charcoal sketch. In 1964 the insurance company Confederation Life commissioned Toronto artist Rex Woods to recreate Harris's 1884 version and presented it to Parliament as a Centennial gift. It now hangs in the Railway Committee Room of the Parliament Buildings.*

Macdonald's mood after the comprehensive success at Quebec City was confident to the point of being cocky. Within a fortnight of the conference's end, he was treating Confederation as if it were already an accomplished fact and was looking beyond to the administrative details of a post-Confederation government. On November 14, 1864, he wrote to Premier Tilley of New Brunswick, "Have you thought over the formation of the Govt— the Federal Govt I mean?—i.e. as to the number and composition of the Executive, the number and nature of the Departments & the general system of administration?" He made the same request to Nova Scotia's Tupper the same day, adding, "I intend to commence next week to draft the Bill to be submitted for the consideration of the Imperial Govt."

His personal correspondence communicated the same assurance. A day after his letters to Tilley and Tupper, in a letter to Judge James Robert Gowan, Macdonald claimed the entire constitution as "mine." In another letter at this time, he declared, "We

---

* A nine-foot-long oak-and-basswood table in the Saskatchewan Legislative Library at Regina may be the same one around which the Quebec City delegates bargained for the resolutions. It was used in the Privy Council at Ottawa from 1865 to some date in the 1883–92 period, when it was brought to Regina. It probably came to Ottawa from Quebec City, and so may have been used at the Confederation conference, but no certain connection has been established.

do not pretend that it is at all perfect, or even symmetrical, but it was the result of a series of compromises which were necessary to secure the support of all classes."

To heighten his high spirits, events kept breaking his way. Midway through the Quebec Conference, the delegates heard worrisome news that two dozen Southern Confederates hiding in Canada had staged a cross-border raid on the northern Vermont town of St. Albans, taking two hundred thousand dollars from three banks, killing one person and wounding another before fleeing back to Canada. The general commanding the American forces in the region gave his troops an order that if other Confederates made a similar sortie, they were to give hot pursuit right into Canada. President Lincoln refused to confirm the order, which would have breached Canada's neutrality, and waited to see how Canada would respond.

By bad luck, that response could not have been more thoroughly bungled. Most of the Confederates were arrested as soon as they arrived back in Canada from St. Albans. On December 13, their preliminary trial came up before Montreal magistrate Charles-Joseph Coursol. The defence lawyer made a convoluted argument for the prisoners' temporary release; a confused Coursol assented, and the Confederate raiders instantly vanished. American newspapers, and many American politicians, were certain it was an anti-North plot. Four days later Washington gave notice that all Canadians would have to have passports to enter the United States. Privately, Macdonald expressed his fury at "the unhappy and mistaken decision of Coursol." To an inquiring businessman, Macdonald's response was nuanced adroitly. On the one hand, Macdonald wrote, there was no reason why "individuals or incorporated companies like Railways should not join in their exertions with Americans from the Western Frontier to procure its [the passport order's] withdrawal." On the other, "it would be extremely impolitic, and, indeed, defeat our object, if the Canadian Government went on its knees to the United States government." Macdonald then gave the businessman a lesson in governance: an intervention by the Canadian government itself, he wrote, "would give Mr. Seward [the secretary of state] an exaggerated idea of the inconvenience and loss suffered by Canada and it [the order] would be kept up as a means of punishment or for purposes of coercion."

In fact, the released raiders were quickly rearrested and retried by a different judge, who subsequently ruled (very likely after being prompted by Macdonald) that they should be extradited to the United States.* To forestall future raids, Macdonald called up two thousand volunteers to stand guard along the border. As a further precaution, he organized a detective force, headed by Gilbert McMicken, "a shrewd, cool and determined man who won't easily lose his head," to provide intelligence on what was happening across the border. The flap died down, although, as always, not without calls by American newspapers, especially the New York *Herald*, for Canada's annexation, if necessary by force. Of lasting consequence, though, was the decision by Congress not to renew the Reciprocity Treaty when it reached its due date in 1866, in reaction to what was seen to be Canadian favouritism towards the South. The combination of this cross-border free-trade pact, together with the immense demand generated by American military mobilization, had led to the growth of Canada's economy at a faster rate than ever before in the nineteenth century.[†]

---

* To further mollify the Americans, the Canadian government compensated the St. Albans banks for their losses with thirty thousand dollars in banknotes and forty thousand in gold.

† In June 1864, the value of the Canadian dollar reached $2.78, a peak never even approached since.

The immediate consequences of this mini-crisis, though, were all positive. Even the passport rule was soon withdrawn. As always, an external threat drew people together. Further, the St. Albans affair reminded Canadians of the threat about to be posed by the imminent victory of the North over the South. About the war itself, Macdonald now insisted on the strictest neutrality, urging it on a colleague with just a hint of regret: "We can't help the South[,] and a naked expression of sympathy would do it no good and greatly injure us." Nevertheless, the fact remained that once the American Civil War ended, the vast Federal armies might be demobilized—or, perhaps, mobilized to march northwards.

To this threat, actual or perceived, two responses were possible: Confederation, which would signal Canada's will to survive; as well, a helping hand from Britain. Macdonald now set out to secure both.

NINETEEN

Parliament vs the People

—~—

If we do not represent the people of Canada,
we have no right to be here.
John A. Macdonald

T
he sweeping success of the Quebec Conference was
followed by the double afterglow of a triumphal
tour of Canada by the Maritime delegates and the
plaudits for the accomplishment expressed by
British newspapers from the *Times* on down. Macdonald's
response to all this praise was to go on a prolonged binge. He performed like a tightly wound spring that, once released, flies all
over the place and then collapses in a heap.

The post-conference tour, which had the dual purpose of
showing Canada to the Maritimers and showing off the
Maritimers to Canadians, began in Montreal with a gala dinner
hosted by Cartier. To encourage the delegates to complete their
good work, the program of toasts included the verse "Then let us
be firm and united / One country, one flag for us all; / United,
our strength will be freedom / Divided, we each of us fall." The
cavalcade then moved to Ottawa, where Macdonald was to act as
host. It began well: the crowds were huge and they escorted the

visitors in a torchlight procession to the Russell Hotel, where they were to dine. As the gala's principal speaker, Macdonald got to his feet, said a few words, then stopped and fell silent.* Galt had to fill up the vacuum with an extemporaneous speech. Macdonald rejoined the group when it left by train for Kingston, with succeeding stops planned at all the communities— Belleville, Cobourg, Port Hope—on the way to Toronto, where Brown would be host. But Macdonald never left Kingston. It's safe to guess that he spent most of his time at Eliza Grimason's tavern, periodically collapsing into the bed kept for him there.

As all who knew him realized well, Macdonald, from this period on, would every now and then go on one of these binges and be unable to do anything until they were over. Then suddenly he would reappear as though nothing had happened, as full of vigour and zest as ever. His constitution was a minor marvel. Macdonald did enjoy walking, but he never undertook any strenuous exercise. He ate lightly, not because he drank heavily as is frequently the case, but because he always ate lightly. A photograph of Macdonald taken at around this time—in 1863 by the famed William Notman of Montreal, and the front cover of this book—portrays him as lean and fit and impressively erect.† The photo also captures perfectly the distinctive quality of his eyes— amused, observant, commanding. It may have been Notman's magic (all the more magical because he used only natural light),

---

* In his report on the Charlottetown and Quebec conferences, published in 1865 under the title *The Union of the British Provinces*, the pro-Confederation Prince Edward Island delegate Edward Whelan dealt delicately with Macdonald's performance: "Illness induced by fatigue from assiduous devotion to public affairs, compelled him to curtail his observations."

† It's possible there was a concealed brace behind Macdonald, as was often used to enable a client to last out the minute and a half or more of motionlessness required for the exposure.

but absolutely nothing about the photo suggests a public figure with a single care in the world, least of all that of his having become, if irregularly, an out-of-control public drunk.

After Macdonald had finished wrestling with whatever devils were assailing him, he went right back to the job at hand. With the Quebec Conference over and a constitution agreed on, the way ahead was clear. Macdonald needed now to get approval for the Confederation scheme first from Canada's legislature, and then from the legislatures of the key Maritime provinces, Nova Scotia and New Brunswick. As the climactic step, he needed the approval of the Parliament at Westminster. Thereafter, he could come back home with Confederation's constitution in his pocket.

One intervening step was required, though. The British press had indeed been laudatory, but it had also expressed some disquieting notes. The *Edinburgh Review*, while applauding the accomplishment, had gone on to describe it as the "harbinger of the future and complete independence of British North America," while the *Saturday Review* judged the achievement as "not so much a step towards independence as a means of softening the inevitable shock." The *Times*, in its more orotund way, declared that while "nothing could be more in correspondence with the interests and wishes of this country" than Confederation, nevertheless "the dependency that wishes to quit us has only to make up its mind to that effect." What Macdonald needed, then, was an official stamp of approval to Confederation from the Imperial government that could be waved in front of the Canadian and Maritime legislatures, and, as an additional reassurance, a cessation of talk in London about possible Canadian independence.

For this vital but delicate mission, Macdonald chose Brown. It was a deft choice. Brown's key qualifications were that he wasn't Macdonald and that he was the leader of Canada's largest party. He would carry in his person to London the message that support for Confederation was widespread. He would also allow Macdonald to get on with his immediate task of assembling the legislature and of figuring out how to secure as quickly as possible its agreement to the scheme.

For Brown, this transatlantic trip had to be one of the most agreeable he ever made, not least because Anne went along with him. They travelled first to Edinburgh, and then Brown went on alone to London.

On December 3, 1864, Brown called on the colonial secretary, Edward Cardwell, who received him almost as a brother. Cardwell had already drafted a memorandum setting out his views on the Quebec Resolutions; this, if Brown approved of it, he intended to dispatch to the governor general in Ottawa and to the Maritime lieutenant-governors. Brown not only approved but was ecstatic. "A most gracious answer to our constitutional scheme. Nothing could be more laudatory—it praises our statesmanlike discretion, loyalty and so on," he wrote afterwards to Macdonald.

Cardwell had one more bit of news of even greater import to pass on. Confederation, he told Brown, was a subject "of great interest . . . in the highest circles." Brown immediately picked up the reference that Queen Victoria herself wanted Confederation for her distant colonies. He was so overcome by this confidence that he asked whether the Queen might come to Canada to open the first post-Confederation Parliament. Cardwell's reply, no doubt couched in the correct circumlocutory phrases, was that Victoria, a grieving widow ever since the recent death of her beloved Prince Albert, was so emotionally shattered that it was "totally out of the question" for her even to open Parliament in next-door Westminster.

Nothing else was denied Brown, and so by extension Canada's Confederates. He went to Prime Minister Lord Palmerston's country house in Hampshire and took a long stroll with the prime minister through the gardens. He met the foreign secretary and the rising political titan and fellow-Liberal William Gladstone. A bit carried away, Brown afterwards told Anne of his encounter with Gladstone: "Though we had been discussing the highest questions of statesmanship—he did not by any means drag me out of my depth." Then hastily he added, "Don't for any sake read this to Tom or Willie, or they will think I have gone daft."

Brown did have one concern to report to Macdonald: "There is a manifest desire in almost every quarter that ere long the British colonies should shift for themselves, and in some quarters evident regret that we did not declare at once for independence." The cause, Brown said, was "the fear of invasion of Canada by the United States," an affront that might compel Britain, for the sake of honour and of face, to make the futile gesture of intervening to try to save its colony. In fact Brown and Macdonald would have been even more concerned had they known of a letter sent at this time to Governor General Monck by the junior minister for the colonies, C.B. Adderley. In it, he reported, "Gladstone said to me the other day: 'Canada is England's weakness, till the last British soldier is brought away & Canada left on her own. We cannot hold our own with the United States.'"

Britain was onside all right, but in its own way.

Brown landed back in Canada on January 13, 1865. Two days earlier, Macdonald had passed a significant milestone—he'd reached the age of fifty. He either paid no attention to his birthday or marked it by consuming a bottle in his room in some boarding house. But for cronies, Macdonald was now alone. Hugh John, at the age of fifteen, was distant from his father, both because he had been brought up by Margaret and James Williamson in Kingston and because he was now beginning to feel the strain of being the son of a famous father. That fall, Hugh John entered the University of Toronto as an undergraduate.*

Macdonald in his prime. This photo was taken by the famous William Notman of Montreal in 1863. The two minutes of motionlessness required for a photograph at the time did nothing to dim his energy and vivacity.

At this same time Macdonald was becoming increasingly concerned about the condition of his law practice. His law partner Archibald Macdonnell had died the previous spring, and ever since Macdonald had been discovering just how deeply his company was in debt, with some of the debts resulting from transactions of highly questionable probity, but for which he would be personally responsible. Brown, in one letter to Anne at this time, confided that "John A.'s business affairs are in sad disorder, and need more close attention."†

Macdonald's two escapes from solitude now were the Confederation project and drink.

---

* That Hugh John should have gone to university at the age of fifteen was not in the least unusual. Some undergraduates then were a year younger. No high schools existed until the 1870s, and bright students were prepared for university entrance exams in special schools. See A.B. McKillop, *Matters of Mind: The University in Ontario, 1791–1951.*

† As must have galled Macdonald, Brown at this time made himself wealthy for life by selling his farm and lands in southwestern Ontario for a handsome $275,000.

The Legislative Assembly met unusually early that year—on January 17, following Macdonald's request to Governor General Monck. The members would need the extra time to debate and, all going well, approve the seventy-two Quebec Resolutions. Thereafter would come the debates in the New Brunswick and Nova Scotia legislatures about the same draft resolutions to establish Confederation.

As if in anticipation of his impending triumph, Macdonald was advised of a tribute soon to be extended to him—he was to be given an honorary degree by Oxford University, the first Canadian to be so recognized.* It is probable, although not certain, that Monck also gave Macdonald early notice that, when it came time to form a government for the new nation (in about a year, it was generally expected), he would invite him to be its first prime minister. At Quebec City, Macdonald had raised himself to the status of the irreplaceable man; he was about to become *the* man.

About winning approval of the draft constitution from Canada's Legislative Assembly, Macdonald had no qualms. "Canada on the whole seems to take up the scheme warmly," he wrote to Tilley. About opinion in his own Upper Canada, he was absolutely right: the only naysayers were a few Tory Conservatives worried that Confederation might weaken the country's ties to Britain. In Lower Canada the prospects were more mixed, yet still predominantly

---

* Macdonald had received his first honorary degree in 1863 from Queen's University; it was also the first honorary degree awarded by Queen's, which he had helped to found.

positive. *Rouge* leader Antoine-Aimé Dorion had already published an anti-Confederation manifesto charging that the Quebec Resolutions would produce not a "true confederation" of sovereign provinces but a disguised legislative union in which the provinces would be mere municipalities and so unable to protect their electorates. As an example of the way Confederation lurched along, one step forward, one back, Galt at this same time was reassuring audiences of his fellow Lower Canada English-speakers that, precisely because the provinces would be merely "municipalities of larger growth," controlled by a strong central government, there was no need for them to worry about being reduced to a minority in a French-dominated province. Fortunately, none of Cartier's *bleu* members had blinked at any of these concerns, and this was all that really mattered in Lower Canada—soon to become Quebec.

And then some of them did blink. The cause wasn't a real problem but an apparent one—in politics, no different from a real problem. The Throne Speech read by Monck at the opening of the legislature included a call for Canadians to "create a new nationality." This ambition was logical enough: everywhere, the reason for creating new nations, as in Italy, which had come into existence just four years earlier, was either to create a new nationality or to liberate an old one from oppression. McGee had been calling for years for a "new nationality." During the Quebec Conference, Prince Edward Island delegate Edward Whelan had got so caught up in the national vision that he dismissed his own province as "a patch of sandbank in the Gulf." Even the cautious Oliver Mowat got into the nationalist spirit, although his exuberance may have been for show because, right after the conference, he announced he was leaving politics to become a judge in the chancery court. (Macdonald filled the vacant Reform cabinet slot by appointing the little-known W.P. Howland.)

The problem was that all this talk about a Canadian nation and a Canadian nationality threatened the national distinctiveness of Canadiens. Adroitly, Dorion moved a resolution calling on members to disavow plans for a new nationality. It was defeated, predictably, but it gained the support of twenty-five French-Canadian members. If Dorion could find another hot button, he might yet be able to whip up an anti-Confederate storm in Quebec.

On February 3, Macdonald moved that the House adopt the Quebec Resolutions. He made a brief explanatory statement, following up three days later with a two-hour speech. Subsequently, all the leading pro-Confederates—Brown, Cartier, Galt and McGee—had their say, as well as some of the far smaller number of anti-Confederates, notably *rouge* leader Dorion and Independent Conservative Christopher Dunkin. All these words, filling 1,032 double-columned pages, became known as the Confederation Debates.

It was in his short statement that Macdonald made his key new contribution to the Confederation project. He had already anticipated the now well-known difficulty of implementing a new constitution or of making major changes to an existing one: that all those unhappy for any reason particular to themselves can vote No, and that all the Noes may add up to a deal-breaking majority, even though the reasons for many of them contradict each other. In Canada—inevitably—there was a further problem. Any division in an overall vote on a constitution can cause frictions to national harmony; a division caused by confrontations between races or religions, though, can shatter national unity. Two values were thus put into conflict—democracy and national unity. Macdonald's choice, naturally, was for national unity over democracy.

⌒

In his statement of February 3, Macdonald set out first to reduce to a minimum the extent of the legislature's debate on the constitution. Rather than a discussion and a vote on each of the seventy-two clauses, there should be only a single vote, for or against the entire document.* The entire Confederation package "was in the nature of a treaty," he said;† each of its clauses had already been fully discussed and either agreed to or amended after compromises. "If the scheme was not now adopted in all its principal details as presented to the House," he informed the members, "we could not expect it to be passed this century."

That mission accomplished, Macdonald moved on to his main argument: approval by the legislature's members was all that was needed for the constitution to be passed. "If this measure received the support of the House," he said, "there would be no necessity of going back to the people." There was no need, that is, for the people to say what they felt, either in an election or in a plebiscite.

That Macdonald wanted to avoid delay and division was the immediate, practical motive for his stance. But it was by no means the only one. He believed also, entirely genuinely, that the

---

* Before his speech, Macdonald had already rejected a suggestion by Brown that he should move a series of resolutions on the scheme.

† This purely tactical use by Macdonald of the term "treaty" was later seized on by advocates of the "Compact Theory" of Confederation. They held that it was a compact or treaty negotiated between the provinces, with the federal government set up by them to perform certain functions. But the provinces, as colonies, had no power to negotiate anything. Further, Ontario and Quebec didn't exist before Confederation and had no one to negotiate on their behalf. A supposed compact or treaty that no one signed, and whose two largest participants (representing four-fifths of the population) didn't exist, is difficult to take seriously.

decision was the exclusive responsibility of the members of Parliament whom the people had elected to represent them, rather than that of the public at large. Canada's constitution was to be for the people, but not of the people.

On the same day that he spoke, Macdonald sent a letter to a supporter, John Beattie, setting out the philosophical justification for his policy. The constitutional package, he pointed out, had received "general if not universal favour." The government had the right, therefore, "to assume, as well as the Legislature, that the scheme, in principle meets with the approbation of the Country, and as it would be obviously absurd to submit the complicated details of such a measure to the people, it is not proposed to seek their sanction."

Today, after the Meech Lake and the Charlottetown accords, no politician would advance such an argument, except one wishing to commit instant political suicide. Oddly, though, the constitutional change cherished most highly by the majority of Canadians, that of the Charter of Rights and Freedoms, was never submitted for approval in a referendum.

In the mid-nineteenth century, however, nothing that Macdonald said was in any way novel or shocking. Then, representative democracy was the norm. He was taking his stand on the side Edmund Burke had taken in his famous declaration to the electors of Bristol: "Your representative owes you, not his industry only, but his judgment; and he betrays, instead of serving you, if he sacrifices it to your opinion." It was the duty of elected members to make the decisions they judged the best; it was the duty of voters to elect those they judged best able to make those decisions.

Today, most of that is an archaism. On almost all occasions

now, MPs make the decisions that their party has already decided they should make. Voters today insist on contributing themselves—the system is known as direct democracy—to the making and the implementing of decisions. It could be said that the era of the divine right of kings was followed, comparatively briefly, by an era of the divine right of Parliament, and this is now giving way to an era of the divine right of the people.

The mid-nineteenth century, though, was still the era of parliamentary supremacy. The Canadian version of it might have been small and parochial, yet it was a branch of the majestic Mother of Parliaments in London stretching back, often gloriously, at times bloodily, over the centuries. And the Canadian version had won for its people the great victory of Responsible Government. Its debates were widely followed, and reported nearly in full, in the newspapers. Its leading men—Macdonald, Cartier, Brown and McGee—were national celebrities, the only ones there were then. The widespread distaste for "partyism," or for disciplined, organized parties, reflected the presumption that individual members would—certainly should—speak out for and vote for their personal beliefs, even their conscience, rather than just the partisan interests of their party. The doctrine of parliamentary supremacy was as much a part of all people's upbringing as were the doctrines of their particular Christian faith. When Macdonald said, "Parliament is a grand inquest with the right to inquire into anything and everything," everyone, except perhaps the dwindling number of populist Grits, would have agreed.

The alternative doctrine of democracy not only had few supporters but was widely suspect. A prime reason was that democracy was an American idea. To Canadians, what was happening south of the border was not democracy but mob rule. Canadians, by contrast, assumed that they themselves enjoyed real liberty because their ultimate ruler was a constitutional monarch rather than an elected president who might become a dictator. That their head of state was essentially powerless was the reason, so hard for Americans to comprehend, why anti-democratic Canadians were genuinely convinced that they enjoyed more real freedom and liberty than their neighbours. Nor were critics of democracy without good arguments: in France it had led to the Terror, then to the dictatorship of Napoleon; in the United States, to the Revolution, then to the Civil War. And Macdonald's arguments were persuasive. The Confederation project had got this far only because of "a very happy concurrence of circumstances which might not easily come again." He appealed to members to "sacrifice their individual opinions as to particular details, if satisfied with the government that the scheme as a whole was for the benefit and prosperity of the people of Canada."

As thought Macdonald, so did almost everyone else. If, in Macdonald's judgment, Americans were subject to "the tyranny of mere numbers," to the Toronto *Leader* U.S. presidents were "the slave of the rabble," to the *Globe* democracy was "one of those dreadful American heresies," and to Brown American elections were a sham, because "the balance of power is held by the ignorant unreasoning mass." McGee, during his speech in the Confederation Debates, said, "The proposed Confederation will enable us to bear up shoulder to shoulder, to resist the spread of this universal democracy doctrine." In Lower Canada politicians thought the same way; so, still more vociferously, did the Catholic hierarchy. In Canada there were conspicuously no great debates about democracy as there had been in Britain during each of its Reform Laws.*

---

* Although democracy, as a grand theory, had few supporters in Canada, the country's political system was quite respectably democratic in practice. While the franchise was limited to property-owning males, as in Britain, there were many more of them here than there, and the vote was extended to Roman Catholics and Jews much earlier here. Walter Bagehot, the great British political

There nevertheless was a debate in Canada's Legislative Assembly about whether a constitution should be sanctioned by the people or only by those few who happened to be members of the legislature. A Reform backbencher, James O'Halloran, addressed the issue directly. "When we assume the power to deal with this question, to change the whole system of government, to effect a revolution peaceful though it may be, without reference to the will of the people of this country," he said, "we arrogate to ourselves a right never conferred upon us, and our act is a usurpation." He went on, describing the people as "the only rightful source of political power." Another backbencher, Benjamin Seymour, supported O'Halloran,* as did a few newspapers, such as the Hamilton *Times*, which declared forthrightly, "If their [the people's] direct decision on the confederation question is unnecessary . . . we can imagine none in the future of sufficient importance to justify an appeal to them. The polling booths thereafter may as well be turned into pig-pens, and the voters lists cut into pipe-lighters."

A second debate on the issue of democracy occurred after the Confederation Debates had ended, when a Conservative member, John Hillyard Cameron, moved a motion calling for an election to be held before the constitution was enacted. The motion was defeated easily. The brief debate that followed, though, inspired Macdonald

---

analyst, wrote in *The English Constitution* (published in 1867) that while "the masses in England are not fit for elective government," because too little educated, "the idea is roughly realized in the North American colonies."

* O'Halloran's speech is quoted in that excellent source book *Canada's Founding Debates*, edited by Janet Ajzenstat. One chapter, "Direct Democracy: Pro and Con," contains an extended analysis of both sides of the argument. O'Halloran himself suffered one serious handicap as an advocate of democracy: he had been educated at the University of Vermont and had served in the U.S. Army, all of which put him under severe suspicion.

to muster his most extended and considered arguments to justify parliamentary supremacy over the will of the people.

The only way to determine the people's will on a single issue would be to hold a referendum, declared Macdonald. In a letter to a supporter, Saumel Amsden, he argued that a referendum would be "unconstitutional and anti-British"; anyway, "submission of the complicated details to the Country is an obvious absurdity." In the Parliament, he based his argument on the nature of Parliament itself. "We in this house" he told the members, "are representatives of the people, not mere delegates, and to pass such a law would be robbing ourselves of the character of representatives." The idea itself was dangerous, because "a despot, an absolute monarch" could use referendums to win public approval "for the laws necessary to support a continuation of his usurpation." The strength of Macdonald's feelings came through in his unaccustomed eloquence: "If the members of this house do not represent the country—all its interest, classes and communities—it never has been represented. If we represent the people of Canada . . . then we are here to pass laws for the peace, welfare and good government of the country. . . . If we do not represent the people of Canada, we have no right to be here."* Macdonald genuinely believed what he was saying; as a desirable bonus, his argument ensured that the Quebec Resolutions would be approved as quickly as possible.†

---

* Macdonald used the phrase "peace, welfare and good government" rather than the now familiar "peace, order and good government." See Chapter 22 for a fuller explanation of this iconic phrase.

† Macdonald—predictably—could switch his arguments against democracy to suit his political convenience. In one letter he denounced constituency nominating conventions as "immoral and democratic," but then went on to advise his preferred candidate that "if a respectable and influential body of delegates is likely to be called together, you must exert every energy to have your friends chosen."

One other factor may have influenced Macdonald's arguments against democracy: he knew that referendums produce losers as well as winners, and that turning some people into losers always comes at a cost. Macdonald had anticipated this point in the speech he delivered at the beginning of the conference in Quebec City. The effect of the constitution, he told the delegates, would be to create "a strong and lasting government under which we can work out our constitutional liberty as opposed to democracy, and be able to protect the minority by having a powerful central government. . . . The people of every section must feel they are protected." One of the constitution's purposes would be specifically to protect minorities—religious, ethnic and linguistic. Here Macdonald was feeling his way towards the thoroughly modern and pre-eminently Canadian concept that democracy must balance its own defining rule—the will of the majority—with the needs, and the rights, of minorities.

Contemporary sensibilities are still bruised by Macdonald's exclusion of Canadians from any say in making their own constitution. If he had included them, though, it might not have made that decisive a difference. Then, no more than 15 per cent of adults in Canada had the vote. And the turnout might well have been low. A systematic search of Macdonald's correspondence during the key years of 1864 and 1865 reveals how few letters he sent out expressing his views about and arguments for the constitution. The explanation is disconcerting: he wrote few letters about the constitution because he received very few asking for his thoughts. The truth is that at the same time they were excluded from constitution making, Canadians willingly excluded themselves. Moreover, there was always the risk that a referendum might indeed have made a decisive difference: Confederation might well have lost.

Macdonald's main speech, two hours in length, given on February 6, wasn't one of his best. He was tired, suffering an illness of some kind that was caused or exacerbated by heavy drinking. Anyway, he had said everything many times before. He declared that he had always favoured a legislative union—"the best, the cheapest, the most vigorous, and the strongest system of government we could adopt"—but accepted that a federation of some kind was needed to protect "the individuality of Lower Canada." In addition, both of the Maritime provinces now committed to Confederation were not prepared to "lose their individuality as separate political organizations."

He did broach one fresh topic of potentially great importance. Some Canadians, Macdonald noted, opposed Confederation out of fear that "it is an advance towards independence." He himself had no such concern; he did, though, expect the transatlantic relationship to change. "The colonies are now in a transition state. Gradually a different colonial system is being developed— and it will become[,] year by year, less a case of dependence on our part, and of overruling protection on the part of the Mother Country, and more a case of healthy and cordial alliance. Instead of looking on us as a merely dependent colony, England will have in us a friendly nation to stand by her in North America in peace or in war."

Among all the speakers in the six-week debate, no one identified the dilemma inherent in Canada's ongoing relationship with Britain with more devastating accuracy than Christopher Dunkin.* Small and whip-smart—perhaps too smart for his own

---

* As noted earlier, Dunkin predicted that the constant cry of the provinces would be "Give, give, give." On defence, he commented with equal acuity, "The best thing Canada can do is to keep quiet and give no cause for war." Dunkin joined Macdonald's cabinet in 1869.

good, because he generated more bright ideas than his hearers could absorb—Dunkin asked rhetorically, "What are we doing? Creating a new nationality, according to the advocates of this scheme. I hardly know whether we are to take the phrase as ironical or not. It is a reminder that, in fact, we have no sort of nationality at all about us. . . . Unlike the people of the United States, we are to have no foreign relations at all to look after . . . therefore, our new nationality, if we could create it, could be nothing but a name." Cruelly, but unanswerably, Dunkin commented, "Half a dozen colonies federated are but a federated colony after all."

In response to the contradiction identified by Dunkin—of creating a nation that would have no nationality—Cartier did his best, very possibly, since he was no intellectual, by repeating ideas suggested to him by Macdonald. "When we were united together, if union were attained, we would form a political nationality, with which neither the national origin nor the religion of any individual would interfere," said Cartier. Some complained that Canada was too diverse, but, he continued, "the idea of unity of races was utopian—it was impossible. Distinctions of this kind would always exist. Dissimilarity in fact appeared to be the order of the physical world, of the moral world, as well as in the political world." Britain itself was composed of several nations. Likewise in Canada, the English, French, Irish and Scots would each, by their "efforts and success[,] increase the prosperity and glory of the new confederacy." In his rough way, Cartier was talking about a nation whose unity would be its diversity.

Cartier's principal purpose was to mollify Quebecers' anxieties about a "new nationality." Nevertheless, his comments were one of perhaps only two genuinely original insights to emerge during the prolonged debate. The other insight has almost vanished from the history books, but it merits being revived. Its author,

Alexander Mackenzie, that worthy but dull rawboned Scot, later a Liberal prime minister, commented in the midst of an otherwise routine speech, "I do not think the federal system is necessarily a weak one, but it is a system which requires a large degree of intelligence and political knowledge on the part of the people."

As the days passed, it became clear that those opposed to the scheme, principally the *rouges*, had nothing to suggest in its place. A mood of inevitability took hold. At times, there were only twenty members in the chamber. In the description of the *Stratford Beacon*, the House had deteriorated to "an unmistakably seedy condition, having as it was positively declared, eaten the saloon keeper clean out, drunk him entirely out, and got all the fitful naps of sleep that the benches along the passages could be made to yield."

The vote on the main motion was called at last, at 4:30 a.m. on Saturday, March 11, 1865. The result was 99 to 33. The Nays included nineteen French Canadians—a half-dozen fewer than those who had voted six weeks earlier for Dorion's motion opposing a "new nationality."

Except for the legislatures in New Brunswick and Nova Scotia, Confederation was now a done deal.

Four weeks later, the long agony south of the border ended when General Robert E. Lee called on Lieutenant General Ulysses S. Grant at Appomattox Court House, Virginia, bringing with him the signed surrender of the Army of Northern Virginia. Thereafter, the North began demobilizing its vast armies with remarkable speed. Fear of an invasion northwards receded rapidly, in Canada as well as in Britain. In Macdonald's judgment, either the huge Northern armies, "full of fight," would invade almost immediately or, if not, "we may look for peace for a series of years."

One substantive concern did remain. Among those soon to be released from the Northern armies were tens of thousands of Irishmen, all now trained in the arts of war. A new word entered the Canadian political vocabulary—*Fenian* (from the Fenian Brotherhood, originally created in 1858 for the purpose of liberating Ireland). Macdonald charged his intelligence chief, Gilbert McMicken, to keep a close eye for any possible cross-border raids. He took seriously the declarations by Fenian leaders that one effective way to deliver a blow at Britain would be to attack the lightly guarded Canada. "The movement must not be despised," he wrote to Monck. "I shall spare no expense in watching them."

Before the Confederation Debates ended, other news—this time deeply discouraging—reached Macdonald. It came from New Brunswick's small capital of Fredericton. The result of a provincial election there, even though not yet completed, was almost certainly going to be the defeat of Premier Leonard Tilley's pro-Confederation government. Shortly afterwards, Nova Scotia's premier, Charles Tupper, sent word to Macdonald that support for Confederation was slipping fast there.

Patching these pieces back together now became Macdonald's principal mission. It would remain so for far longer than he, or anyone, imagined.

TWENTY

The Administration
of Strangers

~

[Take a Nova Scotian to Ottawa], where he cannot view
the Atlantic, smell salt water or see the sail of
a ship, and the man will pine and die.
Joseph Howe, Nova Scotia anti-Confederate leader

The news from New Brunswick, once it had been handed over to Macdonald from the telegraph office, was far worse than the initial reports. Premier Leonard Tilley had not merely lost the government; he had lost his own seat. His party had not just been defeated but trounced, winning fourteen seats against the twenty-seven captured by the incoming anti-Confederation premier, Albert James Smith. Even if Nova Scotia could be kept on side—Charles Tupper by now was thoroughly gloomy—there would be no continuous chain of provinces extending out to the Atlantic. With such a gap in its middle, Confederation would be all but unattainable; without it, Britain and the United States would have no reason to believe that Canadians possessed the will to be a nation.

In the House, Macdonald accepted without argument the choice that New Brunswickers had made; the result, he admitted, represented a "declaration against the policy of Confederation."

In contrast to D'Arcy McGee, who claimed that American money had determined the outcome, Macdonald made only a glancing reference to that possibility. He remained defiant, though, rejecting "any signs of weakness, any signs of receding on this question," and telling Tupper, "there was nothing left for us but the bold game." To one alarmed supporter he counselled, "stick with the ship until she rights." He was particularly concerned that George Brown might use the setback to argue once again for his "mini-federation," applying only to the United Province of Canada. Macdonald was able to forestall that. In private, though, he let his frustration show, telling a Prince Edward Island supporter that Tilley had been "unstatesmanlike" to allow an election to happen without first putting the Confederation scheme to his legislature to ensure that "the subject had been fairly discussed and its merits understood."

Nova Scotia premier Charles Tupper. He was the only Father of Confederation with a university education (Edinburgh, in medicine). He was bold and blustery, an even stronger advocate of a centralized Confederation than Macdonald.

By the end of March, he was already planning a counterattack. "We will endeavour to convince the Catholic Bishop of the benefits to be derived from Confederation," he told Tupper, while he himself would arrange "to get the communication you speak of from the Orange Grand Lodge to the same body, in New Brunswick." These tactics were premature, though. The news soon got bleaker. On April 10, 1865, Tupper informed his legislature in Halifax that "under existing circumstances, an immediate Union of the British North American Colonies has become impractical." He stopped trying to bring the issue to a vote. Inevitably, anti-Confederates in Canada itself joined in. *Rouge* leader Antoine-Aimé Dorion declared triumphantly, "This scheme is killed. I repeat that it is killed." And a new player now came onto the stage. He was Joseph Howe, a former Nova Scotia premier and easily its most exceptional politician of the century. He was also the strongest anti-Confederate that Macdonald would ever face.

Howe was the third of the three Maritime politicians who were by now becoming familiar names to newspaper readers across the country. The others were Tupper and Tilley. Since both men would have long terms in post-Confederation Ottawa, a snapshot of each will suffice for now. Tupper was a medical doctor—ebullient, bombastic, bold. He practically challenged observers to employ purple ink while describing him, as in "broad-shouldered, self-contained, as vigorous-looking as Wellington's charger" and "oratorical and obstetrical"—these latter words by Lord Rosebery, the son of a British prime minister. Tupper was not just pro-Confederate but an ultra Confederate: he outdid even Macdonald in his advocacy of a full legislative union with minimalist provinces, rather than merely the kind of centralized confederation Macdonald aspired to. Tilley was a druggist, and a most successful one. Never popular because of a self-righteous streak, particularly as a

New Brunswick premier Leonard Tilley. He led the fight for Confederation in his province, and for a time lost it.

Joseph Howe, the anti-Confederate leader in Nova Scotia. He was the one "anti" to propose a serious alternative. The odds were against him and he lost, but Macdonald later praised him as "the most seminal mind" he had met.

prohibitionist, he was widely respected for his intelligence and integrity. It's because of Tilley that for a long time, as we shall see, our title was that of a dominion. Between them, Tupper and Tilley began the tradition of the Maritimes exporting its political talent to Ottawa.

Of all the men who fought against Confederation, and so against Macdonald, Howe was the one Macdonald respected the most. Years later, he told his secretary Joseph Pope that Howe possessed "the most seminal mind" he had ever met. Yet Howe was the tragic figure of Confederation. He opposed it, and lost. The true source of his pain, though, was that he lost his faith in Britain. His father, John Howe, who had been living in the United States at the time of the rebellion by the American colonies, had been the only member of his family to come north as a Loyalist. He passed on this almost mystical attitude towards Britain to his son.

Self-educated, Howe edited a journal, the *Novascotian*, which was way ahead of its time in calling for such grand notions as "more of rational freedom" and, as early as 1838, for a union of the British American colonies. Howe sent letters to the colonial secretary suggesting how best to reform the Empire, into a sort of super-confederation of Britain and its colonies strikingly similar to the concept developed decades later as Imperial Federation. Elected to the legislature, Howe took up the cause of Responsible

Government and played a major role in its attainment in 1848, a few months ahead of the United Province of Canada. He became premier, a post he lost to Tupper, regained and then lost again to Tupper in 1860. Short of money, he accepted a minor patronage post as a fisheries commissioner. In 1864 he gave a fiery speech to the touring group of Canadian businessmen and journalists organized by McGee, calling for a sea-to-sea union; the alternative, he said, was to "live and die in insignificance."

Then, in January 1865, Howe burst out as a fully fledged anti-Confederate. He wrote eleven long articles, the "Botheration Letters," which played a substantial part in stoking Nova Scotian fears of what Confederation might bring. Disappointment at his own career was a factor: when his poorly paid patronage job came to an end, Howe would face virtual penury at the age of sixty. Jealousy of Tupper, who had forced him out of politics, was also a factor; invited to be a Nova Scotia delegate to the Charlottetown Conference, Howe refused, saying he wouldn't "play second-fiddle to that damn'd Tupper." He assumed that the conclave would fail, then watched from the sidelines as Confederation took off—and Tupper with it. Howe's core reason for opposing Confederation was his love of country—far less for Nova Scotia than for Britain. As he wrote, "I am a dear lover of old England, and to save her would blow up Nova Scotia into the air or scuttle her like an old ship."

He opposed Confederation so fiercely because he feared it would tug Canada, and so Nova Scotia, away from the mother country. He talked more often about Britain than about his own province, as in his speech in Yarmouth in May 1866: "You go down to the sea in ships, and a flag of old renown floats above them, and the Consuls and Ministers of the Empire are prompt to protect your property, and your sons in every part of the world." And, in another speech, "London [was] large enough—

London, the financial centre of the world, the nursing mother of universal enterprise, the home of the arts, the seat of Empire, the fountainhead of civilization." Who could think of giving all that up for a capital in Canada's backwoods "with an Indian name and any quantity of wilderness and ice in the rear of it"?

When Howe did talk to Nova Scotians about themselves, it was about their past. To take any Nova Scotian to Ottawa, "away from tidewater . . . where he cannot view the Atlantic, smell salt water or see the sail of a ship, and the man will pine and die." Rule by Canada, he said, would be "the administration of strangers." And he simply didn't believe that so polyglot and divided a country as Canada could possibly work: "The builders of Babel were only a little more ambitious than these Canadian politicians."

Howe's interventions made a difference. But the prime source of Maritimers' hostility to Confederation was something quite different and almost unresolvable. This was that they were so distant from Canada and so near, relatively, to Britain. In his speech in Halifax after the Charlottetown Conference, Macdonald had said, jokingly, that Canada was almost as far from the Maritimes as from Australia. (Later, Howe remarked, entirely correctly, that the Maritimes were no nearer to Canada than was Britain to Austria, across half of Europe.) Less than 3 per cent of Canada's exports went to the Maritimes, and the return flow was even smaller. A letter from Halifax took as long to reach Ottawa as it did to cross the Atlantic to Liverpool. There were no Canada–Maritime rail or road connections; just the St. Lawrence River, and it only in summer. Few Canadians had any commercial or personal reasons to make the laborious journey; nor, in reverse, did Maritimers. The *Acadian Recorder* of Halifax summed it all up: "We don't know each other. We have no facilities or resources to mingle with each other. We are shut off from each other by a wilderness, geographically, commercially, politically and socially.

We always cross the United States to shake hands." By contrast, any Maritimer could travel to England in one of the steamships that now made the voyage in as little as ten days.

Differences in self-perception widened the physical distance. The Maritime provinces were small: 350,000 inhabitants in Nova Scotia, 250,000 in New Brunswick, 80,000 in Prince Edward Island. But they were already mini-nations. Just as in the United Province of Canada, they had Responsible Government. In politics, they were ahead in some respects: New Brunswick had the secret ballot, and Nova Scotia had experimented with universal suffrage. It was the Maritimers who, at Charlottetown and Quebec City, had taken the innovative step of including opposition members in their delegations.

Maritimers felt themselves superior to Canada, looking dubiously on its jumble of immigrants and its disturbing qualities of dynamism and brashness—an almost mirror image of the way Canadians viewed the United States.* They were, in other words, defensively superior. British North America's first real theatre had opened in Halifax in 1787, and its first literary periodical began there twelve years later. The Royal Navy, with its base in Halifax, gave the small city a distinct social life. Confederation, if it happened, would bring the Maritimes no new gifts except the Intercolonial Railway, which would create short-term jobs but over time bring new competition for the small and inefficient local business class. Tupper warned Macdonald that "a great body of the trading men comprising the most wealthy merchants" opposed Confederation.

Just as critical, all three Maritime provinces were booming, due chiefly to Reciprocity with the United States and the demand

---

* Howe himself on one occasion argued that "deadly weapons, so common in the streets of Montreal, are rarely carried in Nova Scotia, except in pursuit of game."

created by the Civil War. These, too, were the great days of the sailing ship: one in three ships entering Boston Harbor started out from Nova Scotia. That Maritimers were living on borrowed time was not yet realized, with the steam engine, the screw propeller and the iron hull all soon to turn even the finest wood and sail ships into museum pieces. Why risk any of this prosperity, they argued, for what Howe called "this crazy Confederacy with a mongrel crew, half-English, half-French"? Why give up John Bull for Jack Frost?

There was a good reason to make such a switch, one that Howe undoubtedly realized as it became the principal cause of his anger and his anguish. John Bull was showing clear signs of wanting to get rid of the Maritimes by thrusting them into the arms of Jack Frost. Confederation would enable Britain to distance itself from Canada, most certainly so militarily. Of lesser consequence, yet still useful, Confederation would enable Britain to rid itself of the Maritimes—except for the vital Halifax base, which was considered as important to the Empire as Gibraltar or Malta.

As Howe would have been the first to understand, and so have wanted to rage against the dying of the light, the Maritimes in the end had nowhere to go other than into a union with Canada. Alone, they would be lost. The only alternative was Maritime Union, something New Brunswick and Prince Edward Island feared even more than union with "mongrel" Canada. Ottawa, unlike Halifax, was at least not next door.

The Maritimers who struggled against Confederation were major contributors to their own defeat. They failed to unite themselves, so they never spoke with a single, magnified voice. They trusted Britain. They failed to do their homework until it was too late. At the Quebec Conference, Brown wrote dismissively that "we hear much talkee-talkee" from the Maritimers, "but not very much administrative ability." And they deluded themselves that they could outfox Macdonald.

Before Macdonald appears back on stage, it's necessary to describe the scenery against which this particular act unfolded. This backdrop was not something physical but a force far more substantial—a psychological attitude that had hardened into an utter conviction.

⌒

During the twenty-first century, Canadians have come to define themselves by their tolerance—a quality now accepted almost universally as the feature that makes us a distinct people. The acceptance of difference—indeed, its outright celebration—has gained a talismanic power among contemporary Canadians. To be tolerant is to be a Canadian. To be intolerant is not just to be personally racist or exclusionary, but to possess the attribute of someone who is not a real member of the Canadian community.

The equivalent talismanic virtue in nineteenth-century Canada was loyalty. To be disloyal, even to doubt the centrality of the importance of loyalty, was to be something less than a full Canadian. Expressions of disloyalty divided the community and threatened its identity. Loyalty distinguished the nation from its neighbour even more definitively than tolerance does today. Canada was loyal; the United States was disloyal, or had been when it rebelled. No other cross-border differences needed to be identified or constructed.[*]

---

[*] Over time, as may be only a coincidence, there has been a displacement of one nationally unifying virtue by the other. In the nineteenth century, there was little tolerance in Canada—hence the sectarianism and open religious hatreds. Today, there is little loyalty to institutions, from marriage to employers.

The object of Canadians' loyalty was Britain, the Empire, the Crown, personified so alluringly by Queen Victoria. Even more so, Britain was exemplified by such institutions as the parliamentary system and the judicial system, and by British values of fair play, a stiff upper lip and a man's words being his bond, no matter whether they were for real or just for boasting.

Loyalty wasn't only about being British. Loyalty was a cardinal virtue—its near kin being fidelity—and extended to loyalty to family, to the marriage vows (there were incomparably fewer divorces in Canada than in the United States), to friends, to tribe or clan or community, and to religion (Canadians who exchanged one faith for another faith were called "perverts"). As the educator Egerton Ryerson put it, "it is a reverence for, and attachment to, the laws, order, institutions and freedom of the country."

Being loyal was seen as synonymous with being God-fearing. Ryerson observed that if "a man does not love the King, he cannot love God." And the Reverend J.W.D. Gray informed his parishioners that the "spirit of *submission to lawful authority* . . . lies at the foundation of your loyalty to your earthly Sovereign."

The potency of the ethic of loyalty, conjoining as it did an earthly sovereign with a heavenly one and with the rule of law, was overwhelming. It made Canadians not just proud to be who they were (and not to be Americans) but ebulliently, braggartly proud. There was not the least shyness about Canadians' loyalty. Flags were waved, songs were sung and public figures competed in their expressions of devotion to Crown and Queen. Canadians in the mid-nineteenth century may well have been more patriotic than were Americans, but to the mother country rather than to their own country. Macdonald, the great loyalist, heightened the stakes, and advanced his partisan cause, by accusing his opponents of "treason."

It all began with the Loyalists. There were only about fifty thousand of them, but their spirit defined Upper Canada, Nova Scotia, New Brunswick and Prince Edward Island, and the far larger number of British immigrants who followed took over the torch from them. That torch was the Loyalist Myth—the chronicles of their suffering and sacrifice for the sake of their loyalty to the Crown. It was much embellished, as all national foundational myths always are. In his book *The Sense of Power*, historian Carl Berger makes two perceptive points. One is that "nationalistic history was just as much an instrument for survival for the British-Canadian Loyalists as it was for the French-Canadians." The other is that the Loyalists brought with them not so much British institutions as "its inner spirit"—assumptions such as "the primacy of the community over individual selfishness, society conceived as an organism of functionally related parts . . . religion as the mortar of the social order, and the distrust of materialism." The British connection has long vanished, but it takes only a short dig down to the sedimentary layer once occupied by the Loyalists to locate the sources of a great many contemporary Canadian convictions and conventions.

Perhaps the most eloquent expression of the force of loyalty in Canada among English Canadians was made by a British Columbia Legislature member, T.L. Wood, in a debate about possible entry into Confederation. "The bond of union between Canada and the other provinces bears no resemblance to the union between England and her colonial possessions," Wood said. "There is not natural love and feeling of loyalty. The feeling of loyalty towards England is a blind feeling, instinctive, strong, born with us and impossible to shake off."

If the loyalty of English Canadians was so potent and deeply rooted because it was instinctual, that among Canadiens was as strong, even if unemotional, precisely because it was self-interested and calculated. Cartier summed it up during the Confederation Debates when he said that the reason the Canadiens "had their institutions, their language and their religion intact today, was because of their adherence to the British Crown." Back in 1846 Étienne-Paschal Taché had famously proclaimed that "the last cannon which is shot on this continent in defence of Great Britain will be fired by the hand of a French Canadian." Here resided the magical, however paradoxical, effect of the creed of loyalty among Canadians: being loyal to another nation and to an absent monarch kept Canadians loyal to each other.

Macdonald, to return to the theme of this book, was not merely a loyalist: he embodied it in his very person. In his 1883 biography of Macdonald, the journalist J.E. Collins wrote that "more than any other Canadian statesman . . . [he] taught us the duty of loyalty." In his lifelong battle to keep Canada un-American, Macdonald's most potent instrument was Canadians' loyalty to Britain. No less valuable was the particular nature of his own loyalty to Britain.

His was fiercely loyal, of course; but there was no deference in his posture. Macdonald was exactly the kind of colonial, or foreigner, who could break through English reserve and snobbery simply because there was not a trace of colonial cringe about him. As the journalist Nicholas Flood Davin, himself a British immigrant, observed, Macdonald was "the type of politician who has never failed to delight the English people—the man who, like Palmerston, can work hard, do strong things, hold his purpose, never lose sight for a moment of the honour and welfare of his country, and yet crack his joke and have his laugh. . . . There is nothing viewy about Sir John Macdonald." In short, whenever in Britain, Macdonald regarded himself as an equal, and he was accepted as one.

Only when the British Empire began to fade and fall apart did loyalty lose its magnetic appeal to Canadians; thereafter, as was incomparably more challenging, Canadians had to find reasons to be loyal to themselves.

In the task of turning around public opinion in the Maritimes, loyalty constituted Macdonald's secret weapon. In Nova Scotia, loyalty to Britain, beginning with that of the tortured Joseph Howe, was even deeper than in Canada. In New Brunswick, attitudes were more ambiguous. After an 1864 visit there, the editor of the Kingston *British American* wrote, "They are more American [than Canadians]—more democratic in their tastes—have more of the 'free' swagger in their manners . . . more flash-dressed ladies at Theatres and Concerts."

What Macdonald now had to do was make certain that Maritimers understood what it was that Britain wanted of them—to join Canada. This, therefore, is what he proceeded to do.

TWENTY-ONE

The Turn of the Screw

⌒

The left arm is then extended a little, and the Queen laid her
hand upon it which I touched slightly with my lips.
Alexander Tilloch Galt, describing his presentation to the Queen

S ometime in the spring of 1865, Macdonald figured out
how to haul the Maritime provinces onto the side of
Confederation. He would appeal to their sentiments
about Britain. To do that, a Fathers of Confederation
mission would call upon the Great White Mother.

No real reason existed for Macdonald and the other Canadian
leaders to go over to London. In the legislature, Macdonald
described the group's purpose as "to take stock . . . with the
British Government"—about as vague a description as he could
concoct. For a time Macdonald even protested that he was too
busy to go. This excuse was blatantly untrue, because he was due
to go to Oxford to collect his treasured honorary degree. But once
Macdonald had committed himself to the trip, a doubting Brown
agreed to go along as well. The actual topics to be discussed while
they were in London were not easy to compile: the Imperial government had already made clear its wholehearted support for
Confederation, and although there were defence matters to go

over—the Canadian government had just voted one million dollars for new defence works—no one in London had the least interest in provoking the United States by new military projects. Nevertheless, off went the Big Four—first Cartier and Galt in a ship that made a stopover in Halifax, giving them time for discussions on railway matters there, and then Macdonald and Brown shortly afterwards on a different vessel. The real purpose of their mission was to use the Imperial government to get the Maritimers to turn around and face in the right direction.

The softening process has already begun. The colonial secretary, Edward Cardwell, after his meeting with Brown the previous December, had dispatched to Canada the laudatory memorandum on Confederation that had so pleased his visitor. Still more useful was the covering note attached by Cardwell to the copies he sent to the Maritime lieutenant-governors. "Our official dispatch," he wrote to Arthur Gordon in New Brunswick, "will show you that Her Majesty's Government wish you to give the whole [Confederation] scheme all the support and assistance in your power." Britain's general policy, he explained, was "to turn the screw as hard as will be useful, but not harder." Two discrete turns of the screw were then applied. Gordon was reminded that his career depended on his shepherding New Brunswickers towards voting for Confederation. His counterpart in Nova Scotia, Sir Richard MacDonnell, who had made no secret of his opposition to Confederation, was pulled out completely and sent to Hong Kong. He was replaced by a soldier hero, Sir William Fenwick Williams, who knew how to take orders. Less successfully, Prince Edward Islanders were warned that the bill for the salary of their lieutenant-governor might be transferred from London to Charlottetown, but this pressure made them only more truculent than they already were.

For the Big Four, the reception in London was at least as agreeable as had been the earlier one for Brown alone. The Colonial Office chose the moment of Macdonald's arrival to send word to the Maritime capitals that Maritime Union was no longer discussible; all that was left on the Maritimes' negotiating table, therefore, was Confederation.

The quartet did have diligent discussions with the appropriate British politicians on matters such as defence, Confederation, the prospects for Canada's renewing the Reciprocity Treaty with the United States and the future of the Hudson's Bay Company and the North-West. At the only meeting that actually mattered, none of these topics was raised. That was the meeting with Her Majesty.

On May 18 the four went excitedly to Buckingham Palace in a carriage that picked them up at the Westminster Palace Hotel. On arriving, they discovered, to their mixed pride and terror, that Queen Victoria had asked for them to be presented first. "Dukes and Duchesses had to give way and open up a passage to us," Brown reported to Anne. The procedure that followed was a trifle more complicated: it involved, as Galt described it to his wife, going "down on the right knee (a matter involving, in my own case, a slight mental doubt as to the tenacity of my breeches), the left arm is then extended a little, and the Queen laid her hand upon it which I touched slightly with my lips." That ordeal completed, the quartet was kept together so the Queen could engage them in small talk, including an exchange with Cartier in French. Then she glided away.

Back across the Atlantic went a report that amounted to a command: Her Majesty and her Canadian ministers were as one.

Earlier, the four had spent little time at the Westminster Palace Hotel, because night after night they were out dining at

Queen Victoria. The last British monarch with real political influence, she used it to give Confederation the push it needed to overcome Maritime opposition.

the mansions of dukes and lords and cabinet ministers and railway magnates, or they went to balls where coiffed, bare-shouldered ladies exhibited a remarkable interest in the details of Canadian politics, economics and culture. No less deeply interested in Canadian doings was the Prince of Wales. He had them over to dinner at Buckingham Palace, drew them into an inside room filled with a specially selected group of one hundred of the two thousand guests, and while chatting with them smoked cigars and showed off his new Turkish dressing gown. (In an exercise in re-gifting, Galt was given one of these cigars, which earlier had been presented to the prince by the King of Portugal.) Less interested in the Canadians and in Canada was Bishop Wilberforce, who, as Brown reported to Anne, asked "whether Darwin believed that 'turnips are tending to become men.'"

They also went to the Epsom Downs on Derby Day, taking with them a hamper of food and wine from Fortnum and Mason. The *Times*'s famed war correspondent from the Crimean War, William Russell, took them around, getting them into one of the most socially fashionable of tents, where they sipped turtle soup and champagne cup. They took in the races (Macdonald won twenty guineas) and gazed, as Galt reported to his wife, at "the sights of the course, gypsies, music, mountebanks, games of all kinds, menageries of savage animals, and shows of Irishmen disguised as savage Indians." On the jam-packed road driving back, they used the roof of their carriage as a mobile platform from which to fire dried peas through a peashooter at passersby, who, as was customary, fired back balls of flour. Brown and Macdonald also went together to the opera *Lucrezia Borgia*.

That was it. Official replies to their queries about specifics such as defence were exasperatingly vague. There was one significant shift in their own attitudes, though. The people they had met, Brown reported home, "are a different race from us, different ideas, different aspirations, and however well it may be to see what the thing is like, it takes no hold on your feelings, or even of your respect." Galt was more easily impressed, writing back, "We were treated as if we were ambassadors and not as *mere Colonists*," yet even he added warily, "it bodes no good no matter how flattering it may be."

Three of the four returned home on June 17. Macdonald stayed a week longer to go up to Oxford for his honorary degree of Doctor of Common Law. "This is the greatest honour they can confer, and is much sought after by the first men," Macdonald reported in delight to his sister Louisa. He made it back to Canada early in July.

~

While little or nothing specific had been accomplished, things could hardly have gone better. Before the Canadians left, Cardwell gave Governor General Monck the green light to employ "every proper means of influence to carry into effect without delay the proposed confederation." Above all, Confederation had been given de facto Royal Assent.

The Confederation project now resumed its forward motion, if still creakily. A shift in Maritime public opinion began. To help it along, Cardwell began to dangle before the Maritimers the possibility of improvements in the terms agreed to in the Quebec Resolutions. Those most attracted by this bait were the Maritime Roman Catholic bishops, who set out to secure guarantees for their separate schools.

On closer scrutiny, Confederation's election defeat in New Brunswick turned out to be less crushing than it had first seemed. The Saint John *Telegraph* calculated that the vote had been 15,979 for the anti-Confederate Smith against 15,556 for Tilley. A key by-election was due that fall. To help New Brunswickers make the right judgment about what to do, Tilley wrote to Macdonald, estimating first that victory would require "an expenditure of 8 or ten thousand dollars," and then asking, "Is there any chance of the friends in Canada providing half the expenditure?" On the back of this letter, Macdonald scribbled to Galt, "Read this. What about the monies?" Later, Charles Brydges of the Grand Trunk Railway reassured Macdonald that he had "sent the needful to Tilley" and had "kept all our names here off the document." Down went Canadian money; in came the votes for the pro-Confederate candidate.* By the fall, New Brunswick's Lieutenant-Governor Gordon was able to brag to London, "I am convinced I can make (or buy) a union majority in the Legislature."

A new problem had arisen. On July 30 Étienne-Paschal Taché died, sending Macdonald his last poignant note: "J'aimerais à vous voir encore une fois avant le long voyage que je vais bientôt

---

* Brown very generously contributed five hundred dollars to the by-election fund and wrote, "[I] will not be behind if further aid is required."

entreprendre." The day after Taché's funeral, Monck asked Macdonald, as the most senior of the quartet, to head the ministry. Brown, when called in to see Monck, would have none of it; while denying he had any "personal aspirations whatever," he pointed out that his own Reformers were twice as numerous as Macdonald's Conservatives. He and Macdonald then met one on one. They reached no meeting of minds, despite an offer by Macdonald to step down for Cartier. Given that those two were joined politically at the hip, Brown naturally rejected it. Eventually they reached a compromise: the new premier would be an anonymous, long-serving Canadien, Sir Narcisse-Fortunat Belleau. He was sworn in on August 7.

Then came another complication. Brown, always quick to identify a slight, had already complained that Macdonald had given Galt public precedence over him. He also harboured suspicions—justified, no doubt—that Macdonald and Cartier were dispensing patronage that ought to have been his to allocate. From that point on, Brown refused to speak to Macdonald, dealing only with Cartier.

The malaise continued. A mid-summer government statement on Confederation made to the legislature in August had nothing new to say. Macdonald himself was often absent, supposedly on doctor's orders, but in fact because he was drinking heavily.

Yet while Macdonald was drinking far too much at the worst possible time, his antennae remained as alert as ever. In July a large conference was held in Detroit, organized by the Detroit Chamber of Commerce, to discuss and if possible reverse Washington's decision to end the Reciprocity Treaty with Canada in the spring of 1866. No fewer than five hundred American businessmen attended, as well as fifty Canadians, all worried deeply by the impending loss of cross-border trade.

During the meeting the American consul general in Montreal, J. R. Potter, chose to declare in his speech that the entire problem could be resolved by the United States annexing Canada. News of this extraordinary behaviour by the principal representative of the U.S. Government in Canada took time to reach Ottawa. Macdonald invented an occasion for himself to deliver a speech in Ottawa (press releases didn't exist then), and on September 28 gave his reply in a way that revealed a great deal about his personal feelings on Canada's future in North America. First he talked about Confederation, actually a bit optimistically: "The union of all the Provinces is a fixed fact." Then he talked about himself: "The mere struggle for office and fight for position—the difference between the 'outs' and 'ins' have no charms for me," he said, "but now I have something worth fighting for—and that is the junction of Her Majesty's subjects in all British North America as one great nation." Macdonald knew fully what his own leitmotif was.

As fully, Macdonald now knew precisely what he was doing for himself. The month before, in a letter to Monck on June 26, 1866, he described Confederation as "an event which will make us historical." He then added, almost as if warning Brown to stay out of his way, "—not with my will would another person take my position in completing the scheme for which I have worked so earnestly."

As was now inevitable, relations between Macdonald and Brown went from bad to worse. In November, Brown took umbrage at Galt's having been sent alone to Washington to try (unsuccessfully) to negotiate an extension of the Reciprocity Treaty. Macdonald got Galt to explain that his mission had been unofficial and that, on a second trip, a Reform minister would accompany him.

A parting could no longer be prevented. On December 17 Brown sent in his resignation. Afterwards, he wrote to Anne, "Thank Providence—I am a free man once more." Macdonald got Galt "*without fail* to prepare at once" an account of what had happened between him and Brown so he could show it to the other Reform ministers, in the hope that he could convince them to stay rather than leave with Brown. The tactic worked: there were no other defections from the Great Coalition, and a third Reformer took Brown's place in the government.

The long, intensely personal duel between Brown and Macdonald had reached its end. The clash of personalities made their parting inevitable, as did the fact that their objectives were fundamentally at odds. Brown wanted a "mini-federation" within just the United Province of Canada, to separate the French and the English. He had exulted at the end of the Quebec Conference that French-Canadianism had been extinguished and was delighted when he heard in the spring of 1865 that New Brunswick's pro-Confederation government had been defeated in the election. This result, he wrote to Anne, "is a very serious matter for the Maritime provinces, but magnificent for us." Macdonald's purpose, by contrast, was a transcontinental nation, with Confederation as its essential first building block, one based on a pact of trust between French and English. Brown's last comments about Confederation before it actually happened, during a debate in the legislature in the summer of 1866, showed how distant he was from Macdonald. There, Brown condemned as "a most inconvenient and inexpedient device" any attempt to use the constitution "to bind down a majority . . . to protect a minority"; rather, he argued, the majority should be left free "to act according to their sense of what is right and just."

Nevertheless, Brown fully deserved McGee's encomium to him for having displayed "moral courage" in bringing his followers with him into the Great Coalition government that would bring about Confederation. While many of his political views were narrow, Brown was an exceptional public figure. There was even an expansiveness to his later explanation for quitting: "I want to be free to write of men and things without control. . . . Party leadership and the conducting of a great journal do not harmonize." Most certainly he deserved from Macdonald a great deal more than the crabbed, ungracious compliment he later paid him: "[Brown] deserves the credit of joining with me; he and his party gave me that assistance in Parliament that enabled us to carry. confederation."

From this point on, the tide began to turn decisively. Through the winter, New Brunswick's Premier Smith and his government progressively lost their way. By the spring of 1866 he had been pushed back so far onto the defensive that the Throne Speech actually contained a description of Confederation as "an object much to be desired." Not long afterwards, his government was defeated in the House and an election called. At that instant, there appeared exactly the political reinforcements that Macdonald most needed: the Fenians appeared on New Brunswick's borders.

In fact, Canada-U.S. relations had improved considerably by this time, if for the worst of all possible reasons. The previous April, just one week after Lee's surrender at Appomattox Court House, President Lincoln had been assassinated while attending a play at

Ford's Theater in Washington. Unanimously, Canadian politicians and the press recognized that a giant had been struck down, and they mourned the loss to the United States as well as to the world. The day after, the Toronto *Globe* appeared with its front page bordered in black; Toronto sent two municipal representatives to attend the funeral, and during the two hours that the service was being held, church bells throughout the country pealed unceasingly while ships in the ports of British North America lowered their flags to half-mast. The most moving and the most deeply grieving services for Lincoln were those held in the small wooden churches of Canadian blacks.

At the same time, the rapid demobilization of the North's armies provided relief from the threat of a possible invasion. Just one lingering cause for alarm remained: demobbed soldiers had been allowed to buy back their rifles for six dollars; noticeably, many of those doing so had been Irish Americans. Macdonald was kept well briefed about the Fenians' doings by his intelligence chief, Gilbert McMicken. At least as much, he was kept well briefed by the Fenians themselves. They were talkative, boastful, combative (with each other) and, while brave soldiers individually, hopeless as an organized force. They did have one good marching song: "Many battles have been won / Along with the boys in blue / And we'll go and capture Canada / For we've nothing else to do."

As St. Patrick's Day, March 17, 1866, approached, nervousness mounted in Canada. Some ten thousand militia men were mobilized. Nothing happened. Then on April 7, the streets of the Maine seaport of Portland were suddenly crowded with Irishmen, most carrying revolvers and with long knives in their belts; they went on to the town of Eastport to hold a "convention." Their objective was the island of Campobello, New Brunswick. Two British warships hastily sailed from Halifax, followed by two troopships from Malta. Soon there was a mini Royal Navy fleet off the Maine coast, together with some five thousand British and New Brunswick militia soldiers. The Fenians straggled out of Eastport, leaving behind unpaid hotel bills and around fifteen hundred rifles. Actual action was limited to one boatload of Fenians who made it to an offshore Canadian island and burned down a customs warehouse.

That the Fenian raid had been a fiasco didn't change its consequences but only multiplied them. Canada had been threatened. Britain had fulfilled its obligation to rush to its aid. Most disturbingly, American authorities had allowed the invasion to be attempted from its territory (no Fenian was ever charged afterwards for violating the neutrality laws). Everything that had happened reinforced the argument that Confederation was essential to national security.* Governor General Monck sent home the word that the militia's performance had ended forever the accusation so often hurled at the North American colonies of "helplessness, inertness and dependence." Indeed, the Fenian expedition had been so counterproductive that some people speculated that Macdonald had stage-managed the entire affair with McGee's help.† Not a scrap of evidence suggests that was so. There was, though, something ominous. One of McMicken's detectives reported he had been told that "one thousand dollars is offered in gold to anyone that will bring in D'Arcy McGee's head."

For the time being, Macdonald could not have asked for more than he already had. In Nova Scotia, Tupper was able finally to get the Legislative Assembly to approve a pro-Confederation resolution, which cleverly asked not for approval of Confederation but only for

---

* The militia's adjutant general, Colonel Patrick MacDougall, later wrote that the Fenians had functioned as "invaluable, though involuntary, benefactors of Canada" by giving its people "a proud consciousness of strength."

† The Fenian who had actually proposed the raid was accused of being a Canadian agent and expelled from the movement.

Nova Scotia delegates to take part in negotiations that could "effectually assure just provision for the rights and interests of Nova Scotia."*

A month later, Tilley won the New Brunswick election, winning even more decisively—33 seats to 8—than had his anti-Confederate opponent the previous year. One factor was the support of the Roman Catholic bishops. But money talked even more loudly than did the faith. In June Tilley had written to Macdonald, "Telegraph me in cipher saying what we can rely on. . . . It will require some $40,000 or $50,000 to do the work in all our counties." A few days later, he wrote again, even more urgently, "To be frank with you, the election in this Province can be made certain if the *means* are used." He suggested that the exchange of cash be made outside the province, in Portland, Maine. Monck then got into the act, telegraphing Macdonald: "I think it is very desirable that he [Galt] should undertake the journey to Portland." In counterpoint, Galt wrote to Macdonald, saying, "That *means* had better be used—I think we *must* put it through," adding that he would go to Portland together with Brydges in order to meet with Tilley and consummate the exchange. The use of the "means" did achieve its end. This exercise, undertaken for the higher cause of Confederation and one fully approved by a governor general of the highest probity, introduced Macdonald to the art of extracting election campaign funds from a large railway company.[†]

---

* Anti-Confederates argued that a referendum should be held before any final commitment to Confederation was made, but Tupper retorted that the same legislature had approved negotiations to create a Maritime Union—with no provision for a referendum.

† New Brunswick's Governor Gordon, as so often, summed up the electoral chicanery perfectly: "Confederation has hardly any friends here, but it will be carried by large majorities nonetheless."

Review Extra.

Fenians are coming

(BY TELEGRAPH.)

PORT COLBORNE,
JUNE 1, 1866.—3.30 p. m.

Refugees from Fort Erie report the burning of a Bridge 4 miles back of Fort Erie by
the Fenians.

They have possession of Taylor's Heights,
one mile and a half below Fort Erie, near a
place called Waterloo, and the highest land
in the vicinity. They have commenced
throwing up earthworks there, and have
struck towards Brantford road. This you
can rely on.

There were reports this morning about the
capturing of Port Sarnia and Welland Canal.

FROM COBOURG.

The following telegram was received by
Capt. Poole from Brigade-Major Patterson
at Cobourg this afternoon :—

"All the Companies in my District are to
assemble at Cobourg at once. Tell Captains
Kennedy and Rogers, and send word to
Capt. Leigh, Lakefield.

ALEX. PATTERSON,
Brigade-Major."

Cobourg, June 1, 1866.

*The Fenians decisively helped Confederation. As
American Irish trying to end British rule in
Ireland, they invaded Canada—and so reminded
Canadians of the threat to them from the south.*

The Fenians had not yet completed their contribution to Confederation. On June 1, one of McMicken's
detectives sent an urgent telegram
from Welland: "1,500 Fenians landed
at Fort Erie." Inaccurate in some
details, it was correct in substance.
About half that number of Fenians,
many wearing Union or Confederate
uniforms, had been ferried across the
Niagara River led by a capable officer, John O'Neill. Canadian authorities, made complacent by the earlier
fiascos, were slow to respond.
O'Neill's men occupied Fort Erie and
cut the telegraph wires. A clash with
the Canadian militia took place at
the village of Ridgeway, in Welland
County. The ill-trained militia were
overwhelmed, suffering nine killed
and thirty-eight wounded. Another
clash with militia units outside Fort
Erie ended in a second victory for
O'Neill's Fenians. None of the prom-
ised reinforcements from the United States arrived, though, so
O'Neill ferried his troops back across the Niagara River. The U.S.
authorities persuaded them to "abandon [their] expedition
against Canada" in exchange for free transportation to their
homes. The *Globe* proclaimed, "The autonomy of British
America, its independence of all control save that to which its
people willingly submit, is cemented by the blood shed in the
battle." To intensify Canadians' anger, and to magnify their sense

of aggrieved nationalism, three of the militia men killed had been teenaged students from the University of Toronto. Never again would Macdonald treat a threat of Fenian invasion as probable comedy.

~

With approval now from both New Brunswick and Nova Scotia, with Canadians having just shown they were ready to fight for their country and, far from least, with the Imperial government having committed itself to guarantee five million pounds in loans for the Intercolonial Railway, Confederation stretched out ahead like a broad, flat highway.

A bump soon appeared. In London, the government of Lord John Russell went down to defeat on its key Reform Bill. The new prime minister, Lord Derby, would have to replace Cardwell, by now an authority on the Confederation file. The new colonial secretary was announced as Lord Carnarvon, just thirty-six years old, but, as was unusual, happy to have the post because he was a strong believer in the Empire. Carnarvon moved quickly. By July 21 a complete British North America Bill had been drafted in London, and it merely awaited the arrival of the Canadian and Maritime delegates to agree on its details before the document would be submitted to the Westminster Parliament.*

Then came another bump, and a considerably larger one. The Maritimers arrived in London as planned, at the end of July 1866,

---

* This first version of the BNA Act contained only twenty-two clauses and, unlike the Quebec Resolutions and the final act, did not specify the powers of the central government, relying instead on its general enabling power to make laws for "the peace, order and good government."

but neither Macdonald nor any Canadians appeared.

One of the lesser mysteries of the Confederation chronicle resides in Macdonald's failure to exploit the momentum built up by the middle of 1866 to rush a British North America Act through the British Parliament by that fall. There were some technical considerations. The constitutions for the soon-to-be created provinces of Quebec and Ontario had yet to be approved by the Canadian legislature. Also, Macdonald was convinced that the government needed first to lower Canadian tariffs to ease Maritime fears about high taxation before the climactic negotiations began. The new Derby government was weak, though, and the longer the delay, the greater the risk that the political crisis absorbing the British Parliament would halt Confederation's progress and give its critics a chance to regroup.

Macdonald remained gripped in his inertia. He ignored a June 17 warning from Tupper reminding him that an election in Nova Scotia—of which the outcome was far from certain— had by law to be held before May of the next year, 1867. Tupper pleaded, "We *must* obtain action during the present session of the Imperial Parliament or all may be lost." Governor General Monck was at least as anxious. To get Macdonald moving, he sent him a stinging letter on June 21. In it, he bluntly told Macdonald that "valuable time is being lost and a great opportunity in the temper and disposition of the House is being thrown away by the adoption of this system of delay." Monck then showed the mailed fist inside his habitually well-padded glove: "I have come to the delicate conviction that if from my cause this session of Parliament should be allowed to pass without the completion of our portion of the Union scheme . . . that my sense of duty to the people of Canada myself would leave me no alternative except to apply for my immediate recall." A bit disingenuously, he added that he

wasn't mentioning his possible resignation "by way of threat."

Macdonald's reply, one day later,
began by saying that Monck's letter
had "distressed" him greatly. Thereafter, he conceded nothing. "The proceedings have arrived at the stage
that success is certain and it is now
not a question of strategy. It is merely
one of tactic," he wrote. This tactic
involved picking "the proper moment
for projecting the local scheme [the
provincial constitutions]." Macdonald
then showed his own mailed fist:
"With respect to the best mode of
guiding the measure through the
House, I think I must ask Your
Excellency to leave somewhat to my

*Governor General Monck. He and Macdonald
had their disagreements, but they worked well
together, making sure that Tilley had enough
money to win the key election in New
Brunswick for Confederation.*

Canadian Parliamentary experience." The fist having been shown,
Macdonald offered a conciliatory hand: Monck must not resign
because "to you belongs . . . all the kudos and all the position (not
to be lightly thrown away) which must result from being a founder
of a nation." After that delicate reminder of the relationship
between Monck's prospects for future Imperial employment and
the achievement of Confederation, Macdonald ended jauntily, as he
so often did, "My lame finger makes me write rather indistinctly. I
hope you can read this note."

Monck's reply, written the day he received Macdonald's letter,
was almost as deft. While he accepted without question "your
right as a leader of the Government to take your own line," he
nevertheless reserved the right to advise Macdonald against "a
course of conduct which I consider injudicious." He retained his

right to resign should Macdonald continue to "hang back now when all other parties to the matter are prepared to move on." Thereafter, Macdonald moved no faster than before, but some of the tensions each felt had been released. And their relationship remained as cordial as ever, even surviving Macdonald's spectacular misdemeanour of so losing control during one visit to the governor general's residence as to vomit over a newly upholstered chair Lady Monck had installed in her drawing room.*

A major cause of Macdonald's shilly-shallying was the most obvious. He was drinking more heavily, more continually than he had ever done before, at times having to grip his desk so he could remain standing in the House. Tiredness and stress made him vulnerable. So did D'Arcy McGee. Night after night they caroused together at Ottawa's Russell Hotel. After one such binge, while Macdonald managed to make it back to his room, McGee wandered off into the night and was found the next morning curled up on the desk of the editor of the *Ottawa Citizen*. Cabinet finally addressed the matter, one minister calling the behaviour of the pair a "disgrace." In response, Macdonald sought out McGee and informed him, "Look here McGee, this Cabinet can't afford two drunkards, and I'm not quitting."

Both continued to drink heavily. On August 6, Brown, now an ordinary member, reported to Anne that "John A. was drunk on Friday and Saturday, and unable to attend the House. Is it not disgraceful?" The *Globe* went into attack mode: Macdonald had not been sober for ten successive days and was unfit for his duties as minister of militia. In fact, it was not until the legisla-

---

* This crashing fall from grace is reported in the biography by Elisabeth Batt, *Monck: Governor General, 1861–1868*. She hedges her bets by saying that although this story is told by Monck's descendants, it should be remembered that "the Irish were ever loath to spoil a good story for lack of a ha-porth' of exaggeration."

ture had adjourned in September that he began to regain control over his drinking. He was able to handle a mini-crisis caused by Galt's resignation from the cabinet after he failed to win his long-sought guarantees for Protestant education in Quebec. After shuffling the ministry, Macdonald still persuaded Galt to come to London as one of Canada's constitutional delegates. In the meantime, though, McGee in particular continued to drink heavily.

That Confederation was now so close yet still remained vulnerable was undoubtedly a major cause of Macdonald's prolonged drinking. But cool calculation may also have influenced his behaviour. As people kept blaming Macdonald for his misdeeds, they paid less attention to the fact that time was indeed slipping steadily by. And that is precisely what Macdonald wanted to happen.[*] His objective was to shrink to a bare minimum the span of time between the moment when the Confederation delegates finally agreed on a revised constitution and the actual introduction of the document into the British Parliament. The longer the gap between those two events, the greater the risk that Confederation critics would learn of any last-minute changes to the original Quebec Resolutions and demand a reopening of the entire debate on the grounds that Canada's Legislative Assembly had approved a different version of Confederation.[†] Macdonald explained his stratagem to Tilley in a letter on October 6: "The Bill should not be finally settled until just before the meeting of

---

[*] An apt description of what Macdonald was doing would be "ragging the puck," except that hockey was then so new that the phrase had yet to be minted.

[†] In fact, the *Globe* got hold of a summary of the BNA Bill and published it in late February 1867, fiercely attacking the shifts in jurisdiction to favour Ottawa and the increase in subsidies to the Maritimes. By that time, though, it was all too little, too late.

the British Parliament"; the measure had to be "carried *per saltum*—with a rush. No echo of it must reverberate through the British provinces until it becomes law." Premature disclosure could "excite new and fierce agitation on this side of the Atlantic." But, he promised, "the Act once passed and beyond remede, the people will soon be reconciled to it."

Not until the end of November 1866 did the Canadians finally make it to London. They—Macdonald, Cartier, Galt, Hector-Louis Langevin (a rising Quebec *bleu*) and two Reform ministers, William McDougall and William Howland—all stayed at the now-familiar Westminster Palace Hotel, looking out on Westminster Abbey and with the Houses of Parliament across the road.* Already ensconced there were the two five-member Maritime delegations, headed by Tupper and Tilley. In getting them to join this final, climactic phase of a project that by now had been going on for more than two years, Macdonald and the Fenians had played critical roles. For the Maritimes, though, the decisive force had been that of Britain—far less by its "turn[ing] of the screw" than by the irresistible pull of loyalty. In the end, what caused Maritimers to come in was their realization that in order to remain British, they had to become Canadians.

---

* One of the particular attractions of the Westminster Palace Hotel was that it had been equipped with that new technological marvel, an elevator.

TWENTY-TWO

The Man of the Conference

I had a merry Xmas alone in my own room and my
dinner of tea & toasts & drank all your healths.
John A. Macdonald, in a letter to Louisa

The last of the three Confederation conferences began on December 4, 1866, at London's Westminster Palace Hotel, in an elongated ground-floor room used most of the time for lectures and concerts. The delegates' first order of business was to elect Macdonald as chairman. It was his performance here that prompted Sir Frederic Rogers, the senior Colonial Office mandarin, to describe him as "the ruling genius." Hector-Louis Langevin, the senior Canadien after Cartier, sketched out a similar judgment in a letter to his brother: "Macdonald is a sharp fox. He is a very well informed man, ingratiating, clever and very popular. He is *the man* of the conference."

The conference's second item of business was to keep anti-Confederate critics in a state of sullen ignorance by making sure that everything done inside the room stayed there. At Macdonald's urging, the delegates agreed that "no minutes of the various discussions should be taken, and no record, therefore,

The London Conference was the last of the three conferences that drew up the constitution. The Canadians and the Maritimers were quartered at the grand Westminster Palace Hotel—so grand that it had an elevator.

exists of them."* Macdonald also urged the new colonial secretary, Lord Carnarvon, to "avoid any publicity being given to the resolutions," since this might "tend to premature discussion on imperfect information of the subject both in this country and America." A key reason for this manoeuvring was that Joseph Howe had come over to London and was telling everyone he could persuade to meet him that the project should be halted and that Macdonald was a helpless drunkard. Howe himself, though, was now a forlorn figure. The Halifax *Morning Chronicle* dismissed him as "vanity struck," and he even described himself as "lonely, weary and vexed." He was simply being shunted aside.

Until the conference began, Macdonald used his time to get briefed on the latest twists and turns in British politics caused by

---

* Hewitt Bernard did keep some scanty minutes.

the looming crisis over the Reform Bill and to catch up on news at the Colonial Office. He also got to know the colonial secretary. Despite the gap in their ages, they shared a mutual enthusiasm for the Empire and, from this point on, remained lifelong friends. Carnarvon, while fully briefed about Macdonald's "notorious vice," and angered that Macdonald was "occasionally so drunk as to be incapable of official business for days altogether," yet judged him "the ablest politician in Upper Canada" and reckoned that, without him, the entire Coalition would collapse.

In fact, Macdonald succumbed spectacularly to his "vice" on at least one occasion in London. On December 27 he reported to Louisa that "for fear that an alarming story may reach you, I may as well tell you what occurred." He had come back from a weekend at Lord Carnarvon's country house, took the newspapers to his bed to read, fell asleep and awoke to discover his "bed, bed clothes & curtains all on fire." Macdonald tore down the curtains, dousing them with water, then tore the "blazing" sheets and blankets from the bed and stomped out the flames. With Cartier's help, he made certain that the flames were entirely out. Only then did Macdonald realize that his "hair, forehead & hands [were] scorched." But for wearing a thick flannel shirt under his nightshirt, "I would have been burned to death."* A bad wound on Macdonald's shoulder caused the doctor to order him to bed for three days, and he had to stay on in the hotel for an extra eight days. He ended his note jauntily: "I had a merry Xmas alone in my own room and my dinner of tea & toasts & drank all your healths."

---

* Macdonald was wearing so many garments in bed simply because British buildings in those days were heated only by open fires, windows were single paned and doors gaped.

From the start of the conference, Macdonald's objectives were clear. He wanted the work done as quickly as possible to minimize the risk that a defeat of Lord Derby's government on the Reform Bill would force an election and so delay Confederation's passage beyond the May deadline, when Nova Scotia had to go to the polls. If that happened, there was a distinct possibility that Tupper would be defeated, bringing down with him the entire Confederation project. Indeed, to delay the constitution's passage until after May was the specific reason for Howe's presence in London. No less urgently, Macdonald wanted as few changes as possible to the already agreed upon Quebec Resolutions: each change could lead to others being demanded, and to the potential unravelling of the entire package.

Debate itself could not be avoided. Unlike Canada's Legislative Assembly, neither the Nova Scotia nor the New Brunswick legislatures had approved the Quebec Resolutions; their delegates' mandate was to secure improvements, and only then to sanction Confederation's go-ahead. To negotiate around those obstacles, adroitness was required. Tupper initiated a debate about just how binding were the Quebec Resolutions. Delegates argued both sides of the question. At the right moment, Macdonald pulled them together by declaring that both were right, but within definite limits: "We are quite free to discuss points as if they were open," he said, "although we may be bound to adhere to the Quebec scheme." Macdonald thereby managed to quiet restive Maritimers while keeping any actual amendments to a minimum.

A number of changes were made. Immigration and agriculture were redesignated as joint responsibilities of both levels of government; coastal fisheries and penitentiaries were added to Ottawa's list; and the solemnization of marriages was given to the care of the provinces. There was a long debate about whether, and how, additional senators might be created to resolve a deadlock between Parliament's two houses, the Senate and the Commons.* The Maritimes won for themselves an increase in their subsidies from Ottawa, although Tupper, probably from overconfidence, gained far less for Nova Scotia than the less-showy Tilley did for New Brunswick. "Confederation" was agreed on as the official term rather than "federation," but confusingly the term used throughout the resulting act was "union." The names agreed on for the two Canadian provinces were Quebec and Toronto, the latter being changed later to Ontario.

The single substantive change was to strengthen—a little—Ottawa's role as defender of the educational rights of minorities across the country. This correction came about at the insistence of Galt on behalf of the English minority in Quebec, supported by Archbishop Connolly of Halifax, who lobbied on behalf of his separate schools. The change was small: the federal government was granted the power to intervene in educational matters, but only on occasions when there was a need for "remedial laws." Even this limited authority applied only to school systems already in place before Confederation.

All this work was done in a couple of weeks; indeed, twenty-nine of the Quebec Resolutions were dealt with on the first day. Revised clauses were hurried over to the legal draftsmen at the Colonial Office. There, the chief draftsman, F.S. Reilly, complained at one time, "I can't make bricks without clay, to say nothing of straw."

One change that might have greatly altered Canadian history never happened. A year earlier, when Confederation had seemed

---

* The British authorities insisted on adding a provision authorizing the cabinet to appoint extra senators under exceptional circumstances. This power was first used by Prime Minister Brian Mulroney in 1990 to secure passage of the Goods and Services' Tax Bill through a Liberal-dominated Senate.

Inside this room at the hotel, the delegates settled the last clauses of the British North America Act. A top British official described Macdonald as "the ruling genius."

imminent, a legal draftsman at Westminster, Henry Thring, had drawn up draft legislation by which Canada could opt to become independent from Britain at any time by a two-thirds' vote in both the Commons and Senate. At around the same time, a British politician, Lord Bury, who had served in Canada as an aide to the governor general, proposed that an agreement be negotiated that would allow either Canada or Britain to terminate the colonial connection by its government giving a year's notice. So far as can be determined, this possibility was never discussed at the London Conference. Macdonald would very likely have vetoed it, because of his own attachment to Britain and out of concern that it might provoke a backlash in Canada against Confederation. Indeed, Howe at this time was reporting to Nova Scotia anti-Confederates his dismay at "the almost universal feeling . . . that *uniting the provinces was an easy mode of getting rid of them.*" In fact, Canada's status as a colony would not be ended— legally—until the Statute of Westminster in 1931. Had the constitution included from its start an agreed way to achieve independence, it's more likely that the leap to national maturity would have been taken a lot earlier.

The most significant change was one made to prevent another change from happening. All along, Macdonald had intended that the new nation should be called the Kingdom of Canada.* In one speech during the 1865 Confederation Debates, he had gone further, suggesting that the Queen should be represented in the new nation by "one of her own family, a Royal prince, as a Viceroy to rule over us." (The Queen, as it turned out, had been musing similarly about how "dearest Albert had often thought of the Colonies for our sons.")† At one stage during the London Conference, Macdonald tried out alternative titles, writing in the margin of a handwritten draft of the bill: "Province, Dependency, Colony, Dominion, Vice-Royalty, Kingdom." This last title was used in all the drafts of the constitution sent by the delegates to the Colonial Office until early February.‡

---

* Feo Monck, in her diary about the 1864 Quebec Conference, recalled Macdonald telling her teasingly that the new nation might be called "Canadin" and, as might well have actually happened, that "in some speeches he had said that, to please the Nova Scotians, it should be called 'Acadia.'" She concluded, "John A. is very agreeable."

† At the time, it was widely assumed that the likeliest sibling to be sent to rule Canada as its King was the third son, Prince Arthur. He did in fact make it, although in a lesser role. In 1911, Prince Arthur, by then the Duke of Connaught, was appointed governor general, serving until 1916. He died in 1942, at the age of ninety-one.

‡ Quite different, though, was the first draft of the British North America Bill as sent from the Colonial Office to the delegates at the Westminster Palace Hotel. To the fury of the Canadians, this version used the word "colony" throughout, declaring that the provinces were to be "united into one colony." The offending word was struck out and never used again.

Just before the bill's final version—there were seven drafts in all—the nation's title was changed to the Dominion of Canada.* It was done by Prime Minister Lord Derby on the advice of Carnarvon,† who feared that Americans would interpret monarchical nomenclature as a deliberate provocation. There were, in fact, grounds for this worry: the British minister at Washington reported that newspaper speculation that Canada might become a kingdom had provoked "much comment of an unfriendly character." Macdonald never forgot or forgave this dismissal of his dream. In 1889 he wrote to the then colonial secretary, Lord Knutsford, recounting that he had once described to Disraeli what had happened, and that Disraeli's response had been, "It is so like Derby—a very good fellow but who lives in a region of perpetual funk."

The well-known story about "dominion" is that its author was Tilley, who informed the conference delegates that he had come upon in the Bible, in Psalm 72, verse 8, the evocative phrase, "And he shall have dominion also from sea to sea." This account is certainly correct.‡ The full story may have been a bit more complicated. The use of the term "dominion" for such a purpose was

---

* A problem with the chosen title, "Dominion," overlooked by the London Conference delegates, was that no ready translation for the term exists in French. The one most often used, "La Puissance," is hardly satisfactory.

† Carnarvon reached this judgment despite Monck's counter-argument that "Kingdom" would meet "the natural yearning of a growing people to emerge . . . from the provincial phase of existence."

‡ Tilley's authorship was confirmed by his son, also called Leonard, in a letter he wrote on June 28, 1917, on the eve of Confederation's half-century, to the High Court registrar in Toronto. He recounted that his father had told him how he came upon the phrase in his daily Bible reading, and, "When he went back to the sitting of the convention that morning," he had suggested the title, "which was agreed to."

not in fact new. It was applied to the brief confederation of American colonies, known as the Dominion of New England, which lasted from 1686 to 1689. As well, Virginia, until it became a state, was known as "The Old Dominion."

All these details were marginalia. The central fact was that Confederation had been agreed to by all the constituent provinces. The later "compact" theory, that Confederation constituted a treaty negotiated by the provinces, was pure myth; none of them, as colonies, had the power to sign treaties. Lord Carnarvon, on behalf of the enabling power, Britain, explained in his parliamentary speech that the new dominion "derives its political existence from an external authority"—namely, the Imperial government.

The constitution itself, as Macdonald had wanted from the start, amounted to a prescription for a highly centralized confederation, very likely the most centralized confederation ever conceived (not least because it granted to the central government the power to disallow provincial legislation). Indeed, as the historian Peter Waite has written, "One might almost say that Canada has become a federal state in spite of its constitution."* It was indeed plausible, as Macdonald kept saying in private letters, that the provinces might wither away to municipalities.

The fact was, though, the provinces *did* exist. They were accountable to their voters through political mechanisms—of organized parties, elections and parliamentary debates—identical to those of the "senior" government. They were also, as

---

* Waite included this sentence in his 1953 doctoral thesis, "Ideas and Politics in British North America, 1864–66."

was inherent in so vast a country, incomparably closer to their people. As Macdonald had schemed for all along, the federal government was accorded not just extensive powers but all the unassigned powers, and as well a national override power. Yet although the newcomers, Nova Scotia and New Brunswick, lost some of their existing powers on joining Confederation, they still wielded considerable ones. The two reborn "internal" members, Quebec and Ontario, gained powers greater than their institutional ancestors had ever possessed (if only because, back then, all power resided with the governors general).

Macdonald, moreover, failed to anticipate the consequence to his centralized scheme of the absence from federal jurisdiction of one vital power. Post-Confederation, just as before, Canada was still only a colony; responsibility for foreign affairs remained in London. Ottawa, unlike Washington, could not summon up national support on the grounds that it was responsible for Canadians' doings and reputation in the wider world. In the absence of any shared sense of national identity across the country (really, until the 1960s), the vacuum was bound to be filled by provincial identities. This flaw in Macdonald's concept of the new nation was recognized by Goldwin Smith in an almost eerily perceptive article for *Macmillan's Magazine* in March 1865. There he wrote that while "the sentiment of provincial independence among the several provinces of British North America is at this moment merged in the desire of combining against the common danger [the United States] . . . [w]hen the danger is overpast, divergent interests may reappear and the sentiment of independence may revive . . . especially in the French and Catholic province." It was because national identity was pallid for so long that provincial identities commanded so much support.

In no sense was the British North America Act a constitution made for the people. There was nowhere in it any ringing "We, the people" proclamation. It was, instead, a constitution made for governments. Over the decades, the balance between centralization and decentralization of governmental powers has settled down into pretty much what most Canadians want. Pragmatism has triumphed over principle, and muddling through over theory. Macdonald would disagree with the resulting decentralization, but as a pragmatist and as a believer that politics is about people, he would be delighted by the process.

Today, just one part of the British North America Act—now the Constitution Act, 1867—is familiar to any number of Canadians. It is widely known that the Fathers of Confederation defined their new nation by the talismanic mantra of "Peace, Order and good Government." It is also widely known that this self-description contrasts radically with the idealistic but aggressive aspiration laid upon Americans by their constitutional call to "life, liberty and the pursuit of happiness." In fact, this phrase occurs not in the constitution of the American people but in their Declaration of Independence. But it's the contrast between these two rallying cries, and the illumination it provides about national differences, that matter.

Except that most of this is untrue. More exactly, it is true symbolically, but untrue substantively.

The phrase actually contained in the documents laid before the delegates at the Quebec Conference of 1864 (from which came the greatest part of the BNA Act), and at the start of the Confederation Debates in the Canadian Parliament in 1865 and at the London Conference, was "Peace, Welfare and good Government." The second, unfamiliar, term, "Welfare," was used here in the sense of well-being. It was only at the last moment before the constitution was introduced into the Parliament at Westminster that "Welfare" was replaced by "Order."* The actual change was most probably made by the British legal draftsman Francis Reilly; and no evidence exists that Reilly ever discussed his choice of words with Macdonald or with any Canadian.

To get to the heart of the matter, no evidence exists that at any time throughout any of the three Confederation conferences, or during the long debate in the Canadian legislature, anyone paid the least attention to the phrase itself. The more than one thousand double-columned pages of the published Confederation Debates contain only a handful of references to "Peace, Welfare and good Government" (as it then was); moreover, it was raised almost always in discussions about the narrow issue of marriages and divorces.†

The reason why no one paid any attention to the phrase was straightforward: it actually meant very little. It amounted to a kind of legal boilerplate that was inserted routinely into all kinds of British colonial constitutions—from Newfoundland to New Zealand to New South Wales, from Ceylon to the Cape Colony (of South Africa), from Sierra Leone to St. Helena. The use of this

---

* Not until January 23, 1867, does the familiar "Peace, Order and good Government" triad appear in a draft. This version reappears in the later drafts of January 30 and February 2 and then in the actual BNA Act.

† One of the very few substantial references during the entire Confederation process to the phrase "Peace, Order and good Government" was made not by any Father of Confederation but by its godfather, Colonial Secretary Lord Carnarvon. In his speech in the Lords introducing the British North America Bill, he said that the powers of the federal government "extend to all laws made for the 'peace, order and good government' of Confederation"—a term he described as having "an ample measure of legislative authority."

The author has been able to find only one early use of "peace and order" in its contemporary descriptive sense. The anti-Confederate Howe once described

phrase can be dated all the way back to 1689.[*] It appeared in every Canadian constitution before Confederation, from the Royal Proclamation of 1763[†] to the 1841 Act of Union, which conjoined Upper and Lower Canada. The phrase that Canadians now embrace as distinctively their own was thus employed in the service of just about any entity in the Empire for which a constitution was needed. .

Perhaps the most insightful comment ever made about the ways by which national communities acquire their particular character was from British-born international scholar Benedict Anderson. According to him, almost all of them amount to "imagined communities." Few citizens in any of these societies know many other citizens personally, "yet in the minds of each," wrote Anderson, "lives this image of communion." People, that is to say, become what they are by the way that they think they are.

Not long after the Second World War, Canadians took cognizance of the fact that the British Empire was vanishing from the map and that its role as global hegemon had been taken over by the United States. Canada was threatened by being absorbed into this new imperium, of being reduced to a kind of virtual colony. Cross-border differences therefore became central to national existence itself, because if no differences existed, survival became pointless. In 1961 the historian W.L. Morton published *The Canadian Identity*, a book composed of four major lectures that he had given. In this work, Morton expressed the notion of a rad-

---

the Maritimes as "accustomed to peace and order," in contrast to the belligerent, boastful Canadians. And he made this remark back in 1849.

[*] The phrase's origin is most probably in John Locke's *Two Treatises of Government* of that same year of 1689, where Locke described government's purpose as "the Peace, Security and publick good of the people."

[†] The form used in the Royal Proclamation of 1763, the earliest appearance of the phrase in Canada, was "Public Peace, Welfare, and good Government."

ical difference between Canada and the United States from their very beginnings. "Not life, liberty and the pursuit of happiness," wrote Morton, "but peace, order and good government, are what the national government of Canada guarantees." So far as this author has been able to determine, Morton was the first person to present the concept that the "Peace, Order and good Government" of Macdonald's constitution *is* Canada, in the same way that Jefferson's "Life, liberty and the pursuit of happiness" *is* the United States.

Not long afterwards, "Peace, Order and good Government"—known to Ottawa insiders as POGG—was elevated into a defining national invocation. It has gone on to become the one item of our original constitution that almost every Canadian can recite—and holds to fiercely.*

It's as though, when Canadians learned of the phrase "Peace, Order and good Government" for the first time in the sixties, they, in the mysterious way by which the collective will can exert itself, said more or less simultaneously, "That's us." The constitution's real patriation can thus be dated from the early sixties rather than from its formal enactment in 1982. It was during those years that the people of Canada made the constitution—at the very least one vital part of it—*their* constitution. Maybe it's coincidence, maybe it's karma, but Macdonald, as a conservative, could not have defined the purpose of a constitution better than as "Peace, Order and good Government."†

---

* To appreciate why Morton's insight should have had such a consciousness-raising effect, it should be remembered that right afterwards—in 1965—George Grant published his seminal *Lament for a Nation*, which itself had so powerful an effect among Canadian nationalists.

† Much of the material for this section was provided by the research staff of the Library of Parliament. A number of the facts are drawn from a groundbreaking article by the historian Stephen Eggleston in the *Journal of Canadian Studies*.

At the time, Macdonald won just about everything he wanted. All the last-minute changes made in London strengthened the power of the central government. The federation would indeed be as close to a "legislative union" as was politically practical. These, though, were tactical accomplishments. In themselves, Confederation and the constitution that necessarily accompanied it amounted to not much more than a political fix of a political problem—"deadlock"—that the politicians, Macdonald included, had created themselves. That purpose could have been achieved as easily, almost certainly more so, by a "mini-federation" encompassing just the United Province of Canada. Such a nation, though, would have been a rump of a nation. What was being created instead was, at least potentially, a continental nation—one that would be, or could be, a real nation, marked at its birth by the extravagant ambition both of its geographical reach and of its commitment to British law and British political institutions. As such, it made a commitment to be and to remain that most improbable of all political communities—an un-American nation within North America. First, Macdonald had imagined a Canadian community of this kind; then, in London, he realized it.

All that remained now were details. Howe took his arguments for delay to as many people as he could secure introductions to in Britain. Lord Carnarvon heard him out politely, but without response; almost all the others showed the same indifference. All that remained between Macdonald and his final triumph was a thin red line of British MPs—few of them interested in the colonies at the best of times, and all of them now totally absorbed by the crisis over the Reform Bill and the prospect of an imminent election.

In Macdonald's circumstances—he knew by now he would soon be invited formally to become the first prime minister of the new nation—many would have gloated or at least have celebrated. Instead, Macdonald stayed close to Carnarvon, fussing and worrying over the last details. His one celebratory gesture was to slip over to France for a few days' holiday when things had quieted down.

Once the delegates had finished their last fixes, Francis Reilly, the legal draftsman, worked overtime through the first week of February to render it into proper parliamentary form. The bill was set in type under conditions of strict confidentiality through the nights of February 6 and 7. On February 12 it was introduced into the House of Lords—there, rather than the Commons, because that's where Carnarvon had his seat. The debate was scheduled for February 19, 1867.

TWENTY-THREE

Two Unions

My diaries as Miss Bernard did not need such precautions but then I was an insignificant spinster & what I might write did not matter; now I am a great premier's wife & Lady Macdonald & "Cabinet secrets and mysteries" might drop unwittingly from the nib of my pen.

Lady Macdonald, in the first entry of her new diary, July 5, 1867

In the brief gap between the last few days of haggling over the clauses of the constitution and the document's actual introduction into the Parliament at Westminster in the form of the British North America Bill, Macdonald found time for one other assignment. He got married. His second wife was Susan Agnes Bernard, the sister of Hewitt Bernard, his principal civil service aide, originally his private secretary, and now head of his staff at the Attorney General's Department—and also his friend and apartment mate at the "Quadrilateral," a house on Daly Street in Ottawa.

Their marriage was a union of mutual self-interest. He, now on the verge of becoming prime minister of the Dominion of Canada, would soon need a hostess and a chatelaine. She, by now aged thirty-one, needed to escape a future of ever-diminishing choices. Besides asymmetric needs, they possessed in common one defining quality: each revelled in the exercise of power. Agnes, in the diary that she began right after the first Dominion

Susan Agnes Bernard. She is still five years away from marrying Macdonald, young and slender here, unlike in later photographs. She appears to be wearing a costume.

Day,[*] expressed her addiction the more self-critically: "I also know that my love of Power is strong, so strong that I sometimes dread it; it influences me when I imagine I am influenced by a sense of right." To Macdonald, power was like a comfortable old suit he had no need to apologize for wearing. "I don't care for office for the sake of money, but for the sake of power; for the sake of carrying out my own view of what's best for the country," he once said.

They differed in quite a few respects, from religiosity, of which Agnes possessed an excess, and he little if at all, to her far greater capacity for physicality, as in the epic ride she would take through the tunnels and curves of the Rocky Mountains on the cowcatcher of a Canadian Pacific Railway engine while, most of the time, her grumpy husband, the prime minister, remained rooted in his seat in the special car laid on for them.

The difference between them that defined their relationship was that, while Macdonald respected Agnes, was always polite and considerate, and never deviated in his loyalty, she adored him, if not at the start of their union, which was in no sense a love match, then soon after, and ever after, completely and joyously and defencelessly. Although strong and confident in so

---

[*] Lady Macdonald's diary covers the years 1867 to 1869 with some regularity, but later entries are few and far between. Her diary is the only known one kept by a Canadian prime ministerial spouse.

many respects, as Agnes Bernard most certainly was, at times not merely cajoling him but outright bullying him, and later ruling Ottawa society like a moralizing martinet, she, in her relationship with Macdonald, seemed always to be running to catch up to him while trying never to show how hard she was trying. "I have found something worth living for—living in—my husband's heart and love," she wrote in the diary. Her most revealing comment about herself to herself was "I often look in astonishment at him," referring, surely, both to astonished delight in his almost infinite variety, and even more to her delighted amazement that he should be hers.

Although the marriage was arranged with speed, the courtship between them extended over more than a half-dozen years and may have included an earlier offer of marriage. The original obstacle to any union was, of course, Macdonald's drinking. Bernard would later tell his fellow deputy minister Edmund Meredith that he had done "everything to dissuade his sister from the marriage." To resolve the obstacle, Bernard got Macdonald to sign a marriage contract that committed him to pay sixteen thousand dollars into a trust for Lady Macdonald, thereby protecting her and any children of theirs, but also benefiting Macdonald, since this money could no longer be claimed by his creditors.* To raise the initial funds, Macdonald sold one hundred acres of land in Kingston and deposited his life-insurance policy into the trust. As dowry, Lady Macdonald brought neither money nor looks. A contemporary described her as "tall, tawny, and . . . rather 'raw-boned' and angular."

---

* Marriage contracts of this kind were quite common—most particularly when the woman was bringing property into the union and would immediately lose control over it to her husband—until the passage of the Married Women's Property Act of 1887.

In later photographs, particularly as she became, at one and the same time, stouter and more commanding, she comes across as stern and censorious. In the one early photograph taken before their marriage, she is much slimmer and, if not exactly attractive, wholly agreeable rather than the gorgon she came to be. One photograph of her inclining backwards over a chair conveys not just her physical exuberance but a clear awareness of her own sexuality. (Mid-nineteenth-century photographs showed women to disadvantage: the long period of motionlessness required for the exposure invested men with a portentous gravitas but diminished women's natural animation.) She was highly intelligent, well travelled, well read, accustomed to social situations and fluent in French. Bilingualism, though, didn't cause Agnes to share Macdonald's partiality to French Canadians: "The French seem always wanting everything, and they get everything," she wrote crossly. She was also strong, determined and thoroughly bossy.

She was born in Jamaica in 1836, the only daughter among the four sons of a wealthy sugar-plantation owner, Thomas Bernard.* Following her father's death from cholera, Agnes and her mother moved to England and then, in 1854, to Barrie, Ontario, where her brother Hewitt was practising law. There, just turned twenty, she revealed her fearlessness about physical adventure by ice-fishing and by tobogganing even at night, "tearing down a steep forest roadway and scudding away, breathless, disheveled and nearly shaken to death, over the frozen surface of some lonely pine-fringed lake," as she later portrayed it in a magazine article. Agnes may have been describing here one of her attractions to Macdonald: her physical boldness and athleticism would have

---

* Her ancestry, through her mother, was Scottish.

reassured him that she would not turn into another wifely invalid like Isabella. The decisive influence on her girlhood had surely been her mother, Theodora, a deeply religious woman of demanding and domineering piety. Theodora's death, in 1875, caused the minister who broke the news to a distraught Agnes to "fear for [her] sanity."

In 1858, Hewitt had become Macdonald's secretary, and the future couple—Macdonald by now a newly bereaved widower—had a brief encounter at a concert in Toronto. Agnes's later recollection was acute: "A forcible, yet changeful face, with such a mixture of strength and vivacity, and his bushy, dark peculiar hair as he leaned on his elbows and looked down." Macdonald's recollection had about it a distinct dollop of his "soft sawder": he praised her "very fine eyes," while taking care to avoid getting their colour wrong by not mentioning it. (Agnes's eyes, like her hair, were in fact a striking jet black.)

When the government moved to Quebec City, the Bernards moved with it. They both attended the Valentine's Day Ball that Macdonald organized with such panache in 1860. Some kind of relationship appears to have developed as a result, with Macdonald later calling on Theodora at Hewitt's suggestion that he meet his mother—his unmarried sister being of course the real reason for the arranged encounter. There were rumours of a marriage proposal made but rejected. While Macdonald was by now famous and powerful, besides being charming and witty, he was also a notorious drunk. It's easy to guess that Theodora put her foot down and that Hewitt, despite his loyalty to Macdonald, confirmed the damning reports. Anyway, Macdonald had no pressing need then for a chatelaine and hostess. In 1865 the distaff Bernards moved on to London, where they occupied a grand house on Grosvenor Square. Of life in England, Agnes commented shrewdly that it was "a delicious country for the rich, but I should hate it for the poor," while the middle class had to "toady and fawn."

She and Macdonald met by happenstance, on December 8, 1866, while both were sauntering down Bond Street. However it happened, the relationship developed with lightning speed, much as it had between Macdonald and Isabella. By Christmas they were engaged.

They wed six weeks later, at St. George's Anglican Church in Hanover Square, on February 16, 1867. (It was a most fashionable church. Two British prime ministers were married there, Disraeli and Asquith, and one American president, Theodore Roosevelt). It was all done so quickly that there was no time for reading the banns, for which a special dispensation had to be secured from the Archbishop of Canterbury. For the occasion, Macdonald wore a "Superfine Black Dress Coat with sleeve linings [and] corded silk

Registration record of the February 16, 1867, marriage of John A. Macdonald, "widower," and Susan Agnes Bernard, "spinster," both being of "full" age.

breast facing," as well as a sword. Agnes wore a long dress of white satin and a veil of Brussels lace. The bridesmaids included the daughters of three of the Fathers of Confederation. After the service, Hewitt Bernard hosted a breakfast for ninety at the Westminster Palace Hotel; the *Ottawa Citizen* reported that "a bunch of violets and snow-drops" adorned each plate. In his speech, Macdonald compared his union with Agnes with the one he was on the verge of completing with the provinces. In the marriage register, Macdonald changed his "profession" from that of "cabi-net-maker," as he'd given in Charlottetown. Here, with surely a twinkle in his eye, he listed it as "Hon-ble"—Honourable.*

The happy couple honeymooned in Oxford. Then they returned hurriedly in time to hear the British North America Bill being introduced into the House of Lords.

Agnes and John A. were always husband and wife, rather than partners in the manner of the Disraelis† or of George and Anne Brown. But they connected intimately at two vital points. Macdonald possessed a first-rate mind: he read omnivorously, had an exceptional memory and would quote in the legislature and Parliament from novelists such as Dickens and Trollope, from Shakespeare, and from parliamentary greats such as Pitt and Peel and Sheridan and Walpole. Agnes, similarly, was highly intelli-gent and read at least as much (certainly more novels, often read-ing them while waiting in his office for him at the end of a long

---

* The details about Macdonald's self-designation as "Honourable" and of the other distinguished marriages at St. George's Church were uncovered by the journalist Arthur Milnes on a research trip to London.

† Disraeli once paid his wife, Mary, the highest-possible matrimonial compliment by telling her she was "more a mistress than a wife." At the end of a long day in the Commons, Disraeli returned home to find Mary had stayed up waiting for him with a bottle of cooled champagne and a pork pie from Fortnum and Mason.

day in the Commons). In the provincial Canada of those days, there weren't many like this pair. Agnes provided Macdonald with an opportunity to stretch his intellectual wings beyond the usual politician's fare of government reports and newspapers and campaign anecdotes. She gave him someone he could talk to about ideas and literature, and about such un-Canadian topics as beauty. They were partners as well in another joint enterprise. It took Agnes a long time, it wasn't in the least easy, and there were many setbacks, but because of her care and watchfulness and bullying, Macdonald eventually broke the grip of alcohol on himself. If the biographer E.B. Biggar is right, Agnes may have extended his life by two decades.

Nevertheless, Macdonald for most of the time was a politician, with political jobs to be done. Agnes, for her part, had to set out now to learn the tasks and tricks of being a political wife. One learning experience came quickly. Just over a week after becoming Mrs. John A. Macdonald, Agnes, accompanied by Lady Carnarvon, was presented to the Queen in a general audience at Buckingham Palace. Macdonald afterwards wrote to Louisa, "My wife likes it from its novelty to her, but it rather bores me as I have seen it all before." His indifference was pure posture; Agnes, though, had yet to learn to pretend that she wasn't impressed.

The passage of the British North America Act through the Parliament of Westminster began, in the House of Lords, on February 12. In his speech, Carnarvon laid it on lavishly: "We are laying the foundation of a great State—perhaps one that at a future day may even overshadow this country . . . we have shown neither indifference to their wishes nor jealousy of their aspirations." Macdonald heard it all from the gallery, with Agnes beside him. He was surely reassured by the almost complete absence of any expressions of dissent. But he must also have been worried that the crisis in the government caused by Disraeli's insistence on introducing a new version of the Reform Bill to extend the franchise yet more widely might cause the government's defeat and Parliament's closure for an election. Even if a breakup were avoided, the crisis would make it ever harder for the British parliamentarians to find the time to deal with so minor a matter as a new constitution for an old colony.

On February 26, the British North America Bill slipped through the Lords, despite the appeals of some members that the measure should be temporarily set aside so that Parliament could address "a prospect which affects its own existence"—namely, the Reform Bill. Just one day later, the bill was hurriedly introduced into the Commons.

A brief moment of release from the pressure came Macdonald's way. He and four of the delegates were presented to the Queen in a private audience. Macdonald knelt and kissed the extended hand. As he later wrote to Louisa, "On rising, she said, 'I am very glad to see you on this mission.'" He told her how loyal Canadians were to the Crown: "H.M. said—'It is a very important measure, and you have all exhibited so much loyalty.'" Queen Victoria could influence many things, but not how Parliament did its business.

In the Commons, responsibility for piloting the bill through the chamber fell to the junior minister for the colonies, C.B. Adderley. To head off attempts to amend specific clauses in the bill, he described the measure as "a matter of a most delicate treaty and compact between the Provinces," thereby providing ammunition for generations of Canadian constitutional lawyers.*

---

* Earlier, Carnarvon, for the same purpose of limiting debate, had called the bill "in the nature of a treaty." *The Daily News* commented tartly that it was, in fact, "merely an inter-colonial project."

Criticism came from the Radical John Bright, an ardent advocate of liberating the colonies to look after themselves. As must have delighted Macdonald, Bright gave an indifferent speech and failed to attract any support.

On March 4 the House went into committee to study the details. Almost no changes were asked for or even mentioned. That same day the crisis over the Reform Bill broke: Disraeli had presented to the cabinet his radical scheme for increasing the franchise—the start of his rise to the prime ministership as the champion of an alliance of the aristocracy and the working class against their common enemy, the new middle class. Three Conservative ministers, Carnarvon among them, resigned in protest at this dangerous sally into democracy.

Adderley, though, remained at his post. Suddenly, it was all over. On Friday, March 8, the bill passed third reading without a single word of debate and with the Commons clerk gabbling through the clauses so fast that few MPs could have understood a word of what it was they were voting on. On March 29 the Queen signed Royal Assent.

In fact, it had all happened too easily and too quickly. An anti-Confederate Nova Scotian watching the scene from the gallery wrote home, "The great body of the house was utterly indifferent, even the [Canadian] delegates seemed chagrined at the lazy contempt with which a thin House suffered their bill to pass unnoticed . . . this utter indifference was more mortifying to me than positive opposition. . . . It showed they considered Colonist beings so little related to them as the inhabitants of some nameless Chinese mud village."

Macdonald, in his 1889 letter to the then colonial secretary, Lord Knutsford, looked back with regret and anger: "This remarkable event in the history of the British Empire passed almost without notice." The British politicians had been "quite unable, from the constitution of their minds, to rise to the occasion." Confederation had been treated "much as if the B.N.A. Act were a private Bill uniting two or three English parishes."* Macdonald's rage at the diminution of his and of Canada's historic achievement was understandable, even if allowance is made for the fact that the obsession of the British MPs with the crisis over their Reform Bill was also valid. Of course, being British, the instant the British North America Bill was done with, the MPs switched to debate enthusiastically a bill to reform the system of funding homes for "Destitute Dogs." D'Arcy McGee understood best what had happened: "Everyone knew the result was a foregone conclusion, and they are not apt in England to debate matters already decided."

There were, inevitably, some serious flaws in the constitution that would govern the Canadian Confederation from its birth. No provision was made for amendments to the constitution. The most vital part of any federation, and always its most contentious—the allocation of different powers to the different levels of government—was done quickly and negligently (no thought given to the status of cities, for example), and with scarcely any debate at all. The Aboriginal people were entirely overlooked. Whereas the Royal Proclamation of 1763 had declared that Indians "should not be molested or disturbed" on their historic hunting grounds, no mention of them was made in the British North America Act, except to identify Indians as a subject of federal jurisdiction.

---

* British MPs were famously uninterested in colonial affairs. On one occasion a debate was held in the Commons to determine why this should be so: few attended, and the debate ended inconclusively.

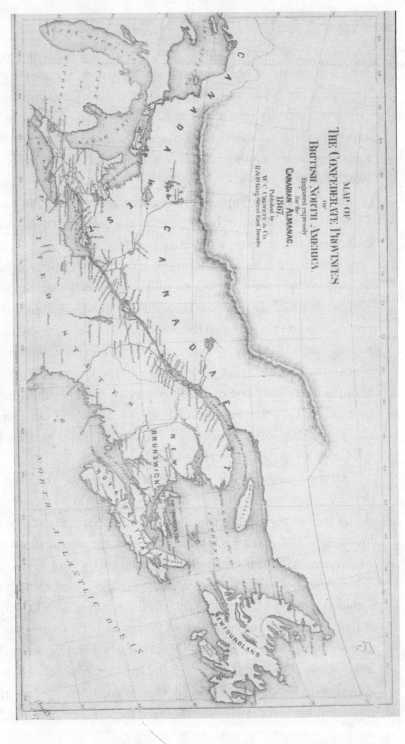

The Canada Macdonald Made

Lastly, two provinces—Prince Edward Island and Newfoundland—remained outside Confederation and so outside its constitution. Typically, the Newfoundlanders said no with a flourish: Confederation was roundly rejected in an election in 1869, with the leading anti-Confederate, Charles Fox Bennett, warning that if they joined, their sons would end up as cannon-fodder, "leaving their bones to bleach in a foreign land."

Still, the act encompassed substantial achievements. It was the first ever constitution to be written by the colonials themselves. It enshrined protection for a minority people, even if only in the limited, permissive form of declaring that the French language "may" be used in Parliament and federal courts. It created a strong central government, and also—not an easy feat to pull off simultaneously—provincial governments with the potential to be strong. It created, or so everyone at the time assumed, a new Canadian common market: Clause 121 provided that "All Articles of the Growth, Produce or Manufacture of any one of the Provinces ... shall be admitted free into each of the other Provinces." It was used later as a blueprint for the 1877 draft confederation of the South Africa Act and for Gladstone's 1886 proposed Home Rule for Ireland.

At the time, all that really mattered was that the deed was done. Canada was about to emerge in the world as a confederation. Once so reconfigured, it could, as its constitution provided for specifically, extend itself right across the entire top half of the continent, initially eastwards, subsequently westwards. This achievement wouldn't make Canada's survival certain, but it would transform Canada's geopolitical character. Until then, the British-American colonies had added up to little more than the accidental detritus of empire—semi-detached statelets somehow left behind in a remote nest of the mother country when the American colonies struck out on their own. In their place there now would be a state with the inherent logic of a community bordered on three sides by salt water and, within these boundaries, stretching out unbrokenly "from sea to sea." The old scattered colonies could never have amounted to more than states in transition; the new one would have the potential to be a permanent state, provided only that its people so willed.

Canadians themselves had created this new state by an exercise of political will that matched almost exactly the one Macdonald had laid down at Quebec City just over two years earlier: "We must, therefore, become important, not only to England but in the eyes of foreign states. And most especially to the United States. . . . The great security for peace is to convince the world of our strength by being united."

The single most important decision taken by Canadians in the nineteenth century was not to form a confederation but, rather, not to become American. Confederation mattered decisively, of course: it was the necessary means to achieve a national unity, and a national ambition, that others would notice and respect. But it was only a means, not an end. That end was a non-American nation-state in North America with enough of the stuff, of will and nerve, to survive—and, no less, with an unbroken connection to Britain. It was, moreover, an uncommonly ambitious nation. Included in its constitution was a pledge—indeed, "a duty of the Government and Parliament of Canada"—to build a railway to Halifax and to the Atlantic, and to begin this construction within six months in order to bind the Maritimes to Canada's heartland. Even more ambitious, and again included in the very constitution of the new nation, was provision for adding to this new nation the vast expanse of "Rupert's Land and the North-Western Territory." It was to be a union not so much of those provinces that joined Confederation but of all the top half of the North American continent.

It was by making this union that Macdonald made us. He made us in the way he had intended to all along—and he made us his way.

TWENTY-FOUR

Idea in the Wilderness

~

A brilliant future would certainly await us were it not for those
wretched Yankees who hunger & thirst for Naboth's field.
John A. Macdonald

Macdonald and Agnes were back in Canada by early May 1867, proceeding directly to Ottawa. They moved into the "Quadrilateral," the large house that Macdonald had shared with Hewitt Bernard and two legislature members (one of them Galt) ever since the government had moved from Quebec City to Ottawa late in 1865. The members moved out, but Bernard stayed on. These departures created room—sort of—for Macdonald and Agnes, and her mother, Theodora, too. In an instant, Macdonald had gone from solitude to being enfolded within the bosom of a family.*

Marriage hadn't altered Macdonald's best-known personal habit. He had made a solemn marital vow to drink less, but not to

---

* That Agnes's mother and brother lived with her at the start of her marriage prompted historian Keith Johnson to write one of the niftiest footnotes in Canadian historiography—"Macdonald had in-laws the way other people had mice."

never drink at all; "less," as Macdonald undoubtedly reminded himself while taking this vow, can only be a subjective measurement. Soon after Macdonald was back, Deputy Minister Edmund Meredith noted in his diary, "John A. carried out of the lunchroom, hopelessly drunk. What a prospect Mrs. John A. has before her!" On the brighter side of his condition, Macdonald was now being cared for, and was eating more or less regularly. He didn't have to worry about arranging to get the house cleaned or laundry seen to. And Agnes was there to express her own views about how "less" should be measured.

The Ottawa they had come to, and where Macdonald had so far lived only spasmodically between his many recent trips to England, was a lumber town of just under twenty thousand people. Its principal characteristic was to be the most verbally abused town in the country: visitors and its own citizens competed to excoriate the place. No one was ever able to top journalist Goldwin Smith's well-known dismissal of Ottawa as "a sub-Arctic lumber village transformed by royal mandate into a political cockpit." But many tried their best. Feo Monck, the governor general's sister, made two diary entries about Ottawa, one describing it as "squalid," the other as "beastly."* Governor General Monck himself persisted in forecasting that Ottawa would be abandoned as the capital within a few years. Edmund Meredith, glancing back nostalgically at Quebec City, which he had just left, wrote in his diary, "The more I see of Ottawa, the more do I dislike and detest it. . . . Possibly the place may be fit for habitation in 50 years from now."

Meredith was being no more than a pinch pessimistic. Ottawa had no sewers, no gas system, no water supply. Water, so-called,

---

* When the diary was published in 1873, Feo Monck's "beastly" was toned down to "horrid."

was delivered in barrels by door-to-door carts; the contents of one barrel when opened turned out to include a dead cat. The streets were like country roads, so that even a central street like Sparks challenged shoppers to make it from one side to the other through three inches of mud. No trees were planted anywhere within the town.* The river was chock full of logs; there were huge piles of sawdust on its banks; and the three hundred or more sawmills created an incessant noise. It was a rough town: Irish and French loggers engaged in repeated drunken brawls. The handful of "respectable" people ranged from lumber barons to a few professional men. There was an acute shortage of housing, due to the arrival from Quebec City of the politicians and some 350 civil servants, soon to become federal civil servants. Joseph Howe, the anti-Confederate Nova Scotian, called Ottawa "a shabby imitation of Washington"; the *Ottawa Citizen* responded that he was grossly unfair.

There was another deficiency to Ottawa. It was about to become a one-industry town, that industry being politics. No less so, its entire social life and the vital decisions about who was up or down or in or out, and about what should be talked about and what mattered, would henceforth be determined exclusively by politicians, or by their spouses. Goldwin Smith made a shrewd analysis of the consequences: because Ottawa lacked "the tempering and restraining influences which the mixed society of a real capital affords," he wrote, the result would be "an unadulterated element of professional politicians, devoting their whole time to the undivided work of corruption and intrigue."†

---

* This was by no means a failing only of Ottawa. Anna Jameson, in her *Winter Studies and Summer Rambles in Canada of 1838*, noted, "A Canadian settler *hates* a tree, regards it to be destroyed, eradicated, annihilated. . . . The idea of useful or ornamental is seldom associated here even with the most magnificent timber trees."

† Smith was in fact anticipating things. In 1867, the entire new dominion civil service numbered just 2,660. As for the "professional politicians," only a few

Amid all the dross, there was one shining and quite astonishing exception: the three Parliament Buildings—the East Block, West Block and Centre Block—situated on what was then called Barrack's Hill and soon to be renamed Parliament Hill, looking down at the churning Ottawa River far below and, northwards, out to the distant, dark blue rim of the Gatineau Hills. The site was spectacular, and so were the buildings. "The noblest architecture in North American . . . I know of no modern Gothic purer of its kind," pronounced the novelist Anthony Trollope, happening by on a lecture tour in 1861. Most other visitors agreed with him.

Inevitably, though, there were defects. The buildings were too hot in summer and too cold in winter, because—inexplicably—the air vents had been placed close to the ceiling of each room. The main building, designed originally for the 130 members of the old United Province of Canada Legislature, was already too small for the 180 who would be coming in from the now four provinces. And, predictably, the buildings had cost far more than expected: the original estimate at the start of construction in 1860 had been an impressively exact $688,505; by Confederation Day, 1867, it had risen to just under $2.6 million; by completion, the figure topped $4.5 million, a sevenfold increase from the original estimate. Macdonald's reaction was more practical: the buildings were at least largely finished, even if the towers still lacked roofs, and the Hill had been cleared of all the construction debris. He did complain privately that the tower of the West Block looked "like a cow bell."

---

dozen actually lived in Ottawa. Most members of Parliament got by in boarding houses during the three months or so that Parliament met each year. Not until after the Second World War did Ottawa become a politics-obsessed, one-industry town.

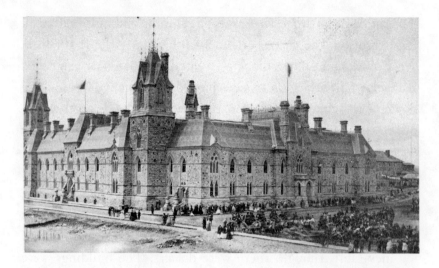

By sheer luck, the magnificent, if magnificently expensive, Parliament Buildings were completed by Confederation Day. This photo shows a military review in front of the West Block, on May 24, 1867.

Nevertheless, the grandeur and scale of the Parliament Buildings cast its defects deep into the shade. By building it, Canadians had pulled off "a visionary, if slightly uncertain, idea in the wilderness," in the words of historian Sandra Fraser Gwyn in her splendid book *The Private Capital: Ambition and Love in the Age of Macdonald and Laurier.* They had, that is, actually dared to dare.

Macdonald's immediate concern on entering the capital that would be his home for the next quarter-century was far less how best to arrange the celebrations for the new country's birthday than—naturally—the politics of Canada's now imminent accouchement. Once Governor General Monck had advised him officially that he would become Canada's first prime minister,

Macdonald knew he would have to form a government. To do that, he would have to form a cabinet. When it assembled, the first item of business would be to call an election soon after Confederation Day. Only after Macdonald had won an election would he become Canada's real prime minister, possessing a mandate rather than just the title.

About his cabinet, Macdonald had long ago settled on its single most important characteristic—it would include Reformers. Their presence would enable him to claim that the old Liberal-Conservative coalition still breathed. At a minimum, the side benefit would be to infuriate the opposition, now more and more calling themselves Liberal-Reformers, or just Liberals; the maximum benefit could be to divide them. Macdonald therefore retained in his new cabinet the three holdover Reformers from the Confederation administration, the most important being William McDougall, originally a Grit, now a Reformer, and well on his way to becoming a Conservative, a progress across the political map that earned him the nickname Wandering Willie. The freshman Maritime provinces would each have two ministers. To further constrain Macdonald's manoeuvring room, Cartier was adamant he would accept nothing less than three posts for *bleu* Quebecers. As well, one Quebec spot had to be kept open for Galt to re-enter the cabinet as finance minister. In these circumstances, no Quebec cabinet seat would be left for Confederation's poet laureate, D'Arcy McGee. Excluding him would be a severe blow to McGee's pride; he had already written to Macdonald that he would "give way neither to Galt, nor to a third Frenchman, 'nor to any other man.'"

To soften McGee's sense of rejection, Macdonald resorted to the device of rejecting another senior member of the Confederation team so that McGee would not twist alone in the wind. His choice was Charles Tupper. Macdonald already owed him a great deal. He now owed him even more, because this Nova Scotian, with great generosity, agreed to stand aside. On Tupper's advice, Macdonald telegraphed an amiable but otherwise anonymous backbencher, Edward Kenny, the unexpected news of his elevation to cabinet. A dry-goods merchant known as "Papa," Kenny had the great virtue of being a Catholic, so could compensate for the exclusion of his co-religionist McGee. Kennedy only just made it to Ottawa from Nova Scotia in time for the swearing-in.* Among the other Maritime representatives was of course New Brunswick's Leonard Tilley.

By his first cabinet choices, Macdonald showed that he understood a cardinal function of Canadian cabinet making: that the duties of the ministers would be not only to run the country but to represent the country to itself. In a tacit admission that the Senate he had just constructed could never serve, unlike its U.S. equivalent, as the regions' representative at the centre, Macdonald fashioned his cabinet into a rough simulacrum of the nation's regions and religions. This practice—ever more finely tuned to accommodate an ever-expanding spectrum of ethnic and other identity claims—has been followed since. Macdonald's handicap was that, while contemporary prime ministers can stretch their cabinets to almost any size, he had to squeeze his choices into a Procrustean bed of just thirteen cabinet portfolios. For himself, Macdonald chose the new portfolio of minister of justice. In a radical change from the past, this post now encompassed the duties of both of the previous attorneys general, for Upper and Lower Canada. The salary for all ministers remained at the pre-Confederation level of five thousand dollars a year.

* Kenny's career continued in anonymity, but of a most agreeable kind. After resigning from the cabinet in 1870, he was appointed a senator and later gained a knighthood.

Composing the cabinet by no means ended Macdonald's tasks as national personnel manager. If Canada needed a government, so, no less, did Ontario and Quebec, neither of which yet existed legally. As well, neither of these two new, but old, provinces had a lieutenant-governor. Macdonald, who had called these officials "chief executive officers," looked on them as key performers in his plan to perpetuate a strong central government that would, besides other accomplishments, reduce the provinces to "mere municipalities." Viewed thus, his choice for Ontario was decidedly odd. Its first lieutenant-governor was Major-General Henry Stisted, a British officer whose most considerable attainment was to have married the sister of the celebrity explorer Sir Richard Burton. Not until one year later, when Stisted resigned and returned to Britain, did the reason for Macdonald's choice become apparent. He then filled this much-sought-after post with William Howland, a Reformer who, by accepting a cabinet post in advance of the 1867 election, had helped insinuate a minimal credibility into Macdonald's claim that his government was a Liberal-Conservative one. Filling the lieutenant-governorship post in Quebec was easy: Macdonald's choice was Sir Narcisse-Fortunat Belleau, who had served Macdonald as titular premier of the Great Coalition. The choice for Quebec's first premier was made by the Quebec Conservatives themselves: he was Pierre-Joseph-Olivier Chauveau, a cultured intellectual who implemented some important educational reforms but was politically a naïf. He too ended up in the Senate, but missed out on a knighthood.

The appointment that took everybody by surprise was Macdonald's choice for the first premier of Ontario. A good deal more useful than being merely surprising, his selection involved one of the most adroit political seductions that Macdonald ever consummated. His choice for the post was his own namesake,

John Sandfield Macdonald. As the first Conservative premier of Confederation's largest province, "Little John" Macdonald harboured two substantial disqualifications: he was a lifelong Reformer (he had firmly rejected earlier attempts by Macdonald to seduce him), and he had been Upper Canada's best-known anti-Confederate. His compensating assets were yet considerable. As a former premier, he commanded credibility. As a Catholic, he brought Irish votes to the Conservatives, federally as well as provincially, along with the other Irishmen Macdonald had already bonded to the party by his alliance with the Orange Order. Most desirable of all, John S. Macdonald's appointment as Ontario premier not only infuriated the Liberals but divided them.

One other political matter needed to be sorted out. Back in London, the British had become convinced, for reasons difficult to comprehend, that when the new dominion was proclaimed officially, the document should include the names of all those who had won the ultimate Canadian lottery of appointment as senators—at that time a life appointment, unlike today's unkind cutoff at the tender age of seventy-five.* Macdonald, looking ahead to the impending first election after Confederation, protested to Lord Carnarvon that "if the list were settled now, every man . . . who is omitted, rightly or wrongly, would vote against the Government." The senatorial announcements were delayed until the fall, safely past the election's date.

The date for the Confederation celebrations was fixed for July 1. Macdonald would have preferred July 15, fearful that not

---

* The super winner of the Confederation senatorial lottery had to have been New Brunswick's David Wark. Called to the Upper House in October 1867, Wark remained a senator for forty years, leaving the chamber only by death in 1905, at the age of 101.

all the preparations could be completed in time, but Monck insisted on the earlier date. He quietly passed the word to Macdonald that he was to receive a knighthood, as Knight Commander of the Bath; the lesser honour of the Companion of the Bath would be accorded to Cartier, Galt, Tupper and Tilley, as well as to "housebroken" Reformers like McDougall and Howland. Of all the people on Monck's list, the most conspicuous, by his absence, was George Brown, now back running the *Globe* and de facto leader of the Reform-Liberals. The list had been compiled on Macdonald's recommendations, and his choices showed him at his least gracious and most vengeful. A year later, Monck wrote to Brown apologizing with great grace: "I will confess to you that I was mortified and disappointed that circumstances rendered it impossible for me to recommend for a share in these distinctions *the* man whose conduct in 1864 had rendered the project of union feasible."

Two of the others, Galt and Cartier, protested strenuously that they too should have been awarded knighthoods. Cartier declined the lesser honour on the grounds that it was an insult to French Canadians for their leader not to have been put in the front rank. Galt similarly refused his reward, telling his wife, "It is an ingracious and most unusual thing to refuse an honour publicly conferred, but if Lord Monck is an ass, I cannot help it." Both Cartier and Galt, as well as several of the others, were eventually awarded the knighthoods they sought, although Galt, always hypersensitive, accepted only after writing to the colonial secretary that he actually opposed all titles and believed instead that Canada should become independent from Britain.

One story that went the rounds was that Macdonald learned from Monck only on Confederation Day itself of his own impending, solitary elevation to the knighthood. Very probably Macdonald was the source of this tale, letting it circulate in order to distance himself from blame for the hurt the incident had caused several of his cabinet colleagues. It's easy to guess that the reason all of them learned of their rewards only at the very last moment was because Macdonald, foreseeing the outcome, had advised Monck to maintain secrecy to the end.

With the Confederation bandwagon now at high speed, more and more people clambered aboard. In June, four of Quebec's five bishops praised Confederation's virtues in pastoral letters that were read for two Sundays from all the pulpits they commanded. Montreal bishop Ignace Bourget, at this time quarrelling with Cartier over his support of the liberal Sulpicians, delayed his pastoral letter until after July 1; in it he enjoined "l'obeissance à l'autorité constituée," a formula that avoided any praise of Confederation.

The most revealing pastoral letter was that of the bishop of Saint-Hyacinthe: he favoured Confederation, he told his flock, because "the fate awaiting us if God suffered us at some future date to enter the great American republic, would be exactly comparable to that of so many tributaries which have come to be swallowed up in the great St. Lawrence." Cartier had made exactly the same point in his speech in the 1865 Confederation Debates: "The question is reduced to this: we must either have a British North American federation or else be absorbed into the American federation." Canadiens had come to accept Confederation because, at the very least, it was better than the probably inevitable alternative of annexation, and at best could—just—prevent that national disappearance. If Macdonald understood this gut sense among French Canadians in a way that few other English-Canadian politicians then did, there was one obvious and decisive reason why: his own gut sense told him the same. Besides instinct, Macdonald by now possessed ample evidence of the United States' mood of expansiveness, northwards.

As Confederation approached, dramatic news came from Washington: the American government had just announced the takeover of a major piece of territory in North America. This territory was Alaska, whose Panhandle, stretching far southwards, cut off much of northern British Columbia from the sea. A steep purchase price of $7.2 million (U.S.) was agreed on between the territory's owner, Russia, and the United States, and the treaty was signed by President Andrew Johnson on March 29—by coincidence the same day that Queen Victoria signed the British North America Act. The New York *Herald* praised the purchase as "a hint" to England that it had "no business on this continent." The New York *Tribune* described it as "a flank movement" on British Columbia by surrounding "a hostile cockney with a watchful Yankee on either side of him." About Confederation itself, the *Tribune* said, "When the experiment of the 'dominion' shall have failed, as fail it must, a process of peaceful absorption will give Canada her proper place in the great North American Republic."

Comments by circulation-chasing editors counted for relatively little. Quite different was the fact that the principal advocates of the Alaska purchase should have been the United States' two well-known annexationists—Secretary of State William Seward and Senator Charles Sumner, the chair of the Senate Committee on Foreign Relations. On April 7, during Senate hearings on the Alaska purchase, Sumner described the takeover as "a visible step to the occupation of the whole North American continent." Seward, in a speech in Boston on the eve of Confederation, said, "I know that Nature designs that this whole continent, not merely the thirty-six states, shall be, sooner or later, within the magic circle of the American Union."

At the same time, a U.S. agent in Canada, E.H. Derby, suggested in a report to Seward that Britain should be asked to cede its possessions in the far west—the then separate colonies of Vancouver Island and British Columbia—as payment for damages to the United States during the Civil War. This damage had been caused by Confederate raiders that had been built in and launched from British ports. From St. Paul, Minnesota, another agent, James W. Taylor, reported to Washington on the steady Americanization of the Red River region of Manitoba; he recommended that "events have presented to the people of the government of the United States the opportunity—let me rather say have developed the duty, of interposing an overture to the people of the English colonies . . . to unite their fortunes with the United States."

These were private communications, about which Macdonald could have no knowledge, although he would have known about the judgment of the *Nor'Wester* newspaper in Red River that "Americanism has become rampant with all classes, ages and conditions." Other private communications, had he been aware of them, would have worried him a good deal more. They would have revealed that similar opinions existed in high places on the far side of the Atlantic. Early in 1867 the foreign secretary, Lord Stanley, wrote to the British ambassador in Washington, Sir Frederick Bruce, to say that Confederation had made Canada even more of a risk to Britain: "Many people would dislike the long boundary line with the United States (they look now to an early separation of Canada)." In March 1867 Stanley wrote again to Bruce: "The Colonies will remain Colonies, only confederated for the sake of convenience. If they choose to separate, we on this side shall not object; it is they who would protest against this idea. In England, separation would be generally popular."

Perhaps most disturbing of all to Macdonald, had he been

aware of it, would have been the private comment by C.B. Adderley, the junior minister for the colonies, who had steered the British North America Act through the Commons: he told some of his colleagues, "It seems to me impossible that we should long hold B.C. from its natural annexation." Nor were these views wholly private. The authoritative *Times* broadcast them by its editorial comment (read, regularly, not just by Canadian officials but no less so by American ones): "We look to Confederation as the means of relieving this country from much expense and much embarrassment." And of Britain's need to pull back its troops still stationed in Canada, the *Times* observed, accurately but embarrassingly, that these served only as "hostages . . . for British good behaviour."

An indication of just how seriously Macdonald took this mood is contained in a letter he wrote shortly before leaving England. Dated April 9, 1867, it was addressed to a prominent English lawyer, Henry Maine, who had received an honorary doctorate from Oxford at the same time as Macdonald the previous June. "I sail in four days for Canada with the act uniting all British America in my pocket," he wrote. "A brilliant future would certainly await us were it not for those wretched Yankees who hunger & thirst for Naboth's field—War will come some day between England & the United States."

In facing this challenge, Macdonald could really count on only one influential political ally who thought as he did. Unexpectedly, that was Galt, highly intelligent but highly volatile too. (There was also the passionate nationalist McGee, except that his political career was now in steep decline because of his insensate drinking.) Back in January 1867, Galt, while still in London and working to get the BNA Act through Westminster, wrote a letter to his wife that indicates a great deal about the threat to Canada from the east as well as the south, or from Britain as well as the United States—at least as that threat was perceived. Galt's letter reveals also an exceptional appreciation of Macdonald's determination to stand on guard for the Canada that was about to be born.

"I am more than ever disappointed at the tone of feeling here as to the colonies. I cannot shut my eyes to the fact that they want to get rid of us . . . and would rather give us up than defend us, or incur the risk of war with that country. Day by day I am more oppressed with the sense of responsibility of maintaining a connection undesired here, and which exposes us to such peril at home. I pray God to show me the right path. But I much doubt whether Confederation will save us from Annexation. Even Macdonald is rapidly feeling as I do." He continued, "Except Macdonald, I know none of the Delegates who really think enough of the future that is before us, and he considers that our present immediate task is to complete the Union, leaving the rest to be solved by time."

Galt had grasped the nature of the "long game" of national survival that Macdonald was playing. It's a shame, in hindsight, that the two never really became partners.

In fact, Macdonald was dead wrong about the readiness of the government of a war-weary America to risk a new conflict, even if against a lion now starting to show signs of its age. The vast armies mobilized during the Civil War had been demobilized down to a minimalist fifty thousand. He was right absolutely, though, that Canada was passing through a period of exceptional peril in which, at the same time that some American leaders were looking expectantly northwards, their equivalents in Britain were doing their best to look the other way. Among possible remedies, Macdonald possessed just one: Confederation itself, or, more exactly, making Confederation serve as a synonym for a nation's will to survive.

As Confederation Day neared, Macdonald wrote to Monck, arguing that it would be "gratifying to the people" if Canada's new national status could be marked by elevating the title of the Queen's representative from governor general to viceroy, the same honorific held by his counterpart in the Empire's "crown jewel" of India. He made the argument that "British North America is now merely a geographical description" and that elevating it to a vice-royalty would reinforce the entity's status. Back from London came word that governor general was as high a title as Imperial protocol could accommodate.

Then, suddenly, there was nothing more for Macdonald to do apart from watch Canada become a Confederation.

Eighteen sixty-seven was something of a banner year for the creation of confederations. There was the North German Confederation, encompassing all the states north of the Main River, which came into being on July 1, and out of which would come Bismarck's Prussian-controlled German Empire. There was, in February of the same year, Austria's *Ausgleich*, or "compromise," which turned the Austrian Empire into the Austro-Hungarian Empire, giving each component state its own parliament and prime minister under a single monarch. And in the wings, rather than on the international stage itself, there was what happened in Ottawa.

July 1, 1867, was "a hot dusty day," as Agnes recorded four days later in the diary she had begun to mark her elevation to Lady Macdonald. She continued in her lively and observant style, "This new Dominion of ours came into existence on the 1st, and the very newspapers look hot and tired with the weight of announcements and of cabinet lists. Here—in this house—the atmosphere is so awfully political that sometimes I think the very flies hold Parliament on the kitchen tablecloths."

As always happens, glitches occurred. The Royal Canadian Rifles assembled on Ottawa's Sparks Street to fire a *feu de joie*, pulled their triggers on command and watched their ramrods, which they had forgotten to remove, make a graceful arc across the street. In Whitby, Ontario, a cavalry troop staged a mock attack on a square of militiamen, but as the Oshawa *Vindicator* reported, "some of them rush[ed] so closely upon the bayonets as to receive severe thrusts."

Inevitably, not everyone regarded the occasion as a festive one. In Halifax, the *Morning Chronicle*, in a front-page editorial edged in black, mourned, "Died! Last night at twelve o'clock, the free and enlightened Province of Nova Scotia," while in Yarmouth, no guns saluted the new nation, the ammunition being preserved for use three days later to mark the United States' Independence Day. The Nova Scotia government went so far as to refuse to allow the Queen's printer in the province to publish the official proclamation sent down from Ottawa by the governor general. In the new province of Quebec, the *bleu* newspaper *La Minerve* reassured its readers that all would be well because Confederation constituted "la seule voie qui nous soit offerte pour arriver à l'indépendance politique."

Although mostly confined to Ontario, there was some genuine excitement, even pride, in the achievement. In Toronto, a whole ox was roasted, carved up and distributed to the poor. In Hamilton, huge bonfires burned for hours on the Mountain. The crowd in Whitby swelled to seven thousand. In town after town there were band concerts, parades, picnics, free ice cream, cricket games, croquet matches and lots of speeches. Montreal sponsored

In Kingston, the Market Square was jammed as the Proclamation was read on July 1, 1867.

a spectacular fireworks display, and there were special celebrations in Macdonald's home town of Kingston. There were artillery salutes everywhere, usually of twenty-one guns, but in Ottawa, starting at midnight, of 101. George Brown stayed up late writing a nine-thousand-word article that filled the *Globe*'s entire front page and many of the inside pages. In fact, Brown had little new to say, expressing himself inelegantly in his opening paragraph: "With the first dawn of this gladsome midsummer morn, we hail the birthday of a new nationality."

At Ottawa, the formal ceremonies were headed by Governor General Monck. He disappointed everyone by turning up in a plain business suit instead of the plumed hat and gold braid people had looked forward to. Accompanied by a single aide, he drove in a carriage to Parliament Hill and then sauntered off to the Privy Council Chamber, where judges, dignitaries, militia officers, senior civil servants and Macdonald were waiting. Monck was sworn in by a judge as the first governor general of the Dominion of Canada, following which he handed over for safe-keeping the new Great Seal of the new nation. Afterwards, Monck, accompanied by the newly sworn-in prime minister, Sir John A. Macdonald, reviewed the troops drawn up on Parliament Hill. That evening there were fireworks displays, and the Parliament Buildings blazed with illuminations.*

Real emotion, though, was rare. Surprisingly, perhaps the most uninhibited expression occurred in the Maritimes. The *New Brunswick Reporter* declared on July 5, "From Halifax to Sarnia, we are one people—one in laws, one in government, one in interests." In these details, little was actually true. Macdonald's description of Canada as only "a geographical expression" was far closer to reality. *The Times* of London came unnervingly close to identifying the limitations and the downright fragility of the new nation: "It supposes a nationality able to command the two oceans it touches, and to raise a barrier of law and moral force extending near three thousand miles between itself and the most powerful and aggressive state in the New World." For such a task, *The Times* added, "we look in vain for the body, the vital organs, the circulation and the muscular force that are to give adequate power to these wide-spread limbs." *The Times* was being a bit severe: Canada's population at birth would be close to four million, a bare tenth of that of its giant neighbour but roughly the same as that of the thirteen American colonies when they had set off on their own national journey.

---

* The celebrations staged by Canadians were outclassed, inevitably, by the great Exposition Universelle held in Paris in that same year of 1867. It attracted ten million visitors. Several Canadian companies even won prizes for their goods; the prize that mattered, though, was the victory by a crew from Saint John, NB, at the World Rowing Championships held on the Seine.

There was a good deal more to the country than just a new administrative interconnectedness across the immense expanses of geography. For the first time anywhere, colonials had written their own constitution. It was an usually difficult constitution to construct, because it was a federal constitution, one of only four in the world—in the United States, Switzerland and the new North German Confederation. And even if still only a colony—as the independent member Charles Dunkin had pointed out, accurately if cruelly—there was something of the stuff of a nation in this curious new entry on the world's stage. Just by achieving Confederation, its citizens had shown they did indeed possess some of the will and nerve it would take to survive.

They possessed another asset. Their leader was Macdonald. Soon his last name would become superfluous: he was about to become known universally as Sir John A. No one else in the country knew politics as well, by a wide margin, as he did. With Lincoln now gone, he knew as much as any leader anywhere about managing a people and a country. He had large and easily visible flaws, and few condemned them more thoroughly than the British-born journalist Goldwin Smith. Yet no one understood better than Smith the sheer impossibility that Macdonald had somehow defied by achieving Confederation. Macdonald, wrote Smith, had been obliged "to hold together a set of elements, national, religious, sectional and personal, as motley as the component patches of any 'crazy quilt,' and actuated each of them by paramount regard for its own interest."

Macdonald hadn't so much created a nation as manipulated and seduced and connived and bullied it into existence against the wishes of most of its own citizens. The best description of the role Macdonald had played came from his friend Judge James Gowan, who called him Confederation's "artificer in chief." By whatever combination of deviousness and magic it took, he had done it. He had made Confederation out of scraps and patches and oddments of thread and string, many frayed and few fitting naturally, but at last it actually existed.

Now that Confederation was done, Macdonald would have to do it all over again. Having conjured up a child-nation, he would have to nurture it through adolescence towards adulthood. How he did this is another story, and its telling, up to his death in 1891, awaits the second volume of this chronicle.

The man who made us, just after he had made us, c. 1868.

Acknowledgements

A great many individuals made important, and in some instances critical, contributions to this work. My first expression of thanks, though, has to be to someone who played no direct part in the process at all—Donald Creighton, author of the two-volume biography of Macdonald, *The Young Politician* and *The Old Chieftain*, published in the mid-1950s. These books are the two greatest achievements in Canadian historiography; no other work even approaches them in the scale of their ambition, in the comprehensiveness and originality of their research and, most distinctively, in the power and persuasiveness of their narrative drive. In later years, Creighton's stature shrank: his opposition to national bilingualism and biculturalism—"francophobic" was one term hurled at him—isolated him from the mainstream. He died in 1979, despairing of Canada's future, convinced that it had become "just a nice place to live . . . but that's all Canada is now." Belatedly, revisionism is under way. The historian Donald Wright is writing Creighton's biography, the first ever of a Canadian historian. Creighton indeed could be difficult—prickly, thin-skinned, hot-tempered, if also generous and hospitable. There's no rule, though, that great artists have to be nice—Picasso is a kind of negative role model. That Creighton was a great historian, there is not the least doubt. He did me the exceptional service of stimulating me, challenging me and at times intimidating me; no writer could ask more of another than to be driven by him or her to stretch to the limit.

All the causes of my other thanks are more conventional. The best way to express them may be in a rough chronological order.

This book exists because Louise Dennys, executive publisher of Knopf Canada / Random House of Canada, and Anne Collins, publisher of Random House, decided jointly to defy one of the embedded rules of Canadian publishing—that Canadians don't read Canadian history. If this book succeeds in its objective of re-introducing Canadians to their past, and so to themselves, with John A. Macdonald performing as a kind of tour guide, these women will have guessed right that rules exist not so much to be broken as to be rewritten. In helping to persuade them to make this decision, my agent John Pearce played a critical role.

Post-Creighton, with infrequent exceptions, works of Canadian history intended for the general reader have most often been written by generalists—first, and forever the foremost, by Pierre Berton, then by Peter C. Newman and Sandra Fraser Gwyn, and today by Charlotte Gray, Christopher Moore, Ken McGoogan and others. All these writers are filling a niche that the professional historians have, largely, stepped back from in order to concentrate on more specific studies. Yet the expertise and the scholarly standards of the professionals remain the foundation on which the generalists must build.

Beyond any doubt, the preceding pages contain errors that I should have excised before surrendering the manuscript or never have put to paper in the first place. That there are not many more is due principally to two individuals. George Ekins, reference librarian at the Library of Parliament, was indefatigably imaginative, not just in looking out for what was wrong but in looking for what I should have known about in the first place—everything from Governor General Head's remarkable memorandum on how Canada should be governed (so reminiscent of Macdonald's own views) to pinning down for me the genealogy of that supposedly distinctive Canadian mantra, "Peace, Order and good Government." My debt to George Ekins is immense, not least because he also read an early draft of the text. My debt to the historian Keith Johnson, now retired from Carleton University and the principal authority on pre-Confederate Macdonald, is almost as considerable. He saved me from multiple embarrassments by reading both the first rough drafts and the near-final text.

Others were as forthcoming. Historian Roger Hall, who played a major role in the process; political scientist David Cameron; social historian Charlotte Gray; and Andrew Smith, just appointed as professor of history at Laurentian University, performed similarly as readers of the early drafts, doing both the grunt work of identifying errors and the creative job of suggesting improvements. Later, I was able to tap the expertise of two historians, Brian McKillop of Carleton University and Donald Smith of the University of Calgary, on important specific topics. Earlier, the geographer Brian Osborne and architectural historian Jennifer McKendry took me on a detailed tour of Macdonald's Kingston. The journalist Arthur Milnes, himself an outstanding researcher, guided me both through Kingston and into Macdonald's personal life. I spent a delightful afternoon with Donna Ivey and Norma Kelly going through their Macdonald memorabilia at his one-time residence, 110 Rideau Street in Kingston.

Those whose job it is to help responded with equal generosity. Maureen Hoogenraad of Library and Archives Canada went out of her way to respond to all my requests. Likewise Paul Banfield, archivist at Queen's University; Robert Paul of the Diefenbaker Canada Centre Archives; Barbara Pilek of the Library of Parliament; and David Brown of LAC's Cartography Division. Those responsible for collections of visual material were every bit as responsive, among them Dorothy Farr of Queen's University's Agnes Etherington Art Centre, Steven McNeil of the National Gallery of Canada, and Heather Home of Queen's University Archives.

It goes without saying that none of those mentioned above bears any responsibility for errors that may remain.

Research is the fun part of any undertaking of this kind; writing is a self-imposed sentence to hard labour interspersed with the occasional epiphany. There can be few more agreeable ways of researching than sitting in Library and Archives Canada poring over a book or learned journal, or the contents of a cardboard box, and every now and then looking out through the ceiling-high windows at the Ottawa River below and the far-off blue line of the Gatineau Hills. The exceptional Robarts Library of the University of Toronto has no views at all but instead offers the stimulation of students scurrying about in search of data to stuff into essay assignments, and the side benefit of researchers being allowed to explore the stacks and so, sometimes, to come upon an unknown book that may contain long-sought details about some scene or personality. An additional research asset I enjoyed was the work done for me by archival consultant Elizabeth Vincent. A medical friend, Dr. Byron Hyde, applied his expertise to trying to diagnose the mysterious illnesses of Isabella. A brother-in-law, Gordon Fulton, took the photograph of me that's on the back cover.

This work went through multiple drafts. Anne Collins first suggested ways to reshape chapters to better fit the narrative through-line. Rosemary Shipton, senior editor for Knopf Canada and Random House Canada, then took over, initially performing the same function and becoming almost a partner in the process of revision and rewriting; working with her was a delight. My copy-editor, Alexander Schultz, and my proofreader, Alison Reid, saved me from yet more embarrassments of detail and grammar.

The person I'm indebted to by far the most is Carol Bishop-Gwyn. During the three years the project took, and most especially during the nine, obsessively focused months of the actual writing, she protected me from daily reality by weaving a cocoon around me and only occasionally interrupting to interpose a hand between me and the screen and, after the premonitory warning "Earth to Richard," bringing me up to date on the latest misdemeanour of the dog or on the social obligation that started half an hour earlier. (A comparable sustaining role was performed by a dear friend, Moira Dexter, during my intense research stints in Ottawa.) Carol was also a full partner in the project itself. All the illustrations are of her choosing, her one regret about them being that the mid-nineteenth century predates both the widespread use of photography and the development of newspaper cartoons. The dedication better expresses my thanks.

A Notes on Sources

These source notes are comparatively short. One reason is that the bibliography of books and articles used during the research is so long. More to the point, the endnotes that customarily identify the sources for quotations and other information in the text have been placed on the website of Random House Canada—to save some trees and to lighten this book's heft.

The purpose of these source notes is comparatively modest—to steer readers who are interested in going more deeply into particular topics towards material that should be useful to them. As a side benefit, this approach enables me to identify writers whose insights set me off in especially productive directions. These notes are therefore indicative rather than definitive. They also use the short-form reference style, so readers should consult the bibliography for the full reference.

For the detailed source notes, see the website at www.randomhouse.ca/johnamacdonald.

Overview

The essentials of John A. Macdonald's story can be found in fewer than ten books. The times themselves—political, social and economic—are recounted in the Canadian Centenary Series, the relevant volumes being Careless's *The Union of the Canadas, 1841–1857* and Morton's *The Critical Years, 1857–1875*. Two contemporary works are invaluable: Biggar's *Anecdotal Life* and Pope's *Memoirs*. The foundation text is, of course, Creighton's *The Young Politician*. Johnson's *Affectionately Yours* is insightful about relationships within the family. Waite's *Life and World* is an elegant essay that includes some interesting information about daily life. Waite, again, in his *Life and Times of Confederation* has provided the best detailed account (if rather Maritime-centric) of the way we were made.

Chapters 1–3 (*Youth*)

Besides Pope, Biggar and Creighton, there's some useful information in Pennington Macpherson's otherwise vacuous biography. Johnson's article, "British Immigration to North America, 1815–1860," is a good source for that topic, with reinforcement provided by Harper's article, "Image and Reality in Early Emigrant Literature." The best review by far of Kingston's past is Tulchinsky's *To Preserve and Defend*. On conditions in early-nineteenth-century towns, nothing comes close to Fingard's article, "The Winter's Tale." A good account of pioneer life is contained in Harris's *Canada Before Confederation*; Susanna Moodie, Catharine Parr Traill and Anna Jameson are musts. About the Scots, Herman's *How the Scots Invented the Modern World* is a captivating read in itself.

Chapters 4–5 (*Young man*)

The best source for Macdonald's years as a full-time lawyer is Teatero's thesis, "A Dead and Alive Way Never Does." Sources about the general state of nineteenth-century law and of crime and punishment include McGrath's *Crime and Its Treatment in Canada* and Waite's *Life and World*. Information about Macdonald's business ventures comes primarily from Johnson's long article, "Macdonald, the Young Non-Politician." Family information is available in Phenix's *Private Demons*. Macdonald's February 1, 1845, speech on primogeniture is in the *Debates* of the legislature, as are all his other contributions up to 1856.

Chapter 6 (*Marriage*)

The prime source is the family letters in Johnson's *Affectionately Yours*. Additional material is in Phenix's *Private Demons* and in Cohoe's articles in

Historic Kingston. Prevailing attitudes towards death are well described in Luella Creighton's *Elegant Canadians*.

Chapters 7–8 (*Early politics*)

Donald Creighton is especially good on this period, while Stewart's *Origins* serves almost as a foundation text. The "miracle" of the revival of post-Durham French Canada is recounted well by Wade's *The French Canadians*, by Monet's *The Last Cannon-shot*, and by Heintzman in his article "The Political Culture of Quebec." A good comparison of French and English attitudes is contained in Morton's *Shield of Achilles*. Bodelson's *Studies in Mid-Victorian Imperialism* and Shippee's *Canadian-American Relations* are useful (if a bit dated) on issues such as Responsible Government and Reciprocity; up to date is Hyam and Ged Martin's *Reappraisals*. The *Dictionary of Canadian Biography* is the place to go for mini-biographies, amplified by sources such as, on Ogle Gowan, Akenson's biography, *Orangeman*; and, on Baldwin, Careless's essay in *Pre-Confederation Premiers*. Ged Martin's "Sir John Eh?" explores Macdonald's speech habits, including whether he had a Scots accent.

Chapter 9 (*The "Big Tent"*)

The (former) National Library's two volumes of Macdonald's letters to the end of 1861, and its third, unpublished, one are an essential source in the years up to Confederation. Much of the argument about Macdonald's ability to speak French is in Ged Martin's "The Canadian Question." The principal source on George Brown is, of course, Careless's *Brown of the Globe*. Willison's *Reminiscences* are a wonderful read.

Chapter 10 (*"Forms Are Things"*)

The argument that Macdonald was a competent administrator is made by Sowby in her thesis, "Macdonald the Administrator," and by Johnson in his article, "John A. Macdonald." Bellomo's "Upper Canada Attitudes towards Crime and Punishment (1832–1851)" is a fine source on exactly that topic. Good material on Macdonald's judicial appointments is contained in Stewart's article "Macdonald's Greatest Triumph."

Chapters 11 and 13 (*Political manoeuvres*)

Macdonald's political stratagems, especially those concerned with patronage, draw substantively on Noel's *Patrons, Clients, Brokers*, Stewart's *Origins* and Simpson's *Spoils*. The development of organized parties is well described in Underhill's article "National Political Parties." The expansive mood of nineteenth-century Canada is covered exceptionally well in Fallis's essay in Morton, *The Shield of Achilles*; McKillop's *Disciplined Intelligence* is good here, while Keefer's *Philosophy of Railroads* is a delightful read in itself. Macdonald's extravagant Valentine's Day ball is well described in Lena Newman's *Album*. For Macdonald's relationship with women, turn to Willison's *Reminiscences* and to Waite's essay "The Man."

Chapter 12 (*The death of Isabella*)

Johnson's *Affectionately Yours* is the principal source. Dr. McSherry's two articles on Isabella's ailments are a fascinating exercise in historical medical sleuthing.

Chapters 14–15 (*The Americans*)

For a fuller understanding of D'Arcy McGee, see Slattery's *McGee*, along with Burns's article, "The Economic Aspects of the New Nationality." For Galt, the source is Skelton's biography. A fine description of the West's first entry onto the Canadian scene is contained in Zaslow's *Canadian North* and Morton's *The West and Confederation*. The early notions for some form of confederation are reviewed in Upton's article, "The Idea of Confederation." The Prince of Wales's tour is well covered in Radforth's *Royal Spectacle*. For Canadian attitudes to the United States, the essential source is Wise and Brown's *Canada Views the United States*, its one defect being that it's too brief. The source for facts and details on this topic is Winks's *The Civil War Years*. On liquor, Ged Martin's "Macdonald and the

Bottle" is an excellent summary. Burnet's article "The Urban Community and Changing Moral Standards" provides a good overview of the social consequences of widespread drinking.

Chapter 16 (*The Brits*)

The prime source for Canada-British relationships throughout this period is Ged Martin's *Britain and the Origins of Canadian Confederation*. Farr's *Colonial Office and Canada* provides good supporting material. Useful also is Waite's "Cardwell and Confederation" and his *Life and Times of Confederation*.

Chapters 17–18 (*The start of the Confederation project*)

The best sources for the creation of the Great Coalition are Careless's *Brown*, Waite's *Life and Times* and Creighton's *The Young Politician*. Ged Martin's *Britain and the Origins of Canadian Confederation* is also useful. The discussion of Macdonald's ideas is drawn from Preece's article on "Political Philosophy" and from Waite's articles "Political Ideas" and "The Man." The *Reminiscences* of both Willison and Cartwright are useful. The story to Charlottetown can be followed in Morton's *Critical Years* and in Waite's *Life and Times*. Louella Creighton provides some delightful fresh details in *The Elegant Canadians*. Careless's "George Brown and the Mother of Confederation" is first class. At the Quebec Conference, Feo Monck in her journal was an astute observer, as was Mercy Coles, while Waite's "Ed Whelan's Reports" is a lot of fun. A fine overview is provided by Moore's *1867: How the Fathers Made a Deal*. Munro's small work, *American Influences*, has good material on Macdonald's thought processes. Smith's "Canadian Confederation" provides some good insights. Useful also is Ged Martin's *Causes of Canadian Confederation*.

Chapter 19 (*Democracy*)

The familiar sources, such as Waite's *Life and Times*, Whelan's *Confederation of the Provinces*, Careless's *Brown*, Ged Martin's *Britain and the Origins of Canadian Confederation*, are all relevant. A new source of great value, especially on the debate about democracy, is the insightful *Canada's Founding Debates*, edited by Ajzenstat.

Chapters 20–21 (*The Maritimes*)

The Maritime scene is well described in Beck's *Howe* and in Pryke's *Nova Scotia and Confederation*, as well as in Waite's *Life and Times*. There's considerable useful material in Chester Martin's *Foundations of Canadian Nationhood*. The nature of the loyalty issue in Canada is well covered in Berger's *The Sense of Power*, and Mills's *The Idea of Loyalty* is a useful supplement. The Fenian threat is described in Senior's books as well as in Stacey's article "Fenianism." The best way to keep tabs on what Monck was doing is Batt's *Monck*.

Chapter 22 (*The London Conference*)

Moore's *1867* and Waite's *Life and Times* are useful, as is Batt's *Monck*. A good overview of the Confederation pact is contained in Frank Scott's long article, "Political Nationalism and Confederation." The magic moment when "Peace, Order and good Government" became the essence of Canada is in Morton's *Canadian Identity*.

Chapter 23 ("*Two Unions*")

The best source on Macdonald's second courtship and wedding is Reynold's *Agnes*, the first-ever biography of a prime ministerial wife. On matters constitutional, good sources are Peter Russell's *Constitutional Odyssey* and, from the British perspective, Hyam and Martin's *Reappraisals*.

Chapter 24 (*Confederation Day*)

The prime source for descriptions of life in early Ottawa is Sandra Gwyn's *Private Capital*. The rise in cross-border tensions prompted by the purchase of Alaska and by Confederation is well described in Shippee's *Canadian-American Relations*. Skelton's *Galt* contains important relevant material, while Louella Creighton has some charming anecdotes in *The Elegant Canadians* about the celebrations.

Bibliography

BIBLIOGRAPHICAL NOTE

The motherlode of Macdonaldiana is located in the Library and Archives Canada (LAC), in Ottawa. His fonds comprise 805 rectangular cardboard boxes that, if stacked side by side, would stretch 37 metres. By contrast, the collection of Pierre Trudeau extends to 851 metres, or more than twenty times as long, and that of Brian Mulroney to 722 metres. The volume of paperwork generated by and for Canadian prime ministers thus expands to fill the capacity of the technology available to generate it, as well as the number of officials assisting in its production, and also, perhaps, to meet an ever-growing prime ministerial conviction of accomplishment.

Macdonald was well served, nevertheless. He claimed to have kept a copy of every letter he sent (largely true, his personal letters excepted) and to be able to put his hand on every letter he received (substantially untrue, according to his confidential secretary and biographer, Joseph Pope). After Macdonald's death, Pope, besides writing three books about him, devoted his retirement to sorting out what he called Macdonald's "appalling mass of correspondence." Between 1914 and 1917, Pope handed over 714 "bundles" of letters to the then Public Archives. Later rearranged professionally, these letters form the foundation of LAC's collection of Macdonaldiana. There are gaps: during his stints in opposition, 1862 to 1864 and 1873 to 1879, Macdonald wrote and kept little.

Additional material has been added over the years—the most recent, quoted in this book, being Macdonald's letter to a British lawyer on April 9, 1867, expressing his concern about possible American military action against the putative new nation. Gaps have been filled and the collection enriched, but the basic record is pretty much as it was a century ago.

Suggestions have been made that Pope was unduly protective of his former master, particularly because, after handing over his "bundles," he burned the rest. Pope insisted there was nothing in the residue that "could not stand the light of day." This is probably true. Pope, although a fierce defender of Macdonald, included in his books letters and papers that showed him in an adverse light; Queen's University principal George Munro Grant carped in his review of Pope's 1894 biography that it contained information about public figures that "contribute[d] nothing of the slightest consequence to our knowledge of the man or of the times."

All this material about Macdonald resides in the LAC cardboard boxes bearing the descriptor MG26-A. Besides Macdonald's outgoing letters (preserved in the form of copies of the originals, then stored in "letter-boxes"), the collection includes incoming letters from close to one hundred individuals with whom Macdonald corresponded regularly, and also his memoranda to the governor general and to the cabinet, state papers and ephemera such as railway tickets and programs for state occasions.

One invaluable aid to researchers exists now, as wasn't the case for Donald Creighton, who had to work entirely from the original handwritten letters and before the invention of the photocopier. In the early 1960s, the then National Library committed itself to publishing all of Macdonald's annotated correspondence. Two volumes were completed, covering the years 1836 to 1861. In the mid-1970s the project was halted for lack of funds. In fact a third volume, extending to mid-1867, was all but completed by this time; its contents are in the archives—Vol. 589, Macdonald Fonds. In addition, Pope published a selection of Macdonald's correspondence containing some 750 letters, as well as those in his Memoirs. The historian Keith Johnson (editor of the National Library volumes) has published in the book *Affectionately Yours* the 205 extant letters exchanged between members of Macdonald's family.

To any researcher these materials are all an immense boon. But they are incomplete. For Macdonald's entire post-Confederation term, nothing has changed since Creighton's day (laptop computers and photocopiers notwithstanding). Macdonald's later letters are available on microfilm, but often these are almost unreadable due to the passage of time and the poor quality of the original technology.

Here, Macdonald has been served less well than have two contemporaries of lesser consequence to Canadians. As a result of a federal grant, the writings of Louis Riel have been published. As the result of another federal grant, Queen's University in Kingston, which owes its existence in part to Macdonald, is engaged in publishing the writings of British prime minister Benjamin Disraeli (the seventh volume came out in 2006, with about as many still to go). Yes to Riel, of course. Yes likewise to Disraeli, Queen's having acquired a valuable collection of his writings. But why not Macdonald's life record? (The author must declare an "interest," since the research for Volume Two of this work will be a good deal slower.)

A last observation in this bibliographical note. Primary sources, such as original letters, are of course the vein of gold for which every historian searches. In fact a great many of the secondary sources listed in the succeeding pages contain primary material that their authors have panned, either from Macdonald's original "appalling mass" of material or from other contemporary sources. The great majority of the books and articles and theses by professional historians listed below postdate Creighton's research of the 1950s. This author thus has been able to peer both ahead and backwards by standing on the shoulders of a great many first-rate post-Creighton researchers. Whenever it seemed appropriate, a particular author has been mentioned in the text or in a footnote. The purpose of this note is to thank all the others who have helped do the work from which this book has emerged.

PRIMARY SOURCES

Almost all of Macdonald's outgoing letters up to Confederation Day have been published in LAC's (then the National Library) two volumes for the period 1834 to 1861 or can be easily accessed in the intended third volume for the period 1862 to May 1867.

An additional important source of pre-Confederation material is contained in LAC's volumes of correspondence between Macdonald and particular individuals. Among these collections, the most important are Narcisse-Fortunat Belleau, E.W. Biggar, William Hume Blake and George Brown, all packed into Vol. 188 of the MG26-A Macdonald Fonds; Alexander Campbell, Vol. 194; George-Étienne Cartier, Vol. 202; Richard Cartwright, Vol. 204; Alexander Galt, Vol. 216; Archbishop Lynch, Vol. 228; D'Arcy McGee, Vol. 231; Gilbert McMicken and Allan MacNab, jointly, Vol. 246; Étienne Taché, Vol. 273; Leonard Tilley, Vol. 276; Charles Tupper, Vol. 282.

Other pre-Confederation volumes in the Macdonald Fonds are grouped under the heading of "Subject Files." Among these are Quebec Conference, Vol. 46; London Conference, Vol. 47; B.N.A Act drafts, Vols. 48, 49; Fenians, Vol. 56–58; Governors General Head, Vol. 74, and Monck, Vol. 75; Minutes of Council, Militia and Defence, Vol. 103; Intercolonial Railway, Vol. 120; Reciprocity, 1865–66 (Vol. 145); Visits to England, Vol. 161.

Other relevant private papers, mostly in the LAC collection, are George Brown, LAC (MG24-B40); Isaac Buchanan, Hamilton Public Library; Edward Cardwell, Public Records Office, London (30/48); Alexander Campbell, Ontario Archives (F-23); Mercy Coles, Diary, LAC (MG24 B66); Alexander T. Galt, LAC (MG27-ID8); James Gowan, LAC (MG27–1E17); John Rose (Macdonald Papers, Vol. 258–59); and Charles Tupper, LAC (MG26-F).

PARLIAMENTARY DEBATES/SPEECHES

Debates of the Legislative Assembly of United Canada, 1842–1856. (Transcripts of subsequent legislature debates to 1867 are in the process of being published by the Parliamentary Library.)

Parliamentary Debates on the Subject of the Confederation of the British North America Provinces, 3rd Session, 8th Provincial Parliament of Canada. Quebec: Hunter, Rose & Co., 1865.

Address of the Hon. John A. Macdonald to the Electors of the City of Kingston, with Extracts from Mr. Macdonald's Speeches Delivered on Different Occasions in the Years 1860 and 1861. No Publisher, 1861.

An invaluable selection of material on both the Confederation Debates and the equivalent debates in the provinces (Nova Scotia, New Brunswick, Prince Edward Island, Newfoundland, Manitoba, British Columbia) is contained in Janet Ajzenstat, ed., *Canada's Founding Debates* (Toronto: Stoddart, 1999).

OFFICIAL SOURCES

Specific relevant official sources are quoted in the notes for each chapter, such as, in Chapter 13, Governor General Head's memorandum on what it takes to govern Canada. In fact a great many documents and official communications of the period are in readily available books and articles. Among these:

Bliss, Michael. *Canadian History in Documents, 1763–1966.* Toronto: Ryerson Press, 1966.

Browne, G.P. *Documents on the Confederation of British North America.* Toronto: McClelland & Stewart, 1969.

Doughty, Arthur G., ed. "Notes on the Quebec Conference, 1864" *Canadian Historical Review* I, no. 1 (1920).

Elgin, James Bruce, Earl of. *The Elgin-Grey papers, 1846–1852.* Edited by Arthur G. Doughty. Ottawa: Printer to the King, 1937.

Forbes, H.D., ed. *Canadian Political Thought.* Toronto: Oxford University Press Canada, 1985.

Granatstein, J.L., and Norman Hillmer. *First Drafts: Eyewitness Accounts from Canada's Past.* Toronto: Thomas Allen, 2002.

George Brown to his wife, 13 Sept. 1864, (George Brown Papers, pp. 1029–36), *Canadian Historical Review* 48, no. 1 (1967): 110.

Morton, W.L. *Monck Letters and Journals, 1863–1868: Canada from Government House at Confederation.* Toronto: McClelland & Stewart, 1970.

Ormsby, W.G. "Letters to Galt Concerning the Maritime Provinces and Confederation" *Canadian Historical Review* 34, no. 2 (1953).

Pope, Joseph, ed. *Confederation: Being a Series of Hitherto Unpublished Documents Bearing on the British North America Act.* Toronto: Carswell, 1895.

Reid, J.H. Stewart, Kenneth McNaught, and Harry S. Crowe. *A Source-book of Canadian History.* Toronto: Longmans, Green, 1959.

"Sir Edmund Walker Head's Memorandum on the Choice of Ottawa as the Seat of Government of Canada" Notes and Documents, *Canadian Historical Review* 16 (1935).

Smith, Wilfrid. Introduction to "Charles Tupper's Minutes of the Charlottetown Conference" *Canadian Historical Review* 48, no. 1 (1967).

Waite, Peter B. "Ed Whelan's Reports from the Quebec Conference" *Canadian Historical Review* 42, no. 1 (1961).

———. *Pre-Confederation.* Canadian Historical Documents Series, vol. 2. Scarborough, Ont.: Prentice-Hall of Canada, 1965.

Whelan, Edward. *The Union of the British Provinces, a Brief Account of the Several Conferences Held in the Maritime Provinces and in Canada, in September and October, 1864,* on the Proposed Confederation of the Provinces. Charlottetown, 1865.

NEWSPAPERS

The complete reports of the Toronto *Globe* for the period 1844 to 1867 are available on-line at the Toronto Public Library website, www.tpl.toronto.on.ca.

Extensive extracts from newspaper reports of the period are contained in: Silver, Arthur I. "Quebec and the French-Speaking Minorities, 1864–1917." Ph.D. thesis, University of Toronto, 1973.

————. *The French-Canadian Idea of Confederation, 1864–1900.* Toronto: University of Toronto Press, 1982.

Waite, Peter B. *The Life and Times of Confederation, 1864–1867: Politics, Newspapers, and the Union of British North America.* Toronto: University of Toronto Press, 1962. (Included is an extensive list of all relevant newspapers for the period, pp. 334–38.)

SECONDARY SOURCES

BOOKS ABOUT MACDONALD AND FAMILY
CONSULTED DURING THE RESEARCH

(A prime source of biographical and related material about all of the major figures of the time is the authoritative *Dictionary of Canadian Biography*, vols. 7 to 14.)

Adam, G. Mercer. *Canada's Patriot Statesman: The Life and Career of the Right Honourable Sir John A. Macdonald.* Based on the work of Edmund Collins, revised. Toronto: Rose, 1891.

Angus, Margaret. *John A. Lived Here.* Kingston: Frontenac Historic Foundation, 1984.

Biggar, E.B. *Anecdotal Life of Sir John Macdonald.* Montreal: Lovell, 1891.

Bliss, Michael. *Right Honorable Men: The Descent of Canadian Politics from*

Macdonald to Chrétien. Toronto: HarperPerennial Canada, 2004.

Collins, Joseph Edmund. *Life and Times of the Rt. Hon. Sir John A. Macdonald, Premier of the Dominion of Canada.* Toronto: Rose, 1883.

Creighton, Donald Grant. *John A. Macdonald.* Vol. 1, *The Young Politician,* and vol. 2, *The Old Chieftain.* Toronto: Macmillan of Canada, 1952.

————. *John A. Macdonald, Confederation and the West.* Winnipeg: Manitoba Historical Society, 1967.

Johnson, J.K. *Affectionately Yours: The Letters of Sir John A. Macdonald and His Family.* Toronto: Macmillan of Canada, 1969.

————. "John A. Macdonald." In *The Pre-Confederation Premiers: Ontario Government Leaders, 1841–1867,* edited by J.M.S. Careless. Toronto: University of Toronto Press, 1980.

————. *John A. Macdonald: The Young Non-Politician.* Ottawa: CHA Papers, 1976.

————, ed. *The Letters of Sir John A. Macdonald, 1836–1857.* Ottawa: Public Archives of Canada, 1968.

Johnson, J.K., and Carole B. Stelmack, eds. *The Letters of Sir John A. Macdonald, 1858–1861.* Ottawa: Public Archives of Canada, 1969.

Maclean, W.F. "The Canadian Themistocles." *Canadian Magazine* 4 (1894): 253–60.

Macpherson, J. Pennington. *Life of the Right Hon. Sir John A. Macdonald.* Saint John, N.B.: Earle Pub. House, 1891.

Newman, Lena. *The John A. Macdonald Album.* Montreal: Tundra Books, 1974.

Parkin, George R. *Sir John A. Macdonald.* T.C. & E.C. Jack, 1909.

Phenix, Patricia. *Private Demons: The Tragic Personal Life of John A. Macdonald.* Toronto: McClelland & Stewart, 2006.

Pope, Joseph. *Correspondence of Sir John Macdonald.* Toronto: Doubleday, Page, 1921.

————. *The Day of Sir John Macdonald: A Chronicle of the First Prime Minister of the Dominion.* Toronto: Brook, 1915.

————. *Memoirs of the Right Honourable Sir John Alexander Macdonald, First Prime Minister of the Dominion of Canada.* Toronto: Musson, 1894.

Reynolds, Louise. *Agnes: A Biography of Lady Macdonald.* Toronto: Samuel Stevens, 1979.

Smith, Cynthia M., with Jack McLeod, eds. *Sir John A.: An Anecdotal Life of John A. Macdonald.* Toronto: Oxford University Press, 1989.

Swainson, Donald. *Macdonald of Kingston: First Prime Minister.* Toronto: A Personal Library Publication, produced exclusively for Nelson, 1979.

————. *Sir John A. Macdonald: The Man and the Politician.* 2nd ed. Kingston: Quarry Press, 1989.

Waite, Peter B. *Macdonald: His Life and World.* Toronto: McGraw-Hill Ryerson, 1975.

————. Introduction to Donald Grant Creighton, *John A. Macdonald: The Young Politician, the Old Chieftain.* Toronto: University of Toronto Press, 1998.

Wallace, W. Stewart. *Sir John Macdonald.* Toronto: Macmillan of Canada, 1924.

Wilson, Keith. *Hugh John Macdonald.* Winnipeg: Peguis Publishers, 1980.

GENERAL WORKS CONSULTED

(Abbreviations: Canadian Historical Association—CHA; Macmillan of Canada—Mac-C; McClelland & Stewart—M&S; McGill-Queen's University Press—M-Q UP; Oxford University Press—OUP; University of Toronto Press—UTP)

Abrahamson, Una. *God Bless Our Home: Domestic Life in Nineteenth Century Canada.* Toronto: Burns & MacEachern, 1966.

Ajzenstat, Janet. *The Once and Future Canadian Democracy: An Essay in Political Thought.* Montreal: M-Q UP, 2003.

————, ed. *Canada's Founding Debates.* Toronto: Stoddart, 1999.

Ajzenstat, Janet, and Peter J. Smith. *Canada's Origins: Liberal, Tory, or Republican?* Ottawa: Carleton University Press, 1995.

Akenson, Donald H. *The Orangeman: The Life and Times of Ogle Gowan.* Toronto: Lorimer, 1986.

Aldous, Richard. *The Lion and the Unicorn: Gladstone vs Disraeli*. London: Hutchinson, 2006.

Batt, Elizabeth. *Monck: Governor General, 1861–1868*. Toronto: M&S, 1976.

Beck, J. Murray. *Joseph Howe*. Vol. 2, *The Briton Becomes Canadian, 1848–1873*. Kingston: M-Q UP, 1982.

————. *Joseph Howe, Anti-Confederate*. Ottawa: CHA booklets, no.17, 1968.

Berger, Carl. *The Sense of Power: Studies in the Ideas of Canadian Imperialism, 1867–1914*. Toronto: UTP, 1970.

————, ed. *Approaches to Canadian History*. Toronto: UTP, 1967.

Bissell, Claude T., ed. *Our Living Tradition: Seven Canadians*. Toronto: Published in association with Carleton University by UTP, 1957.

Black, Edwin R. *Divided Loyalties: Canadian Concepts of Federalism*. Montreal: M-Q UP, 1975.

Bliss, Michael. *Northern Enterprise: Five Centuries of Canadian Business*. Toronto: M&S, 1987.

————, ed. *Canadian History in Documents, 1763–1966*. Toronto: Ryerson Press, 1966.

Bodelsen, C.A. *Studies in Mid-Victorian Imperialism*. New York: H. Fertig, 1968.

Bonenfant, Jean-Charles. *The French Canadians and the Birth of Confederation*. Ottawa: CHA booklets, no. 21, 1966.

Bourne, Kenneth. *Britain and the Balance of Power in North America, 1815–1908*. London: Longmans, 1967.

Brown, Craig. *Upper Canadian Politics in the 1850s*. Toronto: UTP, 1967.

Buckner, Phillip. *Atlantic Canada before Confederation*. 3rd ed. Fredericton: Acadiensis Press, 1998.

————. *The Transition to Responsible Government:* British Policy in British North America, 1815–1850. Westport, Conn.: Greenwood Press, 1985.

Bumsted, J.M., ed. *Interpreting Canada's Past*. Vol. 1, *Pre-Confederation*. 2nd ed. Toronto: OUP, 1993.

————. *The Scots in Canada*. Ottawa: CHA, *Ethnic Groups in Canada*, 1982.

Calder, Jenni. *Scots in Canada*. Luath, 2003.

Callahan, James Morton. *American Foreign Policy in Canadian Relations.* Toronto: Mac-C, 1937.

Careless, J.M.S. *Brown of the Globe.* Vol. 1, *The Voice of Upper Canada 1815–1859,* and vol. 2, *Statesman of Confederation 1860–1880.* Toronto: Mac-C, 1959, 1963.

———. *Careless at Work: Selected Canadian Historical Studies.* Toronto: Dundurn Press, 1990.

———. *Colonists & Canadiens, 1760–1867.* Toronto: Mac-C, 1971.

———, ed. *The Pre-Confederation Premiers: Ontario Government Leaders, 1841–1867.* Toronto: UTP, 1980.

———. *The Union of the Canadas: The Growth of Canadian Institutions, 1841–1857.* Toronto: M&S, 1967.

Carty, R. Kenneth, and W. Peter Ward, eds. *National Politics and Community in Canada.* Vancouver: UBC Press, 1986.

Cartwright, Richard, Sir. *Reminiscences.* Toronto: Briggs, 1912.

Collard, Edgar Andrew. *Canadian Yesterdays.* Toronto: Longmans, Green, 1955.

Colquhoun, A.H.U. *The Fathers of Confederation: A Chroncile of the Birth of the Dominion.* Toronto: Brook, 1916.

Conrad, Margaret, and Alvin Finkel. *Canada: A National History.* Toronto: Longman, 2003.

Cook, Ramsay. *The Maple Leaf Forever: Essays on Nationalism and Politics in Canada.* Toronto: Mac-C, 1971.

Cornell, Paul G. *The Alignment of Political Groups in Canada, 1841–1867.* Toronto: UTP, 1962.

———. *The Great Coalition.* Ottawa: CHA booklets, no. 19, 1971.

Creighton, Donald Grant. *John A. Macdonald, Confederation and the West.* Winnipeg: Manitoba Historical Society, 1967.

———. *The Road to Confederation: The Emergence of Canada, 1863–1867.* Toronto: Mac-C, 1964.

Creighton, Donald Grant, et al. *Confederation: Essays.* Introduction by Ramsay Cook. Toronto: UTP, 1967.

Creighton, Luella. *The Elegant Canadians.* Toronto: M&S, 1967.

Dent, John Charles. *The Last Forty Years: Canada Since the Union of 1841.* 2 vols. Toronto: G. Virtue, 1881.

Dickason, Olive Patricia. *Canada's First Nations: A History of Founding Peoples from Earliest Times.* Toronto: M&S, 1992.

Dickinson, John A., and Brian Young. *A Short History of Quebec.* Montreal: M-Q UP, 2000.

Dyck, Harvey L., and H. Peter Krosby, eds. *Empire and Nations:* Essays in Honour of Frederick H. Soward. Toronto: UTP, 1969.

Dyer, Gwynne, and Tina Viljoen. *The Defence of Canada: In the Arms of Empire, 1760–1939.* Toronto: M&S, 1990.

Easterbrook, W.T., and Mel Watkins, eds. *Approaches to Canadian Economic History: A Selection of Essays.* Ottawa: Carleton University, 1991.

Errington, Jane. *The Lion, the Eagle, and Upper Canada: A Developing Colonial Ideology.* Kingston: M-Q UP, 1994.

Farr, David M.L. *The Colonial Office and Canada, 1867–1887.* Toronto: UTP, 1955.

Finlay, J.L. *The Structure of Canadian History.* Toronto: Prentice-Hall, 1997.

Forbes, H.D., ed. *Canadian Political Thought.* Toronto: OUP, 1985.

Francis, Daniel. *National Dreams: Myth, Memory and Canadian History.* Vancouver: Arsenal Pulp Press, 1997.

Francis, R. Douglas, Richard Jones, and Donald B. Smith. *Origins: Canadian History to Confederation.* Toronto: Harcourt Brace Canada, 2000.

Frankfurter, Glen. *Baneful Domination: The Idea of Canada in the Atlantic World, 1581–1971.* Don Mills, Ont.: Longman Canada, 1971.

Garner, John. *The Franchise and Politics in British North America, 1755–1867.* Ottawa: UTP, 1969.

Glazebrook, G.P. de T. *A History of Canada's External Relations.* Toronto: OUP, 1950.

———. *A History of Canadian Political Thought.* Toronto: M&S, 1966.

———. *A History of Transportation in Canada.* 2nd ed. Toronto: M&S, 1967.

Goodwin, Doris Kearns. *Team of Rivals: The Political Genius of Abraham Lincoln.* New York: Simon & Schuster, 2005.

Granatstein, J.L., and Norman Hillmer. *First Drafts: Eyewitness Accounts from Canada's Past*. Toronto: Thomas Allen, 2002.

Greer, Allan, and Ian Radforth, eds. *Colonial Leviathan: State Formation in Mid-Nineteenth Century Canada*. Toronto: UTP, 1992.

Guillet, Edwin. *Early Life in Upper Canada*. Toronto: Ontario Publishing Co., 1933.

Gwyn, Sandra. *The Private Capital: Ambition and Love in the Age of Macdonald and Laurier*. Toronto: M&S, 1986.

Hamelin, Marcel, ed. *The Political Ideas of the Prime Ministers of Canada*. Ottawa: Les Éditions de l'Université d'Ottawa, 1969.

Hammond, M.O. *Confederation and Its Leaders*. Toronto: McClelland, Goodchild & Stewart, 1917.

Harris, R. Cole, and John Warkentin. *Canada Before Confederation: A Study in Historical Geography*. New York: OUP, 1974.

Herman, Arthur. *How the Scots Invented the Modern World: The True Story of How Western Europe's Poorest Nation Created Our World and Everything in It*. New York: Three Rivers Press, 2001.

Hitsman, J. Mackay. *Safeguarding Canada: 1763–1871*. Toronto: UTP, 1968.

Hodgetts, J.E. *Pioneer Public Service: An Administrative History of the United Canadas, 1841–1867*. Toronto: UTP, 1955.

Hodgins, Bruce W., Don Wright, and W.H. Heick, eds. *Federalism in Canada and Australia: The Early Years*. Waterloo, Ont.: Wilfrid Laurier University Press, 1978.

Horn, Michiel, and Ronald Sabourin, eds. *Studies in Canadian Social History*. Toronto: M&S, 1974.

Hyam, Ronald. *Britain's Imperial Century, 1815–1914: A Study of Empire and Expansion*. London: Batsford, 1976.

Hyam, Ronald, and Ged Martin. *Reappraisals in British Imperial History*. Toronto: Mac-C, 1975.

Jameson, Anna. *Winter Studies and Summer Rambles in Canada*. Toronto: M&S, 1923.

Keefer, T.C. *Philosophy of Railroads and Other Essays*. Edited by H.V. Nelles. Toronto: UTP, 1972.

Knaplund, Paul. *The British Empire, 1815–1939*. London: H. Hamilton, 1942.

Langton, Anne. *A Gentlewoman in Upper Canada: The Journals of Anne Langton*. Toronto: Clarke, Irwin, 1950.

Langton, John. *Early Days in Upper Canada:* Letters of John Langton from the Backwoods of Upper Canada and the Audit Office of the Province of Canada. Edited by W.A. Langton. Toronto: Mac-C, 1926.

Lower, Arthur. *Canadians in the Making: A Social History of Canada*. Toronto: Longmans, Green, 1958.

———. *Colony to Nation: A History of Canada*. Toronto: Longmans, Green, 1946.

MacNutt, W. Stewart. *New Brunswick: A History, 1784–1867*. Toronto: Mac-C, 1963.

Martin, Chester. *Foundations of Canadian Nationhood*. Toronto: UTP, 1955.

Martin, Ged. *Britain and the Origins of Canadian Confederation, 1837–67*. Vancouver: UBC Press, 1995.

———, ed. *The Causes of Canadian Confederation*. Fredericton: Acadiensis Press, 1990.

McGrath, William Thomas. *Crime and Its Treatment in Canada*. Toronto: Mac-C, 1976.

McInnis, Edgar. *Canada, a Political and Social History*. Toronto: Holt Rinehart, 1982.

McKendry, Jennifer. *With Our Past Before Us: Nineteenth-Century Architecture in the Kingston Area*. Toronto: UTP, 1995.

McKillop, A.B. *Contours of Canadian Thought*. Toronto: UTP, 1987.

———. *A Disciplined Intelligence: Critical Inquiry and Canadian Thought in the Victorian Era*. Montreal: M-Q UP, 1979.

Mills, David. *The Idea of Loyalty in Upper Canada, 1784–1850*. Kingston: M-Q UP, 1988.

Minhinnick, Jeanne. *At Home in Upper Canada*. Toronto: Clarke, Irwin, 1970.

Moir, John S., ed. *Character and Circumstance: Essays in Honour of Donald Grant Creighton*. Toronto: Mac-C, 1970.

————. *The Church in the British Era, From the British Conquest to Confederation.* Toronto: McGraw-Hill Ryerson, 1972.

Monck, Frances E.O. *My Canadian Leaves: An Account of a Visit to Canada in 1864–1865.* London: Bentley, 1891.

Monet, Jacques. *The Last Cannon-shot: A Study of French-Canadian Nationalism, 1837–1850.* Toronto: UTP, 1969.

Moodie, Susanna. *Six Years in the Bush: Or, Extracts from the Journal of a Settler in Upper Canada, 1832–1838.* London: Simpkin, Marshall, 1838.

Moore, Christopher. *1867: How the Fathers Made a Deal.* Toronto: M&S, 1998.

Morris, James. *Heaven's Command: An Imperial Progress.* London: Faber & Faber, 1973.

Morton, W.L. *The Canadian Identity.* 2nd ed. Toronto: UTP, 1973.

————. *Contexts of Canada's Past: Selected Essays of W.L. Morton.* Edited by A.B. McKillop. Toronto: Mac-C, 1980.

————. *The Critical Years: The Union of British North America, 1857–1873.* Toronto: M&S, 1964.

————. *Manitoba: The Birth of a Province.* Winnipeg: Manitoba Record Society, 1965.

————. *The West and Confederation.* Ottawa: CHA booklet, 1968.

————, ed. *Monck Letters and Journals, 1863–1868: Canada from Government House at Confederation.* Toronto: M&S, 1970.

————, ed. *The Shield of Achilles: Aspects of Canada in the Victorian Age.* Toronto: M&S, 1968.

Muise, D.A., ed. *A Reader's Guide to Canadian History.* Vol. 1, *Beginnings to Confederation.* Toronto: UTP, 1982.

Munro, William Bennett. *American Influences on Canadian Government.* Toronto: Mac-C, 1929.

Newman, Peter Charles. *Company of Adventurers: How the Hudson's Bay Empire Determined the Destiny of a Continent.* Toronto: Penguin Canada, 2005.

Nicholas, H.G. *Britain and the U.S.A.* Baltimore: Johns Hopkins Press, 1963.

Noel, S.J.R. *Patrons, Clients, Brokers: Ontario Society and Politics, 1791–1896.* Toronto: UTP, 1990.

Osborne, Brian S. *Kingston: Building on the Past.* Westport, Ont.: Butternut Press, 1988.

Owram, Doug. *Promise of Eden: The Canadian Expansionist Movement and the Idea of the West, 1856–1900.* Toronto: UTP, 1980.

Pentland, H. Clare. *Labour and Capital in Canada, 1650–1860.* Toronto: J. Lorimer, 1981.

Pope, Maurice. *Public Servants: The Memoirs of Sir Joseph Pope.* Toronto: OUP, 1960.

Porter, Bernard. *Absent-Minded Imperialists: Empire, Society, and Culture in Britain.* New York: OUP, 2004.

Prentice, Alison. *Canadian Women: A History.* Toronto: Harcourt Brace, 1996.

Preston, Richard A. *The Defence of the Undefended Border: Planning for War in North America, 1867–1939.* Montreal: M-Q UP, 1977.

———. *Canadian Defence Policy and the Development of the Canadian Nation, 1867–1917.* Ottawa: CHA booklets, no. 25, 1970.

Pryke, Kenneth G. *Nova Scotia and Confederation, 1864–74.* Toronto: UTP, 1979.

Radforth, Ian Walter. *Royal Spectacle: The 1860 Visit of the Prince of Wales to Canada and the United States.* Toronto: UTP, 2004.

Reid, W. Stanford, ed. *The Scottish Tradition in Canada.* Toronto: M&S, 1976.

Roberston, J. Ross. *Old Toronto: A Selection of Excerpts from Landmarks of Toronto.* Edited by E.C. Kyte. Toronto: Mac-C, 1954.

Ross, George W. *Getting into Parliament and After.* Toronto: W. Briggs, 1913.

Roy, James. *Kingston: The King's Town.* Toronto: M&S, 1952.

Russell, Peter H. *Constitutional Odyssey: Can Canadians Become a Sovereign People?* Toronto: UTP, 1992.

Russell, William Howard, Sir. *Canada: Its Defences, Condition, and Resources, Being a Second and Concluding Volume of "My Diary, North and South."* Boston: Burnham, 1865.

Ryerson, Stanley B. *Unequal Union: Confederation and the Roots of Conflict in the Canadas, 1815–1873.* Toronto: Progress Books, 1968.

Schull, Joseph. *Laurier: The First Canadian.* Toronto: Mac-C, 1965.

Senior, Hereward. *The Fenians and Canada.* Toronto: Mac-C, 1978.

———. *The Last Invasion of Canada: The Fenian Raids, 1866–1870.* Toronto: Dundurn Press, 1991.

———. *Orangeism: The Canadian Phase.* Toronto: McGraw-Hill Ryerson, 1972.

Shaw, A.G.L. *Great Britain and the Colonies, 1815–1865.* London: Methuen, 1970.

Shaw, Matthew, *Great Scots!: How the Scots Created Canada.* Winnipeg: Heartland Associates, 2003.

Shippee, Lester Burrell. *Canadian-American Relations, 1849–1874.* New Haven, Conn.: Yale University Press, 1939.

Silver, A.I. *The French-Canadian Idea of Confederation, 1864–1900.* Toronto: UTP, 1982.

Simpson, Jeffrey. *Spoils of Power: The Politics of Patronage.* Toronto: W. Collins, 1988.

Skelton, O.D. *The Life and Times of Sir Alexander Tilloch Galt.* Toronto: OUP, 1920.

Slattery, T.P. *The Assassination of D'Arcy McGee.* Toronto: Doubleday Canada, 1968.

Stewart, Gordon T. *The American Response to Canada since 1776.* East Lansing: Michigan State University Press, 1992.

———. *The Origins of Canadian Politics: A Comparative Approach.* Vancouver: UBC Press, 1986.

Swainson, Donald, ed. *Oliver Mowat's Ontario.* Toronto: Mac-C, 1972.

Sweeny, Alastair. *George-Etienne Cartier: A Biography.* Toronto: M&S, 1976.

Tansill, Charles Callan. *Canadian-American Relations, 1875–1911.* New Haven, Conn.: Yale University Press, 1943.

Taylor, Charles. *Radical Tories: The Conservative Tradition in Canada.* Toronto: House of Anansi Press, 1982.

Thompson, Samuel. *Reminiscences of a Canadian Pioneer, 1853–1883.* Toronto: M&S, 1968.

Trofimenkoff, Susan Mann. *The Dream of Nation: A Social and Intellectual History of Quebec.* Toronto: Mac-C, 1982.

Tucker, Gilbert. *The Canadian Commercial Revolution, 1845–1851.* New Haven, Conn.: Yale University Press, 1936.

Tulchinsky, Gerald, ed. *To Preserve and Defend: Essays on Kingston in the Nineteenth Century.* Montreal: M-Q UP, 1976.

Underhill, Frank H. *The Image of Confederation.* Massey Lectures, 3rd series. Toronto: Canadian Broadcasting Corp, 1964.

———. *Upper Canadian Politics in the 1850's:* Essays by F.H. Underhill [and others]. Introduction by Craig Brown. Toronto: UTP, 1967.

Wade, Mason. *The French-Canadians: 1760–1967.* Vol. 1, 1760–1911. Toronto: Mac-C, 1968.

Waite, Peter B. *The Charlottetown Conference.* Ottawa: CHA booklets, no. 15, 1970.

———, ed. *The Confederation Debates in the Province of Canada, 1865: A Selection.* Toronto: M&S, 1963.

———. *The Life and Times of Confederation, 1864–1867:* Politics, Newspapers, and the Union of British North America. Toronto: UTP, 1963.

Wallace, C.M., and R.M. Bray. *Reappraisals in Canadian History, Pre-Confederation.* 2nd ed. Scarborough, Ont.: Prentice-Hall Canada, 1996.

Wallace, Elisabeth. *Goldwin Smith, Victorian Liberal.* Toronto: UTP, 1957.

Warner, Donald. *Idea of Continental Union: Agitation for the Annexation of Canada to the United States.* Lexington: Kentucky UP, 1960.

Whelan, Edward. *Confederation of the Provinces.* Pioneer Publishing, 1865.

Whitelaw, William Menzies. *The Maritimes and Canada before Confederation.* Toronto: OUP, 1966.

———. *The Quebec Conference.* Ottawa: CHA booklets, no. 20, 1966.

Wilentz, Sean. *The Rise of American Democracy: Jefferson to Lincoln.* New York: W.W. Norton, 2005.

Willison, John, Sir. *Reminiscences, Political and Personal*. Toronto: M&S, 1919.

Wilson, A.N. *The Victorians*. New York: W.W. Norton, 2003.

Winks, Robin W. *The Civil War Years: Canada and the United States*. 4th ed. Montreal; Kingston: M-Q UP, 1998.

————. *The Relevance of Canadian History: U.S. and Imperial Perspectives*. Lanham: University Press of America, 1988.

Wise, S.F. *God's Peculiar Peoples: Essays on Political Culture in Nineteenth Century Canada*. Ottawa: Carleton University Press, 1993.

Wise, S.F., and Robert Craig Brown. *Canada Views the United States: Nineteenth-Century Political Attitudes*. Seattle: University of Washington Press, 1967.

Young, Brian. *George-Etienne Cartier: Montreal Bourgeois*. Montreal: M-Q UP, 1981.

Zazlow, Morris. *The Opening of the Canadian North, 1870–1914*. Toronto: M&S, 1971.

ARTICLES CONSULTED

(Abbreviations: CHA—Canadian Historical Association; *CHR—Canadian Historical Review*; *CJEPS—Canadian Journal of Economics and Political Science*; *CJPS—Canadian Journal of Political Science*; *JCS—Journal of Canadian Studies*; *OH—Ontario History*)

Abella, Irving M. "The 'Sydenham Election' of 1841" *CHR* 47, no. 4 (1966).

Angus, Margaret. "Health Emigration and Welfare in Kingston, 1820–1840." In *Oliver Mowat's Ontario*, edited by Donald Swainson. Toronto: Macmillan of Canada, 1972.

Atchison, J.H. "Sir John A. Macdonald: Nation-Builder" (review of Donald Grant Creighton, *John A. Macdonald*) *CJEPS*, 1956, no. 4.

Bailey, A.G. "The Basis and Persistence of Opposition to Confederation in New Brunswick" *CHR* 23 (1942).

Barber, William. "The Anti-American Ingredient in Canadian History" *The Dalhousie Review*, 1973–74.

Bellomo, J. Jerald. "Upper Canada Attitudes Towards Crime and Punishment (1832–1851)" *OH* 64 (1977).

Brown, George. "The Grit Party and the Great Reform Convention of 1859" *CHR* 16, no. 3 (1935).

Buckner, Philip A. "The Maritimes and Confederation: A Reassessment" *CHR* Dialogues, March 1990.

Burnet, J.R. "The Urban Community and Changing Naval Standards." In *Studies in Canadian Social History*, edited by Michael Horn and Ronald Sabourin. Toronto: M&S, 1974.

Burns, Robin. "D'Arcy McGee and the Economic Aspects of New Nationality" CHA *Historical Papers* 2 (1967).

Careless, J.M.S. "George Brown and the Mother of Confederation" CHA *Annual Report and Historical Papers* 39 (1960).

———. "Limited Identities in Canada" *JCS*, 1968, no. 1.

Cameron, David. "Lord Durham Then and Now" *JCS* 25, no. 1 (1990).

Chapman, J. K. "Arthur Gordon and Confederation" *CHR* 37, no. 2 (1956).

Cohoe, Margaret. "John A. Macdonald" *Historic Kingston* 38 (1990).

———. "John A. Macdonald—The Family Man" *Historic Kingston* 37 (1989).

Conway, John. "Politics, Culture and the Writing of Constitutions." In *Empire and Nations*, edited by Harvey L. Dyck and H. Peter Krosby. Toronto: University of Toronto Press, 1969.

Cook, Ramsey. "Quebec and Confederation" *Queen's Quarterly*, 1964–65.

Creighton, Donald Grant. "John A. Macdonald and the Canadian West" Historical Society of Manitoba, 1966–67, no. 23.

———. "Sir John Macdonald and Canadian Historians" *CHR* 29, no. 1 (1948).

———. "Sir John Macdonald and Kingston" CHA *Annual Report and Historical Papers* 29, no. 1 (1950).

———. "The United States and Confederation" *CHR* 39, no. 3 (1958).

Cross, Michael S, and Robert L. Fraser. "'The Waste that Lies Before Me': The Public and the Private Worlds of Robert Baldwin" CHA *Historical Papers* 18 (1983).

Duncan, Kenneth. "Irish Famine Immigration and the Social Structure of Canada West." In *Studies in Canadian Social History*, edited by Michiel Horn and Ronald Sabourin. Toronto: McClelland & Stewart, 1974.

Eggleston, Stephen. "The Myth and Mystery of PogG" *JCS* 31, no. 4 (1995–97).

Fallis, Laurence S. "The Idea of Progress in the Province of Canada: A Study in the History of Ideas." In *The Shield of Achilles*, edited by W.L. Morton. Toronto: M&S, 1968.

Feaver, George. "The Webbs in Canada: Fabian Pilgrims on the Canadian Frontier" *CHR* 58, no. 3 (1977).

Fingard, Judith. "The Winter's Tale: The Seasonal Contours of Pre-Industrial Towns in British North America" CHA *Historical Papers* 9 (1974).

Forsey, Eugene. "The B.N.A. Act" *Queen's Quarterly*, 1964–65.

Flynn, Louis J. "Canada's Greatest Scot: Sir John Alexander Macdonald, a Centennial Tribute" *Historic Kingston* 16 (1968).

Gibson, James A. "The Colonial Office View of Canadian Federation, 1858–1868" *CHR* 35, no. 4 (1954).

Gibson, Sarah, and Karyn Patterson. "A Tribute to Sir John A. Macdonald" *Historic Kingston* 33 (1985).

Greer, Allan. "The Birth of the Police in Canada." In *Colonial Leviathan: State Formation in Mid-Nineteenth Century Canada*, edited by Allan Greer and Ian Radforth. Toronto: University of Toronto Press, 1992.

———. "Historical Roots of Canadian Democracy" *JCS* 34 (1999).

Griffith, Rudyard. Speech to Kingston Historical Society, Jan. 11, 2005.

Hall, D.J. "'The Spirit of Confederation': Ralph Heintzman, Professor Creighton, and the Bicultural Compact Theory" *JCS* 9, no. 4 (1974).

Harper, Marjory. "Image and Reality in Early Emigrant Literature" *British Journal of Canadian Studies*, 1992, special edition.

Heintzman, Ralph. "The Political Culture of Quebec, 1840–1960" *CJPS* 16, no. 1 (1983).

———. "The Spirit of Confederation: Professor Creighton, Biculturalism and the Use of History" *CHR* 52, no. 1 (1971).

Hockin, Thomas A. "Flexible and Structured Parliamentarianism: From 1848 to Contemporary Party Government" *JCS* 14 (1979).

Johnson, Keith. "John A. Macdonald and the Kingston Business Community." In *To Preserve and Defend: Essays on Kingston in the Nineteenth Century*, edited by Gerald Tulchinsky. Montreal: McGill-Queen's University Press, 1976.

———. "Sir James Gowan, Sir John A. Macdonald and the Rebellion of 1837" *OH* 60, no. 2 (1968).

Jones, Ellwood H. "Ephemeral Compromise: The Great Reform Convention Revisted" *JCS* 3, no. 1 (1968).

Lockhart, A.D. "The Contribution of Macdonald Conservatism to National Unity, 1854–78" CHA *Annual Report and Historical Papers* 18 (1939).

Lower, Arthur. "The Character of Kingston." In *To Preserve and Defend: Essays on Kingston in the Nineteenth Century*, edited by Gerald Tulchinsky. Montreal: McGill-Queen's University Press, 1976.

———. "Political 'Partyism' in Canada" CHA *Annual Report and Historical Papers* 34 (1955).

MacDermot, T.W.L. "John A. Macdonald—His Biographies and Biographers" CHA *Annual Report and Historical Papers* 10 (1931).

———. "The Political Ideas of John A. Macdonald" *CHR* 14 (1933).

Malcolmson, Patricia E. "The Poor in Kingston, 1805–1850." In *To Preserve and Defend: Essays on Kingston in the Nineteenth Century*, edited by Gerald Tulchinsky. Montreal: McGill-Queen's University Press, 1976.

Martin, Chester. "Sir Edmund Head and Canadian Confederation, 1851–1858" CHA *Annual Report and Historical Papers* 9 (1929).

———. "The United States and Canadian Nationality" *CHR* 18 (1937).

Martin, Ged. "Archival Evidence and John A. Macdonald Biographers" *Journal of Historical Biography* 1 (2007) (on-line: http://www.ucfv.ca/history/JHB.htm).

————. "John A. Macdonald and the Bottle" *JCS* 40 (2006).

————. "Painting the Other Picture: The Case Against Confederation." In *From Rebellion to Patriation: Canada and Britain in the Nineteenth and Twentieth Centuries*, edited by C.C. Eldridge. Aberystwyth: Canadian Studies Group in Wales, 1989.

————. "Queen Victoria and Canada" *American Review of Canadian Studies* 13 (1983).

————. "Sir John Eh? Macdonald: Recovering a Voice from History" *British Journal of Canadian Studies* 17 (2004).

Mathews, Robin. "Susanna Moodie, Pink Toryism and Nineteenth-Century Ideas of Canadian Identity" *JCS* 10, no. 3 (1975).

McRoberts, Kenneth. "Canada and the Multinational State" *CJPS*, 2001.

McSherry, James. "The Illness of the First Mrs. John A. Macdonald" *Historic Kingston* 34 (1986).

————. "The Invisible Lady: Sir John A. Macdonald's First Wife" *Canadian Bulletin of Medical History* 1, no. 1 (1984).

Monet, Jacques. "The Political Ideas of Baldwin and LaFontaine." In *The Political Ideas of the Prime Ministers of Canada*, edited by M. Hamelin. Ottawa: Éditions Ottawa: 1969.

————. "French-Nationalism and the Challenge of Ultramontanism." In *An Introduction to Canadian History*, edited by A.I. Silver. Toronto: Canadian Scholars' Press, 1991.

Morton, W. L. "The Conservative Principle in Confederation" *Queen's Quarterly* 80, no. 4 (1965).

————. "The Formation of the First Federal Cabinet" *CHR* 36, no. 2 (1955).

————. "The International Context of Confederation." In *Interpreting Canada's Past*, edited by J.M. Bumsted. 2nd ed. Toronto: Oxford University Press, 1993.

Ontario Historical Society. "Confederation: The Atmosphere of Crisis and the Ontario Fathers of Confederation." In *Profiles of a Province: Studies in the History of Ontario*, edited by Edith G. Firth. Toronto: Ontario Historical Society, 1967.

Otten, A.A. Van den. "Alexander Galt: The 1859 Tariff and Canadian Economic Nationalism" *CHR* 63, no. 2 (1982).

Paquin, Stéphane. "The Myth of the Compact Theory of Canadian Federation" www.canadahistory.com/sections/paperspaquin.htm

Patterson, Graeme. "An Enduring Canadian Myth: Responsible Government and the Family Compact" *JCS* 12, no. 2 (1977).

Preece, Rod. "The Political Philosophy of Sir John A Macdonald," Nicholas Nyiri and Toivo Miljan, Interdisciplinary Research Seminar, Wilfrid Laurier University Press, 1980.

———. "The Political Wisdom of Sir John A. Macdonald" *CJPS* 17, no. 3 (1984).

Radforth, Ian. "Sydenham and Utilitarian Reform." In *Colonial Leviathan: State Formation in Mid-Nineteenth Century Canada*, edited by Allan Greer and Ian Radforth. Toronto: University of Toronto Press, 1992.

Romney, Paul. "From the Rule of Law to Responsible Government: Ontario Political Culture and the Origins of Canadian Statism" CHA *Historical Papers* 23, no. 1 (1988).

———. "Provincial Equality, Special Status and the Compact Theory of Canadian Confederation" *CJPS* 22, no. 1 (1999).

Scott, Frank. "Political Nationalism and Confederation" *CJEPS*, 1945.

Smith, David. "National Political Parties and the Growth of a National Political Community." In *National Politics and Community in Canada*, edited by R. Kenneth Carty and W. Peter Ward. Vancouver: UBC Press, 1986.

Smith, David E. "Patronage in Britain and Canada: An Historical Perspective" *Journal of Canadian Studies* 22, no. 2 (1987).

Smith, Donald B. "John A. Macdonald and Aboriginal Canada" *Historic Kingston* 50 (2002).

Smith, Goldwin. "The Proposed Constitution for British North America" *Macmillan's Magazine*, 1865, London.

Smith, Jennifer. "Canadian Confederation and the Influence of American Federalism" *CJPS* 21, no. 3 (1988).

Smith, Peter J. "Ideological Origins of Canadian Confederation." In *Interpreting Canada's Past*, vol. 1, *Pre-Confederation*, edited by J.M. Bumsted. Toronto: Oxford University Press, 1993.

———. "The Dream of Political Union: Localism, Toryism and the Federal Idea in Pre-Confederation Canada." In *The Causes of Canadian Confederation*, edited by Ged Martin. Fredericton: Acadiensis Press, 1990.

Stacey, C.P. "Britain's Withdrawal from North America, 1864–1871" *CHR* 36, no. 2 (1955).

———. "British Military Policy in the Era of Confederation" CHA *Annual Report and Historical Papers* 13 (1934).

———. "Confederation: The Atmosphere of Crisis." In *Profiles of a Province: Studies in the History of Ontario*, edited by Edith G. Firth. Toronto: Ontario Historical Society, 1967.

———. "Fenianism and the Rise of National Feeling at the Time of Confederation" *CHR* 12, no. 3 (1931).

Stanley, George. "The Man Who Made Canada, 1865–1867," address to the Public Relations Society of America, Foundation for Public Relations Research and Education, 1963.

Stanley, George F.G. "Act or Pact: Another Look at Confederation" CHA *Annual Report and Historical Papers* 38 (1956).

———. "The Macpherson-Shaw-Macdonald Connection." In *Historic Kingston* 13 (1965).

Stewart, Gordon. "Macdonald's Greatest Triumph" *CHR* 63 *(1982)*.

———. "The Origins of Canadian Politics and John A. Macdonald." In *National Politics and Community in Canada*, edited by R. Kenneth Carty and W. Peter Ward. Vancouver: UBC Press, 1986.

Stewart, Gordon T. "Political Patronage Under Macdonald and Laurier, 1875–1911" *The American Review of Canadian Studies* 10, no. 1 (1980).

Stewart, Wallace. "The Growth of Canadian National Feeling" *CHR*, June 1920.

Swainson, Donald. "Alexander Campbell, General Manager of the Conservative Party (Eastern Ontario section)" *Historic Kingston* 17 (1969).

————. "Sir Henry Smith and the Politics of the Union" *OH* 66 (1974).

Talman, J.J. "The Impact of the Railway on a Pioneer Community" CHA *Annual Report and Historical Papers* 34 (1955).

Trotter, R.G. "British Finance and Confederation" CHA *Annual Report and Historical Papers* 6 (1927).

Turner, Allan R. "Mystery of the Confederation Table" *Saskatchewan History* 10, no.1 (1957).

Turner, Isabel. "Sir John A. Macdonald: The Person" *Historic Kingston* 46 (1998).

Ullmann, Walter. "The Quebec Bishops and Confederation" *CHR* 44, no. 3 (1963).

Underhill, Frank H. "The Development of National Political Parties in Canada" *CHR* 16, no. 4 (1935).

————. "Some Aspects of Upper Canada Radical Opinion in the Decade before Confederation" CHA *Annual Report and Historical Papers* 7 (1927).

Upton, L.F.S. "The Idea of Confederation, 1754–1858." In *The Shield of Achilles*, edited by W.L. Morton. Toronto: McClelland & Stewart, 1968.

Vipond, Robert. "Federal Principle and Canadian Confederation" *CJPS*, 1983.

Waite, Peter B. "Chartered Libertine? A Case Against Sir John A. Macdonald and Some Answers" Manitoba Historical Society, Transactions, 1975–6, Series 3, No. 32.

————. "Edward Cardwell and Confederation" *CHR* 43 (1962).

————. "The Political Ideas of John A. Macdonald." In *The Political Ideas of the Prime Ministers of Canada*, edited by Marcel Hamelin. Ottawa: Les Éditions de l'Université d'Ottawa, 1969.

————. "Sir John A. Macdonald: The Man" *Dalhousie Review*, 1967–68.

Wallace, Elizabeth. "The Origins of the Social Welfare State in Canada, 1867–1900" *CJEPS*, 1950.

Wallace, Carl. "Albert Smith, Confederation and Reaction in New Brunswick, 1852–1882" *CHR* 44 (1963).

Wearing, Joseph. "Pressure Group Politics in Canada West Pre-Confederation" CHA *Historical Papers* 2 (1967).

Williams, Alan F. "Trunk and Branch: A Celebration of Railways in Canada, 1836–1944" *British Journal of Canadian Studies* 15, no. 1 (1990).

Wilson, George. "New Brunswick's Entrance into Confederation" *CHR* 9 (1928).

Wilson, Ian. "Sir John A. Macdonald in History" *Historic Kingston* 41 (1993).

Wise, S.F. "God's Peculiar People." In *The Shield of Achilles*, edited by W.L. Morton. Toronto: McClelland & Stewart, 1968.

———. "John A. Macdonald, House of Commons Man" *Historic Kingston* 42 (1984).

Wright, Donald. "Reflections on Donald Creighton and the Appeal of Biography" University College of Fraser Valley, *Journal of Historical Biography* 1 (2007).

THESES

Best, Henry. "George-Etienne Cartier." Ph.D. thesis, Université Laval, 1969.

Burns, Robin B. "D'Arcy McGee and the New Nationality." Master's thesis, Carleton University, 1966.

Fraser, George Max. "Egerton Ryerson and His Political Relations with Sir John A. Macdonald, 1854–1872." Master's thesis, University of Toronto, 1922.

Gatner, Joseph. "The Defence Factor in Confederation of the British North American Provinces." Master's thesis, University of Ottawa, 1961.

Guest, Henry J. "Reluctant Politician: A Biography of Sir Hugh John Macdonald." Master's thesis, University of Manitoba, 1973.

Hodgins, Bruce W. "Attitudes Towards Democracy During the Pre-Confederation Debates." Master's thesis, University of Toronto, 1955.

Leighton, James. "The Development of Federal Indian Policy in Canada, 1840–1890." Ph.D. thesis, University of Western Ontario, 1975.

Lewis, J.P. "'The Lion and Lamb Ministry': John A. Macdonald and the Politics of the First Canadian Federal Cabinet." Master's thesis, University of Guelph, 2005.

Lockhardt, A.D. "The Early Life of John A. Macdonald, 1815–1844." Master's thesis, Queen's University, 1931.

Owram, Doug. "White Savagery: Some Canadian Reactions to American Indian Policy, 1867–1885." Ph.D. thesis, Queen's University.

Silver, Arthur I. "Quebec and the French Minorities, 1864–1917." Ph.D. thesis, University of Toronto, 1973.

Smith, Francis J. "Newfoundland and Confederation." Master's thesis, University of Ottawa, 1970.

Smith, Peter J. "The Ideological Genesis of Canadian Confederation." Ph.D. thesis, Carleton University, 1984.

Sowby, Joyce. "Macdonald the Administrator: Department of the Interior and Indian Affairs, 1878–1887." Master's thesis, Queen's University, 1986.

Stewart, Alice. "The Imperial Policy of Sir John A. Macdonald." Radcliffe College, 1946.

Teatero, William R. "A Dead and Alive Way Never Does: The Pre-Political Professional World of John A. Macdonald." Master's theis, Queen's University, 1978.

Picture Credits

Agnes Etherington Art Centre, Kingston
Portrait of a young John A. Macdonald by W. Sawyer (p. ii)
Margaret Greene (originally thought to be Isabella Macdonald) (p. 75)

Archives of Ontario
Advertisement in Kingston Chronicle, July 27, 1821, microfilm N17-R1 (p. 27)
Robert Baldwin s2071 (p. 98)
Alexander Campbell s93 (p. 109)

City of Toronto Archives
Isabella Macdonald's bedroom PA121569 (p. 80)
Toronto, 1856 (p. 143)

City of Westminster Archives Centre
Marriage certificate for Agnes Bernard and John A. Macdonald (p. 411)

Library and Archives Canada
Helen Macdonald 68632297 (p. 12)
Oliver Mowatt C008361 (p. 49)
Isabella Macdonald C004815 (p. 60)
The young John A. Macdonald C003813 (p. 62)
Princess Street, Kingston PA062177 (p. 65)
Isabella Macdonald miniature PA121569 (p. 85)

Lord Durham, Edward Hall collection, C00618 (p. 91)

Louis-Hippolyte LaFontaine C005961 (p. 99)

Lord Elgin and family C006728 (p. 100)

Helen Macdonald in old age e007140959 (p. 107)

John Rose PA025959 (p. 114)

Ogle R. Gowan C023504 (p. 115)

Hugh John Macdonald as a baby C004814 (p. 118)

Margaret Macdonald e007140957 (C022818) (p. 134)

James Williamson e007140958 (p. 134)

Louisa Macdonald e007140956 (C022817) (p. 135)

John A. Macdonald C002831 (p. 147)

The Reverend Peter Jones PA215156 (p. 155)

Sir Allan McNab C005317 (p. 162)

George-Étienne Cartier C006166 (p. 178)

Huge John as a young boy C033956 (p. 187)

Grand Trunk Railway PA149747 (p. 194)

D'Arcy McGee CC21541 (p. 217)

Alexander Galt PA013008 (p. 220)

The Prince of Wales PA051553 (p. 232)

Delegates arriving at Charlottetown by Rex Woods PA164727 (p. 303)

Charlottetown Conference room C021421 (p. 305)

Prelude to Confederation by Jarvis Studios, Ottawa C002780 (p. 310)

Étienne-Paschal Taché PA074100 (p. 316)

John A. Macdonald 014918 (p. 342)

Charles Tupper PA026318 (p. 358)

Samuel Leonard Tilley PA026347 (p. 359)

Joseph Howe PA025486 (p. 360)

Queen Victoria CC001590 (p. 373)

Westminster Palace Hotel C010377 (p. 391)

The London Conference by John David Kelly, 1935, reproduced with permission of Rogers Communications Inc. C006799 (p. 395)

Agnes Bernard Macdonald PA118099 (p. 407)

Map of the Confederate Provinces by Chewett (p. 417)

Parliament Buildings, military review, May 24, 1867 PA022399 (p. 424)

John A. Macdonald, 1868 PA025336 (p. 440)

Library of Congress Prints and Photographs Division

Fort Sumter DRWG/US Key, no. 3 (B) [P&P] (p. 240)

William Seward LC-B813-1431 A[P&P] (p. 243)

McCord Museum

Place d'Armes, Montreal M993X.5.107 (p. 94)

Parliament Buildings under construction 1-16295.0 (p. 202)

St. Louis Hotel 1-21099.1 (p. 206)

Wilfrid Laurier MP-0000.1093.8 (p. 284)

Lord Monck 1-4437.1 (p. 386)

McGill University Library, Rare Books and Special Collections

Eliza Grimason (p. 209)

Queen's University Archives

Orange Order arch, Kingston V23-Str-Princess-37 (p. 234)

Kingston, reading proclamation V23-His-Con-2 (p. 437)

Toronto Public Library

View of Quebec City, from William H. Bartlett, *Canadian Scenery Illustrated* (1854) (p. 18)

View of Kingston, from William H. Bartlett, *Canadian Scenery Illustrated* (1854) (p. 21)

View of Hallowell, from William H. Bartlett, *Canadian Scenery Illustrated* (1854) (p. 47)

George Brown T30668 (p. 139)

"Double shuffle" cartoon, 1858 (p. 176)

Grand Trunk Railway poster (p. 193)

Anne Brown (p. 271)

Fenian raid, Port Colborne, June 1, 1866 (p. 383)

Index

TWENTIETH CENTURY VIEWS

The aim of this series is to present the best in contemporary critical opinion on major authors, providing a twentieth century perspective on their changing status in an era of profound revaluation.

Maynard Mack, *Series Editor*
Yale University

WHITMAN

WHITMAN

A COLLECTION OF CRITICAL ESSAYS

Edited by

Roy Harvey Pearce

A SPECTRUM BOOK

Prentice-Hall, Inc., *Englewood Cliffs, N.J.*

Current printing (last digit):

12   11   10   9

© 1962

BY PRENTICE-HALL, INC.

ENGLEWOOD CLIFFS, N.J.

LIBRARY OF CONGRESS CATALOG CARD NO.: 62-9310

Printed in the United States of America

94458-C

Table of Contents

Introduction

by Roy Harvey Pearce

During Whitman's lifetime, the great and immediate power of the man and his poems made any ordered assessment of his work virtually impossible. To read Whitman was to know a man who made himself out to be now visionary, now sage, now prophet, often all three at once—and only incidentally a poet. Or rather: to read him was to discover that poetry as traditionally conceived, mere poetry, no longer counted for much; it had to be made into a means whereby the "simple, separate person" might discover once and for all that he was bound up ecstatically in the "democratic," the community in which he might discover that he was one with all men, therefore one with God. Whitman said this again and again, most insistently after the Civil War, as here, in "A Backward Glance O'er Travel'd Roads" (1888):

> But it is not on "Leaves of Grass" distinctively *as literature*, or a specimen thereof, that I feel [it necessary] to dwell, or advance claims. No one will get at my verses who insists upon viewing them as a literary performance, or attempt at such performance, or as aiming mainly toward art or aestheticism.

In short, Whitman demanded of his readers not just the willing suspension of disbelief, but belief itself.

He proudly yielded to his own demand. He could be bold, furtive, devious, active, passive—for the sake of writing poems which would express all these capacities of man. He sacrificed himself to his own image—which he meant to be an all-inclusive image of man. He postured and posed, acted (sometimes behind the scenes) as his own public-relations man, sounded now a barbaric yawp, now a lyric cry, now an epic salutation, now a prayerful meditation, as his sense of the occasion demanded. He was ambivalent about most things because he had an amazing capacity to yield himself wholly to the moment— and then, as though he were quite another person, to seize himself in the moment of yielding. And so he changed, and through nine editions changed *Leaves of Grass* with himself. *Leaves of Grass was* himself—as he said on one occasion, an attempt "to put *a Person,* a human being (myself, in the latter half of the Nineteenth Century, in America) freely, fully and truly on record." The record would be so free and full (as he said on another occasion) that it would make possible an "aggregated, inseparable, unprecedented, vast, composite, electric *Democratic Nationality.*"

But of course the freedom and fullness of the record have posed a great problem, perhaps *the* great problem, for critics of Whitman: to decide upon the truth, the authentic version of *Democratic Nationality*—indeed, of Whitman. Initially, the problem is biographical; then it is artistic; then moral, or religious, or philosophical. The complete critic of Whitman (so far we have not had him) would have to be something of a philosophical anthropologist: one who could put together biography, critical analysis, and philosophical judgment in a single grand synthesis, centering upon an inclusive and definitive conception of man. Yet, if Whitman's life and work are to be comprehended, the idea of such a complete critic is impossible, since the life and work teach us that nothing is inclusive and definitive—above all, a conception of man. Thus, much of the earlier criticism of Whitman, which aimed at some kind of "completeness," was wrong-headed from the start. The criticism of the sort represented in this collection makes a more positive achievement because its makers assume there is more than one truth about Whitman and further that, it is possible to seize upon that truth, elucidate it, and, if necessary, show how it is superior to other truths. The difficult thing is to get used to the idea that one can never be sure.

The work of Emory Holloway and Gay Wilson Allen, Whitman's chief biographers, has done much to make this positive achievement possible. (Their relevant work is listed in the Bibliographical Note at the end of this book.) The record of Whitman's career was first set down by some of the disciples who flocked to him during the last stages of his career. To them, he was a prophet; and all his devious claims about his life and works were true, were a part of the synoptic gospel that was the final version of *Leaves of Grass.* Critical analysis, in effect considered irrelevant, was virtually impossible; synthesis was everything —the synthesis of the Whitmanian "system." Considerations of "art" and "aestheticism" were also in effect regarded as irrelevant. First Holloway in the 1920's and 1930's, then Allen in the 1940's and 1950's (Allen was aided by the work of Clifton J. Furness, who died before he could publish many of the results of his research), steadily accumulated the data which let them get straight the facts of Whitman's life and works. Their biographical studies are strongest when they are least interpretive. They make it quite clear that there are many Whitmans, not one; that the parts of his life and work can never be added up to a whole. In effect, their studies have freed critics of

Whitman to find a viable relationship between his work as it was taken to be and as it is, perhaps as it should be. Whitman fully expected this; for he wrote in 1891: "In the long run the world will do as it pleases with the book. I am determined to have the world know what I was pleased to do." Critics of Whitman now see clearly that their task is to justify their choice among the various truths about the life and works. If biographical study of Holloway's and Allen's sort is not represented in this collection, it must nonetheless be remembered that many of the essays here collected could not have been conceived, much less written, if such biographical study had not been so masterfully carried out.

In the years between his death and the 1920's, then, Whitman posed an exasperating problem for men of letters—above all, for the poets to whom he had looked forward:

> Poets to come! orators, singers, musicians to come!
> Not to-day is to justify me and answer what I am for,
> But you, a new brood, native, athletic, continental, greater than
> before known,
> Arouse! for you must justify me.
>
> I myself but write one or two indicative words for the future,
> I but advance a moment only to wheel and hurry back in the
> darkness.
> I am a man who, sauntering along without fully stopping, turns a
> casual look upon you and then averts his face,
> Leaving it to you to prove and define it,
> Expecting the main things from you.

The record of the "main things" is the record of American poetry since Whitman; Whitman has been the main force which the poets who have come have had to contend with. The year of Whitman's death, E. A. Robinson addressed a poem to Whitman in which he wondered if poetry were no longer possible except as Whitman had made it possible, if "the master songs" were once and for all "ended." Some years later Ezra Pound wrote a poem in which he made a "truce" with Whitman. (He later changed the word to "pact.") Having freed himself from an oppressively anti-poetic American milieu, Pound felt that he could counter Whitman—and he has been doing so ever since, most notably in the middle of the *Pisan Cantos,* in which he identifies his role with Whitman's: making the modern world possible for poetry. In one of his critical essays of the 1920's, T. S. Eliot attacked what he claimed to be Whitman's moon-mist ideas; yet the *Four Quartets* are charged with Whitmanian echoes and recollections. Hart Crane, attacking Eliot's "pessimism," made Whitman into a culture hero in *The*

Bridge. William Carlos Williams has recently discovered that Whitman was the pioneer who cleared the way for modern poetry, specifically "American" poetry of Williams' free-wheeling sort. Most recently, poets of the barbarian persuasion have discovered in Whitman the one Old Priest whose Grove they will not violate. Once more they look to the "great audience" as a necessary condition for "great poets." And so it goes. The record of American poetry since Whitman is the record of a series of confrontations like these.

The record is especially significant for this collection, because modern criticism has been so closely tied to the making of modern poetry. The modern critic has increasingly found that his task is defined by the achievement of modern poetry; his role has been to justify, in his own way, the poet's way with language and the modes of sensibility it projects, extends, and authenticates. His task, so far as Whitman is concerned, is to try to determine which Whitman (or, as I have said, which truth about Whitman) is the most "useful," which has the most bearing upon the possibilities of poetry in the modern age. Nor is this a matter of mere "art or aestheticism." For in an age whose language is increasingly vitiated by mass communications and all they entail, the possibility of making authentic poems is one with the possibility of speaking out honestly, fully, frankly, wholly—thus of being true to oneself as a simple separate person, yet democratic, en-masse. Whitman, then, was quite right, not only in what he wanted out of poetry, but in the frankly experimental, shape-shifting way he sought what he wanted. His modern critic must discriminate among the various Whitmans and his various truths, and must justify the discriminations with analysis and interpretation.

The essays collected here represent the great variety among such discriminations and the "methods" by which they are justified. I have put at the beginning the pronouncement of the young Ezra Pound and the not-so-young D. H. Lawrence; these essays in effect define the problem of Whitman as a problem at once in criticism and cultural history. They are egregious essays, but no less so than other comparable pieces —the chief examples of which are the essays by John Jay Chapman and George Santayana in the Bibliography cited at the end of this book. (Both the Chapman and the Santayana essays have been recently reprinted and are readily available.) These four writers, from the turn of the century through the early twenties, saw clearly that Whitman's promise was also a threat; that somehow Whitman's conception of man was one with his conception of poetry; and that at bottom the issue posed by Whitman's very existence was, as he himself had declared, the inviting yet dangerous vistas of art and belief open to a world in which democratic institutions gave the means but not the force whereby man might at long last achieve the dignity which was rightfully his. They saw that Whitman was whole-heartedly and compulsively, with no holds barred, the *modern* poet, for whom matters literary-artistic and socio-political had to be one and the same. Quite uncomfortably, they wanted to come to terms with Whitman—but not exactly on his terms.

Between them, the Pound and Lawrence essays define the boundaries of Whitman criticism. Pound's assessment of Whitman's importance has proved to be the enduring one—even for critics who would be unhappy to know how precisely Pound has announced their themes for them. Pound, in an age when Whitman's immediate disciples were still striving for their synoptic gospel, sees Whitman primarily as a poet's father-figure from whom he must free himself even while acknowledging that it is his father who has taught him that freedom is not only possible but necessary. (What Whitman in one of his later essays called that "ultimate vivification" which is at the heart of all genuine poetry, Pound came to call "making it new.") Yet for Pound—and this is the notion brilliantly and impatiently developed by Lawrence also—to see Whitman thus is not yet to see him as he saw himself: changing, growing, picking and choosing, teaching himself (and his readers) how to bear the burden of reality his poetry revealed. In the end his life was a series of *rites de passage,* his poems a series of ritual forms, none necessarily demanding the others.

It is on the whole a sense of freedom to choose among these forms, and thus among Whitman's varying identities, which marks the rest of the essays in this collection. In the section called "The Integrity of *Leaves of Grass,*" I have included essays which make out the integral Whitman to be he of the 1855, the 1860, and the 1892 (that is, the final) versions respectively. The word *integrity* is crucial here, for the different versions of the poem center on a sense of the wholeness and perfectibility of the idea of man from which derive an artistic wholeness and perfection signified by *integrity.* Thus Whitman's art and aestheticism is discovered to be bound up in various forms of his "personalism." The first essay in the group, by John Kinnaird, makes out in the boldest terms the case for the 1855 *Leaves of Grass*—arguing that Whitman was not the sort of poet, or man, to "improve" his spontaneous song of himself. The last essay in the group, that by James Miller, marks a recent tendency to try to recover the Whitman of the synoptic gospel, as though—because of the careful biographical and historical study which has been carried on since the 1920's—we were now in a position to accept Whitman at face value, the face being that of the prophet of cosmic consciousness. My own understanding of the problem urges me to argue against choosing this version of Whitman's "truth"—as it urges me to argue against the anti-intellectualism which demands of poetry that it do more than it can: "save" man. All this is implicit in my own essay— the second one in the group, which argues for the preeminence of the 1860 *Leaves of Grass.* (Because my essay is included, I do not venture here any "interpretation" of Whitman.) In any case, the three essays are there: representing three choices. If he is willing to suspend his disbelief, the reader can take them all. The question is: Is this to gainsay, or to deny, one Whitman at the expense of another?

The section called "The Poet in His Art" contains essays which deal with some of the principal topics in Whitman's work—politics, religion, language, the structure of poetic discourse. The reader will note that the critic, though he focuses on only one of these topics, must perforce deal with them all. Here the question is not so much deciding upon the "truest" Whitman, but seeing how the poet variously dealt with problems raised by his inquiries into himself, his culture, and his art.

A final section contains essays that do not deal exclusively with Whitman. I have followed him in calling this section "Democratic Vistas"—but have gone beyond him in allowing the vistas to open on the past as well as the future. The essays I have included here are rather occasioned by Whitman's life and work than centered upon them. But surely this is as Whitman wanted it. The poetry, in the end, was to occasion a reader's composing his own song of himself. These essays do not quite consist in this; but they do deal with the occasion of Whitman's poetry, its derivation from its own past and present, and its bearing upon not only the poets who have come, but also the readers. All of which is to say, the essays deal with what Whitman's poetry occasions. But then, as all the essays in this collection testify, the great use of Whitman's work—what pushes it beyond art and aestheticism—is that it would teach readers that they too must be poets, constantly composing their lives in a song, so to celebrate their highest humanity: the *possibility* of composing their songs of themselves and so creating something actual, "a *Person* . . . freely, fully and truly on record."

Do we yet know how to read Whitman? We have not yet sufficiently grasped the structure and quality of the several versions of *Leaves of Grass*—and therefore of Whitman's several identities. We have not yet sufficiently understood the role of the poet in nineteenth-century culture as Whitman's career shows it developing. We have not yet learned well enough to comprehend the "organic" structure of Whitman's poems, taken one by one. We still have not learned to do without the kind of perfection he eschewed. Too often we still ask the wrong questions of his verse. Or rather, we still insist that we cannot ask of it as many questions as we might. The range of the essays in this collection—which I think fairly represents the range of first-rate Whitman criticism—shows all this. Perhaps this is Whitman's greatest triumph: that we have not yet got used to him. And yet somehow the tone of our critical ventures seems to imply that we must at all costs *try* to get used to him, to domesticate the barbarian, to domesticate the barbarian in ourselves. Perhaps there *is* one truth about him—that he will always surprise us, catch us unawares, teach us to catch ourselves unawares. Above all in an Introduction, the final words (the last section of "Song of Myself") must be his:

> The spotted hawk swoops by and accuses me, he complains of my gab and my loitering.
>
> I too am not a bit tamed, I too am untranslatable,
> I sound my barbaric yawp over the roofs of the world.
>
> The last scud of day holds back for me,
> It flings my likeness after the rest and true as any on the shadow'd wilds,
> It coaxes me to the vapor and the dusk.
>
> I depart as air, I shake my white locks at the runaway sun,
> I effuse my flesh in eddies, and drift it in lacy jags.
>
> I bequeath myself to the dirt to grow under the grass I love,
> If you want me again look for me under your boot-soles.
>
> You will hardly know who I am or what I mean,
> But I shall be good health to you nevertheless,
> And filter and fibre your blood.
>
> Failing to fetch me at first keep encouraged,
> Missing me one place search another,
> I stop somewhere waiting for you.

The Open Road

"Years of the modern! years of the unperform'd!
Your horizon rise. . . ."

Walt Whitman

by Ezra Pound

From this side of the Atlantic I am for the first time able to read Whitman, and from the vantage of my education and—if it be permitted a man of my scant years—my world citizenship: I see him America's poet. The only Poet before the artists of the Carman-Hovey period, or better, the only one of the conventionally recognized "American Poets" who is worth reading.

He *is* America. His crudity is an exceeding great stench, but it *is* America. He is the hollow place in the rock that echoes with his time. He *does* "chant the crucial stage" and he is the "voice triumphant." He is disgusting. He is an exceedingly nauseating pill, but he accomplishes his mission.

Entirely free from the renaissance humanist ideal of the complete man or from the Greek idealism, he is content to be what he is, and he is his time and his people. He is a genius because he has vision of what he is and of his function. He knows that he is a beginning and not a classically finished work.

I honor him for he prophesied me while I can only recognize him as a forebear of whom I ought to be proud.

"Walt Whitman" (Original title: "What I Feel About Walt Whitman," dated 1 February 1909). First published from manuscript by Herbert Bergman in *American Literature, XXVII* (1955), 59-61. I have made a new transcription of the manuscript, which is in the Yale Collection of American Literature, and have silently corrected some of Pound's obvious first-draft slips. This essay is published by the permission of the Yale University Library and Dorothy Pound, Committee for Ezra Pound.—R.H.P.

8

In America there is much for the healing of the nations, but woe unto him of the cultured palate who attempts the dose.

As for Whitman, I read him (in many parts) with acute pain, but when I write of certain things I find myself using his rhythms. The expression of certain things related to cosmic consciousness seems tainted with this maramis.[1]

I am (in common with every educated man) an heir of the ages and I demand my birth-right. Yet if Whitman represented his time in language acceptable to one accustomed to my standard of intellectual-artistic living he would belie his time and nation. And yet I am but one of his "ages and ages' encrustations" or to be exact an encrustation of the next age. The vital part of my message, taken from the sap and fibre of America, is the same as his.

Mentally I am a Walt Whitman who has learned to wear a collar and a dress shirt (although at times inimical to both). Personally I might be very glad to conceal my relationship to my spiritual father and brag about my more congenial ancestry—Dante, Shakespeare, Theocritus, Villon, but the descent is a bit difficult to establish. And, to be frank, Whitman is to my fatherland (Patriam quam odi et amo for no uncertain reasons) what Dante is to Italy and I at my best can only be a strife for a renaissance in America of all the lost or temporarily mislaid beauty, truth, valor, glory of Greece, Italy, England and all the rest of it.

And yet if a man has written lines like Whitman's to the "Sunset breeze" one has to love him. I think we have not yet paid enough attention to the deliberate artistry of the man, not in details but in the large.

I am immortal even as he is, yet with a lesser vitality as I am the more in love with beauty (If I really do love it more than he did). Like Dante he wrote in the "vulgar tongue," in a new metric. The first great man to write in the language of his people.

Et ego Petrarca in lingua vetera scribo. And in a tongue my people understand not.

It seems to me I should like to drive Whitman into the old world I sledge, he drill—and to scourge America with all the old beauty (For Beauty *is* an accusation) and with a thousand thongs from Homer to

---

[1] [I do not know what this word means, and Mr. Pound has so far declined to answer my inquiries about it. His deep interest in medieval Romance literature (he had originally gone to Europe to do research and writing in the field) impels two guesses: 1. that this is his faulty recollection of a crux word in *Aucassin et Nicolette* (V, 4), "miramie"—which no one really understands but which some Romance scholars guess is a form of "merveille"—i.e., "marvelous things"; 2. that this is a faulty recollection and characteristically Poundian extension of the Spanish "marrano": "marranismo"—a "marrano" being a Jew converted to Christianity in order to save himself from persecution, and "marranismo," by extension, being the quality of protesting too much about religious matters. (The word "marranism," from "marranismo," exists in Renaissance English with roughly this meaning.)—R.H.P.]

Yeats, from Theocritus to Marcel Schwob. This desire is because I am young and impatient. Were I old and wise I should content myself in seeing and saying that these things will come. But now, since I am by no means sure it would be true prophecy, I [would] fain set my own hand to the labour.

It is a great thing, reading a man, to know, not "His Tricks are not as yet my Tricks, but I can easily make them mine" but "His message is my message. We will see that men hear it."

Whitman

by D. H. Lawrence

Post mortem effects?
>But what of Walt Whitman?
>The "good grey poet."
>Was he a ghost, with all his physicality?
>The good grey poet.
>Post mortem effects. Ghosts.
>A certain ghoulish insistency. A certain horrible pottage of human parts. A certain stridency and portentousness. A luridness about his beatitudes.

DEMOCRACY! THESE STATES! EIDOLONS! LOVERS, ENDLESS LOVERS!
ONE IDENTITY!
ONE IDENTITY!
I AM HE THAT ACHES WITH AMOROUS LOVE.

Do you believe me, when I say post mortem effects?

When the *Pequod* went down, she left many a rank and dirty steamboat still fussing in the seas. The *Pequod* sinks with all her souls, but their bodies rise again to man innumerable tramp steamers, and ocean-crossing liners. Corpses.

What we mean is that people may go on, keep on, and rush on, without souls. They have their ego and their will, that is enough to keep them going.

So that you see, the sinking of the *Pequod* was only a metaphysical tragedy after all. The world goes on just the same. The ship of the *soul* is sunk. But the machine-manipulating body works just the same: digests, chews gum, admires Botticelli and aches with amorous love.

I AM HE THAT ACHES WITH AMOROUS LOVE.

What do you make of that? I AM HE THAT ACHES. First generalization.

"Whitman." From *Studies in Classic American Literature* by D. H. Lawrence (New York, 1923), pp. 241-264. Copyright 1923 by Thomas Seltzer, Inc., 1951 by Frieda Lawrence. Reprinted by permission of The Viking Press, Inc., Laurence Pollinger Ltd., and the Estate of Mrs. Frieda Lawrence. [The essay comes at the end of *Studies in Classic American Literature,* after a meditation on American "doom" as it is figured by the conclusion of *Moby Dick.* Thus Lawrence's opening words.—R.H.P.]

First uncomfortable universalization. WITH AMOROUS LOVE! Oh, God!
Better a bellyache. A bellyache is at least specific. But the ACHE OF
AMOROUS LOVE!

Think of having that under your skin. All that!

I AM HE THAT ACHES WITH AMOROUS LOVE.

Walter, leave off. You are not HE. You are just a limited Walter. And
your ache doesn't include all Amorous Love, by any means. If you ache
you only ache with a small bit of amorous love, and there's so much
more stays outside the cover of your ache, that you might be a bit
milder about it.

I AM HE THAT ACHES WITH AMOROUS LOVE.

CHUFF! CHUFF! CHUFF!

CHU-CHU-CHU-CHU-CHUFF!

Reminds one of a steam-engine. A locomotive. They're the only
things that seem to me to ache with amorous love. All that steam inside
them. Forty million foot-pounds pressure. The ache of AMOROUS LOVE.
Steam-pressure. CHUFF!

An ordinary man aches with love for Belinda, or his Native Land,
or the Ocean, or the Stars, or the Oversoul: if he feels that an ache is
in the fashion.

It takes a steam-engine to ache with AMOROUS LOVE. All of it.

Walt was really too superhuman. The danger of the superman is that
he is mechanical.

They talk of his "splendid animality." Well, he'd got it on the brain,
if that's the place for animality.

> I am he that aches with amorous love:
> Does the earth gravitate, does not all matter, aching, attract all
>   matter?
> So the body of me to all I meet or know.

What can be more mechanical? The difference between life and
matter is that life, living things, living creatures, have the instinct of
turning right away from *some* matter, and of blissfully ignoring the
bulk of most matter, and of turning towards only some certain bits of
specially selected matter. As for living creatures all helplessly hurtling
together into one great snowball, why, most very living creatures spend
the greater part of their time getting out of the sight, smell or sound
of the rest of living creatures. Even bees only cluster on their own
queen. And that is sickening enough. Fancy all white humanity cluster-
ing on one another like a lump of bees.

No, Walt, you give yourself away. Matter *does* gravitate, helplessly.
But men are tricky-tricksy, and they shy all sorts of ways.

Matter gravitates because it *is* helpless and mechanical.

And if you gravitate the same, if the body of you gravitates to all you meet or know, why, something must have gone seriously wrong with you. You must have broken your mainspring.

You must have fallen also into mechanization.

Your Moby Dick must be really dead. That lonely phallic monster of the individual you. Dead mentalized.

I only know that my body doesn't by any means gravitate to all I meet or know. I find I can shake hands with a few people. But most I wouldn't touch with a long prop.

Your mainspring is broken, Walt Whitman. The mainspring of your own individuality. And so you run down with a great whirr, merging with everything.

You have killed your isolate Moby Dick. You have mentalized your deep sensual body, and that's the death of it.

I am everything and everything is me and so we're all One in One Identity, like the Mundane Egg, which has been addled quite a while.

"Whoever you are, to endless announcements——"
"And of these one and all I weave the song of myself."

Do you? Well, then, it just shows you haven't *got* any self. It's a mush, not a woven thing. A hotch-potch, not a tissue. Your self.

Oh, Walter, Walter, what have you done with it? What have you done with yourself? With your own individual self? For it sounds as if it had all leaked out of you, leaked into the universe.

Post mortem effects. The individuality had leaked out of him.

No, no, don't lay this down to poetry. These are post mortem effects. And Walt's great poems are really huge fat tomb-plants, great rank graveyard growths.

All that false exuberance. All those lists of things boiled in one pudding-cloth! No, no!

I don't want all those things inside me, thank you.

"I reject nothing," says Walt.

If that is so, one must be a pipe open at both ends, so everything runs through.

Post mortem effects.

"I embrace ALL," says Whitman. "I weave all things into myself."

Do you really! There can't be much left of *you* when you've done. When you've cooked the awful pudding of One Identity.

"And whoever walks a furlong without sympathy walks to his own funeral dressed in his own shroud."

Take off your hat then, my funeral procession of one is passing.

This awful Whitman. This post mortem poet. This poet with the

private soul leaking out of him all the time. All his privacy leaking out
in a sort of dribble, oozing into the universe.

Walt becomes in his own person the whole world, the whole universe,
the whole eternity of time. As far as his rather sketchy knowledge of
history will carry him, that is. Because to *be* a thing he had to know it.
In order to assume the identity of a thing, he had to know that thing.
He was not able to assume one identity with Charlie Chaplin, for example, because Walt didn't know Charlie. What a pity! He'd have done
poems, pæans and what not, Chants, Songs of Cinematernity.

"Oh, Charlie, my Charlie, another film is done——"

As soon as Walt *knew* a thing, he assumed a One Identity with it. If
he knew that an Esquimo sat in a kyak, immediately there was Walt
being little and yellow and greasy, sitting in a kyak.

Now will you tell me exactly what a kyak is?

Who is he that demands petty definition? Let him behold me *sitting
in a kyak.*

I behold no such thing. I behold a rather fat old man full of a rather
senile, self-conscious sensuosity.

DEMOCRACY. EN MASSE. ONE IDENTITY.

The universe, in short, adds up to ONE.

ONE.

1.

Which is Walt.

His poems, *Democracy, En Masse, One Identity,* they are long sums
in addition and multiplication, of which the answer is invariably
MYSELF.

He reaches the state of ALLNESS.

And what then? It's all empty. Just an empty Allness. An addled
egg.

Walt wasn't an esquimo. A little, yellow, sly, cunning, greasy little
Esquimo. And when Walt blandly assumed Allness, including Esquimo-
ness, unto himself, he was just sucking the wind out of a blown egg-shell,
no more. Esquimos are not minor little Walts. They are something that
I am not, I know that. Outside the egg of my Allness chuckles the
greasy little Esquimo. Outside the egg of Whitman's Allness too.

But Walt wouldn't have it. He was everything and everything was in
him. He drove an automobile with a very fierce headlight, along the
track of a fixed idea, through the darkness of this world. And he saw
Everything that way. Just as a motorist does in the night.

I, who happen to be asleep under the bushes in the dark, hoping a
snake won't crawl into my neck; I, seeing Walt go by in his great fierce
poetic machine, think to myself: What a funny world that fellow sees!

ONE DIRECTION! toots Walt in the car, whizzing along it.

Whereas there are myriads of ways in the dark, not to mention track-less wildernesses. As anyone will know who cares to come off the road, even the Open Road.

ONE DIRECTION! whoops America, and sets off also in an automobile.

ALLNESS! shrieks Walt at a cross-road, going whizz over an unwary Red Indian.

ONE IDENTITY! chants democratic En Masse, pelting behind in motor-cars, oblivious of the corpses under the wheels.

God save me, I feel like creeping down a rabbit-hole, to get away from all these automobiles rushing down the ONE IDENTITY track to the goal of ALLNESS.

"A woman waits for me——"

He might as well have said: "The femaleness waits for my maleness." Oh, beautiful generalization and abstraction! Oh, biological function.

"Athletic mothers of these States——" Muscles and wombs. They needn't have had faces at all.

> As I see myself reflected in Nature,
> As I see through a mist, One with inexpressible completeness, sanity, beauty,
> See the bent head, and arms folded over the breast, the Female I see.

Everything was female to him: even himself. Nature just one great function.

> This is the nucleus—after the child is born of woman, man is born of woman,
> This is the bath of birth, the merge of small and large, and the outlet again——

"The Female I see——"

If I'd been one of his women, I'd have given him Female. With a flea in his ear.

Always wanting to merge himself into the womb of something or other.

"The Female I see——"

Anything, so long as he could merge himself.

Just a horror. A sort of white flux.

Post mortem effects.

He found, like all men find, that you can't really merge in a woman, though you may go a long way. You can't manage the last bit. So you have to give it up, and try elsewhere. If you *insist* on merging.

In "Calamus" he changes his tune. He doesn't shout and thump and exult any more. He begins to hesitate, reluctant, wistful.

The strange calamus has its pink-tinged root by the pond, and it sends up its leaves of comradeship, comrades from one root, without the intervention of woman, the female.

So he sings of the mystery of manly love, the love of comrades. Over and over he says the same thing: the new world will be built on the love of comrades, the new great dynamic of life will be manly love. Out of this manly love will come the inspiration for the future.

Will it though? Will it?

Comradeship! Comrades! This is to be the new Democracy: of Comrades. This is the new cohering principle in the world: Comradeship.

Is it? Are you sure?

It is the cohering principle of true soldiery, we are told in *Drum Taps*. It is the cohering principle in the new unison for creative activity. And it is extreme and alone, touching the confines of death. Something terrible to bear, terrible to be responsible for. Even Walt Whitman felt it. The soul's last and most poignant responsibility, the responsibility of comradeship, of manly love.

> Yet you are beautiful to me, you faint-tinged roots, you make me think of death.
> Death is beautiful from you (what indeed is finally beautiful except death and love?)
> I think it is not for life I am chanting here my chant of lovers, I think it must be for death,
> For how calm, how solemn it grows to ascend to the atmosphere of lovers,
> Death or life, I am then indifferent, my soul declines to prefer
> (I am not sure but the high soul of lovers welcomes death most)
> Indeed, O death, I think now these leaves mean precisely the same as you mean——

This is strange, from the exultant Walt.

Death!

Death is now his chant! Death!

Merging! And Death! Which is the final merge.

The great merge into the womb. Woman.

And after that, the merge of comrades: man-for-man love.

And almost immediately with this, death, the final merge of death.

There you have the progression of merging. For the great mergers, woman at last becomes inadequate. For those who love to extremes. Woman is inadequate for the last merging. So the next step is the merging of the man-for-man love. And this is on the brink of death. It slides over into death.

David and Jonathan. And the death of Jonathan.
It always slides into death.
The love of comrades.
Merging.

So that if the new Democracy is to be based on the love of comrades, it will be based on death too. It will slip so soon into death.

The last merging. The last Democracy. The last love. The love of comrades.

Fatality. And fatality.

Whitman would not have been the great poet he is if he had not taken the last steps and looked over into death. Death, the last merging, that was the goal of his manhood.

To the mergers, there remains the brief love of comrades, and then Death.

> Whereto answering, the sea.
> Delaying not, hurrying not
> Whispered me through the night, very plainly before daybreak,
> Lisp'd to me the low and delicious word death,
> And again death, death, death, death.
> Hissing melodious, neither like the bird nor like my arous'd child's heart,
> But edging near as privately for me rustling at my feet,
> Creeping thence steadily up to my ears and laving me softly all over
> Death, death, death, death, death——

Whitman is a very great poet, of the end of life. A very great post mortem poet, of the transitions of the soul as it loses its integrity. The poet of the soul's last shout and shriek, on the confines of death. *Après moi le déluge.*

But we have all got to die, and disintegrate.

We have got to die in life, too, and disintegrate while we live.

But even then the goal is not death.

Something else will come.

"Out of the cradle endlessly rocking."

We've got to die first, anyhow. And disintegrate while we still live.

Only we know this much. Death is not the *goal*. And Love, and merging, are now only part of the death-process. Comradeship—part of the death-process. Democracy—part of the death-process. The new Democracy—the brink of death. One Identity—death itself.

We have died, and we are still disintegrating.

But IT IS FINISHED.

Consummatum est.

Whitman, the great poet, has meant so much to me. Whitman, the one man breaking a way ahead. Whitman, the one pioneer. And only Whitman. No English pioneers, no French. No European pioneer-poets. In Europe the would-be pioneers are mere innovators. The same in America. Ahead of Whitman, nothing. Ahead of all poets, pioneering into the wilderness of unopened life, Whitman. Beyond him, none. His wide, strange camp at the end of the great high-road. And lots of new little poets camping on Whitman's camping ground now. But none going really beyond. Because Whitman's camp is at the end of the road, and on the edge of a great precipice. Over the precipice, blue distances, and the blue hollow of the future. But there is no way down. It is a dead end.

Pisgah. Pisgah sights. And Death. Whitman like a strange, modern, American Moses. Fearfully mistaken. And yet the great leader.

The essential function of art is moral. Not æsthetic, not decorative, not pastime and recreation. But moral. The essential function of art is moral.

But a passionate, implicit morality, not didactic. A morality which changes the blood, rather than the mind. Changes the blood first. The mind follows later, in the wake.

Now Whitman was a great moralist. He was a great leader. He was a great changer of the blood in the veins of men.

Surely it is especially true of American art, that it is all essentially moral. Hawthorne, Poe, Longfellow, Emerson, Melville: it is the moral issue which engages them. They all feel uneasy about the old morality. Sensuously, passionally, they all attack the old morality. But they know nothing better, mentally. Therefore they give tight mental allegiance to a morality which all their passion goes to destroy. Hence the duplicity which is the fatal flaw in them; most fatal in the most perfect American work of art, *The Scarlet Letter*. Tight mental allegiance given to a morality which the passional self repudiates.

Whitman was the first to break the mental allegiance. He was the first to smash the old moral conception, that the soul of man is something "superior" and "above" the flesh. Even Emerson still maintained this tiresome "superiority" of the soul. Even Melville could not get over it. Whitman was the first heroic seer to seize the soul by the scruff of her neck and plant her down among the potsherds.

"There!" he said to the soul. "Stay there!"

Stay there. Stay in the flesh. Stay in the limbs and lips and in the belly. Stay in the breast and womb. Stay there, O Soul, where you belong.

Stay in the dark limbs of negroes. Stay in the body of the prostitute. Stay in the sick flesh of the syphilitic. Stay in the marsh where the calamus grows. Stay there, Soul, where you belong.

The Open Road. The great home of the Soul is the open road. Not heaven, not paradise. Not "above." Not even "within." The soul is neither "above" nor "within." It is a wayfarer down the open road.

Not by meditating. Not by fasting. Not by exploring heaven after heaven, inwardly, in the manner of the great mystics. Not by exaltation. Not by ecstasy. Not by any of these ways does the soul come into her own.

Only by taking the open road.

Not through charity. Not through sacrifice. Not even through love. Not through good works. Not through these does the soul accomplish herself.

Only through the journey down the open road.

The journey itself, down the open road. Exposed to full contact. On two slow feet. Meeting whatever comes down the open road. In company with those that drift in the same measure along the same way. Towards no goal. Always the open road.

Having no known direction, even. Only the soul remaining true to herself in her going.

Meeting all the other wayfarers along the road. And how? How meet them, and how pass? With sympathy, says Whitman. Sympathy. He does not say love. He says sympathy. Feeling with. Feel with them as they feel with themselves. Catching the vibration of their soul and flesh as we pass.

It is a new great doctrine. A doctrine of life. A new great morality. A morality of actual living, not of salvation. Europe has never got beyond the morality of salvation. America to this day is deathly sick with saviourism. But Whitman, the greatest and the first and the only American teacher, was no Saviour. His morality was no morality of salvation. His was a morality of the soul living her life, not saving herself. Accepting the contact with other souls along the open way, as they lived their lives. Never trying to save them. As leave try to arrest them and throw them in gaol. The soul living her life along the incarnate mystery of the open road.

This was Whitman. And the true rhythm of the American continent speaking out in him. He is the first white aboriginal.

"In my Father's house are many mansions."

"No," said Whitman. "Keep out of mansions. A mansion may be heaven on earth, but you might as well be dead. Strictly avoid mansions. The soul is herself when she is going on foot down the open road."

It is the American heroic message. The soul is not to pile up defenses round herself. She is not to withdraw and seek her heavens inwardly, in mystical ecstasies. She is not to cry to some God beyond, for salvation. She is to go down the open road, as the road opens, into the unknown, keeping company with those whose soul draws them near to her, accomplishing nothing save the journey, and the works incident to the journey, in the long life-travel into the unknown, the soul in her subtle sympathies accomplishing herself by the way.

This is Whitman's essential message. The heroic message of the American future. It is the inspiration of thousands of Americans today, the best souls of today, men and women. And it is a message that only in America can be fully understood, finally accepted.

Then Whitman's mistake. The mistake of his interpretation of his watchword: Sympathy. The mystery of SYMPATHY. He still confounded it with Jesus' LOVE, and with Paul's CHARITY. Whitman, like all the rest of us, was at the end of the great emotional highway of Love. And because he couldn't help himself, he carried on his Open Road as a prolongation of the emotional highway of Love, beyond Calvary. The highway of Love ends at the foot of the Cross. There is no beyond. It was a hopeless attempt, to prolong the highway of Love.

He didn't follow his Sympathy. Try as he might, he kept on automatically interpreting it as Love, as Charity. Merging.

This merging, en masse, One Identity, Myself monomania was a carry-over from the old Love idea. It was carrying the idea of Love to its logical physical conclusion. Like Flaubert and the leper. The decree of unqualified Charity, as the soul's one means of salvation, still in force.

Now Whitman wanted his soul to save itself, *he* didn't want to save it. Therefore he did not need the great Christian receipt for saving the soul. He needed to supersede the Christian Charity, the Christian Love, within himself, in order to give his Soul her last freedom. The highroad of Love is no Open Road. It is a narrow, tight way, where the soul walks hemmed in between compulsions.

Whitman wanted to take his Soul down the open road. And he failed in so far as he failed to get out of the old rut of Salvation. He forced his Soul to the edge of a cliff, and he looked down into death. And there he camped, powerless. He had carried out his Sympathy as an extension of Love and Charity. And it had brought him almost to madness and soul-death. It gave him his forced, unhealthy, post-mortem quality.

His message was really the opposite of Henley's rant:

> I am the master of my fate.
> I am the captain of my soul.

Whitman's essential message was the Open Road. The leaving of the soul free unto herself, the leaving of his fate to her and to the loom of the open road. Which is the bravest doctrine man has ever proposed to himself.

Alas, he didn't quite carry it out. He couldn't quite break the old maddening bond of the love-compulsion, he couldn't quite get out of the rut of the charity habit. For Love and Charity have degenerated now into habit: a bad habit.

Whitman said Sympathy. If only he had stuck to it! Because Sympathy means feeling with, not feeling for. He kept on having a passionate feeling *for* the negro slave, or the prostitute, or the syphilitic. Which is merging. A sinking of Walt Whitman's soul in the souls of these others.

He wasn't keeping to his open road. He was forcing his soul down an old rut. He wasn't leaving her free. He was forcing her into other people's circumstances.

Supposing he had felt true sympathy with the negro slave? He would have felt *with* the negro slave. Sympathy—compassion—which is partaking of the passion which was in the soul of the negro slave.

What was the feeling in the negro's soul?

"Ah, I am a slave! Ah, it is bad to be a slave! I must free myself. My soul will die unless she frees herself. My soul says I must free myself."

Whitman came along, and saw the slave, and said to himself: "That negro slave is a man like myself. We share the same identity. And he is bleeding with wounds. Oh, oh, is it not myself who am also bleeding with wounds?"

This was not *sympathy*. It was merging and self-sacrifice. "Bear ye one another's burdens."—"Love thy neighbour as thyself."—"Whatsoever ye do unto him, ye do unto me."

If Whitman had truly *sympathised*, he would have said: "That negro slave suffers from slavery. He wants to free himself. His soul wants to free him. He has wounds, but they are the price of freedom. The soul has a long journey from slavery to freedom. If I can help him I will: I will not take over his wounds and his slavery to myself. But I will help him fight the power that enslaves him when he wants to be free, if he wants my help. Since I see in his face that he needs to be free. But even when he is free, his soul has many journeys down the open road, before it is a free soul."

And of the prostitute Whitman would have said:

"Look at that prostitute! Her nature has turned evil under her mental lust for prostitution. She has lost her soul. She knows it herself. She likes to make men lose their souls. If she tried to make me lose my soul, I would kill her. I wish she may die."

But of another prostitute he would have said:

"Look! She is fascinated by the Priapic mysteries. Look, she will soon be worn to death by the Priapic usage. It is the way of her soul. She wishes it so."

Of the syphilitic he would say:

"Look! She wants to infect all men with syphilis. We ought to kill her."

And of another syphilitic:

"Look! She has a horror of her syphilis. If she looks my way I will help her to get cured."

This is sympathy. The soul judging for herself, and preserving her own integrity.

But when, in Flaubert, the man takes the leper to his naked body; when Bubu de Montparnasse takes the girl because he knows she's got syphilis; when Whitman embraces an evil prostitute: that is not sympathy. The evil prostitute has no desire to be embraced with love; so if you sympathise with her, you won't try to embrace her with love. The leper loathes his leprosy, so if you sympathise with him, you'll loathe it too. The evil woman who wishes to infect all men with her syphilis hates you if you haven't got syphilis. If you sympathise, you'll feel her hatred, and you'll hate too, you'll hate her. Her feeling is hate, and you'll share it. Only your soul will choose the direction of its own hatred.

The soul is a very perfect judge of her own motions, if your mind doesn't dictate to her. Because the mind says Charity! Charity! you don't have to force your soul into kissing lepers or embracing syphilitics. Your lips are the lips of your soul, your body is the body of your soul; your own single, individual soul. That is Whitman's message. And your soul hates syphilis and leprosy. Because it *is* a soul, it hates these things which are against the soul. And therefore to force the body of your soul into contact with uncleanness is a great violation of your soul. The soul wishes to keep clean and whole. The soul's deepest will is to preserve its own integrity, against the mind and the whole mass of disintegrating forces.

Soul sympathises with soul. And that which tries to kill my soul, my soul hates. My soul and my body are one. Soul and body wish to keep clean and whole. Only the mind is capable of great perversion. Only the mind tries to drive my soul and body into uncleanness and unwholesomeness.

What my soul loves, I love.

What my soul hates, I hate.

When my soul is stirred with compassion, I am compassionate.

What my soul turns away from, I turn away from.

That is the *true* interpretation of Whitman's creed: the true revelation of his Sympathy.

And my soul takes the open road. She meets the souls that are passing, she goes along with the souls that are going her way. And for one and all, she has sympathy. The sympathy of love, the sympathy of hate, the sympathy of simple proximity: all the subtle sympathisings of the incalculable soul, from the bitterest hate to the passionate love.

It is not I who guide my soul to heaven. It is I who am guided by my own soul along the open road, where all men tread. Therefore, I must accept her deep motions of love, or hate, or compassion, or dislike, or indifference. And I must go where she takes me. For my feet and my lips and my body are my soul. It is I who must submit to her.

This is Whitman's message of American democracy.

The true democracy, where soul meets soul, in the open road. Democracy. American democracy where all journey down the open road. And where a soul is known at once in its going. Not by its clothes or appearance. Whitman did away with that. Not by its family name. Not even by its reputation. Whitman and Melville both discounted that. Not by a progression of piety, or by works of Charity. Not by works at all. Not by anything but just itself. The soul passing unenhanced, passing on foot and being no more than itself. And recognized, and passed by or greeted according to the soul's dictate. If it be a great soul, it will be worshipped in the road.

The love of man and woman: a recognition of souls, and a communion of worship. The love of comrades: a recognition of souls, and a communion of worship. Democracy: a recognition of souls, all down the open road, and a great soul seen in its greatness, as it travels on foot among the rest, down the common way of the living. A glad recognition of souls, and a gladder worship of great and greater souls, because they are the only riches.

Love, and Merging, brought Whitman to the Edge of Death! Death! Death!

But the exultance of his message still remains. Purified of MERGING, purified of MYSELF, the exultant message of American Democracy, of souls in the Open Road, full of glad recognition, full of fierce readiness, full of joy of worship, when one soul sees a greater soul.

The only riches, the great souls.

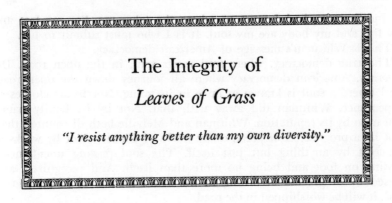

The Integrity of
Leaves of Grass

"I resist anything better than my own diversity."

Leaves of Grass
and the American Paradox

by John Kinnaird

At once the most personal and impersonal of modern poets, only rarely does Whitman confess any anxieties that might belie his pragmatic faith ("What I assume you shall assume") that all human contradictions are but phases of counterpoint in some ultimate music of hope. One of these rare moments occurs in an early poem, "The Sleepers"—a passage the vatic Whitman later deleted from his book—when almost imperceptibly the thematic major wavers, and a half-muted troubled undertone is heard:

> Pier that I saw dimly last night when I looked from the windows,
> Pier out from the main, let me catch myself with you and stay . . .
> I will not chafe you;
> I feel ashamed to go naked about the world,
> And am curious to know where my feet stand . . . and what is this
> flooding me, childhood or manhood . . . and the hunger that
> crosses the bridge between.

"Leaves of Grass and the American Paradox" (Original title: "Whitman: The Paradox of Identity"). From *Partisan Review*, XXV (Summer, 1958), 380-405. Copyright 1958 by *Partisan Review*. Revised by John Kinnaird for publication in this volume, and reprinted by his permission and that of the editors of the *Partisan Review*.

Nothing else that remained in *Leaves of Grass* suggests so much of the original existential Whitman that criticism must continue to recover and understand, particularly since this is the first poet who ever insisted that his book was in reality no book: "Who touches this touches a man." "Childhood or manhood"—presumably the emotions of the bachelor Whitman never crossed the phallic bridge between them; and perhaps his book, like *The Bridge* of Hart Crane, a poet with similar conflicts, should be regarded as his imaginary marriage of worlds: in Whitman's case, a kind of spiritual Brooklyn Ferry (he once called ferries "streaming, never-failing, living poems") on which he could both "stand" in the eternity of imagination and yet move in time, a man like any other, toward a more fully human significance. This would seem to be the first secret of his pose: he is *poised*, perfectly balanced as he moves between possibility and the past—always with the illusion of change as progress, yet never surrendering his freedom to return—between the Long Island shore of his childhood ("Paumanok") and the world of manly ego across the bay, the "Mannahatta" and the American continent that were always for Whitman the waiting and inescapable realities.

Whitman's uncertainty, as the imagery here suggests, was always sexual. The biographical evidence, in itself inconclusive, does seem to confirm what anyone may intuit from the poems: that Whitman was predominantly homosexual in his elementary responses, but never, it seems, in overt conduct and perhaps never in his private relations. But the most important fact is still that ambiguity itself, his uncertainty of sexual will, and this in itself indicates—as seems evident from the autoeroticism in "The Song of Myself"—a suspension, possibly life-long, in some childhood phase of introversion that may never have reached complete inversion. This eroticism, moreover, was further complicated, as Mark Van Doren has noted, by a condition of chronic sensory excitability known technically as *erethisia*. Whitman had an abnormal susceptibility to touch: nearly everyone who knew him well remarked that the skin on his rather large and languorous body seemed unusually soft and pink; in him, as he himself liked to say, was "the flush of the universe." By day he must have felt himself to be, as we have come to know him, the glowing epitome of health—in the American grand manner he established; but by night this same sensuous vitality might easily have abandoned him to an abysmal sense of deprivation, and in such moments, we may conjecture, he became not unlike the wandering sleeper of his poem, lost in an unknown inner "flood" of feeling, a relentless but nameless and impotent longing. This seems to have been the darker necessity animating this secretly lonely and anomalous "caresser of life": as he once confessed in a poem, "I had to let flame from me the fires that were threatening to consume me."

Whitman's adolescence seems almost wholly characterized by indolence and impressionability—a passivity of mind that produced in his youth

a motley and unthinking imitation of the worldly conventions available
to him, and inwardly (we remember his authorship of a temperance
novel) a similarly lazy moral conformity with the great "They" of society across the bay. In his twenties, for instance, he seems to have
taken up the fashionable role of Broadway dandy, sporting a cane and a
boutonnière; and as such this shabby-genteel journalist may have found
a satisfying but transient sense of identity in the cameraderie of work, in
the Broadway crowds, at the opera, in debating societies, in Tammany
meetings and rallies—and then in 1846 (the beginnings of his great
change) in the confident stance he develops as the militant "Free Soil"
editor of the Brooklyn *Eagle*. But perhaps all this while—until the
seven obscure years, 1847-55, when *Leaves* began to materialize in his
notebooks—Whitman never knew his latent sexual identity; and if it
is true, as Malcolm Cowley thinks, that what provoked Whitman's
poetic metamorphosis was some first fully satisfying—or profoundly
disturbing—sexual experience, then what we encounter may be the
crucial anomaly in a life that seems almost definable as a reversal of
the normal development of self-consciousness. For perhaps it was only
after reaching maturity in the world that Whitman discovered that
sexual illumination of the life-processes normally experienced—without,
of course, a correspondingly awakened mind—in late adolescence. This
discovery of what might have seemed to him a kind of renascent innocence would have been received, again paradoxically, by a mind of experience; and the images it evoked in the release that became the poetry
were not primarily, therefore, those of some long-lost adolescent enchant-
ment (as with Sherwood Anderson, perhaps) but those from the public
world itself, from the commonplace life of a petit bourgeois "failure"
already well on in his thirties, his hair already beginning to gray. And
coming, moreover, so late in life, this revelation of sexual fulfillment
would almost certainly have been conjoined with the first intimations
of death. Thus it was, perhaps, that it became forever impossible for
Whitman to dissociate mind from flesh, sex and death, experience and
psyche, body and soul, one's temporal from one's immortal identity—
associations, in fact, so extreme in Whitman that while they intensify
his luminous feeling for death they nevertheless limit, by their emotional
oversimplification, his vision of death as personal mortality. Only, I
think, by assuming some such strangely revolutionary experience, possessing Whitman with an almost religious intensity—and bringing with
it, however bitter the shock, its own joy and power of redemption—can
one account for that extreme identification of the spiritual essence of
life with the organic modes of its birth and dissolution (and for his view,
too, of the poetic imagination as, to quote Richard Chase, "a mode
of the sense of death") that lies at the heart of his sensibility and which
gives his verse its universality of appeal—even to temperaments so distant as the Latin or the Catholic mind: his sense, namely, of an infinite

promise in the body, his belief in the flesh as the sacred and definitive human substance.

"I cannot understand the mystery," Whitman had written in his notebook in 1847, "but I am always conscious of myself as two—as my soul and I—and I reckon it is the same with all men and women." This, the ambivalence Whitman had always known—of "childhood and manhood," of private "soul" and worldly "I"—ceased to be a mute and paralytic conflict and became his lyrical dialogue, his antiphonal "song of myself," when he felt and could express their unconscious struggle as the rhythmic energy of Eros, as not only the human but the elementary organic mystery of change and possibility in the world. And so strong was his sense of power in at last being able to find in images of non-self a relativity for his mystery, that at first it seems to have been enough for Whitman simply to "celebrate" his inward paradox:

> I am satisfied—I see, dance, laugh, sing:
> As God comes a loving bedfellow and sleeps at my side all night and
>   close on the peep of day,
> And leaves for me baskets covered with white towels bulging the
>   house with their plenty,
> Shall I postpone my acceptation and realization and scream at
>   my eyes,
> That they turn from gazing after and down the road,
> And forthwith cipher and show me to a cent,
> Exactly the contents of one, and exactly the contents of two, and
>   which is ahead?

Here and in most of "The Song of Myself" Whitman was content to let even such obscurely troubled questions as this stand rhythmically as their own answers: he would exult in the self as he did in the universe— as perfect and joyous *because* they were insoluble: "the depths are fathomless and therefore calm." But if the divine "touch" of Eros "quivers" him, as he wrote elsewhere in the poem, "to a new identity"— what, then, did his lyrical "acceptation and realization" of this new and otherwise unintelligible "self" mean to the world? In a sense, the thematic problem Whitman now faced was not unlike that of the religious novice: having been converted to the mystery whose integrity 'passeth all understanding,' he must now serve his faith, and he can only communicate it to and with others (and even to himself) as an articulate idea or ritual—which, of course, the original mystery was not. This is the inescapable irony of meaning in the paradox Whitman celebrates; and his peculiarly modern greatness in "The Song" is that he recognizes with an instinctive honesty his enigma for what it is. In his sheer lyrical momentum he is able to play happily with his mystery as both irony and unity; at times he seems even to suggest that human

happiness, like his own comic happiness, is revealed by and is even to
be saved by this sense of the ambiguity of reality, this cosmic joke about
the self-sufficiency of our cosmic ignorance—a joke he directed expressly,
perhaps (as R. W. Flint has recently suggested) at the theological high
priest of his new faith, at Emerson.

Whitman, however, was never consciously prepared to welcome the
ambiguities of poetry as their own justification; and if the joke of his
divine comedy was aimed at Emerson, this was so because it was chiefly
he who gave Whitman the means of resolving his manifold "identity"
problem. "Acceptation," being "enough for myself"—this freedom of
sensibility was now the necessity of his "soul"; but Puritan America
had imbedded in Whitman a conscience far more conventional—in
matters of practical prudence—than this Quakerish Bohemian ever
cared to admit, and an ego conditioned in the Jacksonian age of his
youth still felt the need to satisfy whatever it sensed to be the more
consciously masculine norms, both in ideology and in conduct, of the
paternal American "Mannahatta." Whitman both needed and wished
to return to the 'unreal city' of his experience, even though this return
meant having somehow to find or create, to "assume," a new and—however vicarious—more personalized relation with the American authority
across the bay that had heretofore offered his secret individuality no
means of mediation or self-knowledge. His rebellion, therefore, had to
be both an act of love and an exorcism of his old *alter ego*—a revolt
against American society only in the name of its own ideal culture.
And so it was that when Whitman had his phrenological bumps read—
and learned that he was a manly specimen after all; when he read
Emerson and George Sand and Carlyle and found in them moral and
intellectual confirmation for his mysterious "self": when he discovered
in these and other sources a way to extend magically and mythologically
his rhythmic fantasies of "my soul and I" into an embrace of America—
then, we may conclude, the poet of the notebooks had found a way of
ordering his mystery and was ready and willing to publish.

What Whitman's mythical "assumption" was we may begin to understand, not by appealing at once to Democracy or Transcendentalism or
Panpsychism, but by looking closely at the great structural paradox of
the first *Leaves of Grass*. We find our revealing clue, I think, in the
simple and astonishing fact that in the verse itself such words as
America and *democracy* and *en masse* occur only very rarely—at most
once or twice: we find them acquiring their first significance as determining concepts only in the famous prose Preface, where Whitman he-
raldically announces the coming of the Cosmic Democratic Poet. This
fact is symptomatic of a disparity between the Preface and the earliest
poetry that has never been duly recognized—probably because, like
Emerson (who saw himself in the Preface) and like all readers since,
we begin to read the poetry with elaborate preconceptions of what Whit-

man the poet means—a preconditioning Whitman himself was the first
to establish. If, however, we read the poetry with an uncommitted eye,
we find that we are really never in a consciously American world, but
always within the purely magical universe of Whitman's "self" and its
strange visitations.[1] Whitman reintroduces us kaleidoscopically to what
seems *all* the phenomena of the world, yet now somehow all transfigured: we visit the grass, the sea, oxen, beetles, buzzards, stallions,
molluscs, stars; suicides and murders and childbirths and shipwrecks;
mechanics, sopranos, trappers, prostitutes, slaves, Indians, and Broadway buses and their drivers—but though the creatures of this world may
often as it happens be Americans, we are always within a timeless and
"primeval" democracy; we never find ourselves transported to transcendental realms called "America" or the "New World": we are never
in a world of nationalism and ideology. It is only in the Preface that
we encounter the familiar prophetic utterance we had been led to
expect; only there are we told that "the United States themselves are
the greatest poem," only there do we meet Whitman in the public
phase of his new identity—as the would-be national bard.

This is not to say, of course, that the animus of the Preface differs
radically from the spirit and style of the poetry; but the shift in focus
and intention is clearly there, and indicates the duality of poetic motive
that soon reveals itself as the dialectic of Whitman's career. For it is
always, I think, the habitual *prose* Whitman—the aggressive editor, the
would-be potent male, "of Manhattan the son"—who compulsively wills
his meanings into ideology, who "promulges" vast generalizations, who
"strikes up for a New World" and in doing so compensates for his ego
in the real America. This was the Whitman who by printing his book
accomplished his personal "realization"; but the sensibility with which
it came into being belongs to the anonymous woman and child in him,
to the lonely spirit of "Paumanok," of the earth and the sea and the
darkened beach: the "soul" who "accepts" and "is satisfied," who sym-
pathizes and particularizes and remembers, who knows only dumb
rhythmic images and mutely caresses them. It would be wrong, however,
to identify this recessive self as essentially "the poet" in Whitman; on
the contrary, his poetry owes its expression, and even, in a sense, its
imagination—its unity of word and image—precisely to the tendencies
of his prosaic "I" to dominate with his pragmatic will in language, as he
did politically in the Preface, this otherwise indeterminate lyricism of
his "soul." Whitman, we remember, once called his book a "language

---

[1] Two of the twelve poems in the first edition—later entitled "Europe" and "A
Boston Ballad"—constitute exceptions to this statement. Only in verse form, however
—not in character and subject-matter—can they be said to be integral with the rest of
the volume. I should add that much of what I say here of the early poems is true of
them only as they first appeared—not as later revised by Whitman, which is, unfortunately, the variant of the text almost always reprinted today.

experiment"; and like all successful revolutions in the language of verse
—like the stilnovists' and Dante's, like the Elizabethans', like Dryden's
and Wordsworth's—Whitman's represented a new and necessary assimilation of the modes of poetry and prose: a marriage of mythopoeic or
symbolic motives with the trafficking language of the ordinary world.
And *Leaves of Grass* was just such a success because it "celebrated" a
functionally similar marriage within Whitman: between the compensatory imagination of ego and the dream-fantasies of his unconscious
"soul." The result was to create in the style the figure that was nominally
its author—the novel *persona* or "mask" that gave Whitman his conscious continuity in conceiving the whole of the first edition: a representative "Walt Whitman," in which "soul" and "I" had found a
more than public, a more than private, "identity"; an idea of himself
expressible only as a self-dramatic image, but which, in being dramatic
yet unitary as an image, was also a mythical idea of the world.

In understanding this *persona* at least three dramatic components
must always be distinguished—as Whitman himself suggests when,
bowing into his book for the first time (which, we remember, was otherwise anonymous), it takes him three distinct phrases to properly introduce
himself:

Walt Whitman, an American, one of the roughs, a kosmos

The first of these faces we may readily identify as the Whitman of
Manhattan, the democratic ideologue of the Preface; the second we
recognize as his compensatory masculine image of himself—the cocky,
indolent young workingman of the anonymous daguerrotype frontispiece (actually, and intentionally so, Whitman here seems much more
"rough" in his costume than in his pose or looks); while the third,
the "kosmos," is the most functionally mythical aspect of the *persona*
—the furthest from worldly ego and the closest to his dream life—
the fantastic, serio-comic mask of godhead whereby Whitman resolved in imagination the contradictions of his conscious identity
into a divinely free and conventionally lawless unity of opposites.
This cosmic "self" suggests, of course, his debt to Emerson; but the
stylistic life of Whitman's "kosmos" suggests also a rebellious conspiracy against the romantic transcendentalism from which it derives.
Actually we find this and other Emersonian ideas serving Whitman
as little more than conscious "motifs," while beneath this surface the
value of the divine mask lies precisely in the power it gave Whitman
to escape from Emerson's divine solemnities—from Platonic notions
of the divine; and for a poet this meant a necessary freedom to
transcend the received logic of his metaphors. With part of his mind,
of course, Whitman took Emersonian mysticism seriously, but here
again the value to the poetry lay in his having found a philosophical

authority for regarding the contradictory depths in himself as a microcosm, not of human nature only, but of all reality: he was thus able to accept as an elemental power the essentially androgynous demands of his imagination. Thus assured of an absolute anonymity, his "soul" could now freely wander forth in the infinitudes of imagination, not only as a spirit "maternal as well as paternal, a child as well as a man," but as the vagabond "touch" of Eros and death, as the dynamic Itself of the universe. Now, too, with such a universal soul in its body, the "rough" male *persona*—the incarnate "I" of this "kosmos"—was free to vicariously love and caress not only its own but all bodies and all souls. And if the prose ideologue in Whitman was still troubled by this monstrous indulgence—and the self-defense of the Preface indicates that he was—there was always, as an ultimate justification, the glorious image of the Poet that the intoxicated humanism of the time afforded him. The Poet, wrote the Scottish poet, Alexander Smith—some of whose lines Whitman once quoted as a "grand announcement"—must "reflect our great humanity," must "sprout fragrantly green leaves" like the life-giving Spring, must "sphere the world" with his "heart of love": and in *Leaves of Grass,* thanks to the literalism of Whitman's imagination, this romantic rhetoric became amazingly incarnate—so much so, in fact, that most of Whitman's humanist contemporaries never recovered from their shock of recognition and were never to avow this giant bred by their own idealism.

However much indebted to the existing tradition for his messianic image of the poet-prophet, Whitman knew that he could never adapt the diction and manner of the contemporary romanticism to the vast expressive needs of his "kosmos"—necessities that proved revolutionary enough to overthrow ultimately in English literary culture the pious notion of poetry as a ritual dedicated to an absolute Protestant Good and its ministering angel of Beauty. The literary liberation of Whitman's "soul" became complete—and his *persona* may be said to have properly come into being—when his generalized reaction to conventionality still inchoately represented in the compensatory *imago* of the "rough" ("Washes and razors for foofoos—for me freckles and a bristling beard") joined with his ideological compulsions in willing the act of phallic boldness, the "oath of procreation," that became the metaphor of his "language experiment": "This day I am jetting the stuff of far more arrogant republics."

That seminal "stuff" for Whitman was the potency of the American vernacular, and especially the idiom of the new popular culture filtering in from the West—not so much its monstrosities of diction (he preferred his own "kosmos words") but its flair and grotesquerie and the genius of its slang for symbolic "indirection." Out of the same Jacksonian zeitgeist that had produced in American humor what Constance Rourke calls "the gamecock of the Western wilderness," Whitman fashioned

his primitive "rough" *persona,* and like the gamecock, the proof of
his *charisma* was his ability to talk big, to swagger with words. "I like
limber, lasting, fierce words," he wrote in his *American Primer,*
" . . . strong, cutting, beautiful, rude words. To the manly instincts
of the People they will forever be welcome." And so, then, of course, *he*
would, too: inevitably his egoistic motive recognizes its opportunity.
"Words follow character," he wrote; and if he was to show himself a
"a great user of words," was he not then giving proof that he really had
as the phrenologists assured him, these "natural propensities in himself"?
But when he wrote his first poetry—before, like a ventriloquist, he had
fashioned the visual dummy of the frontspiece for the 'character' of the
voice he was able to 'throw'—Whitman was primarily interested in
accomplishing the anonymous release of his "soul": his *persona* was still
only the unembarrassed voice of his "kosmos"—"gross, hankering,
mystical, nude":

> Flaunt of the sunshine I need not your bask—lie over!

> I too am not a bit tamed—I too am untranslatable

> The last scud of day holds back for me,
> It flings my likeness after the rest and true as any on the shadowed
>   wilds,
> It coaxes me to the vapor and the dusk.

> I believe a leaf of grass is no less than the journey-work of the
>   stars,
> And the pismire is equally perfect, and a grain of sand, and the egg
>   of the wren,
> And the tree-toad is a chef d'oeuvre for the highest,
> And the running blackberry would adorn the parlors of heaven . . .

Such lines as these were not, however, mere somersaults of verbal
bravado, a witty indemnification for a sentimental pantheism or a mind-
less anarchic innocence—"a wild soft laughter," as Carl Sandburg
would have it. The more we attend to them, in fact, the more we observe that they represent in their tonal inference nothing less than the
meaning Whitman has found for the contradictions of the world.
What the playful irony of his voice establishes for us as we read is
the medium of feeling that Whitman imagines as existing between all
beings in the world; for in line after line we learn that what it primarily means to have being of any kind—to have any sort of identity,
animate or inanimate—is to be a manifest challenge, a "mocking taunt"
to all other identities. This irony, however, remains playful because it
expresses not only the oblique point of view of identity, of "each,"

but the loving irony of the poet who, from the omniscient vantage of the "all," represents the experience of being in all its continuity. From the point of view of each identity, existence is essentially ironical: there is nothing quite like itself in the whole world. But although there is a constant chaos and struggle of identities—and consequently suffering, death and defeat (which do *not* go unrepresented in Whitman's world)—the "mocking taunt" is not finally ironic because no identity, whether destroyed or destroying, "countervails" another. Everything has its *thereness,* is "in its place"; has its own body, its own involvement with itself, its own perfection, and is therefore "great." And in having absolute joy or possession of itself, in being individual, it obeys the common "law of perfections": that law of "precision and balance," as he says in the Preface, which was Whitman's own way of enjoying himself and which became, therefore, his principle of perception—the ontology of his vision and the individualistic aesthetic of his "free verse."

What is it, then, to be a self in such a universe? Like all animate identities, Whitman's self finds its positive life in the "dilation and pride" of being, in the will to power; and even love, having its roots, like all emotion, in sexual energy, partakes of this challenge "to be master." The human self, however, is itself a microcosm of struggling identities, in which "body" and "soul" and all the contradictory powers of Whitman's being contend and conspire to woo the secret and elusive beloved, "the Me myself." But the self always escapes from itself as from all other impinging identities, and when it does, the roles are soon reversed: then Whitman's "I" is the pursuer of the miraculous secret of power and love, the mystery whose "mocking taunt" winks back at him from the manifold interplay of the universe. (Here we glimpse the ironic relation that obtains in the poetry between Whitman *in propria persona* and his "kosmos" of Eros, which can only be imagined as existing in the world, and yet when felt or experienced becomes a mystery again by passing into his feeling, into "myself.") The secret thus turns out to be the joy and the style of its pursuit: unlike the romantic secret in *Faust,* the secret may only be sought and felt and loved *as* a secret, for all beings may only share the secret they can never know—the miracle of "touch" or "urge" that "quivers" them all to "identity." To have the self-experience of "identity," then, is not only to imitate the universal life in its expression of energy, but to imitate the universe in its secret balance, to recoil from all extremes and repose upon one's self as a secret, exactly as the body does. (Perhaps this helps to explain, too, Whitman's imagination of death as the perfection of "identity.") Whitman's irony, therefore, being inevitably a self-expression, rises and falls as only a phase of his balance, and must finally yield to the higher paradox of love that Whitman as the poet recognizes. For if "precision and balance" is the law of the body, then there is hope that the power of Eros may also order itself as a self-redemptive law

in the world ("a kelson of the creation is love"), exactly as it does in
his poetry.

This, then, insofar as it yields to analysis, is what I take to be
Whitman's vision of the organic democracy of all things—and it
will be seen at once how radically American this view of the world
is. But the very intensity of Whitman's awareness of his vision seems
to have bred a confusion of values and of the planes of thought and
being, especially when the same voice modulated into the proselytic
will of the Preface attempted to translate a poet's love into the democratic ethos of "sympathy and pride" and poetic "laws of perfection"
into an evolutionary American "fruition." The irony of the "un-
translatable" mystery begins to disappear in the very year of publication,
for in the performance of 1856 Whitman has already begun to lose
the delicate balance of his paradox. The first *Leaves of Grass,* the actual
book, seems to have served Whitman as a kind of mirror, in which the
persona, having acquired objective reality, saw itself for the first time;
and from that moment, as it were, Whitman's love was less for his
democratic mystery than for its American image. It is almost as if
Whitman had looked too long at his own frontispiece, and had then
begun primping to make good on his specifications for an "athletic
bard," forgetting that this new "self" was not its own reality but an
attitude, an imaginative way of speaking, a "language experiment."
What was happening, of course, was what Nietzsche describes as the
"typical velleity" of the artist: "tired to the point of despair of the
eternal 'unreality' and falseness of innermost being," he is tempted
to think that he actually *is* the object he is able to represent, imagine
or express; and then, attempting to have real existence, he "trespasses
on the forbidden ground" of actuality. Almost from the moment of his
first creativity—in his attempt to somehow convert his "mystery" into
a reclamation of ego; in his effort to put on the musical power of his
imaginative experience and *be* the "personality" of his liberating Eros;
in his necessity to find an epic American significance for his rebellious
lyrical impulses—almost at once Whitman's career begins confirming
the truth of Nietzsche's warning.

This American self-consciousness, first stylistically apparent in 1856,
in the third (1860) edition became overwhelming. The writer of most
of these new poems is trying manfully to be the poet of his Preface;
and Whitman was, in fact, so enamoured of the Preface that one of
the new additions, "Poem of Many in One" (later retitled "By Blue
Ontario's Shore"), is almost literally a paraphrase of it—a poem filled
with almost nothing but self-exhortations. This poem really inaugurates
a change in Whitman's style and intention that has never been sufficiently remarked; for in almost all the new poems, even when not
explicitly. "Chants Democratic," some form of incantation has become

the dominant stylistic mode. The difference between Whitman's voice
in the later editions and the "I" of the first *Leaves* might be described
as the difference between a speaker on a platform—or an operatic solo-
ist intoning a recitative (Whitman's own perilous analogy)—and a
solitary "soul" standing up to speak in the silence of a Quaker meeting,
and whose impassioned speech may, as "the spirit moves," modulate into
rhapsodic rhythms of song. The first poems, moreover, had been written
almost conversationally, addressed as an intimate letter to a personal
and private "you"; but Whitman's "you" had now become essentially
plural, the collective democratic conscience of America. And motivating
this new "vocalism" was a change in Whitman's conception of his
book: it was no longer simply the testament of an individual "modern,"
but "the new Bible"—a democratic missal and *vade mecum* for the
entire nation, but especially for teachers, "mediums," "savans," "oratists."
And since the "leader of leaders" was, as the prose Whitman had written,
the native bard, he was now being true to his word:

> Chanter of Personality, outlining a history yet to be,
> I project the ideal man, the American of the future.

Throughout the nineteenth century much of the impulse to poetry
was by way of overt or secret reaction to an abstract humanism or to
bourgeois rationalism; and when he began *Leaves of Grass,* Whitman,
too, had been reacting to an overexposure to ideology: like Wordsworth,
like Mill and Carlyle, his "soul" had protested: "But where am I in all
this?" Yet in seeking a freedom from the slavery of abstractions, his "soul"
sought also to satisfy its craving for love; and by 1860 Whitman had
found a way to anneal both his biological and his ideological compulsions
into the single programmatic purpose of creating an American "Stock-
Personality," a national comradeship, a "One Identity" for "ye partial,
diverse lives." And so intense was this will that Whitman remained
unaware that, in substance if not in form, his poetry was slowly receding
to his habitual prose—an attrition of imaginative power that might, in
fact, be demonstrated almost wholly in terms of the progressive so-
cialization of his once unconscious "soul."

But in the great poems of 1855-56, Whitman remained true to his
instinct for that descriptive law of our literature that Mark Twain
similarly confirmed in our fictional prose—the truth, namely, that
since no "classic" American tradition exists, there can be no significant idiom in our literature that is not a personal voice bearing a
personalized vision; and conversely, there can be no personal voice—
no way of even communicating with ourselves—that is not an individuation of American *speech,* which is incessantly dynamic for this
very reason. "Speech," said Whitman in "The Song of Myself," "is

the twin of my vision"; and if his later folly lay in confounding self-consciously his vision and his American *persona* of speech as the identical "I" of his American "personality," the wisdom of principle in that failure lay in his recognition that the democratic idiom and the personal vision of poetry must live together and cohere dialectically, as they are born together, in the same creative consciousness. If not—if an awareness of modern contradictions is allowed to overcome this sense of our original paradox, then, as is proverbially said of all twins, idiom or vision may cease to be itself when the other dies—and this, as it was Whitman's burden of truth, was also his fate as a poet.

Whitman Justified:
The Poet in 1860

by Roy Harvey Pearce

> Where are we going, Walt Whitman? The doors close in an hour.
> Which way does your beard point tonight?
>> (Allen Ginsberg, "A Supermarket in California")

My title comes from the fourteenth of the "Chants Democratic" in the 1860 *Leaves of Grass*. (This is the poem which finally became "Poets to Come.") The first two stanzas read:

> Poets to come!
> Not to-day is to justify me, and Democracy, and what we are for,
> But you, a new brood, native, athletic, continental, greater than
>> before known,
> You must justify me.
>
> Indeed, if it were not for you, what would I be?
> What is the little I have done, except to arouse you?

Whitman is, he concludes, "the bard" of a "future" for which he writes only "one or two indicative words."

The vision is utopian, of course—and became increasingly so in the 1870's and 80's, when he was calling for, even guaranteeing, a state of things whereby poems would work so as eventually to make for the withering away of poetry. In a preface of 1872 he could claim:

> The people, especially the young men and women of America, must begin to learn that Religion, (like Poetry,) is something far, far different from what they supposed. It is, indeed, too important to the power and perpetuity of the New World to be consigned any longer to the churches, old or new, Catholic or Protestant—Saint this, or Saint that. . . . It must be con-

"Whitman Justified: The Poet in 1860." From *The Minnesota Review*, I (1961), 261-294. Copyright 1961 by *The Minnesota Review*. Reprinted by permission of the editors.

signed henceforth to Democracy *en masse,* and to Literature. It must enter
into the Poems of the Nation. It must make the Nation.

And by 1888 (in "A Backward Glance O'er Travel'd Roads") he could
claim that, contrary to European critical opinion, verse was not a dying
technique.

> Only a firmer, vastly broader, new area begins to exist—nay, is already
> form'd—to which the poetic genius must emigrate. Whatever may have
> been the case in years gone by, the true use for the imaginative faculty of
> modern times is to give ultimate vivification to facts, to science, and to
> common lives, endowing them with glows and glories and final illustrious-
> ness which belongs to every real thing, and to real things only. Without
> that ultimate vivification—which the poet or other artist alone can give—
> reality would seem to be incomplete, and science, democracy, and life itself,
> finally in vain.

These two statements (and they are quite typical) sum up Whitman's
growing sense of the power of poetry, and thus of the poet: Religion,
operating as poetry—and *only* as poetry—can make the nation, vivify
it: or, in the language of a late poem like "Passage to India," "eclaircise"
it.

"In the prophetic literature of these states," he had written in 1871
(in *Democratic Vistas*), ". . . Nature, true Nature, and the true idea
of Nature, long absent, must, above all, become fully restored, enlarged,
and must furnish the pervading atmosphere to poems . . ." And later
in the same essay: "The poems of life are great, but there must be poems
of the purports of life, not only in itself, but beyond itself." Life beyond
life, poetry beyond poetry: This idea came to count for more and more
in Whitman's conception of his vocation, and accordingly, of that of
the poets who were to come. The last edition (1892) of *Leaves of Grass*
is surely the testament of the sort of "divine literatus" whom he had
earlier prophesied. Indeed, he had not only prophesied himself but
made the prophecy come true. But, as he acknowledged, this was not
the only form of his testament. For, when he wrote of the last edition,
"I am determined to have the world know what *I* was pleased to do,"
he yet recognized: "In the long run the world will do as it pleases
with the book." The question remains: How may we use the book so
as to know what we please to do with it? And more: What does the
book, in its structure and function, in its growth, teach us about the
vocation of poet in the modern world? And more: How may it help the
poets who yet are to come discover, and so define, their vocation?

The hard fact—so it seems to me—is that Whitman fails as prophetic
poet, precisely because he was such a powerfully *humane* poet. The adjective makes us flinch, perhaps: but only because, like Whitman, we
have found the beliefs it implies so difficult to hold to that we have

come—if not to seek for the prophetic utterances which will offer us something in their stead, then to discount them as disruptive of the high sense of our private selves on which we ground our hopes for the lives we live. Still, it might be that a close reading of Whitman, the poet of 1860—for it is he whom I suggest we must recover—will teach us what it might be like once more to hold to them. Be that as it may, the record of Whitman's life would suggest that his own power, his own humanity, was at the end too much for him. In any case, when he tried to write prophetic poetry, he came eventually to sacrifice man—that finite creature, locked in time and history, at once agonized and exalted by his humanity—for what he has encouraged some of his advocates again to call cosmic man—the cosmic man of, say, these lines from "Passage to India":

> Passage, immediate passage! the blood burns in my veins!
> Away O soul! hoist instantly the anchor!
> Cut the hawsers—haul out—shake every sail!
> Have we not stood here like trees in the ground long enough?
> Have we not grovel'd here long enough, eating and drinking like
>   mere brutes?
> Have we not darken'd and dazed ourselves with books long enough·
>
> Sail forth—steer for the deep waters only,
> Reckless O soul, exploring, I with thee, and thou with me,
> For we are bound where mariner has not yet dared to go,
> And we will risk the ship, ourselves and all.
>
> O my brave soul!
> O farther farther sail!
> O daring joy, but safe! are they not all the seas of God?
> O farther, farther, farther sail!

It is the idea of that "daring joy, but safe"—everywhere in the poem—which prevents one from assenting to this passage and all that comes before it. The passage of a soul, whether it is everyman's or a saint's, is not "safe," however "joyful." So that Whitman cannot focus the poem on the sort of *human* experience to which one might assent, because one could acknowledge its essential humanity. The figures in the passage proliferate farther and farther out from whatever center in which they have originated, until one wonders if there ever was a center. Probably not, because the experience of the protagonist in this poem is that of cosmic man, who, because he is everywhere, is nowhere; who, because he can be everything, is nothing. *This* Whitman, I believe, is he who mistakes vivification for creation, the ecstasy of cadence for the ecstasy of belief, efficient cause for final cause, poet for prophet. Which is not, I emphasize, the same as conceiving of the poet *as* prophet.

Whitman's genius was such as to render him incapable of the kind of discipline of the imagination which would make for the genuine sort of prophetic poetry we find in, say, Blake and Yeats: of whom we *can* say that they were poets *as* prophets; for whom we can observe that poetry is the vehicle for prophecy, not its tenor. Whitman is at best, at *his* best, *visionary,* and sees beyond his world to what it might be—thus, what, failing to be, it is. Blake and Yeats are at best, at *their* best, *prophetic,* and see through their world to what it really is—thus, what, pretending not to be, it might be. Visionary poetry projects a world which the poet would teach us to learn to acknowledge as our own; it comes to have the uncanniness of the terribly familiar. Prophetic poetry projects a world which the poet would teach us is alien to our own yet central to our seeing it as it really is—a world built upon truths we have hoped in vain to forget. We say of the visionary world that we could have made it—at least in dream—work. We say of the prophetic world that we could not possibly have made it, for it was there already. The ground of visionary poetry is indeed dream—work and magical thought; the ground of prophetic poetry, revelation and mythical thought. Thus the special language of prophetic poetry—one of its most marked formal characteristics—must, by the definition of its purpose, be foreign to us (for it reveals a world, and the strange things in it, hidden from us); yet, by the paradox of prophecy, it is a language native to us (for the things it reveals, being universal—out of the realm of day to day time, space, and conception—put all of us, all of our "actual" world, under their aegis). We can "understand" that language because its grammar and syntax are analogous to our own; understanding it, we assent to—and perhaps believe in—the metaphysical system which its structure and vocabulary entail; trying to account for its origin, we agree with the poet that he has been, in some quite literal sense, "inspired."

Now, when the mood came over him—as it did increasingly—perhaps Whitman did claim to have been "inspired" in this literal sense. But even so, his later work fails as prophetic poetry (for that is what it is meant to be) precisely because, like the earlier work, it projects not a world to which the poet stands as witness, but one to which he stands as maker. Yet he asks of the world projected in the later work that, in accordance with the requirements of prophetic poetry, it have the effect of revelation; that its language be at once of and not of our workaday world; that it imply what in *Democratic Vistas* he called a "New World metaphysics." Yet the editions of *Leaves of Grass* from 1867 on fail of the centrality and integrity of properly prophetic poetry: fail, I think, because the poet mistakenly assumes that poetry, when it is made to deal with the universe at large, *becomes* prophecy. For all his

revisions and manipulations of his text, for all his enlargement of his
themes, the later Whitman is but a visionary poet. And, since he asks
more of it than it can properly yield, the vision, and consequently the
poetry, even the conception of the poet, get increasingly tenuous. A certain strength is there, of course. But it is the strength of an earlier
Whitman, who perhaps prophesied, but could not bring about, his own
metamorphosis from poet to prophet. His genius was too great to let him
forget that, after all, it was *poets* who were to come.

True enough, he wrote, toward the end of "A Backward Glance O'er
Travel'd Roads":

> But it is not on "Leaves of Grass" distinctively as *literature,* or a specimen
> therefor, that I feel to dwell, or advance claims. No one will get at my
> verses who insists upon viewing them as a literary performance, or attempt
> at such performance, or as aiming mainly toward art or aestheticism.

One says: How right, how sad, how wasteful! For, ironically enough,
Whitman's words characterize the *failure* of the 1892 *Leaves of Grass.*
And one turns to the earlier Whitman, I daresay the authentic Whitman,
whose verses did aim mainly toward art and aestheticism: toward a
definition of the vocation of the poet in that part of the modern world
which was the United States.

For me, then, the most important edition of *Leaves of Grass* is the
1860 edition; and its most important poem is "A Word out of the Sea"
(which, of course, became "Out of the Cradle Endlessly Rocking" in
later editions.) Here Whitman may be best justified: as a poet. The
burden of this essay will be to justify Whitman's way with poetry in the
1860 volume; to show how the structure and movement of this volume
and of some of the principal poems in it (above all, "A Word out of
the Sea") are such as to furnish a valid and integral way for a poet
dedicated to saving poetry for the modern world, thus—as poet, and
only as poet—dedicated to saving the modern world for poetry. The
Whitman of the 1860 *Leaves of Grass* would be a sage, a seer, a sayer.
But he speaks of only what he knows directly and he asks of his speech
only that it report fully and honestly and frankly, only that it evoke
other speeches, other poems, of its kind. The poems in this volume do
justify Whitman's claims for poetry in general—but in terms of what
he may in fact give us, not of what he would like, or even need, to give
us. The strength of the major poems in the volume is that they somehow
resist *our* need for more than they present, and make us rest satisfied—
or as satisfied as we ever can be—with what they give. Above all, this
is true of "A Word out of the Sea"—as it is less true, and so characteristic
of the later Whitman, the poet of "Out of the Cradle Endlessly Rocking."

The 1855, 1856, and 1860 *Leaves of Grass* make a complete sequence—
one in which the poet invents modern poetry, explores its possibility as

an instrument for studying the world at large and himself as somehow vitally constitutive of it, and comes finally to define, expound, and exemplify the poet's vocation in the modern world. The sequence, in brief, is from language to argument; and it is controlled at all points by a powerful sense of the ego which is struggling to move from language to argument and which must come to realize the limits of its own humanity, which are the limits of argument. If, as we well know, the poet as envisaged in the 1855 and 1856 *Leaves of Grass* is the counterpart of him of whom Emerson wrote in "The Poet" (1844), the poet envisaged in the 1860 *Leaves of Grass* is the counterpart of him of whom Emerson wrote in his essay on Goethe in *Representative Men* (1850): Not Shakespeare, not Plato, not Swedenberg would do for the modern world, which yet "wants its poet-priest, a reconciler . . ." Goethe was one such: "the writer, or secretary, who is to report the doings of the miraculous spirit of life that everywhere throbs and works. His office is a reception of the facts into the mind, and then a selection of the eminent and characteristic experiences." Note: just a "writer"—(what John Holloway in an important book of a few years ago called the *Victorian Sage*: a philosopher of a kind, but one who constructs his argument according to a grammar of assent). Emerson had concluded:

> The world is young: the former great men call to us affectionately. We too must write Bibles, to unite again the heavens and the earthly world. The secret of genius is to suffer no fiction to exist for us; to realize all that we know; in the high refinement of modern life, in arts, in sciences, in books, in men, to exact good faith, reality and a purpose; and first, last, midst and without end, to honor every truth by use.

The 1860 *Leaves of Grass,* as one of Whitman's notebook entries indicates, was to be a Bible too: "The Great Construction of the New Bible. . . . It ought to be ready in 1859." It was to offer a "third religion," Whitman wrote. And in a way it does; but, for well and for ill, that religion is a religion of man—man as he is, locked in his humanity and needing a religion, yet not claiming to have it by virtue of needing it; not hypnotizing himself into declaring that he has it. (For Whitman a little cadence was a dangerous, if exciting, thing, much cadence, disastrous.) The Whitman of the 1860 *Leaves of Grass* is, *par excellence,* Emerson's "secretary," reporting "the doings of the miraculous spirit of life that everywhere throbs and works." To accept a miracle, to live in its presence, even to try to comprehend it—this is not the same as trying to work one, even claiming to have worked one. And—as the poets who have come after him have variously testified in their puzzled, ambiguous relation to him—Whitman's way with the language of poetry, going against the grain of mass communications and "positivism," may well teach us how to recognize and acknowledge miracles. It cannot teach us how to work them; or even how to earn them. One can well imagine how hard it must be for a poet to go so far with language, only to discover that he can go no farther. Such a discovery constitutes the principal element of greatness in the 1860 *Leaves of Grass,* perhaps the principal element of greatness in Whitman's poetry as a whole.

I have said that in 1855 Whitman "invented" modern poetry. By this I mean only that, along with other major poets of the middle of the century, he participated—but in a strangely isolated way—in the development of romanticist poetics toward and beyond its symbolist phase. (*To invent* may mean, among other things, "to stumble upon.") I do not mean to claim too much for the word *symbolist* here; I use it only generally to indicate that Whitman too came to realize that a poet's vocation was fatefully tied to the state of the language which constituted his medium. He discovered with Baudelaire—although without Baudelaire's (and incidentally Emerson's) overwhelming sense of the problem of "correspondences," that, as regards language, "tout vit, tout agit, tout se correspond." The medium thus had a "life" of its own, and so might generate "life"—the "life" of poetry. Poetry, on this view, thus became *sui generis,* a unique mode of discourse; and the role of the poet became more and more explicitly to be that of the creator: one who might "free" language to "mean"—a creator in a medium, pure and simple. We have in Whitman's early work a version of that conception of poet and poetry with which we are now so familiar: To whom was the poet responsible? Not to whom, the reply ran, but to what? And the answer: to language. And language as such was seen to be the sole, overriding means to establish, or reestablish community. The perhaps inevitable drift—not only in Whitman's work but of that of his contemporaries and of the poets who have come—was toward an idea of poetry as a means of communion, perhaps modern man's sole means of communion, his religion. Professor Abrams (in *The Mirror and the Lamp*) concludes his account of these developments thus:

> It was only in the early Victorian period, when all discourse was explicitly or tacitly thrown into the two exhaustive modes of imaginative and rational, expressive and assertive, that religion fell together with poetry in opposition to science, and that religion, as a consequence, was converted into poetry, and poetry into a kind of religion.

Professor Abrams is speaking about developments in England. In the United States, conditions were somewhat simpler and, withal, more extreme. From the beginning, that is to say, Whitman was sure that the imaginative and rational might well be subsumed under a "higher" category, which was poetry. So that—as I have indicated in my remarks on Whitman and prophetic poetry—for him there was eventually entailed the idea that the New Bible might be just that, a total and in-

clusive account of cosmic man, of man as one of an infinitude of gods
bound up in Nature. It is a nice question whether or not the "symbolist"
dedication to the idea of language-as-communion must *inevitably* lead
to a search for a metalinguistic structure of analogies and correspondences and then to an idea of poetry as religion and religion as poetry.
And it is a nicer question whether or not "symbolist" poetics—with
its emphasis on medium as against matrix, language per se as against
language–in–culture—is characterized by a certain weakness in linguistic
theory. Whitman's work raises these questions; and a full critique of
his work would entail a critique of his theory of poetry, thus of his
theory of language, thus of his theory of culture. But this is not the
place to speak of critics to come, much less to prophesy them.

In any case, we must grant Whitman his special kind of "unmediated
vision." But we are not by that token obliged to grant, or claim for
him a "mysticism"—or for that matter, "an inverted mysticism"; or to
declare that, *ecce,* his poetry is at once *"mystical and irreligious";*
or to see in the Whitman of 1855 a good (prematurely) grey *guru.*
(I cite here the recent claims for this Whitman of James Miller, Karl
Shapiro, and Malcolm Cowley—who confuse, or conflate, this poet with
the one who presided at Camden. And I think of the question, put
with such sweet craziness, by Allen Ginsberg in the line I have used
as epigraph.) At its most telling, Whitman's earlier poetry manifests
what has been called (by Erich Kahler) an "existential consciousness,"
but of a mid-nineteenth-century American sort—its key term, its center
of strength and weakness, being not anguish but joy. Or rather, the
key term is triumph—as suffering, the poet endures, and rejoices:
seeing that it is his vocation as poet to teach men that they can endure.
The freedom which ensues is wonderful, not dreadful.

Thus I take the 1855 and 1856 editions of *Leaves of Grass,* which
most freshly project this mode of consciousness, as stages on the way to
the 1860 edition. In 1855 and 1856 Whitman shows that he has learned
to report truthfully what he has seen; in 1860, that he has learned
to measure its significance for the poet taken as the "secretary"—the
archetypal man. He strove to go beyond this, but in vain. The movement from the 1855 to the 1856 editions is the movement from the
first "Song of Myself" and the first "The Sleeper" (both originally
untitled) to the first "Crossing Brooklyn Ferry (called, in 1856, "Sun-
Down Poem"): the poet first learns to discipline himself into regressing
deeply into his own pre-conscious; then, with his new-found sense of
himself as at once subject and object in his world, he learns to conceive in a new way of the world at large; he is, as though for the first
time, "in" the world. The crucial factor is a restoration of the poet's
vital relationship to language. A good, powerfully naïve account of this
discovery is that in Whitman's prose *American Primer,* written in the
1850's, but not published until after his death:

What do you think words are? Do you think words are positive and original things in themselves? No: Words are not original and arbitrary in themselves.—Words are a result—they are the progeny of what has been or is in vogue.—If iron architecture comes in vogue, as it seems to be coming, words are wanted to stand for all about iron architecture, for all the work it causes, for the different branches of work and of the workman. . . .

A perfect user of words uses things—they exude in power and beauty from him—miracles in his hands—miracles from his mouth. . . .

A perfect writer would make words sing, dance, do the male and female act, bear children, weep, bleed, rage, stab, steal, fire cannon, steer ships, sack cities, charge with cavalry or infantry, or do anything, that man or woman or the natural powers can do.
[Note the insistence on "natural"—not "supernatural" powers.]

Likely there are other words wanted.—Of words wanted, the matter is summed up in this: When the time comes for them to represent any thing or state of things, the words will surely follow. The lack of any words, I say again, is as historical as the existence of words. As for me, I feel a hundred realities, clearly determined in me, that words are not yet formed to represent. . . .

These sentiments generally, and some of these phrasings particularly, got into Whitman's prose meditations. More important, from the beginning they inform the poems. They derive much from Emerson's "The Poet," of course; but they are not tied to even Emerson's modestly transcendental balloon. The power which Whitman discovers is the power of language, fueled by the imagination, to break through the categories of time, space, and matter and to "vivify" (a word, as I have said, he used late in his life—so close to Pound's "Make it new") the persons, places, and things of his world, and so make them available to his readers. In the process—since the readers would, as it were, be using words for the first time—he would make them available to themselves; as poets in spite of themselves.

It is as regards this last claim—that the reader is a poet in spite of himself—that the 1860 *Leaves of Grass* is all-important. For there Whitman most clearly saw that the poet's power to break through the limiting categories of day-to-day existence is just that: a poet's power, obtaining only insofar as the poem obtains, and limited as the poem is limited. In 1860, that is to say, Whitman saw that his Bible was to be a poet's Bible, and had to be built around a conception of the poet's life: his origins, experience, and end; his relation with the persons, places, and things of his world. The 1855 and 1856 *Leaves of Grass* volumes are but *collections* of poems—their organization as rushed and chaotic as is the sensibility of the writer of the *American Primer. Within* individual poems, there is form, a form which centers on the moment in the poet's life which they project. But the 1860 *Leaves of Grass* is an articulated whole, with an *argument*. The argument is that of the poet's life as it furnishes a beginning, middle, and end to an account of his vocation. The 1860 volume is, for all its imperfections, one of the great works in that romantic mode, the autobiography. Or, let us give the genre to which it belongs a more specific name: archetypal autobiography. The 1860 volume is autobiographical as, say, *Moby Dick* and *Walden* are autobiographical; for its hero is a man in the process of writing a book, of writing himself, of making himself, of discovering that the powers of the self are the stronger for being limited. The hero who can say No! in thunder discovers that he can say Yes! in thunder too—but that the thunderation is his own and no one else's.

Now, to say that the 1860 *Leaves of Grass* is quintessentially autobiographical is to say what has been said before: most notably by Schyberg, Asselineau, and Allen. But I mean to say it somewhat differently than they do. For they see in the volume a sign of a crisis in Whitman's personal life; and this is most likely so. Yet I think it is wrong to read the volume as, in this *literal* sense, personal—that is, "private." (The Bowers edition of the surviving manuscript of the 1860 edition clearly shows that Whitman—naturally enough, most often in the "Calamus" poems—wanted to keep the book clear of too insistently and privately personal allusions. He was, I think, not trying to "conceal"—much less "mask"—his private personality but to transmute it into an archetypal personality. I think that it is a mistake to look so hard, as some critics do, for the "private" I.) Thus I should read the volume as not a personal but archetypal autobiography: yet another version of that compulsively brought-forth nineteenth-century poem which dealt with the growth of the poet's mind. (Well instructed by our forebears, we now have a variety of names for the form—all demonstrating how deeply, and from what a variety of non-literary perspectives, we have had to deal with the issues which it raises for us: *rite de passage*, quest for identity, search for community, and the like.) Whitman's problem, the poet's problem, was to show that integral to the poet's vocation was his life cycle; that the poet, having discovered his gifts, might now use them to discover the relevance of his life, his *lived* life, his *Erlebnis*, his *career*, to the lives of his fellows. It is the fact that his newly discovered use of poetry is grounded in his sense of a life lived-through: it is this fact that evidences Whitman's ability here, more than in any version of *Leaves of Grass*, to contain his gift and use it, rather than be used by it. Of *this* volume Whitman said: "I am satisfied with *Leaves of Grass* (by far the most of it), as expressing what was intended, namely, to express by sharp-cut self assertion, One's Self and also, or may be still more, to map out, to throw together for American use, a gigantic embryo or skeleton of Personality,—fit for the

West, for native models." Later, of course, he wanted more. But he never had the means beyond those in the 1860 edition to get what he wanted. And that has made all the difference.

The 1860 *Leaves of Grass* opens with "Proto–Leaf" (later, much revised, as "Starting from Paumanok.") Here Whitman announces his themes and, as he had done before, calls for his new religion; but he gives no indication that it is to be a religion of anything else but the poet's universalized vocation. (My misuse of the word *religion* is his. I mean neither to be victimized nor saved by following him here.) It might yet, on this account, be a precurser to a religion, in the more usual (and I think proper) sense, as well as a substitute for it. "Whoever you are! to you endless announcements," he says. There follows "Walt Whitman," a somewhat modified version of the 1855 poem which became "Song of Myself." It is still close to the fluid version of 1855; strangely enough, it is so over-articulated (with some 372 sections) that it does not have the rather massive, and therefore relatively dogmatic, articulation of the final version. In all, it gives us an account of the poet's overwhelming discovery of his native powers. Then in the numbered (but not separately titled) series of poems called "Chants Democratic," the poet—after an apostrophic salutation to his fellows (it ends "O poets to come, I depend on you!")—celebrates himself again, but now as he conceives of himself in the act of celebrating his world. The chief among these poems—as usual, much modified later—became "By Blue Ontario's Shore," "Song of the Broad Axe," "Song for Occupations," "Me Imperturbe," "I Was Looking a Long While," and "I Hear America Singing." Following upon "Walt Whitman," the "Chants Democratic" sequence successfully establishes the dialectical tension between the poet and his world—the tension being sustained as one is made to realize again and again that out of the discovery of his power for "making words do the male and female act" in "Walt Whitman," has come his power to "vivify" his world in the "Chants Democratic."

The transition to "Leaves of Grass," the next sequence—again the poems are numbered, but not separately titled—is natural and necessary. For the poet now asks what it is to make poems in the language which has been precipitated out of the communal experience of his age. The mood throughout is one of a mixture of hope and doubt, and at the end it reaches a certitude strengthened by a sense of the very limitations which initially gave rise to the doubt. The first poem opens—and I shall presently say more about this—with two lines expressing doubt; later—when the prophetic Whitman couldn't conceive of doubting— the lines were dropped in the poem, which became "As I Ebb'd with the Ocean of Life." The second poem is a version of an 1855 poem, "Great Are the Myths"; and it was finally rejected by Whitman as being, one guesses, too certain in its rejection of the mythic mode toward which he later found himself aspiring. The third poem, which,

combined with the sixth later became "Song of the Answerer" opens
up the issue of communication as such. The fourth, a version of an 1856
poem which eventually became "This Compost," conceives of poetry as
a kind of naturalistic resurrection. It moves from "Something startles
me where I thought I was safest"—that is, in the poet's relation to
the materials of poetry—to a simple acknowledgment at the end that
the earth "gives such divine materials to men, and accepts such leavings
from them at last." The fifth (later "Song of Prudence") considers the
insight central to the poet's vocation. To the categories of "time, space,
reality," the poet would add that of "prudence"—which teaches that the
"consummations" of poetry are such as to envisage the necessary relationship of all other "consummations": The imagination's law of the
conservation of energy. The sixth (which, as I have said, later became
part of "Song of the Answerer") develops an aspect of the theme of
the fourth and fifth; but now that theme is interpreted as it is bound
up in the problem of language: "The words of poems give you more
than poems, They give you to form for yourself poems, religions, politics,
war, peace, behavior, histories, essays, romances, and everything else."
At this depth of discovery there is no possibility of any kind of logically
continuous catalogue of what words "give you to form for yourself."
Poetry is a means of exhausting man's powers to know the world, and
himself in it, as it is. Beyond this, poems

> . . . prepare for death—yet they are not the finish, but rather
>   the onset,
> They bring none to his or her terminus, or to be content and full;
> Whom they take, they take into space, to behold the birth of stars,
>   to learn one of the meanings,
> To launch off with absolute faith—to sweep through the ceaseless
>   rings, and never to be quiet again.

In the seventh poem (later "Faith Poem"), the poet discovers that he
"needs no assurance"; for he is (as he says in the eighth poem, later
"Miracles") a "realist" and for him the real (by which he means *realia*)
constitute "miracles." The poet is led, in the ninth poem (later "There
Was a Child Went Forth"), to a recollection of his first discovery of the
miraculousness of the real: a discovery he only now understands; this
poem, taken in relation to the rest of the sequence, properly anticipates
"A Word out of the Sea." The tenth poem opens, in a passage dropped
from the later version, "Myself and Mine,"—but one which is essential
as a transition in the sequence:

> It is ended—I dally no more,
> After today I inure myself to run, leap, swim, wrestle, fight . . .

Simply enough: the poet, having accepted his vocation and its constraints, is now free—free *through* it; and he must now teach this freedom to others:

> I charge that there be no theory or school founded out of me,
> I charge you to leave all free, as I have left all free.

The rest of the sequence, some fourteen more poems, celebrates aspects of the poet's new freedom as it might be the freedom of all men. (I forebear giving their later titles.) It is the freedom to rejoice in the miraculousness of the real, and has its own costs. The greatest is a terrible passivity, as though in order to achieve his freedom, man had to offer himself up as the victim of his own newly vivified sensibility. Being as he is, the poet sees (in 12) "the vast similitude/which/interlocks all . . ."; yet he must admit (in 15) "that life cannot exhibit all to me—" and "that I am to wait for what will be exhibited by death." He is (in 17) the man who must "sit and look out upon all the sorrows of the world, and upon all oppression and shame"; and he must "See, hear,/be/silent," only then to speak. He declares (in 20); ". . . whether I continue beyond this book, to maturity/ . . . /Depends . . . upon you/ . . . you, contemporary America." Poem 24, wherein the poet completes his archetypal act, and gives himself over to his readers, reads:

> Lift me close to your face till I whisper,
> What you are holding is in reality no book, nor part of a book,
> It is a man, flushed and full-blooded—it is I—So long!
> We must separate—Here! take from my lips this kiss,
> Whoever you are, I give it especially to you;
> *So long*—and I hope we shall meet again.

I quote this last poem entire, because I want to make it clear that the lapses into desperate sentimentality—and this poem is a prime example —are intrinsically a part of Whitman's autobiographical mode in the 1860 *Leaves of Grass,* as they are of the mode, or genre, which they represent. It will not do to explain them away by putting them in a larger context, or considering them somehow as masked verses—evidences of Whitman the shape-shifter. (Speaking through a *persona,* the poet perforce hides behind it.) Confronting the agonies and ambiguities of his conception of the poet, Whitman too often fell into bathos or sentimentalism. Yet bathos and sentimentalism, I would suggest, are but unsuccessful means—to be set against evidence of successful means—of solving the archetypal autobiographer's central problem: at once being himself and seeing himself; of bearing witness to his own deeds. If what he is, as he sees it, is too much to bear; if he is incapable of bearing it; if his genius is such as not to have prepared him to bear it—why then, his miraculism will fail him precisely because he cannot stand too much reality.

Bathos and sentimentalism—and also anxious, premonitory yearnings for something beyond mere poetry—inevitably mar the rest of the 1860 *Leaves of Grass*: but not fatally, since they are the by-products of its total argument. At some point, most foxes want to be hedgehogs. Whitman is a poet who must be read at large. And I am claiming that Whitman can be best read at large in the 1860 *Leaves of Grass*. When he can be read in smaller compass—as in "A Word out of the Sea"—it is because in a single poem he manages to recapitulate in little what he was developing at large. I should guess—as I shall presently try to show—that the large poem, the 1860 volume, is a necessary setting for the little poem, "A Word out of the Sea." That poem (later, I remind my reader, "Out of the Cradle . . .") is one of Whitman's greatest. And I shall want to show that it is even greater than we think. So I must carry through, however cursorily, my glance o'er the 1860 *Leaves of Grass*. There comes next a series of poems ("A Word out of the Sea" is one of them) in which the poet meditates the sheer givenness of the world his poems reveal; he is even capable of seeing himself as one of the givens. But then he must specify in detail the nature of his kind of givenness: which includes the power to give, to bring the given to a new life. Here—after "Salut au Monde," "Poem of Joys," "A Word out of the Sea," 'A Leaf of Faces," and "Europe,"—there is first the "Enfants d'Adam" sequence, and then, after an interlude of generally celebrative poems, the "Calamus" sequence. I want to say of these two sequences only that they are passionate in a curiously objective fashion; I have suggested that the proper word for their mood and tone is neither personal nor impersonal, but archetypal. In contrast, they furnish analogues—directly libidinal analogues, as it were—for the poet's role, seen now not (as in the earlier sequences) from the point of view of a man telling us how he has discovered his gift, put it to use, and measured the cost of using it properly; but seen rather from the point of view of the reader. The *I* of these poems, I suggest, is meant to include the reader—as at once potential poet and reader of poems. So that the "Enfants d'Adam" sequence tell us how it is—what it means, what it costs—to be a maker of poems and the "Calamus" sequence how it is to be a reader of poems—in the first instance the analogue is procreation; in the second it is community. And if Whitman's own homosexuality led him to write more powerfully in the second vein than in the first, we should be mindful of the fact that, in his times as in ours, it seems to be easier to make poems, good poems, even to publish them, than to get readers for them.

Indeed, Whitman announces in the next-to-last of the "Calamus" sequence that we are to be ready for his most "baffling" words, which come in the last poem of the sequence, later "Full of Life Now":

> When you read these, I, that was visible, am become invisible;
> Now it is you, compact, visible, realizing my poems, seeking me,
> Fancying how happy you were, if I could be with you, and become
>   your lover;
> Be it as if I were with you. Be not too certain but I am with you
>   now.

Later Whitman changed *lover* to *comrade*—mistakenly, I think; for, as their function in the 1860 volume shows, the "Calamus" poems were to carry through to completion the poet's conception of his painfully loving relation with his readers.

Having, in the "Enfants d'Adam" and "Calamus" sequences, defined the poetic process itself, as he had earlier defined the poet's discovery of that process, Whitman proceeds variously to celebrate himself and his readers at once under the aegis of the "Enfants d'Adam" and the "Calamus" analogue. (As Lorca said in his "Oda," "Este es el mundo, amigo . . .") Much of the power of the poems, new and old, derives from their place in the sequences. In "Crossing Brooklyn Ferry" and the series of "Messenger Leaves" there are addresses to all and sundry who inhabit Whitman's world, assurances to them that now he can love them for what they are, because now he knows them for what they are. There is then an address to Manahatta—which returns to the problem of naming, but now with an assurance that the problem has disappeared in the solving: "I was asking for something specific and perfect for my city, and behold! here is the aboriginal name!" Then there is an address in "Kosmos" to the simple, separate persons—to each of his readers who is "constructing the house of himself or herself." Then there is "Sleep Chasings" (a version of the 1855 "The Sleepers"), now a sublime poem, in which the poet can freely acknowledge that the source of his strength is in the relation of his night- to his day-time life, the unconscious and the conscious:

> I will stop only a time with the night, and rise betimes
> I will duly pass the day, O my mother, and duly return to you.

And "Sleep Chasings" is the more telling for being followed by "Burial" (originally an 1855 poem which eventually became "To Think of Time"). For in his incessant moving between night and day, the poet manages to make poems and so proves immortal. He makes men immortal in his poems, as he teaches them to make themselves immortal in their acts:

> To think that you and I did not see, feel, think, nor bear our part!
> To think that we are now here, and bear our part!

This poem comes nearly at the end of the 1860 volume. Only an address to his soul—immortal, but in a strictly "poetic" sense—and "So Long!" follow. In the latter we are reminded once again:

> This is no book,
> Who touches this book, touches a man,
> (Is it night? Are we done?)
> It is I you hold, and who holds you,
> I spring from the pages into your arms—decease calls me forth.

We are reminded thus, to paraphrase a recent Whitmanian, that in the flesh of art we are immortal: which is a commonplace. We are reminded also that in our age, the role of art, of poetry, is to keep us alive enough to be capable of this kind of immortality: which is not quite a commonplace.

The central terms in the argument of the 1860 *Leaves of Grass*, I suggest, run something like this: first, in the poems which lead up to "A Word out of the Sea"—self-discovery, self-love, rebirth, diffusion-of-self, art; and second, in the poems which follow "A Word out of the Sea"—love-of-others, death, rebirth, reintegration-of-self, art, immortality. The sequence is that of an ordinary life, extraordinarily lived through; the claims are strictly humanistic. The child manages somehow to achieve adulthood; the movement is from a poetry of diffusion to a poetry of integration. Immortality is the *result* of art, not its origin, nor its cause. The humanism is painful, because one of its crucial elements (centering on "death" as a "clew" in "A Word out of the Sea") is an acknowledgment of all-too-human limitations and constraints. So long as Whitman lived with that acknowledgment, lived *in* that acknowledgment—even when living with it drove him (as it too often did) toward bathos and sentimentalism—, he managed to be a poet, a "secretary," a "sage," a seer, a visionary. His religion was the religion of humanity: the only religion that a work of art can *directly* express, whatever other religion it may confront and acknowledge. *Indirectly*, it can confront religion in the more usual and more proper sense; for it can treat of man in his aspiration for something beyond manhood, even if it cannot claim—since its materials are ineluctably those of manhood—to treat directly of that something-beyond. The burden—someone has called it the burden of incertitude; Keats called it "negative capability"—is a hard one to bear. Whitman, I am suggesting, bore it most successfully, bore it most successfully for us, in the 1860 *Leaves of Grass*.

Which brings me to the most important of the poems first collected in this volume, "A Word out of the Sea." [1] It was originally published separately in 1859, as *A Child's Reminiscence*. Thus far, I have tried to suggest the proper context in which the poem should be read: as part of the volume for which it was originally written; as a turning point in the argument of that book. Note that "A Word out of the Sea" comes about mid-way in the book after "Walt Whitman," the "Chants Democratic," "Leaves of Grass," "Salut au Monde," and "Poem of Joys"— that is, after those poems which tell us of the poet's discovery of his powers as poet and of his ability to use those powers so to "vivify" his world, and himself in it: after his discovery that it is man's special delight and his special agony to be at once the subject and object of his meditations; after his discovery that consciousness inevitably entails self-consciousness and a sense of the strengths and weaknesses of self-consciousness. Moreover, "A Word out of the Sea" comes shortly before the "Enfants d'Adam" and "Calamus" sequences—that is, shortly before those poems which work out the dialectic of the subject-object relationship under the analogue of the sexuality of man as creator of his world and of persons, places, and things as its creatures. I cannot but think that Whitman knew what he was doing when he placed "A Word out of the Sea" thus. For he was obligated, in all his autobiographical honesty, to treat directly of man's fallibilities as well as his powers, to try to discover the binding relationship between fallibilities and powers: to estimate the capacity of man to be himself and the cost he would have to pay. The poems which came before "A Word out of the Sea" have little to do with fallibilities; they develop the central terms of the whole argument only this far: self-discovery, self-love, rebirth, art. Theirs is the polymorph perverse world of the child. In them, death only threatens, does not promise; power is what counts. The turning-point in the poet's life can come only with the "adult" sense of love and death, the beginning and the end of things: out of which issues art, now a mode of immortality. In "A Word out of the Sea" the 1860 volume has its turning-point. Beyond this poem, we must remember, are the "Enfants d'Adam" and "Calamus" sequences, and also "Crossing Brooklyn Ferry" and the "Messenger Leaves" sequence.

The 1860 poem begins harshly: "Out of the rocked cradle." The past participle, unlike the present participle in the later versions, implies no continuing agent for the rocking; the sea here is too inclusive to be a symbol; it is just a fact of life—life's factuality. Then comes the melange of elements associated with the "sea." They are among the

---

[1] The complete text of "A Word out of the Sea" is given in the issue of *The Minnesota Review* in which this essay was originally printed, pp. 273-280, and in a facsimile edition of the 1860 *Leaves of Grass* published by the Cornell University Press, 1961.—R.H.P.

realities whose miraculousness the poet is on his way to understanding. Note the third line (omitted in later versions) which clearly establishes the autobiographical tone and makes the boy at once the product of nature at large and a particular nature: "Out of the boy's mother's womb, from the nipples of her breasts." All this leads to a clear split in point of view, so that we know that the poet-as-adult is making a poem which will be his means to understanding a childhood experience. Initially we are told of the range of experiences out of which this poem comes: the sea as rocked cradle seems at once literally (to the boy) and metaphorically (to the poet) to "contain" the song of the bird, the boy's mother, the place, the time, the memory of the brother, and the as yet unnamed "word stronger and more delicious than any" which marks a limit to the meaning of the whole. This is quite explicitly an introduction. For what follows is given a separate title, "Reminiscence," as though the poet wanted to make quite plain the division between his sense of himself as child and as adult. Then we are presented with the story of the birds, the loss of the beloved, and the song sung (as only *now* the poet knows it) to objectify this loss, so make it bearable, so assure that it can, in *this* life, be transcended. Always we are aware that the poet-as-adult, the creative center of the poem seeks that "word stronger and more delicious" which will be his means finally to understand his reminiscences and—in the context of this volume (I emphasize: in the context of *this* volume)—serve to define his vocation as poet: at once powerful and fallible. The points of view of bird, child, and adult are kept separate until the passage which reads:

> Bird! (then said the boy's Soul,)
> Is it indeed toward your mate you sing? or is it mostly to me?
> For I that was a child, my tongue's use sleeping,
> Now that I have heard you,
> Now in a moment I know what I am for—I awake,
> And already a thousand singers—a thousand songs, clearer louder,
>   more sorrowful than yours,
> A thousand warbling echoes have started to life within me,
> Never to die.

The boy, even as a man recalling his boyhood, does not, as in later versions, at first address the bird as "Demon." He is at this stage incapable of that "or"—in the latter reading "Demon or bird." Even though his soul speaks, he is to discover—some lines later—his special "poetic" relation to the bird. Moreover, as "boy," he holds toward death an attitude half-way between that of the bird—who is merely "instinctive" and that of the man—who is "reflective," capable of "reminiscence." Yet the points of view begin to be hypnotically merged

—*after* the fact. In the boy's "soul" the poet discovers a child's potentiality for adult knowledge; but he keeps it as a potentiality, and he never assigns it to the bird, who (or which) is an occasion merely. Yet having seen that potentiality as such, he can "now," in the adult present, work toward its realization, confident that the one will follow necessarily in due course from the other. Now, in the adult present, he can ask for "the clew," "The word final, superior to all," the word which "now" he can "conquer." I cannot emphasize too much that it is a *"word"* —that the poet is translating the sea (and all it embodies) as prelinguistic fact into a word, knowledge of which will signify his coming to maturity. "Out of," in the original title, is meant quite literally to indicate a linguistic transformation. In the record of the growth of his mind, he sees *now* that the word will once and for all precipitate the meaning he has willed himself to create, and in the creating to discover. And it comes as he recalls that time when the sea, manifesting the rhythm of life and death itself,

> Delaying not, hurrying not,
> Whisper'd me through the night, and very plainly before daybreak,
> Lisp'd to me the low and delicious word DEATH,
> And again Death—ever Death, Death, Death

(Not *Death,* merely repeated four times as in later versions—but *ever,* beyond counting. The prophetic Whitman was bound to drop that *ever,* since for him nothing was beyond counting.)

The merging of the points of view occurs as not only past and present, child and adult, but subject and object (i.e., "The sea . . . whisper'd me"—not *"to* me") are fused. The poet now knows the word, because he has contrived a situation in which he can control its use; he has discovered (to recall the language of the *American Primer* notes) another reality, one that words until *now* had not been formed to represent. He has, as only a poet can, *made* a word out of the sea—for the duration of the poem understood *"sea"* as it may be into *"death"*— *"ever death."* His genius is such as to have enabled us to put those quotation marks around the word—guided by him, to have "bracketed" this portion of our experience with language; and we discover that as language binds in the poet's time, so it is bound in human time.

If the end of the poem is to understand cosmic process as a continual loss of the beloved through death and a consequent gain of death-in-life and life-in-death—if this is the end of the poem, nonetheless it is gained through a creative act, an assertion of life in the face of death, and a discovery and acknowledgment of the limits of such an assertion. And this act is that of the very person, the poet, whom death would deprive of all that is beloved in life. Moreover, the deprivation is quite literally that and shows the poet moving, in high honesty, from the "Enfant d'Adam" sequence to "Calamus." In the 1860 volume, "A Word out of the Sea" entails the "Calamus" sequence. (What if Whitman had, in "A Word out of the Sea," written *comrade* instead of *brother?*)

In any case, at this stage of his career, Whitman would not yield to his longing for such comfort as would scant the facts of life and death. There is, I repeat, that opening *rocked,* not *rocking* cradle; there is the quite naturalistic acknowledgment of the "boy's mother's womb." And there is stanza 31 (the stanzas in the 1860 poem are numbered, as the stanzas of the final version are not):

> O give me some clew!
> O if I am to have so much, let me have more!
> O a word! O what is my destination?
> O I fear it is henceforth chaos!
> O how joys, dreads, convolutions, human shapes, and all shapes.
>   spring as from graves around me!
> O phantoms! you cover all the land, and all the sea!
> O I cannot see in the dimness whether you smile or frown upon me;
> O vapor, a look, a word! O well-beloved!
> O you dear women's and men's phantoms!

In the final version, the equivalent stanza reads only:

> O give me the clew (it lurks in the night here somewhere,)
> O if I am to have so much, let me have more!

The difference between "some clew" and "the clew" marks the difference between a poet for whom questions are real and one for whom questions are rhetorical. The later Whitman was convinced that the lurking clew would find him—and to that degree, whatever else he was, was not a poet. The earlier Whitman, in all humility, feared that what might issue out of this experience was "phantoms"—a good enough word for aborted poems. And often—but not too often—he was right.

Finally, there is not in "A Word out of the Sea" the falsely (and, in the context of the poem, undeservedly) comforting note of "Or like some old crone rocking the cradle swathed in sweet garments, bending aside." Indeed, the sentimentality and bathos of this too-much celebrated line, as I think, is given away by the fact that it is the only simile, the only *like* clause, in the poem. And, in relation to the total effect of the poem, the strategic withdrawal of the *Or* which introduces the line is at least unfortunate, at most disastrous.

I make so much of the kind of disaster, as I think it is, because it became increasingly characteristic of Whitman's way with poetry after the 1860 *Leaves of Grass.* Probably there are poems, written later, which show him at his best; and probably some of his revisions and rejections are for the best. But I more and more doubt it, as I doubt that he had reached his best in 1855 and 1856. I do not mean to take the part of Cassandra; but I think it as inadvisable to take the part of Pollyanna. The facts, as I see them, show that Whitman, for whatever reason, after 1860 moved away from the mode of archetypal autobiography toward that of prophecy. He worked hard to make, as he said, a cathedral out of *Leaves of Grass.* He broke up the beautifully wrought sequence of the 1860 volume; so that, even when he let poems stand unrevised, they appear in contexts which take from them their life-giving mixture of tentativeness and assurance, of aspiration, and render them dogmatic, tendentious, and overweening.

In Lawrence's word, Whitman "mentalized" his poems. To give a few examples of "mentalizing" revisions of 1860 poems: The opening of the third "Enfants d'Adam" poem reads in the 1860 text:

> O my children! O mates!
> O the bodies of you, and of all men and women, engirth me, and I
> engirth them.

In the 1867 version the lines read:

> I sing the body electric,
> The Armies of those I love engirth me and I engirth them.

Another example: the opening line of the fourteenth poem of the same sequence—reads in the 1860 version: "I am he that aches with love"; and becomes in 1867: "I am he that aches with amorous love." (This is the *amorous* which so infuriated Lawrence.) And another example: the opening lines of the fifteenth poem in the sequence—read in the 1860 version: "Early in the morning,/ Walking . . ."; and became in 1867: "As Adam early in the morning,/ Walking . . ." Small examples surely. But note the unsupported and unsupportable claims of "body electric," "armies," "amorous," and the Old Testament "Adam."

A larger—but still characteristic—example is Whitman's revision of the first of the 1860 "Leaves of Grass" sequence, which became "As I Ebb'd with the Ocean of life." The 1860 poem opens thus:

> Elemental drifts!
> O I wish I could impress others as you and the waves have just
> been impressing me.
>
> As I ebbed with an ebb of the ocean of life,
> As I wended the shores I know.

In the poem as it appears in the 1892 edition of *Leaves of Grass*, the first two lines—expressing doubt, as I have pointed out—are missing; the third has been simplified to "As I ebb'd with the ocean of life"— so that the poet is no longer conceived as part of an "ebb." And the fourth line stands as we have it now. Later in the seventh line of the 1892 version, the poet says that he is "Held by the electric self out of the pride of which I utter poems." In the 1860 version he says that he is "Alone, held by the eternal self of me that threatens to get the better of me, and stifle me." And so it goes—all passion beyond spending (unless vivified by a kind of cosmic electroshock), all poetry beyond the mere writing, all life beyond the mere living—since the poet's tactic, however unconscious, is to claim to have transcended that which must have been hard to live with: his extraordinarily ordinary self and the ordinarily extraordinary death that awaits him. Granting the mood and movement of the later editions of *Leaves of Grass*, it is only proper that Whitman would have rejected the eighth poem in the 1860 "Calamus" sequence—which begins "Long I thought that knowledge alone would suffice me—O if I could but obtain knowledge!" and ends, as the poet is brought to confront the readers to whom he would offer his poems, "I am indifferent to my own songs—I will go with him I love . . ."

One more example: this one not of a revision but of an addition to a sequence originating in the 1860 volume. In the 1871 *Leaves of Grass*, Whitman, now wholly committed to making of his poem a series of prophetic books, placed in the "Calamus" sequence the woolly "Base of All Metaphysics," the last stanza of which reads:

> Having studied the new and antique, the Greek and Germanic systems,
> Kant having studied and stated, Fichte and Schelling and Hegel,
> Stated the lore of Plato, and Socrates greater than Plato,
> And greater than Socrates sought and stated, Christ divine having studied long.
> I see reminiscent to-day those Greek and Germanic systems,
> See the philosophies of all, Christian churches and tenets see,
> Yet underneath Socrates clearly see, and underneath Christ the divine I see,
> The dear love of man for his comrade, the attraction of friend to friend,
> Of the well-married husband and wife, of children and parents,
> Of city for city and land for land.

Whitman stuck by this poem until the end, and it went unchanged into the 1892 edition of *Leaves of Grass*, contributing its bit to the "mentalizing" of the whole. And it is only too typical of additions to the book made from 1867 on.

This Whitman begins to take over *Leaves of Grass* in the 1867 edition and is fully in command by the time of the 1871 edition. It is, unhappily, he whom he knew best and he with whom our poets have tried to make their pacts and truces—but, as I think, so that during the uneasy peace they might come to know another (and, as I have tried to show, earlier) Whitman: whose way with the poetry they seem to sense but can never quite get to. The way to that Whitman is not impassable, although working with the Inclusive Edition of *Leaves of Grass* (upon whose variant readings I have depended) is tedious. But there is yet a more direct way: reading the 1860 *Leaves of Grass.*

Meantime we must bring ourselves to say of the Whitman of 1892, the literatus, that he was driven to claim prophetic powers, not to put poetry to their service. Nothing could hold this Whitman back, not even the facts of a poet's life. Indeed, life—his own and life in general —became less "factual," less "real" for him. And—since justification consists in deriving the necessary from the real, of tracing the necessary back to its roots in the real, of showing that the real is necessary—he no longer had a need to justify himself. Well: In this our world, where we too find it increasingly hard to assent to the factually real, where we have got so far as to call the factually real the "absurd," we find it increasingly difficult to hold ourselves back: as do our poets, acting on our behalf. Thus I daresay we need to recover the Whitman of 1860— with his heroic sense of grounding the necessary in the real. He gave us permission to. I am suggesting that we *need* the poet of 1860, the poet of "A Word out of the Sea." I mean to say thereby that our poets need him too. And justifying the need, we must justify him who contrived that his need be archetypal of ours.

America's Epic

by James Miller, Jr.

Did Whitman write the epic for modern America? There have been many who contend that *Leaves of Grass* is merely a collection of lyric poetry, some good, some bad, all of it of a peculiarly personal nature that disqualifies its attitudes and philosophy generally. There have been others who have defended Whitman's book as the embodiment of the American reality and ideal, as a superb fulfilment of all the genuine requirements of the national epic.[1]

What did Whitman believe? The answer may be found in a number of prose works, beginning with the 1855 Preface. It is clear in this early work that Whitman desired *Leaves of Grass* to bear a unique relationship with America: "Here [in America] at last is something in the doings of man that corresponds with the broadcast doings of the day and night. . . . It awaits the gigantic and generous treatment worthy of it." [2] It is generally recognized that the entire Preface is a veiled account of Whitman's concept of his own role as poet. Certainly he includes himself in the category when he asserts: "The poets of the kosmos advance through all interpositions and coverings and turmoils and stratagems to first principles." [3] Although Whitman does not use the term, it is clear throughout the 1855 Preface that he believes his book to have the basic nature and general scope of the traditional national epic.

In *Democratic Vistas*, in the same indirect manner, Whitman again reveals his concept of the nature of his poetry: "Never was anything more wanted than, to-day, and here in the States, the poet of the modern is wanted, or the great literatus of the modern. At all times, perhaps, the central point in any nation, and that whence it is itself really sway'd the

"America's Epic." From *A Critical Guide to Leaves of Grass*, pp. 174-186, by James Miller, Jr., by permission of The University of Chicago Press. Copyright 1957 by The University of Chicago.

[1] See Fern Nuhn, "Leaves of Grass Viewed as an Epic," *Arizona Quarterly*, VII (Winter, 1951), 324-38.
[2] Facsimile of 1855 text of *Leaves of Grass* (New York: Columbia University Press, 1939), p. iii.
[3] *Ibid.*, p. ix.

most and whence it sways others, is its national literature, especially its archetypal poems" (V, 54-55).[4] Whitman was by this time (1871) acutely aware that America had not accepted his book as he had planned and hoped. There can be little doubt that he conceived *Leaves of Grass* as an "archetypal" poem produced and offered to America at its "central point"—a book "sway'd" by the nation and written to sway others. Such a work as Whitman calls for in *Democratic Vistas* is surely the epic of America. And, basically, it is his own work which he desires to be recognized as such.

In "A Backward Glance o'er Travel'd Roads" (1888), summing up the contribution of his own work, Whitman again emphasizes the need of the nation for a commensurate poetry. But no longer is he evasive; his claim is direct: "As America fully and fairly construed is the legitimate result and evolutionary outcome of the past, so I would dare to claim for my verse." The Old World, as the poet points out, "has had the poems of myths, fictions, feudalism, conquest, caste, dynastic wars, and splendid exceptional characters," but the "New World needs the poems of realities and science and of the democratic average and basic equality." And, instead of the "splendid exceptional characters" of the Old World epics, the New World epic will portray simply —man: "In the centre of all, and object of all, stands the Human Being, towards whose heroic and spiritual evolution poems and everything directly or indirectly tend, Old World or New" (V, 54).

Should there be any doubts about the ambition of Whitman to write America's epic, the opening pages of *Leaves of Grass* should dispel them. In "Inscriptions" and "Starting from Paumanok" there are innumerable indications of the epic nature of the work. In the very opening poem, Whitman uses the construction, "I Sing," characteristic of the epic in introducing themes—"One's-Self I Sing," "The Female equally with the Male I sing," "The Modern Man I sing." In this first poem, too, the Muse is mentioned—"Not physiognomy alone nor brain alone is worthy for the Muse, I say the Form complete is worthier far"; but it is not until the second poem, "As I Ponder'd in Silence," that the Muse is invoked, addressed, and reassured. As the poet considers his work, he is visited by the Old World Muse:

> A Phantom arose before me with distrustful aspect,
> Terrible in beauty, age, and power,
> The genius of poets of old lands [I, 1].

This Muse is skeptical, for all past epics countenanced by the "haughty shade" have had as their subject the "theme of War, the fortune of

---

[4] Whitman quotations are where possible identified in the text by volume and page number of *The Complete Writings of Walt Whitman,* ed. Richard M. Bucke *et al.* (New York: G. P. Putnam's Sons, 1902).

battles, / The making of perfect soldiers." The poet welcomes the
challenge and assures the Muse that he, too, sings of "war, and a longer
and greater one than any." In the poet's war, the field is the world, the
battle "For life and death, for the Body and for the eternal Soul." The
central point of this key "Inscriptions" poem is that the poet's book
qualifies as an epic, even under the Old World definition, if sufficient
liberality is allowed in interpreting the terms.

There are other instances in *Leaves of Grass* in which Whitman
calls attention to the epic nature of his book. In "Starting from
Paumanok" he outlines his plan for encompassing in his poetry the
entire nation—"Solitary, singing in the West, I strike up for a New
World." The poems of *Leaves of Grass* are to constitute "a programme
of chants" for "Americanos." The poet advises:

> Take my leaves America, take them South and take them North,
> Make welcome for them everywhere, for they are your own offspring
>   [I, 18].

Whitman's insistence on an intimate and unique relation between his
book and his country appears no more frequently than his appeal to
the Muse. In "Song of the Exposition," the form is epic if the tone is
comic:

> Come Muse migrate from Greece and Ionia,
> Cross out please those immensely overpaid accounts [I, 238].

If in this poem the Muse loses some of her dignity as the poet instals
her amid the drainpipes, artificial fertilizers, and the kitchen ware,
in "By Blue Ontario's Shore" the Muse is transfigured into a "Phan-
tom gigantic superb, with stern visage," who commands the poet:

> *Chant me the poem, it said, that comes from the soul of America,*
>   *chant me the carol of victory,*
> *And strike up the marches of Libertad, marches more powerful yet,*
> *And sing me before you go the song of the throes of Democracy*
>   [II, 107].

It is characteristic of Whitman that he would reverse the Old World
epic practice by which the poet called upon the Muse for help and
would place the Muse in the position of pleading with the poet to
continue his writing so that vital themes would not go unsung.

It is clear from both external and internal evidence that Whitman
thought of his work in epic terms. The extent to which he fulfilled his
epic ambitions, however, may be measured only in terms of his final
achievement. The answer that achievement provides is impressive.

For the hero of his epic, Whitman created the archetypal personality for the New World (the modern man of "One's-Self I Sing"), a man both individual and of the mass. This hero, unlike the hero of past epics, discovers his heroic qualities not in superman characteristics but in the *selfhood* common to every man. Every man in America, according to Whitman, is potentially an epic hero, if he is sufficiently aware of the potentiality of his selfhood, if he celebrates his vital procreative role, and if he is capable of depth of feeling in spiritually complex attachments. In doing and being all these things, the New World epic hero sings the song of himself, acknowledges the parentage of Adam, and finds spiritual fulfilment in "Calamus" comradeship. He accepts, moreover, his New World place in space and position in time. He relishes his home on the rolling earth, and he finds that his appointed position in the unfolding of mystic evolution places him where all time past converges and all time future originates.

Having created his epic hero by broad, free strokes in the first part of *Leaves of Grass*, Whitman next engages him in the usual trial of strength in a great and crucial war on which the national destiny depends. As Whitman's modern man of the New World represents above all a reconciliation of the paradoxically opposed ideals of democracy—individuality and equality (separateness and "en-masse")—so his epic hero paradoxically exemplifies both traits in war. "Drum-Taps" demonstrates the triumph of the American epic hero "en-masse." No individual is singled out from the rest for heroic deeds, but, throughout, the emphasis is on the ranks, the large mass of men welded together in comradeship and a common national purpose. The poet at one point asserts that America has too long "learn'd from joys and prosperity only":

> But now, ah now, to learn from crises of anguish, advancing, grappling with direst fate and recoiling not,
> And now to conceive and show to the world what your children en-masse really are,
> (For who except myself has yet conceiv'd what your children en-masse really are?) [II, 77].

But, as the Civil War proved the heroic quality on an epic scale of America's "children en-masse," the same national crisis also demonstrated democracy's ability to produce individuality of epic proportions. "Drum-Taps" gives way to "Memories of President Lincoln" and that magnificent threnody, "When Lilacs Last in the Dooryard Bloom'd." But the traits of this epic hero are not different from but similar to the traits of the soldiers "en-masse." He is the "powerful western fallen star"; he is the captain of the ship whose loss is universally mourned;

he is the "dear commander" of the soldiers; but he is above all the "departing comrade" who possessed an infinite capacity for love.

In the latter part of *Leaves of Grass*, the mythological background of the epic hero of the New World is completed as he is related to the "resistless gravitation of spiritual law." The entire section of the book from "Proud Music of the Storm" through "Whispers of Heavenly Death" not only presents the New World hero with "religious" convictions and impresses him with the reality of the spiritual world but also provides him with his immortality. Even the gods (like the heroes) in this New World epic are conceived in democratic terms. At the climactic point in "Passage to India" the poet exclaims:

> Surrounded, copest, frontest God, yieldest, the aim attain'd,
> As fill'd with friendship, love complete, the Elder Brother found,
> The Younger melts in fondness in his arms [II, 196].

God is the "final" comrade, the perfect embodiment of those ideal traits earlier invested in the New World epic hero. The relationship to God is not the relationship of a subject to his superior but the relationship of the ideal brotherhood, the perfectly fulfilled comradeship.

In a very complicated way, Whitman's epic embodies at the same time that it creates America's image of itself—the American dream, the American vision, as it reached its climactic elaboration during the nineteenth century. If in retrospect Whitman's faith in science and democracy seems naïve, we must remember that our perspective is a bit jaded. And Whitman's faith was the American faith, his naïveté the American naïveté. In insisting on being the poet of science and democracy and, above all, of "religion," Whitman was not clinging to personal attitudes but was rather defining the nineteenth century's view of the universe and itself and reflecting it in his epic, as the epic poets of the past—Homer, Vergil, Dante, and Milton—reflected their own times in order to become epic spokesmen for their ages. Whitman embraced the modern "myth" of science, democracy, religion, and much more. The question of the "truth" of these nineteenth-century beliefs and attitudes is as irrelevant as the question of the "truth" of Homer's gods or Milton's devils. The relevant fact is that these views were held by an entire culture and the people lived and acted in the simple faith that their beliefs were true.

Leaves of Grass has just claim as America's epic. No attempt before it (and there were many) succeeded in becoming more than awkward imitations of the epics of the past. No book after it can ever again achieve its unique point of view. Coming shortly after the birth of the nation, embodying the country's first terrible trial by fire, prophesying the greatness to be thrust upon these states, *Leaves of Grass* possesses a position of intimate relationship with America that no other work can now ever assume. For better or worse, *Leaves of Grass* is America's, a reflection of her character and of her soul and of her achievements and her aspirations. If *Leaves of Grass* transfigures what it reflects, that is because its poet wanted to dwell not on the reality but on the ideal. If *Leaves of Grass* has its shortcomings and defects, so, surely, does the culture it attempted to embody. But after all the reservations are stated and the qualifications noted, we must confess that the book does measure up. If Whitman's vision exceeded his achievement, the scope of his achievement was still sufficient to win him just claim to the title of America's epic poet.

The Poet in His Art

"I am determined to have the world know what I was pleased to do. . . . In the long run the world will do as it pleases with the book."

Only a Language Experiment

by F. O. Matthiessen

One aspect of Whitman's work that has not yet received its due attention is outlined in *An American Primer,* notes for a lecture that he seems to have collected mainly between 1855 and 1860, using the paper covers of the unbound copies of the first edition of *Leaves of Grass* for his improvised sheets. This lecture, which, as he says, "does not suggest the invention but describes the growth of an American English enjoying a distinct identity," remained, like most of Whitman's lectures, undelivered and unpublished at his death. But he often talked to Traubel about it in the late eighteen-eighties, telling him that he never quite got its subject out of his mind, that he had long thought of making it into a book,[1] and adding: "I sometimes think the *Leaves* is only a language experiment." It will be interesting, therefore, to begin by seeing how much we can learn about Whitman just by examining his diction.

He understood that language was not "an abstract construction" made by the learned, but that it had arisen out of the work and needs, the joys and struggles and desires of long generations of humanity, and that it had "its bases broad and low, close to the ground." Words were not arbitrary inventions, but the product of human events and customs, the

"Only a Language Experiment." From *American Renaissance* by F. O. Matthiessen, pp. 517-32. Copyright 1941 by Oxford University Press, Inc. Reprinted by permission of the publisher.

[1] It was issued as a separate book by Traubel in 1904.

progeny of folkways. Consequently he believed that the fresh opportunities for the English tongue in America were immense, offering themselves in the whole range of American facts. His poems, by cleaving to these facts, could thereby release "new potentialities" of expression for our native character. When he started to develop his conviction that "a perfect user of words uses things," and to mention some of the things, he unconsciously dilated into the loose beats of his poetry: "they exude in power and beauty from him—miracles from his hands—miracles from his mouth . . . things, whirled like chain-shot rocks, defiance, compulsion, houses, iron, locomotives, the oak, the pine, the keen eye, the hairy breast, the Texan ranger, the Boston truckman, the woman that arouses a man, the man that arouses a woman."

He there reveals the joy of the child or the primitive poet just in naming things. This was the quality in Coleridge that made Whitman speak of him as being "like Adam in Paradise, and almost as free from artificiality"—though Whitman's own joy is far more naïve and relaxed than anything in Coleridge. Whitman's excitement carries weight because he realized that a man cannot use words so unless he has experienced the facts that they express, unless he has grasped them with his senses. This kind of realization was generally obscured in the nineteenth century, partly by its tendency to divorce education of the mind from the body and to treat language as something to be learned from a dictionary. Such division of the individual's wholeness, intensified by the specializations of a mechanized society, has become a chief cause of the neurotic strain oppressing present-day man, for whom the words that pour into him from headlines so infrequently correspond to a concrete actuality that he has touched at first hand. For Whitman it was axiomatic that the speakers of such words are merely juggling helplessly with a foreign tongue. He was already convinced by 1847—as he recorded in the earliest of his manuscript notebooks that has been preserved—that "a man only is interested in anything when he identifies himself with it." When he came to observe in the *Primer* that "a perfect writer would make words sing, dance, kiss . . . or do any thing that man or woman or the natural powers can do," he believed that such a writer must have realized the full resources of his physical life, and have been immersed in the evolving social experience of his own time.

Thus instinctively, if crudely, he reached the conviction that "only the greatest user of words himself fully enjoys and understands himself," a conviction surprisingly close to Eliot's, that Racine and Baudelaire, the two chief French "masters of diction are also the greatest two psychologists" among French poets. Whitman thought that all the talk in Racine was "on stilts," and his sole mention of Baudelaire was to quote one of the few beliefs they shared, "The immoderate taste for beauty and art leads men into monstrous excesses." Noting that *Les Fleurs du Mal* appeared only two years after *Leaves of Grass,* Eliot has asked whether any age could have produced "more heterogeneous leaves and flowers?" But his pronouncement that there was for Whitman "no chasm between the real and the ideal, such as opened before the horrified eyes of Baudelaire," did not blind him to Whitman's prodigious faculty "in making America as it was . . . into something grand and significant," "of transmuting the real into an ideal."

Feeling that he had discovered the real America that had been hidden behind the diction of a superficial culture which hardly touched native life, Whitman exclaimed with delight: "Monongahela—it rolls with venison richness upon the palate." He pursued the subject of how "words become vitaliz'd, and stand for things" in an essay in his late *November Boughs* called "Slang in America" (1885). He grasped there the truth that language is the "universal absorber and combiner," the best index we have to the history of civilization. In the *Primer* his cognizance that English had assimilated contributions from every stock, that it had become an amalgamation from all races, rejecting none, had led him to declare that he would never allude to this tongue "without exultation." In the few pages of his printed essay there is more exultation than clarity, particularly in his conception of slang. His starting point is straightforward enough, the statement that "slang, profoundly consider'd, is the lawless germinal element, below all words and sentences, and behind all poetry, and proves a certain perennial rankness and protestantism in speech." But when he equates slang with "indirection, an attempt of common humanity to escape from bald literalism, and express itself illimitably," we are reminded of Emerson's use of the term "indirection" and need recourse to other passages in Whitman for the elusive connotations that he associated with this word.

When he said in his 1855 Preface that the expression of the American poet was to be "transcendent and new," "indirect and not direct or descriptive or epic," he had just been enumerating the kinds of things the poet must incarnate if he was to be commensurate with his people: the continent's geography and history, the fluid movement of the population, the life of its factories and commerce and of the southern plantations. He appears to have thought that the expression of this surging newness must be "indirect" in the sense that it could not find its voice through any of the conventional modes, but must wait for the poet who "sees the solid and beautiful forms of the future where there are now no solid forms." Here Whitman's belief in the way in which the organic style is called into being is seen to converge with his similar understanding of the origin of words. He might have had in mind either or both in his account of the creative process, in another early notebook: "All truths lie waiting in all things.—They neither urge the opening of themselves nor resist it. For their birth you need not the obstetric forceps of the surgeon. They unfold to you and emit themselves more fragrant than roses from living buds, whenever you fetch the spring sunshine moistened with summer rain.—But it must be in yourself.—It shall come from your soul.—It shall be love."

Living speech could come to a man only through his absorption in the life surrounding him. He must learn that the final decisions of language are not made by dictionary makers but "by the masses, people nearest the concrete, having most to do with actual land and sea." By such a route, illogical as it may be, Whitman came to think of slang as indirection, as the power to embody in a vibrant word or phrase "the deep silent mysterious never to be examined, never to be told quality of life itself." When he tried to make his meaning plainer by giving examples of how many "of the oldest and solidest words we use, were originally generated from the daring and license of slang," he showed that what he was really thinking of was something very like Emerson's first proposition about language—that words are signs of natural facts. Whitman's examples are almost identical with those in *Nature:* "Thus the term *right* means literally only straight. *Wrong* primarily meant twisted, distorted. *Integrity* meant oneness. *Spirit* meant breath, or flame. A *supercilious* person was one who rais'd his eyebrows. To *insult* was to leap against. If you *influenc'd* a man, you but flow'd into him." Moreover, as Whitman continued, he expanded into Emerson's next proposition—that natural facts are symbols of spiritual facts—by launching from the word *prophesy* into an enunciation of the transcendental view of the poet: "The Hebrew word which is translated *prophesy* meant to bubble up and pour forth as a fountain. The enthusiast bubbles up from the Spirit of God within him, and it pours forth from him like a fountain. The word prophecy is misunderstood. Many suppose that it is limited to mere prediction; that is but the lesser portion of prophecy. The greater work is to reveal God. Every true religious enthusiast is a prophet."

In such a passage you come up against one of the most confusing aspects of Whitman, the easy-hearted way he could shuttle back and forth from materialism to idealism without troubling himself about any inconsistency. Thinking of "Children of Adam" or of what Lawrence cared for in Whitman, "the sheer appreciation of the instant moment, life surging itself at its very wellhead," we tend to deny that his bond with transcendentalism could have been strong. But it is significant that his earliest quotation from one of Emerson's "inimitable lectures," in a notice for *The Brooklyn Eagle* in 1847, is from "Spiritual Laws" and begins, "When the act of reflection takes place in the mind, when we look at ourselves in the light of thought, we discover that our life is embosomed in beauty." Whitman's response to this kind of idealism was more than fleeting, as we may judge from his marginal note on an unidentified essay on "Imagination and Fact," which Bucke dated to the early fifties. The sentence that struck the poet reads: "The mountains, rivers, forests and the elements that gird them round about would be only blank conditions of matter if the mind did not fling its own divinity around them." Whitman commented: "This I think is one of the most indicative sentences I ever read."

The idealistic strain also runs through his conception of language. Although he asks in his "Song of the Banner at Daybreak":

> Words! book-words! what are you?

and affirms in "A Song of the Rolling Earth":

> The substantial words are in the ground and sea,

nevertheless he proclaims on the first page of his *Primer:* "All words are spiritual—nothing is more spiritual than words." This is the Whitman who could say, "The words of my book nothing, the drift of it everything," the Whitman so concerned with the idea rather than the form that he could take flight into the vaguest undifferentiated generalizations about "Democracy, ma femme," or could write on occasion even of "the body electric" with no sensuous touch of his material:

> O for you whoever you are your correlative body! O it, more than
>   all else, you delighting!

This is the Whitman who has seemed to linguists as though he was trying to get beyond the limits of language altogether. In the view of Sapir, subscribed to by Ogden and Richards, he sometimes is moving so entirely in terms of abstractions that he appears to be "striving for a generalized art language, a literary algebra." In this quality of his work Sapir regarded him as an extreme example of the transcendental drift, an artist whose "expression is frequently strained, it sounds at times like a translation from an unknown original—which, indeed, is precisely what it is." We recall that Emerson's most idealized passages of verse struck Chapman in much the same way.

Thus Whitman seems to show the very dichotomy between the material and the ideal, the concrete and the abstract that we observed in Emerson's remarks on language. Nevertheless, when we look at their poems, it is obvious that Whitman often bridged the gap in a way that Emerson could not. The whole question of the relation of Whitman's theory and practice of art to Emerson's is fascinating, since, starting so often from similar if not identical positions, they end up with very different results. The extent of Emerson's influence has been obscured by Whitman's desire in his old age not to appear to have been too indebted to anyone. In his open letter to Emerson, which appeared in the second (1856) edition, though not subsequently, Whitman did not hesitate to address him as "Master." Speaking of "that new moral

American continent without which, I see, the physical continent remained incomplete," he said: "Those shores you found. I say you have led the States there—have led me there." Long afterwards he told his disciples that he was referring to the experience of having read Emerson after receiving his tribute to the first edition of the *Leaves,* but a more likely account would seem to be the one he gave to J. T. Trowbridge. In this version, based on a conversation in 1860—though not printed until after Whitman's death—the poet "freely admitted that he could never have written his poems if he had not first 'come to himself,' and that Emerson helped him to 'find himself.' I asked him if he thought he would have come to himself without that help. He said, 'Yes, but it would have taken longer.' " Here Whitman dated the fecund reading to the summer of 1854 when he had been working at his trade of carpenter and had carried a book with him in his lunch pail. One day it "chanced to be a volume of Emerson; and from that time he took with him no other writer." As we know, he had been at least acquainted with Emerson's ideas for some years before that, and their working in him may well have been a slower fermentation. He gave his own characteristic expression to the process: "I was simmering, simmering. simmering; Emerson brought me to a boil."

It is not hard to find, for what they are worth, passages in Whitman running parallel to most of Emerson's major convictions about the nature of art. But it would always be salutary to head them with these two from "Self-Reliance" and "Song of Myself": "Suppose you should contradict yourself; what then? . . . With consistency a great soul has simply nothing to do"; and

> Do I contradict myself?
> Very well then I contradict myself,
> (I am large, I contain multitudes.)

At the end of a long paragraph of appreciation of Emerson that Bucke places around eighteen-fifty, Whitman had already observed that "there is hardly a proposition in Emerson's poems or prose which you cannot find the opposite of in some other place." Nevertheless, the main contours of Emerson's doctrine of expression, as we have seen it develop, are unmistakable, and unmistakably Whitman's as well. They can both compress it into headlines: Emerson, "By God, it is in me, and must come forth of me"; Whitman, "Walt you contain enough, why don't you let it out then?" Again, whole essays of Emerson's, notably that on "The Poet," speak eloquently about the very things from which Whitman made his poetry. The two share the same view of the poet as inspired seer, of his dependence for his utterance upon his moments of inner illumination. Yet looking back over forty years, though Whitman reaffirmed that his last word would be "loyal, loyal," he admitted that Emerson's work had latterly seemed to him "pretty thin," always a *make,* never an unconscious *growth,"* and "some ways short of earth."

Whitman's language is more earthy because he was aware, in a way that distinguished him not merely from Emerson but from every other writer of the day, of the power of sex. In affirming natural passion to be "the enclosing basis of everything," he spoke of its sanity, of the sacredness of the human body, using specifically religious terms: "we were all lost without redemption, except we retain the sexual fibre of things." In defending his insistence on this element in his poems (1856), he made clear his understanding of its immediate bearing upon a living speech: "To the lack of an avowed, empowered, unabashed development of sex (the only salvation for the same), and to the fact of speakers and writers fradulently assuming as always dead what every one knows to be always alive, is attributable the remarkable non-personality and indistinctness of modern productions in books." Continuing in this vein he made almost the same observations about conventional society as were later to be expressed by Henry Adams, who, incidentally, found Whitman to be the only American writer who had drawn upon the dynamic force of sex "as every classic had always done." Both were agreed, though the phrasing here is Whitman's, that particularly among the so-called cultivated class the neuter gender prevailed, and that "if the dresses were changed, the men might easily pass for women and the women for men."

Emerson never gave up deploring the want of male principle in our literature, but one reason why it remained remote from his own pages is contained in his pronouncement (1834): "I believe in the existence of the material world as the expression of the spiritual or real." The continuation of his thought reveals the difference of his emphasis from that of the poet of "Crossing Brooklyn Ferry": "and so look with a quite comic and condescending interest upon the show of Broadway with the air of an old gentleman when he says, 'Sir, I knew your father.' Is it not forever the aim and endeavor of the real to embody itself in the phenomenal?" No matter how happily inconsistent Emerson might be on other matters, this basic position of the idealist was one from which he never departed. Whitman was far less consistent in his consideration of the relation between body and soul. He was impressed by a line of John Sterling's, which was also a favorite of Emerson's, "Still lives the song tho' Regnar dies." Whitman added this gloss to it: "The word is become flesh." Just what he implied in talking about language as incarnation, and how he diverged from Emerson, can be followed most briefly in his own words.

In the manuscript draft for the opening section of "Song of Myself," he announced the equalitarian inclusiveness that was destined always to be part of his desire:

> And I say that the soul is not greater than the body,
> And I say that the body is not greater than the soul.

However, that arbitrary equilibrium between the two is far less characteristic of his accents of most intimate discovery than his exultant reckless
feeling in "Children of Adam" that the body "includes and is the soul,"

> And if the body were not the soul, what is the soul?

But in different moods, as in "A Song of Joys," he veers towards the
other pole and seems loosely to approximate Blake in saying that the
real life of his senses transcends his senses and flesh, that it is not his
material eyes that finally see, or his material body that finally loves.
However, he does not pursue this strain very long, and says more usually
that the soul achieves its "identity" through the act of observing, loving,
and absorbing concrete objects:

> We realize the soul only by you, you faithful solids and fluids.

This particular kind of material ideality, suggestive in general of Fichte's,
remains his dominant thought, so it is worth observing how he formulated it in one of his notebooks: "Most writers have disclaimed the physical world and they have not over-estimated the other, or soul, but have
under-estimated the corporeal. How shall my eye separate the beauty of
the blossoming buckwheat field from the stalks and heads of tangible
matter? How shall I know what the life is except as I see it in the flesh?
I will not praise one without the other or any more than the other."

In commenting on the mixture of his heritage, Whitman once remarked that "like the Quakers, the Dutch are very practical and materialistic . . . but are terribly transcendental and cloudy too." That mixture
confronts and tantalizes you throughout his poetry. He is at his firmest
when he says that "imagination and actuality must be united." But in
spite of his enthusiasm for the natural sciences as well as for every
other manifestation of progress, he never came very close to a scientific
realism. When he enunciated, in the eighteen-seventies, that "body
and mind are one," he had then been led into this thought by his reading
of—or about—the German metaphysicians. And he declared that "only
Hegel is fit for America," since in his system "the human soul stands in
the centre, and all the universes minister to it." Following the Civil
War, and increasingly during the last twenty years of his life, he kept
saying that in his *Leaves,* "One deep purpose underlay the others—and
that has been the religious purpose." He often posed variants of the
question, "If the spiritual is not behind the material, to what purpose
is the material?" Yet, even then, his most natural way of reconciling the
dichotomy between the two elements, "fused though antagonistic," was
to reaffirm his earlier analogy: "The Soul of the Universe is the Male
and genital master and the impregnating and animating spirit—Physical
matter is Female and Mother and waits . . ."

No arrangement or rearrangement of Whitman's thoughts on this or any other subject can resolve the paradoxes or discover in them a fully coherent pattern. He was incapable of sustained logic, but that should not blind the reader into impatient rejection of the ebb and flow of his antithesis. They possess a loose dialectic of their own, and a clue of how to find it is provided by Engels' discussion of Feuerbach: "One knows that these antithesis have only a relative validity; that that which is recognized now as true has also its latent false side which will later manifest itself, just as that which is now regarded as false has also its true side by virtue of which it could previously have been regarded as true." Whitman's ability to make a synthesis in his poems of the contrasting elements that he calls body and soul may serve as a measure of his stature as a poet. When his words adhere to concrete experience and yet are bathed in imagination, his statements become broadly representative of humanity:

> I am she who adorn'd herself and folded her hair expectantly,
> My truant lover has come, and it is dark.

When he fails to make that synthesis, his language can break into the extremes noted by Emerson when he called it "a remarkable mixture of the *Bhagvat-Geeta* and the *New York Herald.*" The incongruous lengths to which Whitman was frequently carried in each direction shows how hard a task he undertook. On the one hand, his desire to grasp American facts could lead him beyond slang into the rawest jargon, the journalese of the day. On the other, his attempts to pass beyond the restrictions of language into the atmosphere it could suggest often produced only the barest formulas. His inordinate and grotesque failures in both directions throw into clearer light his rare successes, and the fusion upon which they depend.

The slang that he relished as providing more fun than "the books of all 'the American humorists'" was what he heard in the ordinary talk of "a gang of laborers, rail-road men, miners, drivers, or boatmen," in their tendency "to approach a meaning not directly and squarely" but by the circuitous routes of lively fancy. This tendency expressed itself in their fondness for nicknames like Old Hickory, or Wolverines, or Suckers, or Buckeyes. Their inventiveness had sowed the frontier with many a Shirttail Bend and Toenail Lake. Current evasions of the literal transformed a horsecar conductor into a "snatcher," straight whisky into "barefoot," and codfish balls into "sleeve buttons." But even though Whitman held such slang to be the source of all that was poetical in human utterance, he was aware that its fermentation was often hasty and frothy, and, except for occasional friendly regional epithets like Hoosiers or Kanucks, he used it only sparingly in his poems. Indeed, in some notes during the period of the gestation of his first *Leaves*, he ad-

vised himself to use "common idioms and phrases—Yankeeisms and vul-
garisms—cant expressions, when very pat only." In consequence, the
diction of his poetry is seldom as unconventional as that in the advice
he gave himself for an essay on contemporary writing: "Bring in a sock-
dolager on the Dickens-fawners." He gave examples of "fierce words" in
the *Primer—skulk, shyster, doughface, mean cuss, backslider, lick-
spittle*—and sometimes cut loose in the talk that Traubel reported. But
only on the rare occasions when he felt scorn did he introduce into his
poems any expressions as savagely untrammelled as

> This now is too lamentable a face for a man,
> Some abject louse asking leave to be, cringing for it,
> Some milk-nosed maggot blessing what lets it wrig to its hole.

By contrast his most characteristic colloquialisms are easy and relaxed,
as when he said "howdy" to Traubel and told him that he felt "flirty"
or "hunkydory," or fell into slang with no self-consciousness, but with
the careless aplomb of a man speaking the language most natural to him:

> I reckon I am their boss, and they make me a pet besides.
>
> And will go gallivant with the light and air myself.
>
> Shoulder your duds, dear son, and I will mine.
>
> Earth! you seem to look for something at my hands,
> Say, old top-knot, what do you want?

One of Whitman's demands in the *Primer* was that words should be
brought into literature from factories and farms and trades, for he knew
that "around the markets, among the fish-smacks, along the wharves,
you hear a thousand words, never yet printed in the repertoire of any
lexicon." What resulted was sometimes as mechanical as the long lists in
"A Song for Occupations," but his resolve for inclusiveness also produced
dozens of snap-shot impressions as accurate as

> The butcher-boy puts off his killing-clothes, or sharpens his knife at
>   the stall in the market,
> I loiter enjoying his repartee and his shuffle and break-down.

Watching men in action called out of him some of his most fluid phrases,
which seem to bathe and surround the objects they describe—as this, of
the blacksmiths:

> The *lithe sheer* of their waists plays even with their massive arms.

Or this,

> The negro holds firmly the reins of his four horses, the block *swags*
> *underneath* on its tied-over chain.

Or a line that is itself a description of the very process by which he en-
folds such movement:

> In me the caresser of life wherever moving, backward as well as
> forward *sluing.*

At times he produced suggestive coinages of his own:

> The blab of the pave, tires of carts, sluff of boot-soles, talk of the
> promenaders.

Yet he is making various approaches to language even in that one line.
Blab and *sluff* have risen from his desire to suggest actual sounds, but
promenaders, which also sounds well, has clearly been employed for
that reason alone since it does not belong to the talk of any American
folk. *Pave* instead of *pavement* is the kind of bastard word that, to use
another, Whitman liked to "promulge." Sometimes it is hard to tell
whether such words sprang from intention or ignorance, particularly in
view of the appearance of *semitic* in place of *seminal* ("semitic muscle,"
"semitic milk") in both the 1855 Preface and the first printing of "A
Woman Waits for Me." Most frequently his hybrids take form of
the free substitution of one part of speech for another—sometimes quite
effectively ("the soothe of the waves"), sometimes less so (she that "birth'd
him").

Although it has been estimated that Whitman had a vocabulary of
more than thirteen thousand words, of which slightly over half were
used by him only once,[2] the number of his authentic coinages is not very
large. Probably the largest group is composed of his agent-nouns, which
is not surprising for a poet who was so occupied with types and classes of
men and women. Unfortunately these also furnish some of the ugliest-
sounding words in his pages, *originatress, revoltress, dispensatress,*
which have hardly been surpassed even in the age of the realtor and the
beautician. He was luckier with an occasional abstract noun like *presi-
dentiad,* though this is offset by a needless monstrosity like *savantism.*
The one kind of coinage where his ear was listening sensitively is in such

---

[2] The reported figures, 13,447 and 6,978, are those of W. H. Trimble's unpublished
concordance. The most useful work that has been done on Whitman's diction are
several articles by Louise Pound, particularly "Walt Whitman's Neologisms" (*American Mercury*, February 1925) and "Walt Whitman and the French Language" (*American Speech*, May 1926).

compounds as "the transparent green-shine" of the water around the naked swimmer in "I Sing the Body Electric," or that evoking the apples hanging "indolent-ripe" in "Halcyon Days."

His belief in the need to speak not merely for Americans but for the workers of all lands seems to have given the impetus for his odd habit of introducing random words from other languages, to the point of talking about "the ouvrier class"! He took from the Italian chiefly the terms of the opera, also *viva, romanza,* and even *ambulanza.* From the Spanish he was pleased to borrow the orotund way of naming his country-men "Americanos," while the occasional circulation of Mexican dollars in the States during the eighteen-forties may have given him his word *Libertad.* His favorite *camerado,* an archaic English version of the Spanish *camarada,* seems most likely to have come to him from the pages of the Waverley novels, of which he had been an enthusiastic reader in his youth. But the smattering of French which he picked up on his trip to New Orleans, and which constituted the most extensive knowledge that he ever was to have of another tongue, furnished him with the majority of his borrowings. It allowed him to talk of his "amour" and his "eleves," of a "soiree" or an "accoucheur," of "trottoirs" and "feuillage" and "delicatesse"; to say that his were not "the songs of an ennuyeed person," or to shout, "Allons! from all formules! . . . Allons! the road is before us!" Frequently he was speaking no language, as when he proclaimed himself "no dainty dolce affetuoso." But he could go much farther than that into a foreign jargon in his desire to "eclaircise the myths Asiatic" in his "Passage to India," or to fulfil "the rapt promises and luminè of seers." He could address God, with ecstatic and monumental tastelessness, as "thou reservoir."

Many of these are samples of the confused American effort to talk big by using high-sounding terms with only the vaguest notion of their original meaning. The resultant fantastic transformations have enlivened every stage of our history, from the frontiersman's determination to twist his tongue around the syllables of the French settlement at Chemincouvert, Ark., which ended up with the name being turned into Smackover, down to Ring Lardner's dumb nurse who thought people were calling her "a mormon or something." In Whitman's case, the fact that he was a reader and so could depend upon letters as well as upon sounds overheard kept him from drifting to such gorgeous lengths. His transformations retain some battered semblance of the original word, which, with the happy pride of the half-educated in the learned term, he then deployed grandly for purposes of his own. Often the attraction for him in the French words ran counter to the identification he usually desired between the word and the thing, since it sprang from intoxica-tion with the mere sound. You can observe the same tendency in some of the jotted lists of his notebooks, *Cantaloupe. Muskmelon. Cantabile. Cacique City,* or in his shaping such a generalized description of the

earth as "O vast rondure swimming in space." When caught up by the
desire to include the whole universe in his embrace, he could be swept
far into the intense inane, chanting in "Night on the Prairies" of "immortality and peace":

> How plenteous! how spiritual! how resumé!

The two diverging strains in his use of language were with him to
the end, for he never outgrew his tendency to lapse from specific images
into undifferentiated and lifeless abstractions, as in the closing phrase of
this description of his grandfather: "jovial, red, stout, with sonorous
voice and characteristic physiognomy." In some of his latest poems,
"Sands at Seventy," he could still be satisfied with the merest rhetoric:

> Of ye, O God, Life, Nature, Freedom, Poetry.

In his fondness for all his *Leaves*, he seems never to have perceived what
we can note in the two halves of a single line,

> I concentrate toward them that are nigh, I wait on the door slab,

—the contrast between the clumsy stilted opening and the simple close.
The total pattern of his speech is, therefore, difficult to chart, since it is
formed both by the improviser's carelessness about words and by the
kind of attention to them indicated in his telling Burroughs that he had
been "searching for twenty-five years for the word to express what the
twilight note of the robin meant to him." He also engaged in endless
minute revisions of his poems, the purpose of which is often baffling. Although sometimes serving to fuse the syllables into an ampler rhythm, as
in the transformation of

> Out of the rocked cradle

into one of his most memorable opening lines; they seem almost as likely
to add up to nothing more than the dozens of minor substitutions in
"Salut au Monde," which leave it the flat and formless catalogue that it
was in the beginning.

In a warm appreciation of Burns in *November Boughs*, Whitman said
that "his brightest hit is his use of the Scotch patois, so full of terms
flavor'd like wild fruits or berries." Thinking not only of Burns he
relished a special charm in "the very neglect, unfinish, careless nudity,"
which were not to be found in more polished language and verse. But his
suggested comparison between the Scotch poet and himself would bring
out at once the important difference that Whitman is not using anything

like a folk-speech. Indeed, his phrasing is generally remote from any customary locutions of the sort that he jotted down as notes for one unwritten poem. This was to have been based on a free rendering of local native calls, such as "Here goes your fine fat oysters—Rock Point oysters —here they go." When put beside such natural words and cadences, Whitman's usual diction is clearly not that of a countryman but of what he called himself, "a jour[neyman] printer." In its curious amalgamation of homely and simple usage with half-remembered terms he read once somewhere, and with casual inventions of the moment, he often gives the impression of using a language not quite his own. In his determination to strike up for a new world, he deliberately rid himself of foreign models. But, so far as his speech is concerned, this was only very partially possible, and consequently Whitman reveals the peculiarly American combination of a childish freshness with a mechanical and desiccated repetition of book terms that had had significance for the more complex civilization in which they had had their roots and growth. The freshness has come, as it did to Huck Finn, through instinctive rejection of the authority of those terms, in Whitman's reaction against what he called Emerson's cold intellectuality: "Suppose his books becoming absorb'd, the permanent chyle of American general and particular character—what a well-wash'd and grammatical, but bloodless and helpless race we should turn out!"

Yet the broken chrysalis of the old restrictions still hangs about Whitman. Every page betrays that his language is deeply ingrained with the educational habits of a middle-class people who put a fierce emphasis on the importance of the written word. His speech did not spring primarily from contact with the soil, for though his father was a descendant of Long Island farmers, he was also a citizen of the age of reason, an acquaintance and admirer of Tom Paine. Nor did Whitman himself develop his diction as Thoreau did, by the slow absorption through every pore of the folkways of a single spot of earth. He was attracted by the wider sweep of the city, and though his language is a natural product, it is the natural product of a Brooklyn journalist of the eighteen-forties who had previously been a country schoolteacher and a carpenter's helper and who had finally felt an irresistable impulse to be a poet.

Whitman as Symbolist

by Charles Feidelson, Jr.

"No one will get at my verses," Whitman declared, "who insists upon viewing them as a literary performance, or attempt at such performance, or as aiming mainly toward art or aestheticism." In his conscious literary theory literature is subordinate to sociology, "the United States themselves are essentially the greatest poem," the poet must "tally" the American scene, and the function of poetry is the creation of heroic citizens. Yet it is obvious that a larger principle governs both his poetic and his sociological doctrine; no one will get at his verses who insists upon viewing them as a sociological performance. Whitman intimates that the link between his poems and American life is actually a new method exemplified by both:

> One main contrast of the ideas behind every page of my verses, com-
> pared with establish'd poems, is their different relative attitude towards
> God, towards the objective universe, and still more (by reflection, confession,
> assumption, &c.) the quite changed attitude of the ego, the one chanting
> or talking, towards himself and towards his fellow-humanity. It is certainly
> time for America, above all, to begin this readjustment in the scope and
> basic point of view of verse; for everything else has changed.

The distinctive quality of Whitman's poetry depends on this change of standpoint. In his effort "to articulate and faithfully express . . . [his] own physical, emotional, moral, intellectual, and aesthetic Personality, in the midst of, and tallying, the momentous spirit and facts of its immediate days," his interest is not so much in the Personality or the environment *per se* as in the "changed attitude of the ego." The new method is better defined in the poems themselves than in the critical prose. The ego appears in the poems as a traveler and explorer, not as

"Whitman as Symbolist." Reprinted from *Symbolism and American Literature*, pp. 16-27, by Charles Feidelson, Jr., by permission of The University of Chicago Press. Copyright 1953 by the University of Chicago. The title has been supplied by the editor. [Mr. Feidelson's essay is reprinted here, with his permission, without the notes which buttress and expand his argument. They are to be found on pp. 235-240 of *Symbolism and American Literature*.—R.H.P.]

a static observer; its object is "to know the universe itself as a road, as many roads, as roads for traveling souls." The shift of image from the contemplative eye of "establish'd poems" to the voyaging ego of Whitman's poetry records a large-scale theoretical shift from the categories of "substance" to those of "process." Whitman's "perpetual journey" is not analogous to a sight-seeing trip, though his catalogues might give that impression; the mind and the material world into which it ventures are not ultimately different in kind. Instead, what seems at first a penetration of nature by the mind is actually a process in which the known world comes into being. The "child who went forth every day, and who now goes, and will always go forth every day," is indistinguishable from the world of his experience: "The first object he look'd upon, that object he became, / And that object became part of him." The true voyage is the endless becoming of reality:

> Allons! to that which is endless as it was beginningless,
> To undergo much, tramp of days, rests of nights,
> To merge all in the travel they tend to, and the days and nights they
> tend to,
> Again to merge them in the start of superior journeys. . . .

Here there is no clear distinction among the traveler, the road, and the journey, for the journey is nothing but the progressive unity of the voyager and the lands he enters; perception, which unites the seer and the seen, is identical with the real process of becoming. God, in this context, is a "seething principle," and human society is a flow of "shapes ever projecting other shapes." Whitman's "readjustment in the scope and basic point of view of verse" is actually a transmutation of all supposed entities into events.

A poem, therefore, instead of referring to a completed act of perception, constitutes the act itself, both in the author and in the reader; instead of describing reality, a poem is a realization. When Whitman writes, "See, steamers steaming through my poems," he is admonishing both himself and his audience that no distinction can be made among themselves, the steamers, and the words. Indeed, no distinction can be made between the poet and the reader: "It is you talking just as much as myself, I act as the tongue of you." His new method was predicated not only on the sense of creative vision—itself a process which renders a world in process—but also, as part and parcel of that consciousness, on the sense of creative speech. The *I* of Whitman's poems speaks the world that he sees, and sees the world that he speaks, and does this by *becoming* the reality of his vision and of his words, in which the reader also participates. Most of Whitman's poems, more or less explicitly, are "voyages" in this metaphysical sense. This was Whitman's genre, his "new theory of literary composition for imaginative works." Even in the most personal lyrics of "Children of Adam" and "Calamus," the "one chanting or talking" is not simply the poet; the chant is neither pure self-expression nor pure description; what is talked about is oddly confused with the talker and the talking; and the audience is potentially both the subject and the writer. "Song of Myself," though it breathes the personal egotism of Whitman, makes sense as a whole only when the self is taken dramatically and identified with "the procreant urge of the world."

Consider the last four sections of "Starting from Paumanok"—the entire poem being the "Song of Myself" in miniature. Here at the end of the poem it appears that to start from Paumanok is to start far back of the speaker's birth in the opening line. The beginnings (of the speaker, of America, and of the world) are "aboriginal," as typified by the Indian name; the beginnings, indeed, by a leap of thought, become the perpetual genesis of "a world primal again," announced by the poet's voice. In the following section, with its images of incessant motion, the announcement itself is the genesis of the world; the voice is equated with the becoming of reality. Retrospectively, one sees that the preliminary statement of the poem—"Solitary, singing in the West, I strike up for a New World"—has ushered in a song which not only is addressed to and descriptive of America but also is the vehicle, at once product and creator, of a metaphysical "newness." In the course of the poem the solitary voice of the individual poet has expanded into the presence of an all-inclusive Word—"a word to clear one's path ahead endlessly." And the speaker's union with his hearer is imaged in the final section as the love relationship of "camerados" on the journey. The method of "Starting from Paumanok" does not palliate Whitman's diffuseness and arbitrary choice of material; rather, by depriving him of a static point of view, it is the immediate cause of these defects. Yet the principle behind this poem, the exploitation of Speech as the literary aspect of eternal process, is the source of whatever literary value resides in *Leaves of Grass*.

"This subject of language," Whitman confided to Horace Traubel, "interests me—interests me: I never quite get it out of my mind. I sometimes think the Leaves is only a language experiment." *An American Primer*, Whitman's fragmentary lecture on language, reveals a mind that fed upon words: "*Names* are magic.—One word can pour such a flood through the soul." The sense of language as inherently significant is his meeting ground with Hawthorne, for whom a "deep meaning . . . streamed forth" from the scarlet letter. In both cases attention is deflected from "ideas" and "objects" to a symbolic medium; and in both cases the perception of a meaningful symbol is opposed to another kind of perception, which Hawthorne calls "analysis." Hawthorne would like to reduce the meaning to the rational terms of logical construct or empirical fact; he is plainly uncomfortable at the disturbance of his "sensibilities." In practice, he not only translates symbolism into allegory but also affects a rational style which ties his language down to the common-sense world. Whitman's awareness of words in themselves is stronger, and he is militantly hostile to reason. He proposes "new law-forces of spoken and written language—not merely the pedagogue-forms, correct, regular, familiar with precedents, made for matters of outside propriety, fine words, thoughts definitely told out." He is indifferent to dictionary words and textbook grammar, which he associates with a barren formalism and externality. Fully accepting the intuition at which Hawthorne boggled, he takes his departure from a denial of conventional distinctions: "Strange and hard that paradox true I give, / Objects gross and the unseen soul are one." Since Whitman regards meaning as an activity of words rather than an external significance attached to them, language, together with the self and the material world, turns out to be a process, the pouring of the flood. "A perfect user of words uses things," while at the same time he *is* both the words and the things:

> Latent, in a great user of words, must actually be all passions, crimes, trades, animals, stars, God, sex, the past, might, space, metals, and the like—because these are the words, and he who is not these, plays with a foreign tongue, turning helplessly to dictionaries and authorities.

This kind of speech "seldomer tells a thing than suggests or necessitates it," because to "tell" something would be to suppose something outside the language. The reader is not given statements but is set in action, "on the assumption that the process of reading is not a half-sleep, but, in highest sense, an exercise, a gymnast's struggle." The poem necessarily works "by curious removes, indirections," rather than direct imitation of nature, since "the image-making faculty" runs counter to the habit of mind which views the material world as separable from ideas and speech. Whitman's running battle with the rational assumptions of conventional thought reaches its peak in the hyperbolical "Song of the Rolling Earth," where he identifies all "audible words" with the marks on the printed page and glorifies, by way of contrast, "the unspoken meanings of the earth." In deliberate paradox he asserts that true poems will somehow be made from these inaudible words. The poem expresses the bravado of his conscious attempt to create a wholly symbolic language in the face of intellectual convention. For that is his purpose: the "tallying" of things and man, to which he often alludes mysteriously, is simply the presence of language in each and the presence of each in language. The "language experiment" of *Leaves of Grass*—its promise of "new potentialities of speech"—depends on the symbolic status claimed by the book as a whole and in every part. "From the eyesight proceeds another eyesight and from the hearing proceeds another hearing and from the voice proceeds another voice eternally curious of the harmony of things with man."

The patent symbols of Whitman's best poem, "When Lilacs Last in the Dooryard Bloom'd," are conditioned by the thoroughgoing symbolism of his poetic attitude. As in most elegies, the person mourned is hardly more than the occasion of the work; but this poem, unlike *Lycidas* or *Adonais*, does not transmute the central figure merely by generalizing him out of all recognition. Lincoln is seldom mentioned either as a person or as a type. Instead, the focus of the poem is a presentation of the poet's mind at work in the context of Lincoln's death. If the true subject of *Lycidas* and *Adonais* is not Edward King or John Keats but the Poet, the true subject of Whitman's "Lilacs" is not the Poet but the poetic process. And even this subject is not treated simply by generalizing a particular situation. The act of poetizing and the context in which it takes place have continuity in time and space but no particular existence. Both are "ever-returning"; the tenses shift; the poet is in different places at once; and at the end this whole phase of creation is moving inexorably forward.

Within this framework the symbols behave like characters in a drama, the plot of which is the achievement of a poetic utterance. The spring, the constant process of rebirth, is threaded by the journey of the coffin, the constant process of death, and in the first section it presents the poet with twin symbols: the perennially blooming lilac and the drooping star. The spring also brings to the poet the "thought of him I love," in which the duality of life and death is repeated. The thought of the dead merges with the fallen star in Section 2; the thought of love merges with the life of the lilac, from which the poet breaks a sprig in Section 3. Thus the lilac and the star enter the poem not as objects to which the poet assigns a meaning but as elements in the undifferentiated stream of thoughts and things; and the spring, the real process of becoming, which involves the real process of dissolution, is also the genesis of poetic vision. The complete pattern of the poem is established with the advent of the bird in the fourth section. For here, in the song of the thrush, the lilac and star are united (the bird sings "death's outlet song of life"), and the potentiality of the poet's "thought" is intimated. The song of the bird and the thought of the poet, which also unites life and death, both lay claim to the third place in the "trinity" brought by spring; they are, as it were, the actuality and the possibility of poetic utterance, which reconciles opposite appearances.

The drama of the poem will be a movement from possible to actual poetic speech, as represented by the "tallying" of the songs of the poet and the thrush. Although it is a movement without steps, the whole being implicit in every moment, there is a graduation of emphasis. Ostensibly, the visions of the coffin and the star (Sections 5 through 8) delay the unison of poet and bird, so that full actualization is reserved for the end of the poem. On the other hand, the verse that renders the apparition of the coffin *is* "death's outlet song of life." The poetic act of evoking the dark journey is treated as the showering of death with lilac:

> Here, coffin that slowly passes,
> I give you my sprig of lilac. . . .
> Blossoms and branches green to coffins all I bring,
> For fresh as the morning, thus would I chant a song for you,
>   O sane and sacred death.

Even as the poet lingers, he has attained his end. And the star of Section 8, the counterpart of the coffin, functions in much the same way. The episode that occurred "a month since"—when "my soul in its trouble dissatisfied sank, as where you sad orb, / Concluded, dropt in the night, and was gone"—was a failure of the poetic spring. The soul was united with the star but not with the lilac. Yet the passage is preceded by the triumphant statement, "Now I know what you must have meant," and knowledge issues in the ability to render the episode in verse. The perception of meaning gives life to the fact of death; the star meant the death of Lincoln, but the evolution of the meaning is poetry.

The recurrence of the song of the thrush in the following section and in Section 13 is a reminder of the poetic principle which underlies the entire poem. In a sense, the words, "I hear your notes, I hear your call," apply to all that precedes and all that is to come, for the whole poem, existing in an eternal present, is the "loud human song" of the poet's "brother." But again Whitman delays the consummation. He is "detained" from his rendezvous with the bird—although he really "hears" and "understands" all the time—by the sight of the "lustrous star" and by the "mastering odor" of the lilac. Since both the star and the lilac are inherent in the song of the bird, he actually lingers only in order to proceed. While the song rings in the background, the poet puts the questions presupposed by his own poetizing. How can the life of song be one with the fact of death?—"O how shall I warble myself for the dead one there I loved?" And what will be the content of the song of death?—"O what shall I hang on the chamber walls . . . / To adorn the burial-house of him I love?" The questions answer themselves. The breath by which the grave becomes part of his chant is the breath of life; within the poem the image of the "burial-house" will be overlaid with "pictures of growing spring." The delay has served only to renew the initial theme: the poet's chant, like the song of the thrush, is itself the genesis of life and therefore contains both life and death.

The final achievement of poetic utterance comes in Section 14, when the poet, looking forth on the rapid motion of life, experiences death. More exactly, he walks between the "thought" and the "knowledge" of

death, which move beside him like companions. Just as his poem exists
between the "thought" of the dead, which is paradoxically an act of
life, and the actual knowledge of the bird's song, which embodies both
dying star and living lilac, the poet himself is in motion from the potential to the actual. From this point to the end of the poem, the sense
of movement never flags. The poet's flight into the darkness is a fusion
with the stream of music from the bird:

> And the charm of the carol rapt me,
> As I held as if by their hands my comrades in the night,
> And the voice of my spirit tallied the song of the bird.

As the motion of the poet is lost in the motion of the song, the latter is
identified with the "dark mother always gliding near," and in the
"floating" carol death itself becomes the movement of waves that "un-
dulate round the world." In effect, poet and bird, poem and song, life and
death, are now the sheer process of the carol; as in "Out of the Cradle
Endlessly Rocking," reality is the unfolding Word. The presented song
merges into the "long panoramas of visions" in Section 15, and then the
inexorable process begins to leave this moment behind:

> Passing the visions, passing the night,
> Passing, unloosing the hold of my comrades' hands,
> Passing the song of the hermit bird and the tallying song
>   of my soul. . . .
> Passing, I leave thee lilac with heart-shaped leaves, . . .
> I cease from my song for thee, . . .
> O comrade lustrous with silver face in the night.

But the poetic activity is continuous; the passing-onward is not a rejection
of the old symbols. "Lilac and star and bird twined with the chant of
. . . [the] soul" also pass onward because they are activities and not
finite things. The conclusion of this poem dramatizes what Whitman
once stated of *Leaves of Grass* as a whole—that the book exists as "a
passage way to something rather than a thing in itself concluded."
Taken seriously, in the sense in which there *can* be no "thing in itself
concluded," this notion is not, as Whitman sometimes pretended, a
mere excuse for haphazard technique but the rationale of a symbolistic
method.

Yet "When Lilacs Last in the Dooryard Bloom'd" is a successful poem
only because it does not fully live up to the theory which it both states
and illustrates. The poem really presupposes a static situation, which
Whitman undertakes to treat as though it were dynamic; in the course
of the poem the death of Lincoln, of which we always remain aware,
is translated into Whitman's terms of undifferentiated flow. His other

long poems generally lack this stabilizing factor. Whatever the nominal subject, it is soon lost in sheer "process"; all roads lead into the "Song of Myself," in which the bare Ego interacts with a miscellaneous world. The result is Whitman's characteristic disorder and turgidity. When the subject is endless, any form becomes arbitrary. While the antirational conception of a poem as the realization of language gives a new freedom and a new dignity to poetry, it apparently leads to an aimlessness from which the poem can be rescued only by returning to rational categories. Otherwise, the best that can be expected from Whitman's poetic principle is the "long varied train of an emblem, dabs of music,/Fingers of the organist skipping staccato over the keys of the great organ."

And much worse can be expected. In the last section of "Passage to India," Whitman's most deliberate statement of the process theory, the tone is frenetic even for him:

> Sail forth—steer for the deep waters only,
> Reckless O soul, exploring, I with thee, and thou with me,
> For we are bound where mariner has not yet dared to go,
> And we will risk the ship, ourselves and all.

What begins in Emerson as a mild contravention of reason—a peaceful journey "to some frontier as yet unvisited by the elder voyagers"—becomes in Whitman a freedom from all "limits and imaginary lines,"

> . . . from all formules!
> From your formules, O bat-eyed and materialistic priests.

Thus the looseness of form in Whitman's verse is not merely a technical defect; it is the counterpart of an intellectual anarchism designed to overthrow conventional reality by dissolving all rational order. Moreover, like Hawthorne in the malarial gardens of Rome, Whitman has his *frisson* at this inversion of established values—and without Hawthorne's reservations: "I know my words are weapons full of danger, full of death, / For I confront peace, security, and all the settled laws, to unsettle them." Mixed with the obtrusive health of the "Calamus" poems is a daredevil flouting of convention:

> The way is suspicious, the result uncertain, perhaps destructive, . . .
> The whole past theory of your life and all conformity to the lives
>   around you would have to be abandon'd, . . .
> Nor will my poems do good only, they will do just as much evil,
>   perhaps more. . . .

Nowadays we are too much in the habit of blaming "romanticism" for any irrationality in literature. Certainly the romantic spirit was enamored of a fluid reality, which could not be contained in the old channels, and the romantic often opened the dikes deliberately, just to see what would happen. The Voyager is a romantic figure, the ocean a romantic realm. Yet a distinction is in order. The antirationalism of the romantic voyage is a wilful projection of feeling; the romantic sea is the image of a world subservient to emotion. But the symbolistic voyage is a process of becoming: Whitman is less concerned with exploration of emotion than with exploration as a mode of existence. Similarly, his poems not only are *about* voyaging but also enact the voyage, so that their content (the image of the metaphysical journey) is primarily a reflection of their literary method, in which the writer and his subject become part of the stream of language. It follows that Whitman's hostility to reason has another, more complicated source than the romantic vision of a world suffused with feeling. Like Emerson, he finds the antonym of reason not in emotion but in the "symbolical"; like Hawthorne and Melville, he contrasts "analysis" with "meaning," arithmetic with "significance." For his object is not so much to impose a new form on the world as to adopt a new stance in which the world takes on new shapes. His difficulty is that his method works too well: the shapes proliferate endlessly, and, having deprived himself of an external standpoint, he has no means of controlling them. On the other hand, the occasional violence of his antirationalism is the result of an opposite difficulty: while he would like to be sublimely indifferent to established distinctions, reason fights back as he seeks to transcend it, and he is forced into the position of the iconoclast.

Whitman's Style:
From Mysticism to Art

by Roger Asselineau

Emerson one day confided to a friend that *Leaves of Grass* reminded him at one time of the *Bhagavad-Gita* and the *New York Herald*.[1] Its style is indeed most incongruous. Lyrical flights are to be found side by side with prosaic banalities, mystical effusions with the most familiar expressions from the spoken language. Sometimes Whitman transcribes an everyday scene with extreme simplicity and the greatest transparence:

> The little one sleeps in its cradle,
> I lift the gauze and look a long time, and silently brush away flies
> with my hand.[2]*

Sometimes he heaps up abstract words interminably with an enthusiasm which the reader does not always share:

> Great is Liberty! great is Equality! . . .
> Great is Youth—equally great is Old Age . . .
> Great is Wealth—great is Poverty—great is Expression—great is
> Silence. . . .[3]

"Whitman's Style: From Mysticism to Art." From *L'Evolution de Walt Whitman* (Paris, 1954), pp. 478-492. Translated by Roger Asselineau and Burton L. Cooper. Copyright 1962 by The President and Fellows of Harvard College. Reprinted by permission of the publishers from Roger Asselineau, *The Evolution of Walt Whitman*, Volume II, to be published by the Belknap Press of Harvard University Press.

[1] See Bliss Perry, *Walt Whitman* (1906), p. 276, n. 1.

[2] *LG 1855*, p. 17; *Inc. Ed.*, p. 30; "Song of Myself," §8, ll. 1-2.

* ABBREVIATIONS USED IN THE NOTES: *AL = American Literature; CW = The Complete Writings of Walt Whitman* (New York, 1902), 10 vols.; *CP = The Complete Prose of Walt Whitman*, ed. M. Cowley (New York, 1948); *FC = Faint Clews and Indirections*, ed. C. Gohdes and R. Silver (Durham, N. C., 1949); *Inc. Ed. = Leaves of Grass, Inclusive Edition*, ed. E. Holloway (New York, 1927); *LG = Leaves of Grass; N & F = Notes and Fragments*, ed. R. M. Bucke (London, Ontario, 1899); *SD = Specimen Days; SPL =* Walt Whitman, *Complete Verse, Selected Prose and Letters*, ed. E. Holloway (London, 1921), 2 vols.; *Uncoll. PP = The Uncollected Poetry and Prose of Walt Whitman*, coll. and ed. E. Holloway (New York, 1921), 2 vols.; *With WW in C =* Horace Traubel, *With Walt Whitman in Camden*, 4 vols.; *WWW = Walt Whitman's Workshop*, ed. C. J. Furness (Cambridge, 1928).

[3] *LG 1855*, p. 93; *Inc. Ed.*, p. 465; "Great Are the Myths," §1, ll. 4, 7-8.

Even more, the same verse sometimes brings these two clashing elements together:

> I concentrate toward them that are nigh, I wait on the door-slab.[4]

Too often one passes without transition from the loose, woolly, pretentious language of the journalist who pads his text with big words to the rapid and precise evocation of a concrete detail. It even happens that his best passages are spoiled by the brusque intrusion of a learned word in a very simple context:

> The field-sprouts of Fourth-month and Fifth-month became
> part of him.
> Winter-grain sprouts and those of the light-yellow corn and the *escu-*
> *lent roots* of the garden. . . .[5] [Italics mine.]

The same jarring note is sometimes produced by the unexpected use of a slang term:

> The spotted hawk swoops by and accuses me, he complains of my
> *gab* and my loitering.[6] [Italics mine.]

Thus, most often, the different stylistic elements, instead of being used separately and kept free from all admixture, enter into complex combinations. The concrete passages, in particular, are not always the realistic and perfectly objective little pictures of the sort which we have quoted above. Habitually, the mind of the poet diffuses its own divinity over the void of the external world;[7] grass is not that inert substance which a child carries to him in his fist, but "the flag of [his] disposition, out of hopeful green stuff woven." [8] His sensibility and, all the more, his sensuality often modify the image of things which he gives to us.

> Smile O voluptuous cool-breath'd earth!
> Earth of slumbering and liquid trees . . .

[4] *LG 1855*, p. 55; *Inc. Ed.*, p. 75; "Song of Myself," §51, l. 9.

[5] *LG 1855*, p. 90; *Inc. Ed.*, p. 306; "There was a child went forth," l. 12.

[6] *LG 1855*, p. 55; *Inc. Ed.*, p. 75; "Song of Myself," §52, l. 1. An earlier draft of the passage (p. 583) shows that originally Whitman used a perfectly normal and homogeneous vocabulary and that the introduction of a slang word was therefore conscious and deliberate. When, on the contrary, he introduces a pretentious word into a simple context, he does so inadvertently.

[7] "The mountains, rivers, forests and the elements that gird them round about would be only blank conditions of matter if the mind did not fling its own divinity around them." A sentence in an article entitled "Imagination and Fact" which had appeared in *Graham's Magazine*. Whitman wrote in the margin: "This I think is one of the most indicative sentences I ever read." *CW*, VI, p. 53.

[8] *LG 1855*, p. 16; *Inc. Ed.*, p. 28; "Song of Myself," §6, ll. 3.

> Earth of the vitreous pour of the full moon just tinged with
> blue. . . .[9]

Matter then is dissolved; trees become liquid and contours fluid (these two adjectives *liquid* and *fluid* recur frequently in his verse). One is witness to a mysterious transmutation of the real in which his imagination also intervenes.[10] For Whitman is not content with what he has before his eyes; he wants to evoke, to imply as it were, all the rest of the world, the infinity of space and the "amplitude of time." [11] He soon abandons the stallion whose beauty and dash so much impressed him:

> I but use a moment and then I resign you stallion—and do not need
> your paces, and outgallop them,
> And myself as I stand or sit pass faster than you.[12]

Hence cosmic visions of this sort:

> My ties and ballasts leave me, I travel—I sail—my elbows rest in sea-
> gaps,
> I skirt sierras, my palms cover continents . . .
> I fly those flights of a fluid and swallowing soul,
> My course runs below the soundings of plummets. . . .[13]

He is transformed into a comet and travels round the universe with the speed of light:

> I depart as air, I shake my white locks at the runaway sun,
> I effuse my flesh in eddies, drift it in lacy jags.[14]

This dissolution of himself and this fluidity of the world permit the boldest and most unexpected images:

> My foothold is tenon'd and mortis'd in granite . . .[15]
> . . . a leaf of grass is no less than the jouney-work of the stars . . .
> . . . [I] am stucco'd with quadrupeds and birds all over . . .[16]
> . . . the sobbing liquid of life. . . .[17]

[9] *LG 1855*, p. 27; *Inc. Ed.*, p. 41; "Song of Myself," §21, ll. 17, 18, 20.
[10] See *The Evolution of Walt Whitman* (Paris, 1954), Volume II, Part II, Chapter IV.
[11] *LG 1855*, p. 27; *Inc. Ed.*, p. 41; "Song of Myself," §20, l. 33.
[12] *LG 1855*, p. 35; *Inc. Ed.*, p. 571; "Song of Myself," §32, variant reading of ll. 24-26.
[13] *LG 1855*, p. 35; *Inc. Ed.*, p. 51; "Song of Myself," §33, ll. 5-6 and p. 55, ll. 91-92.
[14] *LG 1855*, p. 56; *Inc. Ed.*, p. 76; "Song of Myself," §52, ll. 7-8.
[15] *LG 1855*, p. 26; *Inc. Ed.*, p. 41; "Song of Myself," §20, l. 31.
[16] *LG 1855*, p. 34; *Inc. Ed.*, p. 50; "Song of Myself," §31, ll. 1, 9.
[17] *LG 1855*, p. 47; *Inc. Ed.*, p. 65; "Song of Myself," §42, l. 15.

The complexity and the discords of his style are not due solely to his lack of education and to his habits as a journalist, they derive also from the duality of his point of view on the world. Sometimes he places himself on the plane of the senses and describes the visible in simple and direct terms; sometimes, as a mystic, he transcends physical appearances and tries to suggest the invisible. As he himself says:

> I help myself to material and immaterial. . . .[18]

Thus is explained the co-existence in his work of descriptive passages and of somewhat obscure lines where he tried to express the inexpressible and translate those mysterious hieroglyphics which all material objects were in his eyes.[19] The problem of the inexpressible haunted him:

> There is something that comes to one now and perpetually,
> It is not what is printed, preach'd, discussed, it eludes discussion and
>   print . . .
> It is for you whoever you are, it is no farther from you than your
>   hearing and sight are from you,
> It is hinted by nearest, commonest, readiest, it is ever provoked by
>   them . . .[20]
> I do not know it—it is without name—it is a word unsaid,
> It is not in any dictionary, utterance, symbol. . . .[21]

How can one resolve this insoluble problem? A frontal attack is impossible. One can only approach it indirectly. And that is precisely what Whitman does. As early as 1855 he understood that in order to evoke "transcendent" reality he had to be "indirect and not direct or descriptive or epic"[22] (what Paul Claudel calls "la divine loi de l'expression détournée"):

> I swear, he said the following year, I see what is better than to tell
>   the best,
> It is always to leave the best untold.[23]

And, in 1860, defining the "laws for creation," he formulated this precept:

[18] *LG 1855*, p. 38; *Inc. Ed.*, p. 55; "Song of Myself," §33, l. 93.
[19] *LG 1855*, p. 16; *Inc. Ed.*, p. 28; "Song of Myself," §6, l. 8.
[20] *LG 1855*, p. 59; *Inc. Ed.*, pp. 180-181; "A Song for Occupations," §2, ll. 17-18, 20-21.
[21] *LG 1855*, p. 55; *Inc. Ed.*, p. 74; "Song of Myself," §50, ll. 4-5.
[22] Preface to 1855 Edition, *Inc. Ed.*, p. 491.
[23] *LG 1856*, "Poem of the Sayers of the Words of the Earth," p. 329; *Inc. Ed.*, p. 190; "A Song of the Rolling Earth," §3, ll. 13-14. See *American Primer*, p. 21: ". . . in manners, poems, orations, music, friendship, authorship, what is not said is just as important as what is said, and holds just as much meaning."

> There shall be no subject too pronounced—all works shall illustrate
> the divine law of indirections.[24]

So, instead of saying, he must suggest[25]—not by means of the music of his verse, as the symbolists tried to do later—it never for a moment occurred to him—but by means of images since "the unseen is proved by the seen." [26] This may lead to a certain obscurity, but a poem must be a beginning and not an end and it belongs to the reader to take up the poet's suggestions and to finish it.[27] In short, Whitman defined here beforehand the fundamental principles of symbolism; and he was still more explicit in *Specimen Days:* "The play of imagination with the sensuous objects of Nature for symbols, and Faith . . . make up the curious chess-game of a poem. . . ." [28] These ideas were not altogether new; they had already broken through in the subjective theories of the romantics and the transcendentalists,[29] but no one had yet applied them

[24] *LG 1860,* "Chants Democratic" no. 13, p. 185 (2); *Inc. Ed.,* p. 324; "Laws for Creation," l. 5.

[25] "The words I myself put primarily for the description of them (*Leaves of Grass*) as they stand at last, is the word Suggestiveness. I round and finish little if anything; and could not, consistently with my scheme. The reader will always have his or her part to do, just as much as I have mine." "A Backward Glance O'er Travel'd Roads," *Inc. Ed.,* p. 531.

[26] *LG 1855,* p. 14; *Inc. Ed.,* p. 26; "Song of Myself," §3, l. 16.

[27] "A great poem is no finish to a man or woman but rather a beginning." Preface to 1855 Edition, *Inc. Ed.,* p. 505.

[28] "After Trying a Certain Book," *SD,* p. 198; *CP,* p. 196.

[29] Emerson had already used the word *indirection.* See F. O. Matthiessen, *American Renaissance,* p. 57. But Whitman may have borrowed it from Shakespeare: see *Hamlet,* II, 1, l. 66: "By indirections find directions out." As to the romantics, Whitman was quite aware of what he owed to them. In "Poetry To-Day in America" (*SD,* p. 249; *CP,* p. 301), he founds his principle of indirect expression in a quotation from Sainte-Beuve. On the other hand, he had underlined the following passages in an article on *The Princess* by Tennyson bearing the date 1848: ". . . the highest art, which is chiefly dependent for its effect upon suggestion, is by no means universally appreciated, as mere skillful imitation is. . . ." "A poet, by becoming openly didactic, would deprive his work of that essential quality of suggestiveness by which activity on the part of the reader is absolutely demanded. . . ."
In an article entitled "Thoughts on Reading," he had underlined the following passages which seem to have exerted a certain influence on his thought: ". . . it is not the idleness with which we read, but the very intensity of labor which our reading calls forth, that does us good. . . . *To think* ourselves into error, is far better than *to sleep* ourselves into truth. . . ." (Cf. this passage in *Democratic Vistas,* *SD,* p. 257; *CP,* p. 258: "Books are to be call'd for, and supplied, on the assumption that the process of reading is not half-asleep, but, in highest sense, an exercise, a gymnast's struggle. . . .") "An author enriches us not so much by giving us his ideas as by unfolding in us the same powers that originated in them. Reading, in short, if it be truly such, and not a mere imparted drowsiness, involves a development of the same activities, and voluntary reproduction of the same states of mind, of which the author was subject in writing." Articles listed in the *Catalogue of the Walt Whitman Collection in the Duke University Library* (1945), p. 78. The very fact that Whitman always kept these articles with him shows how deeply attached he was to the ideas

with as much audacity as Whitman and no poet before him had dared to express his joie de vivre by means of an image as "indirect" as this:

> As God comes a loving bed-fellow and sleeps at my side all night and
>   close on the peep of the day,
> And leaves for me baskets covered with white towels, swelling the
>   house with their plenty.[30]

We have here, it is true, an extreme case where the oneiric character of the evocation and the gratuitousness of the associations almost announce surrealism. Whitman, in general, was reluctant to go in that direction. Comparing himself to Blake about 1868-1870 in an essay which he never had occasion to publish, he wrote:

> Blake's visions grow to be the rule, displace the normal condition, fill the field, spurn this visible, objective life, & seat the subjective spirit on an absolute throne, wilful & uncontrolled. But Whitman, though he occasionally prances off . . . always holds the mastery over himself, &, even in his most intoxicated lunges or pirouettes, never once loses control, or even equilibrium." [31]

The passing from the objective to the subjective plane is thus deliberate and conscious with him, and conscious, too, is his care never to lose contact with objective reality. One is reminded of Wordsworth's skylark which, unlike Shelley's, never forgets in the midst of her wild flight that she has left her nest on the earth; however much Whitman launched his "yawp" over the rooftops of the world, his feet remained firmly planted on the ground.[32]

---

which were developed in them and which he undeniably adopted. He had also underlined in an article from the *American Whig Review* for Jan. 1846 and entitled "A Socratic Dialogue on Phrenology" the following sentence: "We agreed, O Phidias, that it is impossible to speak otherwise than mystically and symbolically concerning the spirit of man." (*Catalogue* . . . p. 75.) The dates of two of these articles show that his thought had already taken this course nearly ten years before the first edition of *Leaves of Grass*. Even while he was writing conventional poems, he was already thinking of another form of art.

[30] *LG 1855*, p. 15; *Inc. Ed.*, p. 554; "Song of Myself," §3, variant reading of ll. 23-24. The passage was later made even more indirect by the suppression of the word *God*.

[31] *FC*, p. 53.

[32] The study of the evolution of Whitman's imagery would reveal nothing special. The drafts which preceded the 1855 text show the chaotic profusion of the original images, but, as early as the first edition, Whitman had to some extent succeeded in simplifying and controlling them. They were never again to be as luxuriant and confused (except in "Calamus" and "Children of Adam" where he purposely took refuge in obscurity in order to tone down the boldness of his subject). This process of clarification and simplification went on during all his career. As a result, at the end of his life, Whitman wrote only very short poems built round a single image. To the last therefore images persisted in his poetry, but they lost in power what they gained in clarity.

The most felicitous passages of *Leaves of Grass* are thus those in which Whitman has succeeded in fusing the diverse elements of his style, those in which he suggests rather than describes and soars rather than trudges through interminable objective catalogues, those, too, in which he takes flight but does not get lost in the clouds. His expression is effective whenever he manages to interweave abstractions and familiar terms as in:

> I believe in those wing'd purposes. . . .[33]

or in:

> Agonies are one of my changes of garments.[34]

These unexpected combinations give a new vigor to his style. But he fails every time he lets one of these elements prevail over the others, notably when he falls into didacticism and preaches in abstract terms his democratic gospel or his personal religion:

> There can be any number of supremes—one does not countervail
>   another any more than one eyesight countervails another, or one
>   life countervails another.
> All is eligible to all . . .[35]
> How plenteous! how spiritual! how résumé! [36]

he went so far as to say in 1860.

Such are the characteristics of Whitman's style in the first two editions of *Leaves of Grass;* but we might have drawn our examples from later editions as well, for until the end his qualities and his faults remained the same. "Grand Is the Seen" written at the end of his career is the exact counterpart of "Great Are the Myths" published in 1855.[37] Is that to say that he made no progress in the interval? Not at all. From 1856 to 1881 he gave himself up to a patient labour of revision of his work which was not in vain and which reveals an increasingly fine artistic sense.[38] Matthiessen claims that these corrections are disconcerting and

[33] *LG 1855*, p. 20; *Inc. Ed.*, p. 34; "Song of Myself," §13, l. 15.

[34] *LG 1855*, p. 39; *Inc. Ed.*, p. 56; "Song of Myself," §33, l. 136.

[35] "Poem of Many in One," *LG 1856*, p. 181; *Inc. Ed.*, p. 287; "By Blue Ontario's Shore," §3, ll. 2-3.

[36] "Leaves of Grass" no. 15, *LG 1860*, p. 234; *Inc. Ed.*, p. 377; "Night on the Prairies," l. 7.

[37] "Great Are the Myths" (1855), *Inc. Ed.*, pp. 465-467; "Grand Is the Seen" (1891), *ibid.*, p. 457.

[38] Killis Campbell is of the same opinion; see his article on "The Evolution of Whitman as an Artist," *AL* VI (Nov. 1934), 254-263. See also Rebecca Coy, "A study of Whitman's Diction," *University of Texas Studies in English*, XVI (Jul. 1936), 115-124.

cannot always be justified,[39] but we do not share his opinion on this point. If some of them appear useless, most of them serve a purpose and can be vindicated.

First of all, as we have pointed out,[40] Whitman in growing old understood that it had been maladroit and tasteless to shock his readers by introducing crude details in contexts where one would not expect to find them. So, without really renouncing his poems which had a sexual inspiration, he gradually eliminated from the others such verses as:

> Have you sucked the nipples of the breasts of the mother of many children? [41]

and:

> And have an unseen something to be in contact with them also.[42]

The first of these lines was suppressed in 1860, that is to say the very year when he added "Calamus" and "Children of Adam" to *Leaves of Grass*.

He very soon also tried to avoid the monotony of certain repetitions and notably coordinating conjunctions which he had over-used in the first edition. Numerous are the *and*'s and the *or*'s which disappeared in 1856.[43] Later he got rid of the *O*'s, realizing that that was a little too facile a method for a lyric take-off. As early as 1867 he suppressed "Apostroph," where they swarmed,[44] and eliminated many others in 1881, in particular in "Out of the Cradle Endlessly Rocking," where one critic in 1860 had counted thirty-five of them.[45] It had taken Whitman twenty

[39] *American Renaissance*, p. 531.

[40] See *The Evolution of Walt Whitman, op. cit.*, Volume I, Chapter VII, pp. 196-198 and Chapter IX, pp. 239-240.

[41] "By Blue Ontario's Shore," *Inc. Ed.*, p. 662, §12, the line which originally followed line 17.

[42] "The Sleepers," *Inc. Ed.*, p. 684, §7, the line which originally followed line 3. The suppression was made in 1881.

[43] Here is a list of some of these suppressions:
"Song of Myself," *Inc. Ed.*, p. 562, §20, ll. 11-12; p. 572, §33, ll. 43, 46-47, 126; p. 573, §34, l. 11; p. 576, §39, ll. 7, 9; p. 578, §42, ll. 19-20; "I Sing the Body Electric," p. 586, l. 24. All these suppressions date back to 1856.

[44] The dispersion in 1867 of "Chants Democratic" to which "Apostroph" served as an introduction in 1860 may have been another reason for suppressing this poem.

[45] See for instance *Inc. Ed.*, p. 638, l. 128. The poem was violently criticized in the *Cincinnati Commercial* when it appeared: "The poem goes on in the same maudlin manner, for a hundred lines or more, in which the interjection 'O' is employed about five and thirty times." The critic then quoted the line: "O I fear it is henceforth chaos!" and treacherously added: "There is no doubt of it, we do assure you." Whitman printed this article in his *Leaves of Grass Imprints*, 1860, p. 59. He also suppressed numerous *O*'s in "A Song of Joys"; see *Inc. Ed.*, pp. 610-611 the lines which originally owed ll. 6, 31, etc.

years to come round to his view. Generally speaking, he attempted to remove all the repetitions which had no expressive value and whose monotony weighted his verse, particularly all the useless *I*'s which came after coordinating conjunctions,[46] as well as the numerous *I swear*'s which in fact added nothing.[47] He also cut out a number of awkward lines of this sort:

> A breed whose testimony is behaviour.[48]

or:

> If you would be better than all that has ever been before, come listen to me and I will tell you,

which in 1867 became:

> If you would be freer than all that has been before come listen to me.[49]

He also suppressed a number of colloquial phrases the incongruity of which in certain passages he now perceived. Thus it was that in 1867 he no longer retained "plenty of them" at the end of the following line:

> If you remember your foolish and outlaw'd deeds, do you think I cannot remember my own foolish and outlaw'd deeds? [50]

"You mean devil" similarly disappeared from "Myself and Mine."[51] The Prince of Wales who had been democratically hailed as "sweet boy" in 1860, became "young prince" in 1881.[52] In "The Centenarian's Story" he avoided the colloquial usage of *good* as an adverb,[53] and in 1871 he eliminated from "Crossing Brooklyn Ferry" "Bully for you!" and *Blab, blush, lie, steal* which were undoubtedly very expressive, but which he now considered too slangy.[54] In 1881 he redoubled his severity with himself and suppressed not only these youthful lines from "Song of Myself":

---

[46] See for instance "Starting from Paumanok," *Inc. Ed.*, p. 551, §11, ll. 17, 19; p. 549, §5.

[47] See for instance "A Song of the Rolling Earth," *Inc. Ed.*, p. 613, §3, l. 10 and §4, second stanza.

[48] "By Blue Ontario's Shore," *Inc. Ed.*, p. 657, §2, l. 4.

[49] *Ibid.*, p. 658, §4, l. 11. For similar changes, see "Passage to India," *ibid.*, p. 653, §15, l. 6 and §16, l. 1.

[50] "A Song for Occupations," *Inc. Ed.*, p. 622, §1, l. 17.

[51] *Ibid.*, p. 633, l. 14; a correction made in 1867.

[52] "Years of Meteors," p. 634, l. 11.

[53] *Ibid.*, p. 607, §9, the line which preceded line 7 of "Terminus."

[54] *Ibid.*, p. 607, §9, the line which followed lines 5 and 7.

> That life is a suck and a sell, and nothing remains in the end but
> threadbare crape and tears.
> Washes and razors for foofoos—for me freckles and a bristling
> beard.[55]

but also these playful lines which he had composed in 1871 to amuse
his audience at the American Institute Exhibition:

> She comes! this famous Female [the Muse]—as was indeed to be
> expected;
> (For who, so ever youthful, 'cute and handsome would wish to stay
> in mansions such as those . . .
> With all the fun that's going—and all the best society?).[56]

But all his corrections did not have such a negative character. He
profited from this minute labour of revision to render his text more
expressive and to choose his words with more care. In particular he
ridded himself of a number of catch-all adjectives like *wondrous* or
mystic,[57] either suppressing them completely, or replacing them by less
vague and more appropriate epithets. Thus, "the mystic midnight" became "the vacant midnight"[58] and "my insolent poems" was changed in
1881 into "my arrogant poems," which is certainly more appropriate.[59]
In "To Think of Time," speaking in the name of the dead, he had at
first written:

> To think of all these wonders of city and country and . . . we taking
> small interest in them. . . .

but even *small* was exaggerated and he replaced it later with *no*. He had
in the same way rather imprudently qualified the trot of the horses of
a hearse as *rapid*; after 1860 he contented himself with *steady*.[60]
  Sometimes he introduced colour adjectives to enhance the descriptive
passages. For example, he added the entire line:

> Scarlet and blue and snowy white,

[55] *Ibid.*, p. 561, §20, the line which followed line 7 and p. 563, the line which
followed line 16.

[56] "Song of the Exposition," *Ibid.*, p. 619, §3, the line which followed line 3.

[57] See for instance "As I Ebb'd with the Ocean of Life," *Inc. Ed.*, p. 639, §3, l. 16
("the wondrous murmuring" became "the murmuring" in 1871) and "When Lilacs
Last in the Dooryard Bloom'd," p. 654, the line which followed line 2 and contained
the adjective *mystic* was suppressed in 1881. See also "Out of the Cradle Endlessly
Rocking," *ibid.*, p. 637, l. 132.

[58] "The Artilleryman's Vision," *Inc. Ed.*, p. 651, l. 2.

[59] "As I Ebb'd with the Ocean of Life," *ibid.*, p. 639, §2, l. 11.

[60] *Inc. Ed.*, p. 685, §3, l. 2 and §4, l. 7.

to "Cavalry Crossing a Ford," [61] and appended the complementary indication "yellow-flower'd" to the rather uninteresting mention of a
cotton wood in a Southern landscape.[62] Almost everywhere dull and banal
expressions gave place to more expressive words. Whereas in 1867 he
merely "sang" on the shores of Lake Ontario, in 1881 he "thrill'd."[63]
"The English pluck" of John Paul Jones's adversaries later became "the
surly English pluck," which is indeed a very apt phrase.[64]

Certain lines were thus completely transformed, like:

> Alone, held by the eternal self of me that threatens to get the better
> of me, and stifle me,

which was, in 1881, changed to:

> Held by this electric self out of the pride of which I utter poems.[65]

The poetic charge of the second version is singularly higher; it is
magnetized, as it were, by the introduction of the adjective *electric*. "I
hear American mouthsongs" was flat and awkward; it became "I hear
America singing" in 1867 and the line now really sings.[66]

He also added some images here and there, for example the line "Thou
but the apples, long, long, a-growing" to "Thou Mother with Thy Equal
Brood,"[67] and realizing the evocative power of the historical present he
substituted it for the preterite in some stories like that of the seafight
between Bonhomme Richard and an English frigate.[68] All these corrections liberated the latent energy of many passages.

But he turned his attention more particularly to titles and first lines
and it was there that he obtained the most spectacular results. While
in 1856 all his titles were of a depressing monotony and an annoying
clumsiness—"Poem of Walt Whitman, an American," "Poem of the
Daily Work of the Workmen and the Workwomen of These States,"
"Poem of the Heart of the Son of Manhattan Island," "Poem of the Last
Explanation of Prudence," "Poem of the Propositions of Nakedness"—
and in 1860 were not much better since most of the poems were simply
numbered, in 1867 he did his best to find picturesque titles. Thus,

---

[61] "Cavalry Crossing a Ford," *Inc. Ed.*, p. 649, l. 6. See also "Thou Mother with Thy
Equal Brood," *ibid.*, pp. 379 and 691, §2, l. 10.

[62] "Song of Myself," *Inc. Ed.*, p. 571, §33, l. 17.

[63] "By Blue Ontario's Shore," *Inc. Ed.*, p. 666, §19, l. 3.

[64] "Song of Myself," *Inc. Ed.*, p. 574, §35, l. 5.

[65] "As I Ebb'd with the Ocean of Life," *Inc. Ed.*, pp. 216, 638-639, §1, ll. 7 and 17.

[66] *Inc. Ed.*, p. 545.

[67] *Ibid.*, pp. 380, 691, §3, l. 12. See also "Out of the Cradle Endlessly Rocking,"
ibid., pp. 215, 638, l. 182.

[68] "Song of Myself," *Inc. Ed.*, p. 574, §35, *passim*. See also "Camps of Green," *ibid.*,
p. 701, l. 21.

"Proto-Leaf," a barbarous expression, was replaced by "Starting from Paumanok" which is concrete and dynamic, and the former "Poem of Walt Whitman, an American" became in 1881, after many meta-morphoses, "Song of Myself," a title which admirably sums up its central theme. The "Poem of the Body" which originally began with:

> The bodies of men and women engirth me and I engirth them . . .[69]

started in 1867 with:

> I sing the body electric . . .

which is singularly more promising. It was that year that he found the title of "One Hour of Madness and Joy," [70] of "Trickle-Drops," [71] of "On the Beach at Night Alone." [72] But it was only later and after much searching that he arrived at "As I ebb'd with the ocean of life," [73] "By Blue Ontario's Shore," [74] "Aboard at a Ship's Helm," [75] "Out of the Cradle Endlessly Rocking," [76] "A Song of the Rolling Earth," [77] etc.

He also took great care in rounding off certain lines whose ends seemed too abrupt—especially, it appears, while preparing the 1881 edition. Thus,

> You shall sit in the middle well-poised thousands of years,

became:

> You shall sit in the middle well-pois'd thousands and thousands of
>   years. . . .[78]

and in the poem entitled "I was looking a long while" the last line:

> All for the average man of to-day,

[69] *LG 1855*, p. 77; "I Sing the Body Electric," *Inc. Ed.*, p. 584.
[70] *Ibid.*, p. 589.
[71] *Ibid.*, p. 594.
[72] *Ibid.*, p. 641. This title was merely the first line in 1867.
[73] *Ibid.*, p. 638. Title added in 1881.
[74] *Ibid.*, p. 656. Title added in 1881.
[75] *Ibid.*, p. 640. Title added in 1871. In 1881 he made an interesting change in line 3. He had originally written in 1867: "A bell through fog on a sea-coast dolefully ringing, An ocean-bell . . ." In 1881, he cut out "A bell," so that we now deal with a raw sensation gradually worked into a perception.
[76] *Inc. Ed.*, p. 636. In 1860 the first line was: "Out of the rocked cradle," but the rhythm was not smooth enough and it was only in 1871 that the line received its present shape.
[77] *Inc. Ed.*, p. 630. Title added in 1881.
[78] "A Broadway Pageant," *Inc. Ed.*, pp. 208, 636, §3, l. 2.

which lacked force and vividness, was changed to:

> All for the modern—all for the average man of to-day,[79]

which is at once more rhythmical and more vehement. Whitman, moreover, took pains not only with his titles and with the ends of lines but also with the ends of his poems. In particular, he added to "A Farm Picture" a last line which has a most happy effect and enlarges to infinity what was originally only a rather banal vignette.[80] And, what was an even more characteristic correction, he introduced into his longer poems, like "Song of Myself," either at the beginning or at the end of the different sections, lines destined to be used, according to the individual instance, as an introduction or a conclusion, in order to prepare the transitions and reinforce the cohesiveness of the whole.[81] In other words, he became increasingly mindful of form.[82]

At the same time, in proportion as his inspiration lost its force, he tended more and more to be content with very short poems for which no problem of composition existed. He had already used this formula as early as 1865 in *Drum-Taps* where he had included a number of short descriptive poems like "A Farm Picture," "Cavalry Crossing a Ford," "By the Bivouac's Fitful Flame," "The Torch," "The Ship," "The Runner," [83] etc . . . or very brief philosophical poems like "A Child's Amaze." From 1881 on, he wrote only poems of this sort, but, refusing to admit the decline of his inspiration, he claimed that in so doing he was deliberately limiting himself in order to conform to a principle posed by Poe, namely "that (at any rate for our occasions, our day) there can be no such thing as a long poem. The same thought," he added, "had been haunting my mind before, but Poe's argument, though short, work'd the sum and proved it to me." [84] He merely omitted to say that, to Poe's mind, the short poem adapted to the capabilities of the modern reader might reach a length of about a hundred lines, as in the

---

[79] *Inc. Ed.*, pp. 325, 678, l. 10. The addition of "and ready" to "A Song of the Rolling Earth," *ibid.*, pp. 191, 631, §4, l. 10, had a similar effect.

[80] *Inc. Ed.*, pp. 233, 645.

[81] See for instance *Inc. Ed.*, p. 533, §1, l. 1; p. 599, §15, l. 66; p. 570, §32, l. 1; p. 571, §33, l. 1; p. 575, §38, l. 1; p. 581, §45, l. 31; p. 583, §50, l. 10.

[82] One could even go further back, to the time when *Leaves of Grass* was gradually taking shape in Whitman's mind. *Pictures* (published by Emory Holloway in 1927) essentially consists of a series of vignettes similar to the ones which are to be found in *Drum-Taps*. The same remark applies to the catalogues. One of the reasons why the later editions do not contain any is that Whitman cut them up, so to speak, and published them in the form of short poems.

[83] This particular poem did not appear in *Drum-Taps*, but in the 1867 edition of *LG*, p. 214.

[84] "A Backward Glance O'er Travel'd Roads," *Inc. Ed.*, p. 530.

case of "The Raven," [85] which was rather far from the few lines with which the author of *November Boughs* now contented himself.

Whitman thus attached more and more importance to form as his poetic material became thinner. Whereas in the Preface to the 1855 edition of *Leaves of Grass* he affected a sovereign scorn for polish and ornaments,[86] and made everything depend on the power of inspiration, ten years later he rejoiced that *Drum-Taps* was "certainly more perfect as a work of art, being adjusted in all its proportions, and its passion having the indispensable merit that . . . the true artist can see it is . . . under control." [87] And it is probably towards this period that he gave himself this advice:

> In future *Leaves of Grass. Be more severe* with the final revision of the poem, nothing will do, not one word or sentence, that is not *perfectly clear*—with positive purpose—harmony with the name, nature, drift of the poem. Also *no ornaments,* especially *no ornamental adjectives,* unless they have come molten hot, and imperiously prove themselves. *No ornamental similes at all—not one: perfect transparent clearness* sanity and health are wanted—that is the *divine style*— O if it can be attained—[88]

It is obvious that he was then very far from the superb assurance he had shown in 1855 and this text proves that all his later revisions were perfectly conscious. As early as 1860 he had begun to understand his error:

> Now I reverse what I said, and affirm that all depends on the aesthetic
>   or intellectual,
> And that criticism is great—and that refinement is greatest of
>   all . . .[89]

Unfortunately it was too late. He could still revise his early poems, but he could not recast them, and, in spite of the progress he achieved, his art remained fundamentally the same. So, at the end of his life, he realized himself the inferiority of his work from the point of view of form. Casting a backward glance over the roads he had traveled he

---

[85] See "The Philosophy of Composition": "Holding in view these considerations, as well as the degree of excitement which I deemed not above the popular, while not below the critical taste, I reached at once what I conceived the proper *length* for my intended poem—a length of about one hundred lines."

[86] "Preface to 1855 Edition," *Inc. Ed.,* p. 530.

[87] Letter to O'Connor, Jan. 6, 1865, *SPL.,* p. 949. But that very year he wrote in "Shut not your doors to me proud libraries" (*Inc. Ed.,* p. 545): "The words of my book nothing, the life of it everything."—which proves that even then he considered his message more important than his art.

[88] *CW,* VI, pp. 32-33. Unfortunately this fragment bears no date. The passages in italics are underlined on the original.

[89] "Says," *LG 1860,* p. 420; *Inc. Ed.,* p. 481, §7, ll. 2-3.

readily acknowledged in 1888 that as far as descriptive talent, dramatic situations and especially verbal melody and all the conventional techniques of poetry were concerned *Leaves of Grass* was eclipsed by many masterpieces of the past.[90] And beating his breast three years later he added: "I have probably not been enough afraid of careless touches, from the first . . . nor of parrot-like repetitions—nor platitudes and the commonplace." [91]

Thus the mystic who, in 1855, had wished to communicate the revelation which he had received and announce to the world a new gospel, by slow degrees became an artist more and more conscious of his imperfections, but, to a large extent, incapable of remedying them. How could he have done it? In spite of his growing respect for art, all discipline seemed to him a useless constraint and all convention a dangerous artifice which risked raising a barrier between his thought and the reader. To art he opposed what he called simplicity,[92] that is to say strict adherence to nature. As a mystic, he was thus able to write: "In these *Leaves* everything is literally photographed. Nothing is poetized, no divergence, not a step, not an inch, nothing for beauty's sake, no euphemism, no rhyme." [93] And, in the same year, as an artist, he on the contrary affirmed the necessity of a transposition: "No useless attempt to repeat the material creation, by daguerreotyping the exact likeness by mortal mental means." [94] This contradiction gives the measure of his predicament. In fact, of course, he had to transpose, but he was not any less convinced that he had remained completely faithful to nature. When in 1879 he traveled in the Rocky Mountains he thought that he saw in their chaotic mass the symbol of his own poems. "I have found the law of my own poems," he exclaimed at the sight of "this plenitude of material, complete absence of art." [95] To art, for him a synonym for artifice, he thus preferred Nature, "the only complete, actual poem," [96] with its disorder, its immensity, its indescribably secret life.[97]

[90] "A Backward Glance O'er Travel'd Roads," *Inc. Ed.*, p. 527.

[91] "Preface Note to 2nd Annex" (1891), *Inc. Ed.*, p. 537.

[92] "Preface to 1855 Edition," *Inc. Ed.*, pp. 495-496.

[93] *CW*, VI, p. 21. This fragment bears the date of 1871.

[94] *Democratic Vistas, SD*, p. 252, *CP*, p. 253.

[95] "An Egotistical Find," *SD*, p. 143, *CP*, p. 142. The same idea is expressed in "Spirit that Form'd This Scene" (1881), *Inc. Ed.*, p. 403.

[96] *Democratic Vistas, SD*, p. 253, *CP*, p. 254. That is why during all his life he meant to write poems capable of producing the same impression on the reader as natural sights. See "On Journeys through the States" (1860), *Inc. Ed.*, p. 8, ll. 6, 13-14, "As I Ebb'd with the Ocean the Crowd," (1860), p. 638, variant reading of the beginning of §1, "A Song of Joys" (1860), p. 149, ll. 4-6 and in 1885, taking up the image of the wave again: "Had I the Choice," p. 425, ll. 5-9. In 1856, he distinguished "real poems," i.e., objects, from the poems written by poets which he called "pictures"; see "Spontaneous Me," *Inc. Ed.*, p. 88, l. 8 and also "A Song of the Rolling Earth" (1856), p. 186, §1, l. 1-14.

[97] He returned repeatedly to this principle of the superiority of nature over art; see in particular· "New Senses—New Joys," *SD*, p. 143, *CP*, p. 142; "Art Features," *SD*,

To this instinctive preference his belief in the unlimited power of inspiration was obscurely related, as well as his faith in the efficacy of the slow germination which precedes the birth of a poem:

> The rhyme and uniformity of perfect poems show the free growth of metrical laws and bud from them as unerringly and loosely as lilacs or roses on a bush, and take shapes as compact as the shapes of chestnuts and oranges and melons and pears and shed the perfume impalpable to form.[98]

In other words, thought and inspiration determine expression, so that what counts in the last analysis is thought and not form which is only its reflection. Whatever its apparent disorder may be, the poem, simply because it grew and matured in the soul of the poet, has the same profound unity and the same beauty as Nature, which was created by God, the supreme poet. The theory was not new. We recognize here the principle of organic unity which Coleridge had borrowed from Schlegel and had discussed many times in his critical writings, in particular in the *Biographia Literaria*, where Whitman may have discovered it. This doctrine suited him perfectly since it authorized him to reject every rule of composition or of prosody.[99]

If it permits one to break free from rules, the theory of organic unity, however, does not exempt the poet from work. It requires much groping to release what is gestating within him. The impression of ease or "abandon," as he said, which Whitman's work gives, was, in fact, the result of careful planning. His simplicity is laboured, and that is why he approved the famous line of Ben Jonson: "A good poet's made as well as born." [100] The first version of *Leaves of Grass*, far from having been written at one sitting, evolved slowly from a considerable number of drafts of the kind which Emory Holloway has published and which represent the work of several years.[101] The short poems of his old age required as much trouble. There exist at the Library of Congress ten different drafts of "Supplement Hours."

An examination of the papers left by Whitman permits a reconstruction of his method. Contrary to poets like Valéry for whom the starting-point is a rhythm or a musical motif, Whitman seems always to have taken off from a word or an idea expressed in prose. His manu-

---

p. 145, *CP*, pp. 144-145: "Capes Eternity and Trinity," *SD*, p. 164, *CP*, pp. 164-165; "Final Confessions—Literary Tests," *SD*, p. 199, *CP*, pp. 196-197.

[98] "Preface to 1885 Edition," *Inc. Ed.*, p. 493.

[99] See *Coleridge's Shakesperian Criticism*, ed. by T. M. Raysor, 1930, I, p. 224 and *Biographia Literaria*, ed. by Shawcross, 1907, II, p. 109. Whitman had reviewed the *Biographia Literaria* in the *Brooklyn Eagle* on Dec. 4, 1847 (*G of the F*, II, pp. 298-299). On the theory of organic unity, see James Benziger, "Organic Unity: Leibniz to Coleridge," *PMLA*, LXVI (March 1951), 24-28 and Gay W. Allen, *Walt Whitman Handbook*, pp. 218-219, 292-302, 409-422, 428-437.

[100] *CW*, VI, p. 189.

[101] See *Uncoll. PP*, and *FC*, pp. 3-7.

scripts show it. This initial material was later elaborated and expressed rhythmically. That is what happened for instance to this list of words which R. M. Bucke published in *Notes and Fragments:* "Perfect Sanity—Divine Instinct—Breadth of Vision—Healthy Rudeness of Body. Withdrawnness. Gayety. Sun-tan and air-sweetness." Out of this material Whitman later made two lines of the poem which eventually became "Song of the Answerer":

> Divine instinct, breadth of vision, the law of reason, health, rudeness
>   of body, withdrawnness,
> Gayety, sun-tan, air-sweetness, such are some of the words of poems.[102]

The germ of "Night on the Prairies" which has been found in his papers also appears in the form of a brief sketch in prose entitled "Idea of a poem." [103] And on another rough draft one can read this revealing injunction: "Make this more rhythmic." [104] Sometimes the first line provoked a rich germination within him and in that case, as the ideas appeared, he noted them down on the first scrap of paper he could find: old envelopes, the backs of proof-sheets, etc., all of which gradually accumulated and soon formed a bundle which he pinned together so as not to lose them. (He often proceeded in the same way when he wrote in prose. . . .) Then he would sort his scraps, add, cut out, change the order of the various fragments, re-arrange them endlessly. When he felt that the process of germination was complete, he placed his pieces of paper end to end and recopied them, or pasted them on large sheets, as he did for "Eidolons," the definitive manuscript of which may be seen at the Boston Public Library.[105] Thus, his method was essentially agglutinative. His poems were composed like mosaics and, as in mosaics, a number of lines or passages are interchangeable.[106] Whitman himself, in the course of the successive editions, did not hesitate to change the order of certain paragraphs. This method of composition explains the looseness and desultoriness of so many of his poems, but it enabled him to gather all the insights that a poetic idea gave birth to in his mind

[102] See *N&F*, p. 93 (40) and "Poem of the Singers of the Words of Poems," *LG 1856*, p. 263; "A Song of the Answerer," *Inc. Ed.*, p. 143, §2, ll. 19-20.

[103] See Oscar L. Triggs, "The Growth of Leaves of Grass," *CW*, VII, p. 125.

[104] *N&F*, p. 38 (118). He differed from Bryant in this respect and noted the fact in one of his common-place books: "William Cullen Bryant surprised me once, relates a writer in a New York paper, by saying that prose was the natural language of composition, and he wonder'd how anybody came to write poetry." *SD*, p. 184, n.; *CP*, p. 204, n. 17.

[105] On his methods of composition, see W. S. Kennedy, *Reminiscences of Walt Whitman* (London: Alexander Gardner, 1896), p. 24—quoted by Furness, *WWW*, p. 118, n. 11. See also Sculley Bradley and John A. Stevenson, *Walt Whitman's Backward Glances* (University of Pennsylvania Press, 1947), pp. 4, 12, 13.

[106] Whitman used the image himself: "Life Mosaic of Native Moments." He had at first thought of using it as a title for *Specimen Days*.

and to respect the slow organic growth of his work. So he used it all his life. It was his way of reconciling his mysticism with his art, of preserving the spontaneity of his inspiration while imposing upon it a certain form.

This loose method was thus one of the constants of Whitman's art. For him the spirit always took precedence of the letter. He said one day to Horace Traubel: "I have never given any study merely to expression." [107] He was right, but he might well have added: "I have thought increasingly of form."

[107] *With WW in C*, III, p. 84.

The New Adam:
Whitman

by R. W. B. Lewis

Whitman appears as the Adamic man reborn here in the
19th century. [JOHN BURROUGHS (1896)]

In his old age, Dr. [Oliver Wendell] Holmes derived a certain
amount of polite amusement from the poetry of Walt Whitman. Whitman, Holmes remarked, "carried the principle of republicanism through
the whole world of created objects"; he smuggled into his "hospitable
vocabulary words which no English dictionary recognizes as belonging to
the language—words which will be looked for in vain outside of his own
pages." Holmes found it hard to be sympathetic toward *Leaves of Grass*;
it seemed to him windy, diffuse, and humorless; but his perceptions were
as lively as ever. In these two observations he points to the important
elements in Whitman which are central here: the spirit of equality
which animated the surging catalogues of persons and things (on its
more earthy level, not unlike Emerson's lists of poets and philosophers,
with their equalizing and almost leveling tendency); the groping after
novel words to identify novel experiences; the lust for inventiveness
which motivated what was for Whitman the great act, the creative
act.

Holmes's tone of voice, of course, added that for him Whitman had
gone too far; Whitman was too original, too republican, too entire an
Adam. Whitman had indeed gone further than Holmes: a crucial and
dimensional step further, as Holmes had gone further than Channing
or Norton. In an age when the phrase "forward-looking" was a commonplace, individuals rarely nerved themselves to withstand the shock
of others looking and moving even further forward than they. Emerson
himself, who had gone so far that the liberal Harvard Divinity School
forbade his presence there for more than thirty years, shared some of
Holmes's feeling about Whitman. When his cordial letter welcoming

Leaves of Grass in 1855 was published in the *New York Tribune*, Emerson muttered in some dismay that had he intended it for publication, he "should have enlarged the *but* very much—enlarged the *but*." *Leaves of Grass* "was pitched in the very highest key of self-reliance," as a friend of its author maintained; but Emerson, who had given that phrase its contemporary resonance, believed that any attitude raised to its highest pitch tended to encroach dangerously on the truth of its opposite.

It would be no less accurate to say that Walt Whitman, instead of going too far forward, had gone too far backward: for he did go back, all the way back, to a primitive Adamic condition, to the beginning of time.

In the poetry of Walt Whitman, the hopes which had until now expressed themselves in terms of progress crystallized all at once in a complete recovery of the primal perfection. In the early poems Whitman accomplished the epochal return by huge and almost unconscious leaps. In later poems he worked his way more painstakingly up the river of history to its source: as, for example, in "Passage to India," where the poet moves back from the recently constructed Suez Canal, back past Christopher Columbus, past Alexander the Great and the most ancient of heroes and peoples, to the very "secret of the earth and sky." "In the beginning," John Locke once wrote, "all the world was America." Whitman manages to make us feel what it might have been like; and he succeeds at last in presenting the dream of the new Adam —along with his sorrows.

A measure of Whitman's achievement is the special difficulty which that dream had provided for others who tried to recount it. Its character was such that it was more readily described by those who did not wholly share in it. How can absolute novelty be communicated? All the history of the philosophy of language is involved with that question, from *The Cratylus* of Plato to the latest essay on semantics; and one could bring to bear on it the variety of anecdotes about Adam's naming the animals by the disturbingly simple device of calling a toad a toad.

Hawthorne conveyed the idea of novelty by setting it in an ancient pattern: allowing it thereby exactly to be *recognized;* and reaching a sharpness of meaning also to be found in Tocqueville's running dialectic of democracies and aristocracies. Whitman employed the same tactic when he said of Coleridge that he was "like Adam in Paradise, and just as free from artificiality." This was a more apt description of himself, as he knew:

> I, chanter of Adamic songs,
> Through the new garden the West, the great cities calling.

It is, in fact, in the poems gathered under the title "Children of Adam" (1860) that we have the most explicit evidence of his ambition to reach behind tradition to find and assert nature untroubled by art, to re-establish the natural unfallen man in the living hour. Unfallen man is, properly enough, unclothed as well; the convention of cover came in with the Fall; and Whitman adds his own unnostalgic sincerity to the Romantic affection for nakedness:

> As Adam, early in the morning,
> Walking forth from the bower refresh'd with sleep,
> Behold me where I pass, hear my voice, approach,
> Touch me, touch the palm of your hand to my body as I pass,
> Be not afraid of my body.

For Whitman, as for Holmes and Thoreau, the quickest way of framing his novel outlook was by lowering, and secularizing, the familiar spiritual phrases: less impudently than Thoreau but more earnestly, and indeed more monotonously, but with the same intention of salvaging the human from the religious vocabulary to which (he felt) it had given rise. Many of Whitman's poetic statements are conversions of religious allusion: the new miracles were acts of the senses (an odd foreshortening, incidentally, of Edwards' Calvinist elaboration of the Lockian psychology); the aroma of the body was "finer than prayer"; his head was "more than churches, bibles and all creeds." "If I worship one thing more than another," Whitman declaimed, in a moment of Adamic narcissism, "it shall be the spread of my own body." These assertions gave a peculiar stress to Whitman's seconding of the hopeful belief in men like gods: "Divine am I, inside and out, and I make holy whatever I touch." Whitman's poetry is at every moment an act of turbulent incarnation.

But although there is, as there was meant to be, a kind of shock-value in such lines, they are not the most authentic index to his pervasive Adamism, because in them the symbols have become too explicit and so fail to work symbolically. Whitman in these instances is stating his position and contemplating it; he is betraying his own principle of indirect statement; he is telling us too much, and the more he tells us, the more we seem to detect the anxious, inflated utterance of a charlatan. We cling to our own integrity and will not be thundered at. We respond far less willingly to Whitman's frontal assaults than we do to his dramatizations; when he is enacting his role rather than insisting on it, we are open to persuasion. And he had been enacting it from the outset of *Leaves of Grass*.

This is the true nature of his achievement and the source of his claim to be the representative poet of the party of Hope. For the "self" in the very earliest of Whitman's poems is an individual who is always moving forward. To say so is not merely to repeat that Whitman believed in progress; indeed, it is in some sense to deny it. The young Whitman, at least, was not an apostle of progress in its customary meaning of a motion from worse to better to best, an improvement over a previous historic condition, a "rise of man." For Whitman, there was no past or "worse" to progress from; he moved forward because it was the only direction (he makes us think) in which he could move; because there was nothing behind him—or if there were, he had not yet noticed it. There is scarcely a poem of Whitman's before, say, 1867, which does not have the air of being the first poem ever written, the first formulation in language of the nature of persons and of things and of the relations between them; and the urgency of the language suggests that it was formulated in the very nick of time, to give the objects described their first substantial existence.

Nor is there, in *Leaves of Grass*, any complaint about the weight or intrusion of the past; in Whitman's view the past had been so effectively burned away that it had, for every practical purpose, been forgotten altogether. In his own recurring figure, the past was already a corpse; it was on its way out the door to the cemetery; Whitman watched it absent-mindedly, and turned at once to the living reality. He did enjoy, as he reminds us, reciting Homer while walking beside the ocean; but this was just because Homer was exempt from tradition and talking at and about the dawn of time. Homer was the poet you found if you went back far enough; and as for the sea, it had (unlike Melville's) no sharks in it—no ancient, lurking, indestructible evil powers. Whitman's hope was unspoiled by memory. When he became angry, as he did in *Democratic Vistas* (1871), he was not attacking his generation in the Holgrave manner for continuing to accept the old and the foreign, but for fumbling its extraordinary opportunity, for taking a wrong turn on the bright new highway he had mapped for it. Most of the time he was more interested in the map, and we are more interested in him when he was.

It was then that he caught up and set to music the large contemporary conviction that man had been born anew in the new society, that the race was off to a fresh start in America. It was in *Leaves of Grass* that the optative mood, which had endured for over a quarter of a century and had expressed itself so variously and so frequently, seemed to have been transformed at last into the indicative. It was there that the hope that had enlivened spokesmen from Noah Webster in 1825 ("American glory begins at the dawn") to the well-named periodical, *Spirit of the Age* in 1849 ("The accumulated atmosphere of ages, containing stale ideas and opinions . . . will soon be among the things that were")—that all that stored-up abundance of hope found its full poetic realization. *Leaves of Grass* was a climax as well as a beginning, or rather, it was the climax of a long effort to begin.

This was why Emerson, with whatever enlarged "buts" in his mind, made a point of visiting Whitman in New York and Boston; why Thoreau, refusing to be put off "by any brag or egoism in his book," preferred Whitman to Bronson Alcott; and why Whitman, to the steady surprise of his countrymen, has been regarded in Europe for almost a century as unquestionably the greatest poet the New World has produced: an estimate which even Henry James would come round to. European readers were not slow to recognize in Whitman an authentic rendering of their own fondest hopes; for if much of his vision had been originally imported from Germany and France, it had plainly lost its portion of nostalgia en route. While European romanticism continued to resent the effect of time, Whitman was announcing that time had only just begun. He was able to think so because of the facts of immediate history in America during the years when he was maturing: when a world was, in some literal way, being created before his eyes. It was this that Whitman had the opportunity to dramatize; and it was this that gave *Leaves of Grass* its special quality of a Yankee Genesis: a new account of the creation of the world—the creation, that is, of a new world; an account this time with a happy ending for Adam its hero; or better yet, with no ending at all; and with this important emendation, that now the creature has taken on the role of creator.

It was a twofold achievement, and the second half of it was demanded by the first. We see the sequence, for example, in the development from section 4 to section 5 of "Song of Myself." The first phase was the identification of self, an act which proceeded by distinction and differentiation, separating the self from every element that in a traditional view might be supposed to be part of it: Whitman's identity card had no space on it for the names of his ancestry. The exalted mind which carried with it a conviction of absolute novelty has been described by Whitman's friend, the Canadian psychologist, Dr. R. M. Bucke, who relates it to what he calls Whitman's "cosmic consciousness." "Along with the consciousness of the cosmos [Dr. Bucke wrote], there occurs an intellectual enlightenment which alone would place the individual on a new plane of existence—would make him almost a member of a new species." *Almost a member of a new species:* that could pass as the slogan of each individual in the party of Hope. It was a robust American effort to make real and operative the condition which John Donne once had merely feared:

> Prince, Subject, Father, Son are things forgot,
> For every man alone thinks he has got
> To be a Phoenix and that then can be
> None of that kind, of which he is, but he.

Whitman achieves the freedom of the new condition by scrupulously peeling off every possible source of, or influence upon, the "Me myself," the "what I am." As in section 4 of "Song of Myself":

> Trippers and askers surround me
> People I meet, the effect upon me of my early life, or the ward and
>   the city I live in or the nation. . . .
> The sickness of one of my folks, or of myself, or the ill-doing or loss
>   or lack of money, or depressions or exaltations,
> Battles, the horror of fratricidal wars, the fever of doubtful news, the
>   fitful events,
> These come to me days and nights and go from me again,
> But they are not the Me myself.
> Apart from the pulling and hauling stands what I am;
> Stands amused, complacent, compassionating, idle, unitary;
> Looks down, is erect, or bends an arm on an impalpable certain rest,
> Looking with side-curved head curious what will come next,
> Both in and out of the game, and watching and wondering at it.

There is Emerson's individual, the "infinitely repellent orb." There is also the heroic product of romanticism, exposing behind the mass of what were regarded as inherited or external or imposed and hence superficial and accidental qualities the true indestructible secret core of personality. There is the man who contends that "nothing, not God, is greater to one than one's self."

There, in fact, is the new Adam. If we want a profile of him, we could start with the adjectives Whitman supplies: amused, complacent, compassionating, idle, unitary; especially unitary, and certainly very easily amused; too complacent, we frequently feel, but always compassionate—expressing the old divine compassion for every sparrow that falls, every criminal and prostitute and hopeless invalid, every victim of violence or misfortune. With Whitman's help we could pile up further attributes, and the exhaustive portrait of Adam would be composed of a careful gloss on each one of them: hankering, gross, mystical, nude; turbulent, fleshy, sensual, eating, drinking, and breeding; no sentimentalist, no stander above men and women; no more modest than immodest; wearing his hat as he pleases indoors and out; never skulking or ducking or deprecating; adoring himself and adoring his comrades; afoot with his vision,

> Moving forward then and now and forever,
> Gathering and showing more always and with velocity,
> Infinite and omnigenous.

And announcing himself in language like that. For an actual illustra‐ tion, we could not find anything better than the stylized daguerreo‐ type of himself which Whitman placed as the Frontispiece of the first edition. We recognize him at once: looking with side-curved head, bending an arm on the certain rest of his hip, evidently amused, com‐ placent, and curious; bearded, rough, probably sensual; with his hat on.

Whitman did resemble this Adamic archetype, according to his friend John Burroughs. "There was a look about him," Burroughs re‐ membered, "hard to describe, and which I have seen in no other face, —a gray, brooding, elemental look, like the granite rock, something primitive and Adamic that might have belonged to the first man." The two new adjectives there are "gray" and "brooding"; and they belong to the profile, too, both of Whitman and of the character he drama‐ tized. There was bound to be some measure of speculative sadness in‐ herent in the situation. Not all the leaves Whitman uttered were joyous ones, though he wanted them all to be and was never clear why they were not. His ideal image of himself—and it is his best single trope for the new Adam—was that of a live oak he saw growing in Louisiana:

> All alone stood it and the mosses hung down from the branches,
> Without any companion it grew there uttering joyous leaves of dark green,
> And its look, rude, unbending, lusty, made me think of myself.

But at his most honest, he admitted, as he does here, that the condi‐ tion was somehow unbearable:

> I wondered how it could utter joyous leaves standing alone there without a friend near, for I knew I could not. . . .
> And though the live-oak glistens there in Louisiana solitary in a wide flat space,
> Uttering joyous leaves all its life without a friend a lover near,
> I knew very well I could not.

Adam had his moments of sorrow also. But the emotion had nothing to do with the tragic insight; it did not spring from any perception of a genuine hostility in nature or lead to the drama of colliding forces. Whitman was wistful, not tragic. We might almost say that he was wistful because he was not tragic. He was innocence personified. It is not difficult to marshal a vast array of references to the ugly, the gory, and the sordid in his verses; brought together in one horrid lump, they appear as the expression of one who was well informed about the shabby side of the world; but though he offered himself as "the poet of wickedness" and claimed to be "he who knew what it was to be evil," every item he introduced as vile turns out, after all, to be merely a particular beauty of a different original coloration. "Evil propels me and reform of evil propels me, I stand indifferent." A sentiment like that can make sense only if the term "evil" has been filtered through a transfiguring moral imagination, changing in essence as it passes.

That sentiment, of course, is not less an expression of poetic than of moral motivation. As a statement of the poetic sensibility, it could have been uttered as easily by Shakespeare or Dante as by Whitman. Many of the very greatest writers suggest, as Whitman does, a peculiar artistic innocence, a preadolescent wonder which permits such a poet to take in and reproject whatever there is, shrinking from none of it. But in Whitman, artistic innocence merged with moral innocence: a pre-adolescent ignorance of the convulsive undertow of human behavior—something not at all shared by Dante or Shakespeare. Both modes of innocence are present in the poetry of Walt Whitman, and they are not at any time to be really distinguished. One can talk about his image of moral innocence only in terms of his poetic creation.

"I reject none, accept all, then reproduce all in my own forms." The whole spirit of Whitman is in the line: there is his strategy for overcoming his sadness, and the second large phase of his achievement, following the act of differentiation and self-identification. It is the creative phase, in that sense of creativity which beguiles the artist most perilously into stretching his analogy with God—when he brings a world into being. Every great poet composes a world for us, and what James called the "figure in the carpet" is the poet's private chart of that world; but when we speak of the poet's world—of Dostoevski's or Balzac's—we knowingly skip a phrase, since what we mean is Dostoevski's (or Balzac's) selective embodiment of an already existing world. In the case of Whitman, the type of extreme Adamic romantic, the metaphor gains its power from a proximity to the literal, as though Whitman really were engaged in the stupendous task of building a world that had not been there before the first words of his poem.

The task was self-imposed, for Whitman's dominant emotion, when it was not unmodified joy, was simple, elemental loneliness; it was a testimony to his success and contributed to his peculiar glow. For if the hero of *Leaves of Grass* radiates a kind of primal innocence in an innocent world, it was not only because he had made that world, it was also because he had begun by making himself. Whitman is an early example, and perhaps the most striking one we have, of the self-made man, with an undeniable grandeur which is the product of his manifest sense of having been responsible for his own being—something far more compelling than the more vulgar version of the rugged individual who claims responsibility only for his own bank account.

And of course he was lonely, incomparably lonely; no anchorite was ever so lonely, since no anchorite was ever so alone. Whitman's image of the evergreen, "solitary in a wide, flat space . . . without a friend a lover near," introduced what more and more appears to be the central theme of American literature, in so far as a unique theme may be claimed for it: the theme of loneliness, dramatized in what I shall later describe as the story of *the hero in space*. The only recourse for a poet like Whitman was to fill the space by erecting a home and populating it with companions and lovers.

Whitman began in an Adamic condition which was only too effectively realized: the isolated individual, standing flush with the empty universe, a primitive moral and intellectual entity. In the behavior of a "noiseless, patient spider," Whitman found a revealing analogy:

> A noiseless, patient spider
> I mark'd, where, on a little promontory, it stood out, isolated,
> Mark'd how, to explore the vacant, vast surrounding,
> It launched forth filament, filament, filament, out of itself,
> Ever unreeling them—ever tirelessly speeding them.

"Out of itself." This is the reverse of the traditionalist attitude that, in Eliot's phrase, "home is where one starts from." Whitman acted on the hopeful conviction that the new Adam started from himself; having created himself, he must next create a home. The given in individual experience was no longer a complex of human, racial, and familial relationships; it was a self in a vacant, vast surrounding. Each simple separate person must forge his own framework anew. This was the bold, enormous venture inevitably confronted by the Adamic personality. He had to become the maker of his own conditions—if he were to have any conditions or any achieved personality at all.

There were, in any case, no conditions to *go back to*—to take upon one's self or to embody. There is in fact almost no indication at all in *Leaves of Grass* of a return or reversion, even of that recovery of childhood detected in *Walden*. Whitman begins after that recovery, as a child, seemingly self-propagated, and he is always going *forth;* one of his pleasantest poems was constructed around that figure. There is only the open road, and Whitman moves forward from the start of it. Homecoming is for the exile, the prodigal son, Adam after the expulsion, not for the new unfallen Adam in the western garden. Not even in "Passage to India" is there a note of exile, because there is no sense of sin ("Let others weep for sin"). Whitman was entirely remote from the view of man as an orphan which motivated many of the stories of

Hawthorne and Melville and which underlay the characteristic adventure they narrated of the search for a father. Hawthorne, an orphan
himself and the author of a book about England called *Our Old Home*,
sometimes sent his heroes to Europe to look for their families; Melville
dispatched his heroes to the bottom of the sea on the same mission.
This was the old way of posing the problem: the way of mastering life
by the recovery of home, though it might require descent to the land of
the dead; but Whitman knew the secret of his paternity.

Whitman was creating a world, even though he often sounds as
though he were saluting a world that had been lying in wait for him:
"Salut au monde." In one sense, he is doing just that, welcoming it,
acknowledging it, reveling in its splendor and variety. His typical condition is one of acceptance and absorption; the word which almost
everyone who knew him applied to his distinguishing capacity was
"absorptive." He absorbed life for years; and when he contained
enough, he let it go out from him again. "I . . . accept all, then reproduce all in my own forms." He takes unflagging delight in the re-
productions: "Me pleased," he says in "Our Old Feuillage"; it is the
"what I am." But the pleasure of seeing becomes actual only in the
process of naming. It is hard to recall any particular of life and work,
of men and women and animals and plants and things, of body and
mind, that Whitman has not somewhere named in caressing detail.
And the process of naming is for Whitman nothing less than the process
of creation. This new Adam is both maker and namer; his innocent
pleasure, untouched by humility, is colored by the pride of one who
looks on his work and finds it good. The things that are named seem
to spring into being at the sound of the word. It was through the poetic
act that Whitman articulated the dominant metaphysical illusion of
his day and became the creator of his own world.

We have become familiar, a century after the first edition of *Leaves
of Grass*, with the notion of the poet as the magician who "orders reality" by his use of language. That notion derived originally from the
epochal change—wrought chiefly by Kant and Hegel—in the relation
between the human mind and the external world; a change whereby
the mind "thought order into" the sensuous mass outside it instead of
detecting an order externally existing. Whitman (who read Hegel and
who wrote a singularly flatulent poetic reflection after doing so) adapted
that principle to artistic creativity with a vigor and enthusiasm unknown before James Joyce and his associates in the twentieth century.
What is implicit in every line of Whitman is the belief that the poet
projects a world of order and meaning and identity into either a chaos
or a sheer vacuum; he does not *discover* it. The poet may salute the
chaos; but he creates the world.

Such a conviction contributed greatly to Whitman's ever enlarging

idea of the poet as the vicar of God, as the son of God—as God himself. Those were not new labels for the artist, but they had been given
fresh currency in Whitman's generation; and Whitman held to all of
them more ingenuously than any other poet who ever lived. He super-
vised the departure of "the priests" and the arrival of the new vicar,
"the divine litteratus"; he erected what he called his novel "trinitas"
on the base of "the true son of God, the poet"; he offered himself as a
cheerful, divine scapegoat and stage-managed "my own crucifixion."
And to the extent that he fulfilled his own demands for *the* poet—as
laid down in the Preface to *Leaves of Grass* and in *Democratic Vistas*—
Whitman became God the Creator.

This was the mystical side of him, the side which announced itself
in the fifth section of "Song of Myself," and which led to the mystical
vision of a newly created totality. The vision emerges from those
lyrical sweeps through the universe in the later sections of the poem:
the sections in which Whitman populated and gave richness and shape
to the universe by the gift of a million names. We can round out our
picture of Whitman as Adam—both Adam as innocent and Adam as
namer—if we distinguish his own brand of mysticism from the traditional variety. Traditional mysticism proceeds by denial and negation
and culminates in the imagery of deserts and silence, where the voice
and the being of God are the whole of reality. Whitman's mysticism
proceeds by expansive affirmation and culminates in plenitude and
huge volumes of noise. Traditional mysticism is the surrender of the
ego to its creator, in an eventual escape from the limits of names;
Whitman's is the expansion of the ego in the act of creation itself,
naming every conceivable object as it comes from the womb.

The latter figure is justified by the very numerous references, both
by Whitman and by his friends, to his "great mother-nature." We
must cope with the remarkable blend in the man, whereby this Adam,
who had already grown to the stature of his own maker, was not less
and at the same time his own Eve, breeding the human race out of his
love affair with himself. If section 5 of "Song of Myself" means anything, it means this: a miraculous intercourse between "you my soul"
and "the other I am," with a world as its offspring. How the process
worked in his poems can be seen by examining any one of the best of
them. There Whitman skilfully brings into being the small world of
the particular poem by introducing a few items one by one, linking
them together by a variety of devices, running back over them time
and again to reinsure their solidity and durability, adding further
items and quickly forging the relations between them and the cluster
already present, announcing at the end the accomplished whole and
breathing over all of it the magical command *to be.*

Take, for example, "Crossing Brooklyn Ferry":

> Flood-tide below me! I see you face to face!
> Clouds of the west—sun there half an hour high—I see you also face
>   to face.
> Crowds of men and women attired in the usual costumes, how curi-
>   ous you are to me!
> On the ferry-boats the hundreds and hundreds that cross, returning
>   home, are more curious to me than you suppose,
> And you that shall cross from shore to shore years hence are more
>   to me, and more in my meditations, than you might suppose.

This is not the song of a *trovatore*, a finder, exposing bit by bit the substance of a spectacle which is there before a spectator looks at it. It
is the song of a poet who creates his spectacle by "projecting" it as he
goes along. The flood tides, the clouds, the sun, the crowds of men
and women in the usual costumes: these exist in the instant they are
named and as they are pulled in toward one another, bound together
by a single unifying eye through the phrases which apply to them
severally ("face to face," "curious to me"). The growth of the world
is exactly indicated in the increasing length of the lines; until, in the
following stanza, Whitman can observe a "simple, compact, well-join'd
scheme." Stabilized in space, the scheme must now be given stabilizing
relations in time; Whitman goes on to announce that "fifty years hence,
others will see them as they cross, the sun half an hour high" (the
phrase had to be repeated) "a hundred years hence, or ever so many
hundred years hence, others will see them." With the world, so to speak,
a going concern, Whitman is able now to summon new elements into
existence: sea gulls, the sunlight in the water, the haze on the hills,
the schooners and sloops and ships at anchor, the large and small
steamers, and the flags of all nations. A few of the conspicuous elements are blessed and praised, in an announcement (stanza 8) not only
of their existence but now rather of the value they impart to one another; and then, in the uninterrupted prayer of the final stanza (stanza
9—the process covers nine stanzas, as though it were nine months) each
separate entity is named again as receiving everlasting life through its
participation in the whole:

> Flow on river! flow with the flood-tide, and ebb with the ebb-tide!
> Frolic on, crested and scallop-edg'd waves!

And so on: until the mystery of incarnation has been completed.

Whitman's Poetic Ensembles

by *Walter Sutton*

> I will not make poems with reference to parts
> But I will make poems, songs, thoughts, with reference to
>   ensemble. . . .

When Whitman wrote of his concern for poetic "ensemble" rather than "parts," he was thinking more of his theme of natural and cosmic unity than of questions of prosody. Yet his words, taken either in or out of their context in "Starting from Paumanok," are also in accord with his poetics. If the "ensemble" is identified with the poem, the statement reveals an interest in the organic unity of the whole rather than in such "parts" as rime or meter, which Whitman, like Coleridge, regarded as superficial aspects of form. In their specific context, the lines express Whitman's insistence that he was singing not just of a day "but with reference to all days"—that he was interested not simply in particulars as such but in particulars as manifestations of the unity of man and nature in a larger scheme. The word *reference* reminds us of Whitman's conviction that the value of his poems lay not so much in their words as in the world of shared experience evoked by their language. It was his custom to identify his poems with their human and natural subjects and to prize the referents of his words more highly than the words themselves. In "So Long" he says of his poetry, "Camerado, this is no book,/ Who touches this touches a man," and in "A Song of the Rolling Earth" he sees "little or nothing in audible words" in the face of "the unspoken meanings of the earth." We find in Whitman a repeated emphasis upon the organic nature of poetic form, but his organicism—unlike much recent contextualist theory—assumes the openness of the poem and the identification of its formal elements with the shared experiences of its readers.   . .

"Whitman's Poetic Ensembles" (Original title: "The Analysis of Free Verse Form, Illustrated by a Reading of Whitman"). From the *Journal of Aesthetics and Art Criticism*, XVIII (1959), 241-257. Copyright 1959 by *Journal of Aesthetics and Art Criticism*. Revised by Walter Sutton for publication in this volume and reprinted by his permission and that of the editor of the *Journal of Aesthetics and Art Criticism*.

Romantic organic theory stimulated the development of the modern free verse movement, but it provides little help to the practical critic of free verse form. The comparisons made by Emerson and Whitman of poetic form and the growth of plants or the movements of the sea testify to their regard for nature and their commitment to the idea that form follows function, but they do not help us order our responses to poems such as Whitman wrote. Even Coleridge's description of the poetic power as manifesting itself in "the balance or reconciliation of opposite or discordant qualities" has proved to be of limited usefulness, since it has been appropriated by critics concerned with a narrow range of structural principles, or "strategies," such as irony, paradox, and tension.

As we confront the problem of ordering the often bewildering complexity of the interrelated formal elements of Whitman's free verse poems (or of any literary work), we are aware of the inadequacy of the conception of any single structural device such as irony or of "parts" such as rime or meter. The poem is, rather, an "ensemble" or complex presenting interrelated patterns of organization that together constitute a "form" only partially apprehended by any one reader.

Although the patterns of organization are necessarily interrelated, they can be identified with one or more of four formal dimensions: sound, syntax, image or event, and meaning. Sound patterns include such devices as rime and meter (often over-emphasized as formal elements of traditional verse), alliteration, assonance, euphony, dissonance, cadence, or onomatopoeia, depending upon the nature of the given work. Syntax has to do with the grammatical relationship of the elements of the poem. It may be involved with the dimension of sound, as when parallel constructions provide riming effects, and it is necessarily involved with questions of meaning. The dimension of image and event includes the imagined events represented by the words of the poem— actions, thoughts, feelings, dreams, as well as sensory experiences—all of which contribute to the integrity of the imagined world of the work. Meaning, which is both conceptual and emotive, exists on two distinguishable levels. On the plain-sense level the events have meaning in terms of the world of the work. On the level of metaphor, the events are value-charged in the consciousness of the reader and invested with meanings and values commensurate with the reader's experience, social and aesthetic. The metaphorical level includes both the argument and theme of the work, however defined, and the individual images and events that support it.

Some such idea of interrelated formal dimensions is necessary for the analysis of the form of Whitman's distinctive free verse poems in *Leaves of Grass*. Of these, the longest and best known—untitled in the first edition of 1855, entitled "A Poem of Walt Whitman, an American," in 1856, and known to us now, since the edition of 1881, as "Song of

Myself"—contains many but not all of the techniques employed by Whitman in such later and more complex poems as "Out of the Cradle Endlessly Rocking," "When Lilacs Last in the Dooryard Bloom'd," and "Passage to India."

As we read "Song of Myself" in its final version, we are aware of certain recurrent organizing devices, the most conspicuous of which are syntactical. Of these, the use of grammatical parallelism and of the sentence, or paragraph, as a containing unit comparable to the stanza in conventional verse, is consistent throughout the poem and contributes to its metrical unity. Both devices may be seen in the first verse sentence-stanza of section 31:

> I believe a leaf of grass is no less than the journey-work of the stars,
> And the pismire is equally perfect, and a grain of sand, and the egg of the wren,
> And the tree-toad is a chef-d'oeuvre for the highest,
> And the running blackberry would adorn the parlors of heaven,
> And the narrowest hinge in my hand puts to scorn all machinery,
> And the cow crunching with depress'd head surpasses any statue,
> And a mouse is miracle enough to stagger sextillions of infidels.

There are other types of parallelism employed in "Song of Myself," but this example illustrates a number of its effects. In the relation of syntax to meaning, it has been observed that grammatical parallelism is an appropriate form for a poet like Whitman with a democratic equalitarian point of view. Yet his equalitarianism is pantheistic as well as political, and the consonance of syntax and meaning is apparent in these lines. The relation of syntax to sound is also apparent, since the repeated initial "And the's" rime. They also echo the parallelism of the King James *Bible* and thus point to a traditional model for Whitman's metrical form, one that is especially important because of his conception of the poet as a seer and prophet who would proclaim the gospel of the truly democratic society of the future.

As for the sound pattern, both alliteration and assonance are important integrating devices. Sound also involves rhythm and stress. Although "Song of Myself" begins with a perfectly regular iambic pentameter line—"I celebrate myself, and sing myself"—and although certain lines and passages approach metrical regularity, most of the verses are irregular in their stress pattern, and conventional scansion is not applicable. Other sound devices, such as onomatopoeia, assonance, and alliteration, are present in "Song of Myself," but they are not as effectively exploited here as in some of the later poems.

In identifying himself with the manifold aspects of American life, Whitman presents a great variety of particular images (the contralto, the carpenter, the farmer, the lunatic, the printer, the quadroon girl, the machinist, the squaw, etc., of section 15, for example). In addition to such apparently unrelated particular images, there are several dominant images basic to Whitman's controlling point of view and to his work as a whole. One is the grass itself (section 6), identified with the principle of life manifested by the persistent life nature cycle and with the impulse to creative expression manifested in the poems themselves as individual "leaves of grass." Another is water, or the sea (sections 17, 22), like the grass a symbol of the life force, containing as a womb-tomb image (both "cradle" and "unshovelled graves") the terminal experiences of the life cycle. Then, too, there is the thematic image of the journey, introduced in section 32 and continued in 44 and following sections. The journey represents the progress, not only of man, but of the physical universe as well. It encompasses the process of evolution, optimistically regarded as directed toward a goal of perfectibility in which man's divine potential is to be realized in the meeting with the "great Camerado," who waits at the end of the journey. It is also the progress of a free nation along the "open road" toward the ideal of democratic community and brotherhood. For the individual, as for the boy disciple who accompanies the poet, it is the journey of life and the quest for truth.

These dominant images are not explicitly interrelated within the poem as events except as we recognize that they are all a part of the experience of the poet, who at the beginning of the poem assumes an identification with all mankind ("And what I assume you shall assume") and who introduces himself in section 24 as

> Walt Whitman, a kosmos, of Manhattan the son,
> Turbulent, fleshy, sensual, eating, drinking and breeding,
> No sentimentalist, no stander above men and women or apart
>   from them
> No more modest than immodest.

This characterization tallies with the portrait of Whitman in workman's clothes that faces the poem in the later editions. The *persona* of the poet as the common man *and* seer who also identifies with all aspects of life helps to explain the apparently fragmented and discontinuous sequence of images and events in "Song of Myself." The device is not entirely satisfactory, however, because it does not require any integration of the particular events or aspects of experience presented. There *is,* of course, a selection of details, as there is in all art, but the rationale of the selection is not apparent. For all the wealth of imagery, the reader is left with a sense of diffuseness and of the lack of an adequate control of form.

This weakness in "Song of Myself" is emphasized by contrast as we turn to "Crossing Brooklyn Ferry," first published in 1856 as "Sun-Down

Poem." Its images and events all relate to a single experience and a single setting: the crossing of the East River by ferryboat, with a view of the river and harbor and of Brooklyn and Manhattan. Within these limits, or within this frame, the sensuous images presented in the opening sections of the poem (1-3) contribute to the sense of verisimilitude. The details of the scene—the soaring gulls, the ships with the flags of all nations, the hills of Brooklyn, the light on the water—reflect the close observation of a coherent experience. Moreover, these complementary images contribute to a sense of the unity of the experience, both for the individual crossing and for crossings separated in time. Image becomes metaphor as the crossing, or transit, is seen to relate both to the life of the individual and to the lives of separate generations. For the many visual images representing the experience of the voyaging poet are all subordinated to the image of the ship, or ferryboat, which crosses the river (of time) from gate to gate (birth and death) and which supplies the poet his perspective as he recognizes the "universality" of his particular experience.

By appealing through sensory images to a sense of shared experience, the poet asserts a sense of unity, or *community,* that provides a bond between individuals of the same generation and between the poet and later generations:

> It avails not, time nor place—distance avails not,
> I am with you, you men and women of a generation, or ever so many
>   generations hence,
> Just as you feel when you look on the river and sky, so I felt,
> Just as any of you is one of a living crowd, I was one of a crowd. . . .

Beyond the identity of experience, there is, for the romantic poet, the recognition of an identity of soul, as well, among all men:

> I too had been struck from the float forever held in solution,
> I too had receiv'd identity by my body. . . .

The images of the harbor scene are again invoked in the conclusion, but in a more exalted mood, as the poet's feeling of alienation, or individuation, is resolved by the assurance of the identity of soul as well as the community of experience. This confidence is also supported by an assertion of the unity of body and soul, for Whitman, unlike the Transcendentalist, regards physical nature as a "necessary film" which "envelops" the soul and without which the soul cannot be known.

The introduction of a set of images relating to a single experience, the speculation upon their meaning, and the re-evocation which resolves the dualism of body and soul represent a new development in Whitman's technique, one that suggests the influence of music upon the poet's conception of form. This device serves to interrelate effects within the dimensions of sound, syntax, and meaning as well as that of the image. The principle involved is comparable to that of rime, if we recognize that in a broad sense rime involves the repetition and resolution not only of sounds, but of grammatical units, sense impressions, and ideas. In this way we see that the repetition of the harbor images involves auditory rime through the repetition of words, visual rime through the images which the repeated words evoke, and conceptual and emotive rime through the associations of the words and images. All contribute to the central theme which they sustain and develop. William Carlos Williams' observation, in "The Orchestra," that "it is a principle of music to repeat the theme" applies to the poem as well.

"Out of the Cradle Endlessly Rocking"—first published in 1860 as "A Word Out of the Sea" and in approximately final form by 1871—is Whitman's most complex and successfully-integrated poem. Several effective new techniques are apparent. One is the use of a triad of images (boy, bird, and sea) through which the poet develops his theme by means of a dramatic colloquy. (A comparable triadic pattern, but without the same dramatic quality, is employed in such later poems as "When Lilacs Last in the Dooryard Bloom'd" and "Passage to India.") There is also a recurrence and resolution in the ordering of images comparable to that in "Crossing Brooklyn Ferry." The influence of music is seen here too in the device, inspired by the model of the opera, of the arias or bird songs, of fulfillment and frustration, which provide interludes of lyric expression of the feelings and emotions aroused by the events presented and analyzed in the narrative and dramatic framework of the poem.

The arias are operative in all formal dimensions: sound (as their lyric intensity enhances the emotive quality of the language of these verses); syntax (as they are set off in relatively self-contained italicized units which provide a complementing of the mood and a counterpointing of the events of the remainder of the poem); image (as they present images from nature—the heavy moon, the sea pushing upon the land—to express the subjective feelings of love and frustration); and meaning (primarily emotive but also metaphorically expressive as the bird's songs of "lonesome love" of the "throbbing heart") brings a realization to the boy, the "outsetting bard," of the relation between suffering and art, of the fact that, for him, poetry is to be a sublimated expression of frustrated love.

The opening section reveals the interrelationship of the four formal dimensions of the poem. It presents a reminiscence of a childhood experience in which the poet, as a boy, saw a pair of mocking birds nesting on the beach. (The impression of love fulfilled which they convey is heightened by the brief "two-together" aria.) The disappearance of the female and the grief of the remaining mate (expressed in the longer aria) introduce the boy to the experience of loss and frustration, which the maturing poet comes to recognize as the basic motive for his poetic expression.

The first verse stanza of the poem brings together images relating to the childhood experience, now interwoven into a symbolic poetic fabric which involves meaning, as metaphor, beyond the context of the events of the remembered experience:

> Out of the cradle endlessly rocking,
> Out of the mocking-bird's throat, the musical shuttle,
> Out of the Ninth-month midnight,
> Over the sterile sands and the fields beyond, where the child leaving
> 　　his bed wander'd alone, bareheaded, barefoot,
> Down from the shower'd halo,
> Up from the mystic play of shadows twining and twisting as if they
> 　　were alive,
> Out from the patches of briers and blackberries,
> From the memories of the bird that chanted to me,
> From your memories sad brother, from the fitful risings and fallings
> 　　I heard,
> From under that yellow half-moon late-risen and swollen as if with
> 　　tears,
> From those beginning notes of yearning and love there in the mist,
> From the thousand responses of my heart never to cease,
> From the myriad thence-aroused words,
> From the word stronger and more delicious than any,
> From such as now they start the scene revisiting,
> As a flock, twittering, rising, or overhead passing,
> Borne hither, ere all eludes me, hurriedly,
> A man, yet by these tears a little boy again,
> Throwing myself on the sand, confronting the waves,
> I, chanter of pains and joys, uniter of here and hereafter,
> Taking all hints to use them, but swiftly leaping beyond them,
> A reminiscence sing.

The images from remembered experience are interwoven into a poetic context. The weaving process, in which the voice of the bird is a "musical shuttle," is suggested by syntactical and sound devices particularly. The repeated introductory prepositions—*out of, over, down from, up from*—serve to indicate the converging movements of an interweaving. The sound pattern of the lines is particularly rich in devices which interrelate the verbal elements of this section. Assonance, alliteration, and internal rime are combined in such sequences as *rocking-mocking, beyond-wander'd, bareheaded-barefoot*. The same qualities, with onomatopoeia as well, are seen in such a phrase as "the mystic play of shadows twining and twisting as if they were alive."

The argument of the poem is also foreshadowed in this section as the poet identifies with the bird, his "sad brother," and sees in the experience of frustration the awakening of his own sense of vocation, the "thousand responses" of his heart and the "myriad thence-aroused words." There is finally the suggestion that the ultimate release from the tension of individual existence (partially resolved through art) is death, "the word stronger and more delicious than any," whispered to the poet by the old crone, the sea. The poet is here identified as the "uniter of here and hereafter," in accordance with Emerson's definition of the poet as the "integrating seer." Whitman's poet is conceived as "taking all hints to use them, but swiftly leaping beyond them," as the images from remembered experience are value charged in the poetic, or metaphoric process.

A reading of the complete poem sustains the reader's impression of an interrelationship of formal elements that can be only briefly suggested here. The sound devices already mentioned are supported by the rhythm of the verses, beginning with the irregularly-stressed but strongly rhythmic opening lines with their intermingled trochees and dactyls, appropriate to both the movement of the sea and the weaving process:

$$ ' \smile \smile \mid ' \smile \quad ' \smile \smile \quad ' \smile $$
$$ ' \smile \smile \mid ' \smile \smile \mid \quad \smile ' \smile \smile ' $$
$$ ' \smile \smile \mid ' \smile \quad ' \smile $$

As for syntax, besides parallelism, which contributes also to the effect of rime, the sentence stanzas provide a periodic control for the rhythm of the individual lines as well as a pattern for the expression of meaning. The events of the childhood experience, ordered by the reminiscing poet, support the theme of the awakening sense of poetic vocation. Meaning is found both on the plain sense level, in the recountal of the child's experience, and on the level of metaphor which rises from this and in which both thought and feeling are involved. Metaphorically, the remembered events relate to the meaning of art and the function of the poet. The theme of the poem embraces not only the maturation process, as the boy is introduced to the experiences of love and death, but also a strongly regressive motive, as the experience of frustration turns the poet's thoughts first to the idea of art as sublimation, then to the welcome recognition of death as a release from tension. Emotive values are most strongly evident in the boy's empathic responses to the bird's songs of love and grief and in the exaltation that accompanies his sense of vocation.

"Out of the Cradle Endlessly Rocking" is one of the most successfully-integrated complex poems in our literature. Its organization easily refutes the blanket indictment of formlessness sometimes levelled against Whitman's poetry because of his tendency to identify and merge with his subjects and to be indiscriminate in the selection of detail. This poem reveals the detachment of the poet and a distancing of subject through the device of the three related central figures who as dramatic characters contribute to the development of the theme. The poem's dramatic quality is heightened by the lyric interludes already discussed. The figures of the boy, the bird, and the sea (as earth-mother) are introduced, the significance of their roles is revealed, and the conclusion of the poem resolves the colloquy as the bird's cries of unsatisfied love and the message of death whispered by the sea are fused with the poet's "own songs awakened from that hour."

Other successful poems in *Leaves of Grass* are more simply organized. Some of Whitman's most effective short poems are the vignettes of Civil War experiences in *Drum-Taps*, first published separately in 1865 and later incorporated into *Leaves of Grass*.

"Cavalry Crossing a Ford" presents a picture of observed war experience:

> A line in long array where they wind betwixt green islands,
> They take a serpentine course, their arms flash in the sun—hark to
> the musical clank,
> Behold the silvery river, in it the splashing horses loitering stop
> to drink,
> Behold the brown-faced men, each group, each person a picture, the
> negligent rest on the saddles,
> Some emerge on the opposite bank, others are just entering the
> ford—while,
> Scarlet and blue and snowy white,
> The guidon flags flutter gayly in the wind.

Imagistic in quality, the poem is of interest primarily as a visual composition conveying the color and other sensuous details of a military action. The pictorial effect is comparable, in its detachment and objectivity, to that of a camp sketch by Winslow Homer. Although there is movement and sound, the pause at the ford provides a relative stasis that enables the observer to focus the scene and compose its details. Although the most conspicuous formal element is visual imagery, the poem is not purely imagistic. The serpent-like column and the brown faces relate the men to primitive nature, and the scene in general conveys a sense of fitness, grace, and competence. The flashing of arms and the clanking of equipment suggest the efficiency of the war machine. This brief glimpse of cavalry campaigning effectively communicates the

impression of adjustment to nature, of excitement, and color. This metaphorical meaning is not developed, however; it rises spontaneously from
a treatment which seems concerned primarily with the level of physical,
primarily visual, experience.

Another poem of the same order is "An Army Corps on the March":

> With its cloud of skirmishers in advance,
> With now the sound of a single shot snapping like a whip, and now
>   an irregular volley,
> The swarming ranks press on and on, the dense brigades press on,
> Glittering dimly, toiling under the sun—the dust cover'd men,
> In columns rise and fall to the undulations of the ground,
> With artillery interspers'd—the wheels rumble, the horses sweat,
> As the army corps advances.

The poem reveals the same concern for sensory detail, the same association of human and physical nature. There is a difference in the quality
of the impressions, however, in keeping with the nature of the subject.
Here is no stasis but rather confusion and movement. The individual
forms do not stand out but rather are absorbed in the masses: "clouds
of skirmishers," "swarming ranks," "dense brigades." Of course, in both
of these brief poems, other kinds of organization are involved besides
that of image and event. The sound pattern is particularly important.
In the third verse, the regular iambic rhythm and the incremental
repetition of the parallel clauses ("The swarming ranks press on and
on, the dense brigades press on") contribute to the sense of the remorse-
less forward motion of a mass within which human identity is lost.

Another brief poem from *Drum-Taps*, "A Sight in Camp in the Daybreak Gray and Dim," also presents a limited and sharp experience
but one which is metaphorically developed as well:

> A sight in camp in the daybreak gray and dim,
> As from my tent I emerge so early sleepless,
> As slow I walk in the cool fresh air the path near by the hospital
>   tent,
> Three forms I see on stretchers lying, brought out there untended
>   lying,
> Over each the blanket spread, ample brownish woolen blanket,
> Gray and heavy blanket, folding, covering all.
>
> Curious I halt and silent stand,
> Then with light fingers I from the face of the nearest the first just
>   lift the blanket;

Who are you elderly man so gaunt and grim, with well-gray'd hair,
and flesh all sunken about the eyes?
Who are you my dear comrade?

Then to the second I step—and who are you my child and darling?
Who are you sweet boy with cheeks yet blooming?

Then to the third—a face nor child nor old, very calm, as of
beautiful yellow-white ivory;
Young man I think I know you—I think this face is the face of the
Christ himself,
Dead and divine and brother of all, and here again he lies.

The three figures are associated with the ages of man; but, as the
third is identified with Christ, we are also reminded of the Savior and
his two companions in death and, by extension, of the Christian Trinity,
which Whitman typically supplants with a secular triadic image of
three soldiers who have died in the common struggle of existence. The
"brownish woolen blanket, / Gray and heavy blanket," is the earth, the
physical nature into which the three forms are merging. The poet, who
lifts the blanket, penetrates the veil of the flesh, of nature, and recognizes the divine potential of the human individual. The syntactical
arrangement of the lines (the recurrent pattern of "I . . . stand, /
Then . . . ," "Then . . . I step . . . ," "Then to the third . . . ," followed respectively by "Who are you . . . ?" "and who are you . . . ?"
and "I think I know you . . .") serves to integrate the verses, to suggest
a symbolic progression, and to develop a suspense which is resolved by
the recognition of the third encounter.

This brief poem is more complex than the two preceding because of
the interrelationship of the levels of image and meaning. The metaphor
of the human victim of war as a Christ figure is clearly suggested, although it is not developed to an extent comparable to the treatment of
Lincoln in the long elegy, "When Lilacs Last in the Dooryard Bloom'd."

The intimate relation of image and meaning can be seen in a short
poem, "The Dismantled Ship," composed late in Whitman's life and
first published in 1888:

In some unused lagoon, some nameless bay,
On sluggish, lonesome waters, anchor'd near the shore,
An old, dismasted, gray and batter'd ship, disabled, done,
After free voyages to all the seas of earth, haul'd up at last and
hawser'd tight,
Lies rusting, mouldering.

Here, as in "Cavalry Crossing a Ford," there is a concentration upon
visual imagery and an avoidance of any direct statement of meaning.
Yet the imagery of this poem, in contrast with that of the other, is immediately recognizable as metaphoric, suggesting the pathos of old age,
its sense of futility and desolation. The reason is that the images used—
ship, voyage, harbor—while they undoubtedly reflect the poet's observed
experience, are also traditional as metaphors of human experience and
thus immediately convey the burden of associated concepts and feelings
which they have accumulated through centuries of use. Furthermore,
the image of the ship had been used by Whitman to suggest a life-quest
in both "Crossing Brooklyn Ferry" and "Passage to India," and the
reader is struck by the contrast in tone in the treatment of this central
image between the confident out-setting of the latter poem ("Sail forth
—steer for the deep waters only, / Reckless O soul, exploring, I with
thee, and thou with me . . .") and the terminus of the voyage in "The
Dismantled Ship."

The interrelated formal dimensions of Whitman's free verse poems
can be distinguished in any poem or literary work. While a high degree
of differentiation and integration of the formal patterns enhances the
interest of a work, complexity cannot be regarded as an arbitrary requirement or criterion. A brief and comparatively simple poem, which
may seem disproportionately developed in any one formal dimension
may be extremely effective.

Also, even relatively simple poems, if successful, will be found to have
a fuller development than is apparent from a casual reading. Thus in
the poem "The Dismantled Ship"—which is syntactically organized as
one sentence—the devices of sound, as well as the visual imagery, contribute to the effect. The long vowels and the interrupting consonants
retard the tempo and support the sense of the sluggishness of age. The
long deep vowels of "unused lagoon," "lonesome," "shore," contribute
to the tone of melancholy. These are the "dark" vowels in terms of mood
as well as of the sound spectrum. The alliteration of *g*'s and *d*'s, the
onomatopoeia of *batter'd,* and the harshness of the *a* sounds all reinforce
the sense of the line, "An old, dismasted, gray and batter'd ship, disabled, done." As image rises into meaning the relationship of "dismasted" to the impotence of age and of "nameless bay" to the problem
of identity as life draws close to its source in nature, becomes apparent.

Whitman's poems demonstrate that poetic form is an open rather
than a closed system. It is susceptible always to re-definition and further
development in the shifting perspective of the reader. The form of the
work is a potential of its verbal structure, and, while we may discuss it
from one viewpoint or another, we can never complete an analysis
which is commensurate with the "complexity" of the work, however
"simple" it may appear upon casual reading. Any analysis which presents
itself as systematic and completely definitive is to that extent false to

the nature of the work and a belittling of it, perhaps to the temporary advantage of the critic.

Whitman is a useful figure to consider in relation to this idea of open and relative form (which applies to prose as well as to verse) because he himself never regarded his poems as "complete" but instead revised them from edition to edition of *Leaves of Grass*. Also, although he wished his poems to tally with the world of nature, he recognized their limitations as verbal abstractions. Yet he also recognized their peculiar power—that as poetic ensembles they related to the larger scheme in ever-changing ways and that they were inexhaustible to interpretation. Consequently the act of reading, or the perception of form, was for him a dynamic never-to-be-completed process. In the 1855 preface to *Leaves of Grass* he spoke of the poet as one who brings his readers to no terminus but who leads them on a continuing quest for the meaning of the forms of art and the common life expressed through them: "Whom he takes he takes with firm sure grasp into live regions previously unattained . . . thenceforward is no rest. . . ."

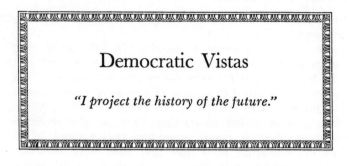

Democratic Vistas

"I project the history of the future."

The Shaping of
the American Character

by Perry Miller

In 1867 Walt Whitman brought out a revision of *Leaves of Grass*. He was constantly revising; this was the fourth version. The first had been in 1855, the second in 1856, the third in 1860. Virtually all approved and respectable critics of the time who even bothered to consider Whitman were hostile; they believed a "poetry" that could be so recklessly revised to be obviously no poetry at all. Nowadays there are many who regard him as our greatest poet; when Lucien Price asked Alfred North Whitehead what, if anything, original and distinctively American this country has produced, the philosopher answered without hesitation, "Whitman." I suspect that Whitman, at this moment, is not so popular as he was thirty years ago; if I am right, then this is a sign of the times, one which I must consider ominous. But be that as it may, Whitman's successive revisions, Whitman being what he was, are apt to come not from a heightened sense of form or from a quest for more precise language, but simply out of his constantly changing sense of the American destiny. He could never make up his mind, though at each point he had to pretend that he did and so declaim with a finality whose very flamboyance betrays the uncertainty.

In 1856 he printed one of his most interesting songs, the one called in the collected works, "As I Sat Alone by Blue Ontario's Shore." In this

"The Shaping of the American Character." From *The New England Quarterly*, XXVIII (1955), 435-454. Copyright 1955 by *The New England Quarterly*. Reprinted by permission of Perry Miller and the editors of *The New England Quarterly*.

version, and again in 1860, the poem is an exaltation of the rôle he assigned himself, the poet-prophet of democracy. But by 1867 he had lived through the central ordeal of this Republic, the war we call variously "Civil" or "Between the States." Something profoundly disturbing had happened to Walt Whitman; it is expressed not only in poems written directly out of his experience, like "Drum-Taps" and "When Lilacs Last in the Dooryard Bloom'd," but in the revisions of previous utterances. In 1856 and 1860, for instance, one line of "By Blue Ontario's Shore" had gone, "Give me to speak beautiful words! take all the rest." In 1867 this became "Give me to sing the song of the great Idea! take all the rest." After the war, he would celebrate the democracy itself, not merely the poet. These changes, commentators theorize, record a chastening of Whitman's egotism; they indicate his belated realization that this country is bigger than any man, even a Whitman, and from the realization he learned humility.

However, the sort of humility one acquires only from discovering that his nation is large and he himself small is by definition suspect. In Whitman, there are some curious additions to the postwar announcement of self-abnegation. This couplet for example:

> We stand self-pois'd in the middle, branching thence over the world;
> From Missouri, Nebraska, or Kansas, laughing attack to scorn.

Or, still more striking, this verse:

> America isolated I sing;
> I say that works made here in the spirit of other lands, are so much poison in The States.
> (How dare such insects as we assume to write poems for America?
> For our victorious armies, and the offspring following the armies?)

Recently a French critic, commenting on this passage, has called it the tirade of a narrow and contemptuous isolationism. Perhaps a Frenchman at this point in history has a reaction different from ours to a boast about the offspring following our victorious armies!

In the light of M. Asselineau's opinion, it is of some significance that Whitman himself, in the 1881 revision of *Leaves of Grass*, suppressed these pieces of strident isolationism. By then he had received further lessons in humility, not from victorious armies but from the stroke that paralyzed him; the last poems, as has often been remarked, show an aspiration toward universality with which the mood of 1867 was in open opposition. However, of one fact there can be no doubt: Walt Whitman, self-appointed spokesman for America, found himself responding in a fashion which may, indeed, be characteristic of the patriot in any country, but has been most conspicuously characteristic of the American: exulting in military victory, he proclaimed that an isolated America has nothing and should have nothing to do with the rest of the world.

This episode in the history of the text is only one out of a thousand which underscore that quality in *Leaves of Grass* that does make it so peculiarly an American book: its extreme self-consciousness. Not only does Whitman appoint himself the poet-prophet of the nation, and advertise to the point of tedium that he sings America, but in the incessant effort to find out what he is singing, what America is, he must always be revising his poems to suit a fluctuating conception. As Archibald MacLeish wrote in 1929 (he as much as Whitman shows how acutely self-conscious about nationality our artists must be), "It is a strange thing—to be an American":

> This, this is our land, this is our people
> This that is neither a land nor a race.

Whether the American public dislikes Whitman or is indifferent to him, still, in this respect he is indeed the national poet Mr. Whitehead called him. So, if we then examine closely this quality of Whitman's awareness, even though we do not pretend to be professional psychologists, we are bound to recognize that it emanates not from a mood of serene self-possession and self-assurance, as Whitman blatantly orated, but rather from a pervasive self-distrust. There is a nervous instability at the bottom of his histrionic ostentation—an anxiety which foreign critics understandably call neurotic. In fact these critics, even our friends, tell us that this is precisely what Americans are: insecure, gangling, secret worriers behind a façade of braggadocio, unable to live and to let live.

Some of the articles in the massive supplement on *American Writing To-Day* which the *Times* of London brought out in September, 1954, are by Americans, but one called "A Search for the Conscience of a People" sounds as though of English authorship; either way, it declares an opinion I have frequently heard in England and on the Continent. Americans, particularly from the early nineteenth century on, have been in search of an identity. "The Englishman," says the writer, "takes his Englishness for granted; the Frenchman does not constantly have to be looking over his shoulder to see if his Frenchiness is still there." The reason for this national anxiety is that being an American is not something to be inherited so much as something to be achieved. This, our observer concludes, is "a complex fate."

Surely it is, as complex for a nation as for a person. Yet what compounds complexity is that all the time we are searching for ourselves we keep insisting that we are a simple, uncomplicated people. We have no social classes, our regional variations are not great compared with those of France or Germany, no weight of tradition compels us to travel in well-worn ruts. From coast to coast we all buy the same standard brands in chain stores built to a standard pattern, we see the same television shows, laugh at the same jokes, adore the same movie stars, and hear the same singing commercials. How, then, can we be complex? Europe is complex—it is civilized, old, tormented with ancient memories; but we are as natural as children. Then, why are we so nervous? Why do we so worry about our identity? One can imagine an English college setting up a conference on the constitutional principles of the Cromwellian Protectorate, or on the issues of the Reform Bill of 1832, but never, I am sure, one entitled, "On Values in the British Tradition." At Oxford and Cambridge those would be so much taken for granted that even to mention them aloud would be bad form, and to insinuate that they needed discussion would become indecent exposure.

As far as I read the history of the West, I find only one other great civilization that faced an analogous predicament, and that was the Roman Empire. Not the Republic: the original Rome emerged gradually, as have the modern nations of Europe, out of the mists of legend, mythology, vaguely remembered migrations of prehistoric peoples. The Republic had traditions that nobody created, which had been there beyond the memory of mankind, atavistic attachments to the soil. But after the murderous Civil Wars and wars of conquest, the old Roman stock was either wiped out or so mixed with the races of the Mediterranean that the Empire had become as conglomerate a population as ours, the social cohesion as artificial. As with us, there was not time to let the people fuse by natural and organic growth over several centuries: Rome was no longer a country but a continent, no longer a people but an institution. The aggregation would have fallen apart in the first century B.C. had not somebody, by main force, by deliberate, conscious exertion, imposed unity upon it. Julius Caesar attempted this, but his nephew and ultimately his successor, Augustus Caesar, did it.

This analogy, as I say, has often struck me, but I should be hesitant to construct so seemingly far-fetched a parallel did I not have at least the authority of Alfred North Whitehead for entertaining it. Actually, it was a favorite speculation with Mr. Whitehead, and I may well have got it from him in some now forgotten conversation. However, it comes back to us, as though Whitehead were still speaking, in Lucien Price's *Dialogues.* Augustus Caesar's foundation of an empire would not, Whitehead agrees, satisfy our ideal of liberty, yet it saved civilization. It is, in the very deliberateness of the deed, a complete contrast to the unconscious evolution of the English constitution. Nobody here, Whitehead remarks, can say at exactly what point the idea of a limited monarchy came in; the conception originated with no one person nor at any specific time, and even today no scientifically precise definition is possible. Though the Roman Empire was not the result of any long-range plan, once it existed, it was recognized as being what it had become, and systematically organized; the British acquired their empire, as the saying goes, in a fit of absence of mind, and have never quite found a way to administer the whole of it. So they surrender to nature and let irresistible forces guide it into forms that are not at all "imperial."

Now Whitehead's point is that the only other creation of a nation and an administration by conscious effort, the only other time statesmen assumed control of historic destinies and, refusing to let nature take its course, erected by main force a society, was the American Revolution and the Constitutional Convention. To read the history of the first sessions of the Congress under President Washington in 1789 and 1790 is to be driven either to laughter or to tears, or to both. Even more than in the first years of Augustus' principate, I suspect, it presents the spectacle of men trying to live from a blueprint. The document prescribed two houses of legislators, a court, and an executive; as men of cultivation they had some knowledge of parliamentary procedure, but beyond such elementary rules of order they knew not how to behave. They did not know how to address the President, and nobody could figure in what manner a cabinet officer was related to the Congress. That is why, although certain customs have been agreed upon, such as "Senatorial courtesy," we do not have the immemorial traditions that govern, let us say, conduct in the House of Commons. Hence, when one of our customs appears to be violated, we behold a Select Committee of Senators trying to find out what the Senate is. We can do nothing by instinct.

As a matter of historical fact, Professor Whitehead might have pushed that moment of conscious decision further back than the Constitutional Convention. Settlers came to the colonies for a number of reasons that were, so to speak, in the situation rather than in their minds, yet none came without making an anterior decision in his mind. They may have been forced by famine, economic distress, a lust for gold or land, by religious persecutions, but somewhere in their lives there had to be the specific moment when they said to themselves or to each other, "Let's get out, let's go to America." The only exception to this rule is, of course, the Negroes; they came not because they wanted to but because they were captured and brought by force. Maybe that is why they, of all our varied people, seem to be the only sort that can do things by instinct. Maybe that is why Willie Mays is the greatest of contemporary outfielders.

Also, the Indians did not come by *malice prépensé*. They are the only Americans whose historical memory goes back to the origin of the land itself; they do not have to look over their shoulders to see if their Indianness is still there. So, they astonished the first Americans by acting upon instinct. One of the most charming demonstrations of this native spontaneity was Pocahontas' rush to the block to save Captain John

Smith from having his brains beaten out. Later on, Indian rushes were not so charming, but even in warfare they exhibited a headlong impetuosity that bespoke an incapacity to make deliberate plans. They could never construct an assembly line or work out a split-second television schedule.

As for Captain John Smith himself, we may doubt that this impetuous adventurer came at first to America out of the sort of conscious decision Whitehead had in mind. To begin with, America meant no more to him than Turkey, and Pocahontas no more than the Lady Tragabigzanda, who inspired his escape from slavery in Constantinople—at least, so he says. But even he, who became a temporary American by accident, after a brief two-years' experience of the land, realized that here lay a special destiny. The initial disorders at Jamestown—which were considerable—convinced him that God, being angry with the company, plagued them with famine and sickness. By the time he was summoned home, the dream of an empire in the wilderness was upon him, and he reviewed these afflictions not as merely the customary and universal rebukes of Providence upon sinners, but as ones specially dispensed for the guidance of Americans. He spent twenty-two years selflessly propagandizing for settlement. By 1624, after he had digested the lesson of his intense initiation, he had thoroughly comprehended that migrating to America was serious business, much too strenuous for those he called the "Tuftaffaty" gentlemen who had come along, as we might say, only for the ride, in the expectation of picking up easy gold from the ground. No: mere tourists, traveling nobles, would not build an empire; it needed people who, having decided to remove, would as a consequence of decision put their backs into the labor. In 1624 he reprinted and emphasized a cry he had written to the company back in 1608, when the lesson was just beginning to dawn upon him:

> When you send againe I entreat you rather send but thirty Carpenters, husbandmen, gardiners, fisher men, blacksmiths, masons, and diggers up of trees, roots, well provided; then a thousand of such as we haue: for except wee be able to lodge them, and feed them, the most will consume with want of necessaries before they can be made good for any thing.

Smith was more prophetic than even he comprehended: America has not time to make people good for anything; they have to be good for something to start with.

The outstanding case of the conscious act of decision was, we all know, the Puritan migration to New England. Whenever we find the religious incentive strong among immigrating groups, something of the same history can be found, but the New Englanders were so articulate, produced so voluminous a literature in explanation of their conduct, and through the spreading of the stock across the continent have left so deep an impress on the country, that the Puritan definition of purpose has been in effect appropriated by immigrants of other faiths, by those who in the nineteenth century left lands of a culture utterly different from the English. The act was formally committed to paper by the "Agreement" signed and ratified at Cambridge in the summer of 1629. The great John Winthrop, the Moses of this exodus, was able to give full expression to the idea even before he set foot ashore; he did it by preaching a lay sermon aboard the flagship of the fleet, on the deck of the *Arabella,* when still in mid-ocean. It was published under the title "A Modell of Christian Charity," in 1630. Chronologically speaking, Smith and a few others in Virginia, two or three at Plymouth, published works on America before the "Modell," but in relation to the principal theme of the American mind, the necessity laid upon it for decision, Winthrop stands at the beginning of our consciousness.

We wonder whether, once Southampton and Land's End had sunk beneath the eastern horizon, once he had turned his face irrevocably westward, Winthrop suddenly realized that he was sailing not toward another island but a continent, and that once there the problem would be to keep the people fixed in the mold of the Cambridge Agreement, to prevent them from following the lure of real estate into a dispersion that would quickly alter their character. At any rate, the announced doctrine of his sermon is that God distinguishes persons in this world by rank, some high, some low, some rich, some poor. Ostensibly, then, he is propounding a European class structure; but when he comes to the exhortation, he does not so much demand that inferiors remain in pious subjection to superiors, but rather he calls upon all, gentlemen and commoners, to be knit together in this work as one man. He seems apprehensive that old sanctions will not work; he wants all the company to swear an oath, to confirm their act of will. This band have entered into a Covenant with God to perform the specific work: "We have taken out a Commission, the Lord hath giuen vs leaue to drawe our owne Articles, we haue professed to enterprise these Accions vpon these and these ends." Because this community is not merely to reproduce an English social hierarchy, because over and above that, more important even than an ordered way of life, it has a responsibility to live up to certain enumerated purposes. Therefore this society, unlike any in Europe, will be rewarded by Divine Providence to the extent that it fulfills the Covenant. Likewise it will be afflicted with plagues, fires, disasters, to the extent that it fails. Profound though he was, Winthrop probably did not entirely realize how novel, how radical, was his sermon; he assumed he was merely theorizing about this projected community in relation to the Calvinist divinity, absolute sovereign of the universe. What in reality he was telling the proto-Americans was that they could not just blunder along like ordinary people, seeking wealth and opportunity for their children. Every citizen of this new society would have to know, completely understand, reckon every day with, the enunciated terms on which it was brought into being, according to which it would survive or perish. This duty of conscious realization lay as heavy upon the humblest, the least educated, the most stupid, as upon the highest, the most learned, the cleverest.

There is, I think all will acknowledge, a grandeur in Winthrop's formulation of the rationale for a society newly entered into a bond with Almighty God to accomplish "these and these ends." However, enemies of the Puritans even at the time did more than suggest that the conception also bespeaks an astounding arrogance. Who was Winthrop, critics asked, and who were these Puritans, that they could take unto themselves the notion that the Infinite God would bind himself to particular terms only with them, while He was leaving France and Germany and even England to shift for themselves? One can argue that coming down from this Puritan conception of America's unique destiny— "Wee must consider," said Winthrop, "that wee shall be as a Citty vpon a Hill, the eies of all people vppon us"—has descended that glib American phrase, "God's country," which so amuses when it does not exasperate our allies. But the important thing to note is that after a century or more of experience on this continent, the communities, especially the Puritan colonies, found the Covenant theory no longer adequate. It broke down because it tried, in disregard of experience, in disregard of the frontier and a thriving commerce, to stereotype the image of America, to confine it to the Procrustean bed of a priori conception. Not that the theology failed to account for empirical phenomena; only, the effort to keep these aligned within the original rubrics became too exhausting. The American mind discarded this notion of its personality because the ingenuity required to maintain it was more than men had time or energy to devise.

The little states suffered many adversities—plagues, wars, crop failures, floods, internal dissension. According to Winthrop's reasoning, the communities could not accept these as the normal hazards of settling a wilderness or augmenting the wealth; they had to see in every reverse an intentional punishment for their sins. By the time they had undergone several Indian wars and frequent hurricanes, a tabulation of their sins would obviously become so long as to be crushing. We can imagine, for instance, what Cotton Mather would have made in his Sabbath sermons, morning and afternoon, each over two hours in duration, of the fact that New England was struck by not one but *two* hurricanes, and that the first, proceeding according to divine appointment, carried away the steeple of his own church, the Old North. He would perfectly understand why, since the population did not immediately reform their criminal habits, even upon such a dramatic admonition, another storm must come close upon the other. Were we still livingly persuaded that we actually are God's country, we would not now be arguing with in-

surance companies or complaining about the Weather Bureau, but would
be down on our knees, bewailing the transgressions of New England,
searching our memories to recall, and to repent of, a thousand things
we have contrived to forget. We would be reaffirming our Americanism
by promising with all our hearts to mend the evil ways that brought upon
us the avenging fury of Carol and Edna.

In pious sections of America at the time of the Revolution some ves-
tiges of the Covenant doctrine remained. Historians point out how
effective was the propaganda device employed by the Continental Con-
gresses, their calling for national days of fasting and humiliations. Historians regard these appeals as cynical because most of the leaders, men
of the Enlightenment, were emancipated from so crude a theology as
Winthrop's. Certainly you find no trace of it in the Declaration of
Independence. Yet I often wonder whether historians fully comprehend
that the old-fashioned religious sanction could be dispensed with only
because the Revolutionary theorists had found a substitute which seemed
to them adequate to account for a more complex situation. Being classicists, they read Latin; while nurtured on authors of Republican Rome,
they were as much if not more trained in the concepts of the empire,
not only in writers like Tacitus and Marcus Aurelius, but in the Roman
law. Which is to say, that the imperial idea, as Augustus made it manifest, was second nature to them. Whether Madison appreciated as
keenly as Whitehead the highly conscious nature of Augustus' statesmanship, he had no qualms about going at the business of constitution
making in a legal, imperial spirit. The problem was to bring order out
of chaos, to set up a government, to do it efficiently and quickly. There
was no time to let Nature, gradually, by her mysterious alchemy, bring
us eventually to some such fruition as the British Constitution; even so,
had time not been so pressing, Madison and the framers saw nothing incongruous in taking time by the forelock, drawing up the blueprint,
and so bringing into working operation a government by fiat. Analysts
may argue that separation of powers, for instance, had in practice if not
in theory come about by historical degrees within the colonial governments, but the framers did not much appeal to that sort of wisdom.
They had a universal rule: power must not be concentrated, it must be
divided into competing balances; wherefore America decrees its individuality through a three-fold sovereign, executive, legislative, and
judicial, and then still further checks that authority by an enumerated
Bill of Rights.

The Revolutionary chiefs were patriots, but on the whole they were
less worried by the problem of working out an exceptional character
for America than the spokesmen of any other period. Patriotism was a
virtue, in the Roman sense, but one could be an ardent American without, in the Age of Reason, having to insist that there were special

reasons in America, reasons not present in other lands, why citizens must inordinately love this nation. Franklin, Jefferson, Madison were as near to true cosmopolitans as the United States has ever produced. But on the other hand, in order to win the war, pamphleteers for the patriot side did have to assert that the Revolution carried the hopes not only of America but of the world. The immense effectiveness of Thomas Paine's *Common Sense*, for example, consisted not so much in its contention that independence of England made common sense but that only America was close enough to Nature, only these simple people were so uncorrupted by the vices of decrepit civilizations, that only here could common sense operate at all.

It is a fanciful speculation, but suppose that the intellectual world of the late eighteenth century had persisted unchanged from 1776 to the present. In that case, through one and three-quarters centuries we should have had a steady and undisturbing task: merely refining on and perfecting the image of ourselves we first beheld in the mirror of the Declaration of Independence. Had there been no Romantic poetry, no novels by Scott, no railroads and steam engines, no Darwin, no machine gun, no dynamo, no automobile, no airplane, no atomic bomb, we would have had no reason to suppose ourselves other than what we were at Concord and Yorktown. We would remain forever formerly embattled farmers listening complacently from our cornfields to the echoes rolling round the world of the shot we fired, without working ourselves into a swivet worrying about whether we should again shoot. However, even before Jefferson and Adams were dead in 1826, the mind of America was already infected from abroad with concepts of man and nature which rendered those of the patriarchs as inadequate as the Covenant theology, while at the same time the nation itself was being transformed by an increase of population and of machines, and so had to rethink entirely anew the question of its identity.

The French Revolution and the Napoleonic Wars, it is a truism to say, aroused all over Europe a spirit of nationalism which the eighteenth century had supposed forever extinct. One manifestation of the new era was an assiduous search in each country for primitive, tribal, barbaric orgins. Germans went back to medieval legends, to the Niebelungenlied, to fairy tales. Sir Walter Scott gave the English a new sense of their history, so that the ideal British hero was no longer Marlborough or Pitt, but Ivanhoe, Rob Roy, and Quentin Durward, while the yeomen suddenly gloried in having come down from Gurth the Swineherd. Realizing that the evolution of English society as well as of the constitution had been organic, natural, spontaneous, illogical, the English renounced reason; they challenged America to show what more profound excuse for being it had than a dull and rationalistic convention. All at once, instead of being the hope of the enlightened world,

America found itself naked of legends, primitive virtues, archaic origins. It might be full of bustle and progress, but romantically speaking, it was uninteresting, had no personality.

Americans tried to answer by bragging about the future, but that would not serve. In the first half of the nineteenth century many of our best minds went hard to work to prove that we too are a nation in some deeper sense than mere wilfulness. At this time Europeans began that accusation which some of them still launch, which drives us to a frenzy: "You are not a country, you are a continent." Not at all, said James Fenimore Cooper; we too have our legends, our misty past, our epic figures, our symbolic heroes. To prove this, he created Natty Bumppo—Leatherstocking the Deerslayer, the Pathfinder, the embodiment of an America as rooted in the soil, as primordial as the Germany that gave birth to Siegfried.

Professor Allan Nevins recently brought out a selection from the five Leatherstocking volumes of the portions that tell the biography of Natty Bumppo, arranged them in chronological order instead of the sequence in which Cooper composed them, and thus reminded us that Cooper did create a folk-hero, achieving in his way a success comparable to Homer's. Modern readers have difficulty with Cooper's romances because they do seem cluttered with pompous courtships and tiresome disquisitions; these were not annoyances to readers in his day (though I must say that even then some critics found his women rather wooden), so that they had no trouble in appreciating the magnificence of his Scout and of Chingachgook. Mr. Nevins says that when he was a boy, he and his companions played at being Natty and Chingachgook; children nowadays do not read Cooper—I am told that if they can so much as read at all, they peruse nothing but comic books—and they play at being Superman and space cadets. But for years Cooper more than any single figure held up the mirror in which several generations of Americans saw the image of themselves they most wished to see—a free-ranging individualist, very different from Winthrop's covenanted saint or from Paine's common-sensical Revolutionary.

Cooper persuaded not only thousands of Americans that he was delineating their archetype but also Europeans. One does not readily associate the name of Balzac with Cooper, but Balzac was an enthusiastic reader of Leatherstocking and in 1841 wrote a resounding review, praising the mighty figures but explaining what was an even more important element in Cooper's achievement:

> The magical prose of Cooper not only embodies the spirit of the river, its shores, the forest and its trees; but it exhibits the minutest details, combined with the grandest outline. The vast solitudes, in which we penetrate, become in a moment deeply interesting. . . . When the spirit of solitude communes with us, when the first calm of these eternal shades pervades us, when we hover over this virgin vegetation, our hearts are filled with emotion.

Here was indeed the answer to the problem of American self-recognition! We may have come to the land by an act of will, but despite ourselves, we have become parts of the landscape. The vastness of the continent, its very emptiness, instead of meaning that we are blank and formless, makes us deeply interesting amid our solitudes. Our history is not mechanical, calculated; it is as vibrant with emotion as the history of Scott's Britain.

On every side spokesmen for the period between Jackson and Lincoln developed this thesis; by the time of the Civil War it had become the major articulate premise of American self-consciousness. Let us take one example. George Bancroft's *History of the United States* had a success with the populace at large which no academic historian today dares even dream of. When he came to the Revolution, he recast it into the imagery of nature and instinct, so that even Jefferson became as spontaneous (and as authentic a voice of the landscape) as Natty Bumppo:

> There is an analogy between early American politics and the earliest heroic poems. Both were spontaneous, and both had the vitality of truth. Long as natural affection endures, the poems of Homer will be read with delight; long as freedom lives on earth, the early models of popular legislation and action in America will be admired.

So, for Bancroft and his myriad readers, the lesson of the Revolution and the Constitution was precisely opposite to what Whitehead sees in the story. Prudent statesmanship, Bancroft says, would have asked time to ponder, "would have dismissed the moment for decision by delay." Conscious effort "would have compared the systems of government, and would have lost from hesitation the glory of opening a new era on mankind." But the common people—the race of Natty Bumppo—did not deliberate: "The humble train-bands at Concord acted, and God was with them."

We can easily laugh at such language. We may agree that Cooper and Bancroft were noble men, patriotic Americans, but to our ears something rings terribly false in their hymns to the natural nation. Perhaps the deepest flaw is their unawareness of, or their wilful blindness to, the fact that they are constructing in a most highly conscious manner an image of America as the creation of unconscious instinct. They apply themselves to supplying the country with an archaic past as purposefully as General Motors supplies it with locomotion. They recast the conception of America into terms actually as a priori as Winthrop's Covenant, and then do just what he did: they say that these spontaneous and heroic terms are objectively true, fixed and eternal. Within them and only them America shall always make decisions, shall always, like the train-bands at Concord, act in reference to their unalterable exactions. We are what we have always been, and so we are predictable. He who acts otherwise is not American.

Behind the Puritan, the Revolutionary and the Romantic conception of social identity lies still another premise; in all these formulations it is *not* articulated. I might put it roughly like this: they all take for granted that a personality, a national one as well as an individual, is something pre-existing, within which an invariable and foreseeable pattern of decision reigns. If, let us say, a man is brave, he will always act bravely. If a nation is proud, chivalric, religious, it will be Spanish; if it is frivolous, amatory, cynical, it will be French. I need hardly remind you that a powerful movement in modern thought has, in a hundred ways, called in question this "deterministic" method. There may be, and indeed there are, physical conditions, such as sex or size, such as climate or mineral resources; but these are not what make the personality we deal with, the nation we must understand. What constitutes the present being is a series of past decisions; in that sense, no act is spontaneous, no decision is imposed, either by the Covenant, by common sense, or by Nature.

In the later nineteenth century, as Romantic conceptions of the universe died out, another determined effort was made to recast the image of America in the language of Darwinian evolution. In this century, as the faith weakened that evolution would automatically carry us forward, we have, in general, reformulated our personality into a creature preternaturally adept in production—the jeep and the know-how. Each successive remodeling retains something of the previous form: we echo the Covenant not only in the phrase "God's country," but when we pray for the blessing of Heaven upon our arms and our industries, we invoke Revolutionary language in our belief that we, of all the world, are preeminently endowed with common sense; we also imagine ourselves possessed of the pioneer virtues of Natty Bumppo, by calling ourselves "nature's noblemen," yet simultaneously suppose ourselves evolving into an industrial paradise, complete with television and the deep freeze. When we try to bundle up these highly disparate notions into a single definition, we are apt to come up with some such blurb as "The American Way of Life."

I am attempting to tell a long story in too short a compass, but I hope my small point is moderately clear. As a nation, we have had a strenuous experience, as violent as that Walt Whitman records; he spent a lifetime trying to put America into his book, to discover himself bedevilled by changing insights, buffeted by unpredicted emotions, rapid shifts, bewildered by new elements demanding incorporation in the synthesis. He who endeavors to fix the personality of America in one eternal, unchangeable pattern not only understands nothing of how a personality is created, but comprehends little of how this nation has come along thus far. He who seeks repose in a unitary conception in effect abandons personality. His motives may be of the best: he wants to preserve, just as he at the moment understands it, the distinctive American essence—the

Covenant, common sense, the natural grandeur, the American Way of Life. But he fools himself if he supposes that the explanation for America is to be found in the conditions of America's existence rather than in the existence itself. A man *is* his decisions, and the great uniqueness of this nation is simply that here the record of conscious decision is more precise, more open and explicit than in most countries. This gives us no warrant to claim that we are higher in any conceivable scale of values; it merely permits us to realize that to which the English observer calls attention, that being an American is not something inherited but something to be achieved.

He says this condemns us to a "complex fate." Complexity is worrisome, imparts no serenity, only anxiety. It keeps us wondering whether we might now be something other, and probably better, than we are had we in the past decided otherwise, and this in turn makes decision in the present even more nerve-wracking. Trying to escape from such anxiety by affixing our individuality to a scheme of unchanging verities is a natural response. Yet our national history promises no success to the frantic gesture. Generalizations about the American character can amount to no more than a statistical survey of the decisions so far made, and these warrant in the way of hypotheses about those yet to be made only the most tentative estimates. However, if my analysis has any truth in it, a backhanded sort of generalization does emerge: he who would fix the pattern of decision by confining the American choice to one and only one mode of response—whether this be in politics, diplomacy, economics, literary form, or morality itself—such a one, in the light of our history, is the truly "Un-American."

An Essay on
Leaves of Grass

by William Carlos Williams

Leaves of Grass! It was a good title for a book of poems, especially for a new book of American poems. It was a challenge to the entire concept of the poetic idea, and from a new viewpoint, a rebel viewpoint, an American viewpoint. In a word and at the beginning it enunciated a shocking truth, that the common ground is of itself a poetic source. There had been inklings before this that such was the case in the works of Robert Burns and the poet Wordsworth, but in this instance the very forms of the writing had been altered: it had gone over to the style of the words as they appeared on the page. Whitman's so-called "free verse" was an assault on the very citadel of the poem itself; it constituted a direct challenge to all living poets to show cause why they should not do likewise. It is a challenge that still holds good after a century of vigorous life during which it has been practically continuously under fire but never defeated.

From the beginning Whitman realized that the matter was largely technical. It had to be free verse or nothing with him and he seldom varied from that practice—and never for more than the writing of an occasional poem. It was a sharp break, and if he was to go astray he had no one but himself to blame for it. It was a technical matter, true enough, and he would stick it out to the end, but to do any more with it than simply to write the poems was beyond him.

He had seen a great light but forgot almost at once after the first revelation everything but his "message," the idea which originally set him in motion, the idea on which he had been nurtured, the idea of democracy—and took his eye off the words themselves which should have held him.

The point is purely academic—the man had his hands full with the conduct of his life and couldn't, if they had come up, be bothered with

"An Essay on *Leaves of Grass*." From *Leaves of Grass One Hundred Years After*, edited by Milton Hindus (Stanford, Calif., 1955), pp. 22-31. Copyright 1955 by the Board of Trustees of the Leland Stanford Junior University. Reprinted by the permission of the publishers, Stanford University Press.

other matters. As a result, he made no further progress as an artist but, in spite of various topical achievements, continued to write with diminishing effectiveness for the remainder of his life.

He didn't know any better. He didn't have the training to construct his verses after a conscious mold which would have given him power over them to turn them this way, then that, at will. He only knew how to give them birth and to release them to go their own way. He was preoccupied with the great ideas of the time, to which he was devoted, but, after all, poems are made out of words not ideas. He never showed any evidence of knowing this and the unresolved forms consequent upon his beginnings remained in the end just as he left them.

Verses, in English, are frequently spoken of as measures. It is a fortunate designation as it gives us, in looking at them, the idea of elapsed time. We are reminded that the origin of our verse was the dance—and even if it had not been the dance, the heart when it is stirred has its multiple beats, and verse at its most impassioned sets the heart violently beating. But as the heart picks up we also begin to count. Finally, the measure for each language and environment is accepted. In English it is predominantly the iambic pentameter, but whether that is so for the language Whitman spoke is something else again. It is a point worth considering, but apart from the briefest of notices a point not to be considered here. It may be that the essential pace of the English and the American languages is diametrically opposed each to the other and that that is an important factor in the writing of their poetry, but that is for the coming generations to discover. Certainly not only the words but the meter, the measure that governed Whitman's verses, was not English. But there were more pressing things than abstract discussions of meter to be dealt with at that time and the poet soon found himself involved in them.

Very likely the talk and the passionate talk about freedom had affected him as it had infected the French and many others earlier. It is said that, when as a young man he lived in New Orleans, he had fallen in love with a beautiful octoroon but had allowed his friends and relatives to break up the match. It is possible that the disappointment determined the pattern of his later rebellion in verse. Free verse was his great idea! *Versos sueltos* the Spanish call them. It is not an entirely new idea, but it was entirely new to the New York Yankee who was, so to speak, waiting for it with open arms and an overcharged soul and the example of Thomas Jefferson to drive him on.

But verse had always been, for Englishmen and the colonials that imitated them, a disciplined maneuver of the intelligence, as it is today, in which measure was predominant. They resented this American with his new idea, and attacked him in a characteristic way—*on moral grounds*. And he fell for it. He had no recourse but to defend himself and the fat was in the fire. How could verse be free without being

immoral? There is something to it. It is the same attack, with a more
modern tilt to it, that undoubtedly bothers T. S. Eliot. He is one of
the best informed of our writers and would do us a great service, if
free verse—mold it as he will—is not his choice, to find us an alternative. From the evidence, he has tried to come up with just that, but
up to the present writing he has not brought the thing off.

The case of Mr. Eliot is in this respect interesting. He began writing at Harvard from a thoroughly well-schooled background and produced a body of verse that was immediately so successful that when
his poem *The Waste Land* was published, it drove practically everyone else from the field. Ezra Pound, who had helped him arrange the
poem on the page, was confessedly jealous. Other American poets had
to take second place. A new era, under domination of a return to a
study of the classics, was gratefully acknowledged by the universities,
and Mr. Eliot, not Mr. Pound, was ultimately given the Nobel Prize.
The drift was plainly away from all that was native to America, Whitman among the rest, and toward the study of the past and England.

Though no one realized it, a violent revolution had taken place in
American scholarship and the interests from which it stemmed. Eliot
had completely lost interest in all things American, in the very ideology
of all that America stood for, including the idea of freedom itself in
any of its phases. Whitman as a symbol of indiscriminate freedom was
completely antipathetic to Mr. Eliot, who now won the country away
from him again. The tendency toward freedom in the verse forms,
which seemed to be thriving among American poets, was definitely
checked and the stage was taken over for other things. I shall never
forget the impression created by *The Waste Land;* it was as if the
bottom had dropped out of everything. I had not known how much the
spirit of Whitman animated us until it was withdrawn from us. Free
verse became overnight a thing of the past. Men went about congratu-
lating themselves as upon the disappearance of something that had
disturbed their dreams; and indeed it was so—the dreams of right-
thinking students of English verse had long been disturbed by the appearance among them of the horrid specter of Whitman's free verse.
Now it was as if a liberator, a Saint George, had come just in the nick
of time to save them. The instructors in all the secondary schools were
grateful.

Meanwhile, Mr. Eliot had become a British subject and removed
himself to England where he took up residence. He became a member
of the Church of England. He was determined to make the break with
America complete, as his fellow artist Henry James had done before
him, and began to publish such poems as *Ash Wednesday* and the play
Murder in the Cathedral, and the *Four Quartets.* Something had happened to him, something drastic, something to do, doubtless, with man's
duty and his freedom in the world. It is a far cry from this to Whit-

man's thought of man as a free agent. The pendulum had gone the full swing.

It is inevitable for us to connect the happenings in the world generally with what takes place in the poem. When Mr. Eliot quit writing, when he quit writing poems, it looked as if he had got to a point where he had nowhere else to turn, and as if in his despair he had given up not only the poem but the world. A man as clever and well informed as he was had the whole world at his feet, but the only conclusion that he reached was that he wanted none of it. Especially did he want none of the newer freedom.

Not that he didn't in his verse try it on, for size, let us say, in his later experiments, particularly in *Four Quartets,* but even there he soon came to the end of his rope. The accented strophe he had definitely given up, as Wagner in the prelude to *Parsifal* had done the same, but to infer from that fact that he had discovered the freedom of a new measure was not true. It looked to me, at least, as if there were some profound depth to his probing beyond which he dared not go without compromising his religious faith. He did not attempt it. It is useful to record the limits of his penetration and the point at which he gave up his attempts to penetrate further. Just how far shall we go in our search for freedom and, more importantly, how shall our efforts toward a greater freedom be conditioned in our verses? All these decisions, which must be reached in deciding what to do, have implications of general value in our lives.

The young men who are students of literature today in our universities do not believe in seeking within the literary forms, the lines, the foot, the way in which to expand their efforts to know the universe, as Whitman did, but are content to follow the theologians and Mr. Eliot. In that, they are children of the times; they risk nothing, for by risking an expanded freedom you are very likely to come a cropper. What, in the words of Hjalmar Ekdahl in *The Wild Duck,* are you going to invent?

Men, offering their heads, have always come up with new proposals, and the world of events waits upon them, and who shall say whether it were better to close one's eyes or go forward like Galileo to the light or wait content in the darkness like the man in the next county? Whitman went forward to what to him seemed desirable, and so if we are to reject him entirely we must at least follow him at the start to find out what his discoveries were intended to signify and what not to signify.

Certainly, we are in our day through with such loose freedom as he employed in his verses in the blind belief that it was all going to come out right in the end. We know now that it is not. But are we, because of that, to give up freedom entirely? Merely to put down the lines as they happen to come into your head will not make a poem, and if, as happened more than once in Whitman's case, a poem result, who is going to tell what he has made? The man knew what he was doing, but he did not know all he was doing. Much still remains to discover, but that freedom in the conduct of the verses is desirable cannot be questioned.

There is a very moving picture of Whitman facing the breakers coming in on the New Jersey shore, when he heard the onomatopoeic waves talk to him direct in a Shakespearean language which might have been Lear himself talking to the storm. But it was not what it seemed; it was a new language, an unnamed language which Whitman could not identify or control.

For as the English had foreseen, this freedom of which there had been so much talk had to have limits somewhere. If not, it would lead you astray. That was the problem. And there was at about that time a whole generation of Englishmen, prominent among whom was Frank Harris, whom it did lead astray in moral grounds, just as there were Frenchmen at the time of the French Revolution who were led astray and are still being led astray under the difficult conditions that exist today. It is the reaction against such patterns of thought that moved Eliot and that part of the present generation which is not swallowed up by its fascination with the scene which draws them to Paris whenever they get the opportunity to go there. For in your search for freedom—which is desirable—you must stop somewhere, but where exactly shall you stop? Whitman could not say.

To propose that the answer to the problem should lie in the verse itself would have been to those times an impertinence—and the same would be the case even now. The Greeks had their Dionysia in the spring of the year, when morals could be forgotten, and then the control of life resumed its normal course. In other words, they departmentalized their lives, being of an orderly cast of mind, but we do not lend ourselves easily to such a solution. With us it is all or nothing, provided we are not caught at it. Either we give ourselves to a course of action or we do not give ourselves. Either we are to be free men or not free men—at least in theory. Whitman, like Tom Paine, recognized no limits and that got him into trouble.

But the waves on the Jersey shore still came tumbling in, quieting him as their secret escaped him, isolating him and leaving him lonesome—but possessed by the great mystery which won the world to his side. For he was unquestionably the child of the years. What was the wave that moved the dawning century also moved him and demanded his recognition, and it was not to be denied. All the discoveries and inventions which were to make the twentieth century exceed all others, for better or worse, were implicit in his work. He surpassed the ritualistic centuries which preceded him, just as Ehrlich and Koch and finally Einstein were to exceed Goethe. It was destined to be so, and the

when a basic change has occurred in our underlying concern
interference in the way it will work itself out.

didn't know anything about this, nor does Mr. Eliot take
considerations nor Father Merton either, but if they had to
satisfactory poetic line it had and still has to be done ac-
his precept. For we have learned, if we have learned any-
the past, that the principles of physics are immutable. Best,
ot approve of what writing has become, to follow in Mr.
eps.

mportant to man's fate that these matters be—if anything
to man's fate in this modern world. At least, you cannot
that have been taken in the past. And you don't know,
o not know, what may come of it. No more than Whitman
is struggle to free verse may have implied and may still
no matter how, at the moment, the world may have for-
he books are not closed even though the drift in the tide
t may at the moment be all the other way. It cannot so
ersed itself. Something is still pending, though the final
thing has not yet crystallized. Perhaps that is the reason
sion. There are too many profitable leads in other asso-
the intelligence for us to draw back now.

the leads which are *not* aesthetic tended to take us in
ntury? By paying attention to detail and our telescopes
es and the reinterpretations of their findings, we realize
ong since broken from the confinement of the more rigid
It is reasonable to suppose that he will in the future, in
setbacks, continue to follow the same course.

mself on the earth whether he likes it or not, with no-
o. What then is to become of him? Obviously we can't
e shall be destroyed. Then if there is no room for us
we shall, in spite of ourselves, have to go *in*: into the
the poetic line, for our discoveries. We have to break
make room for ourselves, whatever may be our tragedy
e may fear it. By making room within the line itself
ns, Whitman revealed himself to be a worthy and
of his age and, to boot, a farseeing one.

New World of which he was a part gave him birth. He had invented
a new way of assaulting fate. "Make new!" was to him as it was to
Pound much later on an imperious command which completely controlled him.

If he was to enlarge his opportunity he needed room, in verse as in
everything else. But there were to be no fundamental changes in the
concepts that keep our lives going at an accepted pace and within
normal limits. The line was still to be the line, quite in accord with
the normal contours of our accepted verse forms. It is not so much that
which brought Whitman's verse into question but the freedom with
which he laid it on the page. There he had abandoned all sequence and
all order. It was as if a tornado had struck.

A new order had hit the world, a relative order, a new measure
with which no one was familiar. The thing that no one realized, and
this includes Whitman himself, is that the native which they were
dealing with was no longer English but a new language akin to the
New World to which its nature accorded in subtle ways that they did
not recognize. That made all the difference. And not only was it new
to America—it was new to the world. There was to be a new measure
applied to all things, for there was to be a new order operative in the
world. But it has to be insisted on that it was not disorder. Whitman's
verses seemed disorderly, but ran according to an unfamiliar and a
difficult measure. It was an order which was essential to the new world,
not only of the poem, but to the world of chemistry and physics. In this
way, the man was more of a prophet than he knew. The full significance
of his innovations in the verse patterns has not yet been fully disclosed.

The change in the entire aesthetic of American art as it began to
differ not only from British but from all the art of the world up to this
time was due to this tremendous change in measure, a relative measure,
which he was the first to feel and to embody in his works. What he was
leaving behind did not seem to oppress him, but it oppressed the others
and rightly so.

It is time now to look at English and American verse at the time
Whitman began to write, for only by so doing can we be led to discover
what he did and the course that lay before him. He had many formidable rivals to face on his way to success. But his chief opponent was,
as he well knew, the great and medieval Shakespeare. And if any confirmation of Shakespeare's sacrosanct position in the language is still
sought it is easily to be obtained when anything is breathed mentioning
some alteration in the verse forms which he distinguished by using
them. He may be imitated as Christopher Fry imitates him, but to
vary or depart from him is heresy. Taken from this viewpoint, the
clinical sheets of Shakespeare as a writer are never much studied. That
he was the greatest word-man that ever existed in the language or out
of it is taken for granted but there the inquiry ends.

Shakespeare presented Whitman with a nut hard to crack. What to do with the English language? It was all the more of a problem since the elements of it could not be presented at all or even recognized to exist. As far as the English language was concerned, there was only to use it and to use it well according to the great tradition of the masters.

And indeed it was a magnificent tradition. At the beginning of the seventeenth century it had reached an apogee which it had, to a great extent, maintained to the present day and of which it was proud and jealous. But when Shakespeare wrote, the laurels were new and had so recently been attained and had come from such distinguished achievements that the world seemed to pause for breath. It was a sort of noon and called for a halt. The man himself seemed to feel it and during an entire lifetime did no more than develop to the full his talents. It was noon sure enough for him, and he had only to stretch out in the sun and expand his mood.

Unlike Whitman, he was or represented the culmination of a historic as well as literary past whose forms were just coming to a head after the great trials which were to leave their marks on the centuries. There had been Chaucer, but the language had come of age since then as had the country. Now America had been discovered and the world could not grow much larger. Further expansion, except in a limited degree, was unlikely, so that the poet was left free to develop his world of detail but was not called upon to extend it. More was not necessary than to find something to do and develop it for the entire span of a long life. But as always with the artist, selection was an important point in the development.

For instance, as his sonnets show, Shakespeare was an accomplished rhymer, but he gave it up early. The patches of heroic couplet which he wrote for the Players in *Hamlet* are among the best examples of that form. Yet his main reliance was on blank verse—though he did, on occasion, try his hand at a triple accent which he rejected without more than a thought. The demands of the age called for other things and he was, above everything else, a practical man.

Practicing for so long a time upon the iambic pentameter, he had the opportunity to develop himself prodigiously in it. Over the years he shows a technical advance, a certain impatience with restraint in his work which makes it loose and verges more toward the conformation of prose. There is a great difference between Shakespeare's earlier and later work, the latter being freer and more natural in tone.

A feeling for prose began to be felt all through his verse. But at his death the form began to lapse rapidly into the old restrictions. It got worse and worse with the years until all the Elizabethan tenor had been stripped away, or as Milton phrased it speaking of his illustrious predecessor:

Sweetest Shakespeare,
Warbled his native wo

With Milton came Cromwell and the
speare was forgotten, together with th
as Whitman today is likely to be fc
verses and all that refers to him.

The interest that drove Whitman
Shakespeare at the end of his life in
written verse, to find more of expres
employed. But the consequences of
drastic and amount in the end to it
of a supreme genius is not easy.

From what has been said thus fa
to imitate Shakespeare; he was par
repeat itself. All imitations of the
empty shells, which have merely t
anything is now to be created, it
if he was to do anything of momen
may have bowed down to the ma
had any meaning at all. And hi
was such that he had no alternati

Though he may not have kno
of the age itself had been brou
which he could not identify any
matter how acute his instincts
chemistry, in physics, in abnor
of the telephone or the disclos
troleum? He knew only, as dic
verse, that something had occu
tional aesthetic and that he co
he acted.

We have to acknowledge at
complex concerns of the worl
the mechanical are likely to s
root. One may be much in ac
in the end a great equalizing
of the advance in the struc
advance in the conception of
no choice in these matters;
changes that are taking plac
And when time itself is cone
that may sound, the constr
accepted with a similar int

about, but
it brooks n
Whitman
it into his
construct a
cording to
thing from
if you do n
Eliot's footst
For it is
is important
retrace steps
you simply d
knew what l
imply for us
saken him. T
of our interes
soon have rev
shape of the
for the regres
ciated fields of
Where have
the present ce
and microscop
that man has l
of his taboos.
spite of certain
Man finds h
where else to g
stand still or w
on the outside
cell, the atom,
the old apart to
and however w
for his inventic
courageous man

Walt Whitman
as American Spokesman

by Richard Chase

[The speakers in the following dialogue, so the author informs us, "in order to give a clear idea of themselves . . . speak, a little artificially, as members of different generations. Yet they all illustrate different facets of the 'interim' or cold-war state of mind which has typified the last ten or fifteen years of American life." "Maggie Motive" is "a glamorous amateur and woman of projects, out of a gay past." "Rinaldo Schultz" is an "optimist, engineer, and newly naturalized American." "George Middleby" is a "solid citizen of the new generation." "Ralph Headstrong" is "a professor, middle aging."—R.H.P.]

MAGGIE: I insist that we talk about Whitman. Rinaldo won't mind. I happen to know that he is fond of Whitman.

RINALDO: Certainly I won't mind. I notice, however, that whenever I talk to the pessimistic and world-weary Americans about Whitman, they think I am a mad European full of naïve optimism and an unexamined belief in progress. They say I have not considered the nature of evil.

GEORGE: But Maggie, you cannot be, as it were, serious in saying that Whitman is funny, I mean as a comic poet is funny. I think of him as uttering vague, humorless, rhetorical assertions about Democracy. Then, too, he keeps solemnly assuring us that he has experienced life to the full, but he never gives us any sense of real experience or knowledge of the actual world. Instead he gives us either empty abstractions or lists of things out of the newspaper morgue, the primer of American history, the dictionary, and the atlas. Of course, he is very "American," but I don't really accept him as spokesman of his country, although I know that many people regard him as such.

"Walt Whitman as American Spokesman" (Original title: "Comedians All"). From *The Democratic Vista* by Richard Chase (New York, 1958), pp. 104-115. Copyright © 1958 by Richard Chase. Reprinted by permission of the author and the publisher, Doubleday & Company, Inc.

MAGGIE: What do you say to that, Rinaldo?

RINALDO: As for Whitman being a comic poet, I believe that he is, although this is certainly not what I would say first about him. First of all he is the celebrant of American material and spiritual progress, of the dynamic, open, productive New World, with all of its brash power. I know that most Americans are ashamed of this side of Whitman, thinking that he is little better than the inspired George Babbitt when he made his passionate speech about the Standardized American to the Boosters Club. But Whitman is not Babbitt, and there is no reason to be ashamed of him, naïve and strident as he occasionally is. It is true that Whitman is very abstract on the one hand and given to making "catalogues" on the other, but I think he makes real aesthetic capital out of this habit of mind. As for being the spokesman of his country, I positively assert that he is—and by no means only as the inspired Rotarian or political prophet but because he reflects many dilemmas and contradictions, many subtle turns of mind and speech that strike me as very American indeed.

MAGGIE: I think George takes him too hard. What is your naïve and unreflecting response to Walt when he says, "I have never read Mill. What did he stand for, teach, saliently promulge?" I wouldn't trade that delicious "saliently promulge" for all the language of *The Golden Bowl*.

GEORGE: It is a delightful oddity, I admit.

MAGGIE: As another test case, what about these lines from "Song of the Exposition" in which Whitman welcomes the muse of poetry as "the illustrious emigre" who has left the fabled haunts of Europe and come to America. She is

> Bluff'd not a bit by drain-pipe, gasometers, artificial fertilizers,
> Smiling and pleas'd with palpable intent to stay,
> She's here, install'd among the kitchen ware!

GEORGE: What do I think of that? Well, that it's a free country and that if Whitman wants to depict the Muse as one of the TV kitchen goddesses of the hard sell, it's all right with me. The lines are amusing. But I should think that you, glamorous amateur, would be the first to object to the rather obvious and deplorable philistinism of taking the erstwhile nymph of the Fountain of Arethuse and plunking her down among the Norges, Hotpoints, and Coldspots.

RINALDO: I think those lines are delightful and witty. I trust my response and leave it to George to worry about philistinism.

MAGGIE: Gaiety and the excellent arrangement of words transmute all, even philistinism. How about the moment in "Song of Myself" when Whitman pauses before embarking on an evolutionary extravaganza and gravely observes: "I find I incorporate gneiss"?

GEORGE: Yes, I remember that. It really is a great comic moment. But the question that bothers me is: When we smile at something Whitman says, are we smiling with him or at him?

MAGGIE: I would stake my soul on its being *with* him in this case, as in most of the Whitman passages I remember best. True, we often laugh at him when he is not laughing at himself—that has unhappily become the standard response to Whitman, though it was not so in my youth. Many of his sillier passages warrant this kind of laughter. Yet at other times, when Whitman is functioning as the great comic poet he is, we laugh *with* him. Sometimes, to be sure, when we laugh with him, we suspect he is not laughing enough—that his comedy is more or less unintentional. But isn't it true that in every great man who has a streak of humor, the humor is partly unconscious?

RINALDO: That is surely true. I can say, too, that Maggie has perfectly expressed the response I have had to Whitman, ever since I had enough English to read him. A good deal of the true quality comes through in German, French, and Italian translation.

GEORGE: Did Whitman ever say he was a comic poet?

RALPH: In effect he did, yes. When one of the Camden friends of his old age called him an incorrigible "comedian" because of something he had said, Whitman replied that "one might end up worse" and declared: "I pride myself on being a real humorist underneath everything else."

MAGGIE: I don't say that Whitman is first and foremost a comic writer. But especially in "Song of Myself" the comic poet is heard—the Dionysian humor of the poet whose room was adorned, as I remember reading, by two pictures, "one of Silenus and one of Bacchus." But aside from any and all argument, Whitman is funny, he makes me laugh, he makes me smile even oftener. So I simply conclude that this reaction is the proper one and that one highroad to an appreciation of Whitman is his humor. Am I right, Ralph? What do you think of Walt?

RALPH: May I turn that question over to Rinaldo?

RINALDO: I think Whitman is not the greatest of your nineteenth-century writers, but that he is the most delightful and valuable. He is an ever-flowing source of inspiration. From what I know of the critics of the last two decades, they have assumed that because in some obvious ways the Whitman influence has been bad, it has been all bad. They have assumed that whatever was good about Whitman has long since been discovered and its influence exhausted. I am bold enough to assert that they were wrong on both counts. We have already, at least for this epoch, assimilated Hawthorne and most of Melville. We have absorbed from them, that is, whatever can do us any good. Whitman is of the future.

RALPH: I agree with that, although in subscribing to what Rinaldo has said, I would not mean to reinstate Whitman as the "focal center" of American culture—the position assigned to him by Van Wyck Brooks and by the 1920's in general. Whitman's occupation of the focal center is too strongly contested by writers very unlike him, notably Melville. Which is one way of saying that our culture is multiform, and has no focal center.

Maggie is playing the sibyl tonight. But her idea that Whitman is a comic poet does not sound sibylline to me. It sounds both obvious and profound. The comic sense, as the theoreticians tell us, is often born of incongruities and contradictions. Any moderately well-disposed reader of Whitman will see that he is very far from stamping out distinctions and inner tensions with his flow of universals and abstractions and his sometimes neurotic desire to "merge" with everyone and everything. Take another test case:

> Do I contradict myself?
> Very well then I contradict myself,
> (I am large, I contain multitudes.)

The tendency used to be to pass this off as mere bravado, or to use it as proof of the self-confessed intellectual and literary incompetence of the poet, or (if one felt favorably toward Whitman) to say that it referred to a Hegelian universe. If one wanted to defend Whitman, in other words, one felt that it was necessary to justify the contradictions of his personality and of his work or to show that he wrote good poetry in spite of them. But nowadays one should be ready to accept his contradictions as integral oppositions and polarities, not of the Hegelian order, but as the elements of a more or less sustained ironic view with which Whitman regarded himself and the world. There is an intermittent but strong comic intent, which not only appears in poems like "Song of Myself" but is carried over into the great elegiac poems—for example "As I Ebb'd with the Ocean of Life," where the poet momentarily faces the ultimate irrationality of the universe while

> the real Me stands yet
> untouch'd, untold, altogether unreach'd,
> Withdrawn far, mocking me with mock-congratulatory signs and
> bows,
> With peals of distant ironical laughter at every word I have written,
> Pointing in silence to these songs, and then to the sand beneath.

To take Whitman as existing in or through his polarities is the first step toward a fuller acceptance and enjoyment of his work. It is the poet who "knitted the old knot of contrariety" that appeals to the reader who is free of the tiresome old prejudices against our greatest poet.

RINALDO: Most of the professors seem to regard Whitman as some sort of philosopher, don't they? They want to "place" him in relation to Neoplatonism, pan-psychism, and God knows what all. No?

RALPH: Yes. The routine academician likes Whitman the "sublime" poet of time and space, Whitman the mystic, the stoic, the Quaker, the cosmic thinker. He pays little attention to Whitman the poet of the self, and is embarrassed by the poet's boastfulness and vaunting Americanism. He explains away or discounts Whitman's poses. He understands Whitman's contradictions, ambiguities, and ironies, not as native to the man, but as inadvertent results of his intellectual naïveté.

Thus when Whitman's official biographer remarks that "this was the real Walt Whitman, undiscriminating, easily stimulated by noise, color, and movement, happy to lose himself in the ceaseless flux of people going and coming," I want to reply: No, that is the mistake of D. H. Lawrence and Santayana and all those who see in Whitman only his "merging" with experience and do not see the recalcitrance with which Whitman could also meet life. The routine academician does not understand the Whitman who described himself as "furtive" and "artful." He does not perceive the alien, neurotic, divided, covertly musing Whitman, the envious, fearful, power-seeking, sagacious Whitman who could stand aside from life and adopt a series of attitudes toward it.

For after all, however much Whitman might pose as a burly proletarian with flowing beard, open collar, and pants tucked in boots, he was in fact a petty-bourgeois intellectual. His life is a series of such paradoxes and symbolic gestures. His charlatanism is a part of the whole man and a part of his work. And, charlatan or not, one of the most consistently remarkable things about him is his ability to make out of his life a series of indestructible ideals, of exemplary acts which belong to any American's cultural heritage. Whitman is only somewhat less recalcitrant to the miscellaneous circumstance of his life as the enfeebled sage of Camden, in his late years, than he had been as the nursing father and hospital visitor of the middle years, or as the proletarian Pan and Christlike carpenter and common man of the period just before the publication of *Leaves of Grass*.

Well, fair Sibyl, what have you to say to all this? Have you a reprise or a summary?

MAGGIE: It appears that Whitman appeals to anyone who reads him with any fresh excitement as the comic poet, the elegist, the singer of the plight and career of the self, the creator both in his personal life and in his poems of various ideal images which we can regard with affection and respect.

GEORGE: But isn't there a danger of being too sophisticated about Whitman?

RALPH: Yes. One can even over-respond to Whitman's own sophistication (he is always setting traps like that), and thus neglect his simplicity, his plain democratic faith, his undistorted intuition of the natural sources of being. However many ironies and ambiguities his recalcitrance to life may generate, one of the ways in which he appeals to us is not in the tensions of his mind but in his "loafing," his flowing, pleasurable intimacy with the world around him. It is easy to smile (but wasn't Walt smiling too?) at the surprised and delighted poet who calls himself a "caresser of life," the musing Dionysus to whom life cries "Ahoy! from the rocks of the river." But it is not so easy, so hectic in us are the distortions of will and intellect, to honor Whitman's receptivity to experience and to recognize the liberating effect it had on a hitherto squeamish American mentality.

GEORGE: I see I must have another look at the Good Gray. Still, I don't suppose you deny there is a lot of awful fustian in him.

MAGGIE: Oh, an immense amount.

RALPH: It was there from the beginning, even in his greatest poem, "Song of Myself." And it got worse as Whitman grew older. Despite his isolation and his relatively small circle of readers, Whitman gradually succumbed to the peculiar pressure a democracy puts on its great writers to become self-publicists, pundits, prophets, theologians, and political oracles.

RINALDO: I have noticed that. Now Faulkner seems in danger of this democratic fate.

GEORGE: Supposing that as I reread Whitman, I should find that you are right about his peculiar excellence, still I should protest that he knew little of the actualities of institutional life, of the life of society.

RINALDO: George is right about that. Walt is too preoccupied with the self as something apart from history and from social and political reality. He thinks of it merely in its ethical, spiritual, and literary relations. In *Democratic Vistas* he simply assumes that history is benign and maternal. One of the things that amazes a European reader is Whitman's belief that America is exempt from all such historical catastrophes as overtook "feudalism"—by feudalism, meaning everything that happened before 1776. In effect, he assumes that America is exempt not only from historical tragedy but from history itself. His sense of things in *Democratic Vistas* is that history really ended at the inception of the Republic, and that from then on change would never be radical but would be merely a matter of gradual unfolding and realization. This view is not only historically unrealistic, as viewed by us unhappy citizens of the atomic age, but it is oddly conservative too.

GEORGE: Yes, I've noticed that. How do we reconcile this conservatism with the usual view of Whitman as the prophet of the future and the "promulger" of those radical changes which were supposed finally to bring about a truly democratic world?

RALPH: Everything Rinaldo says about Whitman's lack of historical realism is true. As for the contradiction between his conservatism and his radicalism, there are many things to be noted, the most obvious being that this contradiction, as I am sure Rinaldo will agree, is extremely common among Americans. One way of getting at it is to notice what Whitman meant by "prophecy." Do you recall what he says in *Specimen Days?* He says "the word prophecy is much misused; it seems narrow'd to prediction merely. That is not the main sense of the Hebrew word translated 'prophet'; it means one whose mind bubbles up and pours forth as a fountain, from inner divine spontaneities revealing God. Prediction is a very minor part of prophecy." Although he is perhaps not speaking directly of social prophecy, what he says here accords with that sense he gives us in *Democratic Vistas* that the purpose of prophecy is to reveal a perfect dispensation already given, but now debased, distorted, or imperfectly realized. Like many, perhaps most, prophets, Whitman employs radically novel emotions, an apparently disruptive philosophical indeterminism, and a new language in behalf of conservative ideals. And thus in *Democratic Vistas* he commits himself to an implied conservatism strangely at odds with his declared principles.

GEORGE: But is there any intellectual substance to his conservatism?

RALPH: No. Whitman's conservatism is real enough as a prophetic attitude and as a form of instinctive prudence. He makes apparent declarations of principle in his later years, such as "I am a conservative of conservatives." But these do not constitute a "position." So that after all, his conservative tendencies as they appeal to us in his poems and dithyrambic prose remain memorable impulses merely, and do not, on the level of ideas, affect in any way the buoyant democratic idealism which also makes itself felt in *Democratic Vistas* or the radical utopian vision of "Song of Myself" or "Song of the Open Road."

So you see, George, the contradictoriness of Whitman's politics is typical of all the "old knots of contrariety" which are found in his personality and his work. In Whitman's mind political radicalism, though dominant, is held in a state of ironic tension with political conservatism. In *Specimen Days*, Whitman noticed a similar conflict in Carlyle, although in Carlyle he found that conservatism dominated; and he spoke eloquently of the "two conflicting agonistic elements" that "seem to have contended" in Carlyle's mind. We will always be wrong about Whitman, the man and his works, if we think of him as in any way monolithic or single-mindedly tendentious, or if we think of him as being merely confused. Whitman too was "agonistic." And it is not out of any love of literary intricacy for its own sake, but in recognition of the facts and because one wants to arrive at a steady and untroubled appreciation of his simplicities, that one tries to conceive of Whitman in his contrarieties.

GEORGE: As I recall, it was Santayana who said that Americans do not regard Whitman as the "spokesman of the tendencies of his country," that he appeals only to the "dilettanti" and that only foreigners regard him as a representative American.

MAGGIE: I love that "dilettanti"! It's so—so *Italian*.

RINALDO: Santayana has hit on an unhappy truth. I do not understand why Americans disown their great spokesman.

RALPH: Obviously Whitman has never been read by a large proportion of his countrymen. And in our drab decade, the literary people have not responded to Walt. But Whitman really is an authentic spokesman for the tendencies of his country. In describing Carlyle as "agonistic" Whitman recognized the fact that to exist in one's contrarieties is not an exclusively American fate. Yet Whitman's writings show his perception that although American democracy offers to the world an appearance of unrelieved uniformity, contrariety is in fact more nearly of the essence of life in America than it has ever been in any great civilization. We now begin to see, perhaps for the first time, the extent to which the life and works of Whitman exemplify what this fate may mean to Americans.

The Poetry of Praise

by Josephine Miles

Often we think of the main tradition in American poetry as that of the intense and cryptic metaphors of Emerson, Dickinson, Frost, and Eberhart, and we think of the very opposite style of Whitman, as almost alien, unexplainable. Under the scrutiny of the metaphysical critics for whom irony and paradox are major criteria of value, the loose clusterings of *Leaves of Grass* seem to become almost an historical anomaly.

What I should like to try is to describe briefly the historical nature of the high style which we see not only in Whitman but also in Anne Bradstreet, in Whittier, in Pound and Hart Crane, especially in many Californians from Charles Erskine Scott Wood on to the active present, to suggest its essential differences in structure and vocabulary from other basic American styles, and to suggest what are its powers for our future. While it is a style that many of us cannot write in, it is one we may become increasingly aware of. In the past year, a number of books have been concerned with it: notably Miller, Shapiro, and Slote's *Start with the Sun*, Wayne Shumaker's *Literature and the Irrational*, and Ernest Tuveson's *The Imagination as a Means of Grace*.

The classical rhetoricians distinguished three sorts of style—the low or colloquial, the middle observational and meditational, the high, ceremonial. Critics today have not regarded these distinctions as useful, because they have wanted to treat all poetry as a function of the first or second low or natural styles. For example, T. S. Eliot, though he has made allowances for Milton, and though he defines three different *voices* in poetry, makes these voices all non-Miltonic, all versions of dramatic colloquial poetry. The high style has been ignored, or at best, since Pope's *Peri Bathous*, has had an unfavorable press. Yet if we think of the high style also as *deep,* not only as empyrean but as subterranean and submarine, I believe we may recognize its serious function for the

"The Poetry of Praise." From *The Kenyon Review*, XXIII (Winter, 1961), 104-125. Copyright 1961 by *The Kenyon Review*. Revised by Josephine Miles for publication in this volume, and reprinted by her permission and that of the editor of *The Kenyon Review*.

present day. To clear and polished surfaces, it adds depths, however murky; to the objectivities of thought, action, and the thing in itself, it adds the subjectivity of inward feeling tumultuously expressed. Like the word *altus* in Latin, which means both high and deep, it relates the gods of the solar system to the gods of the solar plexus. Indeed it is one of the three great modes of poetry through time, and we may look to see how, historically, it has come so strongly into practice in America in its special complex of sound-structure, sentence-structure, and sense.

When American poetry began with the American revolutions of the seventeenth and eighteenth centuries, it was a poetry not of revolt but of enthusiasm, not analysis of America's situation but panegyric for the American land. In a century and a half it has not materially changed; despite the fashions of irony, drama, and complex involvement in the present day, still a prevailing tone is praise; and still a prevailing substance, the country's bounty and beauty. "My country 'tis of thee, Sweet land of liberty, I love thy rocks and rills, Thy woods and templed hills. . . ." These words have prospered and endured longer and stronger than the militant political ones for "Columbia the gem of the ocean" or "Oh say can you see by the dawn's early light What so proudly we hailed at the twilight's last gleaming." Our popular care has been not so much for the America of conflict, trouble, and doubt, as for the America of triumphant abundance. "From the mountains, to the prairies, to the oceans white with foam."

Thinking of the satiric models of the late eighteenth century, of Pope, for example, whom American gentlemen idolized; thinking of America's own native skepticism in the later generation of Emerson and Holmes; and thinking of the jazz of the twentieth century, we may well call into doubt any such generalization about our poetic tradition until we look at its sources.

In the first place, consider the nature or natures of English poetry from which America stemmed, the poetry, that is, of the Renaissance of the sixteenth and seventeenth centuries: we can think what it is like if we think of Chaucer and the Chaucerian tradition: a lively, active, humorous, and intensely human poetry, with people in it, and the sense of their relationships, their stations, high and low, with lords, knights, ladies, kings, fathers and sons living, loving, seeking, giving, taking, telling, in a world of interaction. This world of Skelton, Sackville, the pastoralists and the satirists came to a narrower lyrical focus in two ways: in the specific relation of a courtier to his lady, the poetry of courtly love and Donne's mockery of it; and in the specific relation of the poet to his God, as in the metaphysical verse of Herbert, Herrick, and Vaughan. Speaking either to lady or to God, the poet was colloquial, argumentative, dramatic; the lyric could be the scene from a play; and it was usually more figurative than literal in expression, using irony, exaggeration, and transformation of accepted categories to make its intellectual point. As a whole, this has been called the poetry of wit; there have been many admirers of it but few inheritors in America: none, except perhaps Frost, so close as Hardy or Auden in England.

Concurrent with this verse in the sixteenth and seventeenth centuries ran a kind which was consciously more classical, more objective and observational. It tended to use a long smooth line rather than intricate stanzas, and to describe rather than to argue, in the tradition of Virgil's *Georgics* or of Horace's *Satires*. For a while in England, its function was mainly satiric or deliberative: to mark the fall of a prince in history and cause, to analyze and mock something so specific as political factions or something so general as the foolishness and corruption of mankind; this was social poetry, and its greatest successful exponents were Dryden and Pope, whom the American colonists read avidly in order to keep track of what was wrong in London and the world, as they would read Arnold in the nineteenth century and T. S. Eliot in the twentieth. The more positive and cheerful descriptions of the land and its products, in the Virgilian tradition, grew up more slowly in England and for some reason less richly, but as they grew, served to support and strengthen a third kind of poetry which was just beginning to emerge, and which did not reach full force until the revolutionary and democratic eighteenth century, the poetry of rhapsody, the ode, hymn, dithyramb of praise. Familiar in the Homeric Hymns and in the Odes of Pindar, and powerfully joined by the Hebraic tradition of the Psalms, this was the form which grew in force from Spenser and Sylvester to More and Milton and which provided the whole basis of the vast odes of the eighteenth century, Thomson's pioneering book of *The Seasons*, the work of the Wartons, and Blake's Prophetic Books.

This third kind of English poetry, along with its more classical Virgilian counterpart, was what America brought across the ocean in full force. Not the earlier humanistic verse prevailed here, nor the satiric, nor even the religious and metaphysical work of the seventeenth century, traces of which we see in such early poets as Edward Taylor; but rather the newest, most revolutionary verse which England had to offer, the work of the Whig democrats, of the Protestants, and of the philosophers of benevolence like Shaftesbury and Locke, the work of men not more than a generation older than the first solid poetic group in America; the writers of the new nation, John Trumbull, Timothy Dwight, Philip Freneau, Joel Barlow, and their successors Sigourney, Percival, Drake, and Halleck. These took on wholeheartedly the new vocabulary of English rhapsody, and carried it into the present, while England itself in the nineteenth century nearly abandoned this tradition, returning to it in the twentieth under the leadership of American augmentation and innovation.

This is not the pattern of relationship and development we are usually given by scholars, yet it is a believable one, if we remember some clear distinctions. First, both the religious verse and the social verse of the seventeenth century, which the Puritans might have brought with them directly, with their love of moral criticism and their sense of a personal god, was after all not *their* sort of verse, but indeed the verse they were fleeing, as it was aristocratic and intellectual rather than democratic and enthusiastic. The good Puritan book was the Bible itself, and works most reliant on Biblical language and concept, like Sylvester's translation of Du Bartas' *Divine Week*, for example, meant most to the first tentative and isolated poets of America like Anne Bradstreet. This "tenth muse lately sprung up in America" was more Hebraic than the other nine muses; and sought sometimes the high style of ceremony, not always the low style of colloquy, because she held strongly to Biblical and Pindaric tradition.

Also, the high style seemed suited to the high adventure of America. Remembering that a translation of Ovid's *Metamorphoses* was the first English poetry written on this continent, by George Sandys in Virginia, as early as 1616, we may realize that men's minds were attuned to the idea of marvels and transformations here, of richness and abundance and of a suitably rich diction. Not Horace's mellow humor, not Catullus' sophisticated individuality, but something rarer, if we must be classical, like Ovid or like Virgil, would do better; and nothing was too good.

Thirdly, the political mentor of the constitution makers was John Locke, and it is not unnatural that our poetical mentors should have been his friends and followers, successors to the revolution of 1688, not old-regime roundheads but new parliamentarians, libertarians, latitudinarians, believers in progress and the pursuit of happiness. Here was the psychology of sense and common sense, of the marvels of wonder and imagination; here was the philosophy of men born equal and much alike; here was the cosmic science which followed Newton and Boyle, seeing the universe in wider and wider terms; here was the belief in physical laws and universal truths.

These all fitted together, the alliance of Protestant with Whig in political enthusiasm, the sense of the high style, the philosophy of universals, in encouraging a general ceremonious American style, stressing not what was peculiar or individual, or singular in America, but what it shared with the universe at large, namely, nature itself, in its abundance and splendor. Eighteenth century philosophers and critics had noted that the materials of satire were particularities, the oddities of men, the specific details which stood for trivia; by an inversion of logic, then, the poets in America felt that when they wrote about their country's own singularities they were in a sense mocking her—thus the many satiric poems, half-hearted in their specific characterizations which seemed to lead away from praise, yet eager to record the qualities and characteristics of the American scene.

Here was a dilemma for the poets: how to write a great and noble poem about a special place and situation, America, when universality not specialness was great and noble. The answer came gradually, in the stressing of those traits in which the country was not singular but was, rather, superlative, the traits of natural divine endowment. Once this pattern of emphasis was established, it was not broken even by those later nineteenth century poets who cried for the romantic richness of distinguishing detail: they got no further complexity of human American character nor even more complexity of nature. There was a lot of talk about more bobolinks and grasshoppers for the realism of the scene, but poetry persisted in lofty generality, in the sublime and universal mode which crossed the Atlantic from England and established itself strongly on these shores in philosophic democracy and Protestant theology of praise of the works of God. We are often confused when we look back upon this transit, because we expect a low, modest, and sober plain style from Puritans and democrats. But the eighteenth century democracy of man was based in the universality of sense impressions, the common accessibility of beauty, and the development from sense to soul; the eighteenth century religion of Protestant dissent, while it opposed the artifice of stained glass windows in churches, hailed with joy the art of nature as the most direct revelation of God's handiwork. So the high style of beauty and praise was considered natural.

Just how did this high style sound? We have heard it in the lofty passages of the Bible, possibly in Homer, Pindar, and Lucretius, and in English in Spenser, Sylvester, and Milton. But most precisely we may hear it in that work of their own day, which eighteenth century American poets admired so profoundly and perpetuated so vigorously, James Thomson's poem *The Seasons*. Here are the introductory lines to his "Hymn on the Seasons." Notice the long rolling blank-verse invocation, the progressive round of scene and time, the sense of illimitable and almost inexpressible power, all characteristics of the sublime style.

> These, as they change, Almighty Father! these
> Are but the varied God. The rolling year
> Is full of thee. Forth in the pleasing Spring
> Thy beauty walks, thy tenderness and love.
> Wide flush the fields; the softening air is balm;
> Echo the mountains round; the forest smiles;
> And every sense, and every heart, is joy.
> Then comes thy glory in the Summer-months,
> With light and heat refulgent. Then thy sun
> Shoots full perfection through the swelling year.

The poem continues through the other seasons, and through the farthest reaches of the universe, and ends with a restatement of ineffable power:

I cannot go
Where universal love smiles not around,
Sustaining all yon orbs and all their suns;
From seeming evil still educing good,
And better thence again, and better still,
In infinite progression. But I lose
Myself in him, in light ineffable!
Come then, expressive Silence, muse his praise.

In an early preface to his poem "Winter," 1726, Thomson wrote what he thought about the state of poetry in the early eighteenth century, and what should be done about it. After his own century, more American poets than English believed in him and followed his advice. He said,

Let poetry once more be restored to her ancient truth and purity; let her be inspired from heaven, and in return her incense ascend thither; let her exchange her low, venal trifling subjects for such as are fair, useful, and magnificent. . . . Nothing can have a better influence towards the revival of poetry than the choosing of great and serious subjects, such as at once amuse the fancy, enlighten the head, and warm the heart. [Then he in effect anticipates and rejects the poetry of the Waste Land.] To be able to write on a dry, barren theme is looked upon by some as the sign of a happy, fruitful genius:—fruitful indeed! like one of the pendant gardens in Cheapside, watered every morning by the hand of the Alderman himself. . . . A genius fired with the charms of truth and nature is tuned to a sublimer pitch, and scorns to associate with such subjects. . . . I know no subject more elevating, more amusing; more ready to awake the poetical enthusiasm, the philosophical reflection, and the moral sentiment, than the works of Nature. Where can we meet with such variety, such beauty, such magnificence? All that enlarges and transports the soul! . . .

This was the belief which, though often in milder language, would prevail in American poetry, even into the work of the reformed Alderman of Cheapside, in the sublime passages of his *Four Quartets*, and into more youthful symbolic splendors of Ezra Pound, Hart Crane, and Richard Wilbur. It was a doctrine which met with tough opposition from English sceptics or even classicists from Dr. Samuel Johnson to Coleridge, Arnold, and Hulme; but it was a doctrine which found no great opposition on the new continent, rather a soil fertile for rich growth, with growing transcendentalism and modern imagism not stays but aids.

One might almost call it a doctrine native to America, because even a century before its enunciation by Thomson, it was practiced with enthusiasm by America's first muse, Anne Bradstreet. In her poem, "Contemplations," she writes the stiffer and simpler language of the seventeenth century and of Sylvester, but with the sweeping panegyric spirit of the century to come. Here are the first two stanzas:

> Some time now past in the autumnal tide,
>   When Phoebus wanted but one hour to bed,
> The trees all richly clad, yet void of pride,
>   Were gilded o'er by his rich golden head;
> Their leaves and fruits seemed painted, but were true
> Of green, of red, of yellow, mixed hue.
> Rapt were my senses at this delectable view.
>
> I wist not what to wish, yet sure, thought I,
>   If so much excellence abide below
> How excellent is He that dwells on high,
>   Whose power and beauty by his works we know!
> Sure He is goodness, wisdom, glory, light,
> That hath this under world so richly dight.
> More heaven than earth was here, no winter and no night.

Later in the poem Bradstreet devotes more famous lines to "I heard the merry grasshopper then sing. The black-clad cricket bear a second part"; but these are not so closely American as her general spirit of praise: "More heaven than earth was here, no winter and no night."

In time with the ringing of the Liberty Bell, the positives grew more superlative and competitive, as in Dwight's "Greenfield Hill" (I, 1-41).

> As round me here I gaze, what prospects rise?
> Etherial! matchless! such as Albion's sons,
> Could Albion's isle an equal prospect boast,
> In all the harmony of numerous song,
> Had tun'd to rapture, and o'er Cooper's hill,
> And Windsor's beauteous forest, high uprais'd,
> And sent on fame's light wing to every clime.
> Far inland, blended groves, and azure hills,
> Skirting the broad horizon, lift their pride.
> Beyond, a little chasm to view unfolds
> Cerulean mountains, verging high on Heaven,
> In misty grandeur.

Then there was, in early romanticism and late, free modulation of line-structure and implication—as in Lydia Sigourney's "Tomb of a Young Friend":

> I do remember thee.
>   There was a strain
> Of thrilling music, a soft breath of flowers

Telling of summer to a festive throng,
That fill'd the lighted halls. And the sweet smile
That spoke their welcome, the high warbled lay
Swelling with rapture through a parent's heart,
Were thine.
                    Time wav'd his noiseless wand awhile,
And in thy cherish'd home once more I stood,
Amid those twin'd and cluster'd sympathies
Where the rich blessing of thy heart sprang forth,
Like the moss rose. Where was the voice of song
Pouring out glad and glorious melody?—
But when I ask'd for thee, they took me where
A hallow'd mountain wrapt its verdant head
In changeful drapery of woods, and flowers,
And silver streams, and where thou erst didst love,
Musing to walk, and lend a serious ear
To the wild melody of birds that hung
Their unharm'd dwellings 'mid its woven bowers.
Yet here and there, involv'd in curtaining shades
Uprose those sculptur'd monuments that bear
The ponderous warnings of eternity.

Or Timrod's "The Cotton Boll":

Yonder bird,
Which floats, as if at rest,
In those blue tracts above the thunder, **where**
No vapors cloud the stainless air,
And never sound is heard,
Unless at such rare time
When, from the City of the Blest,
Rings down some golden chime,
Sees not from his high place
So vast a cirque of summer space
As widens round me in one mighty field,
Which, rimmed by seas and sands,
Doth hail its earliest daylight in the beams
Of gray Atlantic dawns;
And, broad as realms made up of many lands,
Is lost afar
Behind the crimson hills and purple lawns
Of sunset, among plains which roll their streams
Against the Evening Star!
And lo!
To the remotest point of sight,

Although I gaze upon no waste of snow,
The endless field is white;
And the whole landscape glows,
For many a shining league away,
With such accumulated light
As Polar lands would flash beneath a tropic day!

At the same time, a larger more social sweep: as in Thomas Holly
Chivers' "The Rising of the Nations":

Millions of millions now are groaning, groaning
    Beneath the grinding weight of Despotism,
While bloody Anarchy, unmindful of their moaning,
    Plunges them deeper into Hell's unsunned Abyssum!
While Earth, now slimed beneath his vile pollution,
    Echoes the wailings of their desolation,
Until the remnant, ripe for revolution,
    Answers the music of their soul's salvation,
Uttered by Liberty upon th' immortal Mountains,
    From all the vallies, out of every habitation—
Coming, like many rills from new-born Fountains
    Fresh opened in the Earth from long-descending rains,
Which, gathering into one great onward rushing river,
    Distending, overflows its banks, till all the plains
Are inundated with its everspreading waters—
    Still gathering volume as it flows forever;—
So did they gather in one mighty multitude,
    As if the Nations from the four great quarters
Of all the earth had migrated in one great flood,
    With one great common sympathy, to overthrow
    This mighty Monarch of the world—this foe
To human greatness—this great Devil to the Free—
This damned Abaddon of the Sons of Anarchy!

The sublime poets were political poets; they were moved by vast
social forces, and exercised a public rhetoric, as Pindar did, for public
purposes. For all of them in America, from Barlow and Trumbull on,
we may let John Greenleaf Whittier do the speaking, for he spoke from
the civil-war torn middle of the century, with a passion we are still
feeling. Here are some stanzas from his "Lines, Suggested by a Visit to
Washington in the 12th Month of 1845":

With a cold and wintry noon-light,
    On its roofs and steeples shed,

Shadows weaving with the sunlight
    From the gray sky overhead,
Broadly, vaguely, all around me, lies the
    half-built town outspread.

Through this broad street, restless ever,
    Ebbs and flows a human tide,
Wave on wave a living river;
    Wealth and fashion side by side;
Toiler, idler, slave and master, in the same
    quick current glide.

Underneath yon dome, whose coping
    Springs above them, vast and tall,
Grave men in the dust are groping
    For the largess, base and small,
Which the hand of Power is scattering, crumbs
    which from its table fall.

Base of heart, they vilely barter
    Honor's wealth for party's place:
Step by step on Freedom's charter
    Leaving footprints of disgrace;
For to-day's poor pittance turning from the
    great hope of their race.

Then, after a vision of the South's anguish, and the nation's highest
purposes, the final exhortation:

Let us then, uniting, bury
    All our idle feuds in dust,
And to future conflicts carry
    Mutual faith and common trust;
Always he who most forgiveth in his
    brother is most just.

From the eternal shadow rounding
    All our sun and starlight here,
Voices of our lost ones sounding
    Bid us be of heart and cheer,
Through the silence, down the spaces,
    falling on the inward ear.

Manifold traits of the sublime style are here: the visionary spirit and
invocative tone, the irregular line length and harmonic use of sound,
the sense of mankind as one great body, with personifiable characteristics,

the exclamations and superlatives, and even the figures, of the restless river, the eternal shadow, and the voice of silence falling on the inward ear. I know none more directly representative of this whole American tradition than Whittier.

While in Whittier we have its representation, in Whitman we have its extreme. More visionary, more invocative, more adjectival, more cumulative and harmonic than any other poet in English, even more than Blake, Whitman is the great, and American, culmination of the sublime tradition. Each of us can recall a dozen or a hundred passages from *Leaves of Grass* which embody these traits we have been thinking of. To begin to quote is not to know where to end. But here is an early passage, "On Journeys through the States," with its free-swinging line and its all-encompassing attitude:

> On journeys through the States we start,
> (Ay through the world, urged by these songs,
> Sailing henceforth to every land, to every sea,)
> We willing learners of all, teachers of all, and lovers of all.
> We have watch'd the seasons dispensing themselves and passing on
> And have said, Why should not a man or woman do as much as the
> seasons, and effuse as much?
> We dwell a while in every city and town,
> We pass through Kanada, the North-east, the vast valley of the
> Mississippi, and the Southern States,
> We confer on equal terms with each of the States,
> We make trial of ourselves and invite men and women to hear,
> We say to ourselves, Remember, fear not, be candid, promulge
> the body and the soul,
> Dwell awhile and pass on, be copious, temperate, chaste, magnetic,
> And what you effuse may then return as the seasons return,
> And may be just as much as the seasons.

Every particular has its place in the list, every list its place in the whole poem, and every whole poem its place in geography and universe. Smallness and greatness are equal in this cycle of meaning. Through Whitman, Emily Dickinson, Marianne Moore and others, America has fostered the sense of size not only in greatness, but in smallness also, in the most minute and loving detail. As Whitman said in "Song of Myself,"

> I chant the chant of dilation or pride,
> We have had ducking and deprecating about enough,
> I show that size is only development.

And therefore the gamut, the interest in degree, of small to large and little to great, in the careful and fond details of the most sweeping verse.

In a particular way, Whitman naturalized the sublime: he located it in individual bodies and souls, not only by specifying the sublime, but by generalizing and expanding the human. Like his contemporaries in America, he fostered the Whig poetizing of earth, sea, and land—the expanses of nature—and then in his own way gave them a human presence, in woman, mother, child; in water, which could be both human and natural, and in the human, natural counterparts of hair and grass. This sharing of physical values, this passiveness of holding and beholding, sleeping and waiting, has been characteristic of much poetry since Whitman—of Pound, Eliot, Lawrence, Crane, Roethke—(See my *Renaissance, Eighteenth Century, and Modern Language in Poetry, 1960*). While for Blake, Keats, and others before Whitman, sublime figures were externalized, for Whitman and those after him they were internalized; earth felt through body, body through earth.

As the historian Bancroft wrote to Prescott in 1848, in terms like Whitman's, "Go forth, then, language of Milton and Hampden, language of my country, take possession of the North American Continent! Gladden the waste places with every tone that has been rightly struck on the English lyre, with every English word that has been spoken well for liberty and for man! . . . Utter boldly and spread widely through the world the thoughts of the coming apostles of liberty, till the sound that cheers the desert shall thrill through the heart of humanity . . ."

I have been making here a number of generalizations which run counter to some standard descriptions of American poetry. I have suggested first that the Protestant-democratic style is not the plain English but the high Biblical style; second, that of two major and almost opposite Romantic styles it was again not the dramatic one of Coleridge but the high one of Thomson and Blake that most affected American nineteenth century romanticism; third, that the prevalent balanced style in America, often called classical, represents a steady and conscious effort at compromise between extremes: between the lowly and plain in poetry, for which the country has so much affinity, and at the other extreme the sublime, the worshipful Sunday poetry early adopted and enthusiastically maintained; and fourth, that when the two nations separated politically at the end of the eighteenth century, it was America, not England, that carried on the eighteenth century poetic tradition, and it is now America which is taking the lead in returning this tradition to England, with an increasing consolidation of interests and powers.

The drama of O'Neill and the fiction of Faulkner each in its own way gives us again this vision of the mystery in the near at hand, and confirms in the sublime style of the prose of America the sublimity of its poetry. The importance of this sublimity will, I think, increase with time. Of all the modes it has been least consciously explored and defined, least critically championed. Yet Dylan Thomas in England and Hart Crane in America have spoken with this voice what Whitman spoke, what the prophets spoke, to the young poets—"Come then, expressive silence, muse his praise."

This American poetry of praise has a long free cadenced line, full of silences, symbols, and implications. It has a cumulative structure, building up to a height of force and feeling, whether in imprecation or in rhapsody. It has a phraseology of resounding sound and of warm responsive sense, suggestive of heights and depths beyond the reach of form or reason. As at its worst it can be dangerously loose, semi-conscious, and irresponsible, at its best it can be powerfully aware of moving forces and meanings. Strong as it was in England in the work of Keats, Tennyson, and Dylan Thomas, it has been more widespread and more central to tradition in America, with added impetus from poets of the Orient as well as of Europe. What can it mean to our future?

It can portend for our poetry a strong sense of ceremony and of public concern, strong personal and passionate comments on public issues, a highly vocal and expressive function of evaluation for the poet—comparable to the role played by Pindar, for example, in his celebration of the Olympic Games—a calling up and praising of great figures of our life—or perhaps of denouncing them, but at any rate of perceiving and portraying them, larger than life, in a great frame of human values and human concerns. It can be not only personal and ambiguous, but social and magnanimous, in the magnanimity of a poetry which transfigures what it values.

Chronology of Important Dates

1819	Walt Whitman born May 31, on a Long Island farm.
1823	Moved to Brooklyn, New York. Father worked as a builder.
1831-1841	Worked as a printer's devil, printer, reporter, schoolteacher, handyman.
1842-1846	Reporter, magazine-writer, small editor and politician in New York City. Published (1842) *Franklin Evans, or the Inebriate,* a tract.
1846	Editor of the Brooklyn *Daily Eagle.*
1848	Discharged from the *Eagle.* Visited New Orleans.
1849	Editor of the Brooklyn *Freeman,* a free-soil journal.
1850-1855	Part-time journalist and homebuilder with father.
1855	*Leaves of Grass,* first edition.
1856	*Leaves of Grass,* second edition—with which began the continuing expansion and revision of the book.
1860	*Leaves of Grass,* third edition.
1862-1864	Went first to Virginia to search for brother George, then to Washington as volunteer nurse in army hospitals. Worked in government offices.
1865	Fired from Department of the Interior on charge that *Leaves of Grass* was indecent. Rehired by Attorney General's office. *Drum-Taps* published.
1866	W. D. O'Connor's *Good Gray Poet,* the first major apologia for Whitman, marked the beginning of his international reputation. His health gradually deteriorating, demands on his time increasing, Whitman continued in Attorney General's office until 1873.
1867	*Leaves of Grass,* fourth edition.
1871	*Leaves of Grass,* fifth edition. *Democratic Vistas.*
1873	Partially paralyzed by mild stroke. Moved to Camden, N.J., where he lived out his life—to be finally at the center of the group of disciples which came to be known as "The Whitman Fellowship."

1876   *Author's Edition: Leaves of Grass* and *Two Rivulets*.

1881   Boston edition of *Leaves of Grass*.

1882   *Specimen Days and Collect.*

1888   *November Boughs.*

1891-1892   "Deathbed Edition" of *Leaves of Grass*.

1892   *Complete Prose Works*. Died March 26 at Camden.

Notes on the Editor and Contributors

Roy Harvey Pearce, the editor of this volume, is Professor of English at The Ohio State University. In addition to many articles and reviews on American Literature and Intellectual History, Professor Pearce has published *The Savages of America* (1953), *The Continuity of American Poetry* (1961), the Introduction to the Facsimile Edition of the 1860 *Leaves of Grass,* and is general editor with William Charvat of the Centennial Edition of the writings of Hawthorne.

Roger Asselineau is Professor of English at the Sorbonne. He is author of *L'Evolution de Walt Whitman* (1954).

Richard Chase is Professor of English at Columbia University. He is author of *Quest for Myth* (1949), *Walt Whitman Reconsidered* (1955), and *The American Novel and its Tradition* (1957).

Charles Feidelson, Jr. is Professor of English at Yale University. He is author of *Symbolism and American Literature* (1953).

John Kinnaird is Instructor in English at Vassar College.

D. H. Lawrence (1885-1930) was the British novelist, poet, and essayist who spent much of the later part of his life in the United States. In a way, *Studies in Classic American Literature* is the richest record of that part of his life.

R. W. B. Lewis is Professor of English at Yale University. He is author of *The American Adam* (1955) and *The Picaresque Saint* (1960).

F. O. Matthiessen (1902-1950) was Professor of English at Harvard University. He is author of *Sarah Orne Jewett* (1929), *The Achievement of T. S. Eliot* (1935), *American Renaissance* (1941), *Henry James: The Major Phase* (1944), *Theodore Dreiser* (1951).

Josephine Miles is Professor of English at the University of California, Berkeley. She is author of *Eras and Modes in English Poetry* (1957) and *Poems: 1930-1960* (1960).

James Miller, Jr. is Professor of English at the University of Nebraska. He is author of *A Critical Guide to Leaves of Grass* (1957) and *The Fictional Technique of Scott Fitzgerald* (1957).

Perry Miller is Professor of English at Harvard University. He is author of *The New England Mind: The Seventeenth Century* (1939), *The New England Mind: From Colony into Province* (1953), *Jonathan Edwards* (1949), *Errand into the Wilderness* (1956).

Ezra Pound now lives in Italy, where he works toward completion of his *Cantos.*

Walter Sutton is Professor of English at Syracuse University.

William Carlos Williams retired from his medical practice a few years ago and has increasingly assumed his rightful position as one of the grand old masters of American letters. His major achievement as a poet is *Paterson* (1946-1958), which is in effect his version of "Song of Myself."

Bibliography

Whitman's Text

The standard edition of Whitman is *The Complete Writings* (New York, 1902), 10 vols., ed. R. M. Bucke, T. H. Harned, and H. L. Traubel. It is, in fact, far from "complete" and is being superseded by *The Collected Writings of Walt Whitman*, ed. G. W. Allen and S. Bradley—of which the first two volumes (containing Whitman's early correspondence) have been issued (New York, 1961). The best among many editions of *Leaves of Grass* is the "Inclusive Edition" of Emory Holloway (New York, 1925 and frequently reprinted) which reproduces the variorum readings of *The Complete Writings*. *The Complete Poetry and Prose*, ed. M. Cowley (New York, 1948, reprinted 1954) is the most readily available edition of its kind. There are facsimile editions of the 1855 *Leaves of Grass*, ed. C. J. Furness (New York, 1939), and the 1860 *Leaves of Grass*, ed. R. H. Pearce (Ithaca, 1961). The 1855 *Leaves of Grass* has also been reprinted, ed. Malcolm Cowley (New York, 1960), and as a Dolphin paperback (New York, 1960). Fredson Bowers has edited *Whitman's Manuscripts, Leaves of Grass: 1860* (Chicago, 1955) and given us the best detailed view we have so far had of a stage in the growth of *Leaves of Grass*. One of the best critical introductions to Whitman's poetry, the text for which derives from the various editions of *Leaves of Grass*, is *Walt Whitman's Poems: Selections, with Critical Aids*, ed. G. W. Allen and C. T. Davis (New York, 1955—reprinted 1959 as an Evergreen paperback).

Biography and Criticism

The number of biographical and critical studies of Whitman is of course enormous. The most judicious recent survey of them is Williard Thorpe's essay in *Eight American Authors* (New York, 1956), pp. 271-318. Below are listed a small selection, representing, along with the essays in this volume, the most important and, from their various perspectives, the most soundly expounded twentieth-century views of Whitman.

Allen, Gay Wilson. *The Solitary Singer*. New York: The Macmillan Co., 1955. The definitive biography.

———. *Walt Whitman Handbook*. Chicago: Hendricks House, Inc., 1946. With its careful bibliographies, this remains the best introduction to the problems raised by Whitman's work.

———, ed. *Walt Whitman Abroad*. Syracuse, N. Y.: Syracuse University Press, 1955. A representative collection of foreign opinion of Whitman, in English translation.

Arvin, Newton. *Whitman.* New York: The Macmillan Co., 1938. The best politically-minded study of Whitman.

Asselineau, Roger. *L'Evolution de Walt Whitman.* Paris: Gregory Lounz, 1954. The first part of this close study of Whitman's "creation" of his biography has been published in English as *The Evolution of Walt Whitman,* Volume I, Cambridge, Mass.: The Belknap Press of Harvard University Press, 1960. Translation of the second part, a selection from which is printed herein, is forthcoming.

Bradley, Sculley. "The Fundamental Metrical Principle in Whitman's Poetry," *American Literature,* X (1938-39), 347-359. The best of the more "traditional" studies of Whitman's prosody.

Chapman, John Jay. "Whitman," in *Selected Writings,* J. Barzun, ed. New York: Farrar, Straus & Cudahy, Inc., 1959, pp. 157-164. Originally published in *Emerson and Other Essays* (New York: Charles Scribner's Sons, 1898), this is one of the earliest balanced assessments of Whitman as at once a threat to and a promise for American life.

Chase, Richard. " 'Go-Befores and Embryons': A Biographical Reprise," in *Leaves of Grass One Hundred Years After,* M. Hindus, ed., Stanford, Calif.: Stanford University Press, 1955, pp. 32-54. The best of the psychoanalytic accounts of the origins of Whitman's genius. Developed into a full-scale historical-critical study in Mr. Chase's *Walt Whitman Reconsidered* (New York: William Morrow & Co., Inc., 1955).

Coffman, Stanley K., Jr. "Form and Meaning in Whitman's 'Passage to India,' " *PMLA,* LXX (1955), 337-349. One of the surprisingly few good formalist explications of a Whitman poem.

Cox, James M. "Walt Whitman, Mark Twain, and the Civil War," *Sewanee Review,* LXIX (1961), 187-193. The best account on the significance of the Civil War for the achievement of Whitman's poetry.

Fiedler, Leslie. "Walt Whitman: Portrait of the Artist as a Middle-Aged Hero," in *No! in Thunder,* Boston: Beacon Press, 1960, pp. 61-75. Originally published as the introduction to the Laurel paperback *Whitman* (New York: Dell Publishing Co., Inc., 1959), this is a free-wheeling assessment of a shape-shifting Whitman who made sure that the joke was on his readers, not excluding Mr. Fiedler.

Foerster, Norman. "Whitman," in *American Criticism,* New York: Houghton Mifflin Company, 1928, pp. 157-222. An interested, cautionary, conservative account of the implications of Whitman's "creed" for modern literature.

Griffith, Clark. "Sex and Death: the Significance of Whitman's 'Calamus' Themes," *PQ,* XXXIX (1960), 18-38. Whitman's Civil War experiences and their role in the sublimation of his homosexuality, thus in the achievement of his poetry.

Holloway, Emory. *Whitman: An Interpretation in Narrative.* New York: Alfred A. Knopf, Inc., 1926. Though superseded by Allen's biography, this remains an exciting and excited account of the discovery of the "real" Whitman.

Jarrell, Randall. "Some Lines from Whitman," in *Poetry and the Age*, New York: Alfred A. Knopf, Inc., 1953. A strenuous Cook's tour through Whitman, marking his acceptance by one of a generation of American poets who heretofore had tended to shun him. In effect, an important "re-discovery."

Matthiessen, F. O. *American Renaissance*. New York: Oxford University Press, Inc., 1941. Both the discussion of Whitman, pp. 517-625 (part of which is reprinted herein) and the book at large are basic compendious studies, knowledge of which is by now a necessary condition to the comprehension of American literature and life in the nineteenth century.

Miller, James, Jr. *A Critical Guide to Leaves of Grass*. Chicago: University of Chicago Press, 1957. The best defense of the "prophetic" Whitman—which in effect mounts an offense, a section of which is printed herein.

Parrington, Vernon Louis. "The Afterglow of the Enlightenment: Walt Whitman," in *Main Currents in American Thought*, Volume III (New York: Harcourt, Brace & World, Inc., 1930), pp. 69-86. The principal "liberal" assessment of Whitman.

Pearce, Roy Harvey. *The Continuity of American Poetry*. Princeton, N. J.: Princeton University Press, 1961. On Whitman, see pp. 63-69, 164-174.

Santayana, George. "The Poetry of Barbarism," in *Interpretations of Poetry and Religion* (New York: Harper & Brothers, 1900, reprinted 1957), pp. 166-216. The "barbarians" are Browning and Whitman. One of the great attacks on Whitman, among other reasons, because Santayana can acknowledge his power. An influential essay, because it directly and indirectly gave rise to so many "defenses" of Whitman.

Saunders, H. S., ed. *Parodies of Walt Whitman*, New York: American Library Service, 1923. The best of these parodies are exercises in exorcism. See also Dwight MacDonald, ed. *Parodies* (New York: Random House, 1960), pp. 143-146, 324, 326, for some more recent examples.

Schyberg, Frederick. *Walt Whitman*, Evie Allison Allen, trans. New York: Columbia University Press, 1951. The best "internationalist" account of Whitman.

Shapiro, Karl. "The First White Aboriginal," in James E. Miller, Jr., *et al. Start with the Sun*. Lincoln, Neb.: University of Nebraska Press, 1960, pp. 57-70. An impassioned plea for the "prophetic" Whitman, coming from a full, frank, free confession of a recent convert.

Spencer, Benjamin T. "Walt Whitman," in *The Quest for Nationality*, Syracuse, N. Y.: Syracuse University Press, 1957, pp. 219-241. A masterful account of Whitman's role in the definition of an autochthonous American literature.

Stovall, Floyd. "Main Drifts in Whitman's Poetry," *American Literature*, IV (1932-33), 3-21. A careful survey of the shifting ideological components of Whitman's work—one of the most valuable of the many descriptive introductions.

Van Doren, Mark. "The Poet," in *Walt Whitman: Man, Poet, Philosopher*, Washington: Reference Department, Library of Congress, 1955, pp. 15-33. A balanced, ordered assessment. In its sweet calmness, one of the best recently written introductions to Whitman.

TWENTIETH CENTURY VIEWS

American Authors